V-BOMBERS

Dr Tony Redding's published work includes:

Bombing Germany: The Final Phase
The destruction of Pforzheim and the closing months of Bomber Command's war
Pen & Sword Aviation (2015)
ISBN 9781473823549

Der Totale Krieg und die Zerstörung von Pforzheim
Verlag Regionalkultur (2017)
ISBN 9783897359604

Flying For Freedom
Mulberry TRS (2008)
ISBN 9780955928000

Revised Edition
Life and death in Bomber Command
Fonthill (2013)
ISBN 9781781552285

War in the Wilderness
The Chindits in Burma 1943-1944
Spellmount (The History Press) (2011, 2015)
ISBN 9780750962179

V-BOMBERS

Britain's Nuclear Frontline in the Cold War

DR TONY REDDING

GRUB STREET • LONDON

To the many V-Force veterans and others who made this book possible

Comradeship
"The Oxford English Dictionary defines defines comradeship as 'friendship between a number of people who are doing the same work or who share the same difficulties or dangers'. Comradeship is in the DNA of all HM Armed Forces and, together with discipline, pride in unit, squadron, ship, regiment, etc, is the glue that binds us together. My service career ended in 1971 with 35 Squadron in Cyprus. Since then we have had some 14 reunions and the old spirit is still there."

Roger Frampton

Published by
Grub Street
4 Rainham Close
London SW11 6SS

Copyright © Grub Street 2024
Copyright text © Dr Tony Redding 2024

A CIP record for this title is available from the British Library

ISBN-13: 978-1-911667-87-2

All rights reserved. No part of this publication may be reproduced, stored in a retrieval system, or transmitted in any form or by any means electronic, mechanical, photocopying, recording or otherwise, without the prior permission of the copyright owner.

Design by Myriam Bell Design, UK
Printed and bound by Finidr, Czechia

CONTENTS

AUTHOR'S NOTE	6
ACKNOWLEDGEMENTS	7
INTRODUCTION	8
1. BRITAIN'S AIRBORNE DETERRENT	10
2. SPECIAL WEAPONS	17
3. POWERED BOMBS AND LAYDOWN BOMBS	32
4. THE V-FORCE MISSION	50
5. DELIVERING THE MISSION	65
6. V-FORCE PILOTS	74
7. NAVIGATORS, AEOS AND GROUND CREW	91
8. ON THE NUCLEAR FRONTLINE	109
9. DESTROYING THE TARGETS	122
10. THE THREAT TO THE AIRFIELDS	145
11. QUICK REACTION ALERT	152
12. CUBA AND LIFE ON QRA	162
13. REDUCING EXPOSURE ON THE GROUND	178
14. GENERATING WEAPON SYSTEMS	196
15. SURVIVING A WAR SCRAMBLE	214
16. LIVING ON YOUR NERVES	231
17. SOVIET AIR DEFENCES	244
18. PENETRATING THE DEFENCES	255
19. ECM AND OTHER COUNTERMEASURES	269
20. ATTACKING TARGETS	280
21. TRAINING FOR A ONE-STRIKE WAR	296
22. SHOULD DETERRENCE FAIL...	318
SELECTED RESEARCH SOURCES AND BIBLIOGRAPHY	327
NOTES TO CHAPTERS	333
INDEX	351

AUTHOR'S NOTE

Following the Nassau meeting between President Kennedy and Prime Minister Macmillan in 1962, the cancellation of the Skybolt air-launched missile and the offer of the submarine-launched Polaris promised the British a modern deterrent based on long-range ballistic missiles carried by a near-invulnerable launch platform.

This outcome was ideal from the British standpoint. The UK would be freed from reliance on a small group of subsonic bombers, armed with inadequate weapons and uncomfortably exposed to destruction on the ground and in the air. The submarine-launched ballistic missile was (and, for the moment, is) the near-perfect small nation deterrent, but the problem was the inevitable wait. It would be at least six years before British Polaris submarines would begin their lone patrols. What could be done, over this period, to stretch the capability and credibility of the V-bombers, to bridge the gap in a world already dominated by inter-continental missiles?

The scope of this book includes a detailed review of the efforts made to bridge this gap, until Britain's strategic nuclear frontline passed to the submarines in mid-1969. It is also about much more: the dedicated aircrew and ground personnel, the aircraft, equipment and weapons and, of course, the V-bombers' long period of supplementary nuclear service alongside the submarines, a period ending, perhaps ironically, in the Black Buck raids of the Falklands War in 1982. Given the main theme of this book, the latter campaign receives only passing reference and the reader is directed to the excellent existing books dealing with this subject – in itself a celebration of the continued capacity of Britain's armed services to make much out of very little.

Returning to the V-Force strategic nuclear role, I have long puzzled over why the extensive literature concerning the Valiants, Victors and Vulcans, the Cold War, the British bomb, the Anglo-American nuclear relationship, etc, contains no detailed account of V-Force capability and credibility and no assessment of its operational capacity, had the Cold War turned hot. This is a significant gap in the literature, given that the V-Force was the cutting edge of UK military posture and international political presence in the very dangerous world of the 1960s and beyond. I hope this book goes some way towards placing on record the immense efforts made to keep us safe during the Cold War years.

Dr Tony Redding
Ash, Canterbury, UK, 2023

ACKNOWLEDGEMENTS

It was suggested that the content of this book was too broad for a lone researcher. It must be said that, early on, I was amongst the doubters! Nevertheless, a start was made, with the research progressing as a PhD project at King's College, London.

The research programme was successful, thanks to the generous help, support and encouragement of many people, including a large group of former V-Force aircrew and ground personnel, together with specialists in areas ranging from operational analysis to the development of British nuclear weapons.

This programme spanned seven years. I am very grateful for the support and interest of many, including Roy Brocklebank (who patiently offered feedback on hundreds of draft pages and kindly consented to write the Introduction to this book), Norman Bonnor, John Huggins, Dr Robin Woolven, Mike Fazackerley, Julian Grenfell and Dr Les Ruskell. I was also fortunate enough to receive a strong response to my call for photographs, with notable contributions from Peter Lawrence, Norman Bonnor and Andy Leitch (who also gave the text a thorough check).

I am grateful for Simon Fowler's assistance in securing official documents from The National Archives and offer my thanks to Fiona Cummings, who used her IT skills to good effect in producing the various drafts – all done without a cross word!

The only reason I moved from project doubter to project believer was through the willing help of many, in what became a collaborative project. Every effort has been made to find and remove errors, but any failures on that front are my responsibility alone.

Three in a row. The 1981 flypast at RAF Scampton to mark the 25th anniversary of the Vulcan. (Anthony Wright)

INTRODUCTION

> ❝ *It cannot be right to acquiesce uncritically, for the rest of human history, in a system that maintains peace between potential adversaries partly by the threat of colossal disaster.* ❞
>
> John Baylis and Kristan Stoddart, citing Sir Michael Quinlan,
> *Thinking about Nuclear Weapons*

The ethos of the V-Force since its inception was a mixture of public disclosure and absolute secrecy. As the United Kingdom's independent national deterrent, it was necessary to demonstrate a capability whilst maintaining the mystery of how this would be achieved. Orders for the three bombers, the Valiant, Victor and Vulcan, were public and many overseas flights demonstrating a global reach were undertaken. As a deterrent, the type of targets in the Soviet Union were publicised but the precise targets, the force routeing and the weapons' effects were closely guarded secrets.

Selected aircrew would assemble at their respective operational conversion units, usually two crews at a time, and be trained to fly their respective aircraft. Once the crew joined their assigned squadron, they would undertake various checks but, most importantly, they would undergo a period of intense study. This would be on an individual crew basis, with no discussion with other crews. They would need to study the Bomber Command War Standard Operations Procedures, the detailed target folders for their assigned targets and pass verbal tests on each target by wing specialists before being declared combat-ready.

Enjoying the sun: Nav/radar Roy Brocklebank's Vulcan at Masirah. Pictured (l/r) are: Flying Officer Dave Major (co-pilot), Roy Brocklebank, Squadron Leader Nigel Baldwin (captain), Flight Lieutenant Tony Ward (AEO), Squadron Leader Frank Guard (nav/plotter) and an unidentified crew chief. (Roy Brocklebank)

On the squadron, attack profiles could be discussed and practised but no crew had knowledge of the routeing of any other crew. For the ground crews, they would prepare the aircraft for routine training flights, be deployed on occasion to dispersal airfields, and, for a few, get to fly on overseas trips. Beyond this, ground crews were as much in the dark as the aircrews. Secrecy extended not just between aircrew and ground crew but to families as well.

Dr Tony Redding has drawn aside this veil of secrecy. Others have published works that give some insight into this secret world, but Tony Redding's work on the nuclear deterrent is unique as he has skilfully combined meticulous research on higher command policy and studies by the Bomber Command Operational Research Branch with first-hand accounts from many aircrews and supporting ground crew who flew or worked on the aircraft. He has examined the viability of the deterrent, from the 'four-minute warning' and the ability to survive a pre-emptive Soviet strike to the crews' ability to reach their targets. Personal tales reveal thoughts about what the crews were told and their faith in their mission and its chances of success should the unthinkable happen.

This work should appeal to both academics and a general readership, especially to aircrews, ground crew, families and, indeed, anyone interested in this tense period of the Cold War.

Roy Brocklebank
Vulcan nav/radar, wing targeting officer, RAF Waddington

1
BRITAIN'S AIRBORNE DETERRENT

> *… we intend as soon as possible to build up … a force of modern bombers capable of using the atomic weapon to the fullest effect. A strong and efficient force of medium bombers is of the greatest importance.*
>
> Cmd. 9075, Statement on Defence, February 1954

THE OBVIOUS COUNTER

On 10 August 1945, the day after the plutonium bomb exploded over Nagasaki, British Prime Minister Clement Atlee established GEN 75, a Cabinet committee charged with establishing Britain as a nuclear power. The world had changed. The obvious counter to an atomic bomb on London was an atomic bomb on the enemy capital. The race to create a credible British nuclear deterrent was under way, with no question over the means of delivery. Nazi Germany's V-2 rocket signposted the future, but Britain remained wedded to the strategic bomber. The national interest required a nuclear weapon system ready by the second half of the 1950s.[1] The bomber was the UK's fastest route to an operational deterrent. There was a belief that missile technologies would not mature until the V-Force had been in service for some time. Yet, by the time this bomber fleet deployed in strength, ballistic missiles had taken centre stage.

During 1946, Air Staff Operational Requirement OR.229 (Specification B.35/46) called for a four-engined bomber able to carry a 10,000-lb bomb at 500 kts at 55,000 ft.[2] Three types emerged, the advanced Vulcan and Victor (responses to B.35/46) and the more conventional Valiant – an 'interim' type (a response to a separate Operational Requirement: OR.231). The decision to build all three, creating the V-Force (or, more formally, the Medium Bomber Force – MBF) echoed the wartime decision to build the Stirling, Halifax and Lancaster four-engined bombers.[3]

During 1953, Air Chief Marshal Sir Ronald Ivelaw-Chapman, Vice-Chief of the Air Staff (VCAS), minuted the Secretary of State for Air, stressing MBF significance and adding: "… for deterrence, the biggest force we can afford is the least we should provide."[4] Later, he added:

> "One thing that is clear … is the overriding importance of the MBF. In peace, it is the force which can provide the necessary power behind our voice in international affairs and in war it is the one force with which we could strike a worthwhile blow against our enemies."[5]

What would that blow consist of? At the time, the priority was to reach out and destroy Soviet nuclear forces capable of striking the UK. A draft paper of 7 July 1955 identified 103 Soviet bomber bases 750–1,500NM from the UK and posing a threat to Britain. This also referred to a 31 May 1955 Bomber Command directive underlining the need to destroy the enemy's will to continue the war by attacking population centres. Seventy-two Soviet cities were considered as targets (37 within 1,500NM of the UK and 35 between 1,500 and 2,000NM).[6] The significance of a mix of both counterforce (military) and countervalue (city) targets was recognised from the first. Eventually, this was reflected in the MBF's two target lists: Plan A (the Single Integrated Operations Plan, or SIOP – the military targets making up NATO's war-fighting programme) and Plan B, the National target list, which maximised the retaliatory threat in the unilateral context by focusing on the biggest Soviet cities. There was deterrent value in having two plans, as it complicated the enemy's assessment task.[7]

Given Britain's parlous post-war condition and the immense cost of building a British bomb and delivery system, the Air Ministry explored unconventional, lower cost alternatives. One, 'Blue Moon', was a crewless 'expendable bomber' capable of reaching Moscow.[8] Blue Moon waned due to the lack of a reliable guidance system. In the final analysis, the need for a workable deterrent was too important for radical experimentation. Many futuristic projects existed on paper, but Bomber Command's daily reality at this time was more akin to World War 2. The early 1950s strategic bombing force consisted of Avro Lincolns, a Lancaster derivative unable to attack Soviet targets.

Nevertheless, operational requirements for the new jet bombers were extremely demanding and, if met, would allow the RAF to leapfrog an entire generation of strategic aircraft. This would take time. Meanwhile, as a stopgap, Bomber Command's heavy squadrons acquired American B-29s, known in RAF service as the Washington. By mid-1952, Bomber Command had over 80 B-29s. There has been some debate as to whether the Washingtons carried atomic weapons (they did not; USAF historian William W. Suit has pointed out that nuclear-armed Washingtons would have violated the provisions of the US Atomic Energy Act 1946).[9] At the same time, the development of a British nuclear weapon *and* the existence of the potential means of delivering it sent a powerful signal into the world community. Simultaneously, Britain's twin-jet, nuclear-capable Canberra pointed the way to the future. This light bomber, arising from specifications including B.3/45, entered service in 1951.

THE NEW BOMBERS

At the strategic level, the British felt it unwise to rely entirely on American weapons and aircraft. Three tenders for the new bombers were progressed and work began under a haze of over-optimistic forecasts and expectations. Tony Blackman commented:

> "Although the new operational requirement for what was to become the V-bombers, conceived in 1947, was clearly going to push the engineering of the day to its limits, the intention was to get the aircraft into service by 1951, which, in itself, demonstrates how little idea the Air Staff had of the task they had laid before the various manufacturers."[10]

In January 1948 Avro received clearance to proceed with Vulcan prototypes (known as Avro 698). This bomber first flew on 30 August 1952. A few weeks previously, Avro had received a contract for 25 production aircraft, soon followed by a second order for 37. The RAF took delivery of its first Vulcan on 20 July 1956. Handley Page's H.P.80 became the Victor, which first flew on 24 December 1952; an initial order for 25 had been placed that June. The first Victor arrived at 232 Operational Conversion Unit (OCU), RAF Gaydon, on 28 November

First of the V-bombers: the Valiant, described as a "gentleman's aeroplane". Taff Foreman's crew on 148 Squadron, RAF Marham (from left to right): Anthony Wright (nav/radar), Ken Lewis (nav/plotter), Taff Foreman (captain), Tony Gale (co-pilot) and Daryl Pace (AEO). (Anthony Wright)

1957. The type entered service in 1958.[11] A total of 217 production Vulcans and Victors were built over a ten-year period. The final V-bomber built, Vulcan B.2 XM657, was delivered in January 1965.

The 'interim' Vickers Valiant first flew on 18 May 1951. A parallel 'insurance' type, the Short Sperrin, did not enter production. The Valiant was the first of the three V-bombers to become operational (February 1955) and saw action in the conventional bombing role during the October/November 1956 Suez conflict (Operation Musketeer). As some Valiants were not fully fitted with the new navigation and bombing system (NBS), the RAF resorted to World War 2-style target marking. It was in 1956 that SA-1 surface-to-air missiles (SAMs) first deployed around Moscow. The more capable SA-2 then appeared; by 1964 there were some 600 SA-2 sites.[12]

Growing Soviet defensive and offensive capabilities were a major challenge to the RAF's new bombers. The 'golden age' of the V-Force in its original high-altitude strategic-bombing role would be very short. This era came to an abrupt end when a Soviet SA-2 Guideline SAM brought down Gary Powers' U-2 from a height of around 70,000 ft on 1 May 1960. Former Vulcan nav/radar Roy Brocklebank has a particular view on this event:

"I think too much is made of the single U-2 shoot-down at 70,000 ft, compared with a high-flying bomber at 56,000 ft. The environment in which the U-2 was shot down was benign. There were no electronic countermeasures (ECM). There were no other penetrating targets. There were no nuclear explosions. The U-2 made considerable ingress into Russian airspace before a successful engagement. Its speed was considerably less than that of a V-bomber, even a Valiant."[13]

Nevertheless, while the Russians may have struggled to destroy the U-2, in the final analysis *they did succeed*.

CREDIBILITY

V-Force operational effectiveness was more than a simple function of force size. RAF Air Historical Branch researcher Clive Richards identified three factors underpinning MBF credibility: the ability to disperse and protect the bomber force in time of war, the development of robust transition to war procedures and the maintenance of a proportion of Bomber Command at a high state of peacetime readiness, "capable of retaliating in the event of a surprise pre-emptive attack".[14]

Credibility demanded round-the-clock, all-weather capability. As Dr Les Ruskell, a former head of the Operational Analysis Cell at UK Joint Permanent Headquarters, Northwood, points out: "The credibility of the deterrent depends not just on the ability to survive to launch and to reach the target, but also to sustain operations even in bad weather." The Royal Aircraft Establishment (RAE) at Farnborough contributed much to V-Force all-weather capability and other factors underpinning operational success, including bomb ballistics.[15]

The major issue surrounding manned bomber delivery of the deterrent was exposure to destruction on the ground. The true measure of V-Force credibility was not its paper strength but, rather, the proportion of the force that would survive pre-emptive attack. The survivors would then run the gauntlet of the Soviet coastal defence belt, fighter, SAM and gun area defences and, finally, point defences concentrated around targets. Furthermore, each British bomber carrying a freefall weapon would be exposed, potentially, to at least two nuclear bursts, one over its home airfield and, subsequently, the detonation of its own weapon over the

Night shift: Vulcan XL386 being serviced on alpha dispersal, RAF Waddington. (Andy Leitch Collection)

Raw power: a striking view from the co-pilot's position – Queen's birthday flypast practice. (Andy Leitch Collection)

target. Whilst the V-bombers would almost certainly arrive after an opening missile exchange, they would be the first strategic bombers attempting penetration.

A SPECIAL PLACE IN WESTERN DEFENCE

A deterrent consisting of a small force of subsonic bombers had obvious operational drawbacks, but the MBF occupied a special place in Western defence, as explained by Baylis and Stoddart. Britain, as a second centre of nuclear decision-making, had significance:

> "... because it complicated the deterrent calculations of the Soviet Union, who had to take heed of the decision-making of a separate government to the United States. This was seen to guard against any decline in the US nuclear guarantee ... Britain could act independently of the US should the situation demand it ... With French withdrawal from the military structure of NATO in 1966, British nuclear weapons came to be viewed as being held 'in trust' for Europe, just in case the Soviet Union perceived that the US might be reluctant to defend Europe."[16]

The emerging V-Force developed a capacity to go to war in two contexts: as part of the NATO war-fighting programme or in a unilateral UK retaliatory strike (the 'National Plan').

WORLD WAR 2'S LEGACY

The British airborne deterrent emerged in a logical way. Firstly, there was a strong national 'affiliation' to the strategic bomber. In the recent past Britain had made a major contribution to the destruction of Nazi Germany through the strategic bombing of cities and other targets. This campaign was pursued in a highly cost-effective manner, as outlined in 1947 by Marshal of the Royal Air Force Lord Tedder, when delivering the Lees Knowles lectures at Cambridge. Over 30 years later, Air Vice-Marshal Stewart Menaul commented:

> "He pointed out that, at the peak of the war, bomber operations took approximately 12 per cent of the direct war effort and averaged over the whole war only seven per cent. In addition to the devastating effects the bomber offensive had on Germany's war-making

capacity, contributing more than any other single factor to their inability to continue the war, Tedder emphasised that the battle for air superiority over Europe, prior to the landing of Allied forces on the Normandy beaches, was achieved not by fighters, but by bombers."[17]

This last observation might be contested by the pilots of P-51 Mustang long-range escort fighters, but it must be true that the huge American formations bombing Germany by day forced the Luftwaffe to commit its dwindling fighter resources, regardless of losses.

Tedder had said:

"I am utterly convinced that the outstanding and vital lesson of this last war is that air power is the dominant factor in this modern world and that, though the methods of exercising it will change, it will remain the dominant factor so long as power determines the fate of nations."

So it was to prove and ballistic missiles – in particular the submarine-launched ballistic missile (SLBM) – became dominant. Tedder's words, however, were delivered at a time when Britain had an extraordinarily advanced and creative aircraft industry, well placed to provide advanced jet bombers to carry the British bomb.

THE ANGLO-AMERICAN RELATIONSHIP

Other factors surrounding the development of the British nuclear deterrent included the extraordinarily close wartime relationship between the RAF and what was then the USAAF (later, the USAF). These ties were strong enough to survive a distinct chill on the political front in the immediate post-war years, when the United States was the sole possessor (albeit briefly) of nuclear weapons. Sir Frank Cooper, a wartime RAF pilot who joined the Air Ministry in 1948 and rose to become Permanent Under-Secretary of State for Defence by the mid-1970s, wrote of this period:

"… the United States adopted a firm policy that it would have a monopoly of nuclear weapons on behalf of the Allies … Strongly held American reservations about Britain becoming a nuclear power were to dog Anglo-American relations for some years to come. In Britain, there was a unity of purpose and determination to build an atomic energy plant with or without American assistance. The only issue therefore was whether the United States would help and so bring the date of acquisition forward. It was to be some long years before full cooperation was restored. Hence Britain had to evolve its own nuclear policy, largely through the Royal Air Force. There is clear evidence that the Air Force wanted to enter the nuclear world in a practical sense as soon as possible and I suggest that it played a major part in developing the theory of deterrence."[18]

THE B-29S ARRIVE IN BRITAIN

It wasn't long before USAF B-29s arrived in Britain. Over two days in mid-July 1948, at the invitation of PM Clement Atlee, 60 B-29s landed at British bases for what was first envisaged as a 30-day training deployment. There was no formal Anglo-American agreement yet Scampton, Marham, Waddington and Lakenheath hosted the six USAF heavy bomber squadrons.[19]

Before these aircraft had actually reached England, their stay was extended to 60 days as part of the Western Allies' response to the Soviet ground blockade of West Berlin. Sixty days then became 90. During November the Air Ministry told Washington that long term use of UK RAF bases by USAF aircraft was 'assumed'. The two governments reached an agreement to this effect.[20] It is easy to understand British eagerness to provide forward bases for American strategic bombers. This meant direct shelter under the American nuclear umbrella. The provision of B-29s for RAF squadrons could be regarded as a *quid pro quo* for use of UK air bases. It drew the two governments together at a time when the US desire for continued nuclear monopoly tended to push them apart in the political context. Naturally, the presence of thousands of American servicemen in Britain made it more difficult to isolate the USA from its European allies and, of course, it was impossible to attack Britain without destroying American personnel and assets.

During the first half of 1949 the USAF regularly rotated heavy bomber units to UK bases for 90-day tours. The aircraft were held on six-hour alert but this was relaxed in May of that year, when the Soviets lifted the Berlin blockade. In August 1949, the detonation of a Soviet atomic bomb signalled new realities. In the UK, the USAF relocated their bombers away from the British east coast, eventually leading to the occupation of Brize Norton, Fairford, Upper Heyford and Greenham Common. Then the outbreak of the Korean War in June 1950 led to a rapid expansion of USAF strength in the UK, facilitated by earlier decisions. During a September 1949 conference in Washington, it was agreed to open up 30 British bases to the USAF: the four main bomber bases, three 'air depots' and 23 other airfields for use by heavy and medium bombers, fighter escorts, reconnaissance aircraft and tankers.[21]

By 1951 the USAF had two main elements in Britain: the B-29s of 7th Air Division and the Third Air Force (responsible for tactical operations and logistics). The American presence continued to grow. By 1955 the USAF occupied around 80 UK installations. The heavy bomber units were upgraded to B-36 and B-47 squadrons. There were some 400 American aircraft and 82,000 USAF personnel and dependants permanently stationed in the UK, but the Eisenhower administration then sought to cut the overseas military spend, leading to a reduction in USAF strength in Britain.[22]

Despite the close relationship between the RAF and the USAF, the UK government did not lose sight of the powerful arguments for a British nuclear deterrent. Indeed, these arguments grew stronger as the Soviet thermonuclear threat to the Continental USA increased, making it less certain that Washington would intervene in a European conflict – especially if this began with conventional warfare only.[23]

Churchill presented these arguments in the House of Commons on 1 March 1955:

> "Unless we make a contribution of our own … we cannot be sure that in an emergency the resources of other powers would be planned exactly as we would wish, or that the targets which would threaten us most would be given what we consider the necessary priority, or the deserved priority, in the first few hours. These targets might be of such cardinal importance that it would really be a matter of life and death for us."[24]

A couple of months later, in June, the Chiefs of Staff (COS) cautioned that it would be "strategically unacceptable" to rely entirely on the United States to provide the deterrent.[25]

2
SPECIAL WEAPONS

> ❝ ... *Safety will be the sturdy child of terror and survival the twin brother of annihilation.* ❞
>
> Sir Winston Churchill, 1955

British scientists had earlier exerted much influence on early developmental work which had ended in the atomic bombings of 1945. This was acknowledged by Vannevar Bush, who had chaired the US National Defense Research Committee. Referring to the July 1941 report from the British MAUD Committee, concerning the feasibility of a uranium bomb, he said:

"There were a number of reports from the Academy of Science about an atom bomb but it was the British report that really made everybody feel that, after all, it probably could be done. Of course, we way underestimated the time and money that would be required. But the first real conviction that the job could be done came from the British report."[26]

The United States enjoyed a short-lived atomic monopoly in the immediate post-war years. The British were denied American assistance in building their bomb; America's closest

A huge bomb: Blue Danube – Britain's first atomic weapon, 24 ft 2 in long and 5 ft 2 in in diameter. The fins extended after release, allowing it to be accommodated in V-bomber bomb bays. (Andy Leitch Collection)

wartime ally was left to begin that formidable task alone. Yet, despite the many difficulties, the British succeeded in developing a family of atomic weapons for delivery by manned aircraft.

These weapons were freefall, with the exception of Blue Steel Mk 1, the 'powered bomb'. Blue Danube, 16 kilotons (kt), was the UK's first nuclear weapon. Miniaturising designs led to Red Beard, a tactical bomb (10–15 kt). After the Grapple trials, pressure for the early introduction of megaton (mt)-class weapons led to five Green Grass large fission warheads used in Blue Danube carcasses, creating an 'interim' weapon, Violet Club – pending production of the intended Blue Danube successor weapon, Yellow Sun 1. Green Grass (500 kt) was later downrated to 400 kt. Yellow Sun Mk 1, the RAF's first practical high yield weapon, was safer. Its successor, Yellow Sun Mk 2, was a true megaton weapon (1.1 mt).

During the 1960s, the V-Force had two principal strategic freefall weapons: Yellow Sun 2 and its long-lived successor, the WE.177B laydown bomb (450 kt). In addition, 40 V-bombers (five squadrons) carried Blue Steel (1.1 mt), whilst 24 Valiants (three squadrons), assigned as the Tactical Bombing Force (TBF) to the Supreme Allied Commander, Europe (SACEUR), carried American Project E weapons, including the B43 laydown bomb.

By the end of 1958, around 58 Blue Danube bombs and five Violet Clubs were available. American E weapons were required as the production of V-bombers outpaced the availability of British weapons. The stockpile increased to around 200 British-made weapons by late-1961.[27]

A decade before, in 1952, Air Marshal Sir Hugh Lloyd, then Air Officer Commanding-in-Chief (AOC-in-C) Bomber Command, wrote: "We've got to get away from this freefalling bomb business as quickly as possible." It was assumed the future V-Force would be armed entirely with stand-off weapons, allowing the bombers to stay outside defended airspace. Yet, 30 years on, at the end of WE.177's greatly extended operational life, the remaining Vulcans were still armed with freefall bombs! Indeed, British fast jets with a nuclear-strike role continued to carry these freefall weapons until the late 1990s. Yet, ironically, British innovation in advanced weapon design had been outstanding during the early post-war years. One example, Blue Boar, was conceived in 1946–47 and, in one variant, was a potential Blue Danube successor. Vickers-Armstrong won a contract for Blue Boar in mid-1950, but this TV-guided stand-off weapon, with a 25NM range, was cancelled in June 1954. The technology of the day was unable to support this all-weather, day or night weapon; difficulties with its command-and-control system could not be overcome.[28]

Avro and other companies produced many advanced concepts for powered weapons, supersonic delivery systems and even designs featuring vertical take-off and landing (VTOL) – which, certainly, would have offered a novel solution to bomber dispersal. Avro proposed a jump-jet Vulcan, the Type 769, armed with the American Skybolt air-launched ballistic missile (ALBM) and with its bomb bay filled with ten lift engines! Barnes Wallis' contributions included a concept for a Mach 4.5 bomber operating at over 90,000 ft – a weapon system suitable for dispersal throughout the Commonwealth.[29]

Early freefall nuclear weapons were relatively unsophisticated; some required last-minute loading (LML) of cores. In addition, the lack of a British freefall weapon for low-level release, at least until late 1966, exposed bombers to SAM defences. As for the stand-off bomb, Blue Steel Mk 1 disappointed. It was liquid-fuelled, difficult to generate, unreliable and required dangerous high test peroxide (HTP). Blue Steel lacked the attributes of a weapon suitable for a rapid response operational environment. What the V-Force needed, from 1963 onwards, was an advanced, solid-fuelled, reliable stand-off weapon with a range of at least 1,000NM. However, long-range Blue Steel Mk 2 was cancelled, as was Skybolt, leaving the five Blue Steel Mk 1 squadrons with a weapon offering only 50 miles range at best when launched at low level.

A VERY BRITISH BOMB ...

Fort Halstead, Kent, and William Penney, Chief Superintendent of Armaments Research, played central roles in delivering the British bomb. Fort Halstead was the initial base for the so-called High Explosives Research Team, charged with building an atomic weapon.[30]

William Penney had contributed to work on the atomic bomb in the United States during the war years. He became indispensable to the British programme when the McMahon Act blocked the sharing of US nuclear information. His team began work on developing a sphere of conventional explosive capable of acting on a plutonium core to trigger a nuclear explosion. Work was also undertaken at the Royal Arsenal, Woolwich, and at Foulness, Essex. Fort Halstead's contributions included the electronic detonators for simultaneous detonation of the bomb's 32 explosive lenses. Klaus Fuchs, head of the Theoretical Physics Division at the Atomic Energy Research Establishment, Harwell, regularly visited Fort Halstead until his exposure as a Soviet spy in 1950.[31] Thanks to Fuchs and others of his kind, the first Soviet bomb detonated on 29 August 1949, far earlier than anticipated in the West.

Britain's first atomic device was packed within the redundant frigate HMS *Plym*. In Operation Hurricane, this was detonated in the Montebello Islands, off the West Australian coast, on 3 October 1952. More devices were then tested (Operation Totem). These were tower detonations on the Australian mainland, in the Great Victoria Desert (October 1953). At this time, the UK government made a request to the Australian government for a permanent test facility and the outcome was the use of Maralinga site, in the Woomera Prohibited Area, South Australia. It was agreed that no fusion weapons would be tested on Australian soil. Following the Operation Mosaic tower test series in May/June 1956 at Montebello, Operation Buffalo involved four tests at Maralinga, including tower, surface and airdrop detonations. The last in the series (September/October 1956) was the first Valiant airdrop of Blue Danube, on 11 October.[32]

BLUE DANUBE AND THE NUCLEAR RAINBOW

Operational Requirement OR.1001, for Blue Danube, the first British atomic weapon, was issued on 9 August 1946. On the first day of that year the Chiefs of Staff had told Prime Minister Atlee that Britain needed "hundreds, rather than scores" of atomic bombs.[33] On 30 July 1947, the Defence Research Policy Committee defined a 'useful deterrent' as a stock of around 1,000 bombs.[34]

Blue Danube was a start. The first live drop in October 1956 released a huge bomb – just over 24 ft long, with a maximum width of 62 inches. Over half its weight consisted of 2½ tons of conventional high explosive. The weapon's six elements each presented distinct problems in development and manufacture: the ballistic casing, the suspension system for the physics

Operation Grapple: Vulcan nav/radar Roy Brocklebank's uncle, Ted Dunne (far left), flew in 49 Squadron Valiant XD822 (captained by Squadron Leader D. Roberts), which made a weapon drop on 31 May 1957. The weapon was Orange Herald with a yield of 720 kt. (Roy Brocklebank)

package, fuses, firing mechanism and detonators, the physics package itself – high explosive outer shell and tamper, core and 'Urchin' (the Polonium 210 initiator) – and, finally, procedures and facilities for handling and storage.[35]

Handling and storage required close attention, to avoid any incident or temperature fluctuations which might crack the high explosive lenses. For normal storage, the temperature range was between 30°C and 12°C, with the rate of change not exceeding 4°C per hour (maximum allowable humidity, 75%). When on the aircraft, the Atomic Weapons Research Establishment (AWRE) required that the total temperature variation over the whole period should not exceed 50°C, the rate of temperature change should not exceed 4°C per hour and the maximum temperature around the weapon should not exceed 25°C above that of the mean temperature of the weapon over the previous seven days or 50°C, whichever is the lesser. AWRE advised that a minimum of -12°C could be tolerated if necessary, but that any simple precautions available to keep this minimum at 0°C should be taken. In short, blankets might be useful to protect weapons.[36]

Blue Danube required LML, with the nav/radar inserting the cartridge from below, making it live just before take-off. Another form of loading, getting this gigantic weapon into the bomb bay, was a challenge. It was even more difficult on a surface not perfectly level. A study concluded that the limits for a hardstanding "should be one degree laterally and 2½ degrees fore and aft".[37] All future hardstandings would be made as level as possible.

Commercial firms, big and small, contributed to Blue Danube and many had no idea of end-use. For example, the bomb's explosive sphere required cushioning by 32 butyl rubber airbags, matching each explosive lens. William Freeman of Barnsley made the airbags, a departure from their usual business – producing hot water bottles. Jonathan Aylen commented:

> "Blue Danube was founded on local knowledge and pragmatic solutions ... Development work was distributed widely. The weapon system was built on the back streets of northern towns, such as Leeds, Barnsley and Mansfield, and in the southern suburbs, such as Ilford, Weybridge and Shoreham, as much as the more familiar sites of Woolwich, Aldermaston and Burghfield."[38]

On 1 November 1952 the Americans detonated their first thermonuclear device. On 16 June 1954 the UK government authorised the production of thermonuclear weapons (announced in the 1955 White Paper on Defence). At the end of that year, the Defence Research Policy

Committee concluded: "The earliest possible achievement of a megaton explosion is necessary to demonstrate our ability to make such weapons, as part of the strategic deterrent against war."[39] The first Soviet hydrogen bomb was tested in November 1955.

Planning for British megaton weapon trials in the Pacific began in 1955, with tests during 1957–58. The British were under pressure to demonstrate a true thermonuclear device before a moratorium of nuclear testing took effect. Valiants of 49 Squadron used Christmas Island as a base, dropping weapons off Malden Island, 400 miles to the south. On 15 May 1957, Valiant XD818 dropped the first British thermonuclear device, Short Granite, housed in a Blue Danube casing. Vulcan nav/radar Roy Brocklebank's uncle, Flight Lieutenant Ted Dunne, was nav/radar in Valiant XD822, which made the second drop on 31 May.[40] In a letter home, dated 7 June 1957, Dunne wrote:

> "… afterwards we turned around to view the cloud towering above us and it looked strangely beautiful in a repulsive sort of way … it wasn't difficult to visualise what the effect would be if one was exploded over the centre of London."

This drop involved a 'small' lightweight Orange Herald warhead, a boosted fission device with a yield of 720 kt. There was a third drop on 19 June. More tests were required – the Antler series at Maralinga and then the final Grapple series: Grapple X (November 1957), Grapple Y (April 1958) and, finally, Grapple Z (September 1958), a series including airdrops with yields in the 2.5/3 mt range.[41] The final Grapple series was conducted on Christmas Island itself, rather than Malden Island. The Grapple tests involved large fission and thermonuclear variants. More thermonuclear design work was found to be required.

Grapple Valiants were finished in anti-flash white, capable of withstanding 72 calories of heat energy per square centimetre. Control surfaces were strengthened, to withstand the weapon's pressure wave. The flight deck and bomb-aiming positions were fitted with anti-flash screens and various cameras and sensors installed.[42]

Of the three V-bomber types, only the Valiant was to drop live nuclear weapons. John Muston, a 49 Squadron nav/radar, dropped the final Grapple hydrogen bomb on 11 September 1958. He remembers Christmas Island as most unattractive – covered with landcrabs and the air full of flies. He had no visual aiming point but, rather, dropped at the end of a timed run from a point on land. It was essential to maintain track and speed:

> "Following the drop we turned 135 degrees, onto our escape heading. We had just levelled out when the bomb went off. We were tail-on to it. We photographed the view from the back.

Awesome: the mushroom cloud rises after John Muston dropped the final Grapple hydrogen bomb on 11 September 1958. (John Muston)

The mushroom cloud reached 60,000 ft, with a column of seawater sucked up to the detonation altitude of 8,000 ft. We had the blinds down, with the pilots flying on instruments."[43]

Muston sought the 'target' visually, rather than on radar, due to a communications breakdown:

"I dropped the weapon in the prone position, from the visual bomb-aiming station. Immediately upon release, I had to scramble out of the nose, return to my seat and strap in before detonation. When the bomb went, I said: 'Bomb away.' I could see it falling – a big black thing. I saw the flash come in around the edges of the blinds. I didn't shut down the electrics. As for the shock wave, I knew what to expect, as we had flown as 'Grandstand' aircraft on previous drops. When it hit you, it felt just like dropping a floor in a lift. There was no great turbulence. A second shock wave reached us eight seconds later, from the blast reflected off the sea. When 40 miles away, we turned and had a good look. I was surprised at the sheer size of the cloud. I wasn't nervous at the time but I sometimes dream of it. The cloud looks just as it did in reality – awesome."

Later, Muston developed concerns about contamination, having married and started a family:

"I was asked to join the Nuclear Veterans' Association. Over the years, some of the grandchildren of the servicemen who took part in the tests were born with defects, such as extra fingers. However, I think the men on the ground were in more danger than those in the air. Today, most of my 49 Squadron comrades have gone – there are only three or four left. I am the sole survivor of the seven nav/radars who dropped the Grapple weapons."

At least one individual was deeply troubled by what he witnessed during Grapple, as remembered by Group Captain Ken Hubbard, commanding 49 Squadron at that time. Following a live drop and subsequent return to the UK, a Valiant captain told Hubbard that his air electronics officer (AEO) had problems with involvement in nuclear weapons. Hubbard interviewed the AEO and told him that his captain knew he held extreme views on the use of nuclear weapons and that he was also involved in the 'Moral Rearmament' organisation:

"I then allowed him to expand on his own views, which, quite obviously, were contrary to the concept of a nuclear deterrent force and indeed extreme to the point of being subversive. Such views were completely unacceptable in any Royal Air Force officer and certainly there was no room for them in the V-Force, particularly in 49 Squadron, with our special task. I was extremely surprised to think that a man with these views could have come through a positive vetting and had no intention of allowing him to taint any of my crews. Having told him that his attitude and beliefs were completely unacceptable, he was suspended from duty and instructed to report back to the Mess and stay away from the squadron until his future was resolved."[44]

This man left RAF Wittering the next day. Hubbard said that he never came across another such case.

THE WEAPONS

Blue Danube, deceptively known as 'Bomb, Aircraft, HE, 10,000 lbs, MC', was first assembled in 1953. No aircraft could carry it until April 1954, when 1321 Flight was formed to integrate Valiant and weapon.[45] Five Blue Danube bombs were available that year, increasing to ten in 1955, 50 in 1956 and 58 in 1957 (when the UK stockpile totalled 928 kt).[46] Blue Danube cost around £500,000 per round and remained operational until 1962.

This bomb was handcrafted, as described by nuclear weapons historian Mike Fazackerley, a former RAF Canberra pilot:

> "Blue Danube can hardly be described as a weapon. It was more a collection of laboratory experiments. Every example was built individually and each completed bomb differed from the next. Blue Danube was very difficult to prepare for a mission and, almost certainly, would have proved quite unreliable to use."[47]

Once armed, Blue Danube had four separate triggers: a primary radar detonation system, barostatic and timer back-ups and, finally, inertia switches to detonate on impact. The barostatic and timer systems were used to overcome radar jamming.[48] Aircrew and ground crew alike referred to Blue Danube as 'The Beast'. Lyle Lark was a member of the ground crew team: "Well, it certainly was a 'beast'. It was huge and seemed to fill the entire bomb bay – which was a massive space. The loading regime involved rigging shrouds around the aircraft during the bombing up."[49]

Violet Club was a step change. This interim megaton weapon consisted of a Green Grass 400-kt fission warhead in a Blue Danube casing. Richard Moore commented on safety issues

Terrifying: Violet Club – the interim megaton weapon. This was a Green Grass fission physics package in a modified Blue Danube casing. (Andy Leitch Collection)

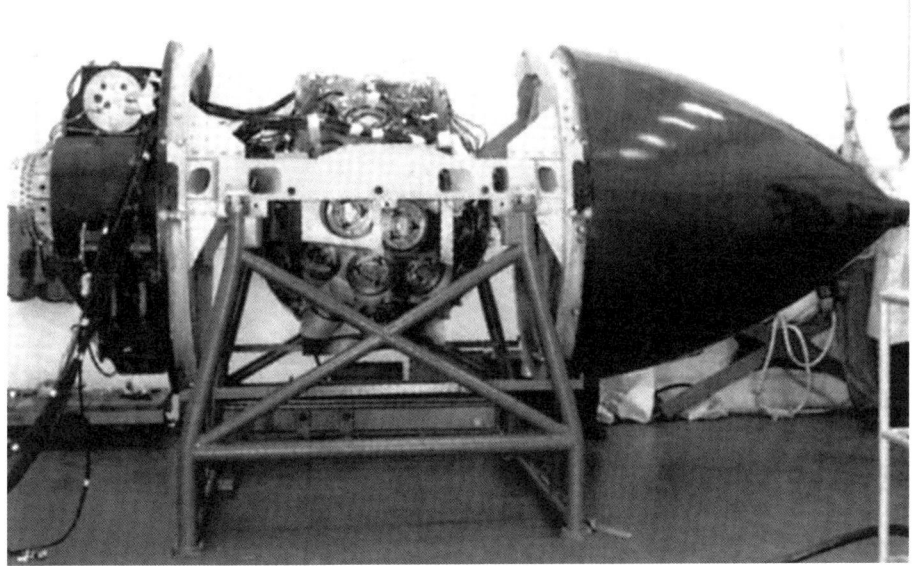

surrounding this large fission weapon and its substantial amount of highly enriched uranium. There was a danger of "super-criticality in the event of an accidental deformation of the warhead".[50]

Violet Club was proposed in August 1956 as a first response to Operational Requirement OR.1136, when it was thought that one of the Grapple warheads could be available before Yellow Sun Mk 1, Blue Danube's intended high yield successor. The first Violet Club reached the RAF in March 1958; five were delivered and by the end of the year a few more may have been assembled, but production then ended in favour of Yellow Sun Mk 1. Violet Club was withdrawn in 1959.[51] Mike Fazackerley described Violet Club as "an improvement of sorts, but it wasn't much better than Blue Danube, with the exception of its much larger yield. Blue Danube and Violet Club demonstrated the importance of what the Americans call 'productionising'."[52]

Those in the know regarded five Violet Clubs as five too many. The evidence suggests that virtually everyone was terrified of this weapon. In a tour de force of British understatement, the DCAS minuted the CAS on 3 March 1958, describing Violet Club as "rather delicate". The Assistant Chief of the Air Staff (ACAS) had written to Bomber Command's AOC-in-C a few days before, commenting that Violet Club was "still in some degree experimental and … subject to a number of serious handling restrictions". It had to be assembled by AWRE personnel on the station from which it would be used; road transport was limited to that required to move it from assembly point to storage building. The integrity of its large hollow sphere of highly enriched uranium, surrounded by a high explosive implosion system, was defended by a filling of 20,000 steel ball-bearings, which increased bomb weight to 11,250 lbs. According to Chris Gibson this exceeded the limit of the Vulcan's bomb release mechanism and so ruled out flight with the safety device in place. There were many associated problems: "Even ground-running of engines was frowned upon … for fear that the bung would fall out, followed closely by 20,000 steel balls." A war sortie with this weapon would require the bung to be removed, allowing the ball-bearings to 'drain' before take-off – which took half an hour at best. The ball-bearings had the unpleasant habit of sticking to the rubber liner within the sphere. Cold weather caused the ball-bearings to freeze together, rendering the weapon useless.[53] Nevertheless, these risks were accepted in order to achieve a 'megaton' capability a few months earlier than might otherwise have been the case.[54]

Mike Fazackerley regards Yellow Sun Mk 1 as the RAF's first practical nuclear weapon: "It represented a big advance in operability, although it still took a lot of time and effort to generate for an operation."[55] Yellow Sun Mk 1 entered the stockpile in 1958 and was withdrawn in 1963. This 7,000 lbs, 400 kt weapon was carried by Vulcan and Victor Mk 1/Mk 1A aircraft.[56] Yellow Sun Mk 1 was a full response to OR.1136 (issued in June 1955, with subsequent issues in 1957 and 1959). The British stockpile included 37 Yellow Sun Mk 1 weapons by 1961.[57]

Whilst a big advance, Yellow Sun Mk 1 also had the risks associated with a large fissile shell surrounded by a sphere of high explosive: the Green Grass physics package – again protected by a filling of ball bearings. This was confirmed by Air Commodore Owen Truelove at an RAF Historical Society meeting in 2001. He recalled a test of mathematical ability and patience: "Yellow Sun Mk 1 had 6,500 ball bearings in it. I know because I dropped them all over the hangar floor and had to personally count every one back in!"[58] Yellow Sun Mk 1 cost £1.2

million per round.⁵⁹ Wing targeting officer Roy Brocklebank adds: "It was necessary to use a Puddling Stick to tamp the balls in. This was a Section 76Z item and therefore a piece of secret equipment. I was told it was actually a broom handle…"

The ball-bearing filling, known rather grandly as the Nuclear Safety Device, prevented a Green Grass collapse and ensuing nuclear detonation. An appendix to an Air Ministry letter of 26 July 1960 gave a stern warning:

> "With the Nuclear Safety Device removed, accidental detonation of the high explosive may result in a nuclear yield approaching the standard yield of the weapon. The Nuclear Safety Device is not, therefore, to be removed except as the final act of weapon preparation, when there is a clear intention to take off on an operational sortie, or when there is a clear indication that such a possibility is imminent."⁶⁰

There was another device (known as the Bar, Insertion) which provided a 'transitional state' of warhead safety, but the appendix warned that "on no account" was it to be regarded as an alternative to the steel balls filling. On a last, cheery note, it concluded: "If the nuclear assembly were crushed, melted or fragments of a broken assembly were collected together, a transient super-critical state might result. Under such conditions, the radiation dose could be lethal within a radius of 30 yards." Care was also required to respect separation distances between warheads. The rule stipulated only one warhead and cartridge per building – with no other fissile material in that space.

Red Beard, a compact tactical weapon, was known (misleadingly) as the Target Marker Bomb. Its warhead was similar to Blue Danube's but much smaller and lighter. There were two marks: the Mk 1 at 15 kt and the Mk 2 at 25 kt. Within the marks there were two types: No. 1, for high altitude delivery by V-bombers and Canberras, and No. 2, for low-altitude bombing system (LABS) delivery by the Buccaneer and similar aircraft. Red Beard entered service in

Red Beard, a tactical atomic bomb for the RAF and Royal Navy. This weapon was 13 ft long and 2.5 ft in diameter. Redesign of the high explosive lenses produced a much smaller physics package than that of Blue Danube. (Andy Leitch Collection)

1962 and continued until superseded by WE.177 tactical variants. Red Beard attracted some radical ideas – including a nuclear Highball, a mid-1950s concept encasing a physics package in a 'bouncing bomb'![61]

Red Beard was still in service in the late 1960s. Peter Moore recalls his arrival at Waddington; he became a 44 (Rhodesia) Squadron co-pilot in mid-1969 (post Quick Reaction Alert [QRA]). He joined an experienced crew of QRA veterans. Moore remembers training procedures for Red Beard tactical weapons:

> "Practising last-minute loading was often amusing. The lead shields that contained the practice plutonium charge had been in use for some time and were showing signs of wear. We were required to practice LML on a regular basis, using a dummy … On one occasion I recall the nav/radar walking over to the lead container (accompanied by another crew member, for the two-man principle); there was a loud clang as the 'plutonium' charge fell out of its case onto the concrete."[62]

Undoubtedly, the tactical variants of WE.177, the successors to Red Beard, were a great improvement.

Yellow Sun Mk 2 was a major advance on Yellow Sun Mk 1. The initial order provided for 24 Yellow Sun Mk 2s, with the 1.1 mt Red Snow physics package, at £500,000 each.[63] Yellow Sun Mk 2 was the principal British freefall weapon from 1961 to early 1967. Red Snow, a modified version of the B28 warhead developed for the American Hound Dog air-launched missile, was a true fusion weapon. Yellow Sun Mk 2 was carried by Vulcans and Victors, until replaced by the WE.177B laydown bomb from late 1966. According to Robert S. Norris and Hans M. Kristensen in that year the British stockpile consisted of 110 Red Beard tactical weapons, 35 Red Beard naval weapons, 86 Yellow Sun Mk 2 thermonuclear bombs, 40 Blue Steel weapons (also with Red Snow warheads) and ten WE.177 bombs.[64]

Mike Fazackerley noted that Yellow Sun Mk 2 "represented a much bigger advance in weapons technology, having benefitted from American expertise in miniaturisation."[65] Its Achilles heel was that it needed an altitude of around 11,000 ft for release, a requirement incompatible with the V-Force's low-level war mission, introduced during 1963–65 following Skybolt's cancellation. Low-flying freefall aircraft carrying Yellow Sun Mk 2 had to 'pop up' into the SAM kill zone to release.

STORAGE, HANDLING AND TRANSPORT

Special weapons required special procedures for storage, handling, transport and loading. Specified separation distances between weapons had to be maintained. Red Beard's minimum separation was 155 ft, whilst aircraft loaded with Yellow Sun Mk 2 had to be at least 150 ft apart.[66] Crews played their part in the ground-safety regime. Roy Brocklebank recalls the procedures followed before a crew boarded. The captain would walk round and make his inspection and the nav/radar and nav/plotter would attend the weapon in the bomb bay:

> "There was a checklist for Yellow Sun. This included a check that the turbine inlet holes were unobstructed and a look at the weapon-control panel. We opened the panel to

check that the ground-impact isolation switch wasn't isolated, as we were going for a groundburst. We would examine the nose for any cracks and check the bomb casing and tail fins for dents or other damage. We also ensured all plugs and sockets were in. Throughout my V-Force operational flying, I never found anything amiss when checking the weapon. They were always in excellent condition."[67]

Despite their awesome power, life with nuclear weapons did have occasional amusing interludes, as illustrated by Valiant co-pilot Dick Fuller:

"I recall the occasion when we had a weather diversion to RAF Valley, in Wales. On landing, we opened the bomb-bay doors, exposing the interior. A curious airman came up and asked what we had on board. I said: 'A nuclear bomb.' He promptly took off at full speed."[68]

In the case of early weapons, the radioactive components were kept apart until the LML procedure, but the Green Grass warhead of Yellow Sun Mk 1 and the later Red Snow for Yellow Sun Mk 2's warhead included high explosive and radioactive material at all times. Bomber Command Armament School (BCAS) engineering officer Michael Hely noted: "This had clear implications for nuclear safety, particularly in storage. You could not, for instance, store two Yellow Suns in the same room ..."[69]

The weapons were held in special storage facilities at depots and airfields, known as Supplementary Storage Areas (SSAs), and a set of strict procedures was developed to govern storage, handling, transport and loading. Weapons were moved around by armed convoys. Storage facilities were built at RAF Barnham, Suffolk, and RAF Faldingworth, Lincolnshire, within Maintenance Command. The latter had a cover story changing its activities to that of a 'gas bottling plant'.[70] Barnham, (a World War 2 ammunition depot, completely rebuilt) had separate domestic and special weapons areas. The nuclear weapons area was known as Top Site. Air Commodore Mike Allisstone arrived at Barnham in April 1960, after a one-week nuclear weapons course at Wittering. He described Top Site, with its two high barbed-wire security fences with electric sliding gates, an inner solid barrier and three 'Goon Towers'. There were armed guards and RAF Police dogs. This part of the complex was floodlit at night. Naturally, there was plenty of local speculation over the purpose of the site: "... locally rumoured to be breeding chimpanzees for a non-existent but convenient UK space programme." Leading off from a

Hidden from prying eyes: fissile core stores at RAF Wittering, with roofs designed to give the appearance of trees – to confuse any Aeroflot flight 'accidentally' straying off route. (Roy Brocklebank)

circular, one-way road inside Barnham's wire, there were three very large storage sheds for weapons and over 50 small huts, each housing a nuclear core – kept securely underground under double locks.[71]

The combination of explosives and radioactives dictated the site layout. Barnham's inner compound, the 'danger area', housed the three storage sheds for the casings and explosives. Four sets of 'igloos' – the individual plutonium core stores (57 in all) – were distributed around the site. Between the outer fences and the secure area's inner concrete panel barrier was a 'free fire' zone patrolled by armed guards. The 'igloo' core stores were shelters 2 m high, fitted with doors, remote alarms, secure door locking and a circular stainless-steel locked safe fitted into the floor. The cores were light enough to be manually handled. The bomb casings, however, required road access and mechanical handling. The casings contained high explosive and were lined with uranium tampers. They were held in the three air-conditioned sheds, surrounded by earth banks. The bombs were stored in a fishbone pattern on trailers, ready to move in the event of fire.[72]

The two-man principle applied: there were always two RAF personnel in charge of handling or releasing a nuclear core. Movements were precise, to maintain separation distance between cores. To release a core from storage required an 'equipper', with the igloo combination, and an 'engineer', with the key to the safe's padlock. They would then walk the core to a load carrier.[73] Each core was kept inside a drum lined with heavy metal. The RAF medics listed those who handled cores as 'radiation workers'.[74] They wore radiation exposure tickets.

The Bomber Command Armament School, established in 1953 at RAF Wittering, introduced Blue Danube and later weapons into service. Its curriculum included convoy safety courses for weapon movements by road. BCAS engineering officer Michael Hely: "Movement of the Green Grass and Red Snow warheads, which incorporated both their conventional explosive and radioactive elements, called for a very high level of safety training."[75] From 1962 onwards, BCAS functioned as a standardisation unit, sending teams to Bomber Command stations in the UK, Germany and elsewhere, to foster high standards in storage, handling and transport of nuclear weapons.

The nuclear weapons convoy commander had a lonely job. Mike Allisstone became a young convoy commander at Barnham:

"… which involved sitting for hours at a time in a modified Morris J2 van with local radio communications, in charge of several six-wheeled Leyland Hippo load carriers and a posse of RAF Police motorcyclists, plus a specially designed fire/technical safety vehicle with an RAF armaments specialist aboard. We plied our trade between, on the 'wholesale' side, No. 94 Maintenance Unit (RAF Barnham) and various Royal Ordnance factories, especially Burghfield, near Reading, the Atomic Weapons Research Establishment at Aldermaston and sundry other suppliers, manufacturers of tail units, etc. some of which went to quite unusual lengths to disguise what they actually did, including operating out of semi-derelict premises, Nissen huts, etc. Our 'retail' operations took us out from the depot to the Supplementary Storage Areas at V-Force stations such as Honington, Wittering and Cottesmore in what was, for us, the south of England, because a sister depot, No. 92 MU (RAF Faldingworth) near Lincoln, tended to deal with V-Force stations in the north. Most stocks of RAF nuclear weapons were held forward in the SSAs and were rotated through the depots for periodic servicing; depot stocks could, we understood, be used for second-strike sorties. I remember hoping that we would be able to get these weapons forward to the frontline airfields and depart again before they became the subject of further attention by Soviet forces, although how long I expected to survive thereafter scarcely entered my head."[76]

On occasion, Allisstone struggled to comprehend his role in a second strike: "… try as I might, I could not imagine the environment I'd be working in – driving through a devastated countryside, trying to find an airfield."[77]

Each weapon's location was controlled by the Air Ministry's E18 Branch, which dealt directly with each depot. Removable cores were transported separately from weapons, to prevent hijackers seizing a viable weapon. There were few motorways in those days – weapons convoys threaded their way through towns. Convoys pulled over if a thunderstorm threatened, but Allisstone was beaten to it on one occasion:

"… one exceptionally vivid flash hit a lamp post right alongside one of the still mobile Hippos just ahead of me, followed immediately by the biggest thunderclap I have ever encountered. The load carrier swerved into the middle of the road and stopped almost dead in its tracks …"

The RAF Police closed the road as Allisstone leapt out and went to the Hippo:

"… the driver was sitting transfixed and completely dumbstruck. We lifted him out of the cab, stiff as a board and still in the sitting position … having seen the flash and heard the enormous explosion just to his rear, he was convinced that the load he was carrying had blown up and that he was dead!"

When Allisstone was promoted to flight lieutenant he became Barnham's stock control officer. As such, he was also responsible for Broken Arrow incident-reporting between road convoys and No. 10 Downing Street. He had occasion to use the link: "… one of our Hippos experienced a runaway engine at the top of a hill on the outskirts of Reading." The cab was abandoned and the now driverless, laden Hippo plunged down the hill and buried itself in the front room of a terraced house at the bottom.

As Allisstone describes:

"Fortunately, the sole elderly occupant was in the back kitchen at the time, from which she emerged, dusty but unhurt, to offer everyone a cup of tea. The only national publicity was a small headline in one tabloid: 'The secret something in widow's parlour.'"

Allisstone's convoy commander on that occasion, Flight Lieutenant (later Wing Commander) Tony Howells, had to borrow change to complete his report, using a nearby public telephone. Allisstone then rang No. 10.

As in all human endeavours (and human nature being what it is), the movement of nuclear weapons always involves risk. Another, later example was a nuclear weapon incident in Germany, involving a containerised WE.177 bomb. This occurred on 2 May 1984. A Board of

Inquiry convened at RAF Brüggen the following day. A number of weapons had been flown to RAF Brüggen in a routine movement. They were placed on trolleys and towed by Land Rovers to an SSA. One weapon was not appropriately secured and slipped off when the carrier negotiated a 180-degree bend at slow speed. The container struck the road and the weapon sustained damage. It transpired that the SSA staff had been moving unsecured weapons on trolleys "as common practice for some considerable time".[78]

In the 1990s, during the final years of the RAF's nuclear capability, WE.177 nuclear weapons were housed away from prying eyes, in weapon storage vaults built into the floor of some Tornado hardened aircraft shelters. The last four WE.177 weapons left Marham's gate on 22 April 1998.[79]

THE NUCLEAR ARMOURY

An October 1964 note on nuclear weapons, from the MoD to the Cabinet Office, judged British nuclear capacity at that time as sufficient to destroy 20 Soviet cities. The MBF in autumn 1964 consisted of four squadrons of Victors (32 aircraft) and nine of Vulcans (72 bombers), with 40 of the 104 aircraft armed (or to be armed) with Blue Steel. There were also 48 Canberras in Germany and 24 Valiants in the UK assigned to SACEUR and armed with American weapons. Interestingly, this note also comments on the successor strategic nuclear force, as then envisaged: *five* submarines (rather than four), each with 16 Polaris A3 missiles. Five submarines would allow two boats on patrol and ready to fire at all times. The keels of the first two had been laid, with two more planned to be laid in 1965 and the fifth in 1966. The first was planned to be operational in June 1968, with the remainder following at six-monthly intervals. This note even referred to a *strategic nuclear role for TSR-2*, with two squadrons of this advanced strike aircraft assigned to NATO and "available, if required, with British high yield weapons, to supplement the strategic nuclear forces".

BCAS continued to train aircrew and ground crew in the storage, servicing and operation of nuclear weapons. Early on RAF Wittering had accommodated a stock of weapons, BCAS, an atomic weapons trials flight and 138 Squadron, the first Valiant unit.[80] As the years passed, each weapon type came to be remembered for different reasons. Yellow Sun Mk 2, the high yield freefall bomb, lacked elegance. BCAS Engineering Officer Michael Hely recalls its blunt nose; this slowed the fall of the weapon and provided a 'crumple zone', protecting the warhead from impact shock: "By keeping the weapon subsonic, the blunt nose also improved the reliability of the barometric fusing system – that was its primary purpose."[81]

LML also became safer and, eventually, this was dispensed with:

"For Blue Danube, a lump of plutonium on the end of a stick of explosive had to be inserted into the warhead – not a nice job on a cold dispersal with the imminent expectation of a four-minute warning of an incoming missile. Red Beard required the insertion of a lump of plutonium without the explosive, which was some improvement. Yellow Sun 1 was a uranium bomb, much nicer than plutonium but it still had the explosive attached. Red Snow and, as far as I know, all subsequent warheads came sealed, so no last-minute handling of fissile material or explosive was involved."

PROJECT E WEAPONS

British-built nuclear weapons were supplemented by American bombs. In December 1956 the CAS, Sir Dermot Boyle, received an offer of American Project E weapons, together with an invitation to coordinate strike plans.[82] Carriage of American weapons raised engineering challenges, involving the design and fit of modified carriers and wiring harnesses. The American weapons supplied included Mk 7 1,650 lbs variable-yield bombs, allocated to NATO-assigned RAF Canberras in Germany. Subsequently, 72 Mk 5 6,000 lbs bombs were also available to the V-Force until March 1962, when Victors and Vulcans ceased carrying E weapons in favour of Yellow Sun 2. The improved B28 1,900 lbs and B43 (laydown) 2,100 lbs bombs were carried by the NATO-assigned Valiants.[83]

E weapons were under dual control (in effect, American guardianship) and held only at certain RAF stations. American Mk 5 weapons first arrived at RAF Honington in September 1958, followed by RAF Waddington and RAF Marham in the final quarter.[84] NATO-assigned Valiants later received 48 B28/B43 weapons, available during the 1960–65 period. Subsequently, NATO Canberras (1965–72) and Phantoms (1972–76) in Germany carried these weapons.[85] Bryan 'Monty' Montgomery, a Valiant nav/plotter (1962–65), recalls that his squadron's American weapons required cores to be loaded on the ground: "We went on a course, to learn how to load them."[86]

Under US law, custodial officers had to "retain physical possession and custody of all US atomic weapons," with transfer to the RAF only on authority from the US Chiefs of Staff, through HQ, Strategic Air Command (SAC).[87] American insistence on dual control meant that E weapons were of limited value; the RAF had to accept obvious disadvantages concerning dispersal and readiness. Vulcan captain John Huggins commented:

> "Before my time, the V-Force could employ American weapons against SACEUR targets, but they could not be accessed readily. The RAF had to rely on an American officer with a key. If war came, it was said that the first job of the RAF duty officer was to shoot the American and grab the key. There would be no time to lose."[88]

These drawbacks and the growing availability of British weapons eventually led to the phase-out of V-Force Project E. However, the 24 TBF Valiants at Marham and assigned to SACEUR continued to carry E weapons until these aircraft were withdrawn from service in January 1965.[89]

3
POWERED BOMBS AND LAYDOWN BOMBS

> *It soon became apparent that more height would not future-proof the V-Force beyond 1960.*
>
> Chris Gibson, *Vulcan's Hammer*

The case for a powered bomb, allowing V-bombers to stay outside point defences, was recognised as early as 1946–47. Weapon launch outside defended airspace was an obvious option for extending V-Force life and early studies were undertaken at the Royal Aircraft Establishment. The goal was a weapon system delivering a thermonuclear warhead by a vehicle 'immune to interception'. The eventual outcome was Blue Steel Mk 1.[90]

Air Vice-Marshal Stewart Menaul described Blue Steel Mk 1 as probably one of the world's most advanced weapons of its time.[91] Chris Gibson, however, wrote that its development was so complex that: "the high technology of 1955 (had) become the old hat of 1963."[92] Blue Steel's speed exceeded Mach 2, with a high-altitude range of around 100NM (some sources claimed 150NM). The accuracy expectation at 150NM was 500 yards. There was a tendency to inflate Blue Steel's operational profile. Certainly, an aircrew recruitment advertisement in the September 1957 issue of *Royal Air Force Flying Review* (p. 30) made misleading claims: "The advent of the stand-off bomb (air-to-ground missile, for dispatch several hundred miles from a target) actually enhances the vital role of the Valiant and other V-bombers for many years to come." This gave a false picture by reference to "several hundred miles" and by portraying the Valiant as an operational Blue Steel carrier (this type's relationship with Blue Steel was confined to the role of carrier during trials). Furthermore, the word "enhances" is certainly open to challenge, given the negative operational experience that would surround Blue Steel.

Gently does it: a Vulcan receiving a Blue Steel stand-off bomb. (Norman Bonnor)

In any event, Blue Steel Mk 1's range at high altitude fell dramatically – to 50NM at best – when launched at low level. On the other hand, its inertial guidance could not be jammed. The Red Snow physics package utilised the American W28 thermonuclear warhead. Blue Steel Mk 1 entered the stockpile in 1962 and remained in service until 1969.[93] A decade after Blue Steel was retired, Air Vice-Marshal Menaul defended its value:

> "Its range, initially, was sufficient to enable the aircraft to stand well outside the SAM defences … but it was realised that it would not enjoy immunity indefinitely … Blue Steel was an interim weapon, leading logically to the air-launched ballistic missile (ALBM), and filled the gap admirably in the high-level role in the interim period."[94]

Unfortunately, the carriers would have to go to war at low level if they were to stand any chance of survival.

Blue Steel Mk 1's Operational Requirement (OR.1132) was issued on 3 September 1954 (only a few months after cancellation of the early concept TV-guided weapon Blue Boar). Blue Steel was expected – by the Air Ministry – to enter service in 1960 (but later, 1961–62, by the Ministry of Supply). With Blue Boar cancelled, Blue Steel was a fresh start.[95] Avro's Weapons Research Division received the development contract for this air-to-surface missile (ASM) from the Ministry of Supply in March 1956. Meanwhile, an Air Staff Target (AST 1140) concerned its planned successor, an advanced powered bomb with a range of up to 1,000NM. This emerged on 28 May 1958 as OR.1159, for the long-range Blue Steel Mk 2.[96]

Blue Steel Mk 1's production contract, placed on 15 December 1960, was for 75 missiles (subsequently reduced to 57). This order for W.105 operational rounds included five "backing rounds" and four proof rounds. An order for 16 W.103A training rounds was also placed. Blue Steel Mk 1 R&D costs virtually doubled within 24 months, from £35 million (October 1958) to £60 million (October 1960). Per round costs (exclusive of warhead) rose from £150,000 to £250,000.[97] The powered bomb was to absorb around eight per cent of total V-Force expenditure.

Emergency operational capability for Blue Steel-armed aircraft of 617 Squadron, the first to receive the Mk 1 powered bomb, was granted in August/September 1962. Blue Steel Mk 1 would be the only stand-off strategic weapon to reach the V-Force. Its planned successor, Blue Steel Mk 2, was cancelled nearly three years earlier, on 1 January 1960, in favour of the doomed Skybolt ALBM. There had been disillusionment over Avro's seeming inability to make Blue Steel Mk 1 more serviceable and reliable (perhaps due to a tendency to allow the Blue Steel Mk 2 project to dominate). In any event, all

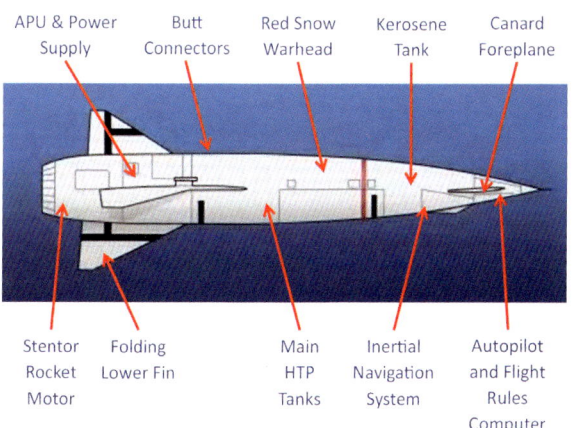

Anatomy of a troublesome child: the Blue Steel Mk 1 stand-off bomb (1.1 mt). (Norman Bonnor)

POWERED BOMBS AND LAYDOWN BOMBS   33

eyes turned to Skybolt and a vision of 72 Vulcans, each carrying two ALBMs and offering an equivalent deterrent threat to that presented by the 144 V-bombers originally agreed by the CDS in August 1957. It seemed straightforward: Blue Steel Mk 1-armed V-bombers would be fully effective until 1966, when Skybolt would open a new chapter – another life extension. RAF nuclear forces historian Humphrey Wynn reflected: "It seemed clear that, early in 1960, the government was thinking in terms of an American weapon – whether Skybolt or Polaris – to succeed Blue Steel."[98] Perhaps in the highest circles, the British, at a deeply confidential level, came to see Skybolt and its troubles as the key to hooking a bigger fish?

Blue Steel Mk 1's tardy entry into service reflected trials-related issues and, most significantly, problems with Red Snow: the warhead would not be ready until March 1962 at the earliest. The powered bomb was surrounded by acute time pressure, given its expected short life on the squadrons before replacement by Skybolt – hoped for by 1966.[99] This was not to be. Meanwhile, another problem loomed: the rapidly expanding Soviet air defences. The ministers of defence, aviation and air met on 26 September 1961 to discuss Blue Steel's problems. Two days later, the Air Ministry sent its assessment of V-Force capabilities against the Soviet defences to the Minister of Defence:

> "… after our meeting on Blue Steel … you mentioned your concern at the latest reports which showed that the Russians are likely to achieve full SAM coverage of their major cities by the end of this year. There is no doubt that the high priority given by the Russians to SAMs has made it more difficult for our bombers to penetrate to their targets. This may mean that in the period before we get Blue Steel we should not be able to achieve quite the same level of destruction as we expected a year or 18 months ago … however, we do not believe that the reduction in the effectiveness of the V-Force will be very serious."[100]

The Air Ministry offered three reasons to support this claim: SAM effectiveness would be reduced by ECM, tactical routeing would avoid known SAM sites and the number of bombers allocated to the most important (and heavily defended) targets would be increased. Interestingly, this Air Ministry assessment raised the issue of low-level attack, to exploit lack of Soviet capability below 5,000 ft, whilst, at the same time, acknowledging the lack of a British low-level freefall weapon at that point. It concluded by stating that the AOC-in-C Bomber Command was:

> "… quite confident that the MBF, even operating without the Americans, is still in a position to destroy the greater part of the targets at which it would be launched. In an operation with the Americans, there should be no reduction in our joint ability to reach the targets, though, of course, Russian SAM capability would necessarily impose heavier casualties on both of us."[101]

Nevertheless, lavish Soviet spending on enhanced air defences continued to fuel Air Staff worries about the V-bombers' ability to penetrate to their targets. What the V-Force really needed was an advanced ASM with a range of 1,000NM, allowing 90% of targets to be attacked without the aircraft entering defended airspace. There was no shortage of ideas for improving Blue Steel Mk 1 – the options had been under review for some time. During a June 1960 meeting between Minister of Defence Harold Watkinson and departmental officials, for example, a concept was discussed for extending Blue Steel Mk 1's range. It was argued that

A proud heritage: Scampton 617 Squadron aircrew at Cottesmore on the occasion of a royal visit. From left to right: Squadron Leader Gordon Blackburn, Flight Lieutenant Chris Adams and Flight Lieutenant Paul O'Gorman. (Andy Leitch Collection)

70% of the missile's fuel was consumed in the climb and only 30% in the cruise. The idea was to use solid fuel boosters for the climb, reserving the main propulsion liquid fuel for the cruise phase, perhaps extending the range to 300NM.[102]

More advanced Blue Steel variants were proposed, including Stage 2 (Mach 4.5 at 85,000 ft with a 240NM range) and, by 1963, Stage 3 (range: 450NM), with a saddle tank and boosters. Later, proposals contemplated ranges of up to 900NM.[103] These ideas came to nothing.

There was a move to push Blue Steel Mk 1 into service earlier by temporary use of Yellow Sun Mk 2 warheads, but the Ministry of Aviation warned that, whilst this would be safe, operational viability "could not be fully guaranteed". A 23 February 1961 minute from the Secretary of State for Air to the Minister of Defence had added that, under this option, a claim of "emergency operational" for Blue Steel could be made by the existing deadline of January 1962.[104] In the event, as mentioned, 617 Squadron did not reach this state until autumn 1962.

Fuel was Blue Steel's primary weakness. The powered bomb was a bi-fuel weapon: its Armstrong Siddeley Stentor twin-chamber rocket engine used high test peroxide (HTP) and kerosene. While HTP's high density allowed more fuel to be carried, it had severe operational disadvantages as an oxidiser. HTP developed a fearsome, well-deserved reputation. It catalysed readily with common materials and a skin splash caused severe burns unless washed off in seconds. Careful handling was essential, requiring special equipment and protective clothing. Water tanks were provided; any operator receiving a splash was expected to jump in.[105] At the strategic level, a liquid-fuelled weapon system had obvious disadvantages in a political and military environment dominated by rapid response.

It was not just a matter of liquid fuel. Many issues dogged Blue Steel, thermal batteries being another example. The Nuclear Weapons Safety Committee refused to accept thermal batteries fitted into readiness Blue Steel missiles. John Baylis pointed out that this undermined QRA:

"In their view, it would only be possible on safety grounds to insert the batteries at the last possible moment before take-off. This, however, was likely to take more than ten minutes to achieve, negating the procedures designed to improve the rapid reaction arrangements of the V-bombers carrying the missile."[106]

Furthermore, as explained in detail by navigator Norman Bonnor, the missile's inertial navigation system (INS) needed time to set up and required delicate handling:

"The aircraft conversion for Blue Steel included the introduction of the ground position indicator (GPI) Mk 6, probably the most accurate analogue aircraft computer ever built. It was the key component for integration of the aircraft system with the INS of the missile. The aircraft could make use of the outputs of the INS until the missile was launched. At last we had an accurate source of true heading, once the INS was aligned. But, here was the rub; the deterrent role of the V-Force involved rapid reaction to the four-minute warning from the ballistic missile early warning system (BMEWS) … hence no time for a conventional 15- to 20-minute ground alignment. Airborne alignments had to be used …"[107]

Reservations grew. The fundamental value of this weapon was questioned. Writing to the Chief of the Air Staff (CAS) Sir Thomas Pike in July 1963, outgoing Bomber Command AOC-in-C Sir Kenneth Cross spelt out Blue Steel's operational inadequacies as he saw them: the chance of a powered launch at the launch point no better than 40% and the probability of a missile reaching the target after launch of about 75%. Of six weapons on readiness, two or at the most three would be launched and the remainder would have to be carried over the target and dropped freefall. "Of those launched, one will probably fail to reach the target." He warned that, in a full-scale generation of 75% of the Blue Steel force during an alert, "the low reliability implies that on present assessment only 14 missiles out of 36 could actually be launched and 11 would reach the target."[108]

On these fundamentals, Baylis offered a blunt summary:

"Having to carry half the number of missiles over their target before launching them destroyed the whole purpose of developing Blue Steel, which was to provide a stand-off capability to overcome rapidly improving Soviet air defences."[109]

THE TROUBLESOME CHILD

The 35-ft-long Blue Steel Mk 1 was designed for release at 40,000 ft. When the rocket ignited, it accelerated to around Mach 3 and climbed to 59,000 ft. It then entered the cruise climb, using Stentor's smaller chamber to reach 70,000 ft. When the rocket cut, the missile began its terminal dive.

Following on from 617 Squadron, 27 and 83 – the other Vulcan squadrons at Scampton – received their missiles, as did 100 and 139 Victor squadrons at Wittering. Julian Grenfell, a 27 Squadron AEO, remembers Blue Steel's arrival: "At first, we saw it as the ideal weapon … we wouldn't have to go through the target defences. The downside was that the weapon wasn't Blue Steel Mk 1. In real terms, it was a productionised test version."[110] Mike Fazackerley agrees: "Blue Steel Mk 1 was a prototype in service … and it was pushed into service very quickly."[111]

Mike Fazackerley pointed out that liquid fuel remained one of the major problems surrounding weapons generation and mating with carrier aircraft: "It was argued that a solid fuel-powered bomb was not feasible, but the Americans proved otherwise." There was a proposal for converting the entire B.2 bomber fleet to carry Blue Steel:

> "This would have meant a massive loss of force flexibility. As things stood, the freefall aircraft had nuclear options, ranging from 10 kt to 1 mt and, of course, they also had the ability to carry US weapons. An extended-range Blue Steel – with wings, boosters and so on – would not have resolved its fundamental problem: it was a liquid-fuelled weapon that was impossible to generate quickly in an emergency."

AEO Julian Grenfell had no fondness for HTP:

> "I got splashed on one occasion and had to jump into the water pit, as I started to smoke. When carrying a 'wet' missile, we watched the HTP temperature gauge. On one sortie the temperature started to rise and we needed an emergency offload. We were on our way back to Scampton and radioed 'Hot Water'. When we landed and shut down, we put on our 'goon suits' but were soon pushed out of the way by a fully equipped ground team. We never found out the cause of that emergency."[112]

Victor nav/radar Norman Bonnor took HTP very seriously, as the nav/radar and co-pilot were responsible for emergency offloading following a diversion, should the HTP begin to overheat whilst airborne.[113]

Blue Steel's entry into service was overshadowed by cancellation of its intended American successor, Skybolt, at the December 1962 Nassau meeting between Kennedy and Macmillan. The canny British prime minister came away with the far more potent Polaris. The advantages of a submarine-based deterrent were summed up by Norman Bonnor: "It is better to be 400 ft down in mid-Atlantic than on an airfield." In the public arena, Skybolt's demise was still raw on 14 February 1963, when a press visit to RAF Scampton was hosted by the AOC-in-C Bomber Command. When introducing the Blue Steel-powered bomb, he managed to avoid mentioning Skybolt.[114]

Arming a V-bomber with Blue Steel tested patience. The weapon had to be removed from storage and fitted with a warhead, the aircraft had to be prepared and missile and aircraft mated (the latter a four-hour process at best). Following post-load checks, the missile would be fuelled with HTP/kerosene and crew combat checks completed. This time-consuming process required several teams and specialised equipment. As Kristan Stoddart remarked, there was plenty to go wrong:

> "There were 471 connectors between the missile and aircraft and all had to work to ensure operation. This meant loading took an estimated two and a half hours before compatibility checks could begin, and if anything was found to be non-functional the entire process had to be repeated."[115]

Blue Steel's problems exercised many minds. Bomber Command chief research officer Tom Kerr acknowledged that its generation took longer and was more difficult than for freefall weapons. He warned that time might be short and that the challenge was to generate as many missiles as possible, including the maximum number in the powered condition. He proposed standard operating procedures (SOPs) for Blue Steel operations and exercises, with clear guidance for generation and dispersal.[116]

One major headache was the time needed to recover fuelled missiles. Given that 18 of 24 missiles arming a wing were brought to 'combat launch' condition, and given the availability of one drying unit (with drying taking at least 24 hours per missile), recovery would take over two weeks! Given four drying units, this could be reduced to about four working days.

Dr Les Ruskell, formerly head of operational analysis at UK Permanent Joint Headquarters, Northwood, observed: "The practical difficulties with fuel seem to have rendered it almost impossible to escape a first strike."

Other problems arose from Blue Steel's sheer complexity. Yet, common sense and ingenuity conquered many difficulties. Norman Bonnor described the intricacies of INS alignment:

"We had to assume a scramble take-off, so we could not start and align the INS on the ground. We started it in the climb and levelled the platform by forcing inertial velocities to equal the Doppler radar (Green Satin) velocities. The Doppler/IN velocity mixing continued whenever the Doppler was locked on … IN alignment in flight took 40 minutes to complete (in the full sense). The initial alignment took six to seven minutes, but two pairs of H2S fixes were required to complete the azimuth alignment.

"In the final preparations for launch, the last position fix was taken on a release point fix (RPF) – the basis for defining the target position. Distances (N/S and E/W in minutes and decimal minutes of latitude and longitude) between the RPF and the target … were set on the GPI Mk 6 and transmitted to the missile during the pre-launch checks, so that the missile guidance and autopilot would know the target position very accurately. As the launch point was approached, the nav/radar used the RPF to make the last corrections, and, once these were accepted, the nav/plotter selected the missile INS to FREE … There were other final actions to perform to launch the missile, including: unfolding the bottom fin at the rear of the missile, arming the warhead, withdrawing the motorised locking pin on the missile release unit, pressurising the kerosene and HTP tanks … The nav/plotter activated the final launch switch and the missile would hopefully fall away under gravity.

"To prevent the rocket motor firing too close to the launch aircraft, a 100-ft lanyard remained attached to the missile and, when this separation distance was reached, a pin was extracted that enabled the kerosene fuel and HTP to flow onto a silver catalyst screen in the Stentor rocket motor. Ignition was almost instantaneous and a thrust of 24,000 lbs was now pushing a missile weighing 16,000 lbs … As it fell away it stayed pretty well under the aircraft and rapidly pointed its nose up until the motor fired (and) rapidly accelerated it to Mach 2.5 in a steep climb, hopefully without colliding with the launching aircraft."[117]

On the ground, armourers, technicians and other ground staff struggled with Blue Steel. Readiness exercises exposed the extent of their problems. In his July 1963 letter to the CAS, outgoing Bomber Command AOC-in-C Sir Kenneth Cross set out some painful realities associated with Blue Steel. Its generation could not be reduced much below seven hours, even in the absence of defects, and could take ten to 15 hours. He was gloomy about future prospects:

"The reliability of the weapon may, of course, improve with more experience, but I am doubtful if we can expect anything significant, particularly in view of its future role at low level, and the dependence for serviceability on the performance of so many associated equipments in the aircraft. No doubt, improvements in performance will occur … but there are so many basic faults in Blue Steel from a readiness aspect that it is very doubtful whether they can be overcome."[118]

Later that year, on 4 October, Sir John Grandy, the new AOC-in-C, attended Scampton to watch a Blue Steel loading and QRA exercise. Subsequently, he wrote to Secretary of State for Air Hugh Fraser, setting out his ideas for turning Blue Steel into a viable weapon. He wanted authority to fuel missiles at readiness, on aircraft with warheads fitted. He wanted the thermal batteries in readiness weapons installed and left there, so avoiding the need for last-minute insertion. He even went so far as to request clearance to fly fuelled missiles, *with warheads loaded*, from main bases to dispersals, to test Blue Steel's ability to tolerate long periods of readiness on dispersal airfields. He wrote again four months later, this time to the Vice-Chief of the Air Staff (VCAS), Air Chief Marshal Sir Wallace Kyle, complaining that no decisions had been taken on his recommendations, made in his letter of 19 November, especially regarding batteries and fuelled/armed missiles on QRA.[119]

Today, when considering Blue Steel's problems, views should be tempered by an allowance for the realities and pressures of the time. In 1999, Professor John E. Allen, a former chief future projects engineer at BAe Kingston, discussed decisions in government, the RAF, RAE and industry "taken in the presence of considerable ignorance of the consequences … Due to the urgency of the Blue Steel project, about 95% of all irrevocable decisions in project design had to be made when only a few percent of the total project data were available."[120]

The RAF was desperate for the stand-off bomb and it was this pressure and the Air Staff's growing alarm at expanding Soviet air defences which contributed to this weapon's immunity from cancellation, despite its very obvious shortcomings. Nevertheless, doubts about Blue Steel's fundamental value were expressed as early as 1959, as outlined in 1984 by Humphrey Wynn:

> "By 1959, when Blue Steel had been under development for five years, there was a lack of confidence about its operational viability by the time it would enter service. A view expressed in October of that year, on the basis of an estimate by the Ministry of Supply that it would be in service early in 1962, was that by 1963 the V-bomber/Blue Steel Mk 1 weapon system was unlikely to constitute a valid deterrent owing to the reducing ability of the aircraft to penetrate to the weapon's required release point."[121]

This, of course, was *long before* Blue Steel's range was cut by two-thirds when the V-bombers were switched to low-level nuclear strike. Yet, Professor Allen took a kindly view of Blue Steel's avoidance of the axe: "When other missile systems of the period are reviewed, it was the flexibility of Blue Steel that enabled it to survive the operational changes when other projects were cancelled."[122]

Blue Steel crews were not envied by freefall crews, as made clear by Rob Williams, a Vulcan captain on IX Squadron:

> "On reflection, I am glad I was not posted to a Blue Steel squadron. The procedures that had to be followed with a 'wet' (fuelled) missile were an absolute nightmare. Blue Steel, in my view, was a dangerous weapon system."[123]

Another Vulcan freefall captain, John Huggins, was no fan: "In my view, the stand-off bomb was useless. It was much better to be in a freefall crew. Blue Steel crews were very much a group apart." Reflecting on Blue Steel's difficulties, he added: "That was always the problem with the V-Force and Britain's independent nuclear deterrent. There was never enough money to fund essential development projects. A stand-off weapon with a 1,000-mile range might have been much more useful."[124]

Another Vulcan captain, Peter Moore, summed it up. When he joined 44 (Rhodesia) Squadron at Waddington in July 1969, Blue Steel was still operated at Scampton: "On flying into Kinloss one day, I witnessed a spectacular HTP off-load fire. Nobody at Waddington wanted to go near a Blue Steel squadron."[125]

Yet Norman Bonnor underlines the stand-off bomb's innovative character at the time:

"Our aircraft with Blue Steel had the first inertial navigation system used by the RAF. Mind you, it was the size of a dustbin! You can hold the modern equivalent in one hand. There were immense challenges faced by those developing the powered bomb – particularly the issues surrounding sustained flight at Mach 2–3. Fabricating the missile in stainless steel proved very difficult. Temperature tolerances were a big factor. On the ground, temperatures could go down to -10°C, with -40 to -50°C at altitude. Yet the missile heated up at the high speeds after launch."[126]

When the V-Force went low level, Blue Steel Mk 1's already modest range was reduced very significantly to just 35–50NM. This brought the carriers much closer to the outer ring of point defences around major targets (a parallel hazard to that faced by freefall aircraft, required to penetrate further in and then 'pop up' to 11,000 ft, inside the SAM kill zone, to drop Yellow Sun Mk 2 weapons). Both factors had a negative impact on V-Force operational effectiveness at low level. In 1967 however, freefall squadrons received WE.177B, a true low-level weapon, albeit one requiring direct overflight of the target. As for the powered bomb, it proved quite straightforward to modify Blue Steel for low-level launch. A contract was signed for the W.200 low-level variant; a low-level trial launch was made at Woomera in November 1963 – the first in a series of 16.[127]

The day of the live firing: Victor XL190 takes off with Blue Steel No. 175 for the first Operation Fresno post-acceptance launch, 27 May 1966. (Norman Bonnor)

Despite Blue Steel's many difficulties, Norman Bonnor made the point that it worked: "I know. I fired one successfully."[128] The original purchase of 57 missiles had included four earmarked for in-service 'proof' firings. Late in 1965, Bomber Command's AOC, 'Bing' Cross, decided that the missile had been in service long enough to begin a series of live launches over Aberporth Bay range, Wales – Operation Fresno. The first proof firing was on 27 May 1966, from a Victor B.2 of 100 Squadron flying at 1,000 ft, at 350 kts.[129] This was XL190, Norman Bonnor's Victor:

> "Our crew was the only command crew at RAF Wittering at that time, which probably accounts for us being chosen to make the first launch. We were expected to do three successful carry-overs across the range before we would be cleared to make the launch. Their radar never locked on to us until about ten seconds before we were due to launch, even with advance knowledge of our height, track and timing! On the day we actually made the launch, they didn't lock on until a few seconds before we dropped the missile, which in a war situation would have been too late. We fired the round into Aberporth Bay, in an area clear of shipping. Blue Steel No. 175 remains on the seabed to this day."[130]

Post-acceptance firings were intended to demonstrate that Blue Steel was successful in squadron use, flown by operational crews and maintained by RAF technicians, rather than R&D trials crews and company personnel. A 139 Squadron crew launched a second missile on 26 August 1966 and the final two were launched by Vulcan crews from Scampton on 31 May and 7 July 1967.[131] The Operational Research Branch report on the first Victor firing states that the launch was made as a direct-ahead attack from low level at 25NM range, with the missile set for a 7,600 ft airburst. The final radial error from target was 410 yards (400 yards to starboard and 80 yards overshoot), described as a "very good result".[132]

What this report didn't mention was the alarmingly close passage of the missile as it fired and entered its climb, as recounted by Norman Bonnor:

> "When the missile released, we performed our escape manoeuvre, pulling around 2.5 g. The missile fell 100 ft on the lanyard and the motor lit up. Blue Steel was a canard design and the motor fired with the missile in a nose-up attitude of around 15 degrees. It was uncomfortably close when it accelerated past us. Our co-pilot claimed it had shot past his right ear! Subsequently, it was decided that it would be best to initiate the turn *prior to release*."[133]

We came back without it! XL190's crew on their return from a Blue Steel live firing. From left to right: John Charlton (AEO), Terry Austin (captain), Jeff Morgan (co-pilot), Norman Bonnor (nav/radar) and Gordon Hagel (nav/plotter). They were joined on the flight by Wing Commander (later Air Chief Marshal) John Curtis, OC Operations (not pictured). (Norman Bonnor)

Another participant in a live-firing has similar memories. Flight Lieutenant Ian McDonald's command crew team, with 27 Squadron at Scampton, included then co-pilot Jon Tye. They were selected for one of the two Vulcan post-acceptance firings:

> "It took ages to launch the thing. We crossed the coast near Galloway, flew across the North of England and did several carry-overs, to check that the aircraft and weapon were ready and that the weather was OK. My job as co-pilot was to map read and look out for the way points running up to the initial point (IP). I remember glancing out of the side window and seeing the Vulcan's shadow on the water. When the launch came, I saw the shadow of the Blue Steel fall away … The Blue Steel went past the nose at incredible speed. It was unbelievably close."[134]

The first powered bombs went to 617 Squadron and, appropriately, a 617 Squadron Vulcan flew the last Blue Steel sortie. A number of Blue Steel Vulcans were converted to the freefall role, around 17 years *after* Bomber Command's then AOC-in-C expressed his desire to "get away" from freefall weapons as soon as possible. Mike Fazackerley is not alone in finding this extraordinary:

> "… it would have been the subject of public controversy, had it not been handled in such a low-profile manner. The RAF managed this by emphasising the restoration of the Vulcan's conventional bombing role. There was no real discussion of a continued nuclear role post-Polaris."[135]

Wittering's Victors were withdrawn in late 1968, for conversion to tankers.

THE LAYDOWN BOMB

Technical challenges also dominated WE.177B's development, in what became the UK's most complex freefall bomb project. The 450-kt, parachute-retarded laydown bomb had to survive a landing after ultra-low-level release from a V-bomber flying at up to 415 kts directly over the target. Following release, the carrier aircraft had barely one minute to make its escape. During an attack, of course, there would be physical constraints. Nav/radar Roy Brocklebank makes the point that countervalue targets (cities) implied buildings, which would "predicate against ultra-low-level release". He remembered the lowest laydown drop height for WE.177B as 50 ft. "I'm not sure of the upper limit, but I think around 1,000 ft." The weapon was required to land tail-first: "On ejection, the rear ram exerted a greater force, which gave the tail-down aspect."[136] According

Compact and catastrophically destructive: WE.177 round. Some V-Force aircrew would have preferred to carry more than one WE.177B, but the quantity of the fissile material available was limited and there was no requirement for multiple nuclear strikes by main force bombers. (Tony Redding)

to Mike Fazackerley, a laydown drop height of 50 ft was probably the design requirement, with 60 ft the minimum in-service delivery height: "Given laydown drop heights of as little as 50 ft and a maximum of 1,000 ft, the duration of the laydown fall would be from two to 16 seconds."[137]

Laydown was a proven concept. American E weapons supplied to the RAF included the B43 laydown bomb, carried by Valiants in the low-level role since 1963. Following Skybolt's cancellation in late 1962 and the decision to switch the entire V-Force to low-level strike, one priority was to replace the Yellow Sun Mk 2 freefall bomb (requiring an 11,000 ft pop-up for release) with a freefall weapon dropped at ultra-low level, under the SAM screen. There was no British inclination to turn to the readily available American B43, which was under dual control. This was not the only factor. Mike Fazackerley maintained that the British did not take American know-how for granted:

> "Whenever possible, the British tried to do better. There were some features of the American weapon which gave cause for concern. The British required more flexibility from a laydown weapon and, furthermore, there were doubts about the high-density packaging system used for the American bomb's parachutes. In any event, an American weapon was not an option at this point. Skybolt's cancellation still rankled – it would have been politically unacceptable to turn to another American weapon to bridge the gap. Dependence on the Americans, at that point, was a non-starter. So, it can be said that WE.177 was a political as much as an engineering statement."[138]

The British, of course, had already accepted another American weapons system, Polaris, to replace Skybolt. Yet, having to rely on the Americans to bridge the gap until Polaris might have been one humiliation too many, at least in the public sense.

The fully realised WE.177 had three variants: the WE.177B strategic weapon, the WE.177A low-yield tactical weapon and the WE.177C high-yield tactical weapon. WE.177 offered extraordinary flexibility. Unlike the mechanical arming and fusing of Yellow Sun and Red Beard, WE.177 had electronic arming, with three 'safety breaks' that had to be closed to achieve detonation.[139] There have been doubts about WE.177B's 'single-point safe' status, but these are dismissed by Mike Fazackerley:

> "This issue has been the subject of heated debate over the years. Some have argued that WE.177 relied on safety systems other than single point. The fact is that WE.177 was a weapon that in fire and accident situations had systems designed to prevent nuclear detonation, which could only result from completion of a long sequence of events. It was always single-point safe."

At the highest military levels, there remained deep divisions between SLBM champions and those still favouring long-term reliance on manned aircraft and air-launched weapons (albeit in more advanced forms). The latter stressed the manned bomber's greater flexibility; the former pointed to the inherent vulnerability of bombers on the ground. Both were right, to some degree. This debate continued into the early 1970s and its echoes travelled across the following decades. There are those, even today, who ask why Britain is the only nuclear power to have abandoned the option of delivery by manned aircraft. Every other nuclear-armed nation has some degree of air capability, with its inherent flexibility. Air Commodore

Edward Jarron, a former Chief of Special Weapons at SHAPE in the early 1990s, saw value in both: "The availability of nuclear-armed aircraft, in addition to the SLBM force, allowed us to engage in a certain amount of nuclear signalling."[140] Certainly, Vulcans are more visible than submarines.

As for WE.177's development and progression into service, there were no arguments, post Skybolt's cancellation, over the need for this dedicated low-level weapon. It avoided the Yellow Sun Mk 2 carrier's climb into the SAM zone for release. WE.177, however, had another crucial advantage – it already existed as a project (albeit progressing at a slow pace until Skybolt was lost). This bomb was conceived as a new tactical weapon (what became WE.177A) for low-level delivery, to replace Red Beard. It then became clear that WE.177 could also meet the need for a high yield strategic laydown bomb (WE.177B), as described by Mike Fazackerley:

"This was the obvious answer. At this time, the RAF played its cards with great intelligence. They seized the moment, acting with a speed that was staggering. Once the development contract for WE.177 was placed with Hunting Engineering, the RAF and government departments left the company alone. They let them get on with it."[141]

It might be argued that precious R&D funds invested in a strategic WE.177 (whilst advanced, still a freefall weapon) would have been better spent on a really determined bid to produce a successful long-range powered bomb, given that the V-Force was to continue in its nuclear role for over a decade post-Polaris handover. This view, however, benefits from hindsight. Mike Fazackerley focused on the view at the time:

"By the mid-1960s, a weapon requiring direct overflight of the target – even at ultra-low level – was not a good option. Rather, it would be best to describe the laydown bomb as the *best available option*. It was seen as faster and less risky to go ahead with WE.177 … Having made the decision to transfer the strategic deterrent to the Royal Navy, had the RAF made a bid for the development of a long-range delivery system, this would have been seen as an attempt to undermine that decision and would have received no political support."[142]

A parallel situation arose with the TSR-2 advanced strike and reconnaissance aircraft. Here, the RAF was less sure-footed, making some serious presentational mistakes. The low key plan to hand down the V-bombers' WE.177B strategic nuclear weapons to TSR-2 squadrons came to nothing with the latter's cancellation. This may have been spurred, in part, by an ill-judged and very public presentation of the TSR-2 prototype in anti-flash white – suggesting an intention to use it in the strategic nuclear role after the handover to Polaris.[143]

WE.177 entered service in late 1966. Its operational lifespan exceeded 30 years. The Defence Evaluation and Research Agency cleared WE.177 variants for use by no less than 18 fixed- and rotary-wing aircraft, from V-bombers, Canberras and TSR-2 (had it entered service) to fast strike aircraft, helicopters as small as the Wasp and even large transport aircraft – the Hercules and VC10.[144] WE.177B was a remarkable engineering achievement; it contained less than 100 lbs of conventional explosive, as against the 5,543 lbs inside Blue Danube. The shock absorption solution (high density polyurethane foam) had to cope with impact velocities of up to 180 ft/sec and deceleration forces of up to 2,000 g. The bomb was designed to 'slap down' tail-first on laydown, with the tail cone taking the lateral shocks. Four parachutes slowed the weapon to a delivery speed of 112 mph.[145] The weapon utilised the RE.179 fusion warhead designed for Skybolt.[146]

This compact bomb (133 in long) weighed around 1,000 lbs. Its fissile material was recovered from obsolete weapons.

The tactical strike/naval variant, WE.177A, had a yield of up to 10 kt (fission first stage/no fusion secondary) and was carried by the Vulcan B.2, Buccaneer, Jaguar and Tornado. WE.177C, another tactical weapon, had a much higher yield (190 kt) – required to destroy airfields and other area targets too large for WE.177A. According to Chris Gibson, this is thought to have utilised some warhead elements from ET.317, the British Polaris warhead, which became available during the Chevaline upgrade (replacing one of the missile's three warheads with penetration aids).[147] The inventory included a peak of 207 WE.177 weapons of all variants. The last examples of WE.177A and WE.177C were withdrawn in March 1998.[148] WE.177C's yield was set at just below the 200 kt limit applying to weapons allocated to SACEUR in the European theatre. In 1962 this limit had been fixed at 10 kt, explaining WE.177A's relatively low yield. Nonetheless, the then CDS, Admiral Sir Peter Hill-Norton, had still struggled to understand why, given the power of the Hiroshima bomb, the RAF would want a larger weapon for an airfield.[149]

The reason relates to the stress of war, according to Mike Fazackerley:

"The RAF lauded the benefits of ultra-low-level strike but also knew that, in the European context, there could be no guarantee of pinpoint delivery. This is why a tactical bomb with a much bigger yield than WE.177A was required. If the weapon misses the aiming point by just a quarter-mile, a much more powerful yield is needed to guarantee destruction. For example, it was calculated that four 10-kt WE.177As would have to be dropped to destroy one airfield. There was a lot of misinformation around – deliberately spread – on the destructive power of nuclear weapons. This was almost always overstated."[150]

In early 1964 the government declared the V-Force fully operational for low-level strike against the Soviet Union. This was disingenuous; most freefall V-bombers had to wait another three years for WE.177B, a true low-level strategic weapon. Mike Fazackerley points out that, during this long wait, the freefall bombers had to soldier on with Yellow Sun Mk 2 and its pop-up delivery:

"The idea of popping up on the outskirts of Moscow says it all! The reason for the long wait had a lot to do with the weapon's sheer complexity – there were only one or two avoidable delays. In total, WE.177B was around six months late … but the wait would have been just as long for Skybolt. Another two or three years with Yellow Sun Mk 2 and the pop-up requirement had been inevitable."[151]

WE.177B first armed QRA Vulcans in October 1966, but were soon withdrawn. They returned after a couple of months. Mike Fazackerley explains the background to this false start:

"WE.177B was pushed into service before its radar fusing system was ready. Indeed, the first weapons had concrete ballast where the radar fuse should have been. Yet this made no real operational difference, as the lack of a radar fuse was immaterial for laydown delivery. Whilst there were delivery problems with radar fuses and also with capacitors for the thermal batteries, the reason for the temporary suspension of production and withdrawal from service was a problem with a German-manufactured mechanical valve in the warhead. The weapon was returned to QRA and production re-started after a temporary fix was identified."

Following Skybolt's cancellation, the Polaris deal and the subsequent grounding of the Valiants, the Interim Plan for the V-Force (until the Polaris handover) provided for 88 aircraft (11 squadrons, nine of Vulcans and two of Victors).[152] This force eventually consisted of 40 Blue Steel-armed aircraft (three Vulcan and two Victor squadrons), together with 48 freefall Vulcans armed with Yellow Sun 2 (succeeded by WE.177B). The Victor was less suited to low-level operations and the requirement for this type to carry WE.177B had been withdrawn in February 1964.[153] The Vulcan freefall force eventually received 53 WE.177Bs (one bomb for each aircraft, plus five operational spares – allowing for maintenance rotation at AWRE). On Blue Steel's retirement in 1970 and the conversion of some carrier aircraft to freefall bombers following the Polaris handover, there were not enough high yield WE.177Bs to arm the enlarged freefall V-Force (56 aircraft, 53 WE.177Bs), but other weapon variants were available. In Cyprus, for example, several low-yield WE.177As were held.[154]

When moving bombs, public considerations were taken into account. Tony Smith, a Vulcan crew chief at Waddington during the 1976–82 period, remembered issues arising from the station's bomb dump being on the other side of the A15:

"There were traffic lights to allow the bombs to be transported across the road. There were usually some Ban the Bomb campaigners around the gate, but they always moved aside to allow the weapons through. The bombs were covered, of course."[155]

Not everyone was prepared to wait, as Peter Moore recalls:

"Waddington's SSA was across the main A15 road. Shapes were moved from the SSA across the road under police fore and aft escort, with the traffic held by traffic lights. One foggy winter's morning an alert was called in the wee small hours. As one weapon convoy crossed the road, a civilian vehicle either hadn't seen or ignored the red lights and managed to get between one of the escort vehicles and the weapon."[156]

The WE.177B stockpile was completed in October 1967. Dual carriage by the Vulcan had been considered.[157] There was no requirement, however, for multiple strategic strikes by aircraft. In any event, the amount of fissile material available was limited. Long-range bomb-bay tanks extended the Vulcan's range and route flexibility. According to Roy Brocklebank, there was still enough room for two WE.177Bs, side by side, with drum tanks fore and aft. He adds: "The double-drum fit enabled us to reach targets such as Kiev and then recover to Turkey … The freefall aircraft QRA targets were essentially peripheral, such as Leningrad, and aircraft required only internal fuel." He noted that a war plan for 1968 required one aircraft for the Leningrad area to have extra fuel capacity as it was routed over Lake Ladoga, to attack the city from the north-east:

"This implied that two aircraft – a QRA bomber and the QRA spare – would need the extra tankage. This would have had a significant impact on aircraft selection for QRA and the station commander, Group Captain Arthur Griffiths, had me request Bomber Command to modify the route to reduce the fuel requirement. This was done."[158]

Every weapon was precious. On 8 August 1967 an RAF Waddington Vulcan, loaded with a live weapon and captained by Flight Lieutenant Ed Shearman, was struck by lightning whilst on QRA. The aircraft was damaged and the weapon was removed to AWRE for inspection.[159] This weapon may have been withdrawn as, subsequently, the number of WE.177B spares was reduced from five to four.[160]

The switch to Polaris was at the halfway point of the V-bombers' long nuclear career. The operational lifespan of the nuclear-armed V-Force post-Polaris handover (1969–82) closely matched the frontline strategic lifespan (1957–69). The V-Force continued as part of the NATO deterrent.[161] Most aircraft remained with Strike Command in the UK, although two squadrons (IX and 35) moved to Cyprus to succeed four squadrons of Red Beard-armed NEAF Canberras.[162]

Deliveries of WE.177A began in 1970 and WE.177C in January 1974, following completion of the WE.177B strategic programme. The longer-range Buccaneers in Germany were given priority for the new WE.177 tactical weapons. Each Buccaneer could carry two WE.177Cs (380 kt) if required, but Roy Brocklebank recalls that aircraft based in Germany and assigned to SACEUR carried only one: "The Supreme Allied Commander, Atlantic (SACLANT) aircraft carried two. I think this reflected the expected vulnerability of the land attack aircraft."[163] In 1976 there remained 48 WE.177B-armed Vulcans (44, 50, 101, IX, 617 and 35 Squadrons), based at Waddington and Scampton and reducing to five squadrons by 1982. It is unclear exactly how the WE.177 rounds were distributed amongst the strike squadrons post V-Force. When the Vulcans retired in 1982, the WE.177B rounds went to the Tornado Force. Meanwhile, some A rounds were converted to C. According to Mike Fazackerley, the most likely distribution was: Buccaneer strike, A and C; Buccaneer maritime strike, A; Jaguar, A and C; Tornado strike, B and C; and Tornado maritime strike, A.[164]

Moscow remained under threat from British-manned bombers for some years after the V-Force. Mike Fazackerley:

> "There was a long-held belief that WE.177B made no appearance in Germany, but this is not the case. The Germany-based RAF Tornado Force had a Moscow capability. Post the Polaris handover and subsequently the V-bombers, the RAF wanted to retain its ability to strike Moscow. This target could be reached by Tornado aircraft equipped with three large drop tanks – one on each wing and a third on the right fuselage pylon, next to the WE.177B on the left fuselage pylon."[165]

It was thought that the Tornado had a good chance of getting through. A 1971 Air Force Department report on current and future air-delivered systems included the comment:

> "… against a level of encounter likely to be typically high, a force requirement of only about two MRCA (as the Tornado was then known) per target will be sufficient to ensure, at a 95% level of assurance, at least one survivor over target … In most cases, a single MRCA would be sufficient for an attack on each city target…"

In 1990, there were 72 UK-based strike aircraft capable of delivering WE.177s. With 12 aircraft per squadron, they consisted of two squadrons each of Jaguar, Buccaneer and Tornado aircraft. In Europe, there were 84 RAF strike aircraft with WE.177 capability – seven Tornado squadrons. Other aircraft would have been mobilised in an emergency from reconnaissance and training units. Over 32 years of operational use, Mike Fazackerley notes 11 safety incidents involving WE.177s (including the aforementioned lightning strike). There were four leaks of tritium gas from weapons (including two at Akrotiri), five falls/slips during loading and a road accident involving a weapon carrier in Wiltshire during January 1987. There was damage to the containerised weapon.[166]

SPYING ON THE V-FORCE

As might be expected, over the years V-Force aircraft, equipment and weapons attracted the attentions of spies and opportunists. They included Vulcan pilot Alastair Steadman, who received a nine-year sentence for attempting to sell secrets, having been caught visiting the Soviet Consulate in London (held under round-the-clock watch).

There was also electronics engineer Michael John Smith, a spy of sterner character who managed to join EMI Defence Electronics, a company with a contract to produce WE.177's XN-715 radar fuse. A member of the Communist Party and recruited by the KGB (codenamed Parellic), Smith slipped through the vetting process, benefitting from confusion with another individual of similar name. He arrived in the quality assurance department in 1976 and supplied enough information to allow Soviet scientists to build a working replica of the fuse. A KGB defector exposed Smith in 1992 and he was sentenced to 20 years. Smith protested his innocence but an investigation of his financial affairs revealed an unexplained sum of over £20,000.[167] The Soviets, apparently, were not impressed with the fuse, regarding it as old-fashioned.

Nicholas Prager also became a spy. The son of a clerk at the British Consulate in Czechoslovakia, he became a British citizen in 1948 and joined the RAF a year later as a radar technician. Recruited by Czech Intelligence, his postings included the Bomber Command Development Unit, RAF Finningley. Given the rather unintelligent codename Marconi, he set about photographing papers from manuals concerning Blue Diver and Red Steer ECM in return for payment. He left the RAF in 1961 and went to English Electric, but was exposed later by a defector. 'One-time pads' were found at his home; he received a 12-year sentence in 1971.[168]

COST AND TIME PRESSURES

British nuclear weapons were products of difficult challenges in terms of design, development and operational need. The common components within each challenge were cost and time pressures. There had to be compromise between what was desired and what was possible. The earliest 'megaton-class' weapons involved compromise between the political need to join the 'thermonuclear club' as soon as possible and acceptance of abnormal levels of risk and restrictions in use. Assembly of Violet Club, for example, required a team of specialists in managing the risks. Both Violet Club and Yellow Sun Mk 1 required special procedures which made them difficult to prepare for operations.

Yellow Sun Mk 2, whilst a major improvement, was compromised to some degree by the need for carrier aircraft to pop up from low level, at the risk of SAM engagement. Red Beard was a compact weapon, but required last-minute loading and had no low-level capability (highly desirable in a tactical weapon). A proportion of Blue Steels worked, but with a very short stand-off range (50 miles at best) at low level. The powered bomb arrived on the squadrons with a depressing catalogue of difficulties. In summary, after Blue Steel Mk 2 and Skybolt were cancelled, the V-Force was left with obsolescent freefall bombs and an inadequate stand-off weapon. At the same time, it should be said that all the key decisions to enhance the credibility of the V-Force during the wait for Polaris were taken decisively, within just four weeks of Macmillan's return from Nassau in December 1962.

By 1963–64 the V-Force needed an advanced, solid-fuelled stand-off weapon with a range of at least 1,000NM. By then, however, it was too late given that responsibility for the UK strategic deterrent would pass to the submarines in four years or so. Seeking a stopgap American air-launched system would have been political poison after Skybolt. The only real option, from time and cost standpoints, was WE.177, a freefall laydown bomb already under development for the tactical role. In this way the V-Force found itself tied to a new freefall weapon in the second half of the 1960s. After Strike Command's formation in 1968, the V-bombers would carry on their supplementary freefall nuclear role into the 1980s.

Looking back, it can be seen that only Blue Danube, Britain's first nuclear weapon, was free of compromise. There was an urgent need for the bomb and that need was to be met, whatever the cost. There was no compromise surrounding the fundamental objective: to become a nuclear power as soon as possible. There is a degree of irony in the way the UK deterrent developed over the years. During the late 1950s and early 1960s, the V-Force carried the strategic deterrent, supplemented by the Thor missile force. In the 1970s and early 1980s, the SLBM submarines carrying the frontline deterrent were supplemented by vintage Vulcans carrying freefall weapons. These freefall bombs were then handed on, in turn, to modern strike aircraft and remained in service until 1998. Mike Fazackerley points out that even 1998 was earlier than planned:

> "It was retired in 1998 due to safety issues. When it went, the decision was portrayed as a political gesture towards disarmament. In reality, engineering trust in the weapon had degraded to a point that it could no longer continue in service. The deterioration would have continued year by year in the absence of this action. There was no specific safety issue, but a generic problem relating to the retention of AWRE expertise in this area and a growing inability to guarantee reliability."[169]

Today, there is no British mixed deterrent, only the Trident submarines – a formidable strategic deterrent with a very tenuous claim to sub-strategic capabilities. Mike Fazackerley sums up a British nuclear posture totally reliant on Trident:

> "A huge amount of capability was lost. The sub-strategic use of Trident is highly questionable. All the evidence suggests that if you need to destroy a hardened target with an inaccurate weapon, you need a very big warhead. The alternative is a reduced yield weapon that is highly accurate. Trident D5 lacks pinpoint accuracy and has a relatively low yield."[170]

4
THE V-FORCE MISSION

> *Since it is accepted that this country could not survive global nuclear war, to devote so small a proportion of our defence expenditure to the prevention of global nuclear war is not excessive, even accepting, for the sake of argument, that the prevention of it is the only role of the V-Force in an age of nuclear sufficiency.*
>
> Secretary of State for Air George Ward, 'The V-bomber force and the powered bomb', memorandum to the Defence Board, 29 October 1958.

BUILDING THE V-FORCE

There is a clear distinction between V-Force war prevention and war-fighting functions. The former was paramount and concerned what the V-Force *could do* rather than what it *might do* in a hot war. Deterrence was the MBF's essential value.

Whilst the V-Force existed to keep the peace, rather than help fight a war without victors, some degree of operational capability to inflict catastrophic damage is the currency of nuclear deterrence. In this context, even relatively 'modest' capacity implies a potential to inflict virtually instant damage at levels of severity so far unrecorded in the history of warfare.

Naturally, the many variables defining an appropriate war-fighting capacity compounded the many difficulties faced by those taking decisions concerning, inter alia, an appropriate V-Force size. In July 1956 the then Chief of the Air Staff (CAS), Air Chief Marshal Sir Dermot Boyle, called for an MBF of 200 aircraft at a Chiefs of Staff (COS) meeting.[171] This was the first reduction. In 1954, the Air Minister, Lord De L'Isle and Dudley, VC, had put the case for 240 V-bombers, backed by Harold Macmillan, then Minister of Defence, the following year. This was supported by the Cabinet Defence Committee and the outcome was Plan K, which looked forward to a force of 240 V-bombers.[172]

V-Force size had been discussed at a COS Committee meeting on 17 February 1953. Those present included the then CAS, Air Chief Marshal Sir William Dickson, who accepted that force size could not be calculated with mathematical precision and that the proposed figure of 240 bombers "was based purely on the minimum effort required to reduce the Russian atomic threat to the UK to manageable proportions". He argued that a figure below 240 would result in a force no longer having "worthwhile hitting power". He also maintained that it was unnecessary to make firm commitments to a 240-strong MBF, as successive rounds of orders (placed two or three years ahead of required delivery) would provide opportunities for readjustment on financial grounds. It would not be until 1955 that orders for the final stage of expansion to 240 would need to be placed. In short, a final decision on size would not be required for around two years.[173]

Baylis and Stoddart charted the very significant decline in this initial ambition of 240 V-bombers. "By 1956 this had been reduced to 184, and then in 1963 to 120. By 1965, prior to the deployment of Polaris, the number had dropped to 88."[174]

At the same time, a deep-seated national pride in the futuristic V-bombers took hold in the 1950s. The V-bombers went to work, 'showing the flag' at the global level from the earliest days. Operation Too Right, the first overseas flight by Britain's new strategic bombers, involved two Valiant Mk 1s of 138 Squadron, based at RAF Wittering. They arrived in Christchurch, New Zealand during September 1955.[175] A round-the-world tour by a Vulcan the following year ended in tragedy – a crash on return at Heathrow Airport. The two pilots ejected (including Bomber Command AOC-in-C Sir Harry Broadhurst) but the four rear crew died.

By late 1957, V-Force expansion gathered momentum. There were seven Valiant bomber squadrons, a Valiant photo-reconnaissance squadron, a Valiant electronic countermeasures (ECM) squadron and two Vulcan B.1 squadrons.[176] Rapid growth continued in 1958. By the end of that year, the MBF included three Vulcan B.1 and two Victor B.1 main force squadrons.[177]

There was a proposal to build only the interim bomber type, the Valiant. In a hot war, however, it was felt that the more advanced types would offer a significant increase in MBF value, given their additional speed and height.[178] In addition, the Vulcan and Victor had significant development potential.

'Worthwhile hitting power' was the mantra for defending V-Force size; this was defined as sufficient power to strike Soviet bomber airfields threatening Britain.[179] Nevertheless, there was always pressure for cuts. An early 1957 paper looked forward to a V-Force of 184 bombers. This was followed by a May 1957 paper embracing the same plan: 120 Mk 2 Vulcans and Victors (for deep penetration targets), 40 Mk 1 Vulcans and Victors (to attack 'fringe' targets) and 24 Valiants – SACEUR's TBF as from 31 December 1959. As the years progressed, 42 Valiants became tankers (Vulcans, from the sixteenth aircraft onwards, and all Victors were equipped to receive fuel). In the early days, this was seen as essential to increase target cover and flexibility in route planning, but flight refuelling was to have little influence on V-Force operations; the tanker fleet's main role became the support of Fighter Command, notably overseas deployment.[180]

Looming over discussions about MBF size was a growing unease about the war-fighting capabilities of subsonic bombers in the missile age. This concern was exceeded only by worries about defending the agreed V-Force programme in London; politicians, civil servants and senior officers of rival services continued to press for further cuts on grounds of cost. Matters came to a head on 2 August 1957, when a smaller V-Force frontline of 144 aircraft was agreed by the Defence Committee. The number of more powerful Mk 2 Victors and Vulcans was to be reduced from 120 to 104.[181]

Plan K, for 240 bombers, had already been declared to NATO and, subsequently, the Minister of Defence told the Defence Committee that there were sound operational arguments for a force of 184 aircraft. Nevertheless, a 144-strong MBF was agreed in August 1957 as an "appropriate compromise" between military and economic considerations. Yet, just over a year later, in October 1958, Secretary of State for Air George Ward found himself having to write to the Defence Board, defending the figure of 144. He reminded the board of the Defence Committee's decision of 1957, accepting 144 aircraft. He also pointed out that only recently (on 16 July 1958) the prime minister had reaffirmed the purpose of the UK's independent nuclear capability:

- To retain our special relation with the United States and, through it, our influence in world affairs and, especially, our right to have a voice in the final issue of peace or war.
- To make a definite, though limited, contribution to the total nuclear strength of the West – while recognising that the United States must continue to play the major part in maintaining the balance of nuclear power.
- To enable us, by threatening to use our independent nuclear power, to secure United States cooperation in a situation in which their interests were less immediately threatened than our own.
- To make sure that, in a nuclear war, sufficient attention is given to certain Soviet targets which are of greater importance to us than to the United States.[182]

Ward then settled to his main task – the defence of the 144-strong V-bomber force:

"To constitute a minimum deterrent and serve the purposes for which it is intended, the V-Force must be operationally viable, i.e. it must be sufficiently large and well-equipped to deliver enough bombs to inflict an adequate measure of destruction in Russia. To be operationally viable, the minimum size of the force should not be less than decided upon a year ago."

Ward argued that all 104 Mk 2 Victors and Vulcans should be armed with powered bombs but, subsequently, cancellation of Blue Steel Mk 2 (January 1960) and, later, the Skybolt ALBM (December 1962) would deny the V-Force more advanced weapons. In 1958, however, these matters were still undecided and, indeed, OR.1159, for long-range Blue Steel, had been issued only in May, a few months previously. Ward pressed his point:

"The Defence Committee decided a year ago to maintain the Mk 2 element of the V-Force at a high level because these aircraft were required to carry first the short-range and then the long-range powered bombs … These weapons are required in order to maintain the capacity of the V-Force to attack deep penetration targets in spite of the expected development of the Russian surface-to-air guided weapon (SAGW) defences. There is no change to this requirement."

This was not the case. The requirement *did* change, as a result of circumstances, within a few years – leaving over half the V-Force as freefall bombers. Meanwhile, Ward thought it prudent to emphasise that the V-Force's *raison d'être* had as much to do with the Americans as the Russians, at both political and military levels:

"A force which is not operationally viable would not enable us to maintain our special relationship with the United States or our influence in world affairs. Nor would it enable us to secure United States cooperation by threatening to use our independent nuclear power if the Americans were tempted to stand aside in a situation in which their interests were less immediately threatened than our own. Both they and the Russians would have reason to believe that if the Russians threatened nuclear attack, we would be bound to yield for lack of the means of retaliation."

Another V-Force cut would be "gravely inconsistent" with the close integration of Bomber Command and Strategic Air Command (SAC) operational plans. Ward also made it clear that retaliation, in the late 1950s, involved a long list of city targets:

> "The effect that could be produced by a bomber force of the size at present planned depends upon the capacity of Russia to absorb punishment. Operational studies suggest that the force at present planned, after allowing for unserviceability and losses, could deliver successfully attacks on 30 to 40 out of 131 major centres of Russian industry and administration with a population of more than 100,000. The larger and more important targets would need more than one bomber to destroy them and the number of targets is progressively increasing … Any reduction in the size of the force would more than proportionately reduce the number of targets that could be attacked. In the first place, a smaller force would still have to attack the larger and more important targets which require more than one bomb. For example, a 25% reduction could halve the number of targets. Secondly, reduction in the size of the attacking force would increase disproportionately the effectiveness of the fighter defences and prevent a larger number of bombers from reaching their targets."[183]

Ward emphasised the need for a sizeable attacking force, to achieve mutual ECM support and prevent the Russians using the more effective 'close control' of defending fighters (as opposed to 'broadcast control', which offers only general guidance on the position of the bombers). Studies suggested that fighters under close control were twice as effective (three times as effective, if bomber numbers could be reduced to 75). Here, Ward issued a blunt warning:

> "The real possibility must be faced that any further reduction in the size of the bomber force would so reduce its effectiveness that no significant proportion would survive to deliver its bombs on target. On operational grounds, therefore, the V-Force should be regarded as already reduced to a minimum, whatever view one takes of the part it should properly play in the strategic conditions of the future, unless one is prepared to contemplate the reduction of the force to military and, hence, political ineffectiveness."

This was dangerous territory, given the fundamental question. In the event of a pre-emptive missile strike, could V-bombers escape in sufficient numbers to destroy major Soviet targets? In March 1955 Air Marshal Sir George Mills, then AOC-in-C Bomber Command, had reported on V-Force progress to the CAS, Marshal of the Royal Air Force Sir William Dickson. At that time the missile threat, whilst recognised, was for the future; for some years, at least, there would be every prospect of those bombers readied for war getting away safely. The early phases of V-Force build-up unfolded. Valiant crews were training at 232 Operational Conversion Unit (OCU), RAF Gaydon, and six of the designated (Class 1) main bases for V-bombers were nearing completion. Meanwhile, a small stock of atomic bombs had been established at RAF Wittering. The AOC could be confident of reasonable warning of an incoming Soviet bomber attack, but the underlying uneasiness remained. He fretted over the vulnerability of his fledgling MBF: "… we can never be a true deterrent force until we can really disperse." The AOC's worries were shared by others. The Vice-Chief of the Air Staff (VCAS) put his concerns on paper:

"… the V-bomber force is being built up primarily as a deterrent and one of the main objects of the deployment plan is to ensure that the enemy realises that the force cannot be wiped out by ten bombs on ten Class 1 airfields."[184]

The Valiant force reached full strength in May 1957, with 59 aircraft (seven squadrons). Some Valiant crews had seen action, participating in attacks on Egyptian airfields during the Suez Crisis. V-bombers would not see action again for over a quarter of a century, until Vulcans and Victors flew their Black Buck sorties during the Falklands conflict. The first Vulcan squadrons formed in 1957 and Victors arrived at 232 OCU. The first Victor squadron began receiving aircraft in April 1958. The Mk 1 Vulcans in squadron service had their Olympus 102 engines upgraded to 104s and these aircraft were then converted to Mk 1As. The upgrade of Victors and Vulcans to Mk 1A standard began in 1959; these bombers received the more powerful engines and improved ECM.[185] Vulcan co-pilot Andy Leitch adds: "Not all Vulcan Mk 1s were upgraded to Mk 1As. The first 15 production aircraft were fitted with Olympus 101s and were not converted. They were used for trials and by the OCU."

The importance of crew continuity was recognised early on. In November 1954, the then VCAS made this point: "Stability of aircrew postings is essential if the MBF is to become really efficient." Long flying tours were deemed necessary – totalling 5¼ or 7½ years, depending on seniority. This would ease the costly training commitment and raise standards overall.[186] There were unfortunate repercussions, however, in future years. Young aircrew seeking sun and adventure were not best pleased at the prospect of spending long years on bases in eastern England; they would come to resent being 'locked in'.

Naturally, each bomber type had its champions. Some aircrew flew tours on two types, or, exceptionally, on all three, and developed distinct preferences. Nav/radar John Muston saw the Valiant as "a gentleman's aeroplane … it was comfortable, with enough room to stretch your legs …"[187] Norman Bonnor rated the Victor as "a superb aircraft … very comfortable in the back compared to the Vulcan." The Victor Mk 1, however, demanded respect when it came to fuel management:

> "This aircraft had only one fuel pump in each of its 21 tanks and we needed to be on the ground when down to 7–8,000 lbs of fuel, having taken off with 76,000 lbs. To go below that could mean a fatal flame-out if required to go round again … That said, the fuel system was a clever design using a 'proportioner' that took fuel from each tank at a rate related to its contents. This meant that the position of the centre of gravity didn't move. Later, the problem was remedied in the Mk 2, when each tank was fitted with two pumps. You could then go down as low as 4–5,000 lbs."[188]

Pilot Tony Cottingham converted from the Valiant to the Victor 2. The latter held a surprise for him: "the lightness of the flying controls on rotation for take-off – my instructor urgently repeated 'Put it down!', meaning I had raised the nose too quickly."

AEO Peter West converted from Valiants to the Vulcan B.2 and went on to join 12 Squadron at RAF Coningsby: "I loved the Vulcan – and 12 Squadron. People talked a lot about the lack of comfort for Vulcan rear crew, but it was a lot more roomy than Economy in a 747."[189] Another Vulcan AEO, Julian Grenfell, remembers his first close-up view of the Vulcan, at

OCU: "It was magic – fast, manoeuvrable and extremely big." There were important things to take into account, however, including 'Coffin Corner':

> "… the Vulcan's fastest speed at altitude was very close to the stall. The Vulcan's aerodynamics are very special and the early test pilots did much to save lives, including mine. The limiting Mach number was 0.975 – the never-exceed speed. At that point, the nose suddenly points towards the ground. You disappear down at very high speed, with both pilots holding the stick into their stomachs. The hope is to reach denser air, but recovery is impossible, as the thicker air would tear off the ailerons, then in the up position."[190]

This problem was addressed by a modification. Subsequently, Julian Grenfell's crew was to manage a recovery in these potentially fatal circumstances. Andy Leitch adds: "The modification was the auto Mach trimmer. The max IMN for the Vulcan was .93 (200 series) or .92 (301)."

Julian Grenfell also recalls that the Vulcan was built to absorb battle damage: "This involved duplicating hydraulic systems and triple wiring the electrics, to reduce vulnerability. The most critical part of the electrical system was the power bay; this was protectively located in the middle of the aircraft."

GATHERING STRENGTH

By early 1960 Bomber Command had 54 Valiants, 24 Victor Mk 1/1As and 24 Vulcan Mk 1/1As.[191] The Mk 2 aircraft would provide the bulk of the strategic frontline from 1962–1969, during the QRA/Blue Steel/low-level period. Humphrey Wynn described how ambitions were much reduced:

> "The plans to have 120 Mk 2s in 15 squadrons were never fulfilled; the UE (unit establishment) for the six Vulcan squadrons and No. 230 OCU in 1963 was 50 and for the two Victor squadrons and No. 232 OCU in the same period 17 – a total of 67. The reason why there were so many fewer Victors than Vulcans was because an order for 57 of the former had been cut by nearly half in mid-1960."[192]

Three squadrons of Valiants (24 aircraft) formed SACEUR's TBF, based at RAF Marham.[193] In the early 1960s there were also the Thor intermediate-range ballistic missiles (IRBMs) – fully deployed as 20 squadrons (60 missiles).

The crew classification system took a firm hold, opening with 'combat' status and rising to 'select star/command'; each crew member had to qualify for the crew, as a whole, to move up the ladder of excellence. Bombing and navigation competitions honed their skills.

In February 1962 Bomber Command listed 36 dispersal airfields approved for operational readiness platforms (ORPs):

- Class 1 (main bases with ORPs and facilities for four aircraft): Finningley, Coningsby, Honington, Scampton, Wittering, Cottesmore, Waddington, Gaydon and Wyton.
- Dispersal airfields with ORPs and facilities for four aircraft: Burtonwood, Bedford, St Mawgan, Ballykelly and Kinloss.

Relaxing at RAAF Butterworth: in 1964 12 Squadron crews reinforced the Far East Air Force in response to the Indonesian Confrontation. This crew connected up their AVS (air-ventilated suits) to cool down. From left to right: Flying Officer Don Chadwick (nav/radar), Flying Officer W. Hennessey (AEO), Flight Lieutenant P. Wighton (nav/plotter), Flying Officer Nick Dennis (co-pilot) and Flight Lieutenant M. Melville (captain). (Nick Dennis)

- Dispersal airfields with ORPs and facilities for two aircraft: Filton, Leconfield, Leuchars, Lossiemouth, Boscombe Down, Pershore, Cranwell, Middleton St George, Yeovilton, Leeming, Llanbedr, Coltishall, Valley, Manston, Brawdy, Lyneham, Wattisham, Stansted, Elvington, Prestwick, Machrihanish and Bruntingthorpe.[194]

This represents a snapshot in time and differs from an earlier list of November 1960 (Treasury/Air Ministry 12-DM 126/127/06) in its composition. The dispersal airfield list was subject to regular changes. Stansted, for example, disappeared from the 1962 list at some point. St Mawgan, accommodating four bombers in the 1962 list, was subsequently reduced to two.

Work continued on new facilities to respond to a Fylingdales ballistic missile early warning system (BMEWS) warning, which could be shorter than four minutes (available from 17 September 1963). The Americans, meanwhile, showed increasing interest in the MBF. A Valiant came seventh overall out of 41 in the 1958 SAC bombing competition in California; one V-Force crew came ninth out of 164 individual crews. The prime minister expressed delight. V-bombers also flew east – Vulcans, for example, landed at RAAF Butterworth, Malaysia, to test reinforcement of the Far East Air Force (FEAF). Valiants flew sorties in the Mediterranean/Far East and visited Mauripur, Pakistan.[195]

RAF THORS

As for the Thor IRBMs, there was a view in some quarters that they were not fully part of the British deterrent, being under dual control. Launch required the turning of two keys (by the RAF missile controller and the USAF authentication controller). The British key (on the prime minister's decision) initiated countdown but could not activate the warhead. The American key (on the president's decision) could activate the warhead but could not launch the missile. In essence, each half of the dual-key control introduced a tactical hold in the countdown sequence, overcome only by political decision. On paper, the 60 Thors in Britain, with megaton warheads and a range of 1,500 miles, were a formidable force. Yet they were vulnerable, being liquid-fuelled and above ground. The missiles, based on wartime airfields, were defended by Bloodhound SAMs. The Thors gave Bomber Command the equivalent of 60 additional V-bombers.[196]

Macmillan saw the UK Thor force as a demonstration of Anglo-American nuclear cooperation.[197] There were dissenting views. Air Chief Marshal Sir Harry Broadhurst, when AOC-in-C Bomber Command, described Thor as "a weapon of doubtful operational value which, in any case, can never be used until our deterrent policy has failed …"[198]

When the V-Force introduced Quick Reaction Alert (QRA), with one aircraft per squadron fully-fuelled, armed and at 15 minutes readiness, the Thors were integrated into Bomber Command's major war exercises. A proportion of the missile force was held at T.15, with targeting controlled through the Bomber Command Operations Centre (BCOC). Bomber Command issued a Thor Readiness Policy on 25 July 1960 (BC/S.91519). This required 60% of the force at standby or available, as a step towards a final readiness capability of 75%. As in the case of the MBF, the Strategic Missile Force operated on a war footing during peacetime.[199]

Thor targets included cities and airfields. The cities targeted increased from 21 to 50 by March 1959 (described in a minute from the Deputy Chief of the Air Staff (DCAS) – AIR 19/964), as the chance of hitting airfields with Thor was judged to be low.[200] The Thors were amongst 105 IRBMs based in Europe; they represented the West's missile frontline for a short period before the US inter-continental ballistic missile (ICBM) force matured. Beyond the 60 Thors in the UK during 1959–63, there were 30 Jupiters in Italy and 15 in Turkey.[201]

By 1963 Thors looked obsolescent, for the same reasons that the British Blue Streak medium-range ballistic missile (MRBM) had been cancelled in April 1960.[202] Yet, RAF Thors had historical significance, as the West's first operational strategic missile system (and, probably, the first in the world). Indeed, during 1961 the RAF began to explore possibilities for extending Thor deployment beyond the existing five-year agreement. In 2001, Wing Commander Colin Cummings listed the system's attributes:

> "The system had proved to be reliable and the crews were well-trained, efficient and effective. The weapon added the equivalent of more than half a dozen V-bomber squadrons to the Order of Battle (ORBAT) and there was a realistic prospect that changes to its propellant, coupled with other modifications, would update the system while reducing countdown time and allowing the missiles to be held, fully-fuelled, a few minutes from launch, without the problems previously encountered with liquid oxygen (LOX)."[203]

This came to nothing. There was little American interest in the idea. With the successful deployment of Titan and Minuteman ICBMs, "Washington no longer needed to have its missiles operated by proxy by its allies". Furthermore, the RAF came to recognise Thor's vulnerability, as it could not be sited underground. Extended operation would be costly without US financial support and Thor's continued inclusion in the ORBAT "would increase pressures for paring down other elements of the RAF's strategic deterrent. Reluctantly, in the late spring of 1962, the Air Council accepted that Thor would have to be withdrawn from service."²⁰⁴

The Thors may have been obsolescent by 1963 but Air Vice-Marshal Stewart Menaul pointed out that no enemy missile force was capable of destroying them in 1959 and an attack by manned bombers would have given plenty of warning. He also maintained that Thor launch sites were small and that "considerably more" than one missile with a megaton warhead would have been required to be sure of knocking out each site. "Thus, when the Thor force became operational in 1958 and for at least two years afterwards, Russia did not have either the number or quality of missiles to destroy it." Menaul maintained that Thor was a viable deterrent at that time.²⁰⁵

THE V-FORCE PEAKS

V-Force strength was expressed in the daily availability of operational aircraft and weapons. Its strength peaked in 1964, with over 180 aircraft, including the Valiants. By 1968 the force was much reduced. Victors were converted to tankers, succeeding the grounded Valiants by mid-1966; this ended a gap in RAF flight-refuelling capability of over six months during 1965.²⁰⁶

Roy Brocklebank described the V-Force at its peak: No. 1 Group wings were equipped with the Vulcan and No. 3 Group wings had Valiants and Victors. The main force in No. 1 Group was deployed in three wings, each with three squadrons of eight aircraft. The Scampton Wing (Mk 2) was equipped with Blue Steel. The Waddington (Mk 1A) and Coningsby (Mk 2) Wings were equipped with freefall weapons. No. 3 Group Victors were also deployed in three wings, but with only two squadrons of eight aircraft each. Victor Mk 1 aircraft were deployed at Honington and Cottesmore and the Mk 2, armed with Blue Steel, was at Wittering. The Valiant, by 1964, was deployed at Gaydon (OCU), Marham (main force) and Wyton, with the photo-reconnaissance (PR) version.²⁰⁷

The Vulcan Mk 2 first appeared at 230 OCU on 1 July 1960. The first operational Vulcan Mk 2 joined 83 Squadron on 23 December 1960. Cottesmore-based 232 OCU received its first Victor Mk 2 on 1 November 1961.²⁰⁸ The advent of the Mk 2s may explain why aircrew detected no erosion of V-Force capability. Certainly, Air Vice-Marshal Michael Robinson noticed no deterioration:

> "We who were in the V-Force in the early 1960s, with our improved Mk 2 versions of the Vulcan and Victor, were not aware of any decline. The pattern of QRA commitments, frequent no-notice alert exercises and the demanding training schedules kept us all very much on our toes."²⁰⁹

Victor captain Jeremy Mudford was impressed by the upgraded aircraft, having been selected for a Victor Mk 2 course in early 1962:

> "We all found the Victor Mk 2 to be vastly superior to the Mk 1 and Mk 1A. The Sapphire had 11,000 lbs of thrust but the Conway in the Mk 2 had 20,000 lbs … the total power available rose from 44,000 lbs to 80,000 lbs. The take-off performance of the Victor Mk 2 was quite extraordinary."²¹⁰

The Mk 2's greater operating height, however, lost its significance when the V-Force went low level, but to some degree the increased range (an additional 200-350NM) allowed for better target coverage (according to Wynn, an increase in the percentage of targets that could be attacked "by as much as 25%") and more opportunities for indirect routeing.[211]

Regarding route planning, human factors occasionally intervened, leading to a less than scientific approach to the challenges. Vulcan nav/radar Roy Brocklebank recalled a visit to the bomber planner (Ops 1A):

> "… he had a large office with a plotting table and, I think, a map chest. I asked him why all the track legs were no more than the 18-inch length of a Douglas navigation protractor – about 180 miles. He replied: 'Someone had taken my straight edge.'"[212]

The Mk 2s were a great advance but they were not perfect. Air Commodore Norman Bonnor, then a Victor nav/radar with 100 Squadron at Wittering, had a surprise:

> "I saw the wing tanks fall off a Victor Mk 2 after heavy rain. There was a problem with the front canopy seals, which allowed water onto the jettison switches and a large spill of fuel resulted. It was a serious event, as this Victor had a live Blue Steel underneath it."[213]

Fatigue problems with the Valiants should have been no surprise. The entire Valiant fleet was grounded in 1965 due to airframe fatigue, but this problem had been known from the very early days. Indeed, in 1957 Valiant WP215, engaged in rocket-assisted take-off trials, had suffered a major main-spar crack, put down to fatigue.[214]

It was hoped that Valiants in the low-level role could soldier on until 1968–70. However, there were numerous reminders of airframe issues involving Valiants flying low-level sorties. This was noted in a 1962 memorandum following a review of the fatigue returns of the Valiant force:

> "… it was established that the SACEUR Valiants had consumed, on average, just under 40% of their fatigue lives. The current average rate of consumption appeared to be about 5½% per annum, but this was with the traditional pattern of flying. With the low-level pattern of flying (involving 1/10 of the flying at a fatigue factor of 10) the average rate of consumption would be about 11% per annum. Hence, the remaining 60% life would last about 5½ years, i.e. until mid-1967."[215]

A visible deterrent: Vulcan XJ784 at Trenton, Ontario, positioned for the Canadian International Air Show at Toronto. (Andy Leitch Collection)

The Vulcan became the mainstay after 1965. The last Mk 2 Vulcan (XM657) was delivered in January of that year.[216] Had Skybolt gone into production, Vulcan Mk 2s would have carried two each, supported by the Blue Steel Victors.[217] With Polaris in prospect, decline set in. The MBF main force in January 1965 consisted of 104 aircraft (32 Victors and 72 Vulcans).[218] The decline continued during 1965, with numbers falling to 88 aircraft (11 squadrons of eight bombers). V-bomber strength remained at this level for some years.

VALUE FOR MONEY

In his October 1958 Memorandum to the Defence Board, defending a V-Force of 144 aircraft, Secretary for Air George Ward presented the V-bombers as tremendous value for money, given that their main role was deterrence and the consensus that Britain could not survive nuclear war:

> "I calculate that the R&D, capital and running cost of the V-Force and its weapons over the next five years will not exceed an average of about £125 million a year, or 8½% of a defence budget of about £1,470 million."[219]

This, however, was a partial disclosure of expenditure. Some months earlier, on 26 February 1958, the chairman of the COS Committee had produced a note on 'nuclear sufficiency and defence expenditure', with an annex on spending on the deterrent (excluding Thor and Blue Streak R&D). This put V-Force and weapons spending (including trials) at £105 million (1958/59), £131 million (1959/60), £125 million (1960/61), £85 million (1961/62) and £70 million (1962/63). However, with the inclusion of main base defence SAGWs, these figures are: £230 million, £254 million, £254 million, £212 million and £207 million respectively. As a percentage of a £1,470 million defence budget, this represented 15½%, 17½%, 17½%, 14½% and 14%.[220]

Yet, even factoring in SAM-related deterrent defence costs, together with expenditure on Thor, this level of investment still appears relatively modest, given UK inability to survive a nuclear catastrophe and, furthermore, taking account of the continued reduction in expenditure on conventional forces permitted by maintenance of the nuclear deterrent.

THE AOC'S DIRECTIVE

Every incoming AOC-in-C Bomber Command received a Command Directive. In February 1965 Air Chief Marshal Sir Wallace Kyle became AOC-in-C and received his directive from the CAS, Air Chief Marshal Sir Charles Elworthy. Kyle was charged with ensuring that enough of his force could survive a war scramble. As AOC-in-C, Kyle could order Alert Condition 3 (full generation of weapon systems) at his discretion, but dispersal required political authority. However, he also received delegated powers to launch a retaliatory nuclear strike, on his own initiative, in the event of war and a total breakdown of communication between Bomber Command and government.

Under the directive heading 'Main Tasks', the new AOC-in-C's first priorities were:

- To serve as the principal national deterrent to general war, by maintaining a capability to meet aggression with immediate nuclear retaliation.

- In the event of unilateral retaliatory action by the United Kingdom against the Union of Soviet Socialist Republics (USSR), to destroy those targets allocated to you in the National Plan.
- In the event of general war, to destroy those targets allocated to you by SACEUR in accordance with his Nuclear Strike Plan.[221]

Kyle's directive recognised the possibility of a catastrophic communications breakdown, should war come. On 15 June 1960, a Cabinet Office meeting of MoD, Air Ministry, Foreign Office and Cabinet Office representatives had discussed procedures for launching nuclear retaliation. A recent exercise (Halberd) exposed a need for improved communications with the prime minister and in Whitehall. The notes from this meeting state: "This was a matter partly of operational effectiveness and partly of the credibility of the deterrent." BMEWS Fylingdales would not be ready until 1963. Assuming, however, at least some degree of warning, the core problem was reaching the prime minister when he was out of London. The meeting concluded that the PM should join the AA: "If his car were linked to the Automobile Association's radio network … messages could be passed to him *en clair* within a minute or so." This solution looked like a bargain: the cost of the equipment in the car was around £200, plus £20 annual rental.[222]

Twigge and Scott offer an aside on the AA link:

"The exact role of the AA in launching Britain's deterrent is less than clear. It is, nevertheless, intriguing that the headquarters of the AA were situated directly opposite the Air Defence Operations Centre in Stanmore."[223]

THE STRANGE STORY OF THE 'POLITICAL SUBMARINE'

The exotic nature of the relationship between nuclear war, the prime minister and the AA is trumped by a stillborn plan to preserve a British 'alternative government' in the depths of the ocean, should Armageddon arrive. Doubts about the survival of cohesive government after a Soviet missile strike produced some unusual proposals; one extraordinary option was discussed in papers written in 1961. Interestingly, these offer clear evidence that the British government, despite its loud protestations over Skybolt's cancellation in late 1962, had long recognised the clear superiority of Polaris.[224]

There had been debate for some time over a long-term successor to the V-bomber/Skybolt combination. Paper S.G. (61) 42 (Revised), written over a year before Kennedy and Macmillan met in Bermuda (when the latter 'supposedly' accepted Polaris as "consolation" for Skybolt's cancellation), had concluded that "the best solution for the UK independent deterrent would be a force of Polaris submarines …" The problem, at that point, was that the Americans were willing to supply Skybolt without strings but, in contrast, wanted Polaris tied to SACEUR.[225]

Nevertheless, the 1961 'Control and Communications' and 'Control after Attack on the UK' papers made clear acknowledgement of the superiority of Polaris. The former linked this to ensuring the survival of an alternative government, tucked away in a dedicated 'political submarine'. This concept, however, was questioned in the second paper, dated December 1961.[226]

It was argued that the earlier paper assumed only a massive nuclear exchange, whereas the later paper considered a reduced form of attack to be "much more likely" (although a handwritten note on Copy No. 15 comments: "Not according to JIC (the Joint Intelligence Committee)." The December paper claimed the Russians would recognise that, in a conventional attack which did not prompt nuclear retaliation, it would be in their interests to spare the primary and/or secondary seats of government, to be able to negotiate. It went on to argue that this seat of government should be within the UK, to ensure it was fully in touch with the situation as it unfolded.

At the same time, the December paper accepted that a massive nuclear attack could not be ruled out, wiping out seats of government in the UK, but that some central authority was required for "establishing national control and cohesion". These needs were behind the earlier paper's political submarine proposals, but the later paper dismissed the concept:

> "The persons in such a submarine would have to embark at the onset of any warning period; they would be collected from various ministries, with no experience of working together as a team. Thereafter they would have limited contact with events and decisions in the UK (particularly if the submarine remains submerged and does not transmit in order to preserve the secrecy of its location). They would quickly get out of touch with the many changing facets of the situation, and would be more and more out of date the longer they were embarked. Thus, a political submarine does not appear to be a particularly good method of meeting the requirement."

Today, both papers appear to have a very loose grip on the realities of nuclear war. The December paper claimed that many other British groups outside the UK would be in a much better position to keep in touch with events. The author pointed to the UK's large embassy in Washington DC, the diplomatic organisation in Paris and high commissioners and support staff in Canada, Australia, etc. commenting that some of these centres might be unaffected: "Thus, in the event of all governmental control within the UK being annihilated, it appears that one of these groups would be very appropriate for taking over control …". A handwritten annotation in the margin dryly asks: "Of what?"

POSITIVE CONTROL

Concerns over a communications collapse and the inability to function immediately following a Soviet missile strike provided the background to the June 1960 Cabinet Office meeting which confronted the worst case: the inability of government to instruct Bomber Command. This meeting concluded that, in a situation of nuclear strike and in the absence of political instructions at the time of breakdown, AOC-in-C Bomber Command should have discretion to launch the V-Force under Positive Control – a system under which the bombers would be required to turn back on reaching the 8 degrees East 'Go/No Go' line in the absence of an authenticated Positive Release (POSREL) message.[227]

The view was that the AOC-in-C should have full responsibility for launching a retaliatory strike if, "despite all efforts by all reasonable means," he was unable to communicate with government and an enemy nuclear attack had occurred. There was no specified waiting time before discretion could be exercised.

Whilst this supplementary directive gave the AOC-in-C 'last resort' powers to launch retaliation, Twigge and Scott considered what might transpire should he become a casualty:

"Although contingency plans existed enabling HQ No. 1 Group at Bawtry 'to assume command in the event of the destruction of HQ, Bomber Command', there is no evidence to suggest that command authority to initiate nuclear retaliation was explicitly delegated to group commanders. Indeed, if the C-in-C considered it necessary to delegate the authority contained in his supplementary directive, 'this should be brought explicitly to the attention of the prime minister and the directive amended as necessary'. It was, nevertheless, noted that the directive did not debar the C-in-C from delegating this authority. This may not have been necessary. In the event of HQ Bomber Command's destruction, the commander of No. 1 Group would then become C-in-C Bomber Command and assume all his command directives, including delegated authority to initiate nuclear retaliation. Thus a Soviet decapitation attack would have the effect of devolving nuclear command authority downward within the command structure."[228]

There was a view that Soviet appreciation of delegation of command authority to the military would both lessen the incentive to mount a decapitation attack and increase the credibility of the deterrent.

Had an authenticated POSREL signal been sent, surviving V-bombers would have crossed the 'Go/No Go' line and pressed home a retaliatory attack. The Positive Control line emerged in late 1957/early 1958.[229] It was defined in a note attached to a letter from the Air Ministry to the Cabinet Office (9 July 1959). It was not a fixed line of longitude but, rather, a contour line running over friendly territory (Norway) or international waters. The average flight time from the bomber bases to the Positive Control line was around 40 minutes. Each bomber would maintain a listening watch. If no authenticated orders to proceed with the attack were received by the time the bomber reached the line, it automatically returned to base. Similar procedures applied to SACEUR-assigned TBF Valiants. The same line would be used under wholly national arrangements.[230]

CONSULTATION *IN EXTREMIS*

On the brink of nuclear war there would be little time for discussion between prime minister and president. London made great efforts to plan and prepare for this situation, by simplifying the process and reserving the decision to launch a nuclear attack to the last possible moment. In early 1962 the issues were set out in a draft memorandum, for discussion with the Americans. Consultation in an extreme emergency would focus, obviously, on the release of strategic nuclear forces. The prime minister would have to approve the use of SAC forces based in Britain and Polaris submarines at Holy Loch. Other subjects included the release of US warheads to British nuclear forces, the employment of tactical nuclear forces under NATO command and, potentially, the use of nuclear weapons beyond the NATO area. The draft discussion document reflected on the challenge: "This constitutes a considerable agenda and will take a considerable time to get through. It would clearly be impossible to complete it in a single conversation in circumstances of emergency." Simplification meant isolating those measures which did not, in themselves, commit nuclear forces to an attack. These could be agreed and authorised separately, in advance of an attack.[231] This memorandum was polished and re-polished; six months later it had still to be presented to the Americans.

How important were British strategic nuclear forces to the Americans? There was a British view that, taken overall, the Americans did not approve of independent nuclear forces, yet the fact remains that the US government and military did a great deal over many decades to support the British independent (or, rather, inter-dependent) deterrent. Indeed, the United States funded a quarter of the original Valiant force, together with four Ministry of Aviation Valiants.[232] The V-Force complicated Soviet calculations of Western capabilities and intentions, with the UK a 'second centre' of nuclear decision-making. There were also operational considerations which, at least in the early years (before the American ICBM force matured), served to magnify the significance of Britain's relatively small retaliatory force, from the American perspective. Given the comparatively short war flights of the V-bombers, together with the 60 Thor missiles, other dual-key nuclear assets (and US nuclear systems based in Britain), the UK occupied a significant frontline position. In a House of Commons debate of 26 February 1959, Defence Minister Duncan Sandys quoted the SAC Commander General Thomas S. Power: "Having regard to Britain's closer proximity, we rely on her V-bombers to provide an important part of the first wave of the Allied retaliatory force."[233]

Behind the scenes, however, a British deterrent built on subsonic bombers continued to be questioned. Operational analysis specialist Dr Les Ruskell reflects:

"I have always felt that the V-Force enjoyed a brief honeymoon period around 1959 and 1960, after which it struggled to keep pace with developments. Despite the various measures introduced to prolong its effectiveness, both technical and tactical, it was a wasting asset."[234]

5
DELIVERING THE MISSION

> *I had no personal qualms about nuclear weapons. They emerged from the 1950s ethos, which was to avoid repeating the errors of the 1930s and attempts to appease Nazi Germany. This time there would be no appeasement.*
>
> Keith Mans, Vulcan co-pilot, 50 Squadron, RAF Waddington

PLAN A AND PLAN B

Everything necessary to launch V-Force retaliation was planned to the last detail, with considerable ingenuity and some degree of ruthlessness. Plan A V-Force targets were SACEUR (NATO) targets, for the most part 'counterforce' military assets, but often located in and around the big cities. Plan B targets were national, identified as 'countervalue' – the big cities themselves. In essence, the Plan A NATO target list was the Allied war-fighting programme (under the Single Integrated Operations Plan, or SIOP), with the V-Force contributing to all-out retaliation by the West, whilst the Plan B (National) target list was an expression of 'pure' deterrence: keeping the peace by projecting the maximum countervalue threat from Britain's limited nuclear stockpile. Everyone struggled to visualise a situation in which the UK *would* wage nuclear warfare without its NATO allies, but the most important fact was that it *could*.

Each V-Force target was assigned one or more 'accounting line numbers' (ALNs). Important targets would receive multiple strikes. Crews were prohibited from discussing their targets amongst themselves. They might well have the same target, with minimum time separation between nuclear bursts. Each crew, in the low-level era, would fight World War 3 alone. The sole objective was to reach and destroy the target. They trained to attack national and NATO targets (a primary and secondary of each target set). SACEUR targets had ALNs in the 100, 200 and 300 series. National targets had ALNs in the 400 and 500 series.[235] National targets included the obvious, such as Moscow, Leningrad, Kiev, and Minsk, although the later focus was on the first and second cities.

A guest of SAC: A Vulcan pictured at Barksdale AFB. (Norman Bonnor)

An October 1958 Air Ministry note to MoD considered the sensitive issue of how many V-bombers might reach their targets. The driver behind this note (as was so often the case) was fear of a further cut in V-Force size and the consequences for operational effectiveness. This rather naive document set out three factors governing the number of bombers reaching their targets: the number of frontline bombers, the number taking off after allowing for unserviceability and, finally, percentage loss en route. It offered some conclusions:

> "The percentage losses en route will depend on the strength and effectiveness of the enemy fighter defences. They will also vary between Mk 1 and Mk 2 V-bombers. Current operational studies suggest that, allowing for 25% unserviceability, a bomber force of 104 Mk 2 and 40 Mk 1 Victors and Vulcans could effectively deliver about 50–60 bombs in the vital first strike. This would imply successful attacks on about 30–40 out of 131 big centres of Russian industry and administration with a population exceeding 100,000. More than one bomb must be delivered against the larger and more important targets."[236]

This note is naive in that it takes account of unserviceability but makes no specific allowance (perhaps understandably) for the likely large-scale destruction of the force on the ground in a ballistic missile strike – an obvious prospect by late 1958.

The key issue was to avoid being caught on the ground. This required Bomber Command to behave more like Fighter Command, with the focus on operational readiness. Training, exercises, maintenance and duty periods became imprinted with the need to generate aircraft within specified time periods and get the aircraft off the ground quickly, so allowing a proportion of the force to survive an attack and continue on, to deliver a retaliatory strike. The eventual result was QRA, an unprecedented peacetime state of readiness for war, persisting until the Polaris handover in 1969 (and with many elements continuing on into the 1970s and beyond – to the present day, in a limited sense).

On 20 May 1959 Sir Kenneth Cross became AOC-in-C Bomber Command. The central V-Force requirement – 75% of aircraft at readiness, armed and dispersed within 24 hours – had been in place for nearly a year and its attainment was proving difficult. A few weeks after assuming command, on 26 June 1959, Cross wrote to the Vice-Chief of the Air Staff (VCAS), Air Marshal Sir Edmund Hudleston, stating that he had just one squadron able to meet the 7 July 1958 readiness requirement, but promising six more by the year-end and a further five by April 1960.[237]

The 7 July 1958 readiness capability reflected the then current expectation of strategic warning. At the tactical level, the MBF was required to maintain 40 minutes' readiness for one month (15 minutes sustained for one week). This required a large network of dispersal airfields, modifications to allow bombers to start up and taxi in the minimum possible time and an increase in manning establishment to provide a two-shift, 18-hour working day and a regime of major exercises to test capability.[238]

Cross applied pressure and work accelerated on measures to improve MBF response times. Turning loops were provided on runway ends at dispersal stations such as Pershore and Leeming, allowing 'stream' take-offs, rather than single aircraft or pairs (shaving up to eight minutes off take-off time for four aircraft). Trials were organised to determine minimum take-off time for a dispersed flight of V-bombers (elapsed time, from scramble order to wheels up, for the first and last aircraft).²³⁹ There was a complete change of mood on MBF stations – with the continuous presence of sufficient personnel to bring a high proportion of aircraft to readiness within 24 hours, 365 days a year.

Timely dispersal was critical. By late 1959 16 airfields were ready for MBF use; a further eight were in an advanced stage of planning and due to be ready during 1960. Another six awaited Treasury approval.²⁴⁰ In June 1961, the Chief of the Air Staff (CAS) accepted a reduction in planned operational readiness platforms (ORPs) from 120 to a more realistic 100 (allowing for 75% serviceability: 14 x four aircraft, 10 x two aircraft (but able to expand to four) and 12 x two aircraft).²⁴¹ One major problem was the inability to disperse aircraft armed with dual-control American weapons under Project E. One result of this was the concentration of the three TBF Valiant squadrons at Marham, their main base, so exposing them to wholesale destruction on the ground.

By early 1960, the AOC-in-C told the Air Ministry his command now met the 75%/24 hours requirement during weekdays, adding: "In order to achieve a readiness capability over weekends and public holidays, 25% of the available aircraft were held at two hours' readiness during these periods …" This report was made after MoD had called for six-monthly updates concerning V-Force readiness, commencing January 1960. Overhanging everything was the threat of a Soviet missile strike and a warning time (given service from an operational BMEWS) that could be less than four minutes – allowing only a proportion of aircraft at advanced cockpit readiness any chance to get off – despite the AOC-in-C's claim of February 1963 the BMEWS *would* (as opposed to *could,* in some circumstances) increase warning time to eight minutes. One outcome of the growing concern was Micky Finn – an alert and dispersal exercise introduced in late 1960. Exercise Mick required generation at no notice but stopped short of dispersal. Exercise Mayflight embraced all aspects of readiness and dispersal, including the scramble, but on a notice basis. Micky Finn was very different – a force war exercise that could be called, at no notice, on a weekday or weekend. It also tested Transport Command's ability to support V-Force dispersal.²⁴²

Streaming at Waddington: Barry Mullen's Vulcan arrives back after a Western Ranger. (Barry Mullen)

The V-Force commitment to readiness for war was paraded to the public as a virtue, but only in a carefully controlled way. There was an acute awareness of the need to avoid over-stimulating the media and alarming the public. The V-Force deterrent role received prominence but little was revealed of its war-fighting plans and capabilities. On 2 December 1960 Air Marshal Hudleston wrote to Bomber Command AOC Sir Kenneth Cross on the sensitive issue of weekend no-notice exercises involving V-bombers. The main concern was the risk of worrying the public. Hudleston made the point that the timing of such exercises should be selected "with close regard to the international situation". He then added:

> "Since we have not as yet used any of the dispersal airfields at weekends, I consider it would be wise periodically to use them on a station or limited basis before we launch a 'weekend' full-scale exercise. The essential purpose of these exercises would be to accustom the local population to weekend flying."[243]

Clearly, the main worry was that the press might get wind of abnormal V-Force activity on a Sunday. The sudden introduction of Micky Finn war exercises at weekends, involving whole RAF commands, might well have sparked unwelcome media interest. Other exercises attracted less attention: group exercises (groupex), command exercises (such as Exercise Yeoman, a major UK air defence exercise) and NATO exercises could be on a large scale but had a character that was more routine. On a daily basis, V-Force crews flew frequent training sorties – 'profiles' (long cross-country flights with built-in exercises and simulated emergencies) and 'compex' (sorties flown in preparation for bombing and navigation competitions). In addition, solitary bombers flew Western Ranger flights to the USA, Goose Ranger flights to Goose Bay, Canada, and Lone Ranger flights east. Very occasionally, a Pacific Ranger was flown to Hickam AFB, Hawaii, and there were the rare round-the-world tours. Squadron-based dispersal was practised in Exercise Kinsman drills – normally involving the dispersal of a flight of two or four aircraft.[244]

BARRIERS TO MISSION DELIVERY

Bombers were vulnerable on the ground and in the air and these exposures intensified from 1960 onwards, given the threat of destruction in a pre-emptive missile strike and destruction in the air at the hands of rapidly expanding Soviet air defences – underlined by the huge Russian investment in new surface-to-air-missile (SAM) sites. In its important report at the close of 1959, the British Nuclear Deterrent Study Group (BNDSG) concluded that Blue Steel Mk 1-armed bombers would become increasingly ineffective after 1965 and that long-range Blue Steel Mk 2 would extend V-Force life by just two or three years after 1965. Even Skybolt would extend V-Force life to only around 1970. It warned that, *irrespective of weapons carried*, the V-Force would remain vulnerable to pre-emptive attack on its bases. In a rather limp concluding comment, it could only claim that "some of the bombers would probably be able to escape".[245]

Much effort was made to reduce MBF vulnerabilities, on the ground and in the air. Inevitably, the early focus was on penetrating the Soviet defences, rather than avoiding destruction on the home airfields, as the main threat to V-Force bases at that time was from bombers. When the Soviet missile threat became dominant, however, vulnerability on the ground received much greater attention. The Joint Intelligence Committee (JIC) eventually assumed that, in the event of an attack, the Soviets would allocate two 500-kt missiles and two 1-mt aircraft-delivered weapons to each MBF airfield.[246]

A deterrent force, of course, is no deterrent if it can be destroyed on the ground. T.C.G. James described the significance of this truism:

> "Its influence can be seen at different levels of policy – from what it was reasonable to assume about advance warning of attack (and the political as well as military indications that an attack might be in prospect) to the precise means of ensuring that the deterrent continued to be credible."

There was no questioning the principle that V-bombers must be capable of dispersing rapidly. Translating this into criteria applicable to dispersal airfields, selecting those airfields and providing facilities to meet the criteria were formidable and expensive tasks. Considerable time and effort was devoted to it, with the Treasury needing to be convinced every step of the way that these measures amounted to adequate insurance and no more.[247]

In 1955 the Air Council had agreed to a force of 240 V-bombers, dispersed over ten Class 1 airfields and 45 other UK airfields (subject to review for factors including ultimate force size).[248] Revision on the latter grounds was required. In late 1957, following agreement on a V-Force of 144 bombers, the revised dispersal plan was based on no more than four aircraft per dispersal site, on a total of 26 airfields, with a full squadron (eight aircraft) remaining on each of seven Class 1 main bases.[249] Later, another six dispersal airfields were added, as approved by the Minister of Defence, to ensure only four aircraft remained on each main base should dispersal be ordered.[250]

The cornerstone of deterrence is preservation of the capacity to retaliate, even after a surprise attack. This grew in importance with the expansion of Soviet capacity to deliver such an attack. Lawrence Freedman summed it up by citing a definition of deterrence by "assured destruction": by "maintaining a clear and unmistakeable ability to inflict an unacceptable degree of damage upon any aggressor … even after absorbing a surprise first strike."[251]

Measures reducing vulnerability on the ground focused on the extremely short warning likely in a pre-emptive missile strike. Scrambling V-bombers required verified warning. Aircraft may be recalled, but launching the V-Force before confirmation that missiles were actually incoming would expose the bombers to destruction as they were restored to readiness upon their return. Many measures were taken to ensure that a proportion of the force would survive a pre-emptive strike, to begin the North Sea crossing and continue on to the targets. They included the elaborate dispersal arrangements and QRA, with part of the force maintained fully fuelled, armed and held at readiness state 15 minutes (RS15).

The response to vulnerabilities in the air focused on electronic countermeasures (ECM). In the early years 'mutual support' barrage jamming was seen as the key to high altitude penetration, but this changed following the loss of Gary Powers' U-2 to a Soviet SAM on 1 May 1960 (although Vulcan co-pilot Andy Leitch remembers barrage-jamming being on the war studies agenda at Cranwell c.1971!). The U-2 was brought down whilst flying well above the V-bombers' maximum ceiling. New and radical measures to improve operational effectiveness were required. It was clear by late 1962, with Skybolt's cancellation, that the

V-bombers would not receive an advanced, long-range weapon allowing them to attack from positions outside heavily defended airspace. During the 1960s – and for over a decade thereafter – the V-Force soldiered on with freefall weapons and, until the end of the 1960s, Blue Steel Mk 1 with its very short range and other inadequacies. The only viable option for continued credibility, given these circumstances, was to switch the V-Force from high-level attack to low-level nuclear strike.

GOING LOW

It would be wrong to suggest that British planners were entirely reactive – propelled only by each fresh development in Soviet offensive and defensive capabilities. By the early 1950s they had already recognised that advanced Soviet radars, SAMs and interceptors would make successful high-altitude attacks by the MBF increasingly difficult and, eventually perhaps, impossible. The advantages of low-altitude attack were acknowledged over ten years before the entire V-Force went low level following Skybolt's cancellation. The Air Staff had first considered the need for a low-altitude bomber (LAB) in June 1951, two and a half years before the first production Valiant flew. A high-speed LAB, to supplement the high-altitude V-bombers, was an expression of elementary military logic. The V-bombers operated at 40,000 ft plus; as Tony Buttler commented, this cast away the full three-dimensional advantage traditionally available to bombers. The Soviets could focus on the narrow, 40,000 ft plus height band, where the V-bombers would become increasingly exposed to SAMs. LAB, however, would force the enemy to spread the defence effort and so ease pressure on the V-bombers.[252]

LAB's Operational Requirement (OR.324) emerged in October 1953, with a war sortie profile of 500 ft or less for 80% of the outbound leg and Mach 0.95 for ten minutes over the target. The weapon was to be an air-to-surface missile. OR.324, however, was cancelled within a year, on grounds of cost and the many technological problems then associated with low-level penetration.[253] Yet, the LAB initiative had real value – it served as a timely reminder of the benefits of going low and this fostered early exploration of V-bomber low-level capabilities.

Inevitably, the early low-level trials involved the Valiant, the first of the V-bombers to enter service. In an undated note, the DCAS reflected:

> "The Air Staff have always regarded a low-level capability as highly desirable as a means of extending the enemy's defence problem and as a possible way of reducing the vulnerability of an attacking aircraft. In 1954 they were obliged to withdraw their requirement (OR.324) for a specialist low-altitude bomber on economic grounds and because the extensive research and development required might have had an adverse effect on other projects. Following the cancellation of OR.324 CAS called for an investigation into the possibility of the V-bombers doing low-altitude sorties."[254]

Serious problems were recognised regarding navigation and accurate bombing at low level. V-bombers had been designed for high-altitude operation and structural strength, to some degree, had been sacrificed in return for optimised performance at height. Those at the top hoped that low-level attacks could be made by night, allowing the speed to be brought down to what could be accepted from the structural viewpoint. However, Valiant low-level trials, beginning in early 1956, soon exposed the severity of reduced fatigue life. This issue was put

On target: a Vulcan attacking a bridge in Italy. (Andy Leitch Collection)

aside when low-level trials were suspended following a decision to focus on preparing the new V-bombers for their primary high-level strategic role. Nevertheless, the Valiant's ability to fly a low-level bombing mission had been demonstrated and this, in itself, was encouraging given recognition that the Valiants would suffer very severe losses at high level. In mid-1956, Air Commodore B. K. Burnett, the Director of Operations (Bomber and Reconnaissance) (D.Ops [B&R]), sent an interesting note to the Assistant Chief of the Air Staff, Operations (ACAS, Ops), referring to American low-level training:

> "… it would probably strengthen Russian convictions that they should build up their defences to counter a low-level threat if they heard of us training in low level as well. Such a deception on our part could be achieved with comparatively little low-level flying over the UK and possibly also over Europe, provided the security measures we took to guard our real intentions were adequate."[255]

Such signalling of V-Force low-level capabilities, if successful, might have had most unfortunate repercussions seven years later, when the decision was taken to give the entire V-Force an exclusively low-level strategic war role.

In the early 1960s, further trials were held to test V-Force ability to find and accurately bomb targets at low level. Trial No. 407, for example, examined the challenges of low-level navigation. This employed a Valiant flying low level from Goose Bay, Labrador, across terrain closely mirroring what would have been encountered during a war sortie.[256] This Bomber Command Development Unit (BCDU) trial, ordered in August 1961, found that the navigation and bombing system (NBS) "functioned extremely well" but had very restricted range at low level – "even prominent features often could not be identified at ranges exceeding about 5NM". The acquisition of Decca roller maps was recommended.[257]

Roy Brocklebank has no recollection of action taken on this front:

"I have no knowledge of roller maps on Vulcans … Decca Navigator depended on fixed ground stations and used the time difference between different stations. Unlike GEE, which used VHF frequencies, Decca used a much lower frequency that could be received at low level. I think that some aircraft based in Germany had the map. The Vulcan Mk 2 had an upgraded Green Satin 2 but this was changed in the late 1960s to a Decca Doppler 72M/J-Band triple beam static system. There was no topographical moving map."[258]

One observation from Trial No. 407 was especially discouraging: "Each low-level sortie produces a certain amount of airframe damage, broken end-cleats and loose rivets, etc. which must be repaired before the next flight."[259]

Trials concerning V-Force system performance continued in Canada; some sorties were flown by ECM trials Vulcan XA895. Trial No. 414 tested some aspects of ECM performance – the measurement of Blue Diver power output (which could not be done over the UK) and also Red Shrimp performance (which could not be carried out over Britain for security reasons).[260]

Views on ultra-low level changed over time and according to circumstances. Decades later, Tornado strike squadrons, trained to attack Warsaw Pact airfields, continued at very low level in their strikes on Iraqi airfields to deliver the JP233 runway denial weapon during the 1991 Gulf War. However, medium level was soon found to be a less risky environment and the campaign evolved into medium-level attacks, eventually delivering laser-guided stores.

NO DEFENSIVE ARMAMENT

V-bombers had no defensive armament. Air Vice-Marshal Stewart Menaul described this issue in these terms:

"… perhaps the most difficult problem and certainly the most controversial … The disparity in speed and ceiling of jet fighters and jet bombers in the early fifties was small, and the RAF believed that the speed and height characteristics likely to be available in their new jet bombers, coupled with an elaborate array of equipment to provide extensive jamming and deception tactics en route to the target, would guarantee a reasonable degree of safety for the bombers."[261]

Ed Jarron, a former Vulcan pilot, shared his thoughts on this thorny subject:

"… as shown in our fighter affiliation training, we could out-turn and out-climb most fighters of the day above 45,000 ft. Our tactic was to turn into the fighter's track and to force it into a turning fight. We always regretted not having an offensive weapon to take them out. However, a large, relatively slow aircraft like the Vulcan was inherently vulnerable at low level."[262]

Bomber Command had fought a long ECM duel with the Germans during World War 2. Stewart Menaul regarded Britain as an ECM pioneer, but electronic warfare (EW) had been much neglected in the immediate post-war period.[263] The V-bombers' arrival triggered a revival but the first of the three types, the Valiant, had very little ECM equipment. Wing Commander Peter West, a Valiant AEO, was far from impressed: "The Valiant's ECM kit was laughable … just terrible. In fact, I think we had better ECM kit during World War 2. The Valiant's tail-warner (Orange Putter) was useless."264

Menaul, in contrast, preferred to focus on Russian difficulties and the geographical issues favouring the MBF:

> "Looking at a map of Russia, it is evident that the Soviets face an enormous air defence problem. The frontier from Murmansk in the north to Odesa in the south is 1,350 miles. In the late fifties, it could be penetrated at almost any point by V-bombers with a high degree of safety … From 1953 onwards, a concerted effort was made to update ECM doctrine, devise new designs and forecast likely developments in defence systems several years ahead, so that countermeasures could be ready … By 1954, the many and varied components of the nuclear deterrent force were in production, including aircraft, weapons, a wide range of complicated radio and radar equipment, bombing and navigation aids and ECM devices."265

The reality was not quite so rosy. There were production delays involving vital items, from ECM to the NBS. In early 1955 the VCAS lost patience and issued a reminder that the Chiefs of Staff saw the MBF as the "primary weapon in the national armoury".266 The Mk 2 bombers were to have radar and fighter control communications jammers, a passive warning receiver and the Red Steer tail-warner. The Mk 1A and Mk 2 ECM outfit consisted of the Green Palm voice communications jammer, two Blue Diver metric jammers for use against ground radars, three Red Shrimps (S-band barrage jammers), a Blue Saga passive warning receiver, the Red Steer tail-warner and Window (chaff) dispensers, at an estimated cost of £1 million per squadron. A 1963 report from the Air Ministry Electronic Warfare Committee (Airborne Offensive Subcommittee) noted that, four years previously, it had been decided that ECM policy long term would focus on noise jamming. The problem here was the absence of a long-term environment – the goalposts were forever on the move.

In October 1961, there had been a revised ECM programme for aircraft earmarked for Skybolt (and, therefore, not required to penetrate Soviet defences). With Skybolt cancelled and the war role switched to low-level attack in early 1963, a new ECM policy was approved that March. The ECM fit seemed little changed: it was to consist of Green Palm, Blue Diver and Red Shrimp noise jammers, Window, and Red Steer and Blue Saga warning equipment. The situation was reviewed again that October, in the case of Mk 2 aircraft in the low-level role, with some variation between freefall and Blue Steel aircraft.267 By that stage, much of the existing ECM had become irrelevant at low level.

Vulcan captain Peter Moore described ECM tactics:

> "The general plan was to fly high level to the edge of the enemy radar cover. Having detected radar pick-up, we would descend, aiming to edge the lobe but not be fully detected … At low level we kept our passive warners on, ready to employ counters when necessary. In my time, we had a new radar warning receiver (ARI 18228) fitted. Active ECM was only employed once we sensed detection."268

Ironically, the modifications to some Vulcans when Skybolt was still in prospect proved useful 20 years later, when the ALBM hard points sported Shrike anti-radiation missiles, together with the AN/ALQ-101D jamming pod, for Black Buck missions.

6
V-FORCE PILOTS

> *If you joined the RAF hoping to fly a Lightning and ended up on QRA, it must have been a bit frustrating.*
>
> Dr Les Ruskell, former head of the Operational Analysis Cell,
> UK Permanent Joint Headquarters, Northwood

Each V-Force squadron of eight aircraft had an establishment of at least 11 crews, each aircraft having five crew members – two pilots, two navigators (nav/plotter and nav/radar) and the AEO. RAF commanders had regarded the V-bombers as an elite force requiring very substantial numbers of aircrew and ground crew. Aircrew training on this scale demanded a huge investment and this had to be protected by requiring an unusual level of continuity. Both aircrew and supporting ground crew were required to serve with the V-Force for at least five years.

Recruitment rapidly developed a head of steam. In 1953 V-bombers received 'super priority' status and large numbers of aircrew and ground crew were sourced and trained in a carefully planned, well-managed programme. Humphrey Wynn described the approach in the early days:

> "Training for pilot and navigator aircrew was mainly to be done at the Canberra OTU. High qualifications were required for acceptance on the V-bomber squadrons. pilots had to have had 2,000 hours' experience as first pilots, plus Canberra experience, or experience on multi-engined jets, though it was recognised that the 2,000 hours criterion would, in the course of time, have to be relaxed."[269]

From Canberra OTU, pilots went to the V-Force Operational Conversion Unit for captains' or second pilots' courses. Navigators were sought for the two subgroups: nav/plotters (principal navigators) and nav/radars (with a role including 'bomb-aiming'). Nav/radars were responsible for the onboard NBS:

> "It was estimated that bomb-aimers and navigators needed at least 100 hours' operating experience on NBS – the core of which was the H2S Mk 9 radar – before they could be considered operationally proficient. Signallers, as fifth crew members, were to be responsible for operating the long-range air-communications equipment, tail-warning radar and RCM (radio countermeasures), later, ECM (electronic countermeasures) fit."[270]

Gary West wanted to fly Canberras but was posted to 232 OCU at RAF Gaydon as a Victor co-pilot, subsequently joining 10 Squadron at RAF Cottesmore. Many new co-pilots were unhappy: "The flying was very curtailed. If you had three flights a fortnight you were doing well. It was not a young man's dream!"[271]

Unlike the crews of World War 2 heavy bombers, V-bomber crews sat close together in a pressurised cabin. During the mid-1950s, the Valiants, followed by the Vulcans and Victors, began to arrive on the squadrons as aircrew progressed through specialised training and crewed up at OCUs. From the first, the V-Force was a highly distinct grouping, with a special status as custodian of the nuclear deterrent. Initially, only mature pilots with plenty of multi-engined experience were sought. Each crew had its core – the so-called constituted crew: the captain and two navigators. They made up the central pool of expertise, supported by the co-pilot and AEO.

The decision not to equip the new bombers with defensive weapons was controversial, but no more so than the failure to provide ejection seats for the three rear crew. A series of accidents would claim some 40 lives. It was extremely difficult for rear crew to leave successfully from a hatch.

As the V-Force grew, it took on a distinct personality – not always to the taste of aircrew posted to V-bomber squadrons. The idea of spending years on bases in Eastern England was less attractive than tours on other aircraft types, promising time in more hospitable climes. Yet at the same time, the late 1950s V-Force, in many respects, did represent cutting edge technology (if one set aside the rapid advance of ballistic missiles).

When the search for highly experienced, elite aircrew for V-Force tours eventually began to falter, a new direction took hold. The premise that the flying had to be done by mature pilots with full logbooks began to unravel. Air Commodore Norman Bonnor provides a context:

"Ideally, most V-Force captains were experienced bomber types with at least two tours under their belts but, within a few years, selection was opened to some of the first co-pilots who had joined the force straight from training and now had up to three years' experience of the aircraft and role. By the mid-1960s, most co-pilots came straight from training and included a proportion of young ground engineers on a flying tour to broaden their appreciation of aircrew needs – an excellent scheme which, unfortunately, was abandoned when their flying training was seen as too expensive for the time they spent on aircrew duty."[272]

INSPIRATIONS

Flying in the RAF promised adventure and glamour for those growing up in a 1950s Britain largely devoid of both. Future Vulcan captain John Huggins was born in Boston, Lincolnshire, in 1947. His father, an RAF engine fitter, spent most of his war in India. His mother was a radar operator attached to a very successful AA (anti-aircraft) site credited with shooting down 11 aircraft. John Huggins expected to go into the services:

"I greatly admired wartime aircrew and I always wanted to fly with the Royal Air Force. It was a time of heroes, from Roy Rogers and Denis Compton to Guy Gibson. Perhaps one in a thousand boys who wanted to be RAF pilots eventually made it. I was just ten when my uncle gave me a copy of Guy Gibson's *Enemy Coast Ahead*. I still have it – an early Book Club edition. From that moment on I wanted to be a bomber pilot. I still watch *The Dam Busters* whenever it is screened. I must have seen it more than a hundred times over the years."[273]

> "I joined the Air Training Corps (ATC) at the age of 13 and went on to win a Flying Scholarship. I had my PPL by the time I was 17. We flew Austers. At that time I was a cadet flight sergeant and flying was the only thing that drove me on. When the film *Those Magnificent Men in Their Flying Machines* was in production, the company wanted me to fly a tiny aeroplane called the Flea, given my small size. Eventually, however, that job was given to a female pilot with more experience."

Inevitably, the day came when young Huggins arrived at Biggin Hill's Aircrew Selection Centre:

> "I was just 17 and the youngest in my group – most were university chaps in their early twenties. During my short visit to Biggin Hill I saw someone walking stiffly towards me. It was one of my heroes – Douglas Bader! I snapped up a salute and said: 'Good morning, Sir.' He turned to me and said: 'I'm not interested in your views on the fucking weather.'"

Bader's personality and his courage were very different things.

John Huggins had to wait for basic training at RAF South Cerney, near Cirencester. Arriving on 10 January 1965 he found himself amongst South Cerney's last intake before station closure.

As a child, future Vulcan captain Roger Smith lived for a period in a house close to the end of RAF Manston's generous runway. In the 1950s, Manston, on the East Kent coast, became an important USAF base – its rich collection of Thunderjets, B-47s and other aircraft did much to encourage his fascination with flying:

> "I joined Ramsgate ATC but we moved in 1958, eventually living in London. Due to the move I had missed out on a flying scholarship. My only ambition at that time was to be a fighter pilot and I tried for Cranwell. In the end I joined in late 1961 via a direct entry commission."[274]

Another future Vulcan captain, Jon Tye, joined the ATC and soloed in gliders but had a competing interest – motorbikes:

> "When I left school I joined Rolls-Royce at Derby as an engineering apprentice. By then, my elder brother was riding competitively for BSA. I took up scrambling and trials and from the age of 17 to 20 I was East Midlands champion at both."[275]

When recovering from a bout of flu, Tye was drawn to an RAF ad in a magazine:

> "Well, I told myself that my view of the world would be confined to a corner of Derbyshire unless I was careful. Flying around in Lightnings and Hunters excited my interest. I applied in 1962 and had an interview at Hornchurch. The three-day selection turned out to be quite intense and there was a problem. The weekend before I had been racing and had a fall – most of the rest of the pack ran over me and I had a cracked rib. When I stripped off for the medical I was black and blue all over. The doctor asked: "What happened?" When I explained, he said that I would not be able to cope with the physical tests. I replied that I wouldn't have the chance to come back. They let me go ahead and, at the end, I was told I was equally able to be a pilot or navigator, but was

totally unsuited to the AEO role. They asked me if I would accept navigator and I said no. It was left at that."

The RAF, however, did not waste promising candidates – they needed aircrew for over 100 V-bombers: "I went straight in as a pilot, on direct entry, and arrived at South Cerney for basic training. I did my initial flying training at RAF Leeming, won the aerobatics prize and came second overall." Tye's next posting was to RAF Valley and the Gnat course.

Vulcan and Victor captain Paul Millikin's father was a wartime Spitfire test pilot who subsequently flew with Bomber Command, completing 53 operations. He received the DFC. His son was just eight when he decided on a future with the RAF.

> "… I had been hooked by films like *The Dam Busters* and *Reach for the Sky*, like many other kids. I joined the CCF and eventually became a cadet warrant officer. As a cadet, I attended Biggin Hill in 1963 and was awarded a Flying Scholarship at Thruxton, which resulted in a PPL. This was a 'licence to kill' – a PPL at the age of 17 with just 30 hours' flying experience on a Piper Colt. Fortunately, I didn't have enough money to ever use my licence!"[276]

Later, Millikin tried for Cranwell and was offered a direct entry commission as a pilot: "This meant a much shorter officer training course prior to pilot training, which resulted in getting to my first squadron 18 months earlier than my ex-Cranwell-trained contemporaries."

Nick Dennis' father also flew operationally with Bomber Command during World War 2, completing 83 operations. Over half the aircrew on his initial training course did not survive. Nick won a flying scholarship; he flew Tiger Moths at Bristol Airport during 1961, logged 21 hours and obtained his PPL. Destined to become a Vulcan captain, he was still doing A-levels when called to the Aircrew Selection Centre, Hornchurch, for leadership and aptitude tests:

> "I passed and reported to No. 4 Flying Training School at RAF Leeming during the following year, 1962. This was the time of all-jet training, on the Jet Provost. I was not a natural pilot. I had to work at it, but the PPL gave me confidence and my father's wartime service was a spur. In fact, I found the Jet Provost, in some respects, easier to fly than the Tiger Moth. Three-point landings in a Tiger Moth could be quite tricky. In contrast, the JP was a nice, easy aeroplane to fly, lovely in formation. We had the Mk 3, which had variable throttle settings, all of which provided the same constant power. The Mk 4 was different, as was the Mk 5, which had pressurisation."[277]

His next posting was to RAF Valley:

> "I was on the last Vampire course. The direct entry cadets got the Vampires; the Cranwell people got the Gnat. Anyway, I loved the Vampire T.11; it performed beautifully in formation. The scenery over Anglesey and Snowdonia was spectacular. It was a delightful time."

Nick Dennis finished on the Vampire in July 1963:

> "I wanted Hunters. I had a quiet manner and didn't shout loud. I thought I'd never get it. We had 20 on our course. The squadron leader called out the postings: ten for the

V-Force and most of the rest for Canberras and Javelins, with one or two creamed off to CFS (Central Flying School) as future instructors. He had called out 18 names. Then he said that the last two, including me, had been picked for Hunters. Sadly, it all went wrong on my final navex. I was late getting a true bearing and, as a result, someone else was given my place. Now I would be flying Vulcans. Much later, with hindsight, I came to realise that this was a good outcome for me."

Vulcan captain Roger Frampton also wanted Hunters, following flying training on Jet Provost Mk 3s and Vampire T.11s. Instead, he was posted to the Valiant OCU at RAF Gaydon and on to 49 Squadron at RAF Marham. Following the grounding of the Valiants, he qualified as a flying instructor and went on to join the Vulcan OCU at RAF Finningley. He became captain of a Vulcan crew and joined 35 Squadron in late 1968. His wife, Mo, has always played an active part in squadron activities and, at the time of writing, remains squadron secretary.

Vulcan captain Dennis Martin's father flew operations in World War 2 as a flight sergeant rear-gunner. His son was interested in aviation but had plans for a medical career and, later as a marine biologist. He prospered, but as a salesman. He married and bought his first house in 1968 at the age of 21. Flying then reared its head and he joined Cambridge University Gliding Club:

"I decided to join the RAF and went to Biggin Hill, where I was told I was too old to become a pilot. The age limit was 23½ and I was nearly 24. I told them it was pilot or nothing else. They obviously agreed with me as a few months later I attended the Initial Officer Training Unit at RAF Henlow, passing out as an acting pilot officer. I was subsequently posted to RAF Church Fenton, attending the 30-hour Primary Flying Course on the Chipmunk T.10. The syllabus allowed 13 hours to solo. My instructor was an old school World War 2 Spitfire pilot; he sent me solo after 7½ hours."[278]

His next posting was to Linton-on-Ouse for flying training on the Jet Provost Mk 3 and 5:

"Again, everything went well. I never failed a test. They wanted to send me to fast jets, but there was a problem – I suffered from airsickness and took pills in secret. I just puked into bags and carried on. I had a very reasonable instructor who agreed not to report my airsickness provided I always completed the sortie. I got quite adept at feeling ill and finishing the sortie anyway."

Dennis Martin now wanted large aircraft rather than fast jets:

"I told them I would prefer the Britannia or Hercules and in the summer of 1973 I arrived at RAF Oakington, to fly Varsities. I finished the course by the year end. I didn't want the V-Force. I *did* want to fly all over the world. The bottom tier of the course – who needed to be co-pilots – would be sent to the V-Force. Even at that point, Victors and Vulcans were regarded as old aircraft. I graduated top at Oakington and went to see the boss for my posting. I became quite grumpy when told I had got Vulcans. Apparently, the V-Force had complained about the quality of the co-pilots they were receiving. That's why some of the top of the group had to go. I didn't know at the time, but that was the best thing that could have happened to me. I thoroughly enjoyed my future flying tours."

First impressions count: "Well, the Vulcan was big, set high off the ground and its cockpit was incredibly small. At first, I couldn't believe it could fly. I began in the OCU simulator at RAF Finningley, doing around 30 hours." However, Dennis had to wait for his place on a squadron. There was a six-month hold and from January to July 1974 he went home to Tadcaster. Never one to sit around doing nothing, he set up a window-cleaning business.

Once again, John Huggins also had to wait. On finishing at South Cerney, Acting Pilot Officer Huggins was posted to Waddington, joining this station's General Duties Flight. It appeared the movie industry was tracking him. As an air cadet on summer camp at Wattisham, the film *633 Squadron* was in the making. Now the cameras were rolling at Waddington:

"When I arrived, they were working on the James Bond film *Thunderball* at this station, with its Mk 1A Vulcans. I was in seventh heaven, strolling around an operational V-Force base.

"I was posted to Church Fenton to begin all-jet training on the Jet Provost. The chop rate on this course was huge. If one flight didn't go well, your next flight was a check flight to decide whether you got the chop or carried on. You had to go solo on the Jet Provost (which had a similar performance to a late mark Spitfire) within 13 flights. You might be given one or two repeats but, after that, you got the chop. We lost half the intake, with some simply unable to cope with the pressure and challenge. Shortly afterwards, the RAF had second thoughts about all-jet training and re-introduced *ab initio* training on Bulldogs, to reduce the failure rate.

"The Jet Provost surprised me. As we took off on that first flight, it reminded me somewhat of a glider. There was no propeller in front and the rate of climb was like a winch launch. It was wonderful. For some reason, the instructors had a lot of confidence in me but, being young, I didn't yet share their feelings. I never had a regular instructor – they were all happy to fly with me. There were some highly decorated World War 2 pilots around; they had a big influence on me and I took it all very seriously. I became determined to fly in what would be as close as possible to an operational environment. I spent many hours 'under the hood', instrument flying.

"The pilot wore a peaked hood, so his vision was confined to the instruments. During the flight, the instructor would put the aircraft through violent manoeuvres, toppling the gyros. The student took corrective action with whatever he had left. By the time I soloed, I had 20 hours more instrument-flying practice than any other student pilot in the group. When in the air I wasn't so much interested in aerobatics per se, but, rather, violent evasive flying of the type you needed in combat. There were plenty of max. rate turns and low-level flying, although we were banned from going lower than 200 ft. The only thing I was never any good at was formation flying … I have always regarded this as dangerous and an unnecessary use of aeroplanes." [279]

John Huggins had ambitions to fly Vulcans but there would be more waiting:

"I was disappointed with a posting to Oakington, near Cambridge, in October 1966. At that time there was a 'training gap'. Older pilots, who had trained during the war or during the immediate post-war years, were used to flying as a crew. The younger pilots, however, had trained on single-engined jets and lacked experience of flying in a crew environment. Oakington addressed this problem. I flew the twin-engined Varsity and was taught how to behave as the captain of an aircraft. Amongst other things, I learnt how to be considerate. Above all, I always remembered my responsibility in leading the crew and keeping them safe. At that time, I thought I would go on to maritime or fly transports, given that Oakington was the Advanced Flying Training School for these multi-engined types."

Certainly, while flying the Varsity Huggins had no guarantee of a V-Force posting. As things turned out, he was the only one of his intake at Oakington to move on to Vulcans. He was posted to 230 OCU at Finningley, where he discovered that V-bombers were individuals:

"The Vulcans had a distinct smell, but this differed from aircraft to aircraft. It was a cocktail of grease, pee, stale food and fuel. Strangely, the big thing that hit me about the Vulcan in a museum was its complete lack of smell."

On leaving OCU John Huggins was promoted to flying officer and joined 101 Squadron. "My father, meanwhile, had been convinced that a boy from a working-class family could never get his wings and become an officer. He refused to believe it until the very moment I got those wings."

Unlike John Huggins, Acting Pilot Officer Paul Millikin had no wish to fly Vulcans. He was posted to RAF Acklington, Northumberland, for all-through jet training on the Jet Provost:

"This was the most popular flying training school in the Royal Air Force as it was purported to have the lowest chop rate for student pilots. Being a long way north, staff and students tended not to go away at weekends, resulting in a great social life and high morale. We were able to concentrate on our flying training. The initial trips in the Jet Provost, despite my PPL training, were as though I had never flown before. I was no star but eventually did OK. Looking back, with some 35 years flying instructor experience, I now see that I was a slow starter – very average in the early days. Having been rather average I was posted to the Varsity for advanced training, rather than the Gnat at RAF Valley.[280]

"On completion of training, I was asked for my preferences for posting. Out of a list of seven aircraft, I, along with most of my contemporaries, got my seventh choice: the Vulcan. At that time, the V-Force was unpopular due to the boring training regime involving mostly high-altitude flying. Additionally, there was no chance of an overseas posting. Fortunately for me, my subsequent posting was to 44 (Rhodesia) Squadron, which was then training in the recently-introduced low-level freefall role."

FAST JETS OR MULTI-ENGINED?

Keith Mans was born into a military family. He applied for an Air Force Scholarship in 1962, arrived at Cranwell in October 1964 and graduated in May 1967. He would become a Vulcan co-pilot:

"This was the era of through-jet training on the Jet Provost. I had already obtained my PPL in 1963 at the age of 17. I learnt to fly on Colts but did my spins in the Auster. I was 19 when I first flew in the Jet Provost. That was in March 1965. I took 12 hours to solo – an average time. I suppose it was like anything else in life: around 10% had innate ability, with exceptional hand/eye coordination. Another 10% had just the opposite. For the 80% in the middle, including me, it was all a matter of application and hard work.[281]

"My first flight in the Jet Provost was less than sensational. I sat on the ejection seat, wearing lots of kit and smothered in straps. It was not very comfortable. I wore an old-fashioned bone dome, with a separate headset. Nevertheless, the JP's performance was that of a late World War 2 fighter, with a speed in the 350–400 mph range."

Keith Mans' father, Major General Rowland Spencer Noel Mans, CBE, welcomed his son's decision to become an RAF pilot:

"He was delighted that I had decided to enter the armed forces and, furthermore, that I was doing something I enjoyed. This was a period when the extraordinary wartime relationship between RAF pilots and the British public still lingered. A pilot had a sort of celebrity status – a certain cachet. Not surprisingly, I wanted to fly fast jets – as did almost everyone else."

Vulcan captain Roger Dunsford's father was a haematologist. They both expected continuity in the medical profession, but things worked out differently: "I became a Vulcan co-pilot, captain and flight commander on various squadrons during the period 1973 to 1984, with over 2,000 hours flying on type."[282]

This alternative future resulted from a chance meeting in a Sheffield pub; Roger Dunsford bumped into his former Scout patrol leader, a couple of years older and a teenage jet pilot at Cranwell. He was advised to apply for a cadetship: "I was just 17 when I went to Cranwell, as his guest, in 1966. I toured the college, saw the fantastic sports facilities and climbed into the cockpit of a Jet Provost." Roger hedged his bets; he applied for a Cranwell cadetship and also an RAF University cadetship and got offers for both. He took up the latter and read Geology at Manchester University:

"I joined the air force in September 1967, as an acting pilot officer. What a great set up! Cadetships were paid £770 in the first year, rising to £1,200 in the final year – far in excess of the basic student grant. At weekends and on 'camps' during the vacations we were taught to fly by the full-time RAF staff of QFIs in University Air Squadron Chipmunks based at RAF Woodvale, near Southport."

On graduating, Dunsford went to Cranwell, was promoted to flying officer and commenced Jet Provost training:

"We started on the JP Mk 3 and I went solo on my ninth flight, with seven hours 40 minutes in the logbook. The JP Mk 5, which we moved onto later in the course, was a slick machine, better streamlined and with a more powerful engine than the Mk 3. I was good enough – but only just – to enter the section of the class selected for fast-jet training. There were around 24 on the Cranwell course. Ten went to fast jets, the next ten to multi-engined aircraft and the rest to helicopters. It was a little more complex than that, as we had some measure of choice and some in the top ten wanted multi-engined or helicopters. For almost everyone hankering after fast jets, however, 'Harriers from carriers' was the ultimate dream. What actually happened was rather different. When we finished the Jet Provost course, in September 1971, there was a backlog of pilots and we went into a 'holding pattern.'"

By early 1972 Roger Dunsford was close to finishing the Gnat Ground School at RAF Valley, but this diminutive aircraft developed a tailplane problem and was grounded. He went on several weeks' 'gardening leave'. Then, in April, he was told he could join the Hunter course, which required another ground school: "During the previous eight months I had done very little flying – only a few backseat rides in ATC Chipmunks. Suddenly, here was the Hunter T.7. Wow! What a lovely aeroplane!"

There were ten RAF and two Jordanian Air Force pilots on the course:

"Well, the Hunter course was a shambles. Everyone was rusty in the air. I flew the T.7, got to a progress check on 25 July and was chopped. I had flown the Hunter for around eight weeks. I felt unlucky rather than resentful – just generally pissed off. It was all very straightforward. The flight commander took me to one side and said: 'It's most unlikely that you will be one of the few going forward to fast jets.' I replied: 'That's no surprise, Sir.' I decided to put the past few months behind me and join a multi-engined course as soon as possible. Overall, from our Hunter course, six were chopped and two were killed (one of the Jordanians and a good friend of mine hit each other, whilst in the Valley circuit). Only four graduated.

"As an aside, my first solo in the Hunter was in WV372, on 3 June 1972. I then flew this aircraft again the following day and again on 6 June. I checked this in my logbook when I saw the tailplane, bearing the markings WV372, being craned out of the wreckage of the Hunter involved in the Shoreham Air Show accident in August 2015, which cost 11 lives."

Some never wanted fast jets. Indeed, future Vulcan captain David Dinmore initially wanted to join the navy! Flying never crossed his mind. Yet, when he reached the sixth form he applied to Cranwell and Sandhurst, as well as Dartmouth, and received offers from all three: "The RAF offered training as a pilot and I entered Cranwell in January 1963."[283]

Having logged 45 hours in Chipmunks, Dinmore progressed to the Jet Provost:

"I graduated in December 1965, having gained my wings and as a pilot officer. This guaranteed a full-service career to 55, if I so wished. I did my advanced flying training in Varsities at RAF Oakington. I never saw myself as a fast-jet pilot and expected a future in Transport Command or Coastal Command. The options after Cranwell were multi-engined aircraft or helicopters. I put down heavy aircraft, then helicopters."

Future Vulcan captain John Reeve joined the RAF Section of the school CCF and went on to win a flying scholarship at Carlisle in 1963: "We flew Huskies, a version of the Auster." This was an RAF-recognised course of 30 hours' flying: "I obtained my PPL. This was worthwhile for the air force, as the training at least identified those who could not fly."[284]

Reeve's sole interest was flying:

"Now, five decades on, I am still instructing on 737 simulators. Many years as an instructor taught me that there is truth in the view that anyone can fly, but many people find it difficult to fly *and* think ahead. The best pilots can do both."

John Reeve reported to the RAF Aircrew Selection Centre, Biggin Hill, in 1963:

"I had been to Biggin Hill before, when interviewed for my flying scholarship. Now the issue was RAF entry. I had my PPL but was short of an O level. At that time, the RAF had a scheme that paid you during two years of A level study. I benefitted and by 1965 I was ready to enter Cranwell for training on Jet Provosts. The transition to jets wasn't difficult. In fact, a Jet Provost is easier to fly in some respects – it had no tail wheel and didn't try to bite you on landing. Looking back, my feeling is that I didn't work hard enough on the ground. However, the prevailing view at Cranwell at that time was that there was no such thing as a bad student – only bad instructors. The student failure rate was just 2%, rather than the 25% of earlier times. There was some logic behind this. In the larger Royal Air Force of the day, aircrew were needed in bigger numbers. There was an argument that, if someone made co-pilot, there was a good chance that, at some stage they would improve."

John Reeve graduated from Cranwell in 1968.

OCU AND THE SQUADRONS

With fast jets off the table, Roger Dunsford still had no V-Force expectations: "Frankly, the Vulcan was not an aeroplane I had considered. After all, it was in the last phase of its service career." His multi-engined training involved the Varsity, with a first flight on 12 October 1972: "As an aircraft I hated it – 'The Pig' or '50,000 rivets flying in close formation' were its less than affectionate monikers." Yet Dunsford finished in the top five and he asked for the Nimrod: "We expressed our preferences, but to no avail. Three of the top five – myself included – were posted to the Vulcan OCU at Scampton."[285]

The first hurdle was the aviation medicine lead-in at RAF North Luffenham, Rutland; decompression, hypoxia and anti-g familiarisation were on the menu:

"Explosive decompression, causing internal gases to rapidly expand and vent, was made all the more fascinating if preceded by a heavy night on Ruddles Ale, served in the Mess. In time-honoured fashion, the members of a new course met each other in the bar at North Luffenham, the evening before the course started. Everybody on the course usually knew which squadron they were going to except the first tourists, that is, all the co-pilots and the occasional young navigator. So, the bar that night was a sort of talent show – the captains (who had the final say) perusing which co-pilot or navigator (if they were short) they would like on their crew. If they had a preference for where they would like to end up, the co-pilots/navigators would try to impress the appropriate captain. To provide a silver lining to my disappointment on being posted to Vulcans, I could think of no better consolation than a posting to 35 Squadron in Cyprus. I sought the captain of that posting and attempted my best audition. We only found out later in the course whether such overtures had borne fruit. In the meantime, we had to get down to the business of learning to fly the mighty triangle."

The Vulcan made a strong first impression on Dunsford, now a flight lieutenant:

"My first thought was, 'Why can't I see anything?' The view from the cockpit was like looking out from inside a letterbox. But, things started to really perk up for me at the Vulcan OCU at Scampton when my instructor, Harry Nelson – a fantastic guy and role model – understood why I had become demoralised. He taught me how to enjoy the Vulcan as an environment – not just an aeroplane but also an opportunity for teamwork with a crew – and enjoy it I did."

Many pilots were taken aback by their first close encounter with the Vulcan. When future captain Nick Dennis finally stood before the aircraft, it made a big impression, in a literal sense:

"I was staggered by its size. I got off the crew coach early on a misty October morning and there it was – the Vulcan looking very imposing in its anti-flash white. My captain was Flight Lieutenant Mike Melville, a nice chap with a Canberra background. He was very fair on his co-pilot, given that I was just a lad. It felt good to be under the wing of such a stable character. The nav/plotter was Pete Wighton – a lovely chap, very solid and totally unflappable. He was an excellent navigator. The nav/radar was Don Chadwick. Don and I got on very well. Our AEO, Bill Hennessy, was from Ireland and fitted in well.

"I made nine flights at 230 OCU, a couple with instructors and the rest with the crew. We graduated in November 1963 and joined 12 Squadron at Coningsby. This freefall squadron was led by Wing Commander Phil Lagesen, a South African. Later, he became AOC No. 1 Group at Bawtry. Lagesen was a real character. At that time I was known for my long hair. On one occasion – AOC's inspection – I went into his office to find that he had a large whip in his hand. He walked around me and said: 'Immaculate, Nick. However, get your hair cut … or the big stick!'

"There were plenty of characters on 12 Squadron. There was Pete West, who was a great cartoonist. He illustrated a whole wall at Coningsby. He painted a large mural in our squadron Nissen hut. The squadron mascot was a fox; he depicted us in groups of five in a hunting scene."[286]

Vulcan captain David Dinmore finished his advanced flying training in September 1966 and was posted to the Vulcan OCU, then at RAF Finningley:

"I had had other ideas, but the V-Force was high profile at the time and the posting looked exciting. Participants on the course soon got to know each other and the captains were required to select their own crews. I had my first flight at OCU in April 1967 and I was impressed by the aircraft. I was later posted to 35 Squadron, RAF Cottesmore. My first flight at Cottesmore was not uneventful. We had trouble getting the undercarriage up – it remained down as we flew circuits to burn fuel."[287]

Time to unwind: Nick Dennis (second from left) returning from a 230 OCU sortie. In the background is a Vulcan in anti-flash white, on the 'Finningley Eight' – eight pans arranged in a curve in front of the hangars. (Nick Dennis)

After a year or so at Cottesmore, David Dinmore completed his time as co-pilot at Akrotiri. In 1971 he joined 44 (Rhodesia) Squadron at Waddington for a two-year tour as captain, before moving to 10 Squadron at Brize Norton for a six-year period flying VC10s – "a much more comfortable aircraft!" He captained the VC10 flying Prince (now King) Charles to Australia and back in 1978. Sadly, a medical issue led to his invaliding-out of the RAF in 1980.

The Vulcan made its mark on Bill MacGillivray, as it did on almost everyone getting to know the aeroplane close up for the first time. His latest instructing tour, on Jet Provosts, ended in June 1969 and he was posted to 230 Vulcan OCU: "I considered myself fortunate. I never went there as a co-pilot." Under a new approach streamlining the co-pilot/captain process, some experienced non-V-Force pilots went straight through as captains. MacGillivray became QFI/training officer on 101 Squadron at Waddington within six months. The Vulcan impressed him from the first:

"I stood underneath it and took a good hard look. It was enormous. At first, I was not that keen on it. I didn't want the large crew environment – I wasn't used to that. My first OCU flight was on 4 August 1969, with three hours 45 minutes logged. This trip covered general handling, effects of controls, low-speed handling, a high-speed run of up to Mach 0.94 and a couple of bomb runs. I was surprised at how pleasantly the big aircraft handled. I did two more trips, covering emergency drills, asymmetric flying and ECM runs, before my first solo flight. Overall, the Vulcan was a lot more responsive than I had expected."[288]

The V-Force crew and frustrated crew chief: an impression from the gifted pen of Pete West, 12 Squadron. (Pete West/Andy Leitch Collection)

Bill MacGillivray's co-pilot was a first tourist:

> "Some co-pilots were restricted by the fact that their captains were first-tour captains, having first done a co-pilot tour and then moving to the left-hand seat. However, given my previous experience as an instructor, I was able to let my co-pilot do more handling than average."

Peter Moore's advancement from Oakington and its Varsities coincided with a drive to prise some of the better pilots out of training and into the V-bombers:

> "I spent six months on Varsities and came second in flying on the Advanced Flying Training (AFT) course. My instructor tried to get me to Valley but I was posted to the Vulcan OCU with a promise that, if I did well enough, I would get an early captaincy. I arrived at 230 OCU, Finningley, in early 1969, having spent eight months at RAF Manston flying Chipmunks with No. 1 Air Experience Flight while waiting for my Vulcan course. During my time at Manston, I met my wife, Judy, who was an air hostess for Invicta Airways."[289]

Progressing from Chipmunks to Vulcans was a big step:

> "On my first Vulcan flight, we passed 10,000 ft in no time at all. My instructor commented: 'You can bring the undercarriage up any time you like.' When I climbed into a Vulcan for the first time I was struck by how small it was inside. You have to swivel sideways to get through the small gap between the front seats. The fuel tray goes up and forward but it is still a tight squeeze and you had to be careful not to snag your personal equipment connector."

Moore was not content and made strenuous but unsuccessful efforts to transfer to Canberras. On finishing OCU in June 1969, he arrived at RAF Waddington to join 101 Squadron. He was unaccompanied. There were no slots for a co-pilot on 101 and he was quickly posted to 44 (Rhodesia) Squadron, in the next hangar. At this time, 44 was struggling with an historical embarrassment and Ian Smith's Unilateral Declaration of Independence flag flew outside the squadron buildings:

"There was a push to take Rhodesia out of our name. It was then pointed out that it had taken a king to put it in. Therefore, it would take a queen to remove it. The fuss then died away. My captain on 44 was Bob Jones. His full given names were Wolfgang Robert Darley, reflecting a German father. He was a solid and stable guy – very capable. He was extremely fair to me, sharing the flying as much as he could. We got on well. The nav/radar was Hugh Thomas, a Welshman who was both likeable and competent. The nav/plotter was Tim Wheatley. He had flown Canberras and was an excellent plotter. The AEO, a Scotsman, completed the team. When I joined the crew, they were well established, with combat status. I was the new boy."

Jon Tye had no problem flying the Vulcan, but was no early convert:

"The positive vetting was straightforward, done by an ex-policeman who came across as a nice bloke. The Sea Survival Course at RAF Mountbatten was rather like being in the Scouts again, although our nav/radar became hopelessly sick in the big dinghy. I was hauled out by helicopter. We were not told much on the Nuclear Weapons Course."[290]

Tye was posted out of 27 Squadron, a Blue Steel squadron at Scampton, in 1967:

"I had a place on the Intermediate Captain's Course but I then received a letter stating that I had been selected, as a 'non-volunteer', for the CFS. At that stage I thought, 'Well, at least I'm out of the V-Force'. Then I was called for a captain's interview with the AOC. He was as mad as fire when I told him about the MoD letter for CFS. Obviously, he should have known about it. Anyway, I went to Little Rissington and spent four months back on Jet Provosts."

Whilst at CFS, Tye was involved in a mid-air collision requiring him to eject:

"I was flying as passenger in No. 4 of the Red Pelicans CFS display team. I was flying with the leader, who was also my instructor. I knew nothing about the plan to try a 'changed lead loop' manoeuvre, a move which, ironically, is completely pointless as it can't been seen from the ground. A collision resulted as we lost sight of each other. The impact was very gentle, but our tail was off and we were gyrating in the sky. I said: 'Should we go now, Derek?' At that point, Derek ejected. Then I went. I ended up with a sore neck for a while, but I was flying again within two to three days."

After CFS, Jon Tye was posted to RAF Syerston and was QFI during the 1967–70 period:

"All my flying was on the JP. It came to a point where I felt I needed a career change. I'd had the Vulcan experience. I was now a QFI. I asked for a career interview in London, as I really wanted the Buccaneer. After all, I had low-level experience and had never gone below 'high average' as a pilot. Yet, I was told: 'No chance. You are going back to the V-Force as an instructor'. I said: 'No – I'm not prepared to do that.' When I reached the door, the last comment was: 'What about a Vulcan captaincy in Cyprus?'"

Another Vulcan tour followed.

SPECIAL COURSES

V-bomber crews (pilots, navigators and AEOs) had to undergo three special courses: sea survival, aviation medicine and nuclear weapons familiarisation. Before his OCU flying began, Roy Brocklebank arrived at RAF North Luffenham in May 1964 for his aviation medicine course:

> "This included the unpleasant experience of being exposed to the equivalent of 56,000 ft unpressurised, for a period of 30 seconds, followed by a simulated 10,000 ft/min. descent to 40,000 ft. After the initial bang your gullet swelled up so much that it was impossible to talk and make yourself understood.[291]
>
> "After suitable pre-training at breathing under pressure we were given 30 minutes of pre-oxygenation to ensure that all the nitrogen in our blood had been purged and thus reduce the risk of bends. Then we were taken, with portable oxygen bottles, into the 'bang chamber'. This was a cylindrical pressure chamber on wheels. Once inside and connected to the chamber's umbilicals, the door was shut with an ominous thud. We sat in the chamber, one at a time, with a doctor who talked us through the procedure again. The pressure was lowered gradually and reduced first to the equivalent of 10,000 ft, at which point we went on oxygen and ran through a series of checks. The pressure was further reduced to a simulated height of 25,000 ft and we were encouraged to release our bodily gases. The doctor withdrew into a small chamber adjacent to ours … A final check, a thumbs up from me and a 5,4,3,2,1 countdown from outside the chamber. Not exactly a bang, more of a whoosh, mainly because sound doesn't travel in a vacuum and the ears were doing other things.
>
> "The chamber filled with mist, pressure jerkin and g-trouser bladders pumped up and counter-pressure at 70 mg mercury was applied. At the same time, a similar pressure was forced through the oxygen mask and into the lungs. At this point, we had to reverse the natural breathing pattern and literally force the air out of our lungs. If you got the swallows you could blow up like Michelin Man. Unlike our bodies, there was no counter-pressure on our heads. Necks and gullets swelled up like a puffer fish … You could not talk and you could not hear, as your eardrums were also drumskin tight. After 30 seconds of this, the controller could open the tap and allow air to bleed back into the chamber, simulating a 10,000 ft per min. descent. After a further 90 seconds, the chamber had reached 40,000 ft and the pressure breathing had dropped off, but we still needed the 100% oxygen. For the first minute or so we had been completely helpless and capable only of controlling our breathing. For real, the pilot would have had to fly the aircraft too."

Before joining his squadron, Roy Brocklebank also attended the Nuclear Weapons Familiarisation Course at RAF Wittering. The Bomber Command Armament School was at the far end of the airfield:

> "We had to go through a police checkpoint and a turnstile gate, empty our pockets of lighters and matches, be tagged and escorted to the school. We were indoctrinated into a special security protocol and then taught how the bombs were built, how they worked and their effects."

John Huggins responded positively to this experience: "I attended an excellent Nuclear Weapons Course, which explained the workings of WE.177, but our instructor refused to reveal the yield. I remember people on that course washing their hands *before* peeing!"

The sea survival training was another memorable experience. They were "pushed unceremoniously off the back of a pinnace into the open water off Plymouth Sound". This was then repeated the following day, with a single-seat dinghy rather than a multi-seat life raft. Roy Brocklebank's course certificate records his 'fortitude and vigour'.

THE CO-PILOT'S LOT

Generally, co-pilot was not the most favoured position in a V-bomber. The individual co-pilot's progress was shaped almost entirely by his captain's personality and the latter's views on sharing the flying. Some were lucky. Dick Fuller was a Valiant co-pilot on 49 Squadron: "As a co-pilot, one of my personal priorities was to get in sufficient take-offs and landings. Fortunately, my captain, Howard Faulkner, was very good and let me do plenty of flying."[292]

In contrast, Tony Cottingham's first captain was "very much old school". The co-pilot was in charge of fuel management, weight and balance:

> "We carried a sort of slide rule device to calculate the centre of gravity, with a fuel check plotted on a graph every half hour. The results would be passed to the captain, who would take a quick look and give a perfunctory nod. The captain did not expect much more of me. My next captain, Tony Caillard, was much more encouraging, both in the air and on the ground."[293]

This was at a time when V-Force captains were expected to have 1,500 hours' experience:

> "I was supposed to spend around 18 months as a co-pilot, then go off to fly Canberras to reach that level. However, a new system was then introduced, which allowed co-pilots to go straight through to the Valiant captain's course after three years. I was amongst the first to benefit from this change. Fortunately, my later captains ensured I had a full share of the flying, to make the transition to captain."

The Valiant was held somewhat in awe as the first of the V-bombers. It was powered by four Rolls-Royce Avon 200 engines, rated at 10,000 lbs thrust each:

> "At full load it could take off on three engines on a 3,000-yard runway, as the squadron commander demonstrated to me. The powered flying controls were complemented by artificial feel, given fairly heavy loading by a pitot air intake on the nose. Full reversion to manual control was possible, with even heavier control loading. The load in manual could be trimmed to neutral by control tabs for each flying surface. A fatal accident was put down to an aileron manual trim tab runaway. As aircraft speed increased after take-off, there came a point when the trim tab over-rode the power control; the aircraft rolled out of control and crashed.
>
> "In cruising flight at high level we generally flew on autopilot, at Mach 0.75 and 38–40,000 ft. The pilots took half-hour turns to monitor it while wearing an oxygen mask in case of decompression of the cabin from the usual 8,000 ft. For a combat mission

cabin height would be set to 25,000 ft and all crew would wear oxygen masks. Ground training with decompression had shown us the effects of anoxia at that height. Climb and descent were flown manually and a few circuits or instrument approaches were flown on most sorties for pilot training.

"In mid-1960 I completed a short course on piloting the Valiant from the left-hand seat, the Intermediate Co-Pilot's Conversion – a course for everything! After that, I flew about a third of the sorties from the left-hand seat, building up first pilot hours. From March to June 1961 I completed the Valiant captain's course and was posted back to Wittering on 7 Squadron, with 1,099 hours total flying in my logbook. Our role was the same as before – main-force V-bomber deterrent – while 49 Squadron was assigned to SACEUR and moved to Marham."

Many pilots didn't want the V-Force and found their wishes counted for little in determining the direction of their flying careers, but there were exceptions. Mike Fazackerley had good fortune from the first. He was attracted to the benefits of an RAF scholarship: "I was accepted for pilot training. I stayed at school until 18, but learnt to fly gliders and powered aircraft. I was sent to a civil flying school at Carlisle. I even managed an exchange trip to America."[294]

Mike joined the RAF in 1971 and flew Jet Provosts at Linton-on-Ouse:

"I wanted to fly Lightnings, having had an earlier opportunity to spend a summer camp at RAF Wattisham, but soon discovered that it takes a particular type of lunatic to do that! In the end, unusually, I was given a choice – Vulcans or Canberras. I went for the Canberra, as this aircraft was closer to my single-seat experience on the Gnat at RAF Valley. The Gnat was a dream to fly."

7
NAVIGATORS, AEOS AND GROUND CREW

> *The significance of the nav/radar role was fully recognised. A quote, attributed to an American officer, was displayed at the Bomber Command Bombing School: 'The navigator/radar is that member of the aircrew who changes a four-engined transport into a weapon of war.'*

Roy Brocklebank, a nav/radar with 12 Squadron and, subsequently, wing targeting officer for three Vulcan squadrons at RAF Waddington, recalls how attitudes towards V-Force crews evolved:

"Initially, navigators (plotter or radar) had to have one tour under their belts. Later, radar operators, like me, were *ab initio*. Early radar operators came from the Lincoln squadrons and did a 12-month course at the Bomber Command Bombing School. My course was one of the first to be squeezed into five months, with the flying on Hastings aircraft. Much later, when the Hastings were retired, *ab initio* radar operators moved straight from the Dominie aircrew trainer to Vulcans."[295]

On graduating from No. 1 Air Navigation School at RAF Stradishall, Brocklebank was posted to the BCBS at RAF Lindholme, for instruction on the navigation and bombing system. He and his contemporaries came from two main streams:

"There were the very few Cranwell officers who had joined the RAF straight from school. They had a minimum of two A levels and had spent three years as cadets before being commissioned. The bulk of the aircrew cadre, in contrast, had required an educational attainment of just five O levels. The RAF was not recruiting rocket scientists! They were drawn at a rate of around 100 per month from the 18–25 age group. They did just four months as cadets before beginning flying training and could arrive on the OCU after about two years' training. In my case, I was 20 when I reached the OCU. Our terms of service were either a short service commission – five, eight or 12 years – on to age 38 or 16 years' service, whichever was longer. We had no expectation of promotion beyond flight lieutenant and to get that we needed to pass a promotion exam with five papers, including air law, operations and, in my case, navigation."

Roy felt some disappointment on emerging as a nav/radar: "My navigational skills were not fully utilised. It was not a 'pure' navigation position, in contrast to the skills required of a Canberra navigator. At that time, the plum navigator role was maritime – on the Shackletons."

Nav/radar Barry Mullen had been inspired by example. His father, Warrant Officer John 'Jack' Mullen, was a wartime rear gunner who refused to accept his lot as a prisoner of the Italians. He was captured when his Wellington was shot down over North Africa: "He escaped several times and eventually ended up in a German-run camp. That didn't stop him. He escaped once again, connected up with a 'rat-line' from the Vatican and made it back to Britain – a home run."[296]

His son was not over-keen on the air force as a teenager, but eventually applied and arrived at Biggin Hill Aircrew Selection Centre. The outcome was an offer of navigator. Barry Mullen was relatively mature at that stage, having reached 23 and with a few years of work experience:

> "On leaving school I got an apprenticeship with the Post Office; they encouraged me to go to university. I was one of the first RAF graduate entrants and went to Cranwell for officer training. This type of entry was the cause of some bad feeling. There were those who regarded graduates as 'instant' flying officers. Yet the barriers went down when we got to know each other – playing sport soon broke the ice. Later, however, I ran into similar hostile attitudes on my first squadron. Graduates were known as 'Green Shielders': we had saved up our 'stamps' to become air force officers."

Mullen found Cranwell a rather alien environment:

> "Strangely, my most vivid memory is of an escape and evasion exercise. This ignored boundaries which, in all probability, should not have been crossed. Our small group was ordered to carry a large pine pole across a remote, dense area of Thetford Forest. We had to make a series of rendezvous points. We slept in the woods, under rough tents of parachute silk. We had to evade search parties sent to find us. At the finish we were being debriefed when a wing commander stormed in and claimed we'd made a mess of everything. We were ordered out once again – this time into a small wood offering no chance of evading capture. Well, they soon caught us. We were blindfolded immediately and received plenty of verbal abuse. About five of us – including me – were picked out for 'special treatment'. We were stripped naked and hoods were put over our heads. We were stood against a wall with our legs apart, waiting our turn for interrogation. I began to shiver. They began using a hard-man/soft-man style of interrogation. I remained naked and blindfolded. At one point, I thought I heard a woman's voice – dignity went out of the window."

Valiant co-pilot Dick Fuller had similar memories:

> "We joined an evasion/escape exercise whilst at Wittering. Previously, we had volunteered to hunt down by car 'evaders' on the North Yorkshire Moors … On one occasion, however, the boot was on the other foot. We took our turn as evaders. We were given a series of objectives and turned loose. We evaded capture but arrived late at the second rendezvous. The powers that be decided we were prisoners and took us into custody at RAF Leeming, where we were stood against a wall with bags over our heads. This went on for 48 hours and I underwent three interrogations. Many of our interrogators sounded American. After many hours I began to hallucinate – I thought I was standing in a cathedral!"

Pilots went to training squadrons and navigators were posted to RAF Finningley. Barry Mullen remembers Finningley's Dominies and Jet Provosts:

> "Trainee navigators had no formal flying instruction but I did have a few flights in the Jet Provost, thanks to an obliging pilot. The navigators' course lasted a year. I was no star but regarded myself as competent. I was happy with the maths, but still inexperienced in the flying environment, unlike those who had come from the university air squadrons."

Vulcan nav/radar Vic Bussereau was another inspired by Paul Brickhill's book, *The Dam Busters*. Decades on, he got his long-standing wish: he flew Tornado GR1s with 617 Squadron at RAF Marham.[297] Bussereau first visited an RAF Recruiting Office whilst still 15; he needed to be 17½ for aircrew. It was suggested that he join the RAF as an apprentice. Instead, he joined a local engineering firm and progressed to an HND in mechanical engineering:

> "At the end of my five-year apprenticeship I still wanted to fly in the RAF but, at the same time, felt a sense of loyalty towards the company, which had supported me through my apprenticeship and allowed me to obtain the HND. So, I stayed for another year and then quietly went off to the RAF Aircrew Selection Centre at Biggin Hill in mid-1964. I was lucky and was offered a supplementary commission of eight or 12 years as a navigator."

HULLAVINGTON AND STRADISHALL

The usual pattern for would-be navigators was attendance at RAF Hullavington (No. 2 Air Navigation School), followed by RAF Stradishall (No. 1 Air Navigation School) for advanced training. John Weller applied unsuccessfully to Cranwell for a place as a flight cadet. Undaunted, he focused on RAF Hornchurch and direct entry: "On 6 April 1962, at the age of 18, I became an acting pilot officer." After basic training at South Cerney, he arrived at RAF Syerston and Flying Training School:

> "After eight hours' flying tuition, my instructor concluded that my talents were wasted and that I should become a navigator. I had a realistic approach to this – if I had carried on I would have probably killed myself. It was my landings. For some reason, I couldn't retain in my memory what I should be seeing during the approach."[298]

John knew he had the aptitude to be a navigator. Following a holding posting, he reported to No. 2 Air Navigation School on 5 November 1962: "This was fine. I enjoyed my eight months in the Varsity. I was getting around 70–80% in the air and 80–90% in the ground exams – enough to seal my fate."

He completed his advanced training at Stradishall: "I spent three months in Varsities and then a month in Meteors, including the NF.14 night-fighter – but flying by day." Then came his posting to RAF Lindholme and the BCBS, so moving closer to becoming a V-Force nav/radar. He flew in the Hastings T.5, with the NBS equipment in the back. His 'targets' included London, Manchester, Liverpool and Glasgow. The aiming points were precise, including, for example, the north-east corner of Newcastle Hospital. They were taught to use 'offsets', one being the bandstand in Hyde Park. On completion of the course, he was posted to the Vulcan OCU at RAF Finningley, then on to IX Squadron in November 1964.

Udai 'Woody' P. N. Fulena was born in Mauritius. His father, a policeman, eventually became chief of police. Smitten with the idea of flying, he applied to Adastral House in

London, received a ticket and arrived in the UK in February 1964. He reported to Biggin Hill for interview and was sent to Cranwell:

> "I went back to London to await results. A few weeks later, a letter was received … I had passed and had been accepted as a navigator. I was thrilled. There were instructions on how to obtain a train ticket in exchange for a warrant, and the train to take to report to South Cerney."[299]

Woody Fulena spent four months at South Cerney. During breaks and bank holidays, cadets invited him to their homes: "It was all very exciting – a huge change in my life. If you think about the Vulcan and then consider that, at that time, a large part of Mauritius had no electricity."

Following basic training, he completed the courses at Hullavington and Stradishall:

> "Fortunately, I had been very good at maths at school and log tables and the circular slide rule (called the 'computer') posed no problems. We trained on Varsities and Valettas (classrooms) and learned how to use the normal and periscopic sextants to take sun, moon and star shots. I graduated from South Cerney in July 1964 and from Stradishall 12 months later. I passed out as best all-round student, clutching a huge trophy offered by Bristol Aeroplane Co. (which had to be given back). My headmaster in Mauritius was very chuffed at the news, which made the local papers."

BOMBING SCHOOL AND THE NBS

Fulena's posting to BCBS, Lindholme, came in December 1965 and he completed the NBS course the following March. By then, he was known as 'Woody' – the instructors having struggled with his Mauritian nickname, 'Udai'. During the wait for 230 OCU he spent time at Bomber Command Headquarters, High Wycombe.

Some nav/radars found the going tough at Lindholme. Alan McLoughlin recalls the exotic targeting: "During our NBS exercises, we attacked targets with fanciful 'Russian' names, customising past and present Lindholme officers. I remember 'attacking' McKaysk, for example."[300] He found some of the training challenging:

> "What saved me was my skill at arithmetic but, otherwise, I was poor at maths and physics. I also demonstrated that I lacked something as a bomb-aimer during the NBS course. On one occasion, I attacked the wrong dam in Yorkshire – an error of nine miles. Of the six in our group, four went to Vulcans and two to Victor tankers. Perhaps my bombing results explain my posting to Victor tankers."

In fairness to Alan, the NBS was not easy to manage:

> "It was a very ancient bit of kit. The NBS was an electro-mechanical system, with all components contributing to accumulating errors when in use. It took a really skilled operator to achieve anything approaching accuracy. My average bombing result was 500 yards from the aiming point, but good nav/radars could do a lot better."

Everyone struggled with the NBS, as recalled by Victor and Vulcan captain John Laycock:

"In the early days the rate of flying was pretty poor, with frequent NBS problems. Many times we attempted to fly but the aeroplane wasn't fit for a fully operational navigational/bombing exercise. Aircraft often failed pre-flight checks. The NBS, with its huge, dustbin-like 'calculators', was still in development."[301]

NAV TEAM CHALLENGES

Norman Bonnor described the challenges in the air:

"The major innovation when compared to earlier medium-bomber aircraft of the RAF was the real time input of accurate drift and ground speed from the Green Satin Doppler radar into the computations of a fully integrated NBS. The NBS was a very complex group of analogue computers … Among its many features were the calculation of forward throw and trail of a selected weapon and the output of accurate steering commands to the computed release point with an automated release signal; gone were the days of 'pressing the tit'. Unfortunately, the system was large and very heavy, involving many 'black boxes', better described as 'black dustbins'. The Green Satin Doppler was very reliable … its velocity and drift accuracy easily met the long-range dead reckoning (DR) requirements of strategic bombing. The same could not be said of the G4B compass. A great deal of effort was devoted to calibrating the compass … but large cross-track navigation errors were still very obvious in the air.

"During sortie planning, the nav/radar used 1:250,000 topographical maps to select suitable radar fix points for the en route phase, and large-scale maps and aerial photographs to study the target area and to select offset aiming points for the target, which, usually, was not a significant individual return on the radar … To help identify the target and related offsets, he would draw an outline with a fine marker pen of the predicted radar echoes on a piece of acetate and, during a bombing run, he would hold this overlay on the plan position indicator (PPI) to 'map match' the radar picture and ensure the range and bearing markers were placed over the correct offset or target using the small joystick controller, the CU626.

"The offset distances were measured or calculated as accurately as possible in yards and set on the NBS as northings and eastings. Here is the second reason why compass errors were so important to the nav team; these offsets were measured against a true north datum, so any error in the true heading used by the NBS appeared directly in the bombing results. For example, using an offset 10,000 yards from the target (not a particularly long one), a degree of heading error would introduce more than 150 yards* bombing error over and above any aiming, ballistics or other errors."[302]

The real problem was the gyro-magnetic compass:

"The crews knew it was the weak link, which is why so much attention was paid to reducing residual deviations by elaborate ground compass swings. On XV Squadron, we elected to air swing the compasses of all our Victor Mk 1A aircraft, using Astro as the

---

*   174 yards, according to Roy Brocklebank.

reference. To our amazement, all eight of the squadron aircraft showed a very similar pattern of errors, with apparent residual deviations of over two degrees on SW headings; no wonder we were suffering large cross-track navigation errors … we started using the air swing deviations and our navigation performance and bombing results immediately improved."

THE OCU EXPERIENCE

For most, OCU provided the first close-up encounter with a V-bomber. In July 1966, Woody Fulena was introduced to the Vulcan: "It was very impressive, with lots of power – a very macho aeroplane. It radiated strength. Inside, of course, it was rather cramped."[303] Others were less impressed – at least initially. Former Valiant nav/radar Anthony Wright converted to Vulcans at 230 OCU: "I arrived at RAF Finningley on 29 April 1965 and found what I had heard about the aircraft was true. The Vulcan was undoubtedly the worst of the three V-bombers in terms of comfort, being able to see out and escape."[304] Nav/radar Jim Walker, however, had no qualms. He went from 230 OCU to 44 (Rhodesia) Squadron at RAF Waddington, arriving in October 1964: "This squadron had Vulcan B.1As. I was quite happy with the Vulcan – it always impressed. It was the ultimate aircraft." Walker had an affinity with the bomber's delta shape, from his days at Sherborne School: "Peter Twiss, who broke the world air speed record in Fairey Delta 2, came to my school to lecture. He was an old boy."[305]

Walker was lucky with his first captain, Wing Commander Mike D'Arcy:

"He was ex-Hunters (OC of 20 Squadron) and he had also flown Spitfires, Typhoons and Mustangs. He had been boss of the Initial Training School at South Cerney and, clearly, was on his way to the top. Phil Leckenby was the co-pilot and he was just 19. The nav/plotter was an Australian, Ted Marmont, who had come from the RAAF Canberra force. The AEO, Jock Lamont, was a 'wee Scotsman' and a bit older than most of us. When we were at OCU I remember Mike looking at the Vulcan B.1A and saying: 'God, I can't fly this.' Well, he did. Later, he went on to command the Queen's Flight. Sadly, Air Commodore Mike D'Arcy died young; he was only 48. When we arrived on 44 (Rhodesia) Squadron, he was promised a 'proper crew'. He refused, saying: 'I'm sticking with these youngsters.' We were together as a crew for 2½ years and there was never a cross word. We achieved command classification."

Roy Brocklebank's experience of crewing up at Finningley was similar to that of many wartime Bomber Command aircrew. They were left to get on with it:

"We all gathered in the bar at RAF Mount Batten on Sunday evening. Amongst this group of strangers were at least two embryo Vulcan crews, including two former co-pilots who would be the new captains. We introduced ourselves and the informal process of crewing up began. One captain, Flight Lieutenant Tris (Tristran) Broadwith, had been posted in from Scampton, the Vulcan Mk 2 Blue Steel base, although his home was at Waddington, which was a Mk 1 Vulcan base. He was planning to go to Coningsby as he didn't want a second tour on Blue Steel. He regarded it as a 'sod of a system' and wanted a freefall squadron. The other captain, Flight Lieutenant Ben McLaren, wanted

Scampton. My choice was easy – I opted for Coningsby as I shared Broadwith's feelings: I didn't want Blue Steel. At the OCU I was Broadwith's nav/radar. He was a pleasant chap and much older – about 26 – with a background as a QFI and instrument ratings examiner. He was very experienced, with a previous tour on Canberras as well as his co-pilot's tour at Scampton."[306]

When at 230 OCU Roy Brocklebank logged 16 flights in the Vulcan, plus a flypast to honour the British Limbless Ex-Service Men's Association. In July 1964 he was posted to Coningsby and 12 Squadron. Brocklebank came to regard 12 Squadron as "unique". The squadron motto is 'Leads the Field':

The line-up: 230 OCU instructors responsible for training nav/radars. Hastings aircraft were fitted out with Vulcan radar. (Barry Mullen)

"Naturally, everyone thinks their squadron is the best, but there is no doubt about it – ours is! We lived in a very social environment. Our squadron mascot was a fox, a reminder of 12 Squadron's association with the Fairey Fox."

It had been the only squadron to fly this sleek inline-engined light bomber in the 1920s. During World War 2, 12 Squadron had two fox shields made, for a pub close to its base at Ludford Magna. Only one shield at a time was displayed. The Red Shield signified 'Ops on' and the Green Shield 'Ops off'. The squadron boss, Bob Tanner, was as Brocklebank describes:

"... a very experienced wartime bomber pilot and a very reasonable chap. I enjoyed my time with the squadron. It had a number of very different traditions. Most squadrons throwing a party would open it to all. However, 12 Squadron's parties were private affairs, held in the squadron building rather than the Mess. Most squadrons present a tankard when you leave but, in 12 Squadron, you had to buy a fox-handled tankard upon joining. If you wanted a drink, you had to bring along that tankard."

Norman Bonnor remembers finding his first captain, David Bywater, at the Gaydon Officers' Mess bar. "He had already completed a tour as the first first-tourist co-pilot on the Victor when it entered service in 1957." Bonnor made the point that: "OCU, of course, only taught you how to fly and use the aircraft." There was no instruction in tactics for the war role:

"We did make a few bombing runs whilst at OCU, but it was fairly simple stuff, using a simulated 'ideal' bomb with no drag component. We 'dropped' it at 40,000 ft and it detonated along track eight miles ahead of the release point. The importance of R/T discipline was stressed at OCU. Expertise was shared; a squadron leader often flew with us while at Gaydon. During some sorties we also had a screened navigator on board, who would help us progress through the exercise. Taken overall, our OCU instructors were very good."[307]

Later, Norman discovered that, at that time, he was a member of the youngest crew in the V-Force, "which meant we made the national press but, more importantly for me, the *Eagle* comic!"

A new V-Force crew arriving on a squadron worked hard to achieve operational (combat) status. They had to complete a series of training sorties, a ground-training programme and undertake target study before being declared combat ready – the first step in a complex series of six-month training cycles to achieve and retain their Bomber Command ranking as a constituted crew. They had to cope with three navigational modes (primary, secondary and limited):

"Primary allowed full use of all aids, including radar fixing, which made staying within about a ¼ mile of track (and timing to better than five seconds) very easy; in fact, the technique was too easy and we hardly needed to practise its use. Secondary assumed loss of the radar picture for fixing, to simulate a more 'stealthy' penetration of enemy defences, so denying the H2S transmissions for airborne interception (AI) fighter or missile homing, but the Green Satin drift and ground speed inputs were still available. This meant using other methods for updating present position, with the emphasis on Astro as the war role demanded autonomy … A good crew would achieve errors of three to five miles at the terminal point of a 1,000-mile navigation stage using the secondary technique. Limited technique took away the Green Satin inputs as a simulated failure, leaving the true airspeed feed and wind vectors set manually on the NBS. This was clearly more difficult, but if the high-level winds were reasonably stable, a good crew would be inside ten miles at the end of 1,000."[308]

WANTING SOMETHING ELSE

Some navigators wanted Canberras, rather than V-bombers, but nav/radar Vic Bussereau had the ultimate prize in mind. He was streamed for fast jets: "I wanted Canberras although when I applied to join the RAF I had TSR-2 as my goal – but the project was cancelled two months after I joined."[309]

He was then selected for the V-Force, rather than Canberras, completed the Lindholme NBS course in early 1967 but had to wait for an OCU place. He spent a couple of months at Bomber Command HQ and strings were pulled to allow him to get away to Boscombe Down for a couple of weeks, where he logged two flights in a Canberra and another in a Meteor. One flight was in the right-hand seat of a T.4 Canberra, on a sortie to photograph the oil tanker *Torrey Canyon*, aground off the Isles of Scilly:

"During the visit to Boscombe Down, when talking to the boss, I said I had wanted to fly in TSR-2. He said: 'Come this way.' I went into the hangar with him and he pointed to a dusty aircraft finished in anti-flash white in the corner, with the two canopies open. It was the second TSR-2 prototype. Upon arrival at Boscombe Down by road, where it was to carry out its initial flights, this prototype suffered severe damage during unloading (it rolled off the low loader). It was then worked on for six months to get it ready to fly. The work was completed and the aircraft was due to fly on the day the TSR-2 programme was cancelled (6 April 1965). It never did fly; however, it was left at Boscombe and I got to sit in the rear cockpit – not many navigators can say that."

During his time at High Wycombe, Bussereau heard he was to be posted to Vulcan Mk 2s at 230 OCU and then 35 Squadron at Cottesmore. He got a tip that, when joining the OCU, he should look out for a certain future Vulcan captain, Flight Lieutenant Rick Wood, who had been noted as a very competent pilot:

"The individual pilots, navigators and AEOs on the course met up for the first time at RAF North Luffenham for aero-med training, where we crewed up informally. I looked out for Rick Wood, found him and said: 'I've been told by High Wycombe that I'm flying with you,' which, of course, was not strictly true. He accepted this with little comment – at the time! Rick Wood was a serious character but a very fine pilot and proved to be a first-class captain, both in the air and on the ground. He had joined the RAF as a sergeant radar operator and flew Javelin night-fighters. Subsequently, he was commissioned as a pilot and completed a Canberra tour in Cyprus. Wood was a man who liked things done properly. The co-pilot was Pete Stannard. We did the first few OCU flights with staff pilots, navigators or even an AEO. On 17 August 1967, however, we had our first flight on our own as a crew. We flew XH558, which, many years later became the last Vulcan to fly."

Nav/radar Bob Sinclair wanted Canberras. He had been in the fast jet stream at Stradishall:

"In the fast jet group, no-one put down the V-Force as first choice. Few wanted Air Defence. Most of us wanted Canberras. The Vulcan meant Waddington, Scampton or Cottesmore. The Victor meant Wittering, Honington or, later, Marham. In contrast, Canberras meant Germany, Cyprus or Singapore. The choice was obvious for those who wanted to see the world."[310]

At the end of Sinclair's course, they gathered in the briefing room:

"We were told where we were going, one by one. Three of us got nav/radar when we had asked for Canberras. We went to tackle the course commander. He said he'd been told to provide six navigators for the V-Force and he'd managed to reduce it to three."

Goose Ranger: Vic Bussereau (then with 35 Squadron) at Goose Bay in September 1968. (Vic Bussereau)

Bryan 'Monty' Montgomery had also felt less than pleased on his arrival at Gaydon, the home of the Valiant OCU. He took a dim view of the lack of a bang seat in the back. Nonetheless, his crew prospered and they climbed the ladder from combat to select star within 18 months. He remembers his time at Marham on 148 Squadron with fondness: "We were a happy community."[311]

CANBERRAS AND SUN

On completing a tour on the Shackletons of 206 Squadron in mid-1959, Robin Woolven was selected for navigator training and commissioning. He expected to become a V-Force navigator and was posted to the BCBS at Lindholme, but was then posted to 231 OCU at RAF Bassingbourn, flying Canberra T.4s and B.2s. Later, he enjoyed the sunshine:

> "I crewed up with a pilot and another navigator. The navigators shared the navigation and bomb-aiming, forming a team of three with the pilot. We finished in March 1961 with a posting to 249 Squadron at Akrotiri, Cyprus. We arrived on the island that May."[312]

This Canberra squadron were target-marking specialists. They trained in high- and low-level bombing techniques, together with shallow dive-bombing for the delivery of red and green 1,000-lb target indicators. Woolven became the squadron's navigation leader and his fellow navigator, Colin Tavner, became bombing leader (or weapons leader). The pilot was Flying Officer Jim Ellis. In December 1961 the squadron upgraded, receiving Canberra B.16s with Doppler radar, GPI and the Morse equipment required for nuclear-armed sorties. Red Beard nuclear weapons were stored on base. Woolven was amused when he found he could read the codeword for release if he held the sealed envelope against the bright light over the B.16's nav station.

The nuclear-armed Canberras at readiness at Akrotiri were protected by armed guards. The wing weapons officer had a training kit for Red Beard:

> "All crew members were required to be competent at LML and there were monthly loading drills. Basically, this involved inserting the weapon's fissile core. This was a device looking rather like an outsized grapefruit, attached to a loading arm about 18 inches long. The aircraft had a system of double locks and insertion of the core required both navigators to go under the bomb bay and locate the entrance for the core. This wasn't easy. The grapefruit was very heavy and the receiving hole in the weapon was offset and awkward to reach. We had to remove the cover from the core port, push in the device, go through a 'double-click' process, remove the loading arm and then replace the cover."

The crews trained in the low-altitude bombing system (LABS). This technique threw the bomb forward as the aircraft performed a violent escape manoeuvre:

> "Delivering a weapon by LABS required some calculations prior to take-off. Various values had to be fed into the analogue system – concerning approach, timing and other issues which determined the distance between the start of the manoeuvre and thus the angle and point of release to the target. The aircraft would fly to an initial point and then make the attack by flying to the release point. This required expertise, as the aircraft had to be flown at a precise indicated airspeed at an exact height, in order to

arrive at the release point at the right time. This was very demanding (the indicated airspeed required was 434 kts!) and crews could achieve the desired results only with a great deal of practice. On approaching the initial point, the bomb-aimer commenced the countdown with the words: 'Pickle, Pickle, Pickle' and the bomb doors opened. The pilot checked speed and height, then gripped the 'pickle', a lever on the control column rather like a bicycle brake. When pressed, the 'pickle' started the final countdown to the point where the pilot pulled back on the stick and the aircraft entered a 3.4 g climb. The navigator selected the switches that ensured the weapon was released automatically at the correct time. The aircraft continued the manoeuvre until inverted; it then rolled out and completed its escape by flying on a reciprocal course in a dive."

The crew began flying LABS sorties with 25-lb practice bombs on 14 March 1962:

"In a war situation, of course, our aircraft would be loaded with Red Beard. Typically, a LABS exercise would involve LABS manoeuvres and an attack on the Episkopi Range. Normally, we would make four runs, dropping a 25-lb practice bomb on each occasion. Although we made four runs before landing, we were always assessed only on the results of the first run – that's the one that counted in crew assessments. One of our nuclear targets was a military complex near Tashkent, off the Silk Road. Our recovery would be to Peshawar, on the North-West Frontier of Pakistan. Obviously, such a long-range sortie depended on good fuel management, with careful calculation of the point at which we could get down to the relative safety of low level, whilst still having sufficient fuel to complete the recovery leg. The Met data was a crucial factor."

Robin Woolven's last flight with 249 Squadron was on 8 November 1963.

Vulcan nav/plotter James Vinales was born in Gibraltar in 1945. His father was Gibraltarian and his mother was Spanish. They wanted him to stay in Gibraltar and become a teacher. In August 1964, however, he attended Biggin Hill Aircrew Selection Centre, passed the aptitude tests and joined the Royal Air Force in January 1965: "I did the advanced navigation at Stradishall. I was not a good student, being rather laid-back and under-confident – perhaps more the latter than the former. However, I was very good at maths and managed some good exam results." Vinales' first operational posting brought him together with 45 Squadron's B.15 Canberras at RAF Tengah, Singapore, armed with Red Beard:

"I spent three years in Singapore, beginning in March 1967. I loved my time in the Far East. When I started to fly in Canberras I began to flourish. I became quite good about halfway through this first tour and had a wonderful three years."

In the longer term, however, James Vinales' operational career would be shaped by the Vulcans of 44 (Rhodesia), 101 and 50 Squadrons, back in the UK.[313]

THE AIR ELECTRONICS OFFICER

Many AEOs had already flown operationally with the Maritime Force or were experienced technicians in ground-support roles. Neil Flowerdew became the RAF's youngest ever direct entry AEO: "I was nearly the last – I had a friend who was last."[314]

Flowerdew had a rather exotic colonial background. He was born in Norfolk but the family moved to Africa within a few months. His parents were accustomed to life in the colonies:

"My grandfather had been chief engineer for Calcutta Railways and, later, India State Railways. My father was born in India and my mother in colonial Canada. During the first half of the 1930s, grandfather was in Africa, building 160 miles of railway through the bush in Nyasaland."

His father served in the RAF during World War 2. Neil joined in August 1964, at the age of 17½:

"Nyasaland was about to become independent, emerging as Malawi. In my early teens, I intended to follow in my father's footsteps and build a future in tea estate management. As Independence approached, it became clear that there was limited scope for a long-term future in Malawi. I felt the need to move. Then a newspaper ad caught my eye. The RAF were looking for AEOs. That headline – 'Scientists in the Sky' – caught my imagination.

"I received an offer from the RAF and my destination was South Cerney, where direct entry aircrew officers received four months' basic training before moving on to their role training – in my case to Topcliffe, then the home of the Flying Training School for AEOs, AEOps and air signallers."

After 12 months at Topcliffe, Flowerdew arrived at the Victor Ground School, RAF Finningley, followed by a posting to the Victor Tanker Training Flight at RAF Marham. He was destined for 214 Squadron, re-formed as the third Victor tanker unit: "The Valiants had gone about 18 months before my arrival on 214 Squadron. Over that period the RAF had to rebuild its flight-refuelling capability, using an interim fit on the Mk 1 Victor."

Barry Masefield moved from maritime and became a Vulcan AEO with 617 Squadron, at RAF Scampton, in 1979. This was a fitting operational posting as the film *The Dam Busters* had increased his early fascination with aeroplanes. His goal, from the first, was 617 Squadron and achieving this required application and patience. He trained as an RAF ground radar technician, entering No. 1 Radio School at RAF Locking, near Weston-super-Mare, in 1959. Three years later he was posted to Wyton as a radar technician. Subsequently, he applied to be a pilot and attended Aircrew Selection at Biggin Hill. He was unsuccessful but was offered AEOp training as an NCO:

"I was disappointed, but AEO/AEOp was a newish trade and I was already streets ahead of everyone else as a qualified radar technician. The plan was to accept AEOp and have another go at selection for pilot at a later date. I never did."[315]

He was posted to Topcliffe for a 12-month course.

"It was demanding, but not particularly difficult. I enjoyed it but suffered air sickness in the Varsities. There were 12 on our course and three of us had been apprentices together. With our radio and radar knowledge, we formed a self-teaching cell. This course focused heavily on how the equipment worked, along with the components – transistors, capacitors and so on. You could fix things in the air in those days. One area beyond the curriculum was electronic countermeasures."

Barry's road to the V-Force and 617 Squadron's Vulcans proved to be long. In 1964 he received a maritime posting, to the Shackleton Conversion Unit at Kinloss. After six months his crew was posted to 204 Squadron at Ballykelly:

> "The Shackleton was a beautiful aircraft, but not much good for anyone prone to airsickness. During our first flight with the OCU, I was on the radar. The radar training area consisted of one master and two slave screens. Unfortunately, they weren't arranged fore and aft but, rather, faced the fuselage wall. Your left shoulder faced the rear and the right faced forward. When flying at extremely low levels (down as low as 80 ft over rough seas) in tight circles chasing a submarine, the gyros in your ear went completely out of kilter."

Masefield was posted to 205 Squadron in Singapore during 1967: "I loved it. I was only 24. I had met my wife in Londonderry and we had just married. For us, Singapore was a three-year honeymoon." In 1970, he returned to Kinloss and 204 Squadron, then reforming. The Nimrod was just entering service:

> "This was a complete revelation to me. I had had only one flight in a Nimrod and I had never felt so ill. Even the most hardened aircrew, who were never airsick, soon became ill in a Nimrod. The main reason was its inherent Dutch Roll. When you looked down to the end of the fuselage, the tail section seemed to be moving in a circle around the centreline. The tail fin was increased in size, to reduce the problem, but the Nimrod still looked, and felt, as though it was corkscrewing its way through the air."

He was posted to St Mawgan, Cornwall, home of the Nimrod OCU. Nimrod NCO operators were classified 'dry' or 'wet'. ECM was the province of 'dry' operators:

> "I became a 'wet' man, as I was a pretty good sonar operator. We sat at our screens, facing the side of an aeroplane much faster than the Shackleton and capable of very tight turns. Our gyros were soon scrambled."

In 1976, after four years on 201 Squadron Nimrods at Kinloss, Barry Masefield was selected for highly secret work under the auspices of the Maritime Acoustics Analysis Unit, analysing the acoustic signatures of surface ships and increasingly quiet Soviet submarines.

In September 1979, after 17 years with maritime, Masefield finally arrived at the Vulcan OCU. He then realised his boyhood ambition, as his next posting took him to 617 Squadron. He was greeted by Wing Commander Henderson, the squadron commander:

> "After a brief welcome, he said: 'I've got just the job for you.' He was right. It involved taking a batch of first-day covers, celebrating the 25th anniversary of the Vulcan, to a residence near Reading. The recipient was none other than Marshal of the Royal Air Force Sir Arthur Harris! The covers were to be signed by the great man, then flown to Australia and on, around the world. I received a warm reception from the former AOC-in-C, Bomber Command. 'Come on in, my boy. Bring in the boxes.' He seemed surprised when aware of how many were involved. They filled four boxes."

Masefield lunched at nearby RAF Benson and returned in the afternoon to pick them up. The job wasn't finished and he waited for completion in Harris' study: "I had never seen anything like it. The memorabilia was extraordinary. I'm sure he'd left a few covers unsigned to give me the chance to have a look round …"

Hugh Prior also spent some years with maritime before becoming a Vulcan AEO:

"I arrived at 230 Vulcan OCU in June 1971. Now I would be flying backwards. I had been ambling along at 150 kts for most of my life. The change in speed was quite significant. Before, I had never got involved in electrics. In the Shackleton, that was the business of the flight engineer. As an AEO in the Vulcan, however, most of the job was about looking after the electrics. I may have joined the V-Force after the handover to Polaris, but it was a very different life for me, with a lot of low flying."[316]

Prior joined 44 (Rhodesia) Squadron at RAF Waddington, as did Geoff Lidbetter, whose father had served in the RAF Regiment during the war. The family were to live close to several airfields, including the famous fighter base RAF Tangmere:

"There were always military aircraft flying around and I made up my mind that I wanted to be a pilot … My father warned me against flying, as I was always prone to travel sickness. Fortunately, in a career spanning nearly 12,000 hours of flying I was never airsick."[317]

He joined the Royal Air Force as a Halton Apprentice in May 1955 and went on to qualify as an armourer. He worked on RAF Swinderby's Venoms and Vampires, maintaining ejection seats: "I did some gliding whilst at Swinderby. Then a QFI based at RAF Syerston asked whether I would like to learn to fly. I went solo in a Tiger Moth, but it was expensive – 30 shillings an hour." Lidbetter was posted to Singapore in February 1960. On arrival he applied for aircrew but was told that he would have to wait until he had completed three years in Singapore and returned to England: "So, I joined the Royal Singapore Flying Club, which operated out of the international airport. I spent most of my money on flying. I got a Colonial PPL, flying Cessnas and Chipmunks."

On returning to the UK in August 1962, he was posted to RAF Middleton St George, near Darlington, as first-line Javelin ground crew. Geoff eventually got an offer to train as a sergeant pilot or air signaller. Then, four months later, a letter informed him that training for NCO pilots and navigators had been discontinued: "The letter went on to ask whether I would be prepared to train as an air signaller. I was very unhappy. I had a chip on my shoulder for years." In any event, Lidbetter accepted the offer and flew in RAF Topcliffe's Varsities:

"I did OK but I wasn't very good at the electronics. I was shocked when I saw the complexity of V-bomber circuit boards. Fortunately, I teamed up with a friendly chap, Andy Nelson, who helped me a lot on the electronics side. I had always stated that I didn't want to go to Coastal Command. In fact, 12 out of our group of 13 went to Coastal. I was the only one to go to Transport Command. My posting was to RAF Thorney Island, a Transport Command OCU, with Beverleys, Hastings and Argosy aircraft."

This was a difficult time for Geoff. He had just met his wife-to-be at Topcliffe and his next posting was back to Singapore. This was evaded by trying again for pilot training. He was unsuccessful but the outcome was a posting to RAF Colerne, near Bath, with 36 Squadron and then 24 Squadron. Subsequently, he was posted to the Shackleton OCU at St Mawgan, Cornwall, then on to RAF Kinloss as a 206 Squadron AEOp. "In doing so, I lost my identity – I became just one of five signallers in a Shackleton crew. I stayed at Kinloss until 1972." By then, the squadron had converted to Nimrods, but his future operational flying would be as a Vulcan AEO with 44 (Rhodesia) Squadron and 35 Squadron.

SUPPORT ON THE GROUND

The maintenance of the V-Force at such a high level of war preparedness would have been impossible without ground support of the highest quality, from ground crew, technicians, armourers and a wide range of specialists. They included Len Hewitt, who attended No. 1 School of Technical Training at RAF Cosford, emerging as an electronics mechanic, navigational instruments. On completing this three-month course, he was posted to Fairford to work on Hercules transports. After 18 months he returned to Cosford for a fitter's course: "I finished there in 1970, at which point my pay doubled, from £16 a week, including marriage allowance, to just over £32 with the advent of the military salary and promotion to junior technician LFitt (NI)."[318]

> His initial posting from the fitter's course was to 30 MU at RAF Sealand, near Chester:

> "This was an 'end of the world' posting and I was relieved to have the opportunity to swap with a chap who had a posting to Waddington. That's how I came to live with the Vulcans of the Waddington Wing. There was a lot of training still to be done. The fitter's course provided only general instruction. At the same time (although I didn't realise it whilst at Cosford) a lot of the kit they used for instruction was actually fitted to the Vulcan."

> The Vulcans made a big impression on Hewitt:

> "Wow! That was my first thought. Having had a first look round, I had a second thought: 'Clearly, this was an aircraft designed never to be worked on.' Having recently spent time with the Hercules, a brand-new aircraft with modern kit, the Vulcan seemed ancient – positively antiquated. I arrived at Waddington in June 1970 and spent nine years there."

> Aircraft are not clones and, occasionally, one aircraft would develop a poor reputation. An example was Vulcan XM606 at RAF Waddington. Len Hewitt was with the ground crew looking after 50 Squadron's aircraft:

> "This was nicknamed 'Sick-o-Sick'. I flew in this aircraft with John Huggins on one occasion. This was a ferry flight. On the way back we went through the acceptance checks at 48,000 ft over Waddington. This involved engine shut-down and relight. When No. 3 engine was shut down it refused to relight. For the landing, I was in the prone position and it looked pretty frightening. When 606 eventually took off again, Huggins went up so fast that the cabin air-pressurisation system couldn't keep up."

> Len also recalls that Waddington Wing had a 'hot' Vulcan during the early 1970s:

"This was a 27 Squadron aircraft fitted with air sampling equipment. It was used to sample the cloud from a Chinese atmospheric nuclear test. Unfortunately, the sampling vents had failed to open. It was then launched for a second attempt. This time it got well and truly irradiated and spent some months parked well out of the way at Scampton. Years later, then at Waddington, it was still having frequent washes and had a bright red warning page at the front of the Form 700."

Having completed two years' first-line servicing, Hewitt was detached to work on low-level modifications to the NBS, before returning to Waddington. Later, after specialised training at RAF Newton, near Nottingham, he was posted to the Vulcan flight simulator at Waddington. Pilots and co-pilots were required for regular simulator work:

"The instructors threw problems at them and tested their ability to cope. Originally, the Vulcan flight simulator had back projection (other, more modern flight sims have totally different video approaches) but this then changed. A new approach involved installing a screen above the simulator and in front of the cockpit, a large curved structure consisting of a frame supporting a polyester film formed into a parabolic mirror, giving crews in the simulator all-round vision."

In September 1958 Ray Gaunt had signed on for nine years. He trained as an air wireless fitter and was posted to Waddington in October 1959. He was impressed by the Vulcans:

"… I spent my first week working on the dustbin wagons, as did all new arrivals. Then I went to the 'Gin Palace', Waddington's Electronics Centre, positioned just inside the main gates. I spent the first few months there. I liked it – there was a good working atmosphere. A sergeant and a team of six fitters worked at the benches."[319]

During the following year, in the summer of 1960, Gaunt finally began working on the aircraft:

"I started with pre-flight checks. On completion, the captain would be invited to sign Form 700, so accepting the aircraft. This routine involved walking around the aircraft, checking that all items were secure, all external aerials were intact and working on any faults. Mostly, this would involve box changes. The faulty box would be removed and taken to the workshop. Some faults were reported by the crew. The offending box was labelled and taken to the 'Gin Palace'."

A year later, Gaunt was put on a prior warning overseas (PWO) roster. He wanted Germany but ended up in Aden which he hated. Relief came in early 1963, with a posting to Scampton – back on Vulcans. "At this point the Cold War became hotter and aircraft were no longer finished in white. Now they were camouflaged." Gaunt was at Scampton until 1966. At that time, he had completed eight of his nine years: "I was supposed to spend the last 12 months in the UK but I was posted to Borneo. I was really pleased with that! There was a war on …"

Taken overall, the V-Force delivered few attractions to Ray Gaunt: "The aircraft would often fly off between 21.00 and 22.00 and return in the middle of the night – around 02.30 to 03.00. The only thing we prayed for was fog." Some felt differently, of course. Cliff Doe joined in January 1961, having applied to be a boy entrant when 15½. He was offered airframe mechanic. By July 1962 he was posted to RAF Waddington and 101 Squadron, but had to wait until 17½ to wear the rank badges of a senior aircraftsman. He lived and worked on a highly active V-Force base, home to 44, 50 and 101 Vulcan Squadrons:

> "Initially, I was in awe of the Vulcan. My first job was to do a 'see-off crew', under the command of a crew chief. Once the captain and crew were satisfied with the pre-take-off checks, the see-off crew of two airmen removed the chocks and power cable, then marshalled the aircraft away from the dispersal as it taxied for take-off. Equipped with a new security pass, I was ushered around and shown the ropes. It came easily to me. I had no problems except for the first time I entered the Vulcan cabin under supervision and sat in the captain's ejection seat – without checking whether the safety pins were in. These were 'live' seats. Boy, did I get a rollicking – I never did that again!"[320]

Cliff Doe progressed to become a V-Force crew chief at Scampton.

As a 1950s teenager, Lyle 'Taff' Lark decided to join the Royal Navy. However, an outing to the cinema to watch *The Cruel Sea* changed his mind: "It put me right off the idea – floating around in the open sea. It would be the Royal Air Force for me." Lark joined the ATC, won a flying scholarship and went solo in a Tiger Moth. He also did some gliding, before attending Hornchurch Aircrew Selection Centre. He passed the aptitude tests, but fate took a hand:

> "I was waiting for my letter. The weather at the weekend was beautiful and I went to see my gliding mates. One of the senior instructors offered a short trip in a Kirby Cadet. I went up on the winch and had a cable break at 800 ft. The glider was trailing an

Leaving Scampton: Wing Commander Tony Atkinson, CO of 35 Squadron, and the crew of XL445 (captain: Flight Lieutenant Clive Allkins), about to depart for Goose Bay. Crew chief Cliff Doe is on the far right. This was his first trip to Goose Bay. (Cliff Doe)

impressive length of steel cable – the cable release had fouled. As I came in, the dangling wire snagged an obstruction and I went in, striking my head hard on the instrument panel. The impact damaged one of my ears and I was declared no longer fit to fly as an RAF pilot. Naturally, I was bitterly disappointed. I walked around with Trafalgar Square on my shoulders for the best part of a year."[321]

He moved on, having decided to specialise in electronics, and became an air radar fitter in 1955, following technical training at No. 2 Radio School, RAF Yatesbury. He was posted to 138 Squadron at Wittering – the first to be equipped with the Valiant. "The squadron was still forming when I arrived in late 1955. The crews had graduated from the Valiant OCU but, as yet, Gaydon had received only three aircraft, finished in anti-flash white." He spent 11 months at Wittering before taking up an exchange posting to Marham, then establishing itself as the base for three Valiant squadrons – 148, 207 and 214 Squadrons:

> "Marham's new Electronics Centre supported all three squadrons. The work included servicing and maintaining the NBS, together with Orange Putter tail-warning radar and the Green Satin system… The Valiant was an amazing technological leap. From all angles, this aircraft was an incredible achievement. Being brand new, equipment serviceability levels were not very good at first. The senior technicians worried that many of the problems were being created by over-testing. If an NBS developed problems during a navigation and bombing exercise, the details would be entered on Form 700. This automatically resulted in around three hours of intensive testing of the NBS – every time. In essence, we were flogging the system to death, causing even more problems in the air. The wing commander, technical, took it up at group level and convinced them that the best approach would be for aircrew and ground technicians to discuss NBS issues before making entries on the Form 700. This meant that any minor problems were dealt with during the normal pre-flight checks, so avoiding the punishing hours of fault-testing. Within six months of this change, serviceability levels improved dramatically. Now the aircraft were completing long-range flights with the NBS equipment remaining online."

Lyle Lark had his share of trips overseas. He went on detachment to Malta. On returning to Marham, he had a pleasant surprise:

> "When I got back, I was told to report the next day. The officer said: 'You're a lucky man. You've been selected to go with the Valiants to America, to represent Bomber Command in the SAC Navigation and Bombing Competition.' Two months later I boarded a Hastings, flying to Iceland, Goose Bay, New York State and down to Florida, where I spent the next four months. We fielded four aircraft, two Valiants and two Vulcans."

8
ON THE NUCLEAR FRONTLINE

> *We were going to drop it on the Russians only if they dropped it on us. If called upon to do so, I would have gone. That was it. We gave it no further thought.*
>
> Paddy Langdown, Vulcan captain

AT READINESS

In July 1958 Bomber Command received its readiness requirements. These were confirmed at a meeting between the Minister of Defence and the Secretary of State for Air:

- Strategic warning: after 24 hours' strategic warning "75% of the MBF should be at readiness, armed and dispersed."
- Tactical warning: "a readiness of 40 minutes should be capable of being sustained for up to one month and/or 15 minutes for one week."[322]

There were incremental requirements for generation: "After strategic warning, medium-bomber aircraft should become available as follows: 20% in two hours, 40% in four hours, 60% in eight hours and 75% in 24 hours." During 1959 Bomber Command worked hard to meet these targets, but admitted that it still had some way to go.

By mid-1960 the ballistic missile threat had put growing pressure on what remained of Bomber Command's 'old ways' – including acceptance of reduced readiness at weekends and during public holidays. From 1 February 1960, 25% of first-line aircraft were maintained at two to three hours readiness during all periods of stand-down. One major problem was the time required to recall personnel. This prompted a decision to retain 25% of the command at readiness during stand-down periods, to provide an alert force and ensure sufficient manpower "to offset, in some measure, the unavoidable delays involved in recalling men who were away on pass". An associated problem was the possible saturation of telephone services. The rate of recall would be "far too slow to enable the planned generation rate to be met".[323] Guidance was sought on a suggestion that civilian radio and TV be used to recall personnel, but this was forbidden during the Cuban Crisis two years later, in the interests of the 'unobtrusive' response required by Prime Minister Macmillan.

The new regime required an increase in manning establishments, to provide for a two-shift, 18-hour working day and enhanced readiness at weekends and on public holidays.[324] Progress accelerated and on 8 February 1960 the ACAS (Ops) sent a report to the VCAS stating that all MBF stations now had a proportion of aircraft and personnel at two hours standby seven days a week and during public holidays.[325] Efforts were made to make weekends on base more acceptable. Sir Kenneth Cross wanted more recreational/gym facilities, but had little success with his call for swimming pools. He maintained that a weekend on the station needed to be made "so interesting and enjoyable that the feeling of hardship largely disappears". However, in a letter to the Chief of the Air Staff (CAS), Sir Dermot Boyle, Cross made a prediction which proved accurate:

> "Restriction on liberty of individuals on such a scale, added to the inconvenience of working an 18-hour/two-shift system, particularly against the background of an almost universal five-day week, is bound to become a real hardship as time goes on."

Ironically, later in 1960 there was a big fuss over a Bomber Command request for more "essential residential telephones". Air Commodore C.G. Stowell complained to the Director of Operations (Bomber and Reconnaissance) (D.Ops [B&R]) on 16 December: "At present I am under fire from headquarters, Bomber Command," following a request for more telephones. "These are in the main to alert personnel under the Alert and Readiness Plan. I have not seen this plan in detail … I am not convinced that essential residential telephones are the answer or that the telephone is the best way to alert personnel." Stowell went on to suggest that Bomber Command had already been "indulged" with extra telephones because of the importance attached to the deterrent.[326]

It is possible that the air commodore might have been less preoccupied with telephones had he had an opportunity to read *The Nuclear Destruction of Britain,* published two decades later. Dr Magnus Clarke made a rare attempt to quantify the consequences of failure to deter a nuclear attack on Britain. He put the immediate effect of a 188-target, 167-mt strike on Britain at 6–8 million immediate fatalities and ten–16 million seriously injured. There would be 31–39 million able-bodied survivors one month after the attack. After three months, there would be a minimum of 20 million dead from all causes, with exhaustion of national food stocks between three and six months after the nuclear strike. Food would become the means of government. Thirty years after the attack, the UK population would have declined to about ten million, mostly living a rural existence.[327]

ON THE NUCLEAR FRONTLINE

V-Force aircrew were in their twenties or early thirties for the most part, although some (especially in the early days) were more mature – in their forties or even fifties. Many did not regard a V-bomber posting as first prize. The younger men enjoyed the traditional pursuits of young flyers. Beyond the serious matters of flying training and target study, they had little thinking time for what many called, irreverently, the 'Nuclear Detergent'. The bomb itself became known as 'the bucket of instant sunshine' or, simply, 'the bucket'. Vulcan co-pilot Keith Mans, with 50 Squadron at RAF Waddington, summed it up:

> "For a young man in the V-Force, the nuclear deterrent element was the most boring part of the job. The really interesting bit was flying long distance – going abroad. Naturally, the most popular destinations were the sunspots, such as Cyprus."[328]

Of course, a long-term V-Force posting at home suited some, especially those establishing families in the UK.

There were some compensations for those on the nuclear frontline. Waddington, for example, had a reputation for the best QRA Mess and restaurant of all the bomber stations.

Operational deployments took crews to the sun. Occasionally, an aircraft deployed to RAF Luqa, Malta, for a period. Crews flew low over the desert when using El Adem bombing range in Libya. Bombing practice over ranges in Libya, Cyprus and Malta involved trips of three or four days. Western Rangers lasted longer – about a week – and often called for low-level sorties over Goose Bay, Labrador, to practise flying over the Arctic tundra. Western Rangers might also involve encounters with USAF radar bomb scoring units (RBSUs) or Nike SAM sites. Many Western Rangers terminated at Offutt Air Force Base (AFB).[329] Early Western Rangers operated out of Lincoln AFB, Nebraska, which closed in 1966.

There were few philosophers on the squadrons. Beyond the round of training, exercises and alerts, crews did not dwell on the possibility that deterrence might fail. They tended to avoid nuclear war as a topic of conversation, both on base and at home. Indeed, it may have been considered bad form to bring up this subject out of the professional context.

AEO Martin Anscombe flew his first sortie with his captain as 50 Squadron's commander on 8 August 1961. Newly-arrived crews buckled down to target study. On a war flight, one of the AEO's many duties was to manage Morse communications. "This was the most reliable of all means of communication for crucial messages, including Positive Release, the message required to cross the 8 degrees E Go/No Go line." Anscombe raised some eyebrows when he rigged a small domestic tape recorder to record Morse transmissions and play them back at slower speed – giving him more time to read them and verify.[330]

During the low-level transition period: 50 Squadron Vulcan Mk 1As on detachment to RAF Luqa, Malta. Two of the eight aircraft are camouflaged. (Martin Anscombe)

Home again: Group Captain M D'Arcy, OC RAF Waddington, welcomes Flight Lieutenant Nick Dennis on his return from the bombing competition at Fairchild AFB, Washington State, 16 October 1969. (Nick Dennis)

Robin Woolven was a nav/plotter with 617 Squadron, Scampton, flying Blue Steel Vulcans:

"So far as I'm aware, everyone around me was completely on-side. We had the weapon, the delivery system and the resolution to use it if we had to. I remember only one case of a man, a young co-pilot, who was moved on from 617 on the grounds of a personality problem, but I believe that had more to do with his sex life than anything else."[331]

Roy Brocklebank recalled an incident at RAF Cottesmore: a co-pilot sought permission to marry a Yugoslav national. He was given a choice: "Marry and lose his security clearance or remain in the V-Force. He married."

Aircrew were subject to positive vetting. Memories of this process are mixed; some found it to be vigorous whilst others remember it as a gentle affair. In 1961, Norman Bonnor was a 22-year-old Victor navigator. His crew were shown films of the aftermath of the Hiroshima and Nagasaki attacks, together with classified films of nuclear tests:

"There was no 'indoctrination', as experienced by Strategic Air Command (SAC) crews, but promotion to flying officer and then flight lieutenant did require success in examinations which included defence studies papers on subjects including deterrence … I also underwent positive vetting before leaving Cranwell. They dredged up the fact that one of my uncles had married a Jewish girl who had escaped from Austria in 1939, to what later became Israel. This issue was examined and then dismissed."[332]

Another nav/radar, Bob Sinclair, remembers his interview, when he was asked: "Do you like the sensation of sand running through your fingers?" He struggled to make the connection with nuclear deterrence. He described the vetting process as "fairly comprehensive" and remembered a young married man with money problems, which got worse. Eventually, he was posted out of the V-Force.

Bomber Command AOC-in-C Sir Kenneth Cross personally interviewed many V-Force aircrew; these were not in-depth encounters, according to Victor captain Jeremy Mudford:

"You could be sure he would ask: 'Do you have a Mess Kit? Do you go to church? Do you play games?' Under his reign, every Wednesday afternoon in Bomber Command was devoted to team sports. Everyone was expected to participate."[333]

Confidence in the deterrent was not absolute, as confirmed by John Huggins:

"Towering over everything was the concept of 'MAD' – 'Mutually Assured Destruction'. In short, if it ever happened, there would be nothing left for anyone. This might seem like a common sense balance of terror but, for some years, it seemed more a question of *when* rather than *if* nuclear war would happen."[334]

Should war have come to the V-Force airfields, ground crews would have been among the first casualties. Aircrew would have had no chance of escaping incoming missiles without the constant commitment of the ground teams. Had the bombers scrambled for war, those remaining on the ground (many with families living at Ground Zero) would have begun their last two minutes of life. John Huggins paid tribute to them:

"Our ground crew were known as 'Waddington PIGs'. 'PIG' was the acronym for the ground crew motto: 'Pride, Integrity, Guts'. They wore a special PIG badge. I got on well with my ground team and always wore a PIG badge with pride."

At least one V-Force ground crew room featured a large Dayglo pig, with the sentiment: "Unloved, unwanted, yet seen around the world." When ground crew visited bars at overseas bases, they would find a spot to plant a small Dayglo pig.

With squadrons run as separate entities, in the days before centralised control of flying and servicing, Roy Brocklebank remembers the competition to launch the first aircraft at 08.00:

"In practice, ground crew would be preparing the aircraft through the night, ready for crew in. The caterers would have been preparing inflight rations and getting ready to serve pre-flight meals any time after 05.00. The crew would assemble in the briefing room at 05.00. With nine bases and 20 plus aircraft all vying for those 08.00 slots, it wasn't going to work. Each station was allocated a number of take-off slots throughout the day, starting at 08.00 and then spread through, with the last planned launch maybe 21.00 that evening. Now, instead of squadrons competing against each other, each station was competing to hit its assigned take-off slots. To that end, the whole process was designed from brief, eat, change, transport, crew in, taxi and rotate at precisely the briefed time."[335]

The post-QRA fly-off also attracted much attention. Each week a QRA aircraft came off-state and was scheduled for a post-QRA fly-off sortie:

"Other than the standard daily pre-flight, as it had undergone on QRA, no other servicing was permitted, except for a rare safety-of-flight issue. Once the weapon was offloaded, the aircraft would be handed to the crew and all eyes were watching to see if it was a goer."

CONFRONTING REALITIES

Given that the number of V-bombers surviving a pre-emptive strike was central to the delivery of sufficient weapons on targets, what were the full implications of a short-warning, hammer-blow missile strike on all MBF airfields? The R-12 intermediate-range ballistic missile (IRBM) (SS-4 Sandal) entered service in 1959 and by the summer of the following year Soviet strategic missile forces were operating 248 R-12 launchers.[336]

Uncomfortable realities were confronted in a May 1960 letter from the then ACAS (Ops), Air Vice-Marshal John Grandy, to the AOC-in-C Bomber Command. Grandy noted that recent intelligence appreciations:

> "… conclude that the Soviets have available a substantial number of IRBMs. The tactical warning available on this missile threat could be as low as three minutes for an IRBM launched on a low trajectory from Eastern Germany, but this amount of tactical warning will not be available until 1963, when the ballistic missile early warning system is expected to be operational."[337]

In effect, Bomber Command could expect little or no warning of low-trajectory IRBM attack for the next three years.

Grandy also referred to the growing Soviet air defence challenge:

> "Successful deep penetration of the Soviet defences is likely to become increasingly complex, since more targets are being protected by the installation of short-range surface-to-air guided weapon (SAGW) systems, to supplement the existing large fighter force. Both an increased ECM capability and Blue Steel Mk 1 should become available to your command within the next 2/3 years, and it is important to study the extent to which these aids to penetration can be maximised."

With this in mind, Grandy proposed forming a joint Air Ministry/Bomber Command working group: "This group would have at its disposal the information available at Air Ministry on future prospects of equipment and weapons, together with the operational experience and knowledge possessed by your command." Six main issues were put forward for joint investigation and action; some were directly significant both in avoiding destruction on the ground and successfully putting weapons on Soviet targets:

- Ways and means of improving the readiness of the current MBF to thwart missile attacks, both with and without the tactical warning offered by BMEWS.
- The implications of keeping a proportion of the bomber force at three minutes (cockpit) readiness on present aircrew/aircraft ratios, and of increasing that ratio.
- The feasibility and desirability of maintaining a limited airborne alert with the currently available MBF.
- A satisfactory presentation of the enemy raid situation to the Bomber Command Operations Centre.
- Implications of the introduction of Blue Steel Mk 1.
- Feasibility and desirability of low-level penetration techniques.

The second point was achieved, in effect, through the emergence of a plan (a new Alert Condition 1) to hold a proportion of the MBF at five minutes' readiness in the context of a major threat of war, with all aircraft dispersed *and some cockpits manned 24/7 by crew rotation (with all checks completed)*. This addressed the missile threat to the greatest extent possible, while action taken on the last point – low-level penetration – reduced the threat from the air defences to the greatest extent possible.

Many innovative measures were taken to reduce the threat of destruction on the ground, mostly contributing to faster scramble times (including construction of ORPs and the introduction of simultaneous engine start [SIMSTART]). Whilst Readiness State 03 was never established as such, RS05 (cockpit readiness) achieved this in practice by requiring crews to be ready for immediate engine start (RS02). Low-level penetration made things much more difficult for the Soviet air defences. Other points of action proved less promising. Various studies of airborne alert had already demonstrated that this approach to force preservation was beyond Bomber Command's relatively modest means. As for Blue Steel Mk 1, its implications certainly deserved scrutiny, given the extreme difficulties faced by squadrons attempting to bring the stand-off bomb into operational service.

While a new realism gradually pervaded Bomber Command, false hopes and excessive optimism lingered. In the early, pre-missile days, the war standard operations plan (SOP) first edition assumed the V-Force would make two or three attacks, rather than one. Having flown their first war sortie, captains landing away were expected to contact base or the resident air attaché for instructions! A note from the Deputy Chief of the Air Staff (DCAS) to the Secretary for Air in February 1958 set out Air Staff expectations of MBF sortie potential (based on 144 aircraft with 75% serviceability and allowing for air and ground losses inflicted by the enemy):

- First strike: 86 aircraft reaching target area and 58 'effective bombs'.
- Second strike: 55 and 35.
- Third strike: 42 and 28.

Low level: across the wilds of Northumberland. (Andy Leitch Collection)

If realised, this would have put 121 weapons on targets. The note commented on estimated losses:

> "It is of course impossible to predict accurately the losses which the enemy could inflict on our bombers. These will depend on tactics, routes, time of day or night, location of the targets and the effectiveness of the Russian defences. Making due allowance for all these factors, however, the best estimate that can be made is that casualties might vary between 54% or even higher for the Valiants to as low as 22% for the Mk 2 Victors/Vulcans with the powered guided bomb. In our calculations we have, in fact, taken a loss rate of 20%, which may be a little on the low side but does not affect the issue very materially. It is of course very unlikely that the air defences would be good in the early stages of a war – as we well know." [338]

Given the likely catastrophic consequences of a pre-emptive missile strike, even with BMEWS and a host of new measures to get bombers off the ground as quickly as possible, plans for second and third strikes eventually melted away. Yet, chronic optimism proved more resilient. Writing in 1993, Sir Frank Cooper (head of the Air Staff Secretariat and, later, Permanent Under Secretary for Defence), made bold claims:

> "The V-Force became genuinely credible as an operationally efficient force which would survive. Its ability to disperse first at home and then overseas, its well-publicised ability to maintain QRA and take off rapidly, the introduction of flight refuelling, coupled with some spectacular long-range flights, all contributed to driving home to the East, and almost as important to the public at large, that the V-bomber force was able to survive aggression and would be able to retaliate."[339]

This was written 24 years *after* the UK strategic deterrent passed from the V-Force to the submarines. Sir Frank's bullish comments contrast with operational realities, reflecting the deeply embedded tendency to make favourable pronouncements about readiness, available warning time, dispersal, war scramble survival and the ability to reach targets. To take just a few of Sir Frank's points: the V-Force had no capacity to launch a strategic retaliatory strike from overseas bases (with the exception of two Vulcan squadrons [16 aircraft] based in Cyprus for several years post-Polaris handover). There was a difficult period, pre-Fylingdales, when the V-Force was exposed to low-trajectory IRBM attack, with very poor prospects of sufficient tactical warning. A war scramble involving QRA aircraft alone would, at best, have put only a very small number of weapons on targets. As for flight refuelling, this proved irrelevant to V-Force strategic capabilities. There were never enough tankers to service V-Force needs, in terms of extended target cover. Vulcan co-pilot Andy Leitch recalls: "Air-to-air refuelling systems were wired off in my day."

REACHING THE TARGET

For those bombers surviving a strike on their airfields, the next challenge was to penetrate the Soviet coastal defence belt. The early plan was to concentrate V-Force aircraft at several crossing points and swamp the local defences. A March 1959 Bomber Command Operational Research Branch report examined the effects of tactical routeing on target coverage. This assumed penetration of the coastal defences via three 'gates' – north (63 degrees N, 22 degrees

E), central (52 degrees N, 10 degrees E) and south (48 degrees N, 13 degrees E), with the central gate offering the most extensive target cover. Following the attack, there were three recovery options: return by entry point, return by direct route or a recovery landing in Cyprus (which increased target cover significantly).[340]

As for weapons, stand-off systems had obvious advantages over freefall bombs. The guided-bomb project Blue Boar was under consideration as early as 1946–47, but difficulties with its TV command and control system could not be overcome; it was cancelled in June 1954. Just three months later, however, OR.1132 was issued for an inertia-guided air-to-surface weapon for the V-bombers. This became Blue Steel Mk 1, the powered bomb, which would allow carrier aircraft to 'stand-off' target point defences. There were Air Ministry hopes that Blue Steel would be in service by 1960, but delivery came in December 1962.[341]

Sir Frank Cooper described 1956 and 1957 as "watershed years" for defence policy, given the shock of Suez, difficult choices over future weapons and, above all, cost pressures in a climate of diminishing resources – despite large cuts in conventional forces on the back of greater reliance on nuclear weapons. He gave a crisp summary of the mood of the times:

> "Looking back, the second half of the 1950s and early 1960s were a difficult period … Cost estimates were widely out. Costs escalated wildly. The Soviet threat was increasing … More than 30 projects were cancelled. Ministers became increasingly frustrated by being unable to get a firm grip on plans and programmes."[342]

The operational need for Blue Steel was obvious, given the rapid expansion of air defences around Soviet cities, but could this complex weapon be made to work? The requirements included an accuracy expectation of 500 yards at 150NM, using autonomous inertial navigation. Doubts about Blue Steel's operational value were expressed as early at 1959. Furthermore, the Air Staff wanted a stand-off weapon with much longer range.[343] A view set out in October of that year, based on an estimate by the Ministry of Supply that Blue Steel Mk 1 would be in service early in 1962, was that by 1963 the V-bomber/Blue Steel Mk 1 weapon system would lose its validity owing to the decline in the ability of aircraft to reach the weapon's required release point. Nevertheless, Blue Steel's production order was placed in December 1960 (eventually finalised at 57 missiles).

This unease reflected wider concerns about the fundamental vulnerability of a bomber-based deterrent. Champions of the bomber regarded missiles as unproven and pressed for a new generation supersonic bomber. Yet, as early as mid-1956, there was a counterview that even supersonic aircraft "would be incapable of operation in defended airspace" by the mid-1960s. Certainly, there were deeply-held concerns about the survival prospects of subsonic bombers in heavily defended airspace.[344] Most advocates of bombers supported the case for the long-range powered bomb (OR.1159, Blue Steel Mk 2) – an option offering greater credibility and a life extension for the V-Force.

LIFE EXTENSION

In mid-1955 A.I. Llewelyn, then Bomber Command's chief research officer, set out options for V-Force life extension.[345] Responding to a reply from the AOC-in-C, Llewelyn (loose minute, 30 August 1955) struck an optimistic tone. He claimed the V-Force "will have a better life than people think", that countermeasures against radars "will really reduce" fighter effectiveness and, furthermore, "the guided-missile defence will take longer and be much less efficient than people think". He added that his priorities at that time included: "a Stage 2 improvement, to get the V-bombers over target at 50,000 ft by 1960." He also favoured a limited low-level capability.

Llewelyn's Operational Research Branch identified six life extension options in its report: aircraft performance, aircraft tactics, force tactics, countermeasures, use of decoys and use of support (e.g. opening attacks by Canberras on reporting and control radars). On aircraft performance, he acknowledged the limited scope for pushing height and speed within buffet boundary limits and the range of the flight. On aircraft tactics, the main choice was high or low. Here, he argued for low-level attacks against "a certain proportion of targets within a restricted range". Force tactics hinged on dispersal in time and space, with limited dispersion the "reasonable compromise".

In the mid-1950s there was time to take considered response decisions; hostile bombers would give ample warning in the very different, pre-ballistic missile world. Llewelyn gave his views:

> "Although statements have been made that the bomber force must retaliate instantly, whether by day or by night, there is no denying the fact that by day the probability that a reasonable percentage of bombers reach their targets is very small. Plans must therefore be based on night attacks if we wish to retaliate effectively and not just make an ineffective gesture."

On countermeasures, Llewelyn referred to radar jammers, chaff (Window), airborne interception (AI) radar jammers and warning equipment: "… the continued survival of the V-Force as the Russian defences improve will depend on the success with which these measures can be introduced and used." The chief research officer was not above referring to "exotics", including concepts for unmanned, ECM-equipped decoys. It was suggested that a decoy would cost only 1/30th of a V-bomber and that scaling back the V-Force by 20 bombers would fund 600 decoys. Unfortunately, these calculations were wrong – they failed to take account of decoy assembly and launch-site costs. This reduced the cost advantage to 1/6th of a bomber. Nevertheless, decoys represented a genuine if undeveloped option for reducing bomber losses.

As might be expected, Llewelyn argued for the powered bomb: "… it would delay the obsolescence of the V-bomber force at least until an effective long-range guided-weapon defence had been introduced." Not only was Blue Steel Mk 1 required, as early as possible, but also air-to-surface missiles (ASMs) with much greater range, yet this need was never satisfied. In any event, a 1959 report, from the British Nuclear Deterrent Study Group, had concluded that long-range Blue Steel Mk 2 would increase V-bomber viable life for only a short period (two or three years post-1965) and that Skybolt was preferable. The following year the Minister of Defence signed a memorandum of understanding for the purchase of 100 Skybolts.

SKYBOLT AND THE FUTURE

With missiles deployed in ever greater numbers, the catastrophic consequences of a pre-emptive strike against the MBF airfields became self-evident. Air Vice-Marshal Menaul acknowledged the threat: "… this demanded new safeguards for the deterrent strike forces

A Skybolt-armed Vulcan: the configuration under test in the transonic tunnel. (Crown Copyright RAE/FAST Archive)

which, in turn, ushered in 'counterforce strategy', which dominated strategic thinking in the early sixties." There was a persistent focus on getting weapons on targets rather than the essential prerequisite – surviving a pre-emptive strike. The Skybolt ALBM was a case in point. Whilst widely regarded as the future of the British deterrent, this weapon system (aircraft, missile and crew) would have become increasingly exposed to destruction on the ground. However advanced the weapon carried, a manned bomber is still a manned bomber, with unavoidable exposure on the ground (unless purpose-designed with airborne alert in mind). Nevertheless, according to Menaul: "Both Bomber Command and SAC were convinced that an air-launched ballistic missile was a logical and desirable step in the development of strategic nuclear forces."[346] As things turned out, it seems that Bomber Command (on the face of it, at least) was more convinced than the Americans, despite the fact that Skybolt would have been less capable in British service, due to Bomber Command's likely inability to adopt SAC-style airborne alert.

This obvious weakness prompted radical thinking by concept teams looking at the use of long endurance aircraft such as Vulcan Phase 6, capable of carrying four Skybolts and with an airborne endurance increased from seven hours to 11½ hours, and a 'military' VC10 transport converted for the Skybolt carrier role.

There was no end to British ingenuity when it came to ideas for making meagre resources go further … and faster. Yet, on 4 April 1957, the government decided not to proceed with the development of a supersonic manned bomber.[347] Nevertheless, Mr A. S. Roger, of Wolves Lane, Palmers Green, London, believed he had an irresistible solution. By 7 August 1960 he was ready and wrote to the Minister of Defence: "Dear Sir, I have been planning for some time a mid-delta wing, three-seat supersonic bomber." This aircraft would be powered by four Bristol Olympus turbojets and carry four 20-mm cannon in a revolving pod under the nose, plus two cannon in the tail and wing points for weapons, including two Skybolts or three Blue Steels. Roger promised a maximum speed of over 850 mph and a range of more than 5,000 miles. His letter described the service ceiling as "secret". Even better: "Production would start early next year."[348] If his proposal was of no interest, Roger suggested that the V-bombers should be equipped with tail turrets.

Roger received a polite acknowledgement of his kind offer. A few weeks later, however, he wrote again:

> "Dear Sir, I thank you for your letter of 11 August, but I regret that due to your lack of interest in the proposals for a supersonic bomber, and for fitting the V-bombers with tail gun turrets, I am afraid I shall have to ask you to cancel the projects. I deeply regret any inconvenience I have caused you."

The 'Roger Bomber' would not be built in 1961. Three days after this last letter, on 11 September 1960, more serious business was afoot: an Anglo-American planning conference on Skybolt.

With Skybolt's cancellation in late 1962, the V-bombers' vulnerabilities remained and continued to grow. The key issue was the number of V-bombers likely to survive a war scramble, rather than its force strength, on paper, pre-missile strike. The most likely combination opening a hot war – very high V-bomber casualties on the ground, followed by heavy losses amongst the survivors attempting penetration – appears to support the case for a mixed deterrent, a combination of bombers and missiles. This had existed for a few years, during the deployment of the Thors, but these missiles were also very vulnerable as stated previously, being above ground and liquid-fuelled. Indeed, these were the very factors which led to the cancellation of the British Blue Streak ballistic missile in February 1960. The Thors

Ready for the crews: XL317 and others at the Cottesmore ORP. (Andy Leitch Collection)

were withdrawn by August 1963. In that year, with no Skybolt and no prospect of Polaris for some years, the question remained: What more could be done to reduce V-bomber casualties on the ground and in the air, in the event of a hot war? A convincing response was needed, to preserve the core retaliatory threat. The solution adopted slowed the inevitable decline in capability and credibility, by combining faster response within shorter warning times and extreme combat tactics – ultra-low weapons delivery.

In retrospect, it can be seen that reliance on manned bombers alone (with the exception of the Thor years) placed Britain in a difficult position. The most appropriate future solution for the UK deterrent was the submarine-launched ballistic missile (SLBM), which offered a large measure of freedom from the threat of destruction before retaliation. The traditional commitment to manned bombers led the British to chase Skybolt, rather than focus entirely on a much more desirable goal: Polaris. Ironically (that is, unless the course of events was 'steered' by the British, using the ALBM as a rudder), the UK won Polaris – without meaningful strings – through the cancellation of Skybolt. This was by far the best possible outcome for the UK, yet it left the problem of a near six-year wait for the submarines – somewhat longer than the prospective wait for the ALBM.

Herculean efforts were made to bridge this gap, by taking more measures to enhance V-Force operational effectiveness, but the fact remained that little could be done to ensure the survival of a significant proportion of the V-Force, in the event of a pre-emptive missile strike. This is why so much attention was devoted to ensuring that the destructive capacity of a relatively small group of war scramble survivors would be maximised, by focusing on the biggest Soviet cities. These measures were progressed in the knowledge that there was no time or budget before Polaris to acquire advanced, long-range stand-off weapons, to allow those few V-bombers surviving a war scramble to attack targets successfully by releasing their weapons from positions outside heavily defended Soviet airspace.

On 15 June 1968 HMS *Resolution* set out on the first Royal Navy Polaris patrol, carrying 16 A-3 missiles, each with three 200-kt warheads. The targeting focus was Moscow, with an upgrade, 'Chevaline', deployed in 1982 and designed specifically to penetrate this city's anti-ballistic missile (ABM) shield. Targeting was transformed in 1994, with the deployment of Trident D5 missiles on board four Vanguard Class submarines. This returned flexibility to targeting due to an increase in deliverable warheads.

# 9

DESTROYING THE TARGETS

> *A capability to kill millions of people became morally neutral because it was reactive. A first strike … was the more heinous crime because that would, almost automatically, trigger a second strike. The crime was to start a nuclear war, not to prosecute it with murderous intensity.*
>
> Lawrence Freedman, *The Evolution of Nuclear Strategy*

MAKING EVERY WEAPON COUNT

Given the modest British nuclear stockpile, the first principle of UK planning was to make every weapon count. The nuclear targeting policy was astute and pragmatic. Great efforts were made to maximise the destructive potential of each weapon in relation to the allocated target (in itself, an explanation for V-Force emphasis on accurate weapons delivery).

The highest standards of navigation and bombing accuracy were essential if destructive power was to be maximised in a retaliatory attack. The viability of the new low-level mission profile depended on the expertise and commitment of bomber crews. The crew classification system set demanding standards of excellence, with select star (command) status extremely difficult to attain and retain. 'Trappers', from the Group Standardisation Unit, were the ultimate arbiters of crew standards. Trapper assessment teams visited MBF bases on an annual basis. Vic Bussereau's second Vulcan tour, with 50 Squadron at Waddington, was cut short. He was posted to Scampton in September 1971 as a nav/radar trapper:

> "The trapper's job was to check the competence of crews and ensure standard procedures were followed. Minute variations, from squadron to squadron, could lead to slight differences of approach. Crew changes, obviously, could have an impact on standardisation. The aim was to fly with all nav/radars at least once every two years. I reported on the individual nav/radar and also the crew in the context of crew cooperation."[349]

Trappers also had the job of exploring the entire squadron:

> "We would take a look at the organisation on the ground – for example, the training records for nav/radars, a check on whether the number of sorties flown complied with requirements and also the number of ground training days. We gave some aircrew ground orals for a couple of hours, encompassing their knowledge of the aircraft systems applicable to their role as well as operational procedures. During my trapping days, I failed only two nav/radars. Failure, in this sense, meant they had to undergo rechecks."

V-Force crews trained to attack Plan A and Plan B targets (see page 65).

Plan B, the core deterrent threat, is the fundamental projection of Britain's nuclear power with the capacity to deter even the most powerful aggressor. In the public arena, Plan B was often discounted, given that the idea of Britain waging nuclear war without its allies was so unlikely as to be hardly worthy of consideration. Yet it remains, to this day, the ultimate expression of UK military and political power and, perhaps, its true significance is undervalued and often misunderstood. Inevitably, given Britain's limited nuclear arsenal, Plan B targets were punitive: 'countervalue' – the major Soviet centres of population. At the same time, Plan A military targets were often near or within major urban areas and, consequently, as Kristan Stoddart pointed out: "… there was little difference between these and the countervalue (city) targets that were the focus of the National Retaliatory War Plan."[350]

Destroying airfields and other military targets might be considered an inadequate response to Britain's total destruction. Many counterforce targets, however, as stated above, were in and around the big Soviet cities; inevitably, a Plan A attack would largely destroy the host cities (at least those not already completely destroyed in the immediate wave of missile strikes). A V-bomber counterforce strike had the potential to inflict catastrophic countervalue damage. From this perspective, both plans were in harmony. Plan A, of course, respected, to some extent, the political niceties of not specifically targeting civilians. Here, Lawrence Freedman drew attention to a comment by T.F. Walkowicz (1955): "… major air bases are frequently located near cities; troops can be concentrated in cities and submarine bases are associated with major seaports. Thus, even counterforce operations will inevitably lead to some destruction of Soviet cities."[351]

Early V-Force targeting had a counterforce emphasis, with priority given to Soviet bomber bases threatening the UK. This was accompanied by countervalue targeting in the national context. Here, the objective was to destroy Russia's major urban areas. Matthew Jones pointed to the logic:

> "This was, after all, the purest way to achieve a deterrent effect: to inflict such a level of destruction on a society and state that it might cease to function in any recognisable manner, making the potential gain of any initial aggression seem insignificant and even ridiculous against the disastrous consequences that would follow as a result … In the strategic environment, where the UK's delivery capabilities were decidedly limited but the power of weapons carried much increased, the attractions of countervalue targeting became steadily more apparent."[352]

The Valiant, the first of the V-bombers, had entered service in February 1955. Jones noted that, two months later, Bomber Command's AOC-in-C, Air Chief Marshal Sir George Mills, was asked to comment on his draft Command Directive. He was not impressed. The priority was to attack the Soviet long-range bomber force. Many air bases were near cities, but Mills preferred the cities proper:

> "… we must be specific in saying that our aim in retaliation is to hurt him where it really hurts …Whoever would be afraid of launching a sudden attack if he thought that the greater part of our retaliation would come back on his airfields?"

Each V-Force crew had Plan A NATO targets and Plan B National targets, together with a priority QRA target. Roy Brocklebank was targeting officer for RAF Waddington's Wing of 24 Vulcans: "There was one QRA target (accounting line number [ALN] 100 series, going up to 119), two Plan A (ALN 200 series), one Plan B (ALN 400 series) and one Plan B follow-on target (ALN 411 or plus)."[353] Targets changed annually (Plan A on July 1 and Plan B on January 1), so presenting crews with fresh challenges. This annual cycle allowed for intelligence updates and changes in targeting policy.

The British allocation of Plan A targets, under the joint SIOP, evolved over the years, as did the Plan B National target list. These changes reflected, inter alia, a shift in policy from instant and massive nuclear retaliation to 'flexible response'. Plan B placed emphasis on an ever-smaller number of the largest Soviet cities. While the British definition of levels of damage unacceptable to the Soviets became increasingly modest in scale, this did *not* solely reflect a decline in V-Force operational capability during the 1960s, but also an evolutionary shift in purpose – towards the unilateral threat of damage *severe enough to undermine the balance between the superpowers.*

From the first, British planners sought to make the most of the UK's relatively modest nuclear stockpile. Their task was to maximise the deterrent threat and, secondly, in the event of war, to maximise damage. Mark Venables set out the realities – for reasons of geography and limited military capabilities, British planners focused on attacking cities, with the fundamental theme being deterrence through punishment.[354]

"Optimisation" of nuclear strike capabilities was the watchword. Undated, but probably written in the third quarter of 1959, Bomber Command's Operational Research Branch produced a seminal report on this subject (Memorandum No. 199): "The effect of delivery accuracy and target allocation on the effectiveness of a nuclear stockpile." Much work was done to understand the mechanisms which would allow the MBF to maximise destructive power:

> "The stockpile ... can be taken to represent the potential destruction of an area of enemy resources. How far the practical results of an offensive using these weapons would fall short of this potential depends on many factors, amongst which are accuracy of delivery, degree of assurance or target coverage required on individual targets, and the disposition of aiming points within a complex target. Lack of accuracy in delivery will always waste some potential damage capability. If the ratio of delivery error to weapon damage radius is more than 1.0, this loss in potential is serious."[355]

The memorandum underlined the need for pragmatic targeting:

> "Economic use of the damage potential of the stockpile and good coverage or high assurance on individual targets are incompatible, so that planning must be a compromise between priority needs and optimum overall use of the weapons available. Disposition of aiming points within a large, complex target is necessary, to prevent the serious over-hitting (and consequent loss of effectiveness elsewhere) which occurs if only one aiming point is chosen. In order to achieve the maximum damage to built-up areas in Russia, the majority of weapons would have to be allocated to the few large towns. This is

particularly the case when delivery accuracy is relatively poor, as with ballistic missiles. In a practical plan, this aim may have to be subordinated to other priorities and when this is so the practical and economically optimum allocations should be compared, to see if some compromise to increase overall effectiveness is not possible."

This report described the rationale behind target allocations, with the destructive potential of a stockpile measured in terms of total area of effect. "For example, the potential of 20 1-mt weapons would be about 250 square miles, if the target system were composed of built-up areas." However, the actual area of destruction caused by the counterstrike "would be very much less than this". Some weapons would fail to explode, others would detonate with less than nominal yield, and, of course, some bombers would fail to reach their targets. Here, the memorandum noted: "These are well-known factors, but there are others, stemming from the way in which it is planned to allocate and deliver the weapons, which are less often considered."

The memorandum used the term "utilisation" to measure the magnitude of weapon effects: "This 'utilisation' is simply the proportion of the nominal destructive area of a bomb which can be expected to be effective in practice when it is used against an area target." As for delivery accuracy, it might be thought that, given the immense power of nuclear weapons, precision is of little consequence. The memorandum, however, describes a more complex reality: "If the target and the damage radius of the weapon are both large compared with the accuracy of delivery, the expected utilisation of the weapon will be high." At the same time, it acknowledged that this was not always the case, adding:

> "The effect of delivery error on bomb utilisation is most pronounced when the target is comparable in size with the damage radius of the bomb, a frequent practical situation. In this case, utilisation falls below 50% unless the delivery error is much less than the bomb damage radius. Any reduction in delivery error which can be made is well worthwhile in this case. If the target is larger than the bomb damage radius, one bomb will achieve almost its full effect unless the delivery error is greater than the bomb damage radius. Against smaller targets, the full potential of the weapon cannot be realised because a proportion of the area of effect necessarily occurs beyond the target boundaries. This initially low utilisation is decreased further if there is any appreciable delivery error."

This does much to explain why Bomber Command placed so much emphasis on accurate delivery of nuclear weapons, despite their enormous power. As the memorandum emphasised: "It is of vital importance to ensure that the accuracy with which weapons are delivered is kept as high as possible if the full potential of the stockpile is to be effective in practice." Roy Brocklebank described the operational expectations of delivery accuracy:

> "When the force was high level only, we had a requirement to achieve certain accuracies in training against realistic simulated targets. These figures varied against crew experience. A new crew who had achieved combat status was expected to achieve a given percentage of scores – from an evasive bomb run – of about 2,000 yards. Where there was no evasion, the accuracy was expected to be in the order of 600 yards for half the attacks. A slightly larger error was permitted against a target that was jamming the H2S radar. After a further six months, a crew might be assessed as combat star, then,

progressively, select and, finally, select star. Progression depended on time together as a crew and accuracy. From memory (after 54 years!), a select star crew might need accuracies in the order of 1,100 yards and 400 yards respectively but to have more bombs within that limit. When the force went low level we had a new training regime: BTR (Basic Training Requirements) … Accuracy levels were now measured in a run of, say, eight out of 10 within the limit. If a crew got eight out of 11 they did not progress to the next level. The equipment was initially estimated to have a 50% accuracy of 400 yards. With certain improvements, the accuracy was around 300 yards. In Cyprus, in one six-month period, the squadron average for practice bombs on a raft target was 300 *feet*."[356]

Roy Brocklebank recalls a mid-1960s RAF study suggesting that severe degradation (75%) of expected peacetime accuracy, due to the "stress of war", should be applied by operational planners.[357] According to Brocklebank, in an attack on an airfield target with a WE.177B laydown bomb, "an accuracy of 400–600 yards was probably achievable".

Vulcan pilot Steve Oddy adds: "In my day, a direct hit was considered to be 200 yards, or less." Accuracy and its degradation in combat remain major concerns in today's military.* When Dr Les Ruskell was head of the Operational Analysis Cell at UK Permanent Joint Headquarters, Northwood, he authored a keynote paper for a Royal Aeronautical Society conference on Test and Evaluation (T&E). This highlighted the effects of real combat and sought to persuade the T&E community to consider these effects when evaluating and comparing systems:

"This seems especially important when comparing some completely novel system never used in anger with more conventional systems. Inevitably, the new systems always seem to be evaluated without addressing any real combat effects, which tends to bias towards the new system over the old."[358]

In the abstract to his T&E paper, Dr Ruskell commented:

"Increasingly, there is a recognition that we need to assess the overall effectiveness of all the elements of systems and to take into account the human dimension, particularly the effects on personnel of the stress of real combat, the fog of war and so forth … part of the test and evaluation process should include an understanding of all the elements, human as well as technical, that contribute to the overall effectiveness of systems."

Dr Ruskell set his comments into a significant context:

"In my time as an operational analyst in military headquarters, we made a lot of use of historical data, in particular the effect of human stress in actual combat and how this affects behaviour and military effectiveness. Looking at effectiveness of troops in defence, from the American Civil War right through to Korea, there is a remarkably consistent degradation factor between controlled trials, exercises and actual combat. Infantry in defence performed about one tenth as well (in terms of casualties inflicted) in combat as they did in exercises. Degradation was less in attack (where non-participation

---

* See David Rowland, *The Stress of Battle – Quantifying Human Performance in Combat*, The Stationery Office, 2006 for an overview of the historical analysis work at the Defence Operational Analysis Establishment, West Byfleet.

is harder for individuals to get away with) or where groups such as gun teams were mustered, and where results were more dependent on the person in charge of the team than on individual members."

Certainly, a five-man V-bomber crew was a team, yet at the same time there would have been inevitable degradation in weapon-delivery accuracy at the climax of a war sortie. Certainly, the realities of war sortie degradation must have influenced operational planners seeking to follow the principles of Memorandum No. 199 and optimise the destructive potential of Britain's limited nuclear stockpile. The achievement of high accuracy was fundamental to optimised utilisation, as made clear by the operational research scientists. The memorandum, in considering the allocation of weapons to targets, stated:

> "The normal procedure in planning is to allocate weapons to a target (taking into account delivery accuracy) so that a certain proportion of the target can be expected to be damaged or so that there is a given assurance of damaging at least some specified proportion of the target area. These two methods, while they differ considerably in concept, are interchangeable in practice, in that they define a number of weapons to be allocated to the target, the end result of this allocation being interpreted either as an expected result or a high chance of achieving some smaller effect."[359]

The memorandum demonstrated how the assumed average utilisation of the bombs allocated varied with the proportion of the target expected to be damaged and with target size, if the accuracy of delivery is known to be equal to the damage radius of the bomb:

> "Against small targets, bomb utilisation is necessarily low, since a major part of the potential effectiveness of the weapons is dissipated beyond the target boundaries. As target size increases, utilisation of the weapon increases to a maximum and is then reduced slightly for the larger targets."

If weapons are all aimed at the large target centre, utilisation is reduced due to over-hitting the central area. This effect is reduced by distributing aiming points across the target area … "it is clear that distributed aiming points are essential if bomb utilisation is to be maintained at reasonable levels on the larger targets."

This suggests multiple strikes on the same large target, with 'Desired Ground Zeros' (DGZs) distributed over various military assets across the greater urban area, to maximise both counterforce *and* countervalue damage – realising both Plan A and Plan B objectives simultaneously. The memorandum warned that very high expectations regarding damage levels drastically reduce utilisation:

> "… if good target cover (which is equivalent to a high assurance of smaller cover) is required, the expected utilisation of the bombs allocated is reduced. For example, if the target has twice the radius of the weapon effect, an increase in planned target cover from 60% to 90% results in a decrease in expected bomb utilisation from 60% to 30%."

So, if the overall plan requires a particular target to be very severely damaged, a reduction in the stockpile's potential total effectiveness must be accepted. Given the core British retaliatory threat – weapons detonating over Moscow and Leningrad – it may be assumed that any concern over utilisation was subordinated to this central operational priority.

The destruction of the largest Soviet cities by British bombers was a common theme of both Plan A and Plan B targeting. Plan A provided for strikes against a number of military targets distributed over the greater target area, to maximise utilisation. These would have been the DGZs in the biggest cities and, if attacked accurately, would have maximised both Plan A and Plan B damage.

MULTIPLE STRIKES ON BIG CITIES

Memorandum No. 199 offers an insight into the strategy of multiple strikes on the largest targets, Moscow and Leningrad – which must have been the absolute targeting priorities, given the likely high V-bomber casualty rate:

> "A distinction should be drawn here between the allocation of many weapons to a target in order to achieve a high level of damage and a similar multiplication of effort as an insurance against non-delivery. In the first instance, which, it should be emphasised, is the case being considered here, it is assumed that all weapons allocated are delivered; in the second, only a proportion of the weapons allocated are expected to arrive and average bomb utilisation will often be determined principally by this proportion. The cost of insurance of this kind must be accepted, because of tactical and strategic priorities. In many cases, however, it should be possible, by appropriate choice of aiming points, to increase the overall effect of the weapons allocated (in the event that more than the expected number arrive), without seriously affecting the assurance of damaging the priority elements of the target. This practical planning problem has to be investigated specifically for each target situation; no general solution is possible."

The memorandum's conclusions reinforce the 'marriage' of Plan A and Plan B outcomes. The UK's limited means (stockpile and delivery potential) dictated the focus on relatively few major targets, the very largest cities:

> "In an operational plan designed specifically to make most effective use of the potential destructive power of the weapons available, the majority would have to be allocated to the larger targets. For example, if the sole object of the plan was to damage as much as possible of the Russian built-up area in towns within bomber range from the UK, without allowing the average utilisation of a stockpile of 200 20-kt weapons to fall below 80%, no fewer than 18 would be allocated to Moscow alone. A further 56 would be allocated to the four next largest towns, so that 36% of the stockpile would be earmarked for five towns. Only 22 further towns would be included in the plan if the expected utilisation were to be kept above 80%."

This is how British targeting evolved, eventually concentrating on the five largest cities (with a QRA and close approach to war focus on the first and second cities). Maximised stockpile utilisation was not an end in itself. It was possible, for example, to mount a counter-argument in favour of staying away from the largest cities in a SIOP attack, as, inevitably, these major targets would have been destroyed in the retaliatory missile strike (with the warheads detonating long before any surviving V-bombers reached their targets).

Logic also suggests a *theoretical* case for distributing the limited UK stockpile over as many cities as possible, as any urban area damaged, to some extent, by a nuclear weapon would remain prostrate for a very long time (in the national context, maximising the UK ability to undermine the balance between the superpowers). However, almost certainly the number of surviving V-bombers would be far too small to achieve this effect in reality. It is not surprising that the very biggest Soviet cities (the seats of power) remained the centre of attention. In practical terms, this was the most appropriate course in the National Plan context (which addressed the remote but not impossible case of Britain acting alone). The overriding factor here is a realisation that only a relatively small group of bombers would be likely to survive a missile attack on their bases *and* successfully penetrate to their targets. The *potential* for a successful unilateral strike against the biggest cities by very few aircraft defines the core of UK deterrence and credibility as a nuclear power at this time.

The UK stockpile in 1959 (the year Memorandum No. 199 was produced) consisted of 58 Blue Danube bombs and 20 Yellow Sun Mk 1 400-kt weapons, a total stockpile of around 9 mt.[360] The ORB report observed:

> "If larger weapons were available, very few could be used against built-up areas without utilisation falling to low levels. For example, if 1-mt weapons (delivered by bomber) were available, only eight could be allocated to Russian towns, two on Moscow and one each on the six next largest towns. To allocate more such weapons for the attack on buildings would necessarily involve a waste of potential effectiveness …"[361]

At the same time, the need to maximise the threat against the biggest cities and provide insurance against large-scale non-delivery due to severe casualties on the ground and in the air must have dominated real world target allocations. In contrast, the Americans and Russians, with their huge stockpiles, had no concerns about wastage of destructive potential on a per weapon basis. The UK was in an entirely different position – every bomb had to count. The memorandum concluded its main theme:

> "… the number of weapons which can be 'economically' employed decreases rapidly with effective damage radius and also with delivery error. As a guide to the yields implied by the damage radii quoted, 1,000 yards is the radius of the 12 psi contour for a 15-kt weapon and a 1-mt weapon gives similar effects at 4,000 yards."

It concluded that, in the case of ballistic missiles, the number of warheads producing near full potential area of damage "would be very small", so that average utilisation of damage potential if a large number were used "would necessarily be small". It argued, consequently, that ballistic missiles were best used on larger targets.

It can be argued that QRA aircraft were Plan B (National) targeted, even if the targets were, officially, Plan A SIOP. The overriding operational need, in projecting and delivering a relatively modest retaliatory threat, was to inflict maximum countervalue damage with few weapons, with DGZs (military centres or not) within the leading two or three cities. The strongest direct evidence for this interpretation is the testimony of a former Waddington targeting officer responsible for managing the targeting of an entire Vulcan Wing of 24 aircraft. Roy Brocklebank knew of plans for a near simultaneous 'assurance' attack by at least five QRA V-bombers (out of a total QRA force of 11 aircraft) on Leningrad, so maximising the chance of at least one weapon detonating on Russia's second city. Logically, Moscow was the most likely target for the remaining six QRA bombers.

Each crew received a time on target (TOT) with a tolerance of plus or minus three minutes. However, Brocklebank notes: "There was a near simultaneous TOT on Leningrad. This QRA target was a primary Plan B countervalue target, second only to Moscow."[362] Commenting on the distribution of weapon-aiming points across Leningrad, he added: "Certainly, the distribution of DGZs around Leningrad met the requirement for target area coverage."[363] He explained how he had arrived at a total of five QRA bombers targeting Leningrad, but with different DGZs: "At least two QRA aircraft from the three squadrons at RAF Cottesmore were covering Leningrad. When I subsequently arrived at RAF Waddington, QRA aircraft from all three squadrons there were also covering Leningrad."[364]

The idea was to swamp the target defences, with the details kept from the crews for obvious reasons (of all former V-Force aircrew contributors to this book, no-one, other than Roy Brocklebank, raised the possibility of TOT convergence as a tactic to enhance the chance of at least one successful attack):

> "The crews were not allowed to discuss their individual targets. They had no idea that they were all tasked to attack the same target, at practically the same time. Separation was down to as little as one minute for Leningrad, in some cases. In other words, attacking aircraft would be destroying other squadron aircraft. The QRA concentration of force was planned to destroy at least one or two very important cities, the equivalent to London and Birmingham."

Given the likelihood of very few V-bombers surviving a pre-emptive missile strike, there were strong operational arguments for targeting *the entire force* at, say, the top five cities (and, ultimately, Moscow and Leningrad exclusively), to maximise the threat from the small group of V-bombers making attacks. This must have exerted an overriding influence on British nuclear targeting policy, which moved from a multiplicity of counterforce and countervalue targets to a handful of the largest cities, with the potential destruction of Moscow and Leningrad as the projected core retaliatory threat. The two leading cities were certainly targets for the powered bomb. Vulcan captain Philip Goodall commanded 27 Squadron at RAF Scampton, equipped with Blue Steel:

> "My crew's target was the Pulkovo Airport at Leningrad … We would climb to high level over the North Sea and then descend over the Baltic Sea, keeping as far to the north as possible and approaching Leningrad over the sea, with the aim of launching our Blue Steel about 50 miles from the city. We would not have the fuel to return to the UK, so would turn port and fly up to Finland or Sweden, presumably with the intention of baling out …"[365]

Moscow was an obvious Blue Steel QRA target, as the stand-off bomb, even with its much reduced range at low level, offered the best available chance of penetrating the Soviet capital's three rings of SAM defences (given a powered launch!).[366]

Roger Smith was a freefall Vulcan pilot:

> "We always assumed that Blue Steel aircraft at Scampton would concentrate on Moscow and Leningrad. We were not aware of the targets and TOT of other crews but it was obvious that there would be more than one aircraft going for the big cities."[367]

Roy Brocklebank adds that Leningrad, a leading Plan B countervalue target, was also a major military target. It was home to the headquarters of the Baltic Fleet and, of course, the Leningrad Air Defence District. Generally, the lower the accounting line number (ALN), the higher the target priority. Brocklebank described the key factor of attack timing:

> "The same target might have different ALNs, with different TOTs, to allow for separation in release times for a multi-weapon strike. The TOT allowed for plus or minus three minutes. On one particular target with a planned ten minutes between strikes, the absolute minimum time separation between detonations was four minutes (equivalent to 28 miles), with a maximum of 16 minutes."

At least, that is what the crews were told:

> "In a multi-weapon freefall attack on the same target, the first aircraft would release, fly on for about 1½ minutes, execute a 180-degree turn, fly low until abeam the target and climb away. This could take it dangerously close to an early second detonation.* One logic for this turn back might have been to take advantage of the local effects of their own bomb."[368]

A more likely alternative explanation (undeclared to crews) would be an attempt to confuse any surviving defences, encouraging them to assume that the returning 'decoy' bomber had yet to release. V-Force veterans discussing this issue appear to have accepted the official explanation. Yet it seems likely, taking account of TOT manipulation, that the true purpose of the return to the cloud was to confuse any surviving defences (although it must be said that, perhaps not surprisingly, no direct documentary evidence for this motive was found by the author).

With each crew having QRA, national and Plan A targets, target study demanded solid application, as recalled by Norman Bonnor:

> "In the NATO SIOP, we had two ALNs to study and prepare: flight plans (nav/plotter), fuel plans (co-pilot), ECM plan (AEO) and target/fix point acetates (nav/radar). The latter were used with the plan position indicator (PPI) screen to enable map-matching … Later, I think the Joint Air Reconnaissance Interpretation Centre (JARIC) prepared something for us using U-2/satellite imagery, which we could add to if we wished."[369]

Roy Brocklebank recalled that some target photographs looked as though they had been enhanced with pen and ink: "I asked the target librarian at JARIC about this and was told they were Luftwaffe photographs updated with later intelligence."[370]

---

* Roy Brocklebank recalls a target assigned to ALN 224: "ALN 214 was assigned an identical track with a TOT ten minutes after 224. Given a speed of six miles per minute it would be at a safe blast range; a turn might take another two minutes and abeam the target at TOT +5. Had he been three minutes late and the other aircraft on time, he would be climbing out two minutes before the second aircraft. Had the second aircraft been early …"

Norman Bonnor confirmed the enhanced JARIC output: "JARIC provided even more when we had to penetrate at low level – route and fix point booklets with fairly complex radar predictions, including hill shading. The more experienced crews were assigned the more important targets."[371]

When operational with 100 Squadron, Norman Bonnor's targets included Tallinn and Riga:

"… or, probably, the air defence centres/fighter airfields nearby. Many of our targets were in the Baltic States. Part of our job was to punch through the Soviet air defences, clearing the way for SAC's B-52s. We were tasked to destroy the coastal belt defences. Consequently, Riga was one of my targets."[372]

Norman Bonnor adds: "Earlier, on XV Squadron, I think Leningrad was one of mine. On the National Plan, my target was always Moscow – but maybe with different aiming points."[373]

Many Strategic Air Command (SAC) bombers would have entered Russia by crossing the Baltic coast, rather than using the 'over the Pole' route. Roy Brocklebank gave an example: "From Loring Air Force Base (AFB) to the Baltic States, they would pass just south of Greenland, then Iceland, south central Norway, southern Sweden and, thence, Russia – virtually the same penetration routes as the V-Force."[374]

Brocklebank confirmed that V-Force war plan targets for crews changed annually. New targets were introduced six weeks before they took effect, to allow primary crews time to prepare the maps and charts and give secondary crews time to become fully familiar with them.[375]

On the squadrons, confidence in the deterrent was strong, but nothing could be taken for granted. Roy Brocklebank remembers a 'bolt from the blue' alert in August 1968, probably linked to the Soviet invasion of Czechoslovakia:

"… I was on the ops desk, covering for the duty ops officer, who was on a lunch break. Two of the squadrons were on ground training days. Suddenly, the 'Bomber Box' burst into life. As I recall, the message was: '*Attention. Attention. This is the bomber controller. Selective generation. Cottesmore, 12 aircraft, Finningley, three aircraft, Scampton, 12 aircraft, Waddington, 11 aircraft*.' Now, I had never heard the term 'selective generation'. We had never had a generation start in normal working hours. I immediately called the OC Ops and we started the generation. We needed to get crews on the road to Finningley PDQ (pretty damn quick) and we also had the possibility that crews could have been drinking at lunchtime. In the event, all crews were available."[376]

Another bolt from the blue was recalled by 27 Squadron Vulcan captain John Reeve:

"… there was a genuine call-out in 1969 which saw the RAF raise its posture after large-scale troop movements were detected a year after the invasion of Czechoslovakia. When the alert came, half of us were in the bar at Waddington and the other half had left for the weekend. In those days, of course, there were no mobiles!"[377]

JOINT TARGETING

Early UK and US planning recognised the possibility of war with the USSR by 1957. The US Department of Defense, however, had a much earlier contingency – the 'Dropshot' plan, ready by 1949, for fighting a pre-emptive war using both nuclear and conventional weapons. The integration of British and American war plans and target lists began in the 1950s, building on the close personal relationships linking Bomber Command and the USAAF during World War 2. As Sir Frank Cooper remarked: "… there can be little doubt now that the arrangements for the USAF to return to Britain were agreed informally between Tedder and Spaatz in 1946 …".[378]

Whilst cooperation with the Americans appeared secure, there were good reasons for the British to pursue self-sufficiency, so far as possible. Almost certainly, the V-Force would be airborne first and first over the targets – so far ahead of SAC as to be "tactically independent". Furthermore, it would take time to achieve full integration and there was some initial uncertainty about the level of cooperation attainable.[379]

Nevertheless, over the years the SAC/Bomber Command relationship continued to deepen. Philip Goodall remembered Colonel Dick Cody, who was to be a kind host when Goodall first arrived on his attachment to SAC. Cody had completed an exchange tour at the RAF Staff College and at Bomber Command. On leaving SAC, Goodall was re-posted to Strike Command HQ, with responsibility for nuclear planning:

> "When I was flying the Vulcan my target had been Leningrad, so I had a close examination to see the total number of nuclear attacks planned on that part of Russia, which, I believe, was something like 15."[380]

In 1957, Bomber Command and the USAF had discovered that all British targets were also covered by SAC. In due course an integrated plan emerged, reflecting the fact that the V-Force would go in first, several hours before the US-based SAC main force. This integrated strike plan took effect on 1 October 1958, with Bomber Command allocated 106 targets: 69 cities, 17 bomber airfields and 20 air defence targets.[381] Cooperation also extended to the supply of US nuclear weapons to the RAF, under the Project E programme.

The Anglo-American relationship continued to progress. A Chiefs of Staff (COS) memorandum, approved on 15 October 1957, set out V-Force strategic target policy. This endorsed the view that in the case of UK unilateral retaliation, attacks should be directed against cities, as "this is the most effective target system for our limited resources".[382]

This focus on countervalue in the unilateral (National Plan) context was fully apparent in the October 1957 COS paper. This considered 131 Soviet cities and towns with a population exceeding 100,000 (54 were graded as of major importance, with governmental, economic and/or military significance). Ten of the potential targets were found to be out of reach.[383]

During the following year, 1958, UK nuclear strike planning envisaged the potential damage inflicted by a 144-strong V-Force as 50% of 40 Soviet cities. It was thought that the destruction of 40 Soviet cities would "render ineffective" over 38 million people, or 30% of the urban population.[384] This scale of destruction came to be seen as greater than necessary. That September, the COS Committee was told by the Air Ministry that the threat to deter Russia from attacking the UK had been reappraised at 30 cities. At that time the Air Staff had concluded that 104 Mk 2 and 40 Mk 1 V-bombers (allowing for unserviceability/losses) could deliver about 50–60 bombs in their first strike against targets on the list of 131 cities. Matthew Jones looked at the potential consequences:

"If the higher figure of 60 bombs was used and several bombs were used against the larger targets, this implied delivery of 35 bombs against 15 cities with populations over 600,000, and 25 bombs on cities which mostly had over 400,000 people (making 40 cities in total)."

The casualties were estimated at the lower figures of 8,000,000 killed and the same number injured.[385]

By 1963, however, following Skybolt's cancellation, the ability to destroy the group of 15 major Soviet cities began to lack credibility. There were three options: leave the gap uncovered until Polaris, 'hire' US Polaris submarines and missiles, or further scale back the 'minimum deterrent' threat. It was in this context that, in late 1963, the intelligence assessment was revised, to a judgement that the Russians would regard the certain destruction of five of their largest cities as an unacceptable risk. Twigge and Scott summed up the prevailing trend:

"In the course of only six years, Bomber Command's ability to threaten the assured destruction of Soviet cities had decreased from over 40 to five – a reduction that reflected Britain's growing inability to maintain a wholly independent second-strike capability."[386]

However, these developments had a much more complex, multi-dimensional character.

The British Nuclear Deterrent Study Group (BNDSG), which first met in July 1959, had adopted the 30–40 cities 'benchmark' capability as a basis for future work. That September the Joint Global War Study Group produced a report for BNDSG based on an attack on 40 cities in 1970. The findings on consequences must have contributed to what could be safely regarded as a minimum deterrent, effective in its purpose. Matthew Jones noted:

"Total deaths from blast effects were estimated at over seven million, with another ten million at immediate risk in target cities from fallout … and a further 23 million people located in nearby areas subject to 'significant' levels of fallout."

The BNDSG's chairman, however, was warned informally that these estimates were, in fact, very conservative: they failed to take account of the full effects of fallout and took no account of deaths and injuries from fire. As Matthew Jones pointed out: "The clear inference was that real casualty figures would be of a far higher order." A British retaliatory strike could drop 40 million tons of explosive equivalent in the first couple of hours of World War 3, rather than just under three million tons dropped by the Allies on Germany during six years of a very long war.[387] In reality, however, the total tonnage equivalent dropped by a handful of V-bomber survivors would have more closely matched that six-year total for Germany (but it would be arriving in the space of a couple of hours!).

As for the benchmark, by January 1962 the Joint Intelligence Committee (JIC) was considering whether 40 cities was still appropriate, or whether it could be reduced to 20 and, in addition, what would be the minimum number for the deterrent to function. *This study assumed no US involvement.* The final report (JIC [62] 10) gave a "point score" to each Soviet city of over 50,000. One point was given for every increment of 50,000, with additional points if the city was a regional administrative centre and/or economic centre, or the location of a significant military headquarters, or served as a major telecommunications hub. The analysis of 40 major cities generated a total of 888 points, the top five accounting for 335 points and Moscow alone receiving 136 points.[388]

Matthew Jones described the outcome. JIC concluded that destruction of the 40 largest cities would be "quite unacceptable" to the Russians and that the destruction of 20 major cities would be "an unacceptable blow at (the) Soviet long-term economy and would seriously weaken the immediate Soviet military potential". As to the final question, what would be the minimum number of cities representing an acceptable deterrent, JIC admitted: "We cannot give a clear-cut answer." However, the central conclusion was that "it would not be unreasonable to say that the Soviet leaders would consider that the certain destruction of their five largest cities would put them at an unacceptable disadvantage in relation to the United States".

This was the crucial point. The 1962 JIC report added:

> "For a British system to constitute an effective deterrent, valid from a Russian point of view, it is enough that the force should, by itself, be capable of significantly altering the balance of power between Russia and the US. We believe that the destruction of 20 of the largest cities in Russia (and even possibly the destruction of a much smaller number) would so alter the Russo/American balance that it would be unacceptable to the Russians and that a British force with this retaliatory capability would constitute an effective deterrent …"[389]

Having received prime ministerial approval, in May 1962 a 15-city benchmark (including Moscow and Leningrad) came into operation for a V-Force then still anticipating Skybolt.[390] With the missile's cancellation, would a V-Force without an advanced, long-range, air-launched weapon be able to present a credible threat of this magnitude?

A steady reduction in the defined minimum deterrent threat did, indeed, reflect a shrinking force capability but, in addition, it mirrored a more refined perception of the significance of the British deterrent's capacity to alter the balance of power between the United States and Russia, in delivering a unilateral retaliatory attack. Baylis and Stoddart viewed the UK concept of minimum deterrence as a "moveable feast which rested in large measure on force levels and military capabilities, rather than being a hard rule based on certainty …"[391] There was, at the same time, a parallel and growing appreciation of the significance of a credible UK nuclear strike potential that could undermine the balance between the superpowers.

By the time Royal Navy Polaris patrols began in 1968, the greater destructive capacity of this system allowed the target list to settle at seven–11 cities, including at least 50% destruction of Moscow and Leningrad, with the remaining cities having populations exceeding 300,000.[392] The 'Moscow Criterion' was key – the assured destruction of the first city, together with a handful of other cities selected in line with the JIC points system.[393]

The Moscow Criterion recognised a natural focus, reinforced if anything by strenuous Soviet efforts to protect the capital with ABMs. Kristan Stoddart spelt out the first city's significance: "… Moscow continued to be the overriding priority because it indicated to the Soviet leadership that whatever defences they were prepared to put up, the UK would defeat them."[394]

The shrinkage in the scale of damage deemed sufficient for effective deterrence was accepted during the six-year wait for Polaris.[395] This was accepted in the knowledge that destruction of the Soviet Union's first city and, possibly, one or more of the other largest cities was achievable (and, therefore, credible), even allowing for the difficulties of V-bombers in surviving a war scramble and, subsequently, penetrating Soviet defences.

Throughout the 1960s the UK maintained this credible core retaliatory threat, centred on the unilateral capacity to destroy one or more of the largest Soviet cities. This threat was real and could not be ignored. This appears to have been the view of the JIC. Indeed, on one occasion it went so far as to suggest, in a draft of its (62) (10) report, "it could well be argued that the certain loss of even one major Soviet city (especially Moscow) would be enough to deter the Soviet Union."[396] This increasingly modest view of the necessary scale of the UK-projected deterrent threat reinforced the case against significant investment in V-Force equipment and a new, long-range air-to-surface missile (ASM). It was felt that a fast war scramble and going ultra-low would suffice to maintain the core threat – delivery of weapons on Moscow and Leningrad – until Polaris arrived.

In this way, the British deterrent developed *and maintained* its independent significance. The V-Force low-level strike mission was potent enough to preserve Britain's status as a third strategic nuclear power and a second centre of Western nuclear decision-making. The V-Force, even with much-diminished capability, provided a continuity of threat into the Polaris era. Then the new SLBM deterrent arrived, with its vast increase in capability. Polaris was the ideal small-nation nuclear deterrent, combining much reduced platform vulnerability with much greater certainty of successful warhead delivery. A key point, of course, is that the continuity of the V-Force threat allowed Britain to maintain its special nuclear relationship with the United States during the wait for Polaris.

RESPONSE POLICIES

The NATO Military Committee's early posture of "instant and devastating" nuclear retaliation was set out in May 1957 (Policy Document MC 14/2), with conventional attack a sufficient trigger.[397]

MC 14/2 was succeeded by MC 14/3, "graduated" or "flexible" response, in January 1968 – the basis of a more sophisticated NATO strategy throughout the 1970s and 1980s. Under MC 14/3, a Soviet conventional attack would be countered by conventional forces, with tactical nuclear weapons used in the event of a breakthrough and strategic nuclear weapons held in last resort.

Response policy and the SIOP evolved over the years, with the Bomber Command/SAC close relationship as its foundation. In the early 1960s, Thors were deployed in the UK and American E weapons armed some Bomber Command aircraft. In October 1962, just a couple of weeks before the Cuban Missile Crisis peaked, ACAS (Ops) sent the Chief of the Air Staff (CAS) a minute on strategic planning by Bomber Command and SAC. This noted that the combined strike plan was subject to the proviso that targets are included "which must be hit in the first strike if the war is to be finished quickly and the damage done to the UK and Western Europe kept as low as possible".[398]

The 1962 edition of the coordinated plan (rewritten annually) took effect on August 1 that year. It introduced a change in target planning for the British, with MBF/Thor attacks on:

- 16 cities.
- 44 "offensive capability" targets, such as airfields.
- ten "defence capability" targets, such as air defence control centres.
- 28 IRBM sites.[399]

This succeeded a plan allocating the British 48 cities, six air defence centres and three bomber bases. The new August 1962 target list may have reflected US Defense Secretary Robert McNamara's "population avoidance" doctrine.[400] However, whilst the new target list gave every appearance of a major shift in emphasis away from cities, many of the 54 offensive/defensive targets were, in all probability, located in and around most of the big cities previously targeted. In any event, the note to the CAS sought to convey a picture of 'no change' and adopted a rather defensive tone:

> "Selection of these targets is by mutual agreement between Bomber Command and SAC and there can be no suggestion of US authorities arbitrarily imposing targets upon the UK strike force. They have been selected to provide the best operational tactical plan. The targets included in current planning fall well within the target system authorised by the Chiefs of Staff. There has, however, been some change of emphasis between the Bomber Command part in the previous and current coordinated plans. The MBF and Thor in the previous plan were directed primarily against cities … In isolation, this could be interpreted as a significant change in the direction of counterforce strategy. However, the coordinated plan for all-out retaliation covers the targets previously allocated to Bomber Command. This plan is therefore fully compatible with the Strategic Target Policy which was formulated against the background of the use of massive retaliation and on the assumption that the Western Powers would not take the initiative and that we would counter actual Soviet aggression."[401]

ACAS (Ops) went on to acknowledge that the Americans had other plans not subject to joint consultation, but claimed these were "compatible" with Bomber Command participation in coordinated action. He then gave reassurance: "There has been no direct suggestion of preemptive action in the joint preparation of plans by Bomber Command and SAC." (The use of "direct" in this sentence is perhaps of interest). He continued: "This line has been confirmed in recent discussions between the Minister of Defence and Mr McNamara." In conclusion, the note stressed that it was "militarily prudent" to have alternative plans. After all, the British had the National Plan. There was, of course, always the thought that the Americans might hold back, in the hope that war could be contained within the European Theatre. Here, the note stated: "Should there be disagreement between ourselves and the Americans … it would still be possible to direct the MBF to concentrate on centres of administration and population, in the case of unilateral action …"

This option also applied to the Valiants assigned to SACEUR and carrying American E weapons in the NATO role. They could also carry British weapons free of dual control. Anthony Wright's Valiant crew was briefed to attack several targets, including national targets, "where the British Red Beard nuclear weapon would have been used if we had to go to war without the USA".[402]

INSIDE THE 'VAULT'

In January 1967 Squadron Leader Roy Brocklebank arrived at RAF Waddington; he became wing targeting officer and vault officer:

> "I was custodian of all the war targets and was responsible for assigning crews to targets every Friday, ready for the following week. The Waddington Wing had three squadrons, each with 11 crews – 33 crews in all. The wing was allocated 24 targets for each War Plan (including different DGZs within large, complex targets). This allowed for leave, sickness and new, non-operational crews. We could have six crews on leave at any given time, plus new crews fresh from OCU and yet to achieve combat status, together with one or more crews who might be non-operational for other reasons. The Waddington target list included Leningrad, Kiev, Riga, Klaipeda and Kaliningrad, although I did find maps for Moscow – earlier, high-level routes. The largest cities, of course, were the most heavily defended. There were other challenges. Kiev, for example, would require two and a half hours at low level going in and another hour and a half at high level getting out."[403]

Each V-bomber main base had a vault, the secure room with a central role in operational readiness. Roy Brocklebank was custodian of Waddington's vault for three years. It was a room with an ordinary outer door fitted with a security lock. There was also an inner steel door with a Sargent and Greenleaf combination lock. Beyond this door was a small vestibule, with two counters presenting a barrier to anyone entering. Crews were never permitted to go beyond the counters. Two blackout curtains concealed the entrance to the inner room. Access to the room was limited to the station commander, the officer commanding operations, the squadron leader operations, the wing AEO, the squadron leader weapons, the two weapons officers, the intelligence officer and the vault officer, or custodian. In practice, the use of the vault was limited to the intelligence officer, the weapons officers and the vault officer.

Immediately inside the vault's inner room, on the wall to the left-hand side, were the 'authentication envelopes' containing the codes for SCRAM (scramble), SCRAMCAN (cancellation of scramble), RELREAD (relaxation of readiness) and POSREL (positive release – authorisation for a retaliatory attack to proceed). One POSREL code, for exercise use, was 'Nourishment'. Later, the POSREL code was changed to a trigraph, such as J9W. Roy Brocklebank described the vault's interior:

> "There were three sets of steel racks. The left rack, bottom shelf, housed the 'nav bags', into which the target material would be packed when issuing to crews. Above were sets of wooden dividers holding the JARIC target folders and the crew-prepared charts and flight plans. There was a 1:3,000,000 navigation chart with the route drawn on, four copies of flight plans (each for a three-month period of the year, based on statistical meteorological data) and four fuel plans, based on the flight plans. Each document was classified Top Secret. Individual notes were not permitted. On the shelves above were the war SOPs, one per crew (33, six for the QRA 'go-bags', plus a master copy – 40 in total). Their contents were ready to be made up into go-bags. There were five editions of the codes; B4 was the active set, but this was subject to change at any time. There were also two filing cabinets in the middle of the room, each containing 18 target sets. These

included targets in the Middle East – later replaced by Far East targets when the Middle East and Far East roles were swapped between Cottesmore and Waddington."

As vault officer, Roy Brocklebank was the custodian of evasion maps printed on silk, an item familiar to World War 2 aircrew:

> "The maps were compressed and came in small packages. We would give crews specific escape locations, but they had to ask for them. Knowledge of the locations and the issue of maps were optional. Around half the crews didn't bother. I had no 'goolie chits' at Waddington, but I know they were in use in later years, during the wars in the Middle East. However, we did have pictures of 'representative tribesmen' and some briefing materials at Waddington. I didn't get involved in specialised survival training when in the UK, but I did attend a lecture on this subject when in Cyprus. It all sounded a bit World War 2, when there was a chance that you could walk out and pick up a French or Belgian escape line. However, if you were hit near Tashkent, how long would it take you to walk out? Escape lines belonged to another era. A new approach had been developed by the late 1960s. The idea was for surviving aircrew to stay very close to specified locations, holing up and waiting for rescue by specialised teams. There were ten such locations in Finland, for example. This, perhaps, was a reflection of American experience in the rescue of shot-down aircrew in Vietnam."

Roy remembers the unworldly advice offered to aircrew in the early 1960s by the *Nuclear Survival Manual* – a thick tome written for insomniacs:

> "It read something like: 'In the event that you are forced to abandon your aircraft, you will probably be contaminated with the effects of your own weapon. When you land, brush off any contamination with a hand brush. In case you do not have a hand brush, use a clump of heather or dried grasses. Then dig a trench about 7 feet long and a couple of feet deep.' With a 3-inch knife? 'Take off your outer garments and bury these at one end of the trench and then bury yourself in the other end. However, if this is in winter, you might need to keep your clothes on. You should now reverse the normal survival drill and eat your ration pack food first, as local food may well be contaminated. Wipe the pack with a clean damp cloth.'"

This book did not survive beyond 1965.[404]

TARGET STUDY

Most factors influencing war sortie outcomes were beyond the influence of crews. Target study, however, was one prominent success factor very much in their hands. When flying as a Vulcan nav/radar, Roy Brocklebank's targets included Leningrad and important military centres, including Arkhangelsk Talagi, south of Severomorsk (headquarters of the Soviet Northern Fleet); Baltiysk, an airbase south-west of Kaliningrad; Baranavichy, an airbase in Belarus and home to interceptors, Tu-16s and, later, a major centre for the Tu-22 'Blinder'; and Starokostiantyniv, in Ukraine, an airbase eventually taken over by the Ukrainian air force in the post-Soviet era. Brocklebank provides a context for target study:

"There were 55 aircrew on each squadron. In general, the old hands tended not to know the new boys. When a fresh crew joined the squadron they went straight into intensive target study, with the squadron's two QRA targets given priority. They teamed up with an operational crew and went through the procedures for a weapon system takeover. An aircraft began in the 'cold' condition. It was then fuelled, serviced and checked by a crew. Once serviceable, it was bombed up, the weapon system was checked and the captain checked and signed Form 700, formally accepting the aircraft, at which point the aircraft would be declared combat-ready. Crews would study each of their allocated targets. A target study session would include studying the target folders and reading up the latest Department of Defense *Defense Intelligence Digest*. Crews were given a random check on each target every half year, using a standard questionnaire produced by Bomber Command.

"Target study was the name of the game: learn and digest the War SOP manual (it had been re-issued in 1965 and comprised 110 pages) and the target folders. The first three sets were for the SIOP. The first target was the one covered by the squadron when on QRA. The second was the crew's individual principal target. Finally, there was a back-up target, in case the primary crew was not available to take their own primary target. Crews never knew who 'owned' the secondary target or who covered their own primary target, although, as crews were from the same squadron you might recognise someone else's work. We were forbidden to discuss this with other crews and we never tried to find out. The rules were enforced in a very British way. We were told it was Top Secret – 'Don't discuss it' – and we never did.

"The target folder had several components. There was a single sheet of paper setting out all the necessary information: the name, bombing encyclopaedia number, SAC ALN and British ALN, its position and the route. Most important was the TOT in minutes, which would give us a clock time based on the 'Execution Hour' broadcast at the time of scramble. It also had instructions: turn port/starboard after launch and earlier missile strike Yes/No. If there was an earlier missile strike scheduled, then crews knew the target appearance was likely to be quite different. However, crews were always keener for that previous strike, as it would suggest severely degraded defences."[405]

On disclosure of pre-strikes or otherwise, Vulcan captain Peter Moore added: "Memory says that all of mine seemed to be secondary attacks."[406] Yet many V-Force veterans are absolutely emphatic in their view that target folders did NOT disclose planned earlier strikes. It is possible, of course, that policy on this issue may have changed over time, but no documentary evidence was found.

Roy Brocklebank recalled that JARIC prepared three strip maps for each target – one flip-style for the pilots and two book-style for the navigators:

"These covered the low-level portion of the route. JARIC had calculated radar fix points and when they would be visible to the radar – the 'Fix Box'. They also had a very small target photograph, which was really of no use at all. The crew drew up a chart, flight plan and fuel plan. We prepared four versions of the flight and fuel plans, using statistical weather data for each season. This was in case we had no time to update the plans for the true weather of the day. We also had climatological data sheets, with the whole USSR divided into broad climate zones. Each sheet set covered all four seasons."[407]

Andy Leitch adds: "The target photograph appeared to be based on a large, vertically-taken recce photo on which model trees and buildings etc. had been constructed in three dimensions. The map/model had then been re-photographed obliquely from the attack direction."

Much emphasis was placed on target study, from the earliest V-Force days. Valiant co-pilot Dick Fuller and his crew, with 49 Squadron during the 1959–63 period, put a great deal of effort into it: "How effective we would have been, in reality, is a matter of conjecture. The Valiant's ceiling was around 45,000 ft, with a speed of Mach 0.82."[408] Target study was taken very seriously on 12 Squadron. Vulcan pilot Nick Dennis remembers it as "no bundle of laughs. We were questioned on our knowledge of the defences, the required escape manoeuvres and other aspects."[409] Everyone knew there would be no time for more target study should the Cold War suddenly become hot. Vulcan captain Roger Dunsford recalls the regular intelligence updates, "tracking the movement of Soviet mobile SAM sites and other defences".[410] Crews were required to follow the pre-determined routes on JARIC maps, which showed the track and radar fixes to be used.

Norman Bonnor had no doubt about target study's significance:

"It was essential to put in the effort … We did most of it while on QRA, to help pass the time. The quality of our target study was assessed by a squadron leader and two flight lieutenants. These assessments were made on a frequent basis … The switch to low level

Navigators: nav/radar Tony Thornthwaite (left) and nav/plotter Barry Mullen in the rear crew simulator at RAF Scampton. (Barry Mullen)

led to a significant increase in the complexity of the target information supplied to crews by JARIC. Nav/plotters and nav/radars, for example, received booklets giving routeing information for specific targets. Target study sessions began with a review of the latest intelligence. Then we buckled down to the main session.

"Curiously, the captain was the one with relatively little to do. The co-pilot concentrated on fuel management issues, the AEO on ECM and the Soviet defences, the nav/radar concerned himself with studying the fix points suggested by JARIC and delivering the weapon on the target and the nav/plotter worked on the route, taking account of statistical information on wind velocities and other weather factors. My first captain was a very calm guy. He'd walk around the room, discussing each of the issues and he'd give the round-up at the end of the session. This all made good sense. During a war flight, it was the captain who had the lowest workload and, therefore, the capacity to confront a sudden emergency."[411]

Bill MacGillivray, a Vulcan captain, had a strategy for escape following weapon release which conflicted with the recommendations made in a report from Bomber Command's Operational Research Branch – further evidence of the command-level failure to ensure all crews were briefed and understood the importance of immediately gaining a height of at least 5,000 ft following release, to avoid reflected shock waves:

"I discussed many things with the crew during target study sessions. We would have stayed low, travelling as fast as possible away from the target upon release … I reckoned we could get around seven miles away before the shock wave hit. We would have been at about 50–60 ft. Apparently, the shock wave rises as it spreads across the ground but, frankly, I still felt we would be turned arse over tit!"[412]

Waddington Wing Roy Brocklebank's targeting responsibilities included monitoring time spent on target study:

"Every month I would send the station commander a letter detailing crews who had failed to complete their study. This was always a very short list and usually a nil return. Had a crew been negligent in completing their study, the station commander would have been on to the squadron commander, etc. I always warned the flight commander in Week 3."[413]

On arrival at RAF Waddington, Brocklebank did some tidying up and made some interesting finds in the vault:

"My predecessor had failed to destroy some old sheets. I got rid of the unused ones but took a look at some examples with routes marked on them. One showed an extremely unusual route. Instead of going north, over Scandinavia, this high-level route went direct to Russia … crossing northern France, through Swiss airspace, into Czechoslovakia and on to the Soviet target. I also remember another pre-low-level example. This involved a Vulcan Mk 1A and the target was Moscow. The approach track was from the north, through the SAM belt, to a point on the edge of the chart and then a 180-degree turn … the next chart to the south showed a simple black dot, surrounded by a triangle, on the Kremlin. This is proof-positive that Moscow, as might be expected, was also a freefall target."[414]

TRAINING FOR WAR

Could the V-bombers have reached their targets? Outcomes would have differed over time. Twigge and Scott considered the position when the emphasis was on bombers, noting the key decisions of 1957, the definition of the V-Force at 144 aircraft and the agreement to coordinate the nuclear strike plans of Bomber Command and SAC. The Joint Planning Staff report "Allied strategic nuclear attack in global war in 1957" (JP [57] 10) formed a basis for UK strategic target policy. The report envisaged a joint first wave strike by 1,500 bombers against 800 targets. The Chiefs of Staff then approved the dual targeting policy for the V-Force – a unilateral strike against Soviet cities and a combined offensive with SAC, targeting a mix of urban and military targets. Twigge and Scott commented: "Later approved by the Defence Committee, these recommendations formed the basis of Bomber Command's Emergency War Plan, which came into operation on 1 October 1958."[415]

As for assessing possible V-Force strike outcomes, the late 1950s and 1960s produced mixed evidence. A positive but misleading picture was claimed concerning British participation in Skyshield, one of two large-scale exercises in the early 1960s involving NORAD (now the North American Aerospace Defense Command) and SAC and testing defences against Soviet air attack. The results showed North American air defences in a poor light, with only some 25% of attackers intercepted. During Skyshield, *all air traffic*, from the Arctic Circle to Mexico, was grounded for up to 12 hours. On 10 September 1961, RAF Vulcans contributed to simulated attacks on the big cities, including New York, Chicago, San Diego, Los Angeles and Washington DC. There has been much confusion over the years about Vulcans and Skyshield and much-repeated claims that Bomber Command "nuked America twice". This is dismissed as an "urban legend" by former Vulcan co-pilot Andy Leitch.

There was no British participation in the 1960 Skyshield, but the 1961 Skyshield included an attack by eight Vulcans. Four flew in from Scotland and another four from Bermuda.[416] The confusion stemmed from British press reports claiming V-Force success in two Skyshields, compounded by the content of initial USAF denials. The 'Target America' story run by the *Daily Express* had as a source an unidentified Vulcan pilot. The affair eventually reached Prime Minister Macmillan's desk in early 1963; he demanded an explanation from the Secretary of State for Air. The response clarified the fact that the Vulcans had participated in Skyshield 1961, when "because of restrictions in the exercise setting, the eight Vulcans taking part were all intercepted – some twice." This outcome conflicted with the good results trumpeted in the press. The *Daily Express* had heard a 'rumour' – a journalist then called the Air Ministry out-of-hours and spoke to the resident clerk "who got drawn into conversation with the reporter".[417]

All V-bomber crews knew they stood more chance at night, in filthy weather. Vulcan pilot Ed Jarron acknowledged that a bright, sunny day would have been a big disadvantage: "In those conditions, perhaps just a handful would have got through, but it would have been a very different story at night – well over half would have dropped their weapons."[418] Once in Soviet airspace, there would have been no room for anything other than the task in hand – staying alive. John Huggins recalls the importance of self-belief:

"The bottom line was that we were confident that a proportion of the V-Force would get through and destroy their targets. In the years following World War 2, the Soviet Union made huge population shifts into the major cities. In the 1960s, these held some 80% of the Soviet population. All the National Plan targets were Soviet cities. The SACEUR targets tended to be key military assets that should already have been hit by missiles … Our crew's targets under the latter plan included Murmansk and Riga."[419]

From the bombers' standpoint, there were discouraging results in Exercise Matador 2, flown on 29 September 1962. This involved four simulated raids on the UK, involving a total of 64 aircraft making a long penetration from the north. The aim was to test the serviceability and effectiveness of the V-bombers' Red Shrimp jammers and Red Steer and Blue Saga warners, gather information on the use of Window and assess the effectiveness of radar and communications jamming. Reporting on the outcome in February 1963, Bomber Command chief research officer Tom Kerr said the jamming was effective, yet Fighter Command intercepted 39 of the 64 bombers at least once, mirroring outcomes in earlier exercises. The 73 participating fighters achieved 92 intercepts. SAM sites claimed to have engaged 31 of the 47 bombers entering the missile zones.[420]

In the ultimate sense, operational effectiveness means the ability to deliver the UK's core retaliatory threat, *however that threat may be defined*. Appropriate targeting is the central component of UK retaliation and that requires a maximised deterrent threat and optimised destructive potential from a small number of megaton-class weapons, should deterrence fail. There was a marked decrease in the number of countervalue (city) targets, but retention of the very largest urban targets, with V-Force deterrence resting on the ability to do damage sufficiently severe to undermine the balance between the superpowers. The fundamental requirement was the potential to make successful attacks on Moscow and Leningrad (the targets for the QRA force, at readiness to provide the UK's minimum retaliatory response). The planners' first priority was to ensure continuity of this core threat until the arrival of Polaris.

10
THE THREAT TO THE AIRFIELDS

> **❝** We are doing all we can to ensure that a surprise attack by the enemy will not cripple the effectiveness of the V-bomber force and its ability to retaliate at once. **❞**
>
> Statement by the Secretary of State for Air, to accompany the
> Air Estimates, 1955–56, February 1956

The V-Force was exposed to destruction on the ground by Soviet bombers and, subsequently, IRBMs. Soviet missiles fired on low trajectories offered very little warning and had a clear potential to wipe out the entire V-Force. Bomber Command lacked the means to preserve some of the force by adopting USAF-style airborne alert. In addition, the V-Force was unsuited to emergency dispersal to remote locations overseas. UK ground alert was the only viable posture for the MBF.

Bomber Command responded with a substantial programme to train, exercise and provide for a transition to war regime allowing some bombers to escape low-trajectory Soviet missiles, despite very short warning and reaction times. Dispersal within the UK was fundamental to ground alert, but organisation and training were subject to certain constraints, not least a prohibition on flights with live weapons.

DEFINING THE THREAT

Could the V-Force be pre-empted? From the first, there were concerns about exposure to destruction on the ground. Low-trajectory Soviet IRBMs began to deploy several years before the BMEWS at Fylingdales Moor commenced operation. Fylingdales' three large domes soon became known as the 'Golf Balls' (replaced in the early

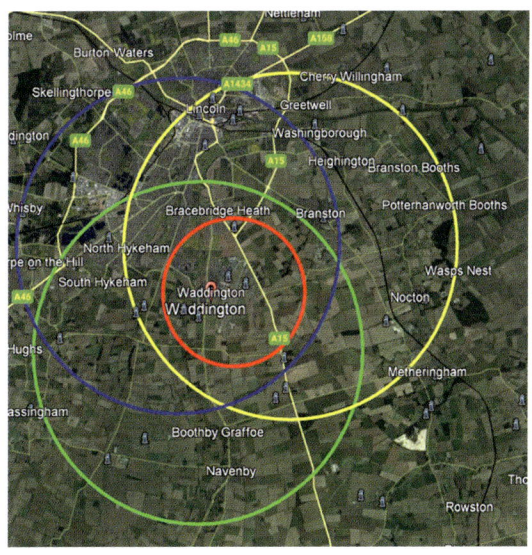

Target Waddington: the red circle is the 1.5NM circular error probable in which 50% of the weapons would land. The three larger circles represent the 1-mt 3.5NM damage radius of weapons. (Roy Brocklebank)

1990s by a more advanced system). Depending on the attack mode, Fylingdales, when ready, might give only 3½ to 4½ minutes' warning. Yet the V-Force adopted 15 minutes' readiness, ostensibly on the assumption that the Soviets would launch for simultaneous burst in the USA and UK – thus granting Britain the significantly longer warning enjoyed by the Americans as a product of geography (that is, at least until the Soviet SLBM fleet grew in size).

British planners initially assumed the Soviets would allocate one missile per MBF airfield, with the possibility of others targeted to catch those V-bombers immediately surviving a war scramble. Subsequent estimates, however, allowed for four weapons per airfield. Assessments of V-Force ability to survive a Soviet missile strike varied from a remarkably optimistic forecast of over 90% of aircraft, made in 1971, to a more realistic 26% or less in a 1962 study. Even the latter figure was based on an unlikely combination of favourable circumstances, with *all crews* at RS05 when the order to scramble came.

The problem of vulnerability on the ground is straightforward, in that any attack scenario would be a surprise, in the sense that the bombers could be scrambled only on detection and confirmation of incoming Soviet missiles. Whilst bombers could be recalled (through the positive release procedure), launching the V-Force before confirmation that missiles were actually on their way would expose the aircraft to destruction on the ground as they were restored to readiness upon return.

REDUCING THE RISK

Many measures were taken to ensure that a proportion of the force could survive a pre-emptive strike, to begin the North Sea crossing and continue to their targets. This called for elaborate dispersal arrangements and a 'minimum response' system known as Quick Reaction Alert (QRA). An obvious response to vulnerability on the ground in a crisis is to disperse to airfields across the UK. Small flights of two or four aircraft per airfield reduced vulnerability, by giving more bombers the chance to take off before the missiles burst (ending long take-off queues on main bases). Given broad scepticism about the credibility of UK ground alert/dispersal, however, more radical solutions were explored, including Strategic Air Command-style airborne alert. This would put QRA V-bombers in the air, rather than sitting exposed on the ground – so ensuring the survival of that part of the force.

Andrew Brookes noted that SAC kept airborne alert aircraft up for 24 hours at a time, from midday to midday, with two refuellings in between: "Each bomber was given 25 targets, all at different ranges from base, the idea being that the crew worked through the targets as their fuel resources dwindled, until they refuelled and then they moved back to the furthest again."[421]

Airborne alert, unfortunately, was inappropriate for the V-Force, due to Bomber Command's lack of means. There were insufficient V-bombers and tankers. The bombers lacked room to carry extra crew for regular extended patrol flights, quite different from the occasional air-to-air-refuelled long-distance flight. Airborne alert in the British context would mean rotating V-bombers every six hours. Andrew Brookes referred to an experiment at RAF Waddington: "Certainly, Waddington managed to fly 64 5½-hour Vulcan sorties round-the-clock during a 14-day exercise, but this imposed such a strain on the station that the airborne alert plan died with Skybolt."

Alpha Dispersal: Vulcan XH503 at RAF Waddington. The board at the nosewheel is thought to indicate that it is armed. (Andy Leitch Collection)

Yet, airborne alert looked so attractive, at least at first glance, that it came to be studied repeatedly – and repeatedly ruled out – over many years. Meanwhile, a second radical survival option was explored: emergency dispersal to remote overseas airfields. Unfortunately, all remote overseas locations required flight refuelling in order to achieve adequate target cover. There were insufficient RAF tankers. This left just one viable option: enhanced ground alert on UK airfields, with measures in place to compress the time required to scramble. The QRA system was adopted, requiring one in eight aircraft to be fuelled, armed and held at RS15 at all times – providing the UK's minimum retaliatory response to surprise attack.

THE SOVIET BOMBER THREAT

An October 1955 briefing (from the ACAS to the CAS) put Soviet medium bomber strength at 81 jets and 853 piston-engined aircraft.[422] The fast-growing Soviet bomber force had been watched with concern for some time. Badger and Blinder medium bombers of the Smolensk Air Army represented a significant threat to the UK.[423]

A September 1953 briefing for CAS had referred to a Joint Intelligence Committee report on a SACEUR study, the latter concluding that no more than three days' warning of attack could be expected. In contrast, as the CAS briefing underlined, the British intelligence appreciation was that "30 days' warning should be received if the Soviet Union were to launch a full-scale attack".[424]

By January 1955, however, the new realism prevailed. In a note, ACAS got to grips with the terminology: "In the past, the term 'warning of attack' has been rather loosely used and one was led to believe that by observing various 'indicators' … we could expect, say, three or four weeks' warning of attack." This new paper, however, appreciated the difference between "preparations for war" and "warning of actual attack". It added: "… 'warning of actual attack' would probably amount to no more than a very short time, made available from the detection of enemy aircraft on Allied radar screens. Under adverse conditions, this time could be as short as 20 minutes." It also made the vital point: "Intelligence does not expect to be able to give the date or hour of the attack."[425]

MBF main bases were defended by SAMs and fighters. When it came to be appreciated that sufficient attackers would still get through to destroy Britain, the role of UK Air Defence switched to a deterrent function – the protection of MBF bases. Later, planners recognised that hostilities might well commence with a period of conventional warfare. This should have raised major questions concerning how to defend the widely dispersed V-Force, as point defences were centred on MBF main bases. Duncan Sandys' April 1957 Defence White Paper placed the emphasis on missiles; the fighter force was to be much reduced. There was a view that fighter and surface-to-air guided weapons (SAGW) defences would become an irrelevance as the strategic missile threat matured. In 1958, however, it was accepted that fighters were still needed to confront the Soviet bomber threat, for as long as that threat continued. An undated note for the CAS, on the future metropolitan fighter force, envisaged SAGW units defending the deterrent increasing from 23 in 1961 to 58 in 1965, whereas the fighter force would reduce from 19 to 13 squadrons over that period. The note considered 13 fighter squadrons "to be the minimum required to give validity to the defence of the deterrent, as a complement to the planned SAGW defences".[426]

An attack on MBF airfields by Soviet bombers was envisaged over three operational zones on a front 200 miles in length:

> "To produce a realistic contribution towards the deterrent, the fighter force should be able to show a potential capability to eliminate or repel between one quarter and one third of this threat before SAGW defences come into action. Anything less than this capability would not be a realistic deterrent as seen through Russian eyes."

Even assuming the highest estimates of fighter lethality, this would require the capability to put at least 40 fighters into engagement with the enemy in each zone. This would need four squadrons (each of 12 aircraft) to cover each of the three zones. Naturally, a fully dispersed V-Force would be much harder to defend. This note acknowledged that only one squadron, plus OCU aircraft, would be available to protect dispersal bases in Scotland.

Investment in fighter defence always triggered challenges, with questions over its effectiveness (although the fighters produced remarkably strong interception results during UK air defence exercises). The prevailing view, however, was pessimistic. In his April 1956 Budget, then Chancellor Harold Macmillan wanted drastically reduced spending on fighters. There was resistance from the prime minister. Instead, Eden agreed to an expenditure review. Macmillan remained a sceptic about fighters when succeeding Eden. The big cuts came in Sandys' April 1957 Defence White Paper, which redefined the fighter role as the defence of MBF airfields.[427] While opposed by Secretary for Air George Ward, savage cuts in the fighter force were confirmed in the 1958 White Paper.[428]

Some of Macmillan's doubts were shared by the Air Staff. In a June 1956 paper, Air Chief Marshal Sir Ronald Ivelaw-Chapman, the Vice-Chief of the Air Staff (VCAS), acknowledged that UK air defences "would be incapable of preventing widespread devastation of the United Kingdom". He also argued, however, that UK air defence was "an essential part of the deterrent".[429] Sandys' 1957 White Paper echoed these themes:

> "It must be frankly argued that there is at present no means of providing adequate protection for the people of this country against the consequences of attack with nuclear weapons; though, in the event of war, the fighter aircraft of the Royal Air Force would unquestionably be able to take a heavy toll of enemy bombers, a proportion would inevitably get through. Even if it were only a dozen they could with megaton weapons inflict widespread devastation."

This is an interesting reflection, as it would also apply, in equal measure, to a small group of surviving V-bombers attempting to retaliate by attacking Russia's biggest cities.

The White Paper recognised the significance of the air defence contribution to deterrence:

> "It is essential that a would-be aggressor should not be allowed to think he could readily knock out the bomber bases in Britain before their aircraft could take off from them. The defence of the bomber airfields is therefore an essential part of the deterrent and is a feasible task."

Nevertheless, the fighter force shrank dramatically as the missile threat grew. Between 1956 and 1958, Fighter Command's strength was cut from around 600 aircraft (1956) to 320, falling further, to 272 in 1960, then to just 140 by 1962.[430]

As for SAGW defences (and regardless of earlier projections), a 1963 response to a USAF request for information on RAF QRA status listed ten UK-based SAM squadrons, each with 32 Bloodhound Mk 1 weapons (20% at ten minutes' alert and 80% at two hours). The SAM sites were at: Woolfox Lodge (62 Squadron), Misson (94), Breighton (112), Dunholme Lodge (141), Woodhall Spa (222), Marham (242), Carnaby (247), Warboys (257), Watton (263) and Rattlesden (266).[431] The first generation Bloodhounds were replaced from 1964 by the more advanced Mk 2, with semi-active homing.

MISSILES AND WARNINGS

In the late 1950s a seven-day strategic warning period was assumed, allowing Bomber Command time to come to readiness to achieve maximum generation of aircraft. The assumed minimum tactical warning was 40 minutes (based on attack by subsonic bombers). Once alerted, the V-Force would be held at 40 minutes – to be sustained for up to 30 days (at 15 minutes, for up to seven days). A 1957 report on Bomber Command's ability to come to alert summarised these early views on readiness, based on assumptions that:

- Aircraft are held fully-fuelled and ready for starting immediately, with bombs in the bomb bay, maintained for a strictly limited period of "great national emergency" – assumed to be a maximum of one month.
- Aircrew maintain a three-watch system: first watch at the aircraft or in a crew room not more than five minutes away; second watch at meals or recreation but able to reach their cockpits fully-dressed in 15 minutes; and third watch sleeping but also able to reach cockpits in 15 minutes. Allowing 15 minutes for checks, starting engines and taxiing, the aircraft should be off the ground in 20–30 minutes.

This paper also referred to other, lower readiness states: three hours standby or half the force at cockpit readiness and half at three hours.[432] The latter state is curious, as a situation serious enough to warrant putting half the force at cockpit readiness appears incompatible with the other half at three hours, even allowing for an attack by subsonic bombers rather than missiles.

Soviet missiles, however, changed everything. As early as 1955, JIC included the destruction of MBF airfields as "one of the enemy's aims within the United Kingdom".[433] In his June 1956 note to the Air Council, Sir Ronald Ivelaw-Chapman warned: "… what would be significant would be if, while we were still reliant upon bombers, the Russians were able to knock them out by ballistic missiles at their airfields before they could take off."[434] The priority target for Soviet IRBMs was the Thor sites, but more weapons became available for striking the airfields when the Thors were withdrawn.

Early warning of missile attack became essential and this led to the construction of BMEWS at Fylingdales Moor, Yorkshire. Operational from September 1963, it joined BMEWS stations at Thule, Greenland, and Clear, Alaska. Squadron Leader Michael Hely spent three years as engineering staff officer responsible for Fylingdales:

> "The site's function was governed by a Joint Operations Plan, which set out the operational priorities. While Fylingdales did supplement Thule and Clear, in that it could detect ICBMs bound for the USA, its *primary* role was to provide a warning of an IRBM attack on the UK … our very clear priority was to identify UK-bound IRBMs …"[435]

Before Fylingdales began operation, Bomber Command received early warning input from the Americans. Bomber Command Headquarters, High Wycombe, was linked to NORAD (North American Air Defense Command), Colorado Springs, allowing the British to share SAC early warning information from 1960.[436] In April 1961, Bomber Command's Operational Research Branch reported on estimates of minimum warning times expected from Fylingdales when in operation. The threats considered were missiles with ranges of 650, 1,000 and 1,500 miles (assuming they would be fired to maximum range in optimum trajectories or in low trajectories, with a 15-degree re-entry angle). The shortest warning from missiles fired from Russia was "approximately 4.2 minutes at Fylingdales Moor when a 1,000 miles missile is fired on a low trajectory over 650 miles range. This would give Kent and areas of Essex, Suffolk and Norfolk just under four minutes."[437] Such a missile would not be detected in the first two or three minutes of flight as it must rise above the horizon for radar detection.

The 'four-minute warning' took firm root in the public mind. Once operational, Fylingdales produced occasional errors. Incidents included a problem leading to QRA crews being brought to readiness. Following a software update, engineers had neglected to re-load the Moon's profile; when the Moon rose, it gave the appearance of a Soviet missile attack.

The US early warning alarm consisted of:

- Alarm Level 3: one double scan (Thule and Clear), one tracked threat object in five minutes, two in 15 minutes and three in 25 minutes.
- Alarm Level 2: two in five minutes, three in 15 minutes and six in 25 minutes.
- Alarm Level 1: three in five minutes, six in 15 minutes and nine in 25 minutes.[438]

The US alarm level was displayed in the Bomber Command Operations Centre (BCOC). According to Operational Research Branch Memorandum No. 285 (February 1964), probable false alarm rates due to environmental conditions at Thule and Clear were:

- Alarm Level 3: one in two years.
- Alarm Level 2: one in 12 years.
- Alarm Level 1: one in 500 years.

As for the probability of false alarms from technical faults/human error, the memorandum merely commented: "NORAD should be able to identify these quickly and pass the information rapidly via Fylingdales to BCOC."

The three UK IRBM alarm levels, for obvious reasons, had different timescales:

- Alarm Level 3: one in two minutes, two in five minutes and three within 15 minutes.
- Alarm Level 2: two in two minutes, three in five minutes and four within 15 minutes.
- Alarm Level 1: three in two minutes, four in five minutes and five within 15 minutes.

Memorandum No. 285 explained the process:

> "If, for example, three threat objects are tracked within two minutes, the alarm levels will be raised through 3 and 2 to the highest alarm level of 1. After two minutes from the tracking of the first object, if no further threat objects have been tracked, the alarm level will fall to 2, after five minutes to alarm level 3 and after 15 minutes will disappear off the display. During this period, the number of objects which are assessed as a threat and have been tracked is displayed and will remain constant on the display until the predicted impact time has elapsed, although the alarm level starts to decrease after two minutes. The number of tracked events is extremely important to the commander-in-chief (C-in-C) or his deputy, as this is the only method of providing an immediate assessment of whether the alarm level 1 has only just been reached or whether a mass raid has been launched."

The memorandum outlined the main types of false alarms. There were three main environmental factors with a potential for triggering false alarms (all with a "very small" probability, particularly at alarm level 1): aurora (conditions would be very short-lived), ducting (very short-lived atmospheric conditions capable of bending the radar beam) and multipath (causing a decrease in reliability and discrimination, but with negligible impact on tracking accuracy).

On the frequency of false alarms from Fylingdales due to technical faults and human error, the memorandum commented: "That will only ever be derived from experience. If human error is the cause, there is an equal likelihood of any of the three alarm levels being raised."

11

QUICK REACTION ALERT

> *We sat in the aircraft, connected by a link to Bomber Command Headquarters at High Wycombe. Five minutes' readiness was called two or three times a week. It wasn't very pleasant to turn out at 02.00 on a winter morning, climb in and get ready to go.*
>
> Dick Fuller, Valiant co-pilot, 49 Squadron

QRA PIONEERS

SACEUR-assigned Valiants were the pioneers – the first V-bombers to adopt QRA. One aircraft per squadron was held fuelled, bombed-up and ready to go at 15 minutes, round the clock. The three squadrons of Valiants assigned to SACEUR were part of No. 3 Group. SACEUR's first Valiant squadron, 207, was assigned on 1 January 1960 and adopted QRA in October of that year.[439]

Two more Valiant squadrons, 49 and 148, were assigned to SACEUR in 1961, fully implementing a decision approved by the Air Council on 15 May 1958. The plan was to make best use of the Valiants, which were to be replaced in the main force by Vulcans and Victors during 1962–63. The Valiants, in turn, replaced SACEUR's Canberras. Other Valiants were used in the tanker role. The 24 SACEUR Valiants replaced 64 Canberras; SACEUR accepted reduced numbers, somewhat reluctantly, due to the value of blind-bombing capability and in the expectation that each Valiant would carry two weapons (the American B28 high-level weapon and, subsequently, from 1 April 1963, the B43 laydown bomb).[440]

Anthony Wright described the scene at RAF Marham, beside the American-armed QRA Valiants:

> "We lived in hutted accommodation. Nearby, our Valiants were parked on pans within a wired-off compound and guarded by both RAF and American police, as our weapons were under dual control. Our accommodation was adjacent, but outside the protected area."[441]

Dick Fuller recalled how life gradually became more serious for operational V-Force crews during the early 1960s: "At Marham, we always had three aircraft with live weapons on QRA for 48 hours at a time. During QRA we went from 15 minutes' readiness to five minutes."[442] Valiant/Victor captain Tony Cottingham remembered QRA developing in stages:

> "At first it was three hours' readiness, which allowed married crew members to be on call at home by telephone … The response time soon became 15 minutes, 24 hours a day. When on duty, crews stayed together, whether in a duty room in the Operations Centre

or at the Officers' Mess … the car was parked nearby, for a quick dash to the aircraft, which was parked on the nearest dispersal to the runway. We could sleep in pyjamas provided the flying suit was nearby. Call-out was by means of a Tannoy message which began with a very loud-ringing phone bell."[443]

When the Valiants were grounded in January 1965, SACEUR lost the three squadrons making up his Tactical Bombing Force. His argument for replacement with Vulcan Mk 1/1A aircraft, then about to leave main force service, was rejected on grounds of cost, supported by a presenting case that SACEUR already had sufficiency of nuclear assets and that TBF's loss would not affect the viability of the deterrent. Andy Leitch adds that, by this time, these aircraft were "very poorly", had used up much of their fatigue lives and became restricted to 250 kts below 20,000 ft (Vulcan Mk 1A Pilot's Notes, Part II, Ch.2, paras 2[a] AL7, Feb 67). SACEUR was told that there would be no Vulcan TBF on 26 March 1965.[444] He had valued Marham's Valiants as they represented his only all-weather blind-bombing assets. He also, of course, regretted the loss of 48 potential nuclear strikes.[445]

QRA had soon been adopted throughout the V-Force. Exercise Macassar (18 September–14 October 1961) trialled main force QRA in a period of tension, testing its ability to maintain some 15 aircraft at 15 minutes' readiness.[446] Two weeks after the conclusion of Macassar, on 31 October 1961, AOC-in-C Sir Kenneth Cross wrote to the VCAS, pressing the case for main force QRA:

"It seems only military common sense to maintain a permanent alert concept of some form, in the face of the growing Russian threat and the need to build up experience to compete with the greatly reduced warning time during the coming years. A permanent alert force also gives us the opportunity of close integration with the Strategic Air Command reflex forces in this country, thus taking full advantage of our combined strengths, and the combined effect of our ECM equipments, especially during the critical phase of penetrating the enemy's outer radar defences."[447]

Preparing for a sortie: night scene at RAF Waddington. (Andy Leitch Collection)

On 7 December 1961 the Air Council approved the QRA proposal to maintain one aircraft per MBF squadron at 15 minutes' readiness.⁴⁴⁸

By January 1963 the main force QRA consisted of 11 Vulcans and Victors: Waddington (3), Honington (2), Cottesmore (2), Wittering (1), Coningsby (1) and Scampton (2). AOC-in-C Bomber Command wanted this increased to 17, as from April 1: Waddington (6), Honington (3), Cottesmore (3), Wittering (2), Coningsby (1) and Scampton (2). This would be followed by a further increase, to 20 QRA aircraft by 1 July, taking in bombers from Blue Steel squadrons. The plan included a trial at Waddington of centralised (rather than squadron-based) flying and servicing.⁴⁴⁹ See Cross' letter below.

Given that a Soviet 'bolt from the blue' was thought unlikely (and, perhaps, impossible to achieve), was there real value in continuous QRA? Would the use of regularly exercised 'Emergency QRA', as a first response to heightened tension, have been less debilitating and, ultimately, more appropriate? In this context, Air Commodore Edward Jarron, a former Chief of Special Weapons at SHAPE, makes an interesting observation: "The most important point here is that permanent QRA is a statement of resolve. It is a matter of nuclear signalling. That is of great importance."⁴⁵⁰

Furthermore, permanent QRA was a response to American doubts about V-Force effectiveness. In 1962 SAC had concluded that it could count on only eight V-bombers being "certainly operational".⁴⁵¹ Sir Kenneth Cross had written to the Chief of the Air Staff, Sir Thomas Pike, in November 1962, outlining his plans for a doubling of the QRA force, to compensate, to some degree, for the phase-out of Thor.⁴⁵²

Sir Kenneth set out his reasons:

> "The phase-out of Thors commencing in April 1963 will progressively reduce the number of weapon systems normally held at immediate readiness (15 minutes) from 68 (54 Thors and 14 aircraft) unless measures are taken to increase the number of aircraft at immediate readiness in the meantime … I think you will agree that in the deterrent role it is systems at readiness that count, and if this needed emphasising then undoubtedly the Cuban crisis did it. We have therefore been examining ways and means of increasing the number of aircraft at readiness as from next April …"⁴⁵³

Cross sent a follow-up letter on 10 January 1963:

> "Detailed studies have now been completed and from 1 April I propose increasing the QRA force to 17 Vulcans and Victors (plus the four Valiants of the SACEUR force), rising to 20 Vulcans and Victors by 1 July, when the Blue Steel squadrons will be able to make their contribution. This plan will enable us to maintain approximately 20% of the force at permanent readiness and will go some way to compensate for the rundown of Thor."⁴⁵⁴

These plans ran into trouble. They were put on ice pending clarification of the position regarding main force assignment to NATO, post-Nassau. Valiants were assigned to NATO from 1960 and, in 1963, the entire MBF was put at SACEUR's disposal (whilst still respecting the paramount national interest). In reality, this move was more political than operational and had very little impact on the squadrons.

Back in the early 1960s, the politically-driven SACEUR/MBF issue was used to stall for time over the call for a larger QRA. Indeed, in a 12 June 1963 note to the CAS (*after* the NATO assignment had been clarified), VCAS expressed the view that plans for a larger QRA should stay on ice; there would be no change to the existing QRA arrangement (one aircraft per squadron).

There was a long-standing reluctance to expand QRA. In December 1961 QRA was about to be introduced at one aircraft per squadron, but the Bomber Command AOC-in-C had proposed going further, to two aircraft per squadron (increasing QRA to 25% of V-Force strength). In a secret annex to the minutes of the 7 December 1961 Air Council meeting, it is stated that CAS took the view that this doubling had "wide implications" and that its consideration should be deferred.[455]

Cross persisted, tabling his somewhat more modest proposal – going from 11 to 17 main force bombers (then, subsequently, to 20 by July 1963). Once again, he found no support. In fact, even existing QRA arrangements (involving one aircraft per squadron) prompted much debate over, for example, the cost of a few extra RAF Police and whether one man could guard two aircraft loaded with live nuclear weapons. One idea here was to use ground tradesmen as guards. Air Marshal Sir John Whitley, the Inspector-General of the Royal Air Force, joined in – proposing several schemes for saving police posts. He went too far, recommending "radically reduced" policing of Thor sites. This, however, was subject to formal Anglo-American agreement; visitors from the Pentagon told the Air Ministry that this agreement could not be re-negotiated. The involvement of American warheads required adherence to the original agreement.[456]

BMEWS AND QRA

The relationship between the ballistic missile early warning system and the V-bomber QRA force was explored in a Bomber Command memorandum of February 1964. This explained the basis for QRA readiness at 15 minutes, but made no attempt to justify its underlying assumptions. The crux of the study was the timing of a Soviet missile launch in a surprise attack, together with, inter alia, the conditions under which a scramble should be ordered – to minimise the chance of responding to a false alarm whilst, at the same time, giving aircraft "a high probability" of escape.[457]

Control procedures for the QRA force were founded on the view that the USSR would launch for "simultaneous impact" in the USA and UK, so providing the UK with a 15–20 minutes warning. In other words, missiles with US targets would launch first. The UK/Western Europe would then benefit from the longer American warning, through the BMEWS/NORAD link. Here, the memorandum commented: "To meet this situation, the QRA force is held at 15 minutes' readiness. The force generally reacts much more quickly than this and, therefore, some aircraft would escape from an attack in which the missiles were launched simultaneously." The memorandum gave no estimate of what "some aircraft" actually meant, although, as Roy Brocklebank points out, some chance of survival in a simultaneous launch strike did exist:

> "To get an assured strike on the base, given a circular error probable (CEP) of five miles, would require all missiles so targeted to actually hit the target area. CEP is only a mean;

a missile could land many miles further away. It was implicit that not all weapons would be on target …"

This document, however, made no attempt to explain why the Russians should be so generous as to offer the British as much warning as the Americans, by adopting a simultaneous impact attack – the staggered launch underpinning the rationale for RS15. In doing so, they would sacrifice the benefits of simultaneous launch in the context of Western Europe. Instead, the memorandum preferred to focus on the risk of erroneous scramble:

> "Recommendations on the criteria used for scrambling the force are made, which safeguard as far as possible against scrambling on a false alarm and yet do not degrade the reaction capability of the force and, hence, the chance that it will escape destruction on the ground and during take-off."

How much time was required for final actions and scramble? The memorandum stated that the best recorded response of an RS15 QRA crew to an RS02 alert (start engines) was four minutes 25 seconds (average: eight minutes six seconds) in autumn 1962 and two minutes 25 seconds (average: six minutes 24 seconds) in autumn 1963 – one of only four occasions when times of less than three minutes were achieved (the crew were in the cockpit, doing checks, in daylight hours).

These figures suggest that, given simultaneous launch rather than simultaneous burst, "some aircraft", in reality, could mean just one or two – given that only 11 would be on QRA and only the most fortunate (at cockpit readiness) would be able to respond instantly to the RS02/scramble order and get off quickly enough. In the case of a low trajectory/simultaneous launch pre-emptive strike, with BMEWS providing only minimal warning, there was a strong possibility (given no QRA aircraft at RS05) that there would be *no survivors* to begin the North Sea crossing. Virtually the entire V-Force would be destroyed in this scenario.

The memorandum acknowledged that a simultaneous launch meant a low probability of escape, but it did not dwell on unpleasantries. Instead, it focused on a simultaneous burst attack – the only scenario really providing enough warning for some of the 11-strong QRA force to get away. Sheltering under the assumption that the Russians would defer launch against the UK for some minutes after launch against the USA, to achieve simultaneous burst, it continued:

> "… it can be seen that if RS02 is ordered as soon as Alarm Level 3 arises, it will take the fastest crew 2½ minutes to reach the end of the runway for take-off. Crews take three minutes or more to reach the end of the runway on 99% of occasions. Clearly, this time can be used for direct consultation between Bomber Command Operations Centre and the Operations Room at Fylingdales, to establish whether the alarm is real or false. If, during this period, Alarm Level 1 has been reached and Fylingdales confirms that the alarm is real, then the scramble order can be given (three minutes after the initiation of Alarm Level 3) with a negligible loss in the reaction time of the force."

The fundamental problem, of course, is that these times mean almost certain destruction in a simultaneous-launch/low-trajectory attack. The bombers require three minutes plus to start engines and position, around one minute to take off and at least one minute to reach survival distance (assuming no second weapon aimed to catch 'escapees') – a process exceeding five minutes and, in all probability, over a minute too long to avoid destruction. Survivors would have to be at RS05 primed for immediate RS02 (engine start), but for most of the time the crews were NOT in the aircraft. Obviously, verification by BMEWS could be academic in a simultaneous-launch/minimum-warning scenario. Should the Soviets launch simultaneously against the UK and USA, Bomber Command would get the minimum warning – around four minutes.

Against this background, it is easy to understand why planners embraced the simultaneous burst/RS15 scenario. According to the memorandum, a simultaneous-burst attack would be detected 7½ minutes to 12½ minutes before detection of the IRBM attack on the UK. This would provide up to 16–17 minutes (perhaps more, allowing for the inevitable spread of impact times) to man cockpits, start engines, taxi, take-off and achieve escape distance. It should be noted, however, that RS15, if inappropriate for a response to a simultaneous launch missile attack, did at least allow the V-Force a daily operating environment with sufficient space for sustainable functioning, although the pattern of force deployment and behaviour in a close approach to war would almost certainly have been very different.

The Bomber Command Operational Research Branch conclusions, assuming the "favourable" attack mode, noted the logic of associating Anglo-American alarm levels, in the context of "deciding the criteria from which the scramble order will be given. This so increases the confidence that the scramble order will not be given on a false alarm that the probability becomes negligible." That said, it was recognised as essential that a scramble could be ordered on the UK alarm level alone, due to the possibility of an attack on the UK alone or the severing of communications between Fylingdales and NORAD. Two critical pieces of information were required to help ensure no scramble on a false alarm: the number of threat objects tracked (a real attack would involve numbers of threat objects far above alarm level values within the first two minutes) and a check with Fylingdales Operations Room, to ensure that a false alarm is discounted (given the additional data available to them).

The memorandum made the point that timings allowed enough room for verification, making a virtue of this:

> "This will take a short time, but there is clear evidence from the practice alerts of the QRA force that three minutes are available from the order to readiness 02 before this state is achieved by the fastest crews. From the current IRBM threat, some 7½ minutes warning of attack is expected. In order to retain a probability of escape, it is essential that the order to scramble be given four minutes before the predicted time of impact. This allows up to three minutes from the first alarm to the time that the scramble order must be given."

Then came a brief, somewhat reluctant acknowledgement of other, more negative possibilities, resulting from simultaneous launch:

> "When the QRA force was introduced, the 15-minute readiness state was fixed so that it had a high probability of escaping from an attack which involved simultaneous impact of missiles on the USA and UK. The EDOM exercise has clearly demonstrated that this can be achieved in practice. For other types of attack, the escape probabilities are relatively small."

The memorandum set out the scramble criteria: USA Alarm Level 1, associated with a UK Alarm Level 3 or higher, in the case of an attack involving simultaneous impact. "The attack on the USA is detected 7½ to 12½ minutes before the IRBM attack on the UK." This is a key assumption. A second is that most QRA aircraft would reach RS02 (i.e. ready for immediate simultaneous engine start [SIMSTART]) *before* the attack on the UK is detected. There would be around seven minutes plus available to escape before first-weapon detonation

Alert and ready: four Vulcans on the ORP. (Norman Bonnor)

and "aircraft have a high probability of escape". The picture is very different for simultaneous launch/detection of missiles fired against the UK and USA. Here, the scramble criteria were UK Alarm Level 1 associated with USA Alarm Level 3 or higher, or associated with a break in Fylingdales/NORAD communication: "Attack detected approximately simultaneously, QRA force will have seven minutes plus from Alarm Level 3. As the QRA force takes, on average, seven minutes to reach Readiness State 02, the probability of escape is relatively small."

Other cases are an attack on the UK alone, or missiles launched against the UK before those against the USA. Here, the scramble criteria was UK Alarm Level 1, with "time to impact" reduced to four minutes:

> "The QRA force will have approximately seven minutes' warning. As the minimum time to reach Readiness State 02 is three minutes, this time can be used to establish the validity of the alarm. If the intelligence data on missile trajectories is correct, then this exactly corresponds with the displayed time to impact decreasing to four minutes. The probability of escape is relatively small."

If the basis of RS15 proved correct on the day and the detected attack is timed for simultaneous impact, QRA aircraft would have relatively good prospects for escape, given an additional 7½ to 12½ minutes of "American warning" (but why would the Soviets grant the UK and the rest of Western Europe this period of grace?). In the event of simultaneous launch, or an attack on the UK alone, the escape probability is low. The memorandum was certainly correct in emphasising that the existing procedure of bringing crews to RS02 on the receipt of any US or UK alarm level was essential, to keep the overall reaction time of the force to a minimum.

No mention was made of the new threat from missile-firing submarines positioned off the UK west coast (these weapons could not be detected, as Fylingdales' aerials covered an arc fixed between 350 degrees and 140 degrees). Obvious priority targets for submarine-launched ballistic missiles (SLBMs) would be MBF dispersal airfields in the north and west. There was no readiness allowance for this threat. As Richard Moore wrote, BMEWS "could not be expected to detect submarine-launched missiles fired towards the UK from the west."[458] Furthermore, an initial mass SLBM launch close to the US seaboards would put many American targets in a similar position to their UK counterparts. In this context, simultaneous burst might be attractive, should the flight times for a substantial weight of attack on continental US and European targets be approximately equal. Indeed, in this scenario, simultaneous launch achieves near simultaneous burst.

WAS PERMANENT QRA THE RIGHT APPROACH?

The V-Force QRA regime was always open to challenge. There were many deployment options. QRA bombers could have been distributed routinely and at random across dispersal airfields (with, perhaps, more frequent visits to those airfields with the longest warning times). The permanent distribution of one QRA bomber per "favourable" dispersal airfield would have maximised the chance of escaping a pre-emptive strike. The amount of organisation, effort and cost required to apply such a regime almost certainly would have been regarded as prohibitive. It would also have required regular flying with live weapons loaded. Another option would have been *occasional* flying with live weapons loaded to the dispersal airfields. Here, it is noteworthy that some senior commanders saw flying with live weapons as acceptable. In October 1963, for example, AOC-in-C Sir John Grandy proposed flying aircraft carrying fully-fuelled Blue Steel, *fitted with live warheads*, from main bases to dispersals, to test the stand-off bomb's ability to withstand war emergency conditions.

Creative thinking on these themes appeared to go so far and no further. According to Wing Targeting Officer Roy Brocklebank: "We never practised or considered converting an Exercise Mick into a Micky Finn (see page 67) … we never considered the full fuel dispersal case." Interestingly, Brocklebank also noted that Hawker Siddeley did eventually clear the Vulcan to land at maximum take-off weight.[459] Fully-fuelled dispersal *was* feasible.

In practice, V-bombers never flew over the UK with live nuclear weapons. This imposed significant restrictions on dispersal exercises and QRA. No documentary evidence was found to suggest that there had been consideration of enhanced V-Force ground alert through

Eager to fly: four Vulcans at RAF Cottesmore. (Andy Leitch Collection)

routine rotation of the QRA force, as single aircraft, to dispersal airfields (with, perhaps, a bias towards airfields in the north and west offering 30 seconds or more additional warning of incoming low-trajectory missiles). Nevertheless, as discussed later in the narrative, the adoption of an ultra-ready Alert Condition 1 requiring up to 30% of aircraft manned at RS05, 24/7 by crew rotation, as early as 1961, is significant. It suggests that aircraft, manned by the most experienced crews and with big city targets, would have been dispersed to geographically favoured airfields when faced with imminent threat of war. The barriers to enhanced dispersal exercises, including deployment during a simulated severe crisis, would have been additional cost and effort. For example, each dispersed QRA duty period would have been immediately preceded by a pre-QRA dispersal flight and regeneration (bomber fully-fuelled and armed), together with additional crews positioned to rotate RS05 QRA duty periods.

In the absence of single-aircraft dispersed QRA (fully-fuelled and armed), a more acceptable option might have been the construction of single weapon stores at some dispersal airfields (with priority for those airfields in the north and west), linked to a requirement for a proportion of bombers coming off QRA to make immediate post-QRA flights to these airfields, so allowing the regular testing of capabilities for reception and generation of weapon systems to combat status. At the same time, a network of single weapon stores would have raised security as well as cost concerns. The prompt dispersal of QRA bombers (one aircraft per dispersal airfield, or more at the most favourable locations) in a time of grave crisis would have been, in effect, a rapid response first step in a wider "trickle dispersal" process. Looking back, Roy Brocklebank felt that Bomber Command "should perhaps have considered rotating crews at RS05 … dispersing with full fuel loads and weapons capable of use".[460]

In the final analysis, the most serious objection to radical solutions would have been QRA founded on dispersal flights with *operational nuclear weapons* – although, by implication, this had already been accepted by the proponents of airborne alert QRA.

In the real world of ground alert, however, even the fundamentals of the existing permanent QRA, centred on the main bases, had to be defended. Permanent QRA, as a concept, was not sacrosanct. This was demonstrated by events in late 1963. The Assistant Chief of the Air Staff (Operations) called a briefing on 17 December concerning QRA and SACEUR's requirements. There were moves afoot to relax some aspects of the 15-minute readiness regime for tactical-strike aircraft. A briefing from the D. Air Plans' office, circulated before the meeting, asked, inter alia, a blunt question:

> "The basis of our case against SACEUR's present QRA requirement is the current intelligence assessment of the Soviet Bloc threat to NATO. A 'bolt from the blue' attack by Russia is now considered to be highly unlikely. On the other hand, in the unlikely event of a surprise nuclear attack being launched by the Soviet Bloc, will the 15 minutes QRA state ensure the survival of a portion of our strike and reconnaissance forces?"[461]

It continued in similar vein (and making a crucial point on likely Soviet attack mode, with a degree of straight-talking rarely seen in such documents):

> "General Parker (Chief of Staff, SHAPE, 1963–69) has stated that there has been no change in the threat. This could be accepted if he refers to the numerical strength of Soviet Bloc forces. However, the likelihood of a large-scale surprise nuclear attack being launched against Europe is the factor that should determine our alert posture, rather than the size of the forces opposing us. General Parker also stated that the 15 minutes alert state was valid as it would be logical for the Russians to coordinate their attack for simultaneous *arrival* of their missiles in the United States and Europe, but this is only one point of view. The Soviets could adopt a simultaneous *launch* for all missiles, with the result that Europe would receive no warning and the Soviets would ensure the elimination of the nuclear strike forces based in Europe, although the USA would still receive 15 minutes' warning from BMEWS."

The Soviet option to strike a huge counterforce blow in Europe by opting for simultaneous, rather than staggered, launch appears more logical than the hope that they would refrain and allow Western Europe's nuclear strike assets to avoid near total destruction on the ground. At the same time, the fact that the continental USA's longer warning would be eroded by expanding Soviet SLBM capacity was ignored. Round-the-clock permanent QRA, as a concept, was questioned by the Director, Air Plans, who went on to put the case for relaxing QRA for tactical (as opposed to strategic) strike forces:

> "We should attempt to get the SHAPE staff to agree to a re-examination of the present QRA and readiness concept for our tactical forces … We should also attempt to convince them that we do not disagree with the possession of a capability to mount QRA and a high overall state of readiness either at random or during a time of international tension. However, we do not consider that the maintenance of the present high alert states throughout the year permit the most effective and efficient employment of our present resources. Some relaxation in readiness state outside times of tension could result in better flying rates and increased training. This could be achieved by avoiding the retention on the ground of four fully serviceable aircraft per NATO squadron … Possible alternatives to the present QRA requirement could be either a reduction in the numbers of aircraft held on permanent alert or, alternatively, a rotation of QRA between squadrons and bases. We should, therefore, endeavour to convince SHAPE that a more flexible alert posture should be adopted for our Tactical Air Forces and methods of achieving this should be devised."

12
CUBA AND LIFE ON QRA

> *I remember thinking it odd when, at a certain point, all the animals in the RAF Regiment dog compound began to howl. I decided to take a bath. Then the siren sounded, signalling the order to go to five minutes' readiness. Usually, the five-minute alert was stood down after a short while, but not on that day. This felt very different. My bath water went cold.*
>
> Dick Fuller, Valiant co-pilot, RAF Marham

Information on the likely outcome of a war scramble was not shared with aircrew and the reasons why are too obvious to state. Vulcan co-pilot Nick Dennis' crew attained combat status with 12 Squadron at Coningsby in December 1963:

"We started QRA and life became pretty restrictive. A QRA during the week lasted 24 hours, but 48 hours at the weekend. We would take over at 09.00 and handover at 09.00. The captains would exchange keys and go-bags at the aircraft. At Coningsby we slept in a wing of the Officers' Mess. Later, at Waddington, we were accommodated in a huge black-painted Nissen hut. Most of the time QRA was boring – it was quite a chore and added a lot of pressure to family life. The crew also took part in overseas reinforcement exercises and so spent quite a lot of time away, when this is added to QRA."[462]

There were no profound thoughts about nuclear war:

"We were very young and, frankly, I thought it impossible that something so catastrophic could happen. Should such an event occur, there wouldn't be much left of civilisation as we knew it – West or East! We thought we had a very good deterrent – no-one would be mad enough to try it out. Yet, any one of those QRA exercises could have been the real thing and we wouldn't have hesitated. We would have gone faster and lower than we had practised and the training over Goose Bay had been very realistic. Had it come to the real thing, everything would have been done more aggressively."

'Woody' Fulena recalled Cottesmore's "very relaxed regime", given its nuclear-armed aircraft on permanent QRA:

"Surprisingly, it was a very open place compared to the barbed-wire enclosures around RAF stations that have been in existence since at least the late 1990s. I remember an occasion when some local schoolteachers turned up unannounced at the Mess bar on a Friday evening. They just felt they'd like to join us and drove from Oakham to Cottesmore guardroom and asked for the Mess! Things were very different then."⁴⁶³

In 1965, Flight Lieutenant Phil Leckenby was co-pilot to the commander of 44 (Rhodesia) Squadron. He recalled how new crews working up to combat status were introduced gradually to QRA:

> "This ensured that inexperienced crews were not saddled with such an onerous operational responsibility until they had acquired a firm foundation of tactical flying by day and night, competence in all modes of weapon delivery, au fait with electronic warfare and fully trained in the complexities of the mighty bomb."⁴⁶⁴

ORGANISING QRA

From the mid-1960s, the QRA force was fixed at 11 aircraft (one per squadron), reflecting a long-term frontline strength of 88 bombers.⁴⁶⁵ V-bomber main bases were left to organise QRA in their own way; approaches differed, as recorded in an October 1962 Bomber Command report:

> "Scampton had two aircraft on QRA for a week or a fortnight, to avoid too frequent weapon changes. The crews did 24-hour QRA (08.30 to 08.30) in rotation. Each crew was on QRA about every fifth day. During the day, they were in the operations block or at the aircraft, moving to caravans near the ops block at night. Each crew had its own car, parked outside the ops block, with the nearest aircraft about 500 yards away … The main runway was shut by air traffic as soon as a warning was received. The taxi distance for the first aircraft was 1,700 yards. By day, if the crew were in the ops block, the go-bag was kept in a safe in the intelligence room; the captain had the key. If the crew left the ops block, the captain took the bag with him. By night, the captain took the go-bag to his room. The ground crew worked a normal two-shift system, but the late shift provided a handling party which stayed behind and slept at the QRA site, whilst the rest of the shift went off duty."⁴⁶⁶

This report (issued only days before the climax of the Cuban Crisis which ran from 16 to 29 October 1962) noted: "Scampton believe that aircraft should ultimately go on operational readiness platforms and that flying clothing be stipulated for the crews by day." Scampton's Tannoy was used to announce alerts by day, with alarm bells sounded during night hours.

Waddington held three aircraft on QRA for about a fortnight, with 11 crews doing 24-hour (09.00 to 09.00) QRA in rotation per squadron. By day, one aircrew officer (out of the three crews) remained at the QRA site, while the others were in the ops block or simulator building next door. At night, an officer slept at the QRA site; the others slept in caravans near the ops block.⁴⁶⁷ Caravans at some dispersal airfields were better than others; the latter were described by Tony Blackman and Anthony Wright. They were green-painted five-man caravans – a very basic shipping container-like structure divided into five small compartments, each with an outward-opening door. Inside each compartment was a narrow caravan-style bunk and a metal wash basin. There was an unprotected metal bar heater.⁴⁶⁸ In later years, at least one station used redundant caravans of this type to house RAF Police dogs.

QRA transport at Waddington consisted of one car per crew and the taxi distance was around 500 yards. Go-bags were kept in the aircraft. The ground crew did 24-hour QRA (08.00 to 08.00), staying at the QRA site by day and QRA caravans by night. Alert by day was by Tannoy and klaxons, with a system of coloured lights on poles in the QRA area. By night, the operations duty sergeant warned the officer on duty at the QRA, who had access to klaxon, bell or voice warning over the Tannoy. The klaxon at the aircrew caravans warned of a cockpit alert, with the bell signalling engine start and/or taxi.[469]

Phil Leckenby recorded his memories of Waddington's QRA, when duty crews were accommodated in Nissen huts:

> "The QRA set-up at Waddington was located at the H-shaped, four-aircraft alpha dispersal, on the north-western side of the airfield … A short distance away from the dispersal was a slightly shabby collection of Nissen huts providing accommodation for crews on QRA. They contained rudimentary dormitories with curtains affording basic privacy, an operations room equipped with an array of telephones and an intercom known appropriately as the 'Bomber Box', a lounge area and a games room equipped with snooker and table tennis tables. As with sailors or prisoners, food took on a disproportionate importance for aircrew whiling away the tedious hours. Meals of generous proportions were taken in the aircrew dining room, predictably known as the 'Greasy Spoon', which was conveniently located nearby in Ops Wing HQ.[470]
>
> "The QRA hut complex was not quite close enough to the aircraft for rapid access on foot, so each squadron had its own QRA vehicle in which they raced to their aircraft whenever the bomber controller raised the alert state from RS15 to RS05 or higher. Response times were critical and crews on QRA were never allowed to roam far from their aircraft. Essentially, they were confined to alpha dispersal, Ops Wing HQ or the QRA hut itself … A service vehicle, often of humble origins, provided transport for a Vulcan crew to its nuclear-armed aircraft. During my time at Waddington, the QRA wagons were changed or upgraded a number of times. The requirements were modest: it had to start without difficulty, accommodate a crew of five with all their flying kit, sport a flashing blue roof light … and be capable of covering short distances to waiting aircraft."

The requirements may have been modest, but they were not always fulfilled. When Vulcan pilot Peter Moore first arrived on 44 (Rhodesia) Squadron, the QRA system had just ended. J2 wagons, however, were still in use for transport to aircraft and they had lost none of their unreliability:

> "Called to 05, my crew jumped into our J2 … we had just crossed the runway by the ORP when the J2 gave its last gasp. As fortune would have it, the 'Sally Ann' sandwich truck was by the ORP, so we jumped out and commandeered Sally Ann's support to get us to Delta. The ladies were amused and delighted to be of such vital help."[471]

There were some instances of 'more haste, less speed', as Peter Moore recalls:

> "As a captain, I once had a nav/plotter who managed to leave the go-bag on the crew bus after we had responded to an increase in the alert state. Moving from 15 minutes'

readiness in the crew room to cockpit alert was always a hasty affair. The alert was Tannoyed, crews grabbed all they needed, drivers went hell for leather to the aircraft and crews boarded as quickly as possible – the aircraft having already been combat-checked with the weapon loaded. In the excitement, the nav had undone the locking chain on the go-bag whilst on the bus, only to leave the NATO Top Secret bag behind. Somewhat fortunately, the cockpit state was not held for long and we had the same bus and driver for the return journey."[472]

A 44 (Rhodesia) Squadron nav/radar, Squadron Leader Hickmore, wrote of inter-squadron rivalry, to see who could get four aircraft aloft in the fastest time:

"It was a hair-raising business. I believe the 44 (Rhodesia) Squadron time was one minute 40 seconds, but at the cost of a crew chief with a broken leg, as he was blown off the pan by the force of the jet wash. The record was one minute 27 seconds, but it was a dangerous operation, particularly for the fourth aircraft, which would struggle to get airborne against the turbulence created by the aircraft ahead."[473]

Peter Moore was fully aware of the hazards:

"I used simultaneous mass rapid start on a few occasions, but we generally opted for 90% and crossfeed. As part of the display scramble team, I was authorised for three-engine take-offs because engines could be slow to fire up on simultaneous engine start and could be subject to used air from lead aircraft – we rolled off the ORP as the engines were winding up."[474]

During his first QRA ground duty at RAF Waddington, Cliff Doe was introduced to Yellow Sun 2: "It was an enormous bomb and didn't leave much room in the bomb bay. We couldn't work around it and had to open the bomb-doors to reach and check the hydraulic reservoir levels." In his experience, ground crew had little contact with aircrew: "They were on the domestic side of the airfield, based in offices annexed to one of the hangars. The ground crew were on Charlie dispersal, with the main runway separating us."[475]

Experiments aimed at improving the efficiency of servicing and technical support were less than successful. In March 1964, MBF squadrons changed from squadron servicing to centralised servicing. Cliff Doe describes the ensuing muddle, when first experienced at Waddington:

"… everyone had to report to Delta and Echo dispersals, from where we were to be managed. It was absolute chaos when we arrived. The only people I knew were the ones with whom I worked on 101 Squadron. It was obvious that there were far too many chiefs. I spent four days in this chaos. Then one of the warrant officers came into the crew room and said: 'I'm afraid no-one's given much thought to the manning of QRA. Until we get this mess sorted out, I want volunteers to work on QRA for the next three months.' By then I'd had enough so I put my hand up. I knew what QRA was like but I just wanted to get away."

QRA offered the disciplined routine that was lost for a period in the switch to centralised servicing:

"When on QRA duties, all trades carried out their daily checks – virtually a before-flight servicing – every morning. If a practice alert went as far as engine start and sometimes with the aircraft taxiing down the runway to simulate the real thing, a further inspection and fuel top-up would be required. We had four-bed caravans on the dispersal and there was a central crew room right next to the dispersal pans. The Vulcans were parked on pans at the end of each leg of an H formation. The QRA operated a two-shift system consisting of 48 hours on shift, then 48 hours off, followed by 72 hours on or off at weekends."

As for centralised servicing, Dave Beane, then a 10 Squadron AEO at Cottesmore, described it as "not a great success, and, subsequently, we reverted to individual squadron servicing". He remembered "one or two 'hangar queens' – they spent a lot of time in the hangar. These aircraft were often robbed of bits, to fix the others and keep them flying."

Maintaining the highest levels of serviceability was a constant challenge and ground crew made personal sacrifices as a matter of routine. Long days and QRA often had a serious, highly negative impact on social and family life. There were strict requirements for aircraft availability – targets for QRA plus four aircraft available, then the next four and so on. Centralised servicing was seen as a way of maximising availability, but often at the cost of important close relationships between aircrew and ground crew. Major servicing had to be split into hourly elements, requiring repeated visits to the hangar to ensure regeneration within the 24-hour envelope. This approach succeeded in demoralising ground crew accustomed to a more personalised system of squadron-based servicing. Some felt a loss of identity and worth.

Bomber Command's October 1962 QRA report noted that RAF Cottesmore (10 and XV Squadrons) held two aircraft on QRA for two to three weeks, parked within a barbed-wire enclosure. Initially, the two Cottesmore squadrons had distinct, squadron-based QRA arrangements. There were six QRA crews at this time on 10 Squadron and three crews shared a week, doing two, two and three days in turn, changing over at 09.00 on the Monday, Wednesday and Friday (for a three-day weekend). There were eight effective crews on XV Squadron, with two crews sharing a week, doing three days and four days (changing at 09.00 on Monday and Friday). This changed from 1 October 1962, when XV Squadron began operating as 10 Squadron. During the day crews remained together and were free to move around the base. At night, they slept in huts 50 yards from the ops block.[476] Roy Brocklebank recalled the layout at Cottesmore:

"The Mess was perhaps 200 yards from Ops. There was a wooden hut complex of three huts plus ablutions about 100 yards from the Mess, in the front and towards the ops block, forming a triangle. When the Vulcan Wing moved to Cottesmore, the first two huts were used as Mess accommodation and the QRA crews took over nine bedrooms in the main Mess. In other words, QRA denied nine Mess members a room in the main Mess."[477]

There was a car for each crew, parked at night at the Mess. The winter months were often uncomfortable and, on occasions, common sense was required when conditions were harsh. Roy Brocklebank remembers a winter alert in the small hours of the night:

"One dark winter night the three QRA crews at Cottesmore were all sleeping in rooms in the Officers' Mess when the alarm went off in my captain's room. Getting up quickly, I dressed in the normal routine: socks, flying suit over pyjamas and into flying boots. Out to the QRA car and we shot out of the garage ahead of the two other crews for the 1½-mile drive to the aircraft. We knew from the colour of the Very cartridge fired from the tower that it was cockpit readiness.[478]

"Once in the cockpit we shut the door, declared cockpit readiness and, with power on, settled down to wait. We were running on external power and brought all the systems up while we waited. Running checks, I realised that the navigation and bombing computer navigation panel meter was frozen. I guessed that it was really frozen and put the anglepoise lamp up against the glass of the display, to thaw it out. Although we had power, other than the heat from the equipment, we had no other heaters. The alert continued so I took off my boots and put on a second pair of socks. Sitting next to me our plotter, Tony Oliver, was shivering visibly. I noticed that his pyjama pants were sticking out of his flying suit; no socks, just slippers. He had my full sympathy but not my spare socks. I think we were at cockpit readiness for well over 45 minutes."

The distance to Cottesmore's aircraft at this time (October 1962), was put at 2,000 yards (or 2½ minutes) from the ops block. Cottesmore's ORP had yet to be completed; when ready, the taxi distance from the QRA site would be a "few hundred yards". However, crews at this base, at this time, could not obtain access from the QRA site to the runway at the ORP end due to obstruction of the perimeter track. Here, the memorandum noted: "The aircraft normally taxi nearly two miles to the other end of the runway." The report adds: "If the tail wind component would be too strong for take-off in this direction, the aircraft taxi to the cross runway. For an exercise, one aircraft joins the main runway, backtracks and prepares for take-off. The second aircraft enters the runway when time has been allowed to simulate the first aircraft clearing. In an emergency, the perimeter track on the far side of the runway could be used but it is not used for an exercise due to the position of a concrete mixer there." It is hard to believe that this situation at Cottesmore was tolerated by the station commander.

The go-bag was kept in a cabinet in the ops room and accompanied the crew to the QRA aircraft (the key was in the cabinet)*. The alerting system was warning bells and/or klaxons at the Officers' Mess, squadron offices, sleeping quarters, ground crew offices and recreation rooms. Aircrew normally reported to the ops room, where they took the go-bag from the cabinet.[479]

RAF Honington maintained two QRA aircraft, usually for a fortnight (one aircraft replaced each week by a third aircraft, which was fully prepared before the aircraft to be replaced was taken off combat readiness). There were 16 operational crews at Honington, each doing 2½-day QRAs, with the weekend crew covering late Friday afternoon to early Monday morning. Days were spent in the ops block, Officers' Mess or sleeping quarters adjacent to the Mess, but they were also free to go together, as a crew, to the simulator or squadron offices. The aircraft were 1–1½ miles away (2½ minutes from the Mess). The taxi distance was 400 yards to the near end of the runway. Go-bags were kept in the aircraft. QRA duty periods for ground crew

---

* Roy Brocklebank adds that, by the mid-1960s, it was common practice to keep go-bags in the locked boxes of the sixth and seventh seats on the aircraft.

were onerous generally and certainly at Honington. Two crew chiefs on each aircraft shared a week, 24 hours on, 24 hours off. The other ranks crew was on duty at the QRA site for five days, with another crew taking over for the weekend. Spells of duty came about one week in seven. The alarm for RS05 was a horn sounded over the Tannoy. The bell was sounded over the Tannoy for engine start or taxi, followed by plain language broadcast over the Tannoy.[480]

In the case of RAF Wittering, when this memorandum was prepared the base held only one aircraft on QRA, for 14 days at a time. Aircrew QRA was 24 hours on, 24 hours off, with two crews alternating for six days of the week (one of the crews doing the remaining day). The crews were held together in the ops block or at various locations during the day and in caravans next to the ops block at night. Transport was by crew coach, kept near to the crew at all times. The aircraft were about three-quarters of a mile distant. The road from the Mess was more "twisty" than the road from the ops block, "with two halt signs and the need to cross the main camp road (therefore difficult at peak hours)." The taxi distance was 300–400 yards to the near end of the runway (nearly two miles to the opposite end of the runway). The go-bag was always with the crew. The alert by day was by plain language over the Tannoy, to the whole station and the QRA site, with supplementary measures. By night, there was always an NCO plus one or two others on duty.[481]

Roy Brocklebank sums up the spartan provision generally made for QRA crew comfort, with no purpose-built alert facilities on main bases or dispersals:

> "Where there was nothing, caravans were provided. These could well have been of World War 2 vintage. No money was wasted on frippery. Some dispersals fared better than others. Ballykelly had better dispersal accommodation than for the resident Shackleton squadrons. We had flush toilets. At Brawdy, I think accommodation was at the opposite end of the airfield. At Pershore, we had caravans. I believe Scampton had caravans sited at ops. Coningsby and Cottesmore used the Messes. In contrast, the alert facility at Goose Bay (Labrador) for the SAC KC-135 tankers was semi-underground, had several exit tunnels and all mod cons – dormitory, messing, recreation, briefing, etc. Had proper facilities been

USAF tankers: KC-135s on alert at Goose Bay. (Andy Leitch Collection)

Plenty of space: the RAF operations room on the American side at Goose Bay. (Andy Leitch Collection)

provided at each ORP or QRA dispersal – suitably sound-proofed, of course – and crews sleeping in flying kit, RS10 could have been maintained, rather than RS15."[482]

Indeed, in an acute crisis, it should have been possible to hold *all* dispersed aircraft not on 24/7 RS05 (by means of crew rotation) at RS07 by the simple expedient of positioning suitably-equipped caravans *next to parked aircraft*. Clearly, the reality was that the quality of accommodation – and the convenience of its positioning – varied greatly across main bases and the dispersal airfields. There was an obvious contrast between RAF austerity and the scale of resources available to the USAF. Andrew Brookes suggested that this contrast between the V-Force and SAC was a matter of style:

"The differences … were largely those of national character – at a V-Force base there were no loud slogans on the gate, proclaiming 'Peace is our profession', no pistol-packing guards everywhere, few dramatic red telephones …"[483]

Yet there was more to it than that. SAC's resources were of a different order of magnitude. SAC aimed to have one-third of its aircraft on ground alert at all times. SAC ground alert began on 1 October 1957 and the arrangements included ten forward bases: four in the UK, three in Spain and three in Morocco, with six B-47 bombers held on alert at each.[484] Later, generous funding provided for continuous B-52 upgrades. In 1972, Philip Goodall wrote a report on his exchange tour with SAC. He described new generation American equipment, including an electro-optical viewing system improving penetration and allowing crews to carry out a pre-strike target assessment, with the option of changing aiming point. He went on to outline the *sixth* upgrade of the B-52's ECM outfit, under the Rivet Ace programme.[485] Given the scale of the budgets allocated to SAC, it is no surprise that crew accommodation and comfort on the USAF nuclear frontline far outstripped that available to their British counterparts.

LIVING THROUGH THE CUBAN CRISIS

Bomber Command's October 1962 report on QRA described, in effect, the minimum responses to war in place at V-bomber main bases during the time of the Cuban Crisis. How ready was Bomber Command during the most dangerous few days of the Cold War? The report, issued just ten days before the crisis came to a head, set out the results of a test of QRA force exercise alert response times over three duty periods: normal (08.30–17.30), normal off-duty (17.30–23.00 and 07.30–08.30) and sleep period (23.00–07.30). The average time from RS15 to RS05 was 4.2 minutes – normal and normal off-duty (6.6 during the sleep period; 5.1 minutes, all periods). The average time from alert to engine start was five minutes (normal duty), 5.8 minutes (normal off-duty) and 7.9 minutes over the sleep period (5.7, all periods). Times required to reach 02 (ready for take-off, wheels rolling) were 7.7, 8.8 and 8.2 (8.1, all periods). It was noted that "average reaction times are all within the alert requirements".[486]

That might be so, but without a continuous RS05 element applying to a dispersed force, the fact remains that a simultaneous-launch/low-trajectory IRBM attack (assuming the required missile numbers were available) would have destroyed most V-bombers on the ground. At this point (October 1962), Scampton and Wittering had yet to introduce SIMSTART, but the equipment was in use at Waddington, Cottesmore and Honington (the Mk 2 aircraft at Wittering and Scampton required modifications, whereas Mk 1 starting trolleys were engineered in-house). This, however, would have made no difference to outcomes, unless the Soviets were illogical enough to mount a simultaneous impact missile attack, so granting enough time for more V-bombers to get away.

That said, in late 1962 – on paper at least – Britain posed a significant nuclear threat to the Soviet Union, as described by Jim Wilson: "One only has to look at the numbers of weapons lined up on each side of the Iron Curtain in 1962 to appreciate just how significant the British strike force was."[487] The more important question, of course, was: How significant would it be *after* a Soviet pre-emptive attack? Nevertheless, the Cuban Crisis arrived "just when the command was reaching the peak of its operational efficiency…", according to Air Vice-Marshal Stewart Menaul, then Senior Air Staff Officer at Headquarters, Bomber Command.[488]

Sir Kenneth Cross, Air Officer Commanding-in-Chief (AOC-in-C) Bomber Command, brought V-bombers and Thor missiles to Alert Condition 3 on Saturday 27 October 1962. Prime Minister Harold Macmillan required all preparations for war to be "unobtrusive". Yet, Twigge and Scott refer to Air Ministry records showing that Alert Condition 3 was ordered by Bomber Command that Saturday lunchtime and remained in force until 5 November.

The Headquarters No. 1 Group operations record book shows receipt of the order from Bomber Command Operations Centre (BCOC) at 13.00 on the 27th.[489] Alert Condition 3 required the

Tight squeeze: loading Yellow Sun Mk 2 into a Victor.
(Norman Bonnor)

maximum number of aircraft to be made combat ready. At main bases, aircraft planned to operate from those bases were to be prepared for operational take-off; the rest were to be armed and prepared for take-off to dispersals (Alert Condition 2).[490] The AOC-in-C went further, as noted by Twigge and Scott:

> "On 29 October, orders were given to double the number of bombers on QRA. At most stations within Bomber Command this would have required six aircraft in total, although at RAF Waddington the number of QRA bombers was trebled by the station commander, resulting in nine fully-armed Vulcans at 15 minutes' readiness. To arm the extra aircraft on QRA, additional Yellow Sun thermonuclear weapons were transported to operational RAF bases from the Faldingworth nuclear storage site in North Lincolnshire."[491]

Preparations to disperse the V-Force were put in hand, with the Air Defence Operations Centre (ADOC) at Bentley Priory informed that Alert Condition 2 (dispersal) would be a 'flash' signal by Bomber Command Headquarters to ADOC and dispersal stations, using the authentication codeword Framework.[492]

While Stewart Menaul wrote of the V-Force's ability to deliver a crushing retaliatory blow, he disregarded the possibility of its wholesale destruction on the ground:

> "The bombers were nearer to Russia by about five hours than aircraft of SAC based in America and Thor's reaction time from the order to launch until impact on target in Russia was about 25 minutes. This represented a very impressive megatonnage (230 megatons on 230 targets, to be precise), most of which would have reached their assigned targets if orders had been given to attack. What is more important, the Russians knew it too."[493]

Some might take issue with Menaul's 230-mt figure and, certainly, his claim that most weapons would have reached their targets, given that the BMEWS had yet to enter service and considering the potentially disastrous consequences of a Soviet pre-emptive strike, magnified significantly in the absence of dispersal. Dr Les Ruskell, an authority on operational analysis, expressed scepticism:

> "… Menaul's assertion that a force which could deliver a 230-mt strike could not be dismissed seems very simplistic. The 230 mt completely ignores the reduction of this figure, possibly down to a few mt (by failure to get airborne within the warning period and attrition en route and over the target) before delivery. This would seem to be him defending the V-Force when others were doubting its continuing effectiveness. Having worked in several military headquarters as an operational analyst, I can testify to the fact that (particularly in an operational context) if a senior officer made an assertion then more junior staff would nod wisely in agreement and would be unlikely to raise a challenge."[494]

Menaul chose to ignore the key fact: that striking power is determined by strength *after* a pre-emptive strike. Yet, commenting on the outcome of the Cuban Missile Crisis 20 years afterwards, he continued in much the same vein:

"… the British contribution in terms of Thor and the V-bomber force, so close to the Russian homeland, was obviously not entirely ignored by Russia in reaching her decision to withdraw the missiles from Cuba. It will be remembered that the combined Allied bomber forces rained down more than two million tons of bombs on Germany in the six years of war 1939–45, devastating almost every major town or industrial complex from the Rhine to Berlin and from the Baltic to the Swiss border. In 1962, Bomber Command alone could have despatched the equivalent of 230 million tons in one raid, enough to destroy every major city or centre of population in the entire Soviet Union. A sobering thought."[495]

Also sobering was the likely reality of, perhaps, only a small number of surviving V-bombers crossing the North Sea with a very small fraction of 230 mt, *before* attempting to penetrate the Soviet defences. Most importantly, it seems reasonable to assume that the main Soviet operational concern over the British threat, at this time, would have been the destruction of all Thor sites before launch. This, taken alone, completely undermines the view that the Soviets would favour "simultaneous burst" – which would have given the Thors time to launch. Yet, in 1980, Menaul continued to talk about the ability to *deliver* 230 mt.

Not surprisingly, Menaul regarded Skybolt, with a British warhead, as a combination of the best elements of manned aircraft and missiles. He was dismissive towards the submarine-based deterrent and continued to ignore the bombers' exposure to destruction on the ground in the missile age. Writing over a decade after the British strategic frontline passed to Polaris, he added:

"To produce a force of submarine-launched missiles with equivalent capability to that of Bomber Command (230 mt) would have required at least 20 submarines at a cost considered beyond Britain's ability to pay in the economic climate then prevailing."

This is a disingenuous statement. Menaul should have compared the *virtually guaranteed* delivery of the attack weight of one Polaris submarine on patrol against the likely smaller delivered tonnage of the few V-Force survivors able to release their weapons (perhaps totalling around 4 mt). Almost certainly, one pre-MIRV (multiple independent re-entry vehicle) submarine – rather than 20 – would have been enough to deliver a heavier blow than a handful of surviving bombers. The SLBM warload of just one submarine would have sufficed to achieve the relatively modest British definition of minimum deterrent, as eventually adopted. Furthermore, in response to an imminent threat of war, a second Polaris submarine could have been readied to fire.

On the squadrons, crews soon noticed the departure from well-established routines as the Cuban Crisis deepened. On 50 Squadron at Waddington, AEO Martin Anscombe saw the Wing QRA aircraft double in number:

"We had six Vulcans fuelled, bombed up and ready on QRA … We ended up with four of the six QRA aircraft on the scramble bays at the end of the runway. We may have gone as far as start engines during that QRA, but we didn't taxi because recovery time taxiing back and refuelling would put the aircraft out of readiness for too long."[496]

Squadron Leader Hickmore, a 44 (Rhodesia) Squadron nav/radar, remembered RS15 aircraft at Waddington then increasing to nine: "Initially, Bomber Command reacted slowly as the

USAF increased the alert state." There was a leave embargo and crews were warned to have overnight bags at the ready:

> "One became even more aware of the density of the SAM sites guarding the approaches to Russia on the route across the Baltic. Crew relaxation involved many undemanding hands of cards, while crew room bridge had a strong following. The aircrew buffet became pivotal for all activities and the catering staff provided excellent meals for 30-plus crews, who seemed always hungry."[497]

Air Vice-Marshal Michael Robinson, a former CO of 100 Squadron (Victors), remembers Cuba as a highlight:

> "For me, as a V-Force squadron commander, a peak of the RAF's nuclear story was reached on the afternoon of Saturday 27 October 1962, when all available Victor aircraft and crews at RAF Wittering were brought to cockpit readiness 05. Each aircraft was loaded with a freefall thermonuclear weapon, the crews had their go-bags, with all the necessary route and target information and authorisation codes … Suffice to say that we remained in our cockpits for several hours before being ordered by the bomber controller to revert to readiness 15. It had been a *long* afternoon."[498]

As expected, there were difficulties preparing the three squadrons of US-armed, SACEUR-assigned Valiants at RAF Marham, as described by Twigge and Scott:

> "… it soon became evident that the USAF custodial officers could not maintain physical control of all the nuclear weapons, as they were only established with sufficient manpower to monitor the QRA compound and the nuclear weapons storage area. Therefore, at the discretion of the commanding officer USAF, control of the weapons was handed over to the base commander. The result was 24 Valiant bombers (each armed with two US nuclear weapons) under the effective operational control of Bomber Command."[499]

HUMAN CONSIDERATIONS

There were also human considerations under a real threat of war. Dick Fuller was a 49 Squadron Valiant co-pilot at Marham. He and his wife went shopping in King's Lynn; on returning they found all aircrew confined to base:

> "Looking back, it seems odd that we were not dispersed. I had told my wife she had to leave the base and drive to her parents, taking our six-month-old daughter. She refused to take me seriously at first, but I told her Marham was certainly a target for Soviet nuclear weapons. Then the PA sounded for the return to 15-minute QRA. That had been a very long 45 minutes! That night Marham's Mess was packed with people having more than one drink. Later, I talked to crews who had been on QRA when it looked like we were going to war. They had been shocked rigid."[500]

Vulcan AEO Peter West was at RAF Coningsby with 12 Squadron when Cuba flared:

"Even when loaded with a live weapon and ready to take off, nobody believed we would actually have to do it. However, I did have a few nightmares afterwards. I was in the aircraft, taking off. There were weapons going off around me. I suppose it was something that just had to be sweated out of me. At that point, we had a family of three very young children, aged five, three and one."[501]

Many constituted crews were very close, rather as a family. They drew together in the wake of Cuba, as recalled by Peter West:

"I don't remember meaningful discussions about the deterrent or the morality of nuclear weapons. Yet, at the same time, I remember our discussion in the crew room after Cuba. We sat down and, over coffee, chatted about how we had reacted to the crisis. We had watched it build on TV. It hadn't been a huge surprise when the doorbell went on that Friday. The RAF policeman standing there told me to get my kit and go to operations as soon as possible. I said to Mary: 'If you hear us take off, it means we are going.' We had never talked about it before. I told her – if she heard us go – to get the kids in the car and drive. Don't pack anything beyond essentials. I told her to make for Skye. When I returned home I felt a bloody fool. How far would she have got before being obliterated?"

In the cockpit, West's crew heard their instructions come over in plain language: "I think we wanted the Russians to hear that we were at readiness 05."

RAF Cottesmore went to a state of high alert during the crisis, with crews manning QRA in their flying kit. Bomb bays were loaded with megaton weapons. Dave Beane was an AEO on 10 Squadron:

"In the language of the day, we were 'hot to trot'. It felt like – and was – a hair-trigger situation. The prevailing view was that we had been trained to go and, if we had to, we would do it and do it well."[502]

In the bomb bay was Yellow Sun Mk 2, the "bucket of sunshine".

Norman Bonnor was also at Cottesmore during the Cuban Crisis. A Victor nav/radar with XV Squadron, he watched the QRA build-up:

View from the cockpit: the ORP at Cottesmore. (Andy Leitch Collection)

"On Saturday 20 October 1962 the Cottesmore aircrew and ground crew were told not to leave the base or the local area. Blue Danube was my first nuclear weapon but, by the time Cuba flared up, we were carrying Yellow Sun Mk 1 (and) in the process of converting to Yellow Sun Mk 2, a true hydrogen bomb with a yield of around 1.1 mt. There were not enough of the new Yellow Sun weapons available at Cottesmore and the decision was taken to load some aircraft with Red Beard, a tactical weapon with a much lower yield. One or two of the seven aircraft XV Squadron generated during the Cuban Crisis week had a Red Beard weapon rather than Yellow Sun loaded.

"We all ended up at cockpit readiness on the final Saturday 27 October. We now had nearly 20 aircraft bombed up and ready to go at Cottesmore. I'm sure we would never have been able to get them all off in time … We held on to the thought that the Soviets would never attack. The West's retaliation would be enough to send them back to the Stone Age. Everything was readied – even the Coastal Command Shackletons were bombed up to attack Soviet shipping around the North Cape. Looking back what is interesting, in retrospect, is that no-one flew that week! The crisis began to unfold on 16 October and my logbook shows that I didn't fly again until 7 November. When the crisis receded, the relief was immense. There was a bit of a party at Cottesmore."[503]

Views differ about flying during the crisis period. Some recall that flying training continued for those yet to become operational. Equally, others have different recollections. Roy Brocklebank notes:

"I was at No. 2 Air Navigation School at the time. I flew a training detail on 19 October. Previous trips were on the 3rd, 8th, 12th, and 18th. This would suggest a trip due on 24/25 October but my next trip was on the 29th – that is, the Monday after."[504]

WHO GIVES THE ORDER?

A Chief of the Air Staff (CAS) meeting on 15 January 1964 considered Bomber Command responses to BMEWS alarm levels. There was much discussion over the delegation of powers to authorise a war scramble; the Bomber Command AOC-in-C was asked to report on a range of issues concerning a war scramble.[505] This meeting was referred to in a letter from the Vice-Chief of the Air Staff (VCAS) to the Assistant Chief of the Air Staff, Operations a month later (17 February 1964). The VCAS' office wrote: "An officer of air vice-marshal rank is now available at all times to speak to the Bomber Command Operations Centre …"[506] The January 1964 meeting arose from a minute from the VCAS of 24 December 1963, on war scramble arrangements. The background was the intelligence estimate of a very low likelihood of a surprise attack and ministerial reluctance to entertain "very hair-trigger" arrangements despite the fact that scrambled aircraft would be under positive control.[507] The 24 December minute from the VCAS to the CAS noted:

"The BMEWS site at Fylingdales will become fully operational during the first quarter of 1964 and I have been considering whether any special measures are needed to ensure that our present arrangements for releasing the deterrent against a 'bolt from the blue' attack are compatible with the reduced warning time which will be provided by Fylingdales.

"In brief, the problem is that Bomber Command constantly maintain a proportion of the MBF, at present 13 aircraft, at 15 minutes' readiness. This QRA force can be airborne in about six to seven minutes from the order to scramble. The minimum warning time (i.e. the time between generation of an alarm level and the time of first impact) from Fylingdales of a Soviet attack is estimated to be between seven and 9½ minutes depending on the range and trajectory of the missiles. Thus, if the QRA force is to react to a 'bolt from the blue' attack, it is necessary that they be given the order to scramble with the minimum of delay. This timing precludes any reference to outside authorities.

"Prior to the installation of BMEWS … the decision to scramble the QRA force against a 'bolt from the blue attack' was related to the reaction of SAC, which, in turn, was based on information provided by the BMEWS sites in the USA. At this time, Bomber Command's procedures were as follows:

a. On receipt of an Alarm Level 3, the duty controller (wing commander/squadron leader) at BCOC brought the QRA force to cockpit readiness.* He also informed the C-in-C or SASO (senior air staff officer), if available, and the duty group captain (operations), who is available throughout the tour of duty at 15 minutes standby.
b. Assuming that the C-in-C or SASO could not be contacted or that they were not able to reach the BCOC by the time the alarm level changed to either 2 or 1, the duty group captain scrambled the force under positive control."[508]

This meant that the QRA force could be launched, in certain circumstances, by a group captain, without reference to higher authority. The American system was very different:

"The decision to scramble the SAC equivalent of our QRA force is never delegated below two-star level, whereas our procedures permit this to be done, in certain circumstances, by a group captain. Such action would be justified if it could be guaranteed that BMEWS will never transmit false alarms and, therefore, the force would only be scrambled against a real attack. It is not possible to give any such guarantee. In addition, it is questionable whether the prime minister intended that the dispensation … should be delegated below senior air rank."

Clearly, one worry was the risk of flying with live weapons, a complete departure from past practice, together with the political and public storm which would certainly surround a false alarm scramble of armed aircraft. Here, the December 1963 VCAS minute commented:

"I think we must anticipate that Fylingdales may generate false alarms and that the QRA force will be scrambled in response. The question is, therefore, whether a group captain should be permitted to authorise such reaction. Although the force would be under positive control and would return to base, unless the AOC-in-C was given political authority to release nuclear warfare, there is always the possibility of an accident. Thus the decision to scramble is of considerable consequence, especially as

---

* This is RS05, rather than the RS02 (start engines) required ON RECEIPT OF ANY US OR UK ALARM LEVEL, according to Bomber Command Operational Research Branch Memorandum No. 285 – what appears to be an error in the VCAS letter to the CAS, 24 December 1963 [i.e. (a) should read: … QRA force to 'RS02', rather than 'cockpit readiness'].

press and Parliament would inevitably learn that the QRA force had been launched on a false alarm. I am sure we would be open to criticism if it then became known that the authority to scramble was given by a relatively junior officer. I consider, therefore, until Fylingdales has been proved beyond reasonable doubt, that the C-in-C Bomber Command should not delegate his authority to scramble the QRA force to officers of less than air rank. This arrangement would be more in keeping with that used by SAC and, in the event of the force being scrambled on a false alarm, it would reduce the risk of political criticism …"

A year passed and this proposal, requiring delegation to no lower rank than air vice-marshal, proved challenging. On May 20 1965 CAS reviewed delegation with the VCAS and the AOC-in-C Bomber Command. A post-meeting note stated:

"The AOC-in-C explained that the arrangement had not proved easy to operate in practice; more important, however, experience showed that the action which had to be taken in the 'bolt from the blue' situation in question was such that no real exercise of judgement was required – successive steps were virtually automatic and admitted of no alternative choice once it had been checked that the information from Fylingdales was genuine and not purely for exercise purposes."

In these circumstances, he believed that continuance of the arrangement in its present form was not justified and that the operational need could be fully met by the duty group captain scheme. CAS accepted this view.[509]

In summary, the missile threat to the MBF could have been countered, to some degree, by airborne alert and/or dispersal to remote bases overseas, in a time of grave emergency, *had Bomber Command been equipped and resourced accordingly*. These options, however, were not available. The challenge, therefore, was to optimise UK ground alert, the sole option available to the MBF.

The key was to make the best possible use of very short warning and reaction times, given the threat from low-trajectory IRBMs. The new Fylingdales BMEWS would offer only around four minutes' warning of a simultaneous launch attack, yet V-Force QRA and main force dispersal and regeneration exercises were based on Readiness State 15 minutes. As has been argued earlier, the latter assumed a Soviet staggered launch for simultaneous burst in Europe and the US (giving the UK the longer "American warning"). No evidence was found, however, explaining why the Soviets would forego the clear advantage of a simultaneous launch attack, with low-trajectory IRBMs, giving a short warning of four minutes or less.

This suggests that only V-bombers held 24/7 at RS05 and poised for RS02 had any real chance of survival, but RS05 could not be maintained for more than a few hours without crew rotation. It follows that the only viable ground alert posture under imminent threat of war would involve holding part of the main force dispersed and at RS05 by crew rotation. This was recognised in 1961. The Cuban Crisis, however, exposed a fundamental weakness of ground alert. Would the political will exist to order dispersal? In October 1962, the V-bombers stayed on their main bases to avoid "provocation" – where they would almost certainly have been destroyed, had war come.

13
REDUCING EXPOSURE ON THE GROUND

> *It should be obvious that what counts in basic deterrence is not so much the size and efficiency of one's striking force before it is hit as the size and condition to which the enemy thinks he can reduce it by a surprise attack – as well as his confidence in the correctness of his predictions.*
>
> Bernard Bradie, "Strategy in the missile age", RAND, 1959

SEEKING A SOLUTION: AIRBORNE ALERT

Many measures were taken to reduce V-Force vulnerability on the ground, but nothing could change the realities of geography and missile flight time. Planners fully appreciated the significance of a key observation from Bernard Bradie: deterrence "dictates primary concern with the survival of a retaliatory force of sufficient size following enemy attack".[510]

This means survival of sufficient capacity to inflict damage at a level judged to be unacceptable to the enemy. In short, this requires maximised delivery of the destructive potential of this post-strike core retaliatory threat – a threat remaining at such a scale as to deter nuclear aggression. Against this background, UK-based ground alert's obvious limitations propelled a search for alternatives. One model already existed: the Strategic Air Command guaranteed minimum response through airborne alert: the maintenance of a proportion of the bomber force in the air, on standing patrol and ready to fly war sorties if so ordered.

Airborne alert, an obvious solution to vulnerability on the ground, was examined repeatedly by British planners. Each evaluation, however, demonstrated lack of viability for the V-Force. Nevertheless, the idea resurfaced repeatedly, reflecting its superficial attraction. Yet, the impossibility of operating V-Force airborne alert was exposed as early as mid-1959. Be that as it may, it was hard to accept that ground alert/QRA was the best available option. Many senior military and political figures refused to accept that reality and, consequently, airborne alert was revisited at a Defence Board meeting in April 1960. In subsequent years, it continued to be resurrected, even as late as the early 1970s, when it was included in rather far-fetched proposals for an air-delivered system to succeed Polaris.

Twelve years earlier, the problems of airborne alert had been spelt out in a Bomber Command operational research report (Memorandum No. 197, July 1959) examining its potential operation during an emergency. This memorandum opened bluntly:

> "As the threat to bomber bases from ballistic missiles increases, straightforward dispersal of the force becomes less effective as a means of ensuring its survival and alternative means must be considered. One such method is to keep a proportion of the force airborne."

This would have been very costly and would have required acceptance of risks associated with the routine carriage of live nuclear weapons over British soil. Significantly, the study found that the normal rate of MBF flying was the equivalent of only one aircraft from every three squadrons continuously in the air (about 4% of strength).[511]

This document confined itself to "practical possibilities" – an airborne readiness system operating for short periods only, in an emergency. It assumed that:

- The force available to provide airborne alert would comprise ten squadrons of bombers and two of tankers, on main bases.
- At any time, 75% of aircraft (bombers and tankers) are available for first-line flying (i.e. 60 bombers and 12 tankers). It was also assumed (rather generously) that 90% of crews were available for operational flying.

The Operational Research memorandum then described the difficulties:

"If bombers were operated in this way, it would be possible to preserve a proportion of the force in the event of an attack on bases, but very few of the aircraft airborne at any time would be operationally effective. The majority would have to land and refuel before setting off on an operational sortie and the problems of recovery and refuelling in the operational environment assumed would be enormous."

In short, most of a small group of bombers airborne at the time of the missile strike would be in no position to proceed with a retaliatory attack. The report outlined other concerns:

"… in practice aircrew fatigue is in any case likely to preclude operation for any length of time at optimum levels … It seems, therefore, that between ten and 15 bombers continuously airborne is the best that can be expected under the conditions of operation assumed. For short periods of time the number could be increased to about 20 by overworking aircrew and accepting abnormal landing risks."

For aircraft airborne and held in a specified area until the 'Go' order, the amount of waiting time available to give that order was very small – less than half an hour – if the bombers were to retain sufficient fuel to complete their war sorties. A theoretical exercise exposed the problems of fuel consumption and range. If the entire available force – 60 bombers and 12 tankers – scrambled simultaneously and were held at a point some 200 miles from base on the way to targets … after an hour's delay about 40 bombers could be given sufficient fuel to continue their sorties, or about 20 after two hours. The memorandum concluded:

Thirsty work: refuelling during Operation Black Buck. (John Reeve)

> "The best operational procedure would be to arrange for a proportion of the force to return to base at intervals, so maintaining a proportion airborne, ready to go, and at the same time ensuring the minimum delay in refuelling the recalled aircraft in preparation for further standby on the ground. In this way, the danger of complete defeat by a spoof attack or false alarm would be reduced."

SAC had the big numbers – aircraft and crews – to make airborne alert work, but this was far beyond Bomber Command's resources:

> "… the concept of airborne readiness is of limited application in Bomber Command … There is, however, a case for demonstrating a capability in this direction, since a bomber airborne in an unknown position over friendly territory is less vulnerable to missile attack than any offensive weapon yet in service and as such constitutes a powerful deterrent."

Airborne alert, as a concept, was readily understood and had immediate resonance. It was the subject of a Commons Question on 19 April 1961. Julian Critchley MP asked the Secretary of State for Air what it would cost to maintain ten per cent of the V-Force on standing airborne alert. Julian Amery offered a creative reply:

> "Because of its capacity for quick reaction to warning of attack, the V-bomber force provides an effective deterrent without recourse to air alert. To maintain a standing air alert with ten per cent of the force would involve not only an increase in flying maintenance costs but also substantial changes in the present organisation of Bomber Command. I am not in a position to say precisely what the cost would be."[512]

That said, the planners quietly went on considering methods which might produce some form of airborne alert in the Skybolt era.

In March 1962 – with Skybolt still in prospect – Bomber Command circulated the findings of a report on aircraft utilisation during continuous airborne alert. This involved both freefall bombers and Blue Steel carriers. Chief research officer Tom Kerr, in his introduction, said that researchers had examined the number of sorties per 24 hours, and hours per month, on Vulcan Mk 2 aircraft required to keep one aircraft airborne when carrying freefall, Blue Steel and Skybolt weapons. The patrol area was a corridor off the Norwegian and Danish coasts. He then summarised Bomber Command's extremely limited airborne alert capability:

> "The number of aircraft which can be kept airborne depends upon the conditions assumed and the aircraft utilisation. Assuming an aircraft carrying Blue Steel, with overload fuel and landing at an alternative base, combined with the present utilisation, one aircraft requires 3.8 squadrons to support it. If the utilisation is doubled, then the number of aircraft on patrol can be doubled. Refuelling in the air does decrease the Vulcan utilisation required, but to save 100 Vulcan hours, 200 Valiant tanker hours are required."[513]

Clearly, airborne alert offered no solution to the threat of V-Force destruction on the ground – the unfavourable mathematics proved inescapable. Nevertheless, the recommendation that it should be practised in future exercises, including the use of tankers to provide insurance against unforeseen delays in the Go order, was supported by the Defence Board. It saw deterrent value in projecting some level of airborne alert capability to the Soviets. One related exercise, the first of its kind, was Trial No. 441, involving Waddington's Vulcan Mk 1/1A aircraft (drawn from 44 [Rhodesia] and 50 Squadrons) during March 1962. An operational research branch memorandum reporting on this trial noted that it was designed to keep one aircraft out of six airborne continuously for 14 days. The study concentrated on aircraft servicing aspects. The main objective was achieved: it was feasible to maintain this capability for a limited period, but this had little relevance to a retaliatory strike.[514]

The fundamental problem – the threat of wholesale destruction on the ground – continued to hover over the airfields. Unpalatable truths had been confronted in a Bomber Command report of November 1961 examining MBF vulnerability to missile attack. The chance of escaping low-trajectory missiles was small and the only valid posture, according to this report, was some form of airborne alert. A circular and persistent line of argument had developed around a solution which might seem obvious but which remained out of reach, at least in the British context.[515]

What drove this constant re-examination, given the negative results from past studies? Part of the answer involves Julian Amery, Secretary of State for Air. In April 1961 he may have answered a Commons Question by dismissing the need for airborne alert, but his true view was the polar opposite. During a meeting with the Chief of the Air Staff and others on 19 February 1962 – to discuss a future replacement for Skybolt by 1975 – Amery pressed hard for airborne alert, choosing to ignore its known futility in the British context. In a note summarising this discussion, Amery confronted the possibility of an attack on the UK with multi-megaton weapons:

> "It would seem reasonable to assume that the Soviets could deliver such an attack from manned aircraft or ballistic missiles, if not at once at any rate in the next year or so. This means that the Soviets will be able, for a much smaller effort than hitherto, to launch an attack which would make our ground alert posture ineffective. This danger has already existed for some time in theory, i.e. if the Russians were prepared to drop several hundred 1-mt bombs on us at one time. It would now become much simpler for them to do so in practice."[516]

Amery continued in a way that suggests he had no real understanding of the issues surrounding airborne alert:

> "If these assumptions are true, then we must be prepared to go over to an airborne alert posture from, say, next year onwards in the event of an emergency. We can, I think, afford to discount the possibility of a Soviet bolt from the blue on the United Kingdom, at any rate in the foreseeable future. But readiness to go to airborne alert in an emergency means, presumably, a level of training amounting to random air alert from now on."

Senior ministers appeared willing to express an honest view of the weakness of ground alert, but only when arguing for their favoured remedies. In any event, their views were rapidly overtaken by events: Skybolt's cancellation, adoption of the submarine-based deterrent and fresh studies further revealing the insurmountable problems surrounding V-Force airborne alert. The capability gap created between Skybolt's cancellation and the arrival of Polaris would be bridged by stopgap measures, a switch to low-level nuclear strike and new initiatives to help at least some bombers escape destruction on the ground: enhanced QRA, dispersal and faster response through initiatives such as simultaneous engine start.

It should have been obvious, from even a cursory glance at V-bomber aircraft, that airborne alert was a non-starter. V-bombers, in contrast to B-52s, had no accommodation for extra combat crew and had relatively poor endurance without intensive tanker support. This is why commercial aircraft – designed and built for high utilisation – were considered as potential Skybolt carriers. One such proposal was for a force of 36 VC10s, each carrying four Skybolts.[517] In the long run, however, all plans for an airborne alert force, capable of delivering the UK's minimum retaliatory attack in response to a pre-emptive strike, came to nothing. The V-Force, on ground alert, would muddle through until Polaris arrived.

NO SOLUTION IN OVERSEAS DISPERSAL

There was another alternative to UK ground alert: dispersal to remote bases overseas. In October 1959 (at a time when a long-range air-to-surface missile was still expected to arm the V-Force), Bomber Command produced a study of target coverage from overseas bases:

> "The main objective of overseas dispersal is to diversify the target system which the Russians must consider by removing a proportion of the deterrent force out of the UK and, at the same time, ensuring that the overseas bases are outside the range of IRBMs. In this way the attraction of a surprise attack on the UK is very much reduced. Overseas bases in Bermuda, Canada, Africa, the Far East and even Australia might be considered, using a combination of staging, flight refuelling and final launching of a long-range guided missile to reach Russian targets. The value of such a deterrent threat would not be diminished because it cannot supply instant retaliation – in fact, since we expect to be attacked first, the primary problem is survival and, provided that this is achieved, retaliation can be sure and at a time dictated by our own requirements."[518]

This study looked at the weapon system in immediate prospect: a Blue Steel-armed Vulcan Mk 2. Assuming fuel in bomb-bay tanks and normal fuel reserves on landing, range was calculated at 3,300NM (slightly more for freefall aircraft carrying more fuel). Vulcan captain Peter Moore makes an interesting point regarding extra fuel provision: "We nearly always flew with bomb-bay tanks – usually saddles. Two drums provided an extra 16,000 lbs of fuel but, because of the weight penalty, the actual gain was only a proportion of this figure."[519]

Range could be increased by using fuel reserves normally allowed for landing. Here, the October 1959 Bomber Command study noted that this would require the crew to bale out over the terminal base:

> "Flight refuelling, using Valiant tankers stationed with the bombers, is another effective method of increasing target coverage, so that there are four main possibilities – a normal landing or a bale out over the terminal base, both with or without flight refuelling. If a second strike is not required, the bombers can land or the crew can bale out over any convenient base in friendly territory … The closer this base is to Russian territory, the greater will be the target coverage available …"[520]

The study examined target coverage available from various overseas bases, using a list of 120 targets, and concluded:

> "… a significant number of targets can be reached from the vicinity of Nairobi by a Vulcan Mk 2 carrying Blue Steel if the crew bale out over Cyprus. Small increases in cover are possible if alternative terminal bases closer to Russia are used … but flight refuelling is required to provide target cover from all the bases considered."

For Vulcan Mk 2s with Blue Steel Mk 1 (around 150NM maximum range at high altitude), they could reach 13 Russian targets from Nairobi and land back in Cyprus, or 45 targets if baling out over Cyprus. These figures increased to 89 and 109 targets respectively, if refuelled. From the Maldives, Blue Steel Vulcans could reach nine targets unrefuelled, but only by baling out over Cyprus on recovery. The position improved dramatically with refuelling, reaching 50 targets with a landing in Cyprus or 99 if bale out was accepted. Salisbury-dispersed Blue Steel Vulcans could reach 34 targets and make a recovery landing, or 54 if bale out was accepted – but only with refuelling in both cases. Refuelling would also be required for bombers if operating from Singapore, allowing only one target to be reached with a recovery landing, but 38 within reach with bale out over Cyprus. Refuelled Vulcans from Ottawa could attack 13 targets and return to land in the UK (49, if bale out was accepted). Aircraft dispersed to Prince Edward Island could reach four targets without refuelling (bale out required); with refuelling they could reach 28 and land back in the UK, or 79 with the bale-out option. Bermuda was a poor option. Even with refuelling, the Vulcans could reach only four targets and land back in the UK (16 if the crews baled out).

Blue Steel Mk 2 (a range of 600NM plus) would have transformed matters, with much enhanced target coverage – especially in the refuelled/bale-out modes. Nairobi was the most advantageous remote overseas location, given a 600NM stand-off weapon and with no refuelling – putting 60 targets within reach with a Cyprus recovery (99, bale out). Not surprisingly, the 1959 study stressed the importance of developing even longer-range weapons: "A range of about 800NM allows most targets in Western Russia to be attacked from outside the defences but 1,200NM would be required to provide complete tactical freedom in choice of the launch point." On the vulnerability of overseas bases, the memorandum commented:

> "The use of overseas bases would increase the deterrent value of the bomber force only if the bombers based there were more difficult to destroy on the ground than those based in the UK. It would be possible to attack the overseas bases considered by means of long-range bombers, or inter-continental ballistic missiles based in Russia, but the operation would be a difficult one (ranges are in excess of 3,000NM) and coordination of such attacks with other vital offensive operations would be a serious problem. A local warning system, in conjunction with adequate communications with the UK, should ensure that bombers based overseas could be scrambled before being attacked by manned bombers."

This memorandum warned against "penny packet" deployments:

"… a sufficient number of bombers must be stationed overseas to provide a serious threat to Russia. If only a token force were deployed, the threat might be assessed as within tolerable limits and the deterrent value … would then be negligible."

At the same time, this report also pointed out that deterioration in accuracy (at that time) over a longer range would mean that a 90% assurance of destruction of a remote base would require many more missiles … (from four 1-mt weapons against a UK base to perhaps 15 or 16 for an overseas base).

This study of overseas dispersal concluded that un-refuelled Blue Steel V-bombers would pose a significant threat only from Nairobi … "and then only if drastic methods of stretching the effective range of the bombers are employed". If Valiant tankers were also deployed, a significant threat from Blue Steel Mk 1 could be projected from Nairobi, the Maldives, Salisbury or Canada, "while some targets can be reached from bases in Bermuda or Singapore".

Given the availability of a 600NM range Blue Steel Mk 2, "flight-refuelled bombers from all the bases considered could provide sufficient cover to constitute a severe deterrent threat to Russia. A weapon having a range of 1,200NM would increase tactical freedom and permit all launchings to be made from outside the Russian defence zone." So, in essence, the absence of a long-range ASM and a larger tanker force ruled out dispersal overseas as a viable option (with the limited exception of Cyprus, where two squadrons (16 aircraft) were deployed, post-Polaris handover, to threaten targets in Southern Russia).

Despite its sober findings, this memorandum recommended further study of dispersal overseas. Ultimately, however, an expanding Soviet missile force and enhanced long-range accuracy eroded any potential advantage associated with the overseas option: aircraft were just as likely to be destroyed on foreign dispersals as they were on UK dispersals.

UK GROUND ALERT: THE ONLY OPTION

Ballistic missiles changed everything, as outlined by Stephen Twigge and Len Scott:

"In 1949, Britain planned on a warning period of three to four months before going to war. By 1960, this had been reduced to 15 minutes. To meet these new conditions, British deterrent policy was re-examined. The outcome was twofold: first, active air defence was effectively abandoned and increased emphasis was placed on early warning and strategic intelligence. Second, in the event of a unilateral British nuclear response, Bomber Command was directed to attack Soviet cities. To implement this strategy and maintain the credibility of the deterrent, further measures were introduced. These included a rapid reaction capability, centralisation of operational control, an unambiguous chain of command, improved communications and the introduction of positive control."[521]

Was this enough? In the absence of airborne alert, the priority was to avoid almost complete annihilation on the ground. The 1960s RAF did its best. With extremely limited means, it sought to preserve the capability and credibility of the V-Force, despite the growing missile threat and the extraordinarily heavy spend on Soviet air defence. Roger Dunsford points to the fact that both sides could not rule out the possibility – albeit remote – that they might fall victim to a first strike:

"… demonstrating that the V-Force was capable of penetrating Soviet defences *in the absence of a prior missile strike by the USSR* remained a critical tool of deterrence throughout the 1970s and (arguably) the early 80s. My experience of Red Flag – successfully penetrating realistic Soviet defences at very low level, at night – in 1979 speaks to exactly that. This aspect of deterrence – forcing the other side into BOTH a defensive and offensive arms race – proved crucial … Many have argued, and I find it very hard to disagree, that it was this massive military expenditure that contributed greatly to their economic woes and, ultimately, to the collapse of the Soviet Union."[522]

Time pressures shaped V-Force ability to generate weapon systems, scramble and fly a war sortie. Bomber Command alert and readiness (BCAR) procedures evolved in response to the growing missile threat. With effect from 1 July 1961, six months *before* the introduction of RS15 QRA across the entire MBF, BCAR was amended. This change replaced precautionary alert, alert alpha and alert bravo with five alert conditions. *There was a new Alert Condition 1, under which 25% of the force could be held at continuous cockpit readiness (RS05)*. Readiness States blue, red and black were substituted with Readiness States 40, 15 and 5 minutes respectively, with the introduction of Readiness State 02 (taxi to take-off position and stand by). Alert Condition 1 recognised the threat of overwhelming destruction on the ground unless a proportion of aircraft could be maintained at 24/7 cockpit readiness RS05 for extended periods during a grave crisis. The five alert conditions˙ were:

5. Normal peacetime conditions.
4. Precautionary alert.
3. Aircraft generation.
2. Aircraft dispersal.
1. 'Partial' 24/7 cockpit readiness (25% of the force at continuous RS05, by means of crew rotation, to be ordered by the Air Officer Commanding-in-Chief [AOC-in-C] in the face of 'imminent risk' of attack).

The 25% proportion consisted of those aircraft covering flight alert targets (priority targets). Squadron and flight commanders were required to ensure continuous coverage of flight alert targets whilst Alert Condition 1 applied. This was done by rotating crews/aircraft. Remaining aircraft, with single crews, were required to adopt the highest state of readiness compatible with adequate crew rest periods, "in order to maintain maximum possible cover on remaining targets. If the number of aircraft and crews available allow more than one crew to be at five minutes' readiness, priority is to be given to holding this state during the four hours before dawn."[523]

Alert Condition 1 (25% at continuous cockpit readiness) was not practised en masse following dispersal. This would have involved prolonged dislocation under exercise conditions (i.e. in the absence of imminent risk of war). However, at least one flight of dispersed V-bombers, on one occasion, did operate an extended QRA at an 'away' airfield, simulating, to some extent, a prolonged war alert.

˙   See Chapter Note 523 and AIR 2/17801 minute from Air Commodore G.R. Magill, D.Ops (Bomber & Reconnaissance) to ACAS (Ops), 12 July 1961.

As for the Soviet missile threat, Waddington Wing Targeting Officer Roy Brocklebank comments:

> "These IRBMs were liquid-fuelled and, like Thor, took time to prepare. They could not sit on the ground for long at readiness. I was told we knew where each was targeted, though how, I didn't know. The IRBMs were deployed in the Baltic States."[524]

Communications intelligence (COMINT) was a valuable tool for warning. Brocklebank made the point that any change in communications policy, such as frequency, code or transmission, could be a warning indicator, yet both NATO and the USSR did not fully come to grips with this issue until a later period.

By 1961, the looming missile threat had prompted Bomber Command's then AOC-in-C, Air Marshal Sir Kenneth Cross, to plan for extending the RS15 QRA system, as already applied to SACEUR-assigned Valiants, to the Thors and the entire MBF, as from 1 January 1962. Furthermore, he had plans to double the initial size of the MBF QRA force. On 7 December 1961 the Air Council had approved the general thrust of his permanent alert plans, but reserved its position on the proposed subsequent increase, from one to two QRA aircraft per squadron by late 1962. Meanwhile, the SACEUR Valiant QRA force at Marham was increased from three to four aircraft and the RAF Germany SACEUR Canberra QRA doubled, from four to eight aircraft (see page 155). However, the AOC-in-C's principal hope, for a much larger V-bomber main force QRA – to compensate, to some degree, for the imminent loss of Thor – came to nothing.[525] The new Alert Condition 1, however, gave him what he wanted in a close approach to war, given political approval.

ADOPTING THE FIGHTER SPIRIT

It took time for those in charge to appreciate fully the value of every second of warning in the missile age, as underlined by an incident described by Andrew Brookes:

> "In 1958, the Vice-Chief of the Air Staff, Air Marshal Sir Edmund Hudleston, commenting on the efficiency of Bomber Command at a Pathfinder Association dinner, revealed with pride that, in a recent surprise alert, the time from bunks to getting airborne in a V-bomber at night had been 11 minutes."[526]

Clearly, things had to change. On 24 January 1961 AOC-in-C Bomber Command's office sent a letter to the Under-Secretary of State (Director of Operations, Bomber and Reconnaissance), Air Ministry, explaining that Headquarters, High Wycombe, had been studying the growing threat from Soviet missiles and the accompanying "drastic decrease in tactical warning time". It commented:

> "Against missiles, the present plan for holding the force at 40 minutes' readiness until the first tactical warning is received is inadequate and it is essential to be able to hold as much of the force as possible at cockpit readiness."[527]

This put the focus on the new ground alert posture, which would be achievable in a national emergency and would soon be introduced in the BCAR, although never rehearsed on a large scale.

The move to an alert condition requiring cockpit readiness (continuous manning) for some bombers was very significant. By the summer of 1961 this was enshrined in the new Alert Condition 1 – the ultimate expression of ground alert. The letter continues:

> "It should be possible to hold about one-third of available aircraft at cockpit readiness (RS05) for about seven days. It should also be possible to hold serviceable Thors, with gyros running, for a similar length of time and, with fully modified missiles, this would allow a launch within ten minutes of the order. These plans will not affect the ability to hold all the bombers at cockpit readiness and the Thors fully fuelled for a matter of hours, should the situation so demand."

The pace of change accelerated. Several senior V-Force posts went to officers with fighter backgrounds, so as to instil Fighter Command's tradition of quick reaction. Indeed, this had begun to take root some years before. During a defence committee meeting on 31 December 1957, Duncan Sandys had been explicit. He said the "real defence" of the V-Force "lay in increasing the state of readiness of the bombers, so that they could take off before they could be destroyed on the ground".[528]

Officers with distinguished fighter careers now filling senior Bomber Command posts included Air Marshal Sir Harry Broadhurst, with an illustrious World War 2 fighter record. He became AOC-in-C Bomber Command in January 1956 and played a significant role in steering change. Air Vice-Marshal Kenneth 'Bing' Cross, with an air defence background, was given No. 3 Group (1956) and went on to become the next AOC-in-C (1959). RAF Cottesmore, the first Victor base, was commanded by J. E. 'Johnnie' Johnson, the top-scoring Western Allied fighter pilot flying against the Luftwaffe in World War 2. Yet, the fighter community held no monopoly – in October 1956 No. 1 Group and its Vulcans went to a noted World War 2 bomber commander, Air Vice-Marshal Augustus 'Gus' Walker (later, Air Marshal and Inspector General of the Royal Air Force).

The V-Force personality began to change. As Minister of Defence, Duncan Sandys pushed hard for that change. At a 21 July 1958 meeting – with Secretary of State for Air George Ward amongst those present – Sandys approved proposals "to enable the bomber force to come to readiness at weekends and holidays no less rapidly than during the week". It was also agreed to "make it possible to bring the force to 15 minutes' readiness for a week in an emergency". In addition, six more dispersal airfields were added to the list of 24 already agreed. This meant that only four (rather than eight) aircraft would be left on each main base after dispersal. Furthermore, George Ward was invited to "report on what could be done to keep part of the force at 15 minutes' readiness for longer than one week in an emergency".[529]

In the early summer of 1959 the Minister of Defence visited RAF Cottesmore. During this visit he asked for a report on MBF readiness. This was prepared by the AOC-in-C Bomber Command and circulated on 1 July. Its summary claimed:

> "Considerable progress has been made during the past year in increasing the retaliatory power at Bomber Command. A coordinated Bomber Command/SAC strike plan has been worked out in detail and is now effective; crews are briefed and trained on their pre-assigned targets for both unilateral and coordinated plans. Eleven more dispersal

airfields have become available for use and equipment is being pre-stocked on them. Most aircraft have been modified and equipped to carry two new types of British weapons and US weapons; there is now a weapon for every operational aircraft.* The force as a whole had been exercised in dispersal and readiness, including weapon preparation. These exercises have shown our plans to be feasible and have enabled detailed improvements to be made."[530]

The new decade, however, opened with doubts about the value of investing in faster take-off times for the V-Force, given the scale of the missile threat and the prospect of exposure to strikes from Soviet submarines positioned off the UK west coast. In July 1961, Air Chief Marshal Sir Thomas Pike wrote to the First Sea Lord, Admiral Sir Caspar John, asking for his support for V-bomber modifications for, inter alia, more rapid take-off:

"I would not dissent from the view expressed by the Joint Intelligence Committee (JIC) that by 1964 missiles fired from submarines could do so from sectors not covered by Fylingdales … whether or not the Russians would use missile-firing submarines against the UK seems to me more problematical, particularly at a time when they do not have parity of weapons with the USA. The submarine gives them the only means of striking the USA without giving some 20 minutes of warning time. Indeed, in the light of the JIC's own assessment of the probable progress of the Russian submarine building programme (35 missile-firing submarines by 1964), I believe we must expect any attack on the UK to come mainly, if not solely, from aircraft and land-based missiles. I am certain that we cannot afford to disregard either the land-based missile or the manned aircraft threat. To counter the first of them, the V-bomber modification programme is of the first importance."[531]

Pike ended on an optimistic note: "Even taking a hypothetical submarine threat into account, the chances of a successful first shot attack on the bomber force, once alerted and dispersed, will always be doubtful."

DISPERSE TO SURVIVE

There was, however, much more at stake than aircraft modifications. There were also concerns over the recently-approved V-Force dispersal plan. In the background was a rather defeatist (and incomplete) argument over the missile threat and V-bomber vulnerability – that given the V-Force was so exposed to destruction, it might as well be destroyed on its main bases and a few dispersal airfields, rather than meet the costs of a full dispersal plan. The debate was muddied by those still optimistic enough to back planning for multiple British nuclear strikes, rather than just one retaliatory sortie.

Some years before, in late 1955, a meeting chaired by the CAS had discussed dispersal against the background of planning for three strikes by a diminishing V-Force, but with only one strike from the dispersal airfields, due to the impracticalities of providing for three full strength strikes from each airfield, "when we clearly could not be certain either of the

---

* Andy Leitch adds that Mk 1 aircraft were built with a wiring harness for Blue Danube. A programme of modifications fitted a harness allowing carriage of the American Mk 5, Red Beard and Yellow Sun. Valiants did not receive Yellow Sun.

distribution of casualties throughout the force or which airfields might be useable". This implied attempted follow-up strikes from main bases only – despite the fact that these bases were obvious priority targets and, therefore, very unlikely to be useable. Logically, as the missile threat matured, there could be only one retaliatory strike. Yet, planning in the second half of the 1950s fell behind this reality. Three lifts were envisaged – a total of 366 sorties, in lifts of 150, 120 and 96. A subsequent initiative considered the second and third lifts flown from a group of 12 specially-prepared dispersal airfields. This could suggest some degree of dispersed weapon storage for second and third strikes. As for dispersal prior to war, the pre-missile era plan was for one squadron to operate from each Class 1 airfield, the rest of the force dispersing, in armed condition, in units of four aircraft. This process was to be completed within 72 hours, with as many bombers as possible brought to 40 minutes' readiness. This had succeeded a requirement for the deployed force to be ready to operate at 1½ hours' notice.[532]

An earlier intention, to operate the entire MBF from ten Class 1 main bases, carried the obvious risk of wholesale destruction on the ground. This led to the dispersal plan (originally ten main bases and 45 other airfields) approved by the Air Council in June 1955.[533] In later years, reduced V-Force size led to a corresponding reduction in the number of dispersal airfields. Roy Brocklebank describes the lack of resources surrounding this issue:

> "The whole dispersal plan was the brainchild of 'Bing' Cross. A huge amount of money had been spent on Bloodhound missiles to protect the Thor sites and the main bases, in addition to, of course, building the bomber fleet. I believe he was then told there was no money for his dispersal plan. He said he could do it and forged ahead with austere dispersals. He must have found the money somewhere to get the ORPs built."[534]

During long-winded debates about the level of dispersal required, cost remained firmly in the driving seat. Historian T. C. G. James set out the main problem on this front:

> "The issue here was how far precautionary measures could go in the interest of effective deterrence, without running into the objection that the objective of expenditure was

Dispersal: Prestwick ORP – XH532, together with XH909. Andy Leitch: "The latest day this photograph could have been taken is 16 July 1964, as 909 crashed on Anglesey on its return trip. All crew baled out successfully." (Pete Middleton via Andy Leitch Collection)

Dispersal: XH498 and a second Vulcan on RAF Valley's two-finger ORP. (Pete Middleton via Andy Leitch Collection)

to avoid war, not to fight it. For the Air Council, this was a genuine issue, and not less because the Treasury was the unseen presence at all its deliberations."[535]

In an ideal world, of course, there would be only one bomber per dispersal airfield, but there were practical as well as financial limits – the number of suitable airfields was finite (as was the number of crews available to sustain round-the-clock cockpit readiness for a proportion of the aircraft). Inevitably, the acceptance of some additional airfields would require acceptance of lower airfield standards.[536]

In searching for suitable dispersal airfields, the planners took in areas in the UK north and west providing slightly longer missile warning. Dispersals were classified as 'near' or 'far' from main bases. The former could be served by road, but far dispersals required air transport support.[537] By early 1960, there had been nine Class 1 airfields: Marham, Waddington, Finningley, Cottesmore, Scampton, Coningsby, Honington, Wittering and Gaydon. In addition, 30 dispersal airfields were planned, of which 16 were available at that time. By 1963, there were seven main bases (Finningley and Gaydon became operational conversion units); the planned allocation of dispersals showed minor changes (e.g. Stansted was dropped as a dispersal and accommodation at St Mawgan was reduced from four to two aircraft). The planned allocation of dispersals at third quarter 1963 was:

- Waddington: Brawdy (2 aircraft), Prestwick (2), Finningley (4), Filton (2), Machrihanish (2), Valley (2).
- Scampton: Burtonwood (4), Lossiemouth (2), Elvington (2), Kinloss (4).
- Coningsby: Yeovilton (2), Llanbedr (2), Bruntingthorpe (2), Ballykelly (4).
- Cottesmore: Boscombe Down (2), St Mawgan (2).
- Honington: Bedford (4), Gaydon (4).
- Wittering: Pershore (2), Lyneham (2), Wyton (2), Leuchars (2).
- Marham: Cranwell (2), Coltishall (2), Manston (2), Wattisham (2), Leeming (2), Leconfield (2) and Middleton St George (2).

Andy Leitch comments that in the initial phase to provide dispersal airfields with provision for four aircraft, some airfields used existing facilities, such as St Mawgan. About a dozen others, especially those airfields with taxiways etc. not strong enough for medium bombers, were given a strengthened hardstanding and taxiway to the threshold of the into-wind runway. When the missile threat was assessed, the time to taxi to the runway was deemed too great and ORPs for two aircraft were constructed in lieu, though at least two airfields, Tarrant Rushton and Shawbury, were deleted (possibly because of their short runways). Some of the ORPs for two bombers were similar to the four-fingered ones at main bases; those on fighter airfields were the existing fighter ORPs modified for two bombers, whilst others had hardstandings constructed over a couple of existing taxiways, such as at Cranwell, St Mawgan and Elvington. This explains why some diversion airfields originally allocated with four aircraft had their allocation of aircraft halved.

The plan, as quoted, provided for the dispersal of 72 aircraft from main bases, with four each (28 in all) remaining on the former (36 airfields, 100 aircraft). It was accepted that, for unserviceability and other reasons, it would be impossible to achieve 100% generation.[538]

Dispersal encouraged the Soviets to allocate more weapons, but gave small flights of dispersed aircraft a better chance of surviving a war scramble (especially flights limited to two aircraft). In a scramble, they would not be caught in take-off queues on the main bases. ORPs facilitated rapid take-off, with aircraft advantageously positioned for scramble. Previously, ORPs were confined to fighter airfields.[539] Dispersal, however, made for more difficult point defence – involving a larger group of airfields with a much wider geographic spread. Conflict might well begin with a period of conventional warfare and the only counter to repeated conventional raids would be repeated "survival scrambles", but this did not feature in major exercises, according to Roy Brocklebank: "Certainly, in the 1960s we never considered the question of survival scrambles. Also, when a Micky Finn was called, we always refuelled to minimum fuel for flight to dispersals. We would have been unable to fly a war mission."[540]

It appears, however, that the significance of survival scrambles was recognised in the post-QRA Polaris era. Vulcan captain Peter Moore remembers such an occasion:

Dispersal: XH479 and XH504 parked on the two-finger ORP at RAF Brawdy. (Pete Middleton via Andy Leitch Collection)

"I'm not sure what the whole of Lincolnshire thought when STC (Strike Command) practised a survival scramble involving every operational aircraft – spectacular breaking cloud to see a sky full of climbing aircraft from Binbrook, Scampton, Coningsby and Waddington. Further south, other aircraft were climbing rapidly."[541]

Tony Cottingham, a Valiant captain, remembers occasional dispersal exercises pre-1965 involving airfields which were not V-Bomber bases:

"We would have three or four aircraft parked on a readiness dispersal with nearby crew quarters, to be at 15 minutes' readiness to scramble for about two days. There could be a call, at any time, to come to five minutes' readiness. All the pre-flight checks, up to engine start, were completed beforehand and the cabin was then locked. On call, the crew ran out to the aircraft, started engines and called air traffic control when ready to taxi."[542]

Dispersal was made more complicated by American E weapons arming Canberras and some heavier aircraft, notably SACEUR's Valiants. The fundamental problem was the dual control issue. E weapons and their American custodians were based at only a few stations; one consequence was the concentration of all three TBF Valiant squadrons at Marham, which increased the risk of their destruction on the ground. In mid-1958, the AOC-in-C Bomber Command expressed concern that refusal to release, or a delay in releasing, E weapons could make it impossible to disperse aircraft.[543]

Project E was active until 1965 in Bomber Command (and much later in the case of RAF Germany). The problem of custodial arrangements and dispersal ended in relation to main force Victors and Vulcans in March 1962, with the arrival of sufficient British Yellow Sun Mk 2 megaton weapons. During the life of the E programme, three supplementary storage areas (SSAs) – at Honington, Marham and Waddington – were occupied exclusively by E weapons. The UK weapons had to be stored at remaining Class 1 airfields and in depots. Humphrey Wynn explained the significance:

"In consequence, UK weapons are not disposed in the best locations to meet the unilateral strike plan, in which aircraft from E stations must be used. Moreover, Yellow Sun weapons must be held at greater concentration than is desirable from safety aspects."[544]

Certainly, American E weapons were a mixed blessing. A letter of 4 August 1959 from the A/ACAS (Ops), Air Commodore P. G. Wykeham, to the Vice-Chief of the Air Staff (VCAS), Air Marshal E. C. Hudleston, noted that, with three SSAs now given over to E weapons and no SSA at Scampton, the only stations on which UK weapons could be held alongside the aircraft were Wittering, Cottesmore and Finningley. "If we consider the case of an enemy attack with a very short period of warning, any delay in releasing E weapons could mean that less than half of the MBF could be rapidly brought to readiness."[545] In July 1960, the Air Council had approved the gradual phase-out of Project E, but it lingered for years.

EXERCISE EDOM

Immediate response when on QRA was practised in Exercise EDOM. Roy Brocklebank described the usual practice at QRA handover:

> "The first question an incoming crew would ask was, 'When was the last practice called?' If it had been more than 24 hours, we would be on edge until the alert was called. As soon as the Tannoy clicked and the magic words 'Attention! Attention!' rang out, the crew were running. You never stopped to find out why. Piling into the staff car, captain driving, we would scorch off across the grass, if necessary, to minimise time to the aircraft. We soon realised the practices were either on the hour or on the quarters. Equally, the bomber controllers realised that we had worked that out. Timings changed to any 10 minutes and then five and, finally, just about any time – bastards!"[546]

The nervous release of a practice alert failed to banish the deeper stress. Sometimes, there would be a second alert within five hours. Brocklebank recalls that, on occasion, it was a case of "more haste, less speed":

> "… to get the shortest reaction time possible, the crew chief would start the engines from outside the aircraft before opening the cabin door. Then the unthinkable happened at Waddington on a Mk 1A. When he was standing on the nosewheel, at full stretch, the key broke off in the lock. There was the nuclear-armed bomber, fully-fuelled, armed, engines running, ready to go and the crew standing outside, looking on. How long could it run at ground idle before running out of fuel?"

On dark winter nights a QRA call-out could feel like torture.

Life on the nuclear frontline had moments of acute tension. Crews were conditioned to follow procedures to the letter. Victor captain Gary West remembers that any departure from the expected was most unwelcome:

> "On a wet and cold winter's afternoon I was on QRA with the crew when the siren sounded. We went to cockpit readiness and then to RS02, so we taxied to the end of the runway and I saw the XV Squadron aircraft move into position on our starboard side. It suddenly dawned on us that no-one had heard the bomber controller use the correct codewords: Exercise EDOM. There was a frightened silence followed by a flood of expletives. After ten minutes or so, we returned to RS15 and, heaving a sigh of relief, taxied back to the pan. The bomber controller had fouled up. He'd forgotten to transmit the codewords."[547]

Nav/plotter Robin Woolven recalled QRA at Scampton, with three Blue Steel-armed Vulcans ready to go: "The boredom was relieved by the alerts – Exercise EDOM. Our QRA aircraft would never taxi with Blue Steel, given the hazards of high-test peroxide (HTP)."[548] Norman Bonnor remembers the "clapped out" Standard Vanguards used for QRA crew transport at RAF Cottesmore: "They were terrible – ancient staff cars, often beyond the point of roadworthiness." He recalled an incident (by no means unique) involving the failure to unplug the sump heater lead. When the car took off, the lead snagged a door jamb and ripped a length of electrical conduit off the wall. This flew across the room, got stuck across a metal window and ripped it out of the frame. The car towed the window to the aircraft. As for the resulting hole in the wall, it snowed that night and the luckless individual with a bed next to it was refused permission to move to another room.[549]

Roy Brocklebank reflected on the variation in QRA routines between squadrons:

> "On most squadrons each crew began a period of QRA standby at 09.00, after the station morning briefing – 'morning prayers'. They would then go to their designated aircraft, remove the previous crew's flight kit, check the target go-bag and the weapon and return to operations for light duties, such as target study or flight preparation for their next training mission. The off-going crew would either stand down or perhaps fly. On my squadron, we had a different deal. Each crew did either a 48-hour duty during the week or a 72-hour duty at the weekend, followed by a 24-hour or 48-hour stand down. This rotation meant we did QRA less frequently and with less disruption to family life. On some wings the crews had to wear uniform but on others they could wear flying suits. All crews ate in the 'aircrew feeder', a flight-line restaurant noted for its high standard of cuisine, frequently better than the regular Messes. The staff here worked a seven-day week in support of both routine flying and QRA. The meals allowance was more than in the Messes. We always arranged to be on QRA over a birthday!"[550]

He described his longest QRA duty: "We did it over an Easter Bank Holiday, 09.00 Thursday until 09.00 the following Tuesday. Five days was just too long."[551]

Every variation in QRA rota design had its champions, as Norman Bonnor recalls:

> "On XV Squadron we had ten crews and, at any one time, one crew would be fresh and yet to be declared combat-ready. Another crew would be on leave and, perhaps, a third would not be available for a variety of reasons. We favoured four-day (Monday–Thursday) and three-day (Friday–Sunday) QRA duties. This meant QRA duty came round every three weeks. The system worked well and we stuck to this regime. On 100 Squadron, however, a 48-hour regime was in place: Monday–Tuesday, Wednesday–Thursday and Friday plus the weekend. It seems each squadron found its own solution."[552]

Whatever solution was reached, crews soon discovered that manning the nuclear frontline dominated their personal lives. If away for more than five hours, they had to ensure the station knew where to reach them. They had to be able to return to base within 24 hours. There were constant reminders of the primary purpose of the V-Force and its association with Armageddon. Roy Brocklebank acknowledged that, to some extent, personal liberty was surrendered:

> "We had been introduced to accounting for our whereabouts upon arrival at OCU by Squadron Leader (later, Wing Commander) J. E. 'Polly' Pollington, who became CO of IX Squadron towards the end of 1964. Later, if going away, we had to put our location in the squadron recall book. This was tested on 12 Squadron, at RAF Coningsby, on 8 September 1964, with our deployment to the Far East during the Indonesian Confrontation. I think one crew member was at Edgbaston, one was shopping in Norwich and two were at Farnborough. They were all tracked down in short order."

The Coningsby Wing moved to RAF Cottesmore in the autumn of 1964:

> "At Cottesmore, my hut was close to the ops block. When there was a call-out, I would dash in, grab the squadron recall book and get to work on the telephone. We used a 'cascade' system. I'd call someone, who would then call others either nearby, or on his

route into the base, and so on … We were required to have at least five complete crews on the station within one hour of the hooter going, allowing for the generation of our QRA spare. Waddington, meanwhile, was required to despatch by road four crews to RAF Finningley, to man OCU aircraft.

"If we were likely to be away from our stated locations for more than 16 hours, we were required to ring operations with fresh contact details. Later, when at RAF Waddington, I discovered that there was a direct line into operations, but few knew of its existence or purpose. I gave it a try, asking the GPO operator for Lincoln Trunk Sub 2 and was immediately connected to Waddington ops. It worked!"[553]

There were occasional glimpses of humanity in the system. Nav/radar Bob Sinclair was posted to 12 Squadron in June 1967, but his stay lasted only to the end of the year:

"I was on QRA on New Years' Eve. We had combat status but were the most junior crew; 12 Squadron disbanded that night. As a special dispensation we were allowed to finish 30 minutes early, at 23.30. We changed from flying kit to DJs and joined the Mess celebrations. The bomber controller had been told not to instigate any alerts after 23.30."[554]

In summary, as discussed earlier in the chapter, the evidence clearly shows that UK ground alert was the only viable MBF posture. Airborne alert lacked viability – although some politicians were content to tout an airborne alert capability which did not exist. The mathematics revealed that one aircraft in the air required 3.8 squadrons to support it and, for much of the 1960s, the V-Force consisted of just 11 squadrons. Equally, dispersal to remote locations overseas lacked viability without more tankers and a long-range stand-off weapon.

Ground alert was the MBF's sole option and the most important decision reducing exposure on the ground was taken back in 1961, with the adoption of an Alert Condition 1 providing for some degree of continuous cockpit readiness in an emergency. The adoption of QRA at RS15 the following year did not conflict with Alert Condition 1, as frequent calls to RS05 cockpit readiness (or a higher alert state) were central to QRA exercises – but in a process which avoided the inevitable disruption resulting from a large-scale Alert Condition 1 exercise.

Alert Condition 1 was V-Force "maximum effort", as there were insufficient crews to maintain much more than 30% of the generated and dispersed V-Force at RS05. However, those aircraft held round-the-clock at RS05, with all cockpit checks completed and ready for RS02 (engine start/taxi), would have allowed a few bombers to survive an IRBM simultaneous launch on low trajectories against the airfields.

It would seem that the lack of documentary evidence of plans to implement Alert Condition 1 in a close approach to war was matched by a lack of detailed briefings for those who would be responsible for the implementation. No aircrew contributor to this book referred to 24/7 manning of some dispersed V-bombers by crew rotation, in response to an imminent threat of war. Later, a new system, replacing Bomber Command alert and readiness, was introduced in 1968, upon the establishment of Strike Command.

14
GENERATING WEAPON SYSTEMS

> *Estimates of Soviet targeting policy changed over time. According to the Joint Intelligence Committee's 1967 list of probable targets in the UK, a total of 32 bomber bases, dispersal airfields and refuelling facilities were estimated to be on the Soviet target list for strikes, each target receiving two 500-kt missiles and two 1-mt weapons dropped by aircraft.*
>
> > "Probable nuclear targets in the United Kingdom, assumptions for planning", JIC, at the request of the Machinery of Government in War Subcommittee of the Home Defence Committee, Annex A, Revised List, 2 November 1967

HOME TRUTHS

The fundamental behind credibility is post-strike capacity. Lawrence Freedman:

> "It had always been accepted that the most reliable deterrent force was that which would permit retaliation even after … surprise attack. This requirement gained in importance as the Soviet capacity for mounting a surprise attack grew and as the concepts of first and second strikes became widely understood."[555]

This led to a definition of 'assured destruction' as the ability to deter a nuclear attack on the USA or its allies by the "clear and unmistakable ability" to inflict unacceptable damage upon an aggressor even after absorbing a surprise first strike.

Consequently the UK's Defence Board met at the Treasury during the late afternoon of 4 April 1960, to discuss the unpleasant realities surrounding the new strategic environment – mass deployment of nuclear missiles by East and West. Those present included Harold Watkinson, Minister of Defence, Duncan Sandys, then Minister of Aviation, George Ward, Secretary of State for Air, and Christopher Soames, Secretary of State for War. General Sir Francis Festing, Chief of the Imperial General Staff, and Air Chief Marshal Sir Thomas Pike, Chief of the Air Staff, also attended. The main business was V-Force vulnerability on the ground; both Sandys and Ward had prepared papers for consideration. Major concerns included the future of the deterrent and the relative merits of a Skybolt-armed V-Force and the British Blue Streak medium-range ballistic missile.[556]

Blue Streak, a surface-launched, liquid-fuelled weapon, was just as vulnerable as the American Thors deployed in Britain. Sandys said the military case for Skybolt rested largely on the claim that the V-Force was less vulnerable to a Soviet first strike than Blue Streak. He told the board that, if invulnerability to pre-emptive attack was militarily essential, the V-bombers were just as vulnerable as Blue Streak and, therefore, also amounted to a 'fire first' weapon. Conveniently, he ignored the positive control attribute of the bombers – a point of some significance. Sandys argued that, with no strategic warning, V-bombers would be concentrated on their main bases, representing only three separate aiming points for a Soviet attack with 3-mt missiles (which were then potential weapons, rather than weapons in service). The document setting out this meeting's conclusions noted that if such missiles were fired on low trajectories, "it was agreed that the whole V-bomber force would almost certainly be destroyed on the ground".

George Ward's contribution also lacked balance. He argued that, according to the JIC, a bolt from the blue attack was unlikely. During a period of rising tension, the V-bomber force would be deployed across 36 main and dispersal airfields and brought to a high standard of readiness, *which could include keeping part of the force on airborne alert*. The Air Staff supported Ward's bold claims regarding airborne alert and, looking ahead, suggested that an airborne alert of 20% of the total force, with each aircraft armed with two Skybolts, would constitute "a significant deterrent". These claims are not without interest given that Bomber Command operational studies had already demonstrated, rather convincingly, that airborne alert lacked feasibility.

In the interests of balance it should be said that Bomber Command's Operational Research Branch was taking a fresh look at airborne alert for a proportion of a Skybolt-equipped V-Force. In his memoirs, Bomber Command's chief research officer, Tom Kerr, described an approach aimed at keeping one V-bomber in a group of four airborne continuously in a time of tension, by means of in-flight refuelling, with each flight lasting 12 hours. He claimed trials had successfully demonstrated that, in an emergency, a continuous airborne patrol by part of a Skybolt-armed V-Force was possible.[557]

As for the existing ground alert, just over two years later Prime Minister Harold Macmillan would decide against V-Force dispersal, despite the very real threat of nuclear war over Cuba.

Sandys went on to claim that 50 Soviet missiles could destroy virtually the entire V-Force, even if dispersed, unless the crews were at cockpit readiness. The Air Staff felt otherwise, telling only part of the story by arguing that four V-bombers could already scramble in four minutes and that this time would improve with Mk 2 aircraft and simultaneous engine starting. They suggested 40% survival even on a short warning. Sandys then went further, claiming that 250 Soviet missiles would be enough to destroy 80% of the V-bombers, on the ground or in the air, even if the crews were in the aircraft, with engines running.

Once again, the Air Staff disagreed, continuing to avoid the full picture and pointing to the possibilities of airborne alert and of dispersing V-bombers more widely in the UK or even to remote bases overseas. The latter argument ignored the obvious political and logistical problems of overseas dispersal and the lack of target coverage without refuelling (already highlighted just six months before in a Bomber Command operational study). As for heightened readiness on ground alert, to reduce exposure to missile strike, 20 V-bombers held permanently at cockpit readiness would be extremely costly, requiring a 50% increase in aircrew and force frontline strength.[558] This ignored the practical way forward, which was eventually adopted – round-the-clock RS05 deployment of part of the V-Force, by a system of crew rotation in an extreme emergency. This formed the basis of a new Alert Condition 1 the following year and as described in Chapter 13.

Setting aside these arguments, in the final analysis V-Force credibility turned on just one number: how many bombers would survive a war scramble? Here, the UK Defence Board considered information obtained from the British Nuclear Deterrent Study Group and the Joint Inter-Service Group for the Study of All-out Warfare. This was pessimistic about the bombers' chances of getting away, given capabilities at that time and the possible use of 3-mt low-trajectory weapons. It was estimated that aircraft on the ground had to be six miles from Ground Zero (three miles in the air) to survive. This was not based on actual megaton burst data but, rather, a scaling up of data on kiloton bursts. A Defence Board Secretariat note gave a summary of timings:

> "Allowing for the detection of a Soviet missile and the communication of the information to the bomber stations (25 seconds), for the bombers to start take-off and get their wheels up (70 seconds) and for the aircraft to fly clear of a 3-mt burst on their base (60 seconds), the total time required between first radar pick-up and a bomber being safely in the air is two minutes 35 seconds."[559]

This is based on very unlikely assumptions: no delays and *all crews* at RS02, with engines running and positioned for immediate take-off when warned of incoming missiles. A low-trajectory missile could mean less than four minutes' warning between detection and detonation. According to the Defence Board Secretariat:

> "On this timing (which assumes all procedures work perfectly and aircrew are at cockpit readiness), only the first bomber taking off from each of the 36 dispersal airfields could get safely away; succeeding bombers would be caught either on the ground or within lethal distance from the burst on their base."

Yet, using these 'highly favourable' assumptions, this note still put a brave face on things:

> "Nevertheless, the successful launching of 36 bombers would represent about 50% of the available frontline of Mk 2 V-bombers, on the current Air Staff assessment that 70% of the frontline would be serviceable at any one time. The achievement of these timings will, however, require considerable improvement in the take-off timings and procedures of the V-bomber force: in a recent Air Ministry exercise, six minutes was required to launch successfully 50% of the participating force."

These expectations still look over-optimistic, to say the least, regardless of that closing qualification. Whilst the Soviet weapons considered were not yet deployed, this outcome relied on a long list of favourable circumstances: prompt dispersal, fast regeneration, swift command decision-making, fast verification of early warning, faultless communications and immediate reaction from crews *already in the cockpit and ready to go*. It was possible for four aircraft to get off in one minute 45 (or even slightly faster), but crews had to be in their cockpits, with engines running and positioned for take-off. Even then, many (probably most) would have been destroyed or damaged by incoming missiles.

Measures such as QRA and SIMSTART optimised the scramble, but nothing changed the fundamental mathematics, should the Russians opt for a low-trajectory surprise attack on the airfields. The V-Force was vulnerable even when dispersed and cockpit ready. There was, however, that one emergency option available to Bomber Command's AOC – part of the force held 24/7 at RS05 – which would increase the chance of a survivor or two on some airfields. Assuming dispersal and regeneration of flights of two or four aircraft, it would have been possible to keep some aircraft at RS05 (up to the very point of engine start), by rotating crews in a much expanded, extreme form of QRA. This would apply the highest possible ground alert readiness state at a time of grave national peril.

The note from the April 1960 Defence Board meeting (together with the conclusions of a March 1962 Bomber Command Operational Research Branch memorandum [No. 241] on MBF exposure to missile attack) look relatively realistic when set against claims made a decade later. In 1971, consideration of a future air-delivered deterrent formed part of the Long Term Strategic Nuclear Working Party's review of options for a successor to Polaris. The Air Force Department's contribution to this study took an extraordinarily optimistic view of the survivability of the existing V-Force at launch: "… scrambles are regularly practised and the average time achieved over the last eight years by the fourth aircraft is one minute 53 seconds." There was, however, no acknowledgement of the significant time required to reach the point where scramble was possible. Equally, there was no mention of the relatively poor prospects for survival identified in past years. On the contrary, the Air Force Department claimed:

> "Studies carried out some years ago, and since updated, show that the chances of scrambling aircraft escaping the effects of incoming nuclear missiles are very high; even assuming the minimum warning time, they are of the order of 92% to 94%."[560]

This rather fanciful Air Force Department paper tended to rely on a favourable expectation – the availability of the longer warning associated with simultaneous impact attack, rather than the short warning simultaneous launch mode. It went on to make a dubious claim:

> "This situation of four minutes' warning from the BMEWS is pessimistic, in that it assumes the UK being attacked first or in isolation, thus giving to the United States positive collateral of nuclear strikes – a strategy unlikely to be adopted by the Soviet Union."

Once again, the central assumptions were all favourable: crews in cockpits and ready to go, with aircraft fully-fuelled and dispersed as planned. By 1971, however, the pressure was off, to some extent, as Polaris then occupied the strategic frontline. Furthermore, the purpose of this Air Force Department paper was advocacy of a *future deterrent* based on manned aircraft. This goes some way to explain the 92%–94% survivability claim for the existing manned bomber force in a short warning strike. In fact, this paper wanted it both ways. Despite an upbeat assessment of the current ability to escape incoming missiles (even given some years of exposure to Soviet SLBMs), the paper continued:

> "If a future air-delivery system were to be decided upon as the main national deterrent, there would be a need to revive a ground-based QRA and, as such a system would not be viable if missiles were launched from submarines close to the United Kingdom, there

would also be a requirement for progression to an airborne alert state in which the aircraft would be scrambled in times of political tension and kept airborne by in-flight refuelling – a procedure which had been shown by studies and trials to be entirely practicable and economical with aircraft of long endurance. The requirement to maintain airborne alert would need to be observed in designing a future air-delivered system."

This is a curious conclusion: ageing Vulcans had no need of airborne alert, yet airborne alert would be essential for a future air-delivered system. This paper ignored past studies drawing negative conclusions about V-Force airborne alert (although, of course, a new system could be purpose-designed with this in mind, given a sufficiently generous budget).

The V-bombers' fundamental flaws included Britain's relatively close proximity to Russia, together with the ten-minute gap between RS15 and RS05 and the small size of the bomber force. For ground alert to be fully viable (i.e. credible), there had to be sufficient strategic warning for the generation, arming, dispersal and regeneration of the bombers, which might take several days to complete in full. Once dispersed and combat-ready, the crews would be at RS15 with, perhaps, a proportion at 24/7 RS05. Assuming a BMEWS four-minute warning, the ideal readiness state immediately prior to the warning would be for the first aircraft of each two or four-strong dispersed flight (24/7 manned by rotation) to be at cockpit readiness poised for RS02 (immediate engine start and a scramble take-off), with an ability to reach escape distance within four minutes of warning (although even this might not be enough to escape SLBMs).

The central problem was that RS05 (with all cockpit checks complete, up to the point of engine start) could be held for only a few hours without crew rotation and, therefore, 24/7 RS05 could involve only a proportion of the force (perhaps a little over 30% at best) at any given time. There were insufficient crews to man for 24/7 RS05 across the entire mobilised force. Furthermore, in a practical sense, *any IRBM attack would be a bolt from the blue*, in that scramble required the verified detection of missiles in flight. Potentially, at the brink of war, crew rotation to maintain part of the dispersed force at RS05 (positioned on those dispersal airfields offering the longest warning time) might yield a modest increase in scramble survivor numbers. Equally, in the absence of commonly applied favourable assumptions, *there might be no survivors*. Credibility, in these circumstances, boiled down to the inability of the Soviets to guarantee *total destruction* of Britain's nuclear strike force.

The best that could be done, at a time of grave threat of war and given a dispersed force of 80 bombers armed and fuelled, would be to man, say, 30% (around 24 aircraft) at Alert Condition 1, the highest possible sustained ground alert readiness. A significant number of aircraft would escape given a 15–20 minute 'American warning'/simultaneous burst attack, but this seems to be an unlikely strategy for the Soviets.[561] There was, however, a chance that a few 'first in the queue' bombers (24/7 cockpit manned) could get away in the much more likely four-minute warning/simultaneous launch attack – *given that missiles would not arrive simultaneously* but, rather, over a period of some two minutes.

Here, Roy Brocklebank makes several important points:

"… I suppose sequential launching over two minutes was not unreasonable. It would also be logical for a launch group of, say, six launchers to have six different targets, with back-up missiles from a different launch group, to allow for Allied pre-launch attacks. Furthermore, given the lack of defensive ABM capability, defence saturation would have been unnecessary but fratricide would have been a significant risk. This may well have demanded a much longer launch window. That window could also be constrained by the threat from counterstrikes."[562]

Fuel was always a worry, recalled Vulcan pilot Ed Jarron, "but I can say that crews were *not* briefed on one-way missions. Every mission had an allocated recovery base".[563]

Yet, some V-Force veterans clearly recollect that, at some stage, they were briefed on targets offering no chance of recovery. Those largely sharing Air Commodore Jarron's views include Roy Brocklebank:

" … the RAF did not plan one-way missions and made detailed plans for recovery … Bomber Command's War Standard Operations Plan (SOP) 1st Edition went into much detail on recovery, much of which was omitted from the 2nd Edition. Yet, the 2nd Edition still had recovery details, with half-hourly IFF (identification, friend or foe) code tables."[564]

At the same time, Brocklebank did concede that the crews of the two Vulcan squadrons in Cyprus were briefed for war sorties requiring bale out after weapon release. The SOP required war sorties to be planned to terminate overhead the designated recovery base at maximum altitude with 4,000 lbs of fuel remaining, but the most likely outcome in some cases was a bale out due to fuel exhaustion. Roy Brocklebank made a point of providing every target folder with a number of suitable alternative airfields, although this was not a stated requirement for target folders.[565]

Bill MacGillivray had found the Wittering nuclear weapons course "quite frightening". In June 2018 he added:

"Our primary target was on the wrong side of Moscow – an industrial and weapons production centre. As we moved up the line, our targets changed. Eventually, we had a target so far away that we would have had just eight minutes' fuel left after dropping our weapon. The target file commented that action, at that point, was at the captain's discretion!"

Peter Moore recalls the fatalistic mood of the time:

"While official policy was that there were no one-way targets, the practical situation was different. My crew took the view that everything was one-way. We would only be airborne post-recognition of a Soviet attack which, most likely, would take out our landing options. We also didn't expect much of the UK to remain in a recognisable state and our families would most probably have been killed. For my deep penetration target, the designated recovery base was Yeşilköy (Istanbul)*. However, to get there we needed to climb soon after weapon release. Collectively, we decided that that was signing our own death warrants. We were going to push on as far as we could at low level, to avoid detection and provide a minimum target opportunity for the defence. While never

---

* Andy Leitch recalls another recovery airfield in Turkey, Ankara Esenboğa.

really believing that we would ever be launched, we reckoned there would be nothing to come back to, anywhere."[566]

GENERATING AIRCRAFT AND WEAPONS

A fully-fuelled and armed V-bomber and crew, combat-ready and at RS15, represented the tip of a very large iceberg. A combat-ready V-bomber required a vast effort on the part of technical personnel, ground crew, armourers and other specialists. Readiness for a retaliatory strike involved so much more than flying. V-Force ground teams strived to meet demanding time targets for aircraft and weapons generation. Exercise Mick challenged the main bases to generate weapon systems within required timeframes. Exercise Micky Finn went further, requiring dispersal and regeneration of the entire V-Force. Roy Brocklebank adds: "Micky Finn dispersal was usually around H+5, to allow for a sizeable quantity of aircraft to get airborne in 15 minutes." Exercise Kinsman tested dispersal at the squadron level. There were also Mayflight exercises. In May 1963, Mayflight VI saw Bomber Command achieve full generation and dispersal for the first time. The Vice-Chief of the Air Staff, Air Marshal Sir Wallace Kyle, recorded the results: "Of the 115 weapon systems available for the exercise, 105 (91%) were generated within eight hours and 100% within 15½ hours." The intention was to disperse 52 weapon systems and all had been dispersed within nine hours 40 minutes. Time targets for the air transport of ground personnel to dispersal airfields were met. All systems had regenerated within 16 hours 25 minutes.[567] Scampton did not participate fully as it was engaged in Blue Steel trials.

Mayflight VI began with a call for force generation, followed one hour later by the order to disperse. Results were an improvement on Mayflight V (1962). During Mayflight VI, the practice readiness states were called three times to cockpit readiness and take-off readiness. A somewhat reduced Thor missile force took part simultaneously (Exercise Redouble); of the 45 missiles available, 44 were counted down to launch at the conclusion. The remaining missile had guidance trouble.

Regular exercises were the essence of V-Force life. Exercise Mick was called on 25 August 1963 (a Sunday) as a no-notice generation test. This eight-hour drill's outcome was described as "impressive". The generation of 65 live weapon systems was expected and 64 (98%) were ready in eight hours (19 aircraft in two hours, 37 in four hours and 57 in six hours).[568]

Generating the stand-off bomb within acceptable times, however, was always a challenge and the exclusion of Scampton, a Blue Steel station, from the May 1963 Mayflight VI must have contributed to the good results. During April 1964 Scampton held the second of a series of trials investigating the problems surrounding Blue Steel generation. The first, on 10 March, called for the generation of four Blue Steel weapon systems. The second, a few weeks later, required the generation of eight systems and the simulation of their "trickle dispersal" in Exercise Nursemaid. Notice was given but no special preparations were permitted. At the start, seven first-line aircraft were available – six of which were serviceable and required only scheduled servicing to be ready for missile loading. The seventh was unserviceable but two second-line aircraft were available and generated for loading Blue Steel. All missiles were loaded prior to fuelling.[569]

Nursemaid highlighted the lengthy procedures required to make aircraft available for missile loading, despite the fact that six were serviceable from the first. Two training rounds had to be offloaded. There were also delays in fuelling missiles, exposing a need for scheduled fuelling prior to loading. Simulated dispersal revealed a need for more effective assessment of regeneration problems. It was decided that the next trial would involve actual dispersal. Meanwhile, of the eight weapon systems generated, only five of the 'powered bombs' were capable of powered launch; the rest would have been dropped freefall. The report on Nursemaid commented:

> " … the first system was declared combat-ready 15 hours and the eighth 32 hours after the start of generation … All eight systems completed the post-load checks successfully in the powered role. The three systems which became unpowered did so because of leaks in the high test peroxide (HTP) system … The times for regeneration varied between four and 14 hours … No times can be quoted for unpowered systems since the work carried out on these made them unrepresentative of the operational system."

Clearly, Blue Steel needed more than a 'nursemaid'. It was not just a question of system complexity:

> "Aircraft became available for missile loading between one and two hours later than planned and between four and six hours later than the times taken to generate freefall aircraft in a typical no-notice exercise. This slow rate of progress was largely the result of bringing only 50% of line squadron men on duty at the beginning of the trial. Lack of manpower prevented integration of scheduled work and was responsible for delays … It is considered that the bulk of line squadron manpower should be brought on duty at the beginning of generation. The missile-loading and post-load teams were not fully employed during the trial because of the slow rate at which aircraft became available. Serious delays, amounting to between five and eight hours, in starting missile fuelling occurred on five of the eight systems generated. Those delays were caused partly in moving aircraft to the dispersals on which missile fuelling was carried out and partly by shortage and poor control of fuelling teams. The division of the available fuelling teams into two equal shifts was not the best deployment for the task in hand. In view of the slow rate of aircraft preparation and the inability to utilise missile-fuelling teams fully in the early part of generation, when all missiles are loaded before fuelling, it is considered that a proportion of missiles should be fuelled before loading to aircraft."

Freefall weapons were very different. According to Waddington Wing Targeting Officer Roy Brocklebank, this station's weapons teams could load and hand over a Yellow Sun Mk 2 hydrogen bomb in minutes. Expectations remained high when the new WE.177B laydown freefall bomb arrived in late 1966:

> "The station commander, Arthur Griffiths, was annoyed (incandescent) when the first WE.177 took about 95 minutes. As there were only six loading teams, such a slow rate would cripple his force generation times. Typically, he expected his 20-aircraft target to be met in under five hours. Eventually, we got the WE.177 time down to 35 minutes."[570]

Fast load times required intelligent planning. The aircraft had both nuclear and conventional roles. Waddington's Vulcans were fitted with panel EP for Yellow Sun Mk 2 or ER for WE.177, but in the conventional role this was replaced with a 90-way panel (which could sequence up to 90 bombs). Roy explained:

> "Role change involved removing the 90-way panel and fitting the nuclear panel. Checking and certifying the wiring and then wire-locking and lead-sealing the weapon switches took time. It became practice to limit the number of aircraft in the conventional role so that on Friday only those scheduled for conventional sorties on Monday morning would be left in the conventional fit."

Returning to Blue Steel, many a good man refused to accept defeat in the face of the missile's idiosyncrasies. There were improvements in generation times and readiness, yet the fact remained that many bombers on Britain's nuclear frontline carried a weapon with serious disadvantages in the 'four-minute warning' world of QRA. There were always doubts, at the highest level, about Blue Steel's value as a positive contributor to V-Force operational effectiveness. A March 1966 Bomber Command memorandum (issued in May) reported on the operational effectiveness of Blue Steel QRA over a six-month period. This complex study was made more difficult by the "impracticability of making a post-QRA flight with a system representative of the state it was in on QRA". The work had to be based on post-QRA ground tests, together with limited checks made whilst on QRA and estimates of likely in-flight "arisings". This drew on evidence from other sources, particularly defects reported during training sorties and tests of missile-system components.[571]

The mean values from post-QRA analysis (at take-off, but including some defects probably arising during the flight) gave:

- 81% probability of successful powered launch.
- 4% probability that a system, nominally powered, would fail after launch.
- 15% probability that an unpowered launch would have to be made.

Taking five QRA systems (one per squadron of eight Blue Steel aircraft), this suggested a likelihood of four powered and one unpowered system, with a small probability that one of the powered systems would fail after launch. The reality, however, was worse:

> "Adding in the estimates of likely in-flight arisings (pre- and post-launch) results in final mean estimates of 65% probability of successful powered launch, 15% probability of post-launch failure and 20% probability of unpowered launch. Once again, in terms of five systems, this means a likelihood of three systems making a powered attack, a fourth system, nominally powered, failing after launch, while a fifth system would make an unpowered attack."

Given only five Blue Steel QRA systems, a change in this outcome would require "considerable alteration of individual probabilities". The causes of unpowered delivery were varied but failure of the Stentor rocket motor "makes a major contribution to the probability of post-launch failure (this has been estimated from manufacturer's tests of returned motors, giving a 12.8% failure rate)". Here, the memorandum noted action taken to improve the motor and also the autopilot – "another major source of unserviceability leading to failed systems". The memorandum's authors stuck to their brief and made no comment on how many of the five Blue Steel QRA systems were likely to survive an attack on their bases and continue to survive until the point of release, powered or unpowered.

The Operational Research Branch also studied the likely effectiveness of the freefall QRA force. This considered reports on aircraft after post-QRA flights or after periods on QRA standby not followed by a flight. The aim was to measure likely operational capability in a hi-lo mission. This September 1965 memorandum focused on the in-service functioning of the navigation and bombing system (NBS). Annex F to this report noted:

> "Of the 137 radar bombing attacks … made on post-QRA flights over the period May 1964–April 1965, 15 (10.9%) were affected by equipment malfunctions. In normal training flights over the same period, there were 7,908 radar bombing attacks, of which 688 (8.7%) had actual (as opposed to simulated) equipment malfunctions. Although the malfunction rate was higher on post-QRA flights, the difference is not significant, since it could arise by chance three times out of ten."[572]

In his covering note to this memorandum, R. J. Monaghan, then Bomber Command's chief research officer, identified the key points:

> "Evidence from post-QRA flights is the more reliable and indicated major degradation of operational capability on 7.7% of occasions. Adding to this the evidence from cases where ground defects caused cancellation of the post-QRA flight brings the total for major degradation up to about 10.5%. Of this, 4% would be from before-flight unserviceability and 6.5% would be from in-flight unserviceability. NBS faults were the major cause on at least 75% of the occasions of unserviceability, with a malfunction rate during flight about the same as that encountered in normal training flights."

Failure rates in both Blue Steel and freefall QRA systems were higher than planners had hoped, given the small overall size of QRA/MBF forces. On this basis, *any* reduction in failures would be significant. At the human level, regardless of hardware limitations, senior officers' expectations of absolute crew commitment never wavered. Radar bombing targets for a sortie were declared pre-flight in squadron authorisation books. Once airborne, crews were required to complete attacks on these targets, regardless of the state of systems. The only exception accepted was the observation of peacetime safety limitations. Crews, therefore, practised a range of 'limited procedure' attacks, including without computer or even without radar picture. The results, given the simulated equipment failures, were often very accurate.

STRUGGLING WITH BLUE STEEL

Blue Steel presented planners, aircrew and ground technicians with a host of problems. Bill Taylor was the co-pilot in Stan Lambdon's 27 Squadron crew at Scampton. They arrived in October 1963, when 27 was still high altitude and armed with Yellow Sun Mk 2. The first Blue Steels came through Scampton's gates within a few weeks; the Lambdon crew flew their first powered bomb training round in February 1964. They could launch Blue Steel from 250 ft but, overall, they were not impressed: "Its serviceability was not terribly good. Mating the weapon to the aircraft raised all sorts of difficulties. 'Wet' rounds were a worry. We had a couple of high temperature incidents with HTP."[573]

Questions over Blue Steel's value on the nuclear frontline persisted. Problems with the powered bomb, highlighted in later operational research studies, should have come as no surprise, given the findings of a report of July 1963. This study, "Blue Steel and QRA", reached some extremely disturbing conclusions. The Air Officer Commanding-in-Chief (AOC-in-C) Bomber Command went so far as to order that this document *should not leave Headquarters, High Wycombe*. The conclusions were so damning that Bomber Command's then chief research officer, Tom Kerr, proposed meeting QRA requirements at Blue Steel bases by deploying freefall aircraft armed with the new laydown freefall bomb, WE.177, when it became available (which it would not be, in any numbers, before early 1967 – well over three years away).[574] The ultimate question was not addressed: had the arming of 40 V-bombers with Blue Steel enhanced or degraded overall V-Force capability and credibility?

This significant study was made just before Blue Steel-armed aircraft joined freefall aircraft on QRA. Kerr noted that freefall QRA aircraft had been "extremely effective" in maintaining less than 15 minutes' readiness. The memorandum then reflected:

"The Blue Steel weapon system (aircraft and missile) is complicated and prone to numerous defects, both on the ground and in the air. In these circumstances, the operational implications of keeping the missile on QRA, with or without fuel, have been examined."

The findings on serviceability of Blue Steel QRA systems made grim reading:

"Assuming that six weapon systems are on QRA, (serviceability data) indicates that 40%, or between two and three, will be launched at the launch point and the remaining four or three will have to be carried to the target and released from a pop-up manoeuvre … Of the missiles launched, about 75%, or two, will follow their correct trajectories and about 25% – about one – will fail before reaching the target area and will be wasted."

These figures did not improve sufficiently over the next few years to make any significant difference in such a small QRA force. Furthermore, no allowance was made for losses from enemy action. Kerr did not shy away from the facts:

"Since three of the fuelled missiles will have become freefall before release, the difference in operational capability between the fuelled and unfuelled missiles rests upon the difference in the probability that three freefall missiles delivered from a pop-up manoeuvre will achieve greater or lesser success than two Blue Steel missiles launched from a stand-off position relative to the target. As the biggest unknown is how much the defences will have suffered by the initial missile strikes, it is impossible to estimate, with any accuracy, the relative success. The difference is likely to be very small. Operationally, therefore, there is little to choose between keeping fuelled and unfuelled missiles on QRA."

It was "strongly recommended" that, initially, QRA missiles should be prepared for freefall use only, followed by the progressive introduction of full preparation of missiles, but unfuelled, for QRA then, ultimately, fuelled QRA missiles. Kerr, however, then went much further:

> "The cost of maintaining a high state of readiness with the Blue Steel weapon system and its predicted unreliability make it extremely important that the use of the laydown bomb be examined as an alternative QRA weapon system for the Blue Steel stations. The inconvenience of having aircraft on one station in two different roles must be weighed against the savings in aircraft and manpower which can be achieved, and a marked increase in the operational capability of the weapon system."

In essence, Kerr was suggesting that Blue Steel was inappropriate as a QRA weapon, given its operational drawbacks and high probability of unpowered use. Why not bend to the facts and adopt an all-freefall QRA? Had this course of action been taken, however, there would have been a long wait for a non-pop-up freefall weapon.

Not surprisingly, Kerr's pragmatic advice fell on deaf ears. Indeed, the struggle to turn Blue Steel into a viable weapon system intensified. By April 1964 Bomber Command had a computer simulation of Blue Steel generation, including inputs on times for each stage of preparation and the probabilities of unserviceability. Scampton provided the model and two periods were allowed for: the second half of 1964, when 'modifications' (presumably, for the low-level role) would reduce the number of missiles and aircraft available and, secondly, mid-1965, when the numbers of missiles and aircraft available on station were likely to peak (24 of each). Kerr's scepticism shone through in his opening remarks to the report on the use of this program:

> "This study has been based on input parameters which take an optimistic view of the state of training and organisation of the men, the recoverability of the weapon systems and the modification of certain limiting parts of the airfield schedules. Considerable effort will be required on the part of all associated with Blue Steel to achieve these predictions."[575]

The chief research officer was correct.

Freefall bombers were armed in a straightforward manner – the weapon was issued and loaded. Arming with Blue Steel, however, involved the issue of the weapon from the missile servicing and storage building, the fitting of the warhead pod, checking compatibility of the weapon with the aircraft and missile fuelling. Each step required specialised teams and ground-handling equipment, at different airfield locations. The computer program focused on the parts of the generation process known collectively as the 'missile airfield pattern': preparation of the missile after issue from the store, its loading to a prepared aircraft, the testing of the aircraft/missile combination and the loading of propellants. A 'secondary airfield pattern' was included for the generation of partly-prepared missiles already fitted with warheads, stored in the SSA on trolleys. In this pattern, the missile was moved to an aircraft dispersal and loaded directly to the bomber. The simulations showed that the principal controlling factor on generation time was likely to be the rate at which aircraft became available for missile loading. The latter was assumed to be that of previous Micky Finn no-notice generation exercises. The computer simulation report concluded:

> "Holding aircraft and missiles at advanced states of readiness gives a valuable increase in generation capability, particularly in the early stages of generation. If aircraft and missiles cannot be made available for this purpose, the first system generated in the powered role will not become available in much less than ten hours."

If serviceability and readiness are set aside, Blue Steel certainly looked a winner. Squadron Leader Robin Woolven makes the point: "Here is this eight-ton missile capable of Mach 3, with an inertial guidance system and a megaton warhead."[576] However, by the time Woolven reached his squadron, in April 1964, the switch to low level was under way, cutting Blue Steel's already meagre range by at least two-thirds, to 50 miles at best. His crew made a large number of simulated Blue Steel attacks:

> "In May 1964 Blue Steel and inertial navigation were new systems, still finding their way. Both were extremely complex and, in the best tradition of the RAF, they were accompanied by training rigs. These were used to take us through increasingly implausible combinations of possible problems that might be met in the air. If we had an operational round to fly, less the warhead, we started up the auxiliary power unit and went through our drills. We did that scores of times. The first time we did it in the air, the missile decided to shut down of its own accord. This resulted in a Court of Inquiry. The nav/radar and I had to attend with an investigating officer from another squadron. We went through the sequence on the training rig and were able to show that the fault was with the system."[577]

Norman Bonnor, a Victor nav/radar with 100 Squadron at RAF Wittering (1964–66), contributed to efforts to make Blue Steel viable. He and his crew were dissatisfied with the procedure for aligning Blue Steel's inertial guidance system: "We soon realised that the Standard Operating Procedure (SOP) had been written during the trials programme in Australia and nobody had considered revising it since the system had entered operational service."[578] They found a way of saving up to 20 minutes:

> "The inertial navigation system (INS) could not be started up and aligned on the ground because, in a war situation, we would have only four minutes' warning to complete a scramble take-off; the SOP, as written, took about 15 minutes to start up the gyros and level the system. We were not supposed to start the SOP until in level flight at our cruising altitude. We couldn't see the point of waiting and felt we should begin activating the system during the climb.
>
> "We went to the servicing bay to watch a technician setting up the system on the bench; he followed a much faster procedure than our SOP. We – that is, the nav/plotter and I – called up a senior scientist at RAE Farnborough, who had been involved in the design, and asked him what he thought of aligning the INS in the climb. He couldn't see a problem. So, we began using the faster procedure in the climb and were soon completing many more practice attacks than other crews. We were asked what was going on by the squadron commander, Wing Commander John Herrington (later, Air Vice-Marshal). He told us to continue ignoring the SOP, adding: 'You must tell all 100 Squadron crews, but don't tell 139.' However, with 100 Squadron outperforming 139, the station commander, Group Captain Lawrence, got involved. He told us to carry on, adding: 'Tell 139, but don't tell Scampton!'"[579]

Bonner has interesting and balanced views on Blue Steel's reliability:

"It has been suggested that only half the Blue Steels would have worked on the day, had that day come. It is true to say that, initially, it was not unusual to find the weapon unserviceable on going out to the aircraft. It did take several hours to mate missile to aircraft, involving the marriage of a whole series of complex butt connections. Frequently, on starting up the system, missile and aircraft would refuse to talk to each other. The mating could take four hours and it was very awkward work, as the Victor sat very low on the ground … We normally flew training sorties with the training rounds, which did not contain a warhead, rocket engine or fuel tanks. It came as quite a surprise when we were ordered to fly with what we called 'wet' rounds … that is fully fuelled with HTP and kerosene but without – of course – a warhead. This had good results, as the reliability of the whole system improved. When the system entered service, the missile/aircraft combination on QRA wouldn't last much more than a week. Yet, as time passed, things did get much better. By late 1965, a Blue Steel aircraft on QRA would be OK for up to the full 30 days expected. Regular flying of operational missiles made a big difference."

TESTING GENERATION: MICK AND MICKY FINN

During 1964, various drills were held to speed up Blue Steel generation, including Exercise Extrude in June and Exercise Imperious in July, involving Scampton and Wittering respectively on a "partial no-notice" basis. The stations were pre-warned that the exercise would be called during a specific week. Blue Steel's problems were compounded by the lengthy periods required for missile recovery after exercises. Bomber Command studied the missile recovery performance at Scampton following the August 1964 Exercise Mick (the first full no-notice generation exercise at a Blue Steel station). Scampton generated 11 missiles, ten of which were loaded to aircraft. It took 28 days to complete the missile recovery, a shorter period than that required for recovery from Exercise Nursemaid that April (see page 202) and Exercise Extrude in June, "but considerably longer than the potential achievement of ten –11 days". The reasons included the wet tests required due to missile leaks.[580] The recovery of missiles at Scampton was reduced to 19 days after Micky Finn 4 that October.[581]

Were these signs of genuine improvement in generation, regeneration and, in the case of Blue Steel, missile recovery? Both Scampton and Wittering took part in an Exercise Mick generation exercise on 11 October 1965. Bomber Command chief research officer R. J. Monaghan described the results as "most encouraging". He added: "Increased holding of pre-fuelled missiles and improved serviceability of aircraft undoubtedly helped in the early stages of generation, but there were delays in the generation of later systems." As for the underlying reasons, he noted that Scampton's troubles involved missiles whilst Wittering's problems were with aircraft, but, in both cases, the common denominator was a shortage of spares.[582]

The October 1965 Exercise Mick was the first-generation exercise involving both Blue Steel stations since the previous March. Maximum weapon-system generation was required. Scampton had 22 aircraft; 14 were available after allowing for QRA, detachments and other commitments. Wittering had 20 aircraft and 12 available (increasing to 13 when an aircraft returned from the manufacturer six hours after the alert). Both stations had 28 missiles and 19 available (each had five fully fuelled and serviceable). In the case of Scampton, another four Blue Steels were unfuelled and serviceable and ten more unfuelled and unserviceable.

At Wittering, six missiles were unfuelled and serviceable and a further eight unfuelled and unserviceable. In all, the two stations generated 27 Blue Steel systems, 24 in the powered and three in the unpowered mode.

Scampton generated 14 weapon systems, 11 powered and three unpowered (one was issued unpowered and two others developed leaks during HTP filling which could not be rectified). Monaghan's report reviewed the results:

> "The generation achievement at Scampton bettered the Bomber Command alert and readiness (BCAR) requirements for the intermediate times of eight, ten and 12 hours after the alert and only just failed (by about 25 minutes) to meet the requirement for the number of systems to be ready within 16 hours of the alert, that is, the latest time for which procedures gave a definite requirement."

As for Wittering, 13 weapon systems were generated, all powered, and the generation achievement met BCAR requirements for the number of systems to be ready within eight, ten, 12 and 16 hours of the alert, although "the generation of some of the later systems was prolonged …"

Problems were identified at both stations. At Scampton, only one of the two missile gantries was serviceable (and this failed twice); filling was dogged by an unusually high number of HTP leaks. Wittering benefitted from a revised airfield pattern, avoiding delays in the use of missile transporters. Further benefits were anticipated from the revised airfield pattern and plans were underway to increase to eight the mandatory holding of pre-fuelled missiles. The persistent problem for both stations, however, was still the lack of a plentiful supply of essential spares.

Whilst some improvements were apparent, Exercises Mick and Micky Finn continued to expose significant differences between freefall and stand-off weapons generation and regeneration performance. Nothing could be done to radically transform Blue Steel's generation process: removal from storage, fitting of the warhead, preparation of the carrier aircraft, mating the weapon and aircraft, post-loading checks, fuelling and aircrew checks. A failed mating meant starting again from the beginning. Even if successful, there was no guarantee that the missile would remain serviceable in the air, in which case it would have to be dropped freefall. In essence, the real problem was that Blue Steel was a liquid-fuelled weapon of great complexity, requiring lengthy preparation, although this process was rationalised.

The uncomfortable contrast between freefall and Blue Steel generation persisted. The first in a long series of Micky Finn no-notice generation and dispersal exercises had been called in December 1961.[583] Nearly three years on, a Micky Finn was called in October 1964. This generated 61 MBF freefall and TBF systems – 85% (52) within ten hours and 97% (59) within the planned 20 hours. Of the 35 systems planned to disperse, 94% (33) had been regenerated within 24 hours of the start of the exercise. As for Blue Steel, 30 weapon systems were available for the exercise – the first full generation of the Blue Steel force. The results offered a sharp contrast to the freefall figures: 47% (14) Blue Steel systems completed initial generation within 20 hours and 86% (26) within 40 hours. The results were described, in a draft minute from the Assistant Chief of the Air Staff (Operations), as "much slower than expected" and "less encouraging" than the freefall outcome – which showed modest improvement over the previous year.[584]

Micky Finn 5, initiated on 5 July 1965, was another major no-notice test of the BCAR plan and the second involving generation, dispersal and regeneration of freefall and Blue Steel systems (but with only Scampton's Blue Steel aircraft participating). The surprise alert came at 03.00. Later, during the early afternoon, Roy Brocklebank's freefall Vulcan crew took off for their dispersal airfield – Ballykelly – where the bomber was refuelled and brought up to RS15. During this exercise, the crew were treated to a bizarre sight:

> "I recall at one point we were in the aircraft as the Joint Inter-Service Hovercraft Trials Unit hovercraft came down the main runway towards the ORP. Its progress was erratic and we were worried that it might lurch into the ORP."

Scampton was challenged to generate the maximum number of Blue Steel systems and disperse to five airfields: Burtonwood, Coningsby, Elvington, Kinloss and Lossiemouth, followed by regeneration to combat-ready. The signal to disperse when ready came at 10.00. Scampton had 24 aircraft on strength; 12 were available – the others were on QRA, detached or overseas. The availability was unusually low, four less than for Micky Finn 4, in October 1964 – in part due to two aircraft attending the Calgary International Air Show and a third aircraft on a 'Goose Ranger' (the latter was back at Scampton in the early evening and, subsequently, was generated).[585]

As for missiles, Scampton had 28 on strength and 20 were available (three more than for Micky Finn 4). Five of the 20 were fully fuelled and serviceable, two were unfuelled and serviceable and 13 were unfuelled and unserviceable. Scampton managed to generate and disperse 13 aircraft, four each to Burtonwood and Kinloss, two each to Elvington and Lossiemouth and one to Coningsby – the most successful result to date, largely due to the highest initial aircraft serviceability achieved so far (50%). This was not matched by regeneration performance at the dispersal airfields, with results "unexpectedly poor" and "far below expectation". A Blue Steel system was considered capable of regeneration within three hours of landing at a dispersal airfield but this was achieved by only four of the 13 systems, the remaining nine taking 3¾–11 hours. Only five out of the expected nine systems were combat-ready within 24 hours and only eight of an expected 11 systems were available within 28½ hours. The final outcome was summed up in the exercise report: "Ten powered and three unpowered systems were ultimately prepared at dispersal airfields within 43½ hours of the declaration of the alert, but one of the unpowered systems was considered usable in the powered role in a war situation."

Bomber Command's response to Blue Steel's relatively poor showing in Micky Finn 5 and the January 1966 Exercise Mick was to devise a new type of no-notice generation and dispersal exercise for Wittering and Scampton. Known as Exercise Finnigan, it was first called on 7 March 1966. This generated 24 Blue Steel systems, 20 (83%) in the powered mode. The results confirmed the powered bomb as an on-going challenge. BCAR requirements for generation were met but the generation of the later systems "was unusually protracted" and reflected difficulties in aircraft preparation. Twenty-three systems were dispersed and regenerated but over half took more than four hours to recover. In the case of Wittering, for example, generation of the last three systems required 40¾, 60¼ and 76½ hours respectively, with regeneration times ranging from 3¾ to 22½ hours.[586] Clearly, the stand-off bomb was a weapon requiring generous political/intelligence warning and an enemy in no particular hurry.

Missile dependability on QRA remained a concern. The maximum permitted QRA time for a fuelled missile was 30 days (extended to 40 days from August 1965). Operational Research Branch Memorandum No. 326 (March 1966) detailed Blue Steel standby periods at Scampton and Wittering during the April–September 1965 period and looked at 44 weapon system QRA periods. There was little difference between the two bases in the average time spent by systems on standby, the overall average being about 17.7 days (similar to freefall station figures). If a missile had been in the wet condition before going on QRA, less than 30 days (or 40) was available to it whilst on standby. There were also the unserviceabilities; there were 15 premature removals in the period and 11 missiles were on standby for less than 13 days.[587]

In July 1966, Bomber Command consolidated Blue Steel exercise performance data. This major review took in the results of 16 generation exercises involving Scampton and Wittering, from the earliest in March 1964 to Micky Finn 6 in May 1966. The early exercises required generation of a limited number of systems from a pre-arranged start-time. Subsequent exercises were no-notice and (with the exception of the first two in 1965) required generation of the maximum number of systems. Six of the 16 exercises also required dispersal. Two major factors influenced system generation performance: changes in missile fuelling and airfield patterns and, secondly, a progressive increase in the number of missiles held in a pre-fuelled state on aircraft pans. Both Wittering and Scampton progressed to hold eight missiles in the pre-fuelled state. Control aids also led to improvements. These were tools to promote timely decision-making and avoid bottlenecks and delays. However, there were limits to improvement. The Operational Research Branch report setting out the review findings (No. 332) summed up the situation:

> "There was a steady improvement in generation achievement in the first 15 to 18 months of the period, but the achievements of the last nine months have been somewhat variable. Regeneration achievement has also improved, though to a lesser extent for Wittering than for Scampton. Both stations had difficulty in regenerating systems within the guiding time of three hours laid down in the BCAR procedure."[588]

The memorandum called for "continuous pressure" to improve in three areas:

- Speedy preparation of aircraft for missile loading (particularly those under the control of the air engineering squadron).
- Implementation, "from the instant of the declaration of an alert", of a simultaneous flow pattern for all fuelled and unfuelled missiles and their associated weapon pods, to ensure a prepared missile availability that should match any rapid aircraft preparation.
- Practice in the use of control aids at all levels of the generation pattern.

Yet 12 months later, in July 1967, Bomber Command shied away from testing the generation, dispersal and regeneration capabilities of Blue Steel and freefall squadrons on an equal footing. During that month, Air Vice-Marshal L. M. Hodges, ACAS (Ops), wrote a note to the private secretary of the Chief of the Air Staff (CAS), commenting on the results of a just-completed Micky Finn: "C-in-C Bomber Command has just telephoned me to say that the exercise has been successfully completed and 66 aircraft were 'scrambled' from dispersal and main bases in under two minutes."[589]

He continued, with no trace of irony:

"The only difference between this exercise and previous ones is that, in this instance, the Blue Steel stations were given the go-ahead 24 hours earlier, in view of their slower force generation. This has meant that the Blue Steel force was able to disperse at about the same time as the freefall force and was better from a morale point of view."

Hodges added: "I think CAS may wish to be aware of the successful conclusion of this exercise."

On balance, the evidence exposes an uncomfortable disparity between the generation/regeneration performance of freefall and Blue Steel squadrons. Immense efforts were made to overcome at least some of Blue Steel's shortcomings but only minor improvements could be achieved. At the same time, in the crucial area of alert and readiness, the adoption of the new Alert Condition 1 and its RS05 crew rotation requirement in a close approach to war demonstrated a clear appreciation of what was needed to maintain the V-Force's core retaliatory threat against Moscow and Leningrad. This decision was of fundamental significance and was taken despite the persistent reluctance of senior ministers and commanders to face up to the operational realities of a subsonic bomber deterrent.

15
SURVIVING A WAR SCRAMBLE

> *ATTENTION. ATTENTION. THIS IS THE BOMBER CONTROLLER FOR BOMB LIST DELTA. SCRAMBLE. AUTHENTICATION WHISKY NINE JULIET.*
>
> Squadron Leader Roy Brocklebank, Wing targeting officer,
> RAF Waddington: "So would start the Third World War in the 1960s."

Much was done to reduce V-Force vulnerabilities on the ground: the introduction of an onerous QRA/exercise regime, measures to improve alert response times and wider recognition of the gravest threat – a low-trajectory, short-warning missile strike on MBF airfields. The severity of this threat was the context for the new Alert Condition 1 as previously described. Under UK ground alert, this was the only way to ensure a chance of escape for at least some of the bombers.

EXERCISING ARMAGEDDON

From 1959 onwards, V-Force stations, squadrons and crews exercised regularly to test readiness for war. Dispersal exercises had begun in May of that year with Mayflight 1, a pre-notified exercise testing the administrative, engineering and operational facilities required by crews to maintain combat status. There was also Exercise Kinsman, a notice drill requiring individual squadrons to fly to and operate from dispersal airfields, so familiarising crews with wartime conditions.

In November 1959 and almost immediately upon joining XV Squadron, John Laycock – then a Victor Mk 1 co-pilot – flew with his new crew from Cottesmore to St Mawgan, Cornwall, on Mayflight 2, a dispersal exercise. It was all very new, including the possibility of being called from his bed for a night alert requiring RS05:

"There was always the possibility of RS02. We would then wait for

The chances of a successful escape were very slim in an IRBM low-trajectory strike. (Steven Jefferson)

the next order or taxi. At Cottesmore we had Standard Vanguard cars and J2 vans to take us to the aircraft. The idea was always to be together as a crew. The Mess, sleeping accommodation and operations block were in a 100-yard triangle. We had our evening meals in the Mess and the cars were always outside. During the night they were parked in a garage behind the Mess, protected from the weather. The drivers responsible for ground transport were also on 15 minutes' readiness."[590]

QRA crews at RS15 always had transport close at hand, even if the aircraft were only a few hundred yards away. QRA alerts were broadcast in crisp terms: "*This is the bomber controller. For the QRA force only. Exercise EDOM. Readiness 05.*" (see page 192) Roy Brocklebank remembers the call being repeated three times:

"You had a maximum of ten minutes to go from RS15 to RS05. The time physically required depended, to some extent, on station layout. At RAF Cottesmore, for example, a night alert meant getting up, dressing, a car drive along a stretch of main road, then a turn down the 'lazy runway' (closed/disused), to complete a half-mile run to the dispersal – followed by a rush to board the aircraft. RS05 required all five crew members to be inside, with the door shut. Achieving that reaction in ten minutes was not an 'automatic satisfactory'. It worked on a par system – like golf. If your par time was 7½ minutes and, one night, it took longer, someone would want to know why. As the Cottesmore crews had some distance to travel to their aircraft and had to use Standard Vanguard estates, a back-up crew bus was provided. The driver was responsible for checking the cars in the garages during the night and then following the QRA cars to the dispersal. Waddington QRA, in contrast, was very close to the dispersal and we could achieve short response times. The maximum time permitted was 13 minutes to 02."[591]

It is remarkable that, having invested huge sums in building the V-Force, paltry funds were not found to provide reliable transport for QRA crews requiring every available second to get off the ground. Phil Leckenby did two tours at Waddington, first as a Vulcan Mk 1A co-pilot, then as a captain on 101 Squadron flying the Mk 2. He recalled the ancient Morris J2 vans:

"What the J2 lacked in elegance it more than made up for in temperament … the woefully undersized engine was notoriously reluctant to start. Even in a summer heatwave, it could be coaxed into life only with difficulty. In wet, cold weather it was a toss-up as to whether the starter motor or the battery would give up the unequal struggle first, leaving the frustrated crew no option but to run to the aircraft as best they could. The second trifling imperfection lay with the J2's column-mounted gear change … the older the vehicle became, the more imprecise was the selection of the three forward gears. As the linkage became worn, first and second gears would become increasingly difficult to engage, leaving the driver with the option of kangarooing uncertainly forward in third or accelerating away ignominiously in reverse.

"I have an enduring memory of a particular QRA exercise which required us to board the aircraft, start up and taxi to the runway threshold … As we ran out of the QRA hut, I caught sight of 50 Squadron's van lurching towards the dispersal in a cloud of blue smoke and a series of hesitant leaps. As we drove off in pursuit, I noticed 101

Squadron's van motionless in its parking slot, its blue light flashing in anticipation and anxious faces peering out of the windows; eventually, it must have coughed into life because soon afterwards we were treated to the bizarre spectacle of their J2 accelerating away rapidly in reverse, weaving an uncertain path backwards to the waiting aircraft." [592]

Speed of response meant life or death in a war scramble. Perhaps the organisers of V-Force ground transport were of Russian heritage?

THE THREAT FROM SPETSNAZ

The risk to the MBF on its airfields was not confined to hostile bombers and missiles. During the 1960s, there was plenty of lurid Sunday newspaper coverage of the threat from Spetsnaz, Soviet special forces. That risk might be real enough on the brink of war. Spetsnaz roles certainly included the destruction of NATO nuclear weapons, although, in the UK case there would have been obvious difficulties regarding insertion (but, equally, there was also the parallel risk from 'sleepers').[593]

Generally, MBF station security was very low key during the 1960s, with poorly protected gates, perimeters and aircraft. There was easy access from public roads adjacent to or even intruding into bases. Roy Brocklebank describes the set-up at RAF Waddington with:

"The Roman Road, High Dyke, running arrow-straight from the A1, through Ancaster, through the southern dispersal and between the domestic site and the technical site. There was a simple crash gate at that southern dispersal. At RAF Coningsby the crash gate on the Old Boston Road was left open. The Old Boston Road continued across the airfield to the QRA dispersals. At RAF Cottesmore, the station road ran straight from the village, through the main gate, past operations and thence with little difficulty to the QRA dispersal."

Veterans' accounts of low levels of protection are supported by contemporary documentary evidence discussing, inter alia, whether one RAF policeman with sidearm and dog could guard two nuclear-armed aircraft and the use of ground personnel in a 'Home Guard' role. During exercises, vital points were guarded by airmen armed with pickaxe handles. Even during the Cuban Crisis, there appears to have been no major tightening of base security. Prevailing attitudes are summed up by Robin Woolven:

"… a former Thor squadron commander told me that on hearing of the Cuban Crisis escalating on the Saturday morning, he personally authorised his RAF police guards to load their weapons but his boss countermanded the order, as 'somebody might get shot'."[594]

The USAF had a different approach. As a 14-year-old air cadet, this author visited Brize Norton in 1963 and saw the heavily-armed jeep patrols racing around, guarding SAC B-47s on their aprons. For its part, Bomber Command appeared to regard the Campaign for Nuclear Disarmament (CND) as more of a threat, followed in the 1970s by the Provisional IRA. TACEVAL, however, brought a change of heart, with more appreciation of the Spetsnaz threat. In the 1980s, armed guards appeared, but it was only in 1999 that the Military Provost Guard Service was established, to provide dedicated armed security at bases.[595]

According to a paper by USAF Major Burton A. Casteel Jr, the Spetsnaz threat was real enough. He described it as "a significant threat to the USAF, whether at home or on foreign soil".596 Equally, the seemingly modest RAF security efforts at MBF bases during the 1960s should not be belittled, as plans for much greater protection in a serious crisis did exist. In 1958, all RAF commands received orders regarding preparations for global war. Procedures included 'State Black', requiring "unobtrusive measures" to safeguard operating forces, including the deployment of light anti-aircraft artillery and RAF Regiment field squadrons, together with preparations for evacuation of families from V-bomber bases.597 The need for effective ground defence was recognised, at least on paper, although there does seem to have been a lack of application, even of an unobtrusive nature, during the Cuban Crisis.

AT THE READY

Phil Leckenby described procedures for starting the aircraft:

> "… the approved engine-start procedure was to brief the crew chief that as soon as he saw the aircrew emerge from the wagon on the edge of the dispersal, he was to press all four start buttons. This could save a precious few seconds, allowing the engines to be winding up whilst the crew clambered into the crew compartment; as soon as the pilots reached the narrow confines of the cockpit, they would open the throttles to the idle gate and the aircraft would be ready to taxi."598

Things did not always go well:

> "The custody of the aircraft key was usually entrusted to the co-pilot. During one exercise call-out the inevitable happened. The kangarooing J2 lurched to a halt on the edge of the pan and the crew chief, who had already started the ground power unit, hit all four start buttons, as briefed. The crew sprinted to beneath the entrance door and waited for the co-pilot to unlock it. The Olympus engines began their noisy wind-up. The co-pilot repeatedly felt around his neck for the key lanyard, but it wasn't there. He then went through a slap-stick comedy routine, furiously patting all the many pockets of his flying suit as he tried to locate the missing key. The penny finally dropped. The hapless co-pilot had committed the cardinal sin of leaving the key on his nightstand in the QRA dormitory where, until a few minutes ago, he had been enjoying a peaceful afternoon nap. Ashen-faced, he was despatched back to the QRA hut to retrieve the key."

A dispersed bomber force would give the Soviets more targets to cover but the primary survival benefit of dispersal was avoidance of the take-off queue. A dispersed flight of four aircraft could take off in one minute 45 seconds or less, assuming crews at RS05 and then RS02. With crew rotation for a portion of the force it would have been possible, if uncomfortable, to maintain round-the-clock cockpit readiness for some aircraft during a period of acute tension – in effect, creating a much enlarged, dispersed QRA force at the highest possible readiness, just short of engine start. This capability, combined with the selective dispersal of these bombers to airfields in the north and west, direct communication with the bomber controller at Bomber Command Headquarters via Telescramble, simultaneous engine start

(SIMSTART) and operational readiness platforms (ORPs), represented "maximum effort" ground alert readiness.

Aircrew certainly appreciated the significance of timely dispersal, but would there be enough time to complete the lengthy generation/dispersal/regeneration process? Ed Jarron regards this as:

> "A realistic assumption and I also think that the proportion of the force surviving a war scramble would have been high in those circumstances. Once dispersed, the crews didn't need 15 minutes. I think the scramble survival rate would have been good."[599]

Equally, it is a fact that, for some unfathomable reason, *crews were not fully briefed on how to maximise their chances of surviving a war scramble.* Surprisingly, the essential survival tactics required during the vital first few minutes in the air were not passed on in any coordinated, formal manner.

Most measures taken to reduce exposure to the missile threat focused on faster take-off times. John Huggins made the essential point:

> "Dispersal meant aircraft could get airborne in the minimum time, without having to queue … Every field had hard-points pre-prepared, with a direct line to High Wycombe. Once on the pad, the aircraft was plugged into the ground point and the bomber controller talked directly to the crew, who maintained radio silence."[600]

Robin Woolven, a Blue Steel Vulcan nav/plotter with 617 Squadron, recalled that when the alert state was raised to cockpit readiness crews hurried to their aircraft and checked in with the RAF police guard and the crew chief:

> "The final external safety connections with the missile would be pulled out by the nav/radar, the aircraft door would be locked and the anxious crew would be listening intently to the bomber controller and the 'pips' assuring us that the line was good."[601]

Reaching escape distance: only aircraft 'first in the queue' and climbing immediately after take-off had a chance of survival. (Peter Lawrence)

Vulcan captain Paddy Langdown remembers the next stage:

> "RS02 was ordered in a similar format to the RS05 message and involved starting all four engines using rapid start (a developed SIMSTART system). This would spin an Olympus engine up to self-sustain speed in seconds. A modern big fan engine today will take about a minute to achieve the same steady state."[602]

Scramble requirements pre-QRA reflected the then dominant threat from manned bombers: 80% of aircraft airborne nine minutes after the scramble order, in favourable circumstances (assuming cockpit readiness), as described in Bomber Command's May 1959 Mayflight 1 exercise report. This document referred to the looming missile threat with unusual candour:

> "Estimates of performance in less favourable circumstances show that, even from a relaxed readiness state, 80% of the force could be expected to be airborne in 14 minutes from scramble order. These reaction times are sufficient to allow unhurried decision in the event of a subsonic bomber attack on this country and are satisfactory in the face of a supersonic threat, but would be inadequate if short-range ballistic missiles were used in quantity against airfields … In order to provide a manned bomber deterrent in the face of a serious ballistic missile threat, much more drastic measures than the present dispersal scheme are needed, such as airborne alert or overseas dispersal. If an effective automatic warning system were available, a ground alert (engines running, on the end of the runway) would provide take-off times compatible with missile flight times, but the difficulties of implementing such a scheme over long periods of time are obvious."[603]

The report made three major recommendations: investigation of the practicalities of "trickle dispersal" on the initial Alert Alpha (generation of maximum aircraft and commencement of preparations for dispersal) – to inject more uncertainty into enemy planning and avoid a sudden drop in force availability; a study of ways to increase the deterrent value of dispersal (by making it impossible for the enemy to accurately forecast the number and location of airfields actually in use); and the use of "refined analytical methods" to optimise the allocation of targets and weapons to crews (with emphasis on efficient switching of the plan from national to coordinated).

This report was produced at a time when Soviet missile strength was modest. However, if dispersal airfields were used only during dispersal exercises, even a modest missile force could hope to destroy the MBF by targeting the main bases alone:

> "It is very important, therefore, that use of the dispersal airfields should be unpredictable and, if possible, virtually continuous, so that at any time an enemy planning an offensive will find that inclusion of the dispersal airfields in his attack plan demands the employment of more missiles than he has available."

That said, the report's authors appreciated that this state of affairs would be short-lived:

> "The number of proposed dispersal airfields in this country is limited and the enemy capability increases with time. It may be important, therefore, within the effective life of the MBF, to introduce alternative methods of decreasing its vulnerability to missile attack."

Early recognition of the essential problem for the 1960s was not accompanied by a solution; the MBF would depend on a potentially very short BMEWS warning, favourable circumstances for launch (after dispersal, regeneration and a proportion of crews at RS05 24/7 advanced readiness), together with, of course, fully optimised "flyaway" procedures.

The July 1960 Mayflight 3 exercise took place at a time when the growing missile threat was receiving more attention. New measures were being introduced, such as SIMSTART and Telescramble, to get the bombers off the ground and clear of their bases before Soviet weapons detonated. The results were set out in an Operational Research Branch post-exercise report which looked forward to the widespread provision of ORPs on the airfields. Mayflight 3 also further explored "trickle dispersal". Taken overall, however, Mayflight 3 indicated that any major improvement in V-Force response times required an uphill struggle.[604]

Mayflight 3 involved 82 aircraft (80% of strength). The initial generation of weapon systems (excluding the effects of dispersal) resulted in 66% and 69% of strength ready within 12 and 24 hours respectively. According to the report:

> "For those aircraft trickle dispersing after Alert Alpha, 50% were dispersed and ready within 10 hours of Alpha and 90% within 24 hours. For those aircraft dispersing in the normal way at Bravo, 50% were dispersed and ready within 4½ hours and 90% within 10 hours of Bravo."

There was no marked improvement in reaction times on previous Mayflight exercises.

On scramble times – from cockpit readiness – 50% of the force reached take-off within 5½ minutes and 90% within 7½ minutes of the scramble order. One conclusion from Mayflight 3 was that times could increase, to about 13 minutes and 20 minutes for 50% and 90% of the force respectively, in "difficult or unexpected circumstances" – such as scrambling from Blue (40 minutes' readiness) or in the case of land-line failure. The report added that further improvement in scramble times from cockpit readiness was unlikely until simultaneous engine start and ORPs were employed. The few aircraft then fitted with SIMSTART saved up to one minute 40 seconds in starting engines (up to two minutes in trials). Telescramble-equipped aircraft saved about 30 seconds on time to engine start.

At this time, some nuclear weapons required last-minute loading (LML) of fissile cores immediately prior to take-off. The report called for more practice of LML and improved procedures. Its conclusions struck a downbeat note: comparison with the results of earlier exercises indicated "small improvements" in generation rates and, to a lesser extent, in scramble times, but "these improvements probably reflect greater familiarity with exercise requirements, rather than improved operational capability".

INTRODUCING SIMSTART

Valiant captain Tony Cottingham recalled that starting engines one by one took about four minutes. Starting with less than a minute between engines ran the risk of blowing the main starter fuse, meaning a long delay while it was changed.[605] Dick Fuller, a Valiant co-pilot, added:

> "Towards the end of my operational flying, SIMSTART was introduced. I remember the huge battery packs. On one occasion, a flight of four Valiants on QRA did a SIMSTART

scramble for Ministry of Defence observers. It was an impressive sight. They put the power on, the plugs pulled out as the aircraft began to roll and in less than two minutes they were climbing away."[606]

Michael Alcock (later, Air Chief Marshal Sir Michael) was instrumental in the development of SIMSTART. As a young man he had joined the Bomber Command Development Unit (BCDU) in 1959 as a National Service technical officer. During that autumn a Squadron Leader Dixon telephoned, on behalf of the command electrical engineer at Bomber Command HQ:

> "The Air Officer Commanding-in-Chief (AOC-in-C) Bomber Command, Air Chief Marshal Cross, had recently returned from the USA, where the USAF had demonstrated simultaneous starting of all engines of, I think, a B-47. The AOC-in-C wanted to know why 'his' V-bombers could not do the same trick. Dixon relayed that question to BCDU's technical officers. After an intense morning's session, pouring over wiring diagrams of the Valiant together with our crew chiefs and SNCO electricians, we called back later that day to say we thought it would be relatively simple to do."[607]

The team acquired a bomb trolley and mounted four engine-starter panels and lots of batteries, wired directly to the starter motors of each engine. The engines were started externally by the crew chief, who hit all four starter buttons in turn (fully simultaneous operation caused failure due to the extreme current demand). Sir Michael recalled the AOC-in-C's reaction on witnessing a demonstration, on 23 December 1959, as "a joy to behold …He turned to Squadron Leader Dixon and ordered the whole V-Force, Valiants, Vulcans and Victors – the lot – to be modified with SIMSTART as soon as possible."

Sir Michael regards SIMSTART as the very foundation of QRA:

> "… it was the BCDU's pioneering work in the field of simultaneous engine starting, leading to the ability to scramble four aircraft in well under four minutes … that had made this a realistic proposition. Thus it was that the V-Force was able to take on its QRA commitment of one loaded weapon system and crew per operational squadron."

There was, however, a snag with early SIMSTART equipment: ground crew had to unplug the starter leads from the undercarriage bays and this required them to stand on the wheels:

> "… it was not unknown for ground crew to be doing that as the aircraft began to move – they called it 'wheel-dancing'. Trial 420 was the last in the series and … allowed us to improve the design, with automatic disconnection of all power supplies."

Eventually, Vulcan Mk 2 aircraft received a system with a starting panel available to the pilot. This had a 'rapid' selector. According to Sir Michael, the Vulcan Mk 2 "could achieve less than 30 seconds to lift-off, almost as quick as Lightning fighters of the time."[608]

A CDS memorandum of July 1961 described SIMSTART as essential, as "the modifications will reduce take-off time from 140 seconds to about 60 seconds and contribute significantly to the credibility of the deterrent against pre-emptive attack by enemy land-based ballistic missiles."[609] The use of the phrase "land-based" here is, perhaps, noteworthy, given the rapid growth of the submarine-launched ballistic missile threat during the 1960s. SIMSTART's total cost across the V-Force was £6.75 million (£4 million for engine-starting, including R&D, and £2.75 million for other equipment and services, including 'snatch' disconnections). The initial costs of Mk 1 SIMSTART were met from existing resources. On 19 July 1961 the Deputy Chief of the Air Staff (DCAS), Air Marshal R. B. Lees, warned the penny-pinchers: "… unless we are prepared to accept an increase of reaction time of at least one minute, no economy is possible."[610] The spend was approved.

HOW MUCH WARNING?

The 'four-minute warning' was a common expression, but the reality was rather more complex. In 1961, Bomber Command took a close look at what could be expected from BMEWS, Fylingdales, when it became operational. An Operational Research Branch study (April 1961) considered attacks by missiles of 650, 1,000 and 1,500 miles range, fired to maximum range in optimum trajectories or in low trajectories with 15 degrees re-entry. The key findings included:

- A low trajectory considerably reduces missile flight time and decreases proportionally the warning time.
- Average time between a missile first entering radar coverage and being detected is ten seconds (average time between two successive 'looks').
- The most westerly bases had an increase in minimum warning time of one to one and a half minutes.[611]

A 1,500-mile-range missile fired to maximum range "should be detected at least 10.5 minutes before impact for targets in Eastern England, this time increasing to 11.3 minutes for targets in the extreme west of the UK". If the same missile could be fired on a low trajectory over 1,000 miles range, warning time would be reduced to between 3½ minutes and 5½ minutes. Launch sites for such firings could be within the borders of the Soviet Union; the use of missiles over a 650-mile trajectory would require launch sites in satellite countries. Given deployment near the East German border, such missiles could hit the UK's most westerly targets. If missiles were fired on low trajectory over 650 miles, warning time would vary between 3½ minutes for East Anglia to five minutes for Northern Ireland.

The critical factor determining warning time was a capability to fire on low trajectories. If low trajectories could not be used and missiles were fired on minimum energy trajectories, there would be significant increases in warning times:

"… Taking a target in the Midlands, the warning time would be 7½ minutes for a 650-mile trajectory, 9.2 minutes for a 1,000-mile trajectory and 10.8 minutes for a 1,500-mile trajectory. There would be an advantage, therefore, from the Russian point of view, in forward deployment of missiles in this case. The smallest warning times from missiles fired from Russia are approximately 4.2 minutes at Fylingdales Moor when a 1,000-mile missile is fired on a low trajectory over 650 miles range. Significant improvement in warning times can only be achieved by using dispersals in the most westerly areas in the UK."

HOW VULNERABLE?

John Huggins recalled the "getaway" in a simulated war scramble:

> "The first aircraft moves out and starts its take-off run. Whilst she is rolling, the next aircraft moves out and starts rolling 15 seconds after the first one releases its brakes. The next one and the fourth one do the same. The total elapsed time is one minute 40 seconds, with the aircraft rolling down the runway two at a time. From brakes off to rotate is 30 seconds in peacetime and slightly less in war. We lifted off at 165 kts. The acceleration on the ground was faster than a Ferrari. The 'decision speed' was 145 kts – the maximum speed for streaming the braking chute."[612]

Crews on dispersal airfields, in the ultimate national emergency, would be expecting the first wave of missiles. John Huggins set the scene: "The aircraft would be blacked out, with anti-flash screens and blinds down." One or both pilots would be wearing eyepatch protection, to save one eye from flash. This was described by Roy Brocklebank as a "sensible precaution" protecting against total blindness.[613]

The chances of surviving a missile strike on the airfields were slim under any scenario other than "simultaneous impact" attack on US and UK targets. Other attack modes ("simultaneous launch" and an attack on the UK in isolation) left Britain with around 3½ to 5½ minutes warning at best. Only crews at RS05, ready for immediate engine start and positioned first for take-off, had any real chance of escape. John Huggins had no illusions:

How would the Cold War end? In 1965, it felt like the world was on the "eve of destruction", in the words of a popular song of the time. Here, a group take in the view at Waddington. The Ford Anglia's registration disc reads May 1965. (Pete Middleton, via Andy Leitch Collection)

"Naturally, we thought about that four-minute warning. It would take, at the very best, at least 15 seconds from early warning to the order for scramble. My fastest ever four-aircraft scramble was one minute 46 seconds. Could we get far enough away to escape the blast from weapons falling on the airfield? Some crews fancied their chances by climbing, but that meant going westwards (taking off into the prevailing wind), then circling to head east. Almost certainly, they would be passing through the nuclear clouds which would have been all that was left of Scampton, Coningsby and the rest. I had another idea. We would go ultra-low and seek shelter from the Lincolnshire Edge, a drop of about 200 ft. We would go down to 50 ft, hoping the blast wave would travel over the top of us. I didn't really think much of our chances. A nuclear detonation creates a huge vacuum and blows a big hole in the upper atmosphere, reaching up to the ozone layer. This vacuum compounds the damage, by sucking back the blast into the centre and flattening the few surviving structures."[614]

In fact, studies demonstrated that the best survival tactic during flyaway was to climb to at least 6,000 ft, even at the sacrifice of some escape distance, to avoid reflected shock waves near the ground.

Bomber Command circulated an important report on MBF vulnerability to missile attack in March 1962. This study, dated November 1961, attempted to answer the fundamental question: Could the bombers escape an attack on the airfields, in a successful war scramble? The report estimated the weight of missile attack required to neutralise the MBF (under various circumstances) and considered the effects of warning time delays in scrambling aircraft, together with survival issues relating to tactics immediately after take-off. Its conclusions were disturbing. This study assumed dispersal over 24 airfields (including main bases) and examined the issues in two parts. The first considered the weight of attack required to neutralise the MBF whilst still on the ground, including estimates of aircraft vulnerability, weapon yield, accuracy and reliability. The second part included estimates of the probability of aircraft survival, in relation to warning times, given assumptions concerning missile trajectory and aircraft reaction times.[615]

Part One considered an attack on aircraft parked on airfields, with assumptions taking account of a range of aiming error, weapon yields of 1, 3 and 10 mt and blast overpressures of 3 psi and 5 psi. This allowed the relationship between yield, overpressure and damage radius to be presented. It was assumed that the V-Force was dispersed, with three aircraft* parked randomly on each airfield. It was recognised that, in actuality, aircraft would be clustered on ORPs, but that was found to make practically no difference to results. On the important matter of airfield separation, the report commented: "Although most of the airfields considered are far enough apart to ensure that each airfield will be attacked independently, there are some which are close enough for one weapon to neutralise aircraft on two or more airfields." Each missile striking an airfield (assuming 1-mt yield) was judged to be "practically certain" to destroy parked aircraft. Assuming a 3.6-mile damage radius and a 1.5-mile circular error probable (CEP):

---

* Dispersed flights, typically, were of two or four aircraft. Presumably, the choice of an even dispersal of flight of three aircraft assisted the study.

> "…there is a 98% chance of neutralising the aircraft … With weapons of higher damage radius or lower CEP, aircraft on more than one airfield may, in some cases, be neutralised by one weapon … The most likely values of the variables involved are a CEP of one mile, an overpressure level of 5 psi and missile reliability ¾. With these values, the number of missiles needed is 36 missiles with 1-mt warheads, 35 missiles with 3-mt warheads or 32 missiles with 10-mt warheads. Because of the very small decrease in numbers with an increase in yield, it seems unlikely that warheads of greater yield than 1 mt would be used in an attack directed solely at aircraft parked on dispersal airfields."

In considering the effects of missile attack on aircraft after take-off, strategic warning of a likely attack was assumed, allowing dispersal and regeneration to readiness, a state of cockpit readiness when the missiles are detected and take-off of a flight of three Vulcan Mk 2s at 30-second intervals … The ability of aircraft to get well away before the missiles burst was limited by the time lag between BMEWS missile detection and the first aircraft starting to move down the runway. The time lag consists of delays in transmitting the warning to the aircraft and the time taken to start engines and taxi to the runway (minimum: 90 seconds). It was assumed that the bombers would achieve a 30-second interval take-off (i.e. with the second aircraft starting to roll on the runway as the first aircraft lifts off) and that the aircraft then climb at maximum rate and start a turn, in either direction, at constant bank, 30 seconds after lift-off, continue to turn "for some arbitrary time" and then fly straight. Turns of 20 degrees and 40 degrees bank were considered. Roy Brocklebank regarded a 40–45-degree turn more likely. An aircraft flying away from the airfield would have its tail on to the bomb – presenting the minimum profile to the blast. A turn was necessary to obtain better distribution and increase survival rate, but this exposed more surface area to blast. The steeper the turn the briefer the greater exposure to blast. It seems that, at the operational level, such considerations were academic, as crews were not briefed on this and other tactics to achieve even spatial distribution. The only immediate turns during a scramble take-off were limited to initial positioning, to avoid turbulence from aircraft directly ahead.

Brocklebank regarded a 30-second stream as improbable, as it "would more likely be ten–15 seconds, so the fourth aircraft would be airborne no more than 60 seconds of No. 1 brakes off (Mk 2s, that is)".[616]

Warning time depended on target location and missile trajectory. An IRBM with 1,000 miles maximum range, launched low trajectory from 650 miles, would provide around four minutes' warning (but nine minutes if launched from maximum range). In short, when a missile is launched from less than its maximum range, it can fly along a much lower trajectory, with a higher average ground speed – producing a very short warning. Airfields in the north and west would receive longer warning. The study allowed for the loss of 1½ minutes warning time (30 seconds delay in transmitting the BMEWS warning and one minute for airfield delays, until the first aircraft is rolling). There were then the assumptions concerning damage radius and aiming error. The damage radius depends on yield and levels of overpressure, gust, thermal and nuclear radiation which the aircraft can withstand. The assumed yield was 3 mt and a value of 1.5 psi overpressure assumed to neutralise aircraft:

> "The exact values of overpressure and gust which are required to neutralise a Vulcan are somewhat doubtful, but the values of 1.5 psi and 100 ft/second used are the best

available estimates, assuming random orientation of the aircraft relative to the direction of the missile burst."

Given these levels of overpressure and gust, levels of thermal and nuclear radiation were not regarded as "critical".[617] The report then continued:

"With these damage criteria, the damage radius of a 3-mt warhead is six miles for aircraft flying at altitudes between 6,000 ft and 40,000 ft. Above 40,000 ft the damage radius drops to about four miles. However, aircraft will not reach this altitude until some nine minutes after take-off, and since warning times considered here are less than nine minutes, this effect is not relevant."

Aircraft attempting to escape by staying low, rather than climbing to at least 6,000 ft, would have been destroyed: "Below 6,000 ft the damage radius rapidly increases to about 12 miles … (the overpressure is doubled by reflection at the Earth's surface)." Roy Brocklebank confirmed this conclusion: "This is the Mach Stem effect. The weapon has its shock front increased by reflection from the ground."[618]

The March 1962 Bomber Command report set out in more detail the consequences of staying low:

"Since the aircraft are assumed to climb at maximum rate, an altitude of 6,000 ft will be rapidly attained (about 1.6 minutes after take-off) and the Mach Stem effect will not be important. If, however, aircraft were to fly for some time at low altitude, the damage radius of the warhead would be doubled and, hence, the area of damage would be quadrupled. Thus, the proportion of the force neutralised will be increased if aircraft fly for any length of time at altitudes below 6,000 ft; in some circumstances, the damage may be increased fourfold."[619]

Surprisingly, given this factor's great significance, it appears that V-bomber captains were not briefed on this subject. Those who decided, at crew level, to stay low would *not* outrun the blast.

This was a major failure on the part of Bomber Command's leadership, given the explicit nature of the conclusions set out in the Operational Research Branch report on vulnerability to missile attack. Taking account of the gross nature of this oversight and/or negligence, it is perhaps not surprising that no documentary evidence was found that addressed these omissions, which further reduced the survival chances of those few bombers which might escape a short warning missile strike. In contrast, the oral evidence is plentiful and compelling. No aircrew contributor to this book recalled a specific warning to *climb immediately* after a war scramble take-off – a tactic *absolutely essential for survival*. Andy Leitch suggests, however, that things may have changed in the 1970s: "I joined the force in 1974 and a high departure was standard. There was never discussion of a low-level departure."

SURVIVING FLYAWAY

Elements contributing to the prospects for safe getaway after take-off included enemy uncertainty over the direction of turn (or flight straight ahead) after take-off, together with considerable variation between airfields regarding the time lag between BMEWS missile detection and aircraft take-off (bombers would not necessarily reach the maximum potential distance from their airfields): "Thus, when missiles explode, an aircraft must be assumed to be anywhere within a certain region around its airfield, determined by the maximum performance of the aircraft and the effective warning time." The area around the given airfield was considered as three regions – an inner region in which three aircraft may be found, a strip around this where only the first two aircraft may be found, and another strip around this where only the first aircraft may be found. "Since the average number of aircraft per unit area is greatest in the central region, this will receive missile cover before the other regions." If there is any delay in transmitting the BMEWS warning to aircraft, the aircraft are more likely to be in the inner region, where there will be a higher density of missile bursts. "Hence, there will be a higher level of damage if the transmission of warning is delayed."

Missiles (1,000 miles maximum range) from 650 miles away offered a warning from 3.6 minutes (at Honington) to 4.6 minutes (at St Mawgan and Lossiemouth):

> "Assuming cockpit readiness and a loss of 1½ minutes from the warning time to wheels rolling at the end of the runway, the first aircraft to take off can fly eight and 17 miles respectively from its airfield. With these short warning times, the 24 airfields are practically independent. There is a little interaction between three pairs of airfields, but this is sufficiently small to be neglected, so that the results of damage to aircraft from single airfields may be applied directly."

The study team assumed that, with one missile per airfield, the enemy would prioritise airfields in the south-east, with the shorter warning times, since these have a higher average density of aircraft:

> "With 24–48 missiles, one missile is allocated to each airfield and a second missile allocated to airfields in the north and west with the longer warning times, since more aircraft will escape the first missile from these airfields. Any further missiles are allocated to the few airfields where there is a chance that some aircraft may escape two missile bursts."

If these missiles are fired from maximum range (1,000 miles), the 8.8–9½-minute warning would allow aircraft to be some 60 miles from their airfields when warheads burst:

> "In this case, there will be considerable interference between airfields, except St Mawgan and Lossiemouth, if aircraft from each airfield may fly away in any direction from their airfields. With aircraft equally likely to fly away in any direction, there will be considerable variation in the expected density of aircraft at different points; there will be regions in which aircraft from as many as 11 different airfields may be found. This is clearly disadvantageous to aircraft, since unless enough missiles are available to cover nearly all the area which may contain aircraft, an unnecessarily high damage level may be achieved by allocating missiles to regions of highest aircraft density. The best distribution of aircraft would be one where the mean density of aircraft is constant."

This ideal could not be achieved but density could be evened out by confining aircraft to sectors (or 'cones') centred on each airfield: "… the sectors being chosen so that they are roughly the same size and overlap by only a small amount, but cover nearly all the area which aircraft can reach." Yet, according to Roy Brocklebank, crews had no awareness of this. "In practice you would just get airborne and head north-east."[620]

This appears to be another example of command oversight and/or negligence in a critical area of war scramble survival, once again ignoring key findings of the Operational Research Branch (ORB) report on MBF vulnerability to missile strike. The conclusions ignored were designed specifically to reduce avoidable V-bomber casualties in the opening few minutes of war. Roy Brocklebank and the other V-Force veterans interviewed have no recollection of the term 'flyaway cones'. Each crew had their own route and no awareness of any other.

Taken overall, the findings of this study were sobering, especially as it was grounded in an unlikely sequence of favourable circumstances (the key one being the improbable assumption that the *entire* dispersed MBF would be at RS05 – rather than the planned but never exercised maximum ground alert of 24/7 cockpit readiness of 30% of the force, by crew rotation under Alert Condition 1). The memorandum continued by stating the obvious:

> "… the percentage of aircraft that escape increases as the warning time increases, and decreases as the number of missiles increases. For warning times less than 3½ minutes, one missile will neutralise practically all aircraft from one airfield. With a four-minute warning time, one missile will do considerable damage, allowing only some 25% of aircraft to escape. The situations for longer warning times, in the eight- to nine-minute range, is quite different. In this case, even with as many as ten missiles round an airfield, some 75% of the aircraft may be expected to escape."[621]

A longer warning – commonly assumed from a Soviet staggered launch seeking simultaneous UK/USA impact – formed the basis of RS15, despite the lack of advantage to the Soviets. This may explain the remarkably high war-scramble survival estimates quoted elsewhere.

The Bomber Command report addressed many critical factors influencing the chance of survival. For example, the difference bank angle made in shorter warning times "may be quite considerable … with a 4½-minute warning time and two missiles round an airfield, 12% of aircraft will escape with a 20-degree bank turn, while 30% will escape with a 40-degree bank turn." Any delay in giving the take-off order (perhaps in an extended effort to verify BMEWS warning) would be costly:

> "If, for example, the warning time is 4½ minutes and one missile bursts over an airfield, the percentage of aircraft that escape will be cut from 55% to practically zero by a one-minute delay in take-off. Although the effect of delays becomes relatively smaller as the warning time increases, it is still not negligible."

As to the threat from low-trajectory missiles from 650 miles, giving only 3½ to 4½ minutes' warning, the report cautioned:

> "… considerable damage can be done to the force with only a small number of missile bursts round each airfield … With 24 missile bursts, one over each airfield, some 28% of the force can be expected to escape, while with 48 missile bursts, two round each airfield, less than 10% of the force can escape. Sixty missile bursts will allow about 5% of the force to escape."

This assumed that the aircraft may take off in either direction: "If this is limited to one direction only, fewer missiles would be needed, since aircraft would be restricted to a smaller area." In these circumstances, one missile over each airfield "will allow less than 12% of the force to escape and two missiles round each airfield will neutralise the whole force". Here (if this is what the report means, in a literal sense), Roy Brocklebank questions the practicalities of take-off in either direction from dispersal airfields, as against main bases with aircraft on dispersals around the airfield:

> "Two aircraft using the runway in opposite directions will take longer to clear the take-off area. The second aircraft would not start rolling until the first had cleared the zone. In this instance, a rapid turn away would be needed."

Either way, it is easy to see why planning and RS15 were based on the UK/US simultaneous burst scenario. Without a US duration warning, the UK V-Force was very close to a sitting duck, a condition eased marginally by the Alert Condition 1 posture of continuous RS05 for some aircraft, by crew rotation.

These numbers were based on successfully launched missiles. Assuming 75% reliability and allowing for failures, it was calculated that 51% of aircraft would survive a 20-missile strike on the airfields, given 3½ to 4½ minutes total warning, take-off in either direction, a 40-degree bank turn and 1½ minutes time lost. The percentage of survivors would fall to 31% (30 missiles), 22% (40 missiles) and 12% (60 missiles). With take-off in only one direction, the numbers would fall to 40%, 16%, 7% and 0%. Longer warning time (missiles from 1,000 miles) and aircraft flying away in designated sectors (cones) would increase the numbers escaping:

> "With an attack of 100 missiles, 70% of the force is expected to escape, while with 250 missiles, 32% of the force would escape. At least 400 missiles are needed to ensure that only 10% of the force escapes, whilst 570 missiles are needed to ensure complete neutralisation of the force."

The effects of 60 seconds' delay in this context were also explored:

> "Although this effect is relatively smaller for long warning times, it is still appreciable. The proportion that escape is decreased by 7% of the force with an attack by 100 missiles and by 13% of the force with 250 missiles."

In reviewing these findings, the report added: "A high state of readiness is extremely expensive to maintain for long periods and therefore the readiness state at any time must be matched to the intelligence evaluation of the threat and assessment of the method of attack."

A weapon fired from 1,000 miles away providing a nine-minute warning (simultaneous launch *but* not low trajectory) would allow 98% of aircraft (independent airfields) to survive, assuming RS05, 1½ minutes to first aircraft rolling and zero delay. A one-minute delay would reduce survival by only 1%, to 97% (with respective figures for two weapons per airfield being 97% and 95%). Roy Brocklebank recalled a brief from Bomber Command intelligence "that the IRBMs were in the Baltic States, which was roughly 1,000 miles back. There was no mention of shorter-range missiles in East Germany."[622]

In the case of a 1,000 miles range weapon per independent airfield, launched from 650 miles at low trajectory (four-minute warning), the report stated that 25% of aircraft might survive, but this could be reduced to zero by a one-minute delay. In a two weapons per airfield case, 10% might survive, assuming no delay (zero with one-minute delay). The report claims that longer warning times of 20, 16 and nine minutes:

> "…are most typical of those which might be expected over the next few years. It can be seen that if the state of readiness is matched against the current threat, one minute's delay in transmitting the BMEWS warning to the crews may be very expensive in lost weapon systems if two to four missiles arrive at their target. It appears therefore that BMEWS warning should be transmitted direct to the crews who then start engines, taxi and take off. Within this period, sufficient time elapses to cancel the warning if it is assessed as a false alarm or hold the aircraft at the end of the runway, engines running, if for some reason the validity of the warning is doubtful. When the warning time falls to that corresponding to missiles fired on a low trajectory over 650 miles range, the escape chance becomes small …"[623]

The report states that in this last situation (surely the most likely) airborne alert appears to be the only real answer. Roy Brocklebank summed up the position on the squadrons succinctly, confirming the lack of disclosure: "Crews were not briefed on this document."[624]

This seminal Operational Research Branch study was based on the simultaneous arrival of missiles, whereas, in reality, arrival would be spread over "at least two minutes". It added that "the results, therefore, as presented, are somewhat pessimistic but, nevertheless, do provide a reliable guide to the changes of survival chance with time, and represent the worst case of simultaneous detonation of all weapons about each airfield".[625]

To summarise, the report concluded that the chance of escape increased if aircraft are thought to be capable of taking off in either direction, turn with up to 40 degrees of bank after take-off, climb rapidly to altitudes above 6,000 ft and use flyaway patterns producing as even a distribution of aircraft in the air as possible. The importance of this package of survival measures appears undeniable, but, unfortunately, no-one seems to have told the crews.

16
LIVING ON YOUR NERVES

> ❝ ... we were all on constant alert ... and, almost unnoticed by us, the constant stress began to tell ... some succumbed to ulcers and we had a least one nervous breakdown on the squadron and, possibly, two suicides. ❞
>
> Tony Blackman and Anthony Wright, Valiant Boys

FRONTLINE STRESS

Air Commodore Edward Jarron, a former Vulcan pilot who was Chief of Special Weapons at Supreme Headquarters, Allied Powers Europe (SHAPE) in 1992, is well qualified to underline the cardinal purpose of the V-Force:

> "The most important fact about the UK deterrent is that it is there to deter, NOT to warfight ... When Chief of Special Weapons at SHAPE I found it necessary, occasionally, to remind the generals that this is the case. I pushed the point at every opportunity. All bets are off when the first weapon flies."[626]

On the V-Force squadrons, bomber crews, for the most part, were confident that the deterrent would deter. Yet the special character of life on the 1960s nuclear frontline penetrated all but the thickest skins. QRA governed life on each squadron from 1962 until the Polaris handover in mid-1969. QRA duty crews constantly exercised, moving up and down the readiness states, but all this came at a price. In a very real sense, they lived in a bubble – a small 'wartime' community living in a country at peace (though fearful that this peace could end, at any time, in a four-minute warning). Vulcan captain Rob Williams was not alone in describing life on QRA as "an absolute bind at the personal level". He added:

> "On IX Squadron we did three days on and four days off. Naturally, you tend to get on each other's nerves when living in such close proximity. We played cards, read books or studied. One AEO, Alfie Price, even became an author."[627]

Dr Price's books include the fine work *Instruments of Darkness*.

> "As part of the strategic plan, we visited many dispersal airfields, including Lossiemouth and Machrihanish in Scotland and St Mawgan in Cornwall, Pershore, Gaydon and Valley. I was rather exuberant at times and, on one occasion, when we were reverted to normal readiness, I decided on a fast taxi back to the dispersal, down the runway. Unfortunately, it was a little too fast and the nosewheel lifted. The station commander took a dim view of this incident."

Perhaps exuberance was a mechanism for coping with constant tension.

NUKES ON BOARD

Many V-Force veterans talk about QRA stress. John Huggins recalled the alarming day when the correct procedures for stand-down, after a real alert, were overlooked:

> "We were ordered to go from 05 to 15 but the stand-down code wasn't given. The Waddington QRA aircraft refused to comply and the crews remained at cockpit readiness. It was a false alarm. I saw the station commander arrive and approach the secure area. He was accompanied by the armaments officer, who was holding the weapon key. I told the armed guard beside our aircraft to warn them not to enter the area. I also told him to shoot them if they got within 50 ft of the aircraft. The procedures were clear: no stand-down without the correct code – which, eventually, was given. We loaded live nukes for QRA and we had the target information with us. As far as we were concerned, we could be going to war."[628]

Security on QRA was always present but low key. Each armed aircraft had an RAF police dog-handler. The guard carried a sidearm. As Roy Brocklebank recalled, security arrangements in the 1960s certainly offered scope for improvement:

> "At Cottesmore we had the occasional intruder. The gates were never closed. On one occasion, a driver got confused, drove through the main gate, continued straight ahead, turned left, headed down a very wide road, turned right onto an even wider road and ended up next to three nuclear-armed aircraft! Quite often, when the station hooter went, a small crowd of local residents would gather on the other side of the perimeter fence to watch the fun. It was all splendidly British. Eventually, two-man control was extended, to cover the police guard. We now had to have someone to 'guard the guard'. Extra RAF police had to be recruited; gradually, security was tightened."[629]

When the alert siren went, it could be a source of annoyance, rather than notice of a free 'air show'. Exercises continued to dominate V-Force life post-QRA, with call-outs often in the middle of the night. Vulcan captain Peter Moore remembers how this excitement was shared with the local community:

> "On base, mobile sirens were towed around, making enough noise to wake the dead, but not always my first AEO! Some Waddington married quarters were located in Birchwood, near the former RAF Skellingthorpe. These off-base quarters were treated to the same wailing wake-up sirens as the main base. I'm not quite sure what the nearby civilian neighbours made of that."[630]

QRA drills were so ingrained that crews developed an almost Pavlovian reaction to alarms. Vulcan nav/plotter Jim Milne remembers one Saturday in the crew room, on QRA: "Ops rang and said they were about to test the bells and that we shouldn't react. Yet, when the bells rang we were out of the door and heading for the Standard Vanguard. We couldn't help ourselves."[631]

Jim Milne also recalled an incident involving failure to use the stand-down code:

"Geoff Dyer was my last captain. We were on QRA with two other aircraft, with doors shut at RS05. Then, after ten minutes, the station operations officer said that it was back to RS15. Geoff told him that he hadn't been released by the bomber controller and that his crew would stay put. Eventually, the group captain intervened. We got out but the groupie said Geoff had been quite right to refuse."

ACCIDENT TOLL

QRA-related stress overlaid the normal but stressful demands of operational flying. Many V-Force aircrew experienced incidents threatening complete disaster. Roy Brocklebank notes that three Vulcan Mk 2s never entered service, reducing the Vulcan Mk 2 frontline to 86, of which a significant number – 14 in all – "were lost through crashes or substantial damage".[632]

Nav/radar Bob Sinclair received a sharp reminder of the random nature of fate whilst on 35 Squadron at Cottesmore:

"We were programmed to fly and allocated an aircraft. Unfortunately, the aircraft was U/S and wasn't going anywhere. Our captain went into planning, to badger for another aircraft. He was told to go away. Subsequently, Pete Tait and his crew took the aircraft we were supposed to take, as their sortie was a check-ride."

They had problems with bomb bay overheating during the sortie. They tried to control it by feeding in cool air. The optimum temperature was set at 15 degrees. If cold air fails and only hot air finds its way into the bomb bay, the temperature could double, to 30 degrees. If the temperature gets too extreme, the aircraft can develop control problems – all the control rods pass through the bomb bay and overheating can make the controls sloppy:

"The only solution is to open the bomb bay, let it cool off and shut the doors – repeating as necessary. Pete Tait had to burn fuel to reach landing weight. They returned to the circuit to carry out practice approaches when the temperature was within limits. On the last circuit they overshot. They informed air traffic and put on full power. Suddenly, there was a bang and the controls went slack. The inboard engine on the starboard side had exploded, destroying the outboard engine. Debris cut the control rods. The aircraft started a descending turn with Tait trying to level up, but to no avail. He told the rear crew of three, plus a screened nav/radar doing a check, to abandon. The aircraft continued its roll and Tait ordered the co-pilot to eject. It was all last-minute stuff. Tait ejected and he went out horizontally. Power lines snagged his parachute and he was able to step out of his harness … There was a Board of Inquiry. It was concluded that the rear crew would have survived if they had had bang seats."[633]

One risk exposure in the Vulcan related to what some regarded as inadequate lubrication of the rear turbines. John Huggins provided some background:

"If there was an explosion due to lack of lubrication, the blades would shatter and destroy the adjacent engine. Furthermore, the 'mixer box' – which translated movement from the control column to the flying controls – was located in the rear of the bomb bay and in line with the engines. This was also exposed to an engine explosion and would be destroyed."[634]

Nav/radar Jim Walker was a member of Vulcan captain Mike D'Arcy's crew. They had a close call when all four engines were lost just after take-off. It was a total electrical failure and the batteries provided a back-up for only minutes. Two aircraft were lost in such circumstances:

> "D'Arcy told us to prepare to abandon. I got out of my seat and went down to the hatch. Strangely, I clearly remember my whole life going into a tunnel in front of my face. Luckily, the AEO got the bus-bars back on line and the engines re-started. We were at 200–300 ft when this happened."[635]

Walker left 44 (Rhodesia) Squadron in September 1968. He was posted to 35 Squadron, Cottesmore, as radar leader:

> "Overall, morale on this squadron was good, but they had just suffered an accident. The co-pilot of the crew I joined, together with his wife, had witnessed it. He then decided he no longer wanted to fly. He was labelled LMF (Lack of Moral Fibre) and posted out immediately. He was just a young bloke and his wife was terrified; living next door to them had been the AEO who'd been killed in that accident."

It might seem surprising that the harsh wartime LMF regime lingered into the late 1960s. The RAF's LMF 'culture', however, was deeply rooted. LMF had been introduced in 1940; there were 4,059 cases during the war years and 2,726 were eventually classified as LMF. Late in the war, with victory in sight, the official line moderated and LMF was then described as the "inability to stand the strain of flying duties". The emphasis on punishment receded, giving way to 'combat stress' and, later, 'post-traumatic stress disorder'.[636]

Nevertheless, as the 1960s began, Air Council-endorsed policy for "disposal of aircrew who forfeit the confidence of their commanding officers" still called for their removal at the earliest opportunity, with a posting to No. 1 Personnel Holding Unit. Officers not exposed to exceptional stress could be called on to resign or find their commission terminated. Logbooks were impounded, to prevent such individuals obtaining commercial licences.[637]

NO EJECTION SEATS FOR REAR CREW

Lack of ejection seats for rear crew contributed to stress. There were sensitive conversations within crews and, in addition, interventions by anxious wives making direct appeals to captains. John Huggins became a 50 Squadron captain; he explained the sequence of abandonment:

> "The co-pilot would eject first, so relieving pressure on the door jacks. The nav/radar would swivel his seat and pull a handle which inflated the seat cushion. This allowed him to get down into the well of the aircraft and reach the door. He had to operate the emergency door handle, open the door and jettison the attached crew ladder. He would then jump, followed by the AEO, with the nav/plotter going out last (he couldn't swivel his seat, so it took him longer to reach the door)."

Their parachutes operated on a static line. With everyone out, the captain then ejected:

> "Captains operated on the basis that they would not leave the aircraft unless the rear crew were out. I promised my crew that I would never leave the aeroplane with them

still in it. This responsibility was underlined, in the most direct way possible, during my tour as a co-pilot – most of which was spent as first pilot. On one occasion, during the Summer Ball at Waddington, I met my AEO's wife for the first time. They were both around 50, whereas I was just 23. She turned to me and said: 'You will look after him, won't you!' There was a standing joke with my nav/radar; he said he always put the pins in my seat and they would stay there until landing! I was always acutely aware of the other guys. I made a point of bringing them down in a timely manner. We never flew around just on my personal whim. The most dangerous part of any flight is in the circuit. You are at, or below, 1,000 ft, with the undercarriage down. It was virtually impossible for the rear crew to survive a bale-out in that situation."

Any volunteers? A Martin-Baker Vulcan rear crew ejection test rig. Andy Leitch explains: "First, the hatch would open. Then the nav/plotter in the middle would be ejected. The other seats are pivoted at the bottom and can slide inwards at the top of the horizontal rail. This would angle the crew member inwards towards the hole before being ejected. This was all in sequence. No individual ejection was possible." (Andy Leitch Collection)

There were difficult debates, behind the scenes, over the possibilities of retrofit. Air Vice-Marshal Nigel Baldwin gave his view at an RAF Historical Society meeting:

"I came to the conclusion long ago that it should have been done because all those pilots who sat in the front had big responsibilities and, I suppose, influencing my thought is that I have stood in a lot of cemeteries. I buried my first Vulcan crew on my first wedding anniversary, with a young wife by my side, and we went on to do that several times in our careers. There is no doubt that I wouldn't have been there, in that old cemetery in Coningsby churchyard in 1964 that day, if there had been five ejection seats in that aeroplane. And so, I am emotionally involved in this question and, looking back on it now, I think you could begin to argue that it was disgraceful that it wasn't done."[638]

This issue and other frustrations combined to produce the toxic atmosphere at an important No. 1 Group anniversary dinner at Waddington in 1965, with behaviour serious enough to warrant formal interviews for everyone. Some aircrew had enjoyed early drinks in a pub. There were more drinks upon arrival at Waddington and behaviour deteriorated rapidly.

Many accidents involved loss of life. Victor captain Jeremy Mudford survived an engine fire costing three lives:

"This was a Victor Mk 1 and its Sapphire engines were not always reliable. The cause in my case was fatigue failure of an alternator drive shaft. Each Sapphire had a large alternator mounted on the airframe, connected by a flexible drive shaft to the engine. In this case, the No. 2 engine drive shaft failed, at the alternator end, leaving a few inches of shaft flailing around in the engine bay, destroying wiring and fuel lines. As fuel contacted hot surfaces, there was a bang and a fire-warning light came up. I activated the fire extinguisher and the engine shut down, but the engine was still turning … and still doing damage. I heard another bang and the adjacent engine caught fire.

"I ordered the crew to bale out. They all succeeded in leaving by the port-side door – but this was on the same side as the fire. Sadly, two of the three were killed by flying fragments from the crippled engines. The third, my AEO, survived and landed safely. When the fire broke out, the aircraft was at 15,000 ft. As the escaping fuel burnt, the centre of gravity moved forward, the aircraft inevitably became nose-heavy and the steepening dive increased almost to vertical. I told my co-pilot to go at about 1,500 ft above the ground. He pulled the blind but his ejection seat failed to fire. I told him to leave by the side door but, sadly, we were very low and he had no time. There was no point in staying – I could see the leaves on the trees. I ejected successfully at approximately 700 ft and 305 kts.[639]

"Later, a Board of Inquiry concluded that the cause was mechanical failure and that no blame attached to the captain. Meanwhile, the Sapphires were modified, including the fitting of a steel shroud over the drive shafts. This didn't apply to the Victor Mk 2s, as their Conway engines were direct drive – there were no drive shafts."

Jeremy Mudford suffered a compression fracture of the spine – two discs were compressed. He has complete recall of those traumatic last moments:

"When I told the crew to go, I remember the huge amount of noise and smoke in the cockpit. The side door was open and we were doing nearly 300 kts at the time. I also remember what seemed like absolute silence after I left the aircraft."

Vulcan crew chief: Tony Smith was a crew chief with IX Squadron at RAF Waddington from 1976 to 1982. (Tony Smith)

Waddington crew chief Tony Smith experienced moments of great sadness in his career. During his first year on IX Squadron one of the Vulcans crashed at Malta. Two crew chiefs were on board and both died. One was making his final trip overseas as he was about to retire. The other was making his first flight in a Vulcan. Tony Smith remembers that he didn't want to go, for family reasons:

> "At the last moment, I told him: 'Don't go – I'll get my gear and take your place.' He thought for a few seconds and said: 'No, I'm going to do it. I'll get it out of the way.' There was a problem with the runway at Malta. It had a lip at the end. The Vulcan hit that lip and the right undercarriage punched through the wing. There was a fire but it was quickly dealt with and the Vulcan continued to climb, leaving an undercarriage leg on the ground. It exploded at a height of around 750 ft. The two in the front ejected; the five in the rear died."[640]

The unfortunate behaviour during the Waddington dinner was an expression of broader discontent. Vulcan captain Roger Smith put his thoughts into words:

> "The V-Force had always been portrayed as an elite. However, by 1965 it had become a force that nobody wanted to go to. Once in, navigators and AEOs found it very difficult to get out of the V-Force, as did many of the more experienced pilots. There were plenty who were fed up by that time and wanted to leave."[641]

COULD THE NUCLEAR NIGHTMARE COME TRUE?

Cases of conscience concerning nuclear weapons were rare and, therefore, were not a major contributor to stress, as confirmed by Cottesmore co-pilot David Dinmore (later, a captain at Waddington): "I was not aware, at that time, of anyone with reservations about the nuclear role." However, he did recall someone who left the air force when in his mid-thirties, to become a Church of England minister. "Later on, I talked to him and he described his calling. That conversation led me to believe that he had some regrets about his past role, but that wasn't apparent at the time."[642] Philip Goodall recorded another case:

> "A while ago I met someone who said that a friend of his had been a Vulcan captain and had decided that he could not accept the responsibility of dropping a nuclear weapon. He was 'retired' from the RAF in days."[643]

On rare occasions, there was that knot-in-the-stomach feeling that the ultimate nightmare might come true. Vulcan nav/radar John Weller, with IX Squadron, had such a moment. On a Tuesday evening in April 1965 it seemed the standard operating procedure (SOP) would be put to the test:

> "When the siren went I was with the Scouts, in my role as an assistant scoutmaster. I was still in my Scout uniform when I arrived at operations. I was told to get my kit on. Was this a Mick or Micky Finn? No – it was the real thing! 'Here's your target!' The BMEWS had picked up incoming missiles. A USAF major on site had been briefed on 'the 12 parameters of retaliation'. Apparently, on this occasion, 11 parameters were met. The

projected target was the sole parameter not met. In fact, a satellite had broken up and the pieces had registered individually. As the fragments were in Earth orbit, rather than a ballistic trajectory, BMEWS couldn't find the predicted targets."[644]

This experience was very uncomfortable, not least because the procedures in place to meet that moment were pushed aside: "I was allocated a crew. That was strange – it was not my crew. I was handed a target, but it was not one of my targets. I pointed this out but was told 'get on with it.'"[645] They were stood down at 21.30:

> "When we were stood down, we went to the bar and drank it dry. There was an acceptance that an attack would come following a build-up. We would have expected to know if we were close to the real thing. We didn't expect World War 3 to start at a minute's notice."[646]

There was always something to worry about, in the air and on the ground. Scampton's operations record book for 1968 records a scare in August, when the station's RAF police dogs appeared to go down with typhoid. The animals were immediately quarantined in their compounds and all other MBF stations were alerted. It was then discovered that the symptoms, although similar to typhoid, were caused by over-feeding. The ORB notes: "Daily issues of meat were controlled and the dogs were fit and back on duty within one week."

BARRIERS TO UPGRADES

Many aircrew and ground crew must have harboured frustrations over the obvious unwillingness to spend money on equipment upgrades, but, as Roy Brocklebank points out, it was not just lack of funding. The small size of the V-bomber fleet acted as a barrier to substantial modification programmes. There were "simply too few aircraft to permit extensive work" without emasculating the frontline. In addition, "a radical upgrade would require a large-scale personnel retraining programme. I saw such a change with the introduction of the Mk 2 Nimrod – the training system could handle just one crew per month."[647]

Scale is important in the context of modernisation projects. Roy Brocklebank notes that Strategic Air Command (SAC) had 2,042 B-47 bombers (operational until 1965) and 744 B-52s (including 102 B-52H aircraft). In contrast, Bomber Command had 46 Valiants, 86 Victor Mk 1 and Mk 2 bombers, 46 Vulcan Mk 1s and 89 Vulcan Mk 2s – totalling 267 aircraft. For much of V-Force operational life, the frontline consisted of just 11 squadrons: a UE (Unit Establishment) of 88 aircraft – eight per squadron.

Brocklebank commented: "From a peak of 18 squadrons (144 aircraft at full strength) in 1964, the number of squadrons reduced to eight in the late 1960s (144 aircraft down to 64 aircraft)." By 1973, seven squadrons remained: IX and 35 in Cyprus, 44 (Rhodesia), 50 and 101 at Waddington and 27 and 617 at Scampton. During that year, 27 was reassigned to the maritime radar reconnaissance role, bringing the number of UK squadrons down to four, plus the OCU.

Roy Brocklebank reinforces his point:

> "I think this proves the command had few aircraft spare for extensive modification programmes … it was a pure numbers game – maintaining the frontline. This did not mean, however, that no modifications were undertaken. The first major modification was the conversion of most of the Mk 1 Vulcans to Mk 1A by adding the ECM suite

(a small number of Mk 1s were not converted to Mk 1A standard). The next major modification to all V-bombers was the change from white overall to the familiar green and grey scheme on the upper surfaces. This was a rapid programme but, nevertheless, required each aircraft to be withdrawn from service. This was a quick fix – the early paint was later replaced with a high gloss polyurethane finish. This was generally applied during other major works and increased the time for aircraft away from the frontline. Modifications during this time included the change from earlier fixed rear crew seats to the swivel seat on the Vulcan Mk 2 and the Victor Mk 2.

"Aside from the continuing work monitoring fatigue and essential main-spar repair and modification, a major programme was the modification of Blue Steel aircraft to freefall bombers. Other modifications included the installation of the terrain-following radar (TFR), a new pitch instrument for pop-up delivery of Yellow Sun, installation and integration of the heading reference system, fitting the X-Band jammer as a replacement for Green Palm, IR decoys, rapid blooming window and Red Steer Mk 2 tail-warning radar. The X-Band jammer was modified for forward radiation, to counter the Gun Dish anti-aircraft artillery (AAA) radar.

"As well as the X-Band jammer, a Red Shrimp S-Band jammer was changed to an L-Band jammer. The Blue Saga S-X-Band detector was first modified from 360 degrees coverage to four quadrants, providing an idea of threat direction. Blue Saga was then replaced with a better passive warning receiver (ARI 18228), giving that later squared shape to the top of the fin. Less obvious but, nevertheless, significant changes were made to the nav bombing system. The largest range scale, ¼ million, was changed to ⅛ million as an aid for the Fishpool mode, to detect fighters below the aircraft. The smallest scale, 1:1 million, was increased to 1:2 million for the MRR role. This allowed the operator to shift the screen centre to the edge of the display and double the area visible when compared to 1:1 million.

"This shows there was a continuing work programme taking aircraft from the frontline, repairing, modifying and improving all the time … and these are only the ones which I am aware of from my time on the Vulcan. Seductive as it might have been to strip out the old ECM and install a new suite, strip out the tried and trusted navigation and bombing system and install a modern radar, and to provide an active air defence, time out of service would have reduced the aircraft available to the frontline quite significantly."

THE PRESSURE ON INDIVIDUALS

Many V-Force aircrew completed two or more V-bomber tours; they lived for six years or more with the onerous 1960s QRA regime. The general rule was no alcohol for eight hours before flying and, theoretically at least given the ever-present possibility of call-out, only very moderate consumption unless stood down.

There were no concessions recognising the hardships and stress of long-term V-Force duty – experienced by both aircrew and ground crew. Married officers were not entitled to a marriage allowance until reaching the age of 25. They could not be allocated a married quarter. Those wishing to marry had to seek permission. Young married aircrew had to watch the money. Peter Moore remembers the small financial advantage to being a junior Vulcan captain:

"At some point in the distant past a question had been asked in the House of Commons about lowly-ranked officers captaining nuclear-capable aircraft. This was denied by the minister and an order was promptly made that flight lieutenant was the minimum rank for captaincy. All flying officer captains were given acting rank, provided they had passed the B promotion exam. I was a flying officer when I arrived back on the squadron as a captain and had passed the exam, so I got paid acting rank for a year or so, until my substantive promotion came through. As I had married at 22 years of age – under the recommended age – I didn't qualify for the marriage allowance, so the enhanced pay was welcome."[648]

Another Vulcan captain, John Reeve, adds:

"…pay was bad in the V-Force. You could get more driving a bus for Lincoln Corporation than flying a V-bomber! The co-pilot's pay in the early 1970s was £3,500 a year. In 1976 I was paid £400 a month. We had a ½% pay rise while I was instructing at Cranwell. Then there was a substantial increase during the last years of the Labour Government. Pay levels remained just about tolerable during the 1980s, under Mrs Thatcher. I bought my first house in 1974 and, if we had had another child, my wife and I would have been classified as 'in poverty'. My wife was a nurse – if she hadn't worked, I don't know how we would have coped."

Yet, John Reeve and many others risked all during the Falklands War. His crew was selected as lead for Black Buck 1, targeting the runway at Port Stanley. The aircraft failed to pressurise and Martin Withers' reserve crew took over. John Reeve and his team flew Black Buck 2.

There was also, of course, the occasional stroke of luck. Norman Bonnor's posting to 100 Squadron at RAF Wittering introduced him to its vibrant social life:

"Most people had rented or had bought properties in the surrounding area and, for this reason, Miggs and I were able to move into married quarters for the first time, even though I had yet to reach the required age of 25."[649]

At this time, there were social barriers in place. In general, officers were expected to avoid fraternising with NCOs and other ranks. There was also the constant pressure on aircrew to perform to the highest standards, within an aggressively competitive environment. Some blossomed but others had a very different experience.

V-Force morale is a complex issue. Naturally, it varied according to the individual and his circumstances. Yet the oral evidence gives a vivid impression of forces acting on morale in the 1960s V-Force. Co-pilots, for example, often had a tough time; some were held back by difficult captains or squadrons with a reputation for slow advancement. Many aircrew, posted to the V-Force against their wishes, failed to warm to the role, yet went on to complete two or even three tours.

Nuclear weapons may have had little direct influence on morale, but the same cannot be said for Eastern England's long, bleak winters. QRA, exercises and other commitments put relationships under strain, aggravated by an awareness that separation and divorce might have severe and even career-ending consequences.

Flying hours were subject to strict control. Furthermore, the system could be very unfair. Hard-won select star/command status, for example, could be lost through the posting of one of the team, rather than any misdemeanour or failing. Occasionally, efforts were made to introduce flexibility, by turning a blind eye to a sortie flown with a 'guest' covering for a missing crew member. However, the system had a rigid character and displayed little or no pragmatism, as confirmed by Roy Brocklebank, who spent several years as wing targeting officer and vault officer at RAF Waddington:

> "… every bombing run was recorded on the Bomber Command Form Stats 2222 (Quadruple Two). The form had the first pilot's name and the bomb aimer's, either the nav/radar or the nav/plotter, depending on whether it was a radar or visual attack. In addition to my role as vault officer, I also worked in the weapons office as weapons analysis officer. One day we got a very stiff letter from Bomber Command claiming that our submissions were wrong – that attacks claimed as constituted crew were carried out by non-constituted crew members and so on. We had to go through every form and refute every allegation."[650]

It took Brocklebank and two others three long days to finish the job.

There were occasions when morale really suffered, particularly following accidents involving the loss of rear crew, due to the lack of ejection seats. Some aircrew also failed to push aside unease about a war mission to penetrate Soviet defences in an aircraft lacking defensive armament.

There was, however, a wider negative dynamic at work here: the conflict between constant readiness for war and a deep-seated conviction, on the part of most, that deterrence would hold and that a war sortie would never be flown. This could foster apathy, resentment and a lack of willingness to challenge inadequacies such as poor accommodation, unreliable transport to the aircraft and weaknesses in electronic countermeasures (ECM). Roy Brocklebank remembers the inadequate accommodation situation at Cottesmore, a station set up for two squadrons but the base for three:

> "As a consequence, many were accommodated in wooden huts. Our senior officers appeared to do nothing to improve matters. At Waddington I was again assigned a hut at the back of the Mess. I had an old multi-strand electric fire fastened to the wall. Quarters were often damp …"

That said, many aircrew enjoyed their V-Force tours, relished the pervasive competitive spirit, met the high expectations from above and took pride in climbing Bomber Command's challenging ladder of excellence. They achieved well-deserved recognition amongst their peers and repeatedly demonstrated that skill, nerve and extreme combat tactics could overcome many inadequacies.

At the same time, stress respected no rank, undermining some in relatively senior positions. Air Vice-Marshal Nigel Baldwin flew in the 1960s V-Force:

> "I recall that when I was a flight lieutenant captain of 35 Squadron at Cottesmore, our station commander had a nervous breakdown and disappeared. It happened again some years later when I was at Waddington; during my two years there as a squadron commander, two other wing commanders had nervous breakdowns and, during an earlier stint, as a squadron leader, a staff officer to the Senior Air Staff Officer (SASO) at Strike Command. These

things seemed to be happening to wing commanders and group captains right across the service. What I don't remember happening, however, is flying officers and flight lieutenants having nervous breakdowns. With the insouciance of youth – or whatever it was – perhaps we/they just didn't worry too much. Looking back on it now, one can see that the real pressures were applied at the wing commander/group captain level."[651]

Perhaps the strain at this level centred on the obvious flaws in the system: the extent of exposure to destruction on the ground and the endless penny-pinching overhanging the V-Force as it struggled to deliver its mission throughout the 1960s. Even the fundamentals came under threat. The 1962 Defence Review estimated V-Force expenditure in the coming decade at around £500 million and the deterrent remained under constant scrutiny by those searching for potential savings. Many battles were fought to preserve the essentials, including dispersal across 36 airfields. This plan was defended in a September 1962 Air Ministry position paper. This looked at the worst case – IRBMs fired on low trajectory and no "American Warning", but, rather, 4-6 minutes – yet it still repeated frequently-assumed but unrealistic escape probabilities. These were based on all dispersed aircraft at cockpit readiness or even RS02. However, the paper did make the valid point that full dispersal was crucial if even a few aircraft were to escape destruction. It argued that fewer airfields would likely increase the number of missiles targeted on each airfield and so widen the area of destruction around each base:

> "If the area of destruction is allowed to extend beyond a certain point, it will be impossible for any bombers to fly clear in time, however rapid their reaction … 36 dispersal airfields are the fewest which will afford a reasonable minimum of immunity to pre-emptive attack."[652]

It must have been taxing to constantly engage in 'combat' with those holding the purse-strings. There is more than a hint of exasperation in this paper's reference to SACEUR TBF Valiants concentrated at Marham: "To keep 24 aircraft and their associated nuclear weapons concentrated at a single airfield makes no military sense at all …"

Indeed, it argued that this made a case for *increasing* the number of dispersal airfields beyond 36 (whilst, at the same time, it recognised the limits imposed by economics and

RCAF Cold Lake, 1980: delivering bombs for RAF Buccaneers participating in Exercise Maple Flag. (Anthony Wright)

airfield availability). Nevertheless, it added that the Air Staff had decided to add the Valiants to the dispersal force. However, adding TBF Valiants to dispersal detachments (setting aside difficult issues with E weapons) could have had the effect of reducing the survival chances of MBF Vulcans and Victors (unless, of course, the Valiants were always positioned last in the queue for a scramble take-off). In conclusion, the Air Ministry paper warned that any saving from reducing the number of dispersal airfields would be very small – a fraction of 1% of total investment in the V-Force – and would cause "extremely heavy" operational penalties.

RELIEF IN THE AIR

As for frontline aircrew, at least they had the release of flying, including Ranger flights overseas and occasional air defence exercises at home and abroad. Testing the ability to defend UK airspace and Bomber Command's operational capabilities offered the crews added interest and experience, but the number and scale of these exercises declined sharply in the ten years to the mid-1960s. Overall, there was a steep reduction in the flying effort, duration and exercise area from the late 1940s to mid-1960s. There were 600 sorties in 1948, a peak of over 1,000 in 1955, then a slump to only 40 sorties flown in 1964, in a single raid.[653] One problem here was the massive growth in civilian air traffic.

When training to penetrate defended airspace, mock attacks on the UK were always impressive in the early days, as recalled by John Laycock:

> "We'd have 20 aircraft in line astern, at ten-mile intervals, flying up the North Sea. They would all turn west and begin to head towards their UK targets. The Hunters and Javelins would then come up and try to intercept us."[654]

The infrared (IR) decoys proved very effective in fighter affiliations: "The flares were fantastic. If we were unlucky enough to get a fighter approach from the rear and lock-on with a heat-seeker, the flares would almost certainly have proved successful."

Lively encounters provided an outlet for frontline stress and were not always confined to 'friendlies'. John Laycock knew of a brush with the Russians:

> "I'd heard that one RAF pilot on a special mission had been chased by a Russian fighter over the Barents Sea. The V-bomber was on a maritime reconnaissance mission and over international waters. The Vulcan was light, with around half a fuel-load. When the MiG-21 'Fishbed' approached, the captain just pulled the Vulcan into a vertical climb, on full power, and put a wing over. He ended up behind the MiG-21!"

During a tour, however, aircrew had to accept and accommodate the ever-present risk of a catastrophic accident. Bill Taylor, a 617 Squadron Vulcan captain, had a very close call on 6 April 1967. He and his crew were in XL385 when they suffered a severe fire:

> "There was a problem with the high-pressure and low-pressure compressors of No. 2 engine. The imbalance caused No. 2 to fall to pieces, destroying the adjacent engine. We were rolling* at the time. We were six – we had a 16-year-old CCF cadet on board. I told everyone to get out. The aeroplane was a write-off."[655]

---

*   On the runway, taking off.

17
SOVIET AIR DEFENCES

> *However good the Soviet air defences might be, would they be confident that they were capable enough to stop every bomber delivering on target? Would they risk even one weapon detonating over Moscow or Leningrad? In conventional warfare a 20% chance of kill might not sound great to the attacker, but it might seem high if you are the target.*
>
> Dr Les Ruskell, former head of the Operational Analysis Cell,
> UK Permanent Joint Headquarters, Northwood, UK

PVO'S AIR DEFENCE NETWORK

Soviet air defences posed a major challenge to the credibility of a deterrent consisting of a small force of subsonic bombers. A CIA intelligence assessment of late 1962 warned:

> "The significant improvements in the Soviet air defence system … will progressively reduce the chances of successful attacks by manned bombers. Successful penetration by manned bombers will therefore require increasingly sophisticated forms of attack."[656]

PVO-Strany, the Soviet air defence forces, presented a layered defence: surface-to-air missiles (SAMs), fighters, guns and various radars for early warning, target acquisition, tracking and fire control. Robert Hewson made the telling point that during the 1940s and 1950s:

> "Russia actually spent far more on building its air defence system than it did on nuclear weapons … For the modest number of British V-bombers faced with a massive array of Soviet air defences, there was no guarantee of survival at all."[657]

Initially, PVO focused on the point defence of cities threatened by attack from high-flying bombers. A parallel Soviet programme sought to develop ABM capabilities. PVO's defence against bombers was based on high-altitude SA-2 SAMs and fighters operating under close control. It built a coastal defence belt of SAMs with fighter barrier patrols in front and behind, area defence by long-endurance fighters, mobile SAM sites and gun batteries, and concentric rings of point defence SAMs protecting big cities and other vital targets.

Following Soviet success in bringing down Gary Powers' U-2 and, subsequently, the cancellation of Skybolt, the V-Force went low level, presenting PVO with an entirely novel challenge. It would take years to reconfigure defences built largely to combat high-level attackers. Gradually, however, Soviet SAMs and fighters with low-level capabilities emerged – the SA-3 Goa missile became a significant threat to low-level penetrators. The

High-altitude killer: the SA-2 Guideline SAM. (Norman Bonnor)

V-Force responded with extreme combat tactics – attacking below 300 ft. This was regarded as an effective counter to improving Soviet defences (which, in a hot war, would almost certainly have already suffered severe degradation in the initial missile exchange). In 1981 there were still some 2,000 Goa launchers in the PVO's inventory.[658]

Ultra-low penetrators trained to dip below SA-3's envelope, leaving both SAMs and guns with extremely brief engagement windows. Soviet fighters were dismissed as having little or no ultra-low capability. Low-level strike appeared to offer the MBF a meaningful life extension. Roy Brocklebank recalls a convincing demonstration of the advantages:

"At our ECM lecture on 230 OCU in 1964 the AEO lecturer started with an overhead projector (OHP) display – just the square with the white light on the screen: 'This is the cover from just four 'Bar Lock' radars at high level.' He then took a bag of old one penny pieces and put them on the OHP. There were lots of white gaps. This illustrated graphically just how many radars would be needed to give radar cover at low level and, even so, there were gaps."[659]

Bomber Command studies demonstrated that, outside the target area, the interception of low-level bombers was largely a matter of chance. Past experience of low-level attack underlined the advantage of flying raids with single aircraft, going as low as possible and avoiding chance sightings by keeping clear of airfields and targets other than the desired target. Risks increased with penetration distance; attack routes had to reflect the point where the target could be reached by the shortest penetration.

"Short" is a relative term, a point well made by Roy Brocklebank, who examined low-level deep-penetration routes in some detail: "I had a look at routes from southern Sweden on straight-line tracks. Moscow would be 745NM. Our own deep penetration target was Kiev – about 675NM, with an immediate high-level climb, to recover to Turkey." Another of Brocklebank's deep targets, in Turkmenistan, would have been around 1,000NM: "I remember looking at the low-level route book, a line straight as a die north-east across page after page of the booklet, only the colour of the map changing to relieve the boredom. Hopefully, the sortie would have been boring too."[660]

Most deep targets required extra fuel. Roy Brocklebank provided more details:

"The Vulcan had three different bomb-bay fuel tanks available. The Blue Steel aircraft could carry two saddle tanks, the A forward and the E aft. These tanks were profiled to fit snuggly over the Blue Steel missile. The A held 5,744 lbs and the E 5,768 lbs of

Avtur. There were also drum tanks with a capacity of 7,960 lbs. I don't believe there were enough drum tanks to go round.

"Freefall aircraft could carry an A, A and E or one or two drum tanks … Blue Steel aircraft had the A and E fit to give them the extra range at low level to reach the deeper targets, such as Moscow. The double-drum fit enabled us to reach other targets, such as Kiev, and then recover to Turkey.

"The freefall aircraft QRA targets were essentially peripheral targets, such as Leningrad, and aircraft required only internal fuel. I noted that the new War Plan for 1968 required an aircraft for the Leningrad area with at least an A tank as it was routed over Lake Ladoga to attack Leningrad from the north-east. Had we accepted this, it would have required one QRA aircraft to have an A tank *and* the QRA spare also to have an A tank. This would have had a significant impact on aircraft selection for QRA and the station commander, Group Captain Arthur Griffiths, had me request Bomber Command to modify the route, to reduce the fuel requirement. This was done."

The 1962 CIA study, commenting on rapidly expanding Russian air defences, stated:

"The USSR had continued to devote large-scale efforts to improving and modernising its air defense system. We estimate that, in recent years, air defense has absorbed about one fifth of the Soviet military expenditure … Defenses against hostile aircraft, especially against medium- and high-altitude bombers, have been greatly strengthened in recent years by the widespread deployment of SAM systems, improved interceptors with AAMs (air-to-air missiles) and advanced equipment for air defense warning and control …For defense against aircraft, the Soviets now rely primarily upon SAMs employed near important fixed targets, and upon fighters deployed to cover approach routes as well as gaps between missile-defended locations. We estimate that, in mid-1962, SAM sites were operational in defense of more than 200 target areas in the USSR, including principal cities and other targets of economic and military importance. … we estimate that in mid-1962 about 750 sites were operational … we now estimate that the Soviets will deploy a total of some 1,000-1,200 SA-2 sites in the USSR."[661]

In 1971, just over a decade after Gary Powers' U-2 was shot down, an Air Force Department paper estimated:

"In the Western Air Defence Districts of the USSR, there is a total of 738 SAM sites and 2,423 aircraft in the air defence role. In addition, there are some 4,000 AAA (anti-aircraft artillery) guns belonging to the army. At first sight, the sheer numbers of the air defence weapon systems appear to be formidable, but these must be seen in perspective against the vast geographical area of the country, which tends to dilute the overall defensive capability and to force a concentration of effort in the more sensitive areas."[662]

COUNTERING THE HIGH-FLYING BOMBER

Recognising the growing Soviet threat, British interest in airborne electronic reconnaissance revived in 1948, having been moribund for several years following the end of World War 2. The U-2 overflights began in the late 1950s; spy satellites did not emerge until the mid-1960s.

In the interim, early British Electronic Intelligence (ELINT) operations involved Lancaster and Lincoln bombers based in Iraq. In September 1948 they began flying sorties along the Soviet border, listening to signals traffic. During the 1950s, the Central Signals Establishment assumed a major role in electronic reconnaissance, in conjunction with No. 90 Signals Group's four squadrons of Lincolns, Washingtons, Mosquitos and, later, Canberras and Meteors. The large aircraft flew long-range missions; they could carry bulky electronics and had the necessary generating capacity. Sorties were structured to provoke Soviet air defence reaction; a Washington of 192 Squadron first established that the Soviets had airborne radar intercept capability, recording an airborne interception (AI) radar-equipped MiG-15.[663]

These missions were known as Air Ministry operations or special duty flights. The Lincolns and Washingtons retired, succeeded by Comets and specially modified Canberra B.6 aircraft. Much later, the Comets were succeeded by Nimrod R.1s. The missions probed for gaps in radar coverage and attempted to identify how long the defences took to respond to a threat, how command and control was exercised and information on the specific characteristics of each radar type. By the mid-1950s, specially equipped Valiants began exploring Soviet defences.[664]

Jeremy Mudford had flown Hunters with 34 Squadron during the mid-1950s. Subsequently, he was posted to the Victor OCU as a co-pilot and then joined the Radar Recce Flight at Wyton. The first three production Victors were earmarked to replace the Radar Recce Flight's Canberras: "We flew occasional sorties around the peripheries of the Soviet Union, along the Baltic and southern coasts. Our flight plans were printed on rice paper. I suppose the idea was to eat them if in danger of capture!"

PVO's early development involved extending ground-based defences to ever higher altitudes and, secondly, deploying a force of heavily-armed interceptors. The perceived threat was from individual or small cell penetrators. Milestones included entry into service of the SA-1 and SA-2 SAMs (1956 and 1958 respectively) and the Su-9 Fishpot fighter (1959). PVO concentrated on all-weather interceptors, mostly equipped with two AAMs. A RAND Corporation paper by James T. Quinlivan noted:

> "High-altitude bomber penetration could be aided by electronic countermeasures against the radars of aircraft and SAMs, but the appearance of nuclear warheads at SAM sites made it clear that ECM would be a winner at high altitude only if it could induce large miss distances. In the West, there was general agreement that subsonic high flyers were obsolete."[665]

Yet, the PVO itself had problems dealing with ultra-high altitude reconnaissance intrusions, as suggested by the struggle to shoot down Powers' U-2. The RAF played a major role in high-altitude reconnaissance overflights from the very beginning, with the development of an extended wing Vampire fighter. This reached 59,446 ft in March 1949. Then the Canberra twin-jet bomber arrived. An American photo-reconnaissance expert, Lieutenant Colonel Richard S. Leghorn, prompted English Electric to send a team to Dayton in 1951, with a plan to develop an ultra-high altitude Canberra variant for intelligence missions over the Soviet Union. This had a planned capability to photograph up to 85% of targets in both the USSR and China.[666]

One outcome was the USAF RB-57D 'Big Wing Canberra', first flown in early 1955. Martin delivered 20 of these aircraft. Under Project Robin, a modified Canberra left a West German airfield in 1953, photographed a missile launch site in the Soviet Union and landed at a base in Iran. It came close to being lost to flak batteries. Then the U-2 arrived; an example overflew Leningrad and Moscow in one flight on 5 July 1956.[667]

Squadron Leader John Crampton flew North American RB-45 Tornado reconnaissance sorties in the 1950s. Crampton described a 1954 sortie, as they photographed targets until they were south-south-west of Moscow:

> "… where we turned for the home run, still photographing, until we had to dog-leg south towards Kiev to photograph more targets. It was then that we were very nearly hit by heavy predicted flak. It was as if 500 anti-aircraft guns … were fired simultaneously. When that lot went BOOM right in front of us, about 30 seconds flying time away, I was astonished … I was under the impression that we were undetected and, anyway, we had been told at the briefing that the risk of flak, at our height and speed, was minimal. You can't trust anyone!"[668]

The Russians proceeded with the mass deployment of SAMs and the introduction of interceptors and gun systems with higher engagement altitudes. James T. Quinlivan commented: "Throughout the period of high-flyers, the primary Soviet emphasis was on the creation of a system of point defence of critical facilities, primarily with the new SAMs, backed up with interceptors."[669] Quinlivan added that, by the early 1960s, with the arrival of new fighters and SAMs, PVO had some confidence in delivering point defence against high-flying penetrators. Border SAM belts and coastal airfields provided linear barrier defence, while an enlarged radar network and improved data-handling of the command-and-control network provided a "true zone defense". This assumed penetrators would fly in high enough and remain within individual radar coverage long enough to allow completion of an interception.

COUNTERING LOW-LEVEL PENETRATORS

Even before the U-2 loss in 1960, RAF planners recognised that new weapons and tactics were required to penetrate mature SAM defences. The weapon of choice was the stand-off air-to-surface missile (ASM), released in undefended airspace. Quinlivan noted the change in emphasis:

> "The Americans developed the Hound Dog missile, with a stand-off range of some 500NM, while the British developed Blue Steel, with a range of about 200NM [sic]. During the same period, both air forces also introduced low-altitude bomber penetration tactics – which did not rely on technology as much as the skill and courage of the aircrew."

The Russians might have coped with the ranges of first-generation stand-off weapons, had the carriers remained at high altitude, but low-altitude penetration changed that outlook completely. Quinlivan described the challenge faced by the Soviets:

> "The RAF low-level penetration threat against the Soviet Union dates from the early 1960s, when the Valiant component of the British V-bomber force was assigned to operational control of SACEUR. Rather than modernize the Valiants with ECM equipment intended to retain a high-altitude penetration capability, the Valiants were

given a low-altitude penetration mission. The low-altitude penetrator completely negated the PVO system of defense. The then current SA-2 variant probably had no capability whatsoever against aircraft below 5,000 ft. The interceptors then in inventory had no ability to 'look down' and detect bombers flying against an earth background. But the situation was even more complicated for the interceptor force than the end-game detection. The limited time a low-level penetrator would be within the horizon-limited detection range of any particular radar precluded the launch and vectoring of an interceptor from ground alert. Given the limited endurance of the interceptors then in inventory, Soviet interceptors could only carry out intercepts from ground alert, rather than an airborne CAP (combat air patrol)."

SOVIET SAM DEFENCES

Soviet SAMs were tested in a full-scale proxy war: Vietnam. Some 7,658 Soviet SAMs were supplied to North Vietnam and there were around 5,800 combat launches. At the conclusion of the Linebacker II bombing campaign (18–29 December 1972), the SA-2 shoot-down rate against B-52s was 7.52% (15 B-52s were shot down and five were badly damaged, for 266 missiles).[670] The SA-2 standard site consisted of six single-rail launchers arranged in a hexagon, together with the Fan Song missile control radar and the Spoon Rest early warning radar. SA-2 had a 200-kg warhead with a 50% circular error probable (CEP) lethality radius of 60m.[671]

The Russians responded to the low-level threat with large-scale deployment of the SA-3 SAM, with low-altitude capability, to reinforce both point and barrier defences. Quinlivan noted that the SA-3 role was to re-establish point defence against low-level penetrators:

"In order to cover a fixed site against low-altitude penetrators, many SA-3 launchers and engagement radars were required. Such a defense had the disadvantage that the horizon-limited detection and even smaller engagement radius guaranteed only a single engagement with a transiting bomber. This limited engagement opportunity contrasted with the multiple engagement opportunities high-flying penetrators provided to SA-1s and SA-2s. Modifications to existing SA-2s … included changes in the fire control to accommodate optical guidance and improve low-altitude performance. Meanwhile, the low maximum altitude capability of the SA-3 (about 40,000 ft) demanded that high-altitude SAMs be kept in place because penetrating bombers could still penetrate at high altitude if the Soviets did not defend that altitude band."[672]

Dispersal of nuclear forces, to threaten areas with weaker air defences, were, in effect, a form of economic warfare, as pointed out by Roy Brocklebank: "When we were deployed to Cyprus, that was a game-changer, with the USSR having to extend its border SAM coverage by several hundred miles – an economic win for us."[673]

PVO's requirement for a new generation SAM capable of engaging both high-altitude and low-level penetrators was issued in the late 1960s/early 1970s but the resulting SA-10 Grumble was not deployed until 1980. This system combined the capabilities of SA-2 and SA-3.[674]

In its 1971 paper to the Long Term Strategic Nuclear Working Party, the Air Force Department was extraordinarily optimistic about Vulcan survival in a dense SAM environment – even allowing for the fact that this paper was part of a submission advocating a future British air-delivered nuclear weapons system, despite the overwhelming dominance of ballistic missiles:

> "Against SAM defences, the Vulcan's chances of penetration are high; the only SAM credited with a kill capability at the height at which the Vulcan would fly is SA-3. The engagement zone at 500 ft is between 3.3 and 5.7NM and the single shot probability of killing an aircraft penetrating this zone is about 0.2, given an alerted SAM crew. For an aircraft at 300 ft, the height which the Vulcan could maintain over sea or reasonably flat terrain by night or in IMC (instrument meteorological conditions), the probability is, at most, 0.05 and this would require ideal conditions for the SAM crew, such as:
>
> • An alert and well-trained crew.
> • A good early warning 'feed-in'.
> • All equipment working perfectly.
> • No terrain-screening of the SAM radar.[675]

> "At 200 ft or below, the Vulcan's penetration height in clear-day conditions, the SA-3 system would have no capability. The positions of SA-3 sites are known and aircraft would be routed well clear of them wherever possible. At places where they can only be avoided by a narrow margin – on the coast or near the target, for instance – the aircraft would fly as low as possible and certainly not above 300 ft."[676]

There would certainly be a "narrow margin" when crossing the enemy coast. This fact was brought home to Roy Brocklebank:

> "Just before the inception of a new War Plan, with several Waddington aircraft planned to fly between two SA-2 coastal sites, the updated master list of defences listed two new SA-3 sites. These were gap-fillers between adjacent SA-2 sites. The planned penetration tracks were as close as 1.8NM to one site and about 3.2NM to the other. I alerted No. 1

A stern test: preparing for an evening take-off at Nellis AFB, Red Flag 1982. (Anthony Wright)

Group Ops 1, who, in turn, contacted Bomber Command. It was decided to leave the plan as was."[677]

Each SA-3 site was capable of launching a salvo of two missiles, the interval between firings in the salvo being around five seconds. A second salvo can be fired after about 30 seconds. This study assumed a complex of five sites for city defence. Getting down to 300 ft was important. For a Vulcan flying at night at 500 ft at cruise speed, within the SA-3 threat zone, kill probability for a single SA-3 site was put at 0.46 (or 0.76 for a five-site complex).[678]

FIGHTER DEFENCES

Returning to fighters, Julian Grenfell, an electronic warfare specialist and former Vulcan AEO, reflects:

> "You should *never* discount a weapon system because it was said to have no capability … The AEO would be listening to his RWR (radar warning receiver). He would react to what the RWR was telling him, not to some manual back at base!"

At the same time, Grenfell added: "In the event of nuclear strikes before the bombers got to the target runs, the situational awareness of Soviet command centres would be very poor; units would most likely operate autonomously."[679]

The breezy, optimistic tone of the 1971 Air Force Department paper continued with regard to fighters:

> "… the Soviets lack continuous radar early warning and tracking capabilities at low level for the employment of fighters, using the traditional close-control technique to which they are wedded; and, secondly, there is no evidence that they operate, exercise or train at heights below 1,500 ft. Thus, on present form and until the Russian fighters show definite signs of really concentrating on low-level air defence, they do not present a significant threat."[680]

The close-control system was based on each fighter being homed onto one bomber target. Tom Kerr, Bomber Command's chief research officer (1960–64), recalled:

> "We were always surprised that the Russians persisted with the close-control system, opening the possibility that if the communication channel could be jammed, the means of controlling the interception would be lost. Their reasoning may have given priority to knowing exactly where their own fighters were, as quite a few of them defected to the West, particularly to Scandinavia."[681]

In the 1971 paper, fighters were assumed to mount barrier patrols at low level across the direction of threat: "Since they are unable to use their conventional pulse AI radars at low level, they would be forced to rely on visual detections, followed by gun or missile attacks, thus limiting any fighter capability to clear daylight conditions." Allowance was made for low-level degradation of missile effectiveness and the use of infrared decoys by the Vulcans.[682]

Julian Grenfell agreed that there were some grounds for optimism, as fighters of the late 1960s would have found it difficult to engage a low-level, camouflaged and manoeuvring

Battle practice: Vulcans against the rocky panorama at Nellis. (Anthony Wright)

target employing chaff and jammers.[683] However: "Even though the probability was low for engagement by a fighter, it was still a weapon system that would kill you. PVO had lots of fighters!"[684]

James T. Quinlivan's 1989 paper took a similar line:

"The look down problem drew most of the attention. PVO first received the MiG-23 (Flogger), an aircraft developed for the tactical forces, which had a radar with some depressed angle capability. Later, MiG-25 aircraft were modified to the same standard. The modifications improved the end-game performance of the interceptors, assuming the interceptor could be brought to the end-game situation. Providing the interceptor with a 'look down/shoot down' capability in the end-game engagement was a challenging technical problem, but it was a problem that could be solved given sufficient effort. That effort could come from either the radar engineers of the Soviet design bureaus or the overseas intelligence officers of the GRU. Both paths were followed and the results appeared in PVO inventory with the Foxhound (MiG-31) and Flanker (Su-27).

"A more challenging problem was changing the command-and-control system so that close-control intercepts could be brought to end-game on the basis of the intermittent coverage of different radars. With low-altitude penetration tactics, even a subsonic bomber is within the coverage of any particular radar for only minutes. The most direct approach to solving this problem is the 'interneting' of radars so that a penetrator's continuous time in radar coverage is made long enough to permit completion of a controlled intercept. Another Soviet effort in this area was the development of airborne warning and control aircraft. The higher altitude of the airborne radar platform permits greatly expanded coverage regions against even low-altitude targets, provided the target can be detected in ground clutter."[685]

There were moves to push forward the air defence boundary – perhaps reaching the bombers before they began low-altitude penetration. That resulted in the Soviets' introduction of the long-range Tu-28 Fiddler and the Tu-126 Moss AWACS (airborne warning and control system) aircraft, together with "the preferential basing of the Tu-28s along the northern periphery of the Soviet Union".[686] The Tu-28 was a long-endurance 'loiter' supersonic fighter, armed with a powerful radar and long-range AAMs.[687]

Taken overall, however, Soviet fighter defence in the 1960s allowed individual pilots little freedom of action, as explained by Julian Grenfell:

> "The whole of Soviet air defence was procedural … fighter pilots were not allowed autonomous operation; the fighter controller told the pilot which type of engagement to fly and would state a missile or guns engagement. If the fighter pilot did not receive instructions, nothing would happen!"[688]

SOVIET GUN DEFENCES

The 1971 Air Force Department paper stated that PVO had discarded gun defences (beyond weapons for local-site defence) in the early 1960s:

> "However, there are a number of army divisions in known barrack areas in Western USSR Military Districts and these have AAA and SAMs for their own defences. They form part of the second echelon reinforcements for the Soviet forces in East Germany and in crisis or in conflict they would move to the forward areas. It is believed that the guns which are owned by the army would be taken with them. Nevertheless, to cater for the unlikely event of them staying behind, it is planned to avoid all places where the deployment of any available gun defences would be expected – army installations, airfields, SAM and radar sites, towns and soft ballistic missile sites … As it is not entirely certain that the list of likely AAA-defended sites is exhaustive, it is assumed that 5% of the army guns are in unknown positions randomly distributed over the military districts to which they belong. Penetration probabilities have been calculated on this basis."[689]

For obvious reasons, low-flying penetrators would be well-advised to avoid airfields with defences including 57-mm S-60 gun batteries, each consisting of six to eight guns, a Firecan S-Band fire-control radar and a PC6 predictor. A 1968 RAF Strike Command report on low-level defence penetration (in a limited war/non-European context) commented:

> "A Soviet fighter airfield battalion consists of three batteries and deployment is normally in a circular pattern … a search radar with a low-level capability is associated with each battery, to provide, whenever possible, a degree of radar early warning of target approach … In front of the gun sites, visual observation posts are likely to be established, to supplement radar early warning."[690]

The S-60 sites were semi-fixed rather than mobile. The batteries had Firecan or Flapwheel J-Band radar control. According to this Strike Command study:

> "The guns of a Soviet complex would probably open fire at maximum range (about 3NM) by firing in short bursts. This would give the gunner a chance to make any adjustments considered necessary. As the aircraft approaches, the bursts would become longer and, since it is necessary to allow the guns to cool from time to time, the open fire times are staggered so that only one gun at a time needs to be stood down for cooling. The equipment is primarily designed for firing at targets flying straight and level but attempts are made to improve the chances of hitting manoeuvring aircraft by modifying the muzzle velocity correction. This is done at the predictor by switching the time

function from 15 seconds to six seconds so that the predictor provides a solution more quickly but less accurately. The fire may also be dispersed artificially by using a different target speed setting on each pair of guns."

An annex to the Air Force Department 1971 paper considered the AAA threat in more detail. The army inventory included 57-mm S-60 guns with Firecan or Flapwheel radar, together with the 57-mm ZSU/57/2 with no radar, the ZSU/23/4 with Gun Dish radar and the 23-mm ZU/23 with no radar. The ZSU/23/4 Gun Dish combination was a major threat to low-level attackers but the scale of its deployment was unknown at the time of the study.[691]

ZSU 23/4 was known by the Soviets as Shilka. It was described in a 1981 Sandia report as "a most impressive and highly dangerous weapon system". While it had a maximum rate of fire of up to 4,000 rounds per minute (1,000 rounds per barrel), "the more practical rate is about 200 rounds per minute per barrel (800 rounds per minute for four barrels), fired in 50-round bursts of about 3¾ seconds." Sandia quoted an important source: "In 1973 Israeli pilots learned from experience that to remain in the sights of the Shilka at 2,150–2,750 yards for 35 seconds is lethal and shorter exposures at closer ranges provide the same unwelcome result."[692]

The Air Force Department paper pointed out that there was some doubt as to whether the guns of the field armies would fire on V-Force aircraft, given the short reaction times and lack of tactical warning from surveillance radars. Nevertheless, it based its narrative on the worst case – that all guns able to fire do so.[693]

It can be seen that British planners, at least publicly, largely discounted Soviet SAM defences at ultra-low level (given the avoidance of known sites), and also dismissed the fighter threat due to lack of low-level capability. They took the view that ultra-low penetration presented Soviet defenders with a set of problems which could not be solved. Most V-bomber crews, however, had no doubt about the greatest threat, as confirmed by Victor and Vulcan captain John Laycock:

"In penetrating those defences, the most dangerous threat was the ZSU four-barrelled cannon – which was bloody lethal. We would be right in its threat zone, at 500 ft or less, and we had no idea where these mobile units would be sited on the day. It would take a run of 50–100 miles to fully clear the coastal defence belt."[694]

This weapon's Gun Dish was a J-Band tracking radar; the Vulcan had no J-Band jammer.

18

PENETRATING THE DEFENCES

> *Whatever happened, it would not be good for us. We knew the Soviets' defences were improving all the time, with better radars, missiles and fighter aircraft. Certainly, in the event of war, I wasn't going to win! A sort of fatalism developed amongst V-bomber crews. It was not a feeling that the Soviets were superior to us, but more a sense that no-one would come off well.*
>
> Bryan Montgomery, Valiant nav/plotter, 148 Squadron

GETTING THROUGH TO THE TARGET

Before the V-Force went low level in 1963–64, the intention was to strike Russia with cells of high-flying bombers benefitting from mutual electronic support. V-Force ECM and tactics were tested in Spellbound exercises – Bomber Command pitted against Fighter Command. The results were not encouraging for the bombers, with high levels of ECM unserviceability and poor defensive outcomes. When reporting (June 1961) on the first three trials penetrating UK airspace, Bomber Command chief research officer Tom Kerr was sufficiently concerned to make an unusual suggestion: "In these circumstances, we request that this report be shown only to those who have a 'need to know' details of the results and the performance of the equipment."[695]

The last in the series, Spellbound 14 (14 bombers opposed by 15 fighters), was flown on 26 April 1962, with shocking results. The defending fighters intercepted 79% of the bombers at least once (two bombers were intercepted four times; only three bombers were not intercepted).[696] As Roy Brocklebank points out: "This always presented a problem for analysts. Would the three not intercepted have been intercepted had the overkills not taken place?"[697] Brocklebank believes that UK Air Defence exercises should have been re-designed, with the fighters regarded as Russian, using Russian tactics: "Instead, we always played 'Red', using tactics that ensured UK Air Defence got the maximum number of kill opportunities."

Spellbound had no place for tactical ingenuity on the part of the bombers and, typically, the fighters had a field day. With the Spellbound series completed, Tom Kerr reported and did his best to be upbeat. Whilst acknowledging that ECM design faults, unserviceabilities and a shortage of the correct aerials had marred the first six exercises in the series, he went on to claim that Spellbound did much rapidly to enhance knowledge of the ECM equipment's servicing and operation. In war, of course, much would depend on the experience of the enemy's radar operators. As for Window, Kerr was dismissive: "Window dispensed in the confusion role during the Spellbound exercises was probably more of a help than a hindrance to the (fighter) controllers."[698]

Problems were compounded by lack of realism in Spellbound exercises. Roy Brocklebank offered an example of what could be achieved when bomber crews took matters into their own hands, making life much more difficult for opposing fighters and their controllers. This concerned Kingpin 65, a simulated penetration of UK airspace flown on 22 June 1965:

> "We took off at 11.25 local and flew to Bergen before tracking south down the Danish coast. We then swung right for the UK. We were not at the front but definitely at the top. We were at about 52,000 ft. For this exercise, our precise H2S frequencies had been recorded, to provide information for the UK Air Defence radar passive detectors. We kept our radars off. As I had nothing to do, I did lookout using one of the periscopic sextants. I saw lots of contrails heading towards the UK and lots of opposing contrails that swung in behind their targets. We were not intercepted."[699]

In the round, Spellbound exposed serious weaknesses concerning ECM, Window and the very high level of fighter interceptions achieved. These problems were not shared with V-Force crews. However, everyone must have been aware that the prospects were poor for high-altitude penetration. Then came the dramatic shift, from 50,000 ft plus to 500 ft and lower.

Whilst aircraft and weapons had changed radically over two decades, a Bomber Command study of the early 1960s suggested that the fundamentals governing survival in enemy airspace at low level were little changed on World War 2. This September 1963 memorandum was prepared as the V-bombers were switching to low-level nuclear strike. The study drew heavily on Bomber Command's experience in World War 2, together with the outcome of post-war exercises during the periods 1946–53 and 1958–59. This report reflected:

> "… with the current change in Bomber Command tactics, interest in low-level operations has increased considerably … No attempt has been made to assess the effectiveness of modern air defences against low-flying aircraft, but most of the problems existing ten and 20 years ago are still present."[700]

With the exception of the final months of World War 2 – when the Luftwaffe was much reduced – Bomber Command undertook relatively few deep penetration, low-level daylight raids. The data available demonstrated that losses to fighters were governed by raid size and penetration depth. Loss rates for raids of 20 or more aircraft were "appreciably greater" than for single aircraft (with small groups, of up to five aircraft, suffering no greater losses than single aircraft). Post-war attempts at close control of fighters as low-level interceptors achieved no real success. The report added: "Due to the general difficulty the defences have in tracking aircraft at low level, it follows that changes in track could confuse the defences even more so." The report continued:

> "Chance appears to play a very large part in the success of fighters in intercepting low-level aircraft. It follows that the greater the density of fighters in the area of low-level operations, the greater is the risk to the attacking aircraft. In particular, the post-war exercises have demonstrated how, by avoiding fighter airfields by 10–20 miles, the interception risk is reduced considerably."

The effects of height on risk exposure were difficult to assess, but "there appears to be no real variation in the losses suffered for aircraft flying between 100 and 500 ft". This view changed when the SA-3 low-level-capable surface-to-air missile was fully deployed. As for speed:

> "Generally, it appears that the faster the bomber flies, the less the risk, but the real factor is the command of speed which the defending fighters have over the bombers. Provided the fighters can outpace the bombers by 50 kts or more, the conversion rate of sightings to combats will be high."

On the threat from light flak, there was little data on wartime low-level penetration losses or from peacetime exercises, but the report made several rather obvious observations: losses would depend on the number of guns/firepower, the height of the attackers (defining the engagement time) and the element of surprise.

On penetration depth, post-war exercises (1948–1953) revealed that the interception risk per 10 miles of penetration by a low-flying bomber "is 0.04 when the targets are airfields and 0.01 when non-airfield targets are attacked and when airfields are avoided by at least 20 miles on the route to the target". This was based on an average fighter density of three per 100 square miles, an efficient ground observer network providing raid reporting and no precision type of control but provision of raid information allowing more efficient defence patrols. Lack of a ground-observer network reduced interception risk by a factor of three. Interceptions and combat losses, of course, are different things: "With the present-day fighter armament, the probability of converting an interception into a successful combat will lie somewhere between 10% and 40%."

Whilst this study was, essentially, an historical review, few challenges for the defences had been solved by 1963: "The only parameter which has shown any change … has been an increase in speed, which is more marked in the case of defending fighters than that of the attacking bombers." Yet, this comment excludes another change of more profound consequence – the immeasurably greater destructive power of the weapons carried and, thus, the extraordinarily high price of failure to intercept *and kill each penetrator* before weapon release. Even the remarkably high interception rates achieved in UK post-war exercises would have left some bombers to deliver their weapons and wreak havoc.

The Operational Research Branch study made a powerful case for low-level attack. It stated that, in a non-ECM environment, a single high-level aircraft runs a 95% interception risk after 250 miles' penetration of radar cover. In contrast, "there has been no progress whatever in the precision control of fighters at low level. Low-level fighter defence appears to be still essentially one of barrier patrols and of patrols in the target area." Naturally, low-level deep penetrators surviving the attack phase then faced continued

Low means low: as demonstrated by this Vulcan at Biggin Hill in 1971. (John Huggins)

exposure during the recovery flight, perhaps aggravated by the need to climb to conserve fuel. At the same time, in the context of a one-strike nuclear attack, kills made after weapon release were valueless to the defenders. Furthermore, this report did not consider the rapid growth in Soviet SAM defences – the review was historical in character and, at the same time, the bulk of Soviet SAM defences then consisted of high-altitude SA-2 sites. Nevertheless, it did comment: "… in the future, this type of defence will probably constitute the greatest threat to low-level aircraft." In the V-Force, 500 ft would soon be regarded as dangerously high.

According to this report, the main lessons for low-level strike were: fly raids with single aircraft, fly as low as possible and, inter alia, confound raid reporting and avoid chance sightings to the maximum degree by avoiding airfields and targets other than the desired target. As for the results of post-war exercises, the report's Appendix C commented: "There is considerable evidence to state that interception of low-level aircraft is a matter of chance, the risks increasing with penetration. Against non-airfield targets, the risk was 5% per 50 miles penetration." It then continued:

> "When many of the operational uncertainties of low-level defence are reduced or eliminated, resulting in a high degree of control of a small defended area, then the interception rate can be as high as 70 to 75% (the 1958–59 exercise results)."

COULD THE V-FORCE SUCCEED?

There was always an undercurrent of doubt as to whether the V-Force could survive a pre-emptive missile strike with sufficient strength to go on and deliver a meaningful retaliatory attack. The primary vulnerabilities were exposure to destruction on or around the bases and, secondly, the lack of a long-range stand-off weapon – forcing some surviving bombers to make a perilous deep penetration into heavily defended airspace. Yet the V-Force survived its critics, although, according to one senior source, Peter Hudson: "It was a near thing." He described how Sir Robert Scott, chairman of the British Nuclear Deterrent Study Group, "separately minuted the Minister of Defence in July 1961, without the Air Ministry's knowledge, that 'the time has come to consider … giving up control of British nuclear weapons and their delivery systems … and negotiate the best terms possible with the Americans in return for handing over control to them.'" This proposal came to nothing, but Hudson observed that the very fact that this advice was given at all indicated "the cross-currents running at the time".[701]

In sharp contrast, only a month before Sir Robert's note, Air Vice-Marshal T. O. Prickett, Assistant Chief of the Air Staff, Operations, presented a gleaming vision of the V-Force. In a Guidance Memorandum on deterrent policy, circulated to all RAF commands, he wrote:

> "The V-bombers have no superior in the world today among bombers of their range, and the present defence system of the potential adversary could not hope to seal off his vast airspace so completely as to prevent enough of them striking home to wreak enormous damage."[702]

Prickett's note acknowledged that point protection of vital targets "is bound to become more effective", but entry into service of Blue Steel would meet this challenge and provide "continuing validity". He then added: "We must expect that eventually the effectiveness of the opposing defences will further develop to the point where even area penetration will become very difficult and costly." However, at this time Skybolt was still in prospect – a solution avoiding penetration of defended airspace. "With this weapon, to which no practicable defence is in prospect, the V-bombers' ability to hit their targets will be preserved until at least the end of the decade."

Interestingly, Sir Robert's minute and Air Vice-Marshal Prickett's memorandum both avoid uncomfortable truths. Sir Robert ignored the full implications of the political chasm which would open up, should Britain "surrender" its nuclear deterrent to the Americans (regardless of endless and often pointless debates about the quality of its "independence"), at a time when the Cold War was edging towards climax. What would have been Britain's position during the Cuban Crisis, in the absence of the V-Force? Equally, Prickett lauded the power of the V-Force, whilst ignoring the fact that in a Cold War turned hot, most of its strength would have been vapourised on the ground, or destroyed in the air in the immediate vicinity of its airfields.

LOW-LEVEL PENETRATION

When Skybolt was cancelled in December 1962, V-Force crews accustomed to flying at over 50,000 ft were suddenly expected to fly very low in large aircraft designed to do exactly the opposite. Many relished the challenge, having tired of long, uneventful flights at high altitude. Air Commodore Norman Bonnor, then a Victor nav/radar, described a typical hi-lo-hi training flight for Blue Steel-armed aircraft: a climb to 40,000 ft plus and a 1,000NM high-level navigation exercise (navex), "followed by the descent for a 500NM low-level navex (250/350 kts at less than 500 ft, including a simulated missile launch at 300 ft) and a high-level recovery leg."[703]

Successful low-level attack depended on V-Bomber aircrew accepting the inherent risks of training for war at 300 ft or lower. "Low flying" was a flexible term – much depended on the captain's attitude and the confidence and experience of his crew. Vulcan captain Nick Dennis describes the challenge:

> "When low flying at night the nav/radar gave a running commentary. If terrain-following radar (TFR) had been introduced earlier, it would have saved lives. When we eventually got TFR, it was basic – just a yellow indicator oscillating on the director horizon as the terrain changed. It was very difficult to follow with any accuracy. Tragically, one crew hit the top of the Brecon Beacons, flying in white-out conditions without TFR."[704]

He had a close call himself during poor winter conditions:

> "We were flying over the Cheviot Hills, across a snow-covered landscape. When letting down, I found I couldn't distinguish between sky and ground. Happily, a tree then came into view and it had no snow beneath. That was my ground marker."

Vulcan nav/radar John Weller's crew were confident of flying a successful war sortie:

> "We would be very low, using TFR, although we didn't fly lower than 500 ft at night in peacetime. I think our chances would have been improved by weapons detonating all over Russia – with the EMP (electromagnetic pulse) knocking out many of their radars."[705]

"Footloose on the Goose": low level – at 250/300 ft agl. (Andy Leitch Collection)

Many former aircrew recall the excitement of flying ultra-low over the Arctic tundra of Goose Bay, Labrador. Wing Commander Peter West, MBE, was a 12 Squadron Vulcan AEO. His captain, Squadron Commander Bob Tanner, took "low level" literally: "When we flew low, we never went higher than 250 ft; Bob preferred 110 ft during our regular visits to Goose Bay – 'footloose on the Goose!'"[706]

Nav/radar Jim Walker and crew did a great deal of low flying in Vulcan Mk 1As: "Initially, we flew at 500 ft, or 1,000 ft at night. Things were different when we reached Goose Bay." His captain, Mike D'Arcy, went down as low as 50 ft! "When we flew over the sea, we picked up a crust of salt." His other captains had different ideas: "My second captain was more cautious than D'Arcy and the third was more nervous. Anyway, we were cleared to fly down to 250 ft at 375 kts on occasions, such as in major exercises." D'Arcy and crew didn't think much of the '2H' attack – the pop-up with Yellow Sun 2. Jim Walker remarked, with a degree of understatement: "That would have been pretty dangerous." Things changed when the WE.177B laydown weapon arrived, although danger certainly remained; this laydown bomb would have been dropped in a 2F attack whilst directly overflying the target at ultra-low level:

> "We would have been travelling at 600 ft per second and reckoned to be six miles away at detonation. I always understood we would keep low, going flat out, rather than make an attempt to climb out. If the weapon airburst, you couldn't get away. However, we were going for a WE.177 groundburst and this would have contained the energy to some degree."[707]

At the other end of the scale, Walker's Vulcan, on one occasion, was hit by enemy ground fire. D'Arcy and crew flew into Aden. When they landed, a .303 bullet was found in the wing.

"Someone had fired on us on the approach. We then found we couldn't get into the Officers' Mess. It had been blown up by a bomb and the chef had been killed."

Roy Brocklebank joined 12 Squadron in June 1964, but it was some months before a low-level sortie was flown. During the remaining months of 1964, this crew ventured overseas (BC/12/Libya), then spent the December period in the Far East, in response to a deterioration in the Indonesian Confrontation. When back in the UK, they began flying low level: "… on 15 January 1965 we did the UK/LL from EP6 to 12; EP6 would have been South Wales and thence north towards West Freugh – though we were not yet cleared for pop-up attacks."[708]

The intense training continued to unfold. On 9 February, Brocklebank's crew completed a 1,500-mile tactical profile flight: a 500-mile primary navigation leg using the navigation and bombing system (NBS), then entering UK/LL at EP1, on the south coast, and terminating at Ouston, near Newcastle: "The low level (night) portion would have been about 650NM … The low level would have been at heights of 1,500–4,000 ft, as we lacked both equipment and skills to fly lower in safety."

The routine progressed with several low levels terminating at Ouston Gate: "The significance of Ouston Gate was to allow the radar bomb scoring unit (RBSU) on the airfield to pick us up as we passed …" The initial point for a pop-up attack would be reached: "… we would turn about 90 degrees port, initiate a climb at about ten miles from the target, level at about 11,000 ft and 'release' the bomb at about two miles, over Newcastle."

A change in weapon system began in the first half of 1965, with flights including Trial 505 sorties flying test rounds of the WE.177B laydown bomb (450 kt). The Yellow Sun 2 pop-up sorties remained significant, however; WE.177B did not become fully operational until early 1967. In the final weeks of December 1965, having returned from a Western Ranger to Goose Bay, Roy Brocklebank's crew flew their first Yellow Sun trips terminating at West Freugh range, south-east of Stranraer:

> "This was the first time we could practise the 2H attack: accelerate to 350 kts, pull up at about 18,000 yards, climb at a 14-degree angle – later changed to 18,450 yards and 15 degrees – and release the bomb in the climb on passing 10,500 ft at about two miles. We were not permitted to practise the escape manoeuvre. I still remember the process for booking West Freugh … I would ring Stranraer 2501 on the GPO line, ask for 76 and then rattle off call-sign, target number, time on target and then hang up. Time after time the response was: 'This is Stranraer 2502'. I lost count of the number of times the GPO put me through to a little old lady in Stranraer. She was always so polite and probably totally confused."

In due course, the pending arrival of WE.177B laydown weapons influenced sortie planning, but simulated ultra-low-level strikes with the new bomb had yet to begin. On 20 April 1966, however, Roy Brocklebank's crew flew Exercise Coop and attacked Juvincourt, a French airfield, adopting laydown tactics despite the absence, at that time, of published procedures regarding height and speed. They were intercepted by a French Vautour fighter near the initial point: "We went through the target at a speed near 420 kts. This was before we knew the maximum peacetime speed was 350 kts and the war speed was 375 kts, with a one-off ten-minute dash at 415 kts. It was certainly bumpy." Roy Brocklebank added:

> "In the April 1966 exercise we went U/S after we had taxied for take-off. We were ordered to leave our aircraft on the operational readiness platform and take the spare. We boarded and departed. The aircraft was covered in snow but we were assured that it would come off at about 25 kts. True enough, as we reached 25 kts we hit a snowbank on the runway, where all the other aircraft had dropped their snow. From declaring we were U/S to getting airborne in the spare was 16 minutes."

From the early years of the V-Force, there were concerns about "over-familiarisation" in the training programme, arising from repeated use of static RBSUs and their associated targets. This could lead to consistently high scores, prompting the introduction of another system to back up ground radar assessment of attacks. The second scoring method used the plan position indicator (PPI) of aircraft to score attacks, with assessment by nav/radars and bombing analysis staff reviewing photographs of the PPI taken at or just subsequent to release.[709]

This second assessment method was explained in a Bomber Command Research Branch report prepared by a 'bombing assessment team'. This described PPI analysis as "complementary and essential" alongside the ground radar-scored attack. The latter gave the most accurate measure of the actual bombing error, so determining the effectiveness of the bomb-aimer's technique, his bombing error and the equipment errors. However, the report added that, as the RBSUs are all located on static sites and have a limited range, complete radar cover of these areas is soon built up at all stations: "over the years, the precise location of all bombing responses becomes well known, until a stage is reached where the more expert crews are obtaining consistently good results, the limitations of accuracy of which are those of the equipment." This explains the occasional challenge of simulated attacks on unfamiliar continental airfields:

> "It has been recognised that first run attacks on unknown targets on the Continent simulate closely the problems of PPI interpretation where previous radar cover is unlikely to exist, as in the case of many operational targets. Where there is no RBSU, the only method of assessing bombing accuracy is by photographic analysis."

This paper set out a methodology for PPI analysis, dealing with the key issues affecting effectiveness: quality of photograph, the accuracy of available mapping, the accurate calculation of the forward throw of the bomb and the method applied – the analysis procedure, as described in the paper.

GOING IN

A late 1960s Strike Command report on low-level penetration by the Vulcan force recognised the difference between a war sortie taking the aircraft to its performance limits and "acceptable training levels, which … will be based upon a performance envelope lying well inside the maximum permissible limits." This study concerned penetration in conventional, non-European conflicts. It assumed a range of speeds, from about 225 kts to 375 kts IAS (indicated air speed), and that aircraft endurance would give a degree of freedom of choice of penetration route. As for minimum height, Vickers Armstrong had studied risk at a nominal clearance height of 200 ft during work on the TSR-2 programme, given a peacetime criterion of terrain-following being permitted to cause only a 5% increase in aircraft accident rate from all causes. This concluded that 150 ft "could be satisfactory on the same basis or even 100 ft could be acceptable for peacetime flying," given system developments. From this report, together with the results of an earlier American study by the Wright Air Development Division, the Strike Command Development Unit commented:

> "… it seems reasonable to conclude that the safe clearance altitude is a function of aircraft speed and that an altitude of 200 ft at a speed of M.0.5 should be possible for short periods, with 300 ft sustainable for longer periods of time."[710]

Crews had a variety of views on the chances of successful penetration. Vulcan navigator Paul Hickley thought it would have been "extremely easy", as "certainly in the 1960s, 1,000 Minuteman and Atlas missiles would have arrived two hours before the V-Force and the Soviet Union would have been a smoking ruin …"[711]

A July 1963 Bomber Command study on Blue Steel and QRA had concluded: "The targeting of ICBMs is now so extensive that missile strikes on or near the QRA targets can be expected and the effectiveness of the defences – both fighters and SAMs – considerably weakened."[712] As for whatever defensive capability remained, Julian Grenfell points out that going low significantly reduced the early warning range and, hence, the warning of incoming attackers. The early warning radar's intermittent 'paints' of the target made the handover to acquisition radars more difficult, while height-finding and tracking by fire-control radar was more difficult, as SA-2 could not engage lower than 5,000 ft – but this was much reduced later.[713] Grenfell acknowledged, however, that SA-3 Goa did much to plug the gap in the defences.

The fact remained that the penetration of hostile airspace, flying ultra-low across a country submerged in a tidal wave of nuclear bombardment, would test even the most courageous to the very limit. Remembering the early years, Dick Fuller recalled his profound doubts about hi-lo-hi:

> "Our range gave a maximum flight time of around seven hours, but when you fly low you burn fuel at one hell of a rate. All our targets were in Western Russia and I didn't have much hope of penetrating successfully. Naturally, our routes in were based on intelligence and designed to avoid the defences, but I was more worried about the nuclear flashes and clouds from other bombs. After all, many important targets were earmarked for multiple strikes. As for getting back, we were supposed to return to Marham. We didn't give that much thought. Certainly, we all believed that the losses going in and coming out would be tremendous. There was a tendency to over-estimate the capabilities of the Soviet air defences – we gave them credit for being a lot better than they were. Nevertheless, our Valiants were sitting ducks."[714]

The September 1971 Air Force Department paper for the Long Term Strategic Nuclear Working Party offered views on the likely effectiveness of a V-Force strike: "Taking into account all the potential capabilities of the Russian air defence systems, the probability of a single aircraft surviving each type of defence and reaching its target has been calculated." This paper included a table referring to "four representative – but not particularly easy – targets which are at present allocated to the RAF alone". (Target identities were removed from the source document, imposing obvious difficulties in interpretation.) Single aircraft survival probabilities were given as follows:[715]

PENETRATION DISTANCE	SA-3	FIGHTERS (BY DAY ONLY)	GUNS	OVERALL
215NM	1.0	0.61	0.98	0.60
530NM	1.0	0.36	0.95	0.34
450NM	1.0	0.60	0.96	0.57
105NM	0.98	0.73	1.0	0.71

In considering the probability of kill (assured kill = PK1), the first shot PK may be 0.46 but this changes with a second (also with PK 0.46) – with the possibility of Hit/Miss, Miss/Hit, Hit/Hit and Miss/Miss.

Generally, losses from fighters and guns increase with penetration distance, but SAM casualties, according to this study, would be almost non-existent amongst penetrators flying at extremely low level. In addition, this paper stressed lack of evidence for Soviet fighters operating below 1,500 ft. The assumptions on the Soviet fighter defences are those in the 1971 National Retaliatory War Plan study, but with numbers and types of fighters at each base updated. These changes were minor and required no recalculation of losses to fighters. This included the following combat lethalities:

- Pair of gun-armed fighters: 0.40
- Single gun-armed fighter: 0.23
- Fighter with two AAMs (other than Alkali missile): 0.22
- Fighter with four AAMs (other than Alkali missile): 0.35
- Fighter with four Alkali missiles: 0.08.[716]

The problems with the 1971 paper are that, on the one hand, it was 'selling' a future air-delivered system to succeed Polaris and thus had every reason to present optimistic views on the chances of survival and successful penetration by ageing Vulcans, whilst, at the same time, it skirted the problem of making a realistic allowance for the severe degradation of the Soviet defences following a retaliatory missile strike. Here, the paper offered a bare comment (but still a relevant observation in the context of unilateral response): "The effect of Polaris strikes on the defences is considered negligible."[717]

The paper's Annex A gives a maximum damage radii (for 50% probability of moderate damage) from a Polaris burst (assuming optimum height of burst), as: jet fighters: 3.6NM; apartment-type buildings: 5.2NM; trucks, rocket-launchers, fire-control equipment: 2.5NM; and artillery: 1.35NM.[718]

James T. Quinlivan gave a wider view of the missile threat to Soviet air defences:

"In 1964 the Strategic Air Command ICBM force of 931 missiles first equalled the alert bomber force. Besides representing a significant change in the form of a strategic attack, the missile force presented a new threat to the operating environment of the air defense. Missile attacks presented the Soviet air defense with the question, 'What, exactly, would be left for a strategic air defense to defend after an initial missile exchange?' PVO would thus have to survive an initial suppression attack before it could begin its defense of the homeland. PVO ability to survive a nuclear missile attack was problematic."[719]

In assessing the Vulcan's ability to penetrate Soviet defences in the early 1970s, the Air Force Department's paper assumed adverse conditions for survival: daylight and good visibility. Yet, it remained upbeat, claiming: "We can avoid or fly below the effective envelopes of all SAM defences." Whilst ignoring the true severity of the V-bombers' main problem – launching successfully – it concluded: "… in spite of the nature and numbers of the Soviet air defence weapons systems, it is possible for the aircraft to penetrate to their targets with a good chance of delivering at least one weapon on each."[720]

PENETRATION BY DAY

There was always an acute awareness of the greater risk to V-bombers in daylight. Many aircrew assumed a war sortie would be flown in daylight, given the UK–US time difference and the potential advantage to the Soviets of launching a pre-emptive missile strike for impact in the US Mid-West during the small hours of the night. For some years, exercises with UK home defence fighters had produced alarming results for daylight penetrators. In October 1958, for example, Exercise Sunbeam involved several attempts to break through the fighter defences – with each attack regarded as a possible first raid at the outbreak of war. The analysis was based on interceptions in which one or more fighters could have made a firing pass (with 'interception' NOT synonymous with 'kill'). Sunbeam was a major exercise, involving 150–300 aircraft attacking the UK east coast in waves, from north of the Thames to the Orkneys. The raiders included aircraft from Bomber Command, 3rd Air Force, 2nd Allied Tactical Air Force (ATAF), 4th ATAF and NATO national air forces. Bomber Command participated in all six day raids, flying 16 Valiant and 70 Canberra sorties, with no ECM, at heights from 37,000 ft to 45,000 ft, and opposed by Hunters and Javelins. The results were shocking, providing real evidence that the Valiants were, indeed, "sitting ducks". Bomber Command's exercise report faced the truth: "There is no doubt that under the conditions of this exercise the fighter defences were able to intercept some 90% of the attacking Bomber Command aircraft. This is the highest average interception rate in any peacetime exercise."[721] The figure for the preceding year (Exercise Vigilant, 1957) was 44%.

There were just two Valiant day raids (both on the first day):

> "… the Canberra and Valiant raids penetrated in the same general area but whereas the Valiants suffered 100% interception, only 70% of the Canberras were intercepted … the most striking difference lies in the number of interceptions reported by the aircraft. Valiants reported 3.1 interceptions each, whereas the Canberras reported only 1.2 interceptions per aircraft."

The appalling result for the V-bombers was attributed largely to the greater visibility of the anti-flash white-painted Valiants. The 1959 report on Sunbeam concluded:

> "The conversion of such an interception rate into 'losses' is a matter of speculation. With conventional gun armament, the lethality of combat is expected to be in the region of 0.2 to 0.3. Bearing in mind the multiple interceptions which were effected (average of 2.3 per bomber) the 'kill' rates would have been high, around 50% … The worst 'losses' would have been a raid of six Canberras, where one or none of the aircraft would have survived."

On that basis, the high-altitude jet bombers of the late 1950s would have fared no better than the RAF's Fairey Battle light bombers, massacred over the Meuse bridges when the Germans overran France in 1940. The Sunbeam report acknowledged: "From the bomber's viewpoint, the above conclusions are very pessimistic." Some factors, however, worked in favour of the defences: there was no ECM, no concentration of the attacking force in an attempt to swamp local defences, and raid times were generally known and repetitious (although the impact on the 90% interception rate "would be a matter of conjecture").

When using ECM, chaff, decoys and vigorous evasive measures in affiliations with fighters, it could be a very different story for the more advanced and powerful V-bombers, although, by the early 1960s they were increasingly vulnerable to SAMs when at high altitude. The Vulcan, extraordinarily manoeuvrable at high altitude, held unpleasant surprises for fighters. AEO Peter West discussed high-level performance:

> "A Vulcan at high level could out-manoeuvre any fighter. Whether high or low, however, it was hard to break missile lock. Nevertheless, a decent pilot and AEO certainly had a chance. On one occasion, flying with Bob Tanner on a fighter affiliation, we were limited to 'gentle manoeuvring' at no higher than 40,000 ft. At a certain point the Sea Vixen pilot said he had to return due to his fuel state. Bob asked him whether he fancied an all-out last go. Bob then got onto the fighter's tail and, once there, the Sea Vixen couldn't shake us off."[722]

Equally, the Vulcan could be highly aggressive when low. Roy Brocklebank confirmed its ability to turn the tables on an attacking fighter:

> "When at Waddington, our Vulcans practised evasive manoeuvres when chased by Sea Vixens. The Sea Vixen would come up behind the Vulcan. It would be detected by the Red Steer Mk 2 tail-warning radar … it could detect a simulated missile launch out to five miles. The normal release distance at low level was around two miles. We would wait until the simulated missile launch was detected, then drop chaff and decoys, go into a rapid climb to at least 1,000 ft, execute a 90-degree turn and then return to very low level before reverting to the original track. We would leave behind a bank of violent turbulence. During the trials of this evasive manoeuvre, the turbulence was found to be powerful enough to flip over the following Sea Vixen onto its back."[723]

Visual contact, of course, was the key to low-level detection in daylight. Here, the Vulcans suffered the disadvantage of trailing black smoke. A solution was sought; 617 Squadron's operations record book for August 1968 noted trials of a smoke suppression product. Another fluid, C12, was also tested; it was said to have been used with considerable success in Vietnam.[724] Andy Leitch remembers aircraft being fitted with better burners in the engines, to produce less smoke.

Smoke suppression had real significance for daylight survival, given that Russian fighter pilots with expended armament were expected to ram bombers. A Soviet document on air defence (1958) had a dedicated section on ramming:

"Soviet military doctrine requires the destruction of the enemy without fail before he reaches his target ... atomic and hydrogen bombing is a question of life and death for the great masses; therefore, it must be averted at any price, under any conditions. If a fighter pilot has expended his supply of shells and rockets, but failed to destroy the enemy (he) must resort to ramming. If he does not resort to ramming, his commander can 'recommend' it to him."[725]

PENETRATION BY NIGHT

V-bombers had a better chance of successful penetration at night and/or in bad weather. The V-bombers became increasingly vulnerable by day during the 1960s, but retained their potency at night for many years – well into the 1970s. This point was made, in convincing style, by V-Force aircraft participating in the USAF's Red Flag, widely regarded as the most realistic simulated combat flying environment anywhere in the West. The positive outcomes achieved by British crews, flying obsolescent aircraft with ageing equipment during the late 1970s, support the view that V-bombers would have been even more capable at night during the preceding decade.

Roger Dunsford flew Vulcans during the 1973–84 period. In early 1978 he was captain of an elite command crew on 44 (Rhodesia) Squadron. They were selected for Strike Command's Red Flag team that year, to fly against the best weapons and systems fielded by the Soviet Union:

Red Flag battle practice, November 1978: Cliff Doe and Vulcan XL444 (captain: Flight Lieutenant Pat Hewitt), ready to depart Scampton for Nellis AFB. (Cliff Doe)

"As work-up for Red Flag, we did a lot of low-level night flying out of Goose Bay. My logbook shows that we flew a night Red Flag exercise in the United States starting on 27 November 1978 – pretty late in the Vulcan's life, when many considered it obsolescent, if not obsolete. This was centred on Nellis AFB, Nevada. The opposition came from fighters of the USAF Aggressor Squadron, which made use of Soviet radar technology and tactics in simulating Soviet aircraft. There were 'Soviet' SAM and gun batteries out in the desert, similarly trained and equipped to complete the full suite of Soviet air defences. They were dedicated to reproducing, as accurately as possible, a realistically hostile environment against which to test our own technology and tactics. Four Vulcans flew that exercise and all four 'delivered' their weapons on a simulated Soviet headquarters. Each sortie was minutely scrutinised in the debrief, using the USAF's highly sophisticated analytical methods, which showed every detail of what worked and what did not. It was a great confidence booster to have confirmation that, if we ever had to do it for real, we had a realistic chance of success, provided it was at night."[726]

The 1963–64 switch to low level greatly increased V-Force war-fighting potential and, as underlined by Roger Dunsford, this lingered to some degree far into the 1970s:

"… the Vulcan was an aircraft full of surprises. The Americans had a big shock when we flew that first Red Flag exercise at night … Despite their best efforts – using the latest Soviet fighter, SAM and anti-aircraft artillery technology and techniques – our aircraft came through unscathed! By the late 1970s we were no longer a viable day-bombing force, but it was a very different story at night. The Red Flag results made the Americans realise that British V-bombers were not a spent force for night attacks against less heavily defended but, nevertheless, operationally vital targets which Polaris did not cover.

"We flew at ultra-low level at night, getting the very best out of the first generation TFR, in contrast to higher flying, third-generation TFR-equipped F-111s. The latter were trained to fly down to only 1,000 ft at night, using their advanced, swept-up TFR. We made the most of the crew's teamwork and 'steam-driven' TFR to go below 500 ft at night – sometimes down to 250 ft. That was a genuine surprise to most USAF observers – we could get more out of less … Even at the end of the 1970s, V-bombers at night posed a real threat to the Russians."

19
ECM AND OTHER COUNTERMEASURES

> *When we went low level, we still needed the radar warning receiver to pick up the AAA and portable missile threats, together with the fighters with low-level capability. Our big problem was the multi-barrelled 23-mm gun. It could tear an aircraft to bits, as the Americans found out in Vietnam. It wasn't for nothing that they called Hanoi 'Dodge City'. It was part of my job to ensure we never got into its cone of fire.*
>
> Peter West, Valiant/Vulcan AEO

Air Marshal Sir Frederick Sowrey defined Electronic Warfare (EW) as: "exploitation of the electromagnetic spectrum and the denial of its use to the enemy."[727] Electronic countermeasures (ECM) included: "deception" (inserting false data), "confusing" (inserting redundant information, to delay and confuse) and "overloading" (an interference signal). A measure to overload may not confuse; indeed, overloading may clarify an otherwise confused situation.[728]

When the German war ended in Europe during May 1945, ECM (then known as RCM – radio countermeasures) took a back seat. Later, the needs of the V-Force provided a stimulus. Its ECM outfit was defined by 1954: a centimetric radar jammer, a communications jammer, a metric radar jammer, a proximity fuse jammer, a warning receiver for dispensing Window and automatic Window dispensers. This led to the operational V-Force ECM fit, including the Red Shrimp barrage jammer (ARI 18076), the Green Palm communications jammer (ARI 18074) and the Blue Diver early warning radar jammer (ARI 18075).[729]

Green Palm would jam Soviet fighter ground-control communications. Roy Brocklebank described its function:

> "It was believed that Russian fighters had only a four-channel VHF box. Although we could jam any one of the four channels, all aircraft were briefed to jam the same channel – Channel 3, I think – which was the recovery channel, thus denying the fighters vector information to find their airfields when low on fuel."[730]

It was hoped that ECM would ensure that a reasonable proportion of the surviving bombers would penetrate well-defended airspace. In 1964, despite the cancellation of Blue Steel 2 and Skybolt, together with expansion of Soviet air defences, Bomber Command's Operational Research Branch still expressed optimism on this front:

> "In the air exercises around 1950 the Bomber Command raids which penetrated Fighter Command used ECM on one night and not on the next night. This enabled an estimate

to be made of the overall effectiveness of ECM. It is interesting to note that ECM in those days provided a 40% reduction in the interception rate of the bombers and this figure was in broad agreement with the results of the last war. It is believed that 50% is about the maximum degradation which ECM will achieve in the operational environment."[731]

This paper was presented at a NATO conference in London during August 1964. It summarised the Operational Research Branch analysis of peacetime air exercises. The benefits of ECM may have been significant in 1950 but subsequent exercises challenging UK air defences produced very worrying outcomes for the bombers.

Tom Kerr, who headed Bomber Command's Operational Research Branch, recalled battles between Headquarters, High Wycombe, and the Air Staff in London, marked by vitriolic correspondence. One memorable fight concerned Bomber Command's desperate need for broadband jammers to protect Mk 2 V-bombers from Soviet SAMs. MoD refused to find the money – around £2 million – to equip Mk 2 bombers with these jammers. Kerr, in blunt mode, proposed a radical solution. Each bomber cost £1 million. Why not cancel two aircraft and spend the money on the jammers? "The suggestion was not welcome. The Bomber Command staff were determined to win the Whitehall battle … Some six months later we did win …" The ECM bulge was fitted to the Vulcan.

A 1963 report on MBF ECM, from the Air Ministry Electronic Warfare Committee, noted that, four years previously, it had been decided that ECM policy long term would focus on noise jamming. This was followed in October 1961 by a revised ECM programme for aircraft earmarked for Skybolt (and, therefore, not required to penetrate Soviet defences). With Skybolt cancelled and the MBF war role switched to low-level attack, as from early 1963, a new but not entirely appropriate ECM policy was approved that March. The ECM fit would consist of Green Palm, Blue Diver and Red Shrimp noise jammers, Window and the Red Steer and Blue Saga warning equipment. This situation was reviewed again in October 1963, in the case of B.2 aircraft in the low-level nuclear-strike role, with some variation between freefall and Blue Steel aircraft.[732]

There were concerns about ECM serviceability in war, including significant unknowns surrounding the impact of electromagnetic pulse (EMP) on airborne electronic systems. Roy Brocklebank recalled the general lack of knowledge of EMP, despite a long series of nuclear tests:

"In 1966 we received a two- or three-page request for anyone who might have knowledge of EMP. Given that the majority of V-Force aircrew were your typical five GCE men (and physics not necessarily being one of them), I don't think there was much response."[733]

ECM'S STOP-START DEVELOPMENT

With hindsight, it can be seen that V-Force ECM developed in a stop-start manner. Air defence exercises in the mid to late 1950s had demonstrated that V-bombers would need all the help they could get to achieve successful high-level penetration. Yet the first V-bombers had only rudimentary ECM, according to Dick Fuller:

"We had no flares on board. The electronic jammers were pretty unsophisticated, but we had techniques for detecting fighters or missile launches. It was then a question of violent evasion – a variation of the 'corkscrew' of World War 2 vintage. This was a steep turn to the left, a vigorous pull-up, followed by a steep right turn."[734]

ECM installation accelerated in 1960; by late 1962 most Vulcan and Victor aircraft had the equipment. Until then, it was thought that Skybolt, launched outside defended airspace, would greatly reduce the future need for ECM. Consequently, second generation ECM projects, including an advanced comprehensive jammer, were cancelled. Subsequently, however, Skybolt itself was cancelled. Then, the V-Force war role switched to low-level strike and this appeared to reaffirm the case for not proceeding with new generation ECM.[735]

Window, anti-radar foil strips first used in World War 2, had several potential roles. Aircraft could lay a Window corridor or screen, to mask other air activity, or Window could be dispensed randomly to confuse ground radars. Trials and exercises produced disappointing results for Window in these contexts, although in the 'chaff' role – deflecting threats to a specific aircraft – it was much more promising. Trial No. 512 (1966) tested low-level use of Window against a fire-control radar. Bomber Command's then chief research officer, R. J. Monaghan, was heartened: "The results of this trial were very encouraging, in showing that Window was remarkably effective in breaking lock, both in low-level flight and in pop-up simulated attacks."[736]

Trial No. 512 investigated the effects on AA No. 3 Mk 7 (S-Band) tracking radar, when the target Vulcan dispensed Type 26 Window at low level during level flight and in a simulated pop-up to 3,000 ft. The AA No. 3 Mk 7 was considered a "near equivalent" to some Soviet AAA fire-control radars. This trial took place at West Freugh Range. Type 26 Window was dispensed for 15-second periods at three rates: continuously at 30 bundles/minute, a burst rate of three bundles per second for one second, with an interval between bursts of two seconds and a burst rate of five bundles per second for one second, with an interval between bursts of two seconds. The report concluded: "The surprising result of this trial is the comparative ease with which unlocking was achieved at low level."

PROTECTING THE AIRCRAFT

There could be conflict between air force and AEO priorities. Wing Commander Peter West listed the AEO's three functions: traditional wireless communications, monitoring electrical systems and, thirdly, EW: "… largely overlooked, ignored, suppressed by the air force." Yet West regarded protecting the aircraft as his primary role: "I didn't like flying in the Valiant. It was a lovely aircraft, well-built, but it had no EW equipment of any note at all … The Vulcan had an excellent electronic suite which was becoming better all the time."[737]

The first level of protection was provided by the nav/plotter, rather than the AEO, as this involved evasive routeing:

"We relied totally on good intelligence and it still fills me with admiration how our intelligence services … managed to provide all this information, including the sounds of the Soviet radar systems. The first sound you are likely to hear … is just 'zu-zum' and, a minute's pause, 'zu-zum'. These were the big early warning radars … you picked them up at approximately twice the range that they pick you up."

This was because of the bounceback:

"Then you start hearing the more interesting and more intense and urgent sounds ... I remember one Soviet fighter of the 1960s that sounded as though it had got a Latin American beat. We nicknamed it 'scan-can' and it went 'bumpadum-bumpadum'. When you heard that you were right to be concerned, because it meant he was searching for you and he was close. But the thing you waited for was a steady note – 'bizzzzzzzz' – which meant he had locked on and then you have really got to move."

There were echoes of World War 2 and the interaction between gunner and pilot:

"The important thing then is to give your pilot commentary – let him know where the threat is coming from. His action then is to turn into the direction of the threat, exactly as it was done with gunners and pilots in Lancasters, Halifaxes, Wellingtons, etc."

LOW-LEVEL ECM

In a sense, the inadequacies of first-generation V-bomber ECM were addressed at a stroke with the switch to low level. From that point on, what counted was electronic silence, giving little or no warning to SAM sites and gun positions as the solitary, low-flying attackers sped across the flat Russian terrain towards their targets. Crews would respond only to direct threats as and when they arose. It took some time to make appropriate changes to high-altitude ECM practices. In July 1963, with the conversion to low level under way, Tom Kerr wrote a note on ECM and bomber defence. This was pessimistic about the value of Red Steer and Blue Saga warners, at high *and* low level:

"At low level, the main defence of the bomber is to remain low and undetected. In clear conditions, the 50% chance of sighting is probably about ten miles range, varying from zero at about 15 miles to 100% at about five miles ... there is little a bomber can do once sighted and attacked visually. Under instrument conditions, the bomber flying 500 ft to 1,000 ft above ground level, there is only a small probability that a fighter will detect the bomber. The fighter's task is an extremely difficult one as it not only has to keep clear of the ground but simultaneously to search for the bomber. It is unlikely, therefore, that it will be able to get below the bomber and look up, in the hope of a detection in an uncluttered AI picture."[738]

Kerr did not hold back:

"The bombers' warning equipments are unlikely to be of much value. Blue Saga will hear all the AI fighters within 30 to 40 miles and up to high altitudes, which are orientated correctly towards the bomber and on a direct line of sight. Red Steer will have over half of its extremely limited cover (a 45-degree cone) unusable due to ground clutter, presenting an extremely difficult problem in detecting the fighter. Even when detected, the peculiarities of the display will make the assessment of its position extremely difficult. The greatest safety of the bomber will be obtained by descending to a lower altitude, if possible ..."

As an aid to low-level flying, Vulcan co-pilot Keith Mans found the terrain-following radar (TFR) "very clever". He explained:

> "When flying over a hill you had to push down at the top but, inevitably, you would balloon – going higher than you needed to and increasing the risk from SAMs. Our TFR took care of that. It anticipated reaching the top, avoided the balloon and, in doing so, reduced our exposure to SAMs."

AEO Julian Grenfell continued to apply his EW knowledge, coming up with the idea of a C-Band forward-looking antenna, to counter acquisition radars. He also proposed an ECM modification "that took the pulse from Fan Song and shifted it, in effect presenting Fan Song with a false range". This was not taken up. Crews were not being briefed on the capabilities of new Soviet SAM systems appearing from the mid-1960s onwards, including SA-8 Gecko (entering service in 1971), as there were no EW systems to counter them:

> "The SA-8 had a capability down to 80 ft and the only answer was jamming in phase. Yet there was no V-Force capability against semi-active and active pulse Doppler. Remarkably, we'd had the answer to this years before, in the so-called comprehensive jammer, but that was cancelled in 1960."[739]

CONCERNS OVER ECM QUALITY

Very tight timescales and a determination to avoid expenditure on the V-Force during its final years on the strategic frontline contributed to lack of interest in ECM at the top, despite the fact that V-bombers had no defensive armament. Time and budget pressures, set against the huge investment made in Soviet air defences, generated pessimistic attitudes – even as early as May 1960, when Bomber Command's then acting chief research officer, R. Bruce, wrote in blunt terms:

> "The warning systems provided for bomber aircraft as part of the ECM fit and the proposed alterations in the future do not represent a satisfactory solution to the real problem of providing a bomber with adequate warning of enemy fighters or missiles. The great weakness with our present set-up is the problem of interpretation, which becomes critical if one talks about missiles attacking bombers. I cannot believe that suitable equipment which will solve this 'defence of the bomber problem' could be made available during the next four to five years and, therefore, I suppose we must begin to forget the potential value of such equipments, which would be invaluable today but of limited value after 1965."[740]

This bleak summary formed part of the background to the long squeeze on V-Force equipment upgrades. By 1963–64, it was argued that ECM upgrades had no place in low-level nuclear strike, with Polaris just a few years away. Aircrew lived with the situation and AEOs tended to be phlegmatic. Nothing much changed. AEO Dave Beane was still flying operationally several years *after* the Polaris handover:

> "As AEO I had the usual mix of active and passive ECM systems. They were as up-to-date as they could be, given that ECM – by their very nature – are always a step behind the threat they are supposed to counter."[741]

AEO Barry Masefield, operational during an even later period, had a different outlook:

"As for ECM, there had been no recent upgrade when I arrived on the V-Force at the end of the 1970s. The chance of a successful retaliatory strike in Vulcans had been much diminished by that time. We had fallen further and further behind."[742]

Roger Dunsford noted that the Americans, relatively free of funding pressures, took a different approach:

"Eventually, there came a time when some Americans saw the V-bombers as a spent force – an obsolete weapons platform. Yet, there remained a feeling of respect for the British ability to make a great deal out of very limited resources. The US had thrown money at the B-52 – the same generation as the Vulcan – by installing the latest EW suites and arming it with cruise missiles in order to make it a viable weapons platform … We could not afford to do the same with the Vulcan; we were always looking for innovative ways to improve our capability by constantly adapting the equipment, procedures and training on the frontline squadrons."[743]

Not all V-Bomber AEOs kept quiet about inadequate ECM. Those prepared to speak out included Vulcan AEO Hugh Prior:

"The ECM wasn't up to much. There were Green Palm VHF and UHF jammers and Red Shrimp, to jam SA-2 radars, but SA-2 was the least of our worries. The real threat came from SA-3, SA-6, SA-7 (a handheld weapon) and the ZSU gun. We had nothing to counter these weapons. Taken overall, nothing had been done to bring Vulcan ECM into the 20th century. I got annoyed when I found that many AEOs appeared to be satisfied with this state of affairs. We were checked out on a regular basis but this was largely concerned with the electrics. ECM appeared to be very secondary. To be fair, I also remember that some aircraft then had equipment to jam behind and in front, to interfere with SA-3 and gun radars, and there was general agreement that our infrared decoys (IRDs) and chaff were good."[744]

When the V-bombers went low level, they carried Type 22 Window (X-Band, against fighters) and Type 150 delayed-action Window (DAW). According to Roy Brocklebank, the main purpose of DAW "was to sow confusion during the high-level recovery phase".[745] DAW was parachute-deployed and burst well behind the aircraft. There were IRDs, fired in bursts of four at high level and two at low level. There was also rapid-blooming Window (RBW X-Band (I-Band)) chaff:

"Type 22 was dropped to the formula 5-10-2, if I recall correctly. This was five bundles per second for ten seconds, at two-second intervals. At this rate, we experienced 'stripper runaways'. The stripper had to open the cardboard packet, to enable the Window to bloom. Failure was reduced at 3-10-2."

Hugh Prior asked the all-important question for the period after handover to Polaris:

"Could we have flown a successful retaliatory strike? In the 1970s, crossing the coastal defence belt would have been like threading your way through a string of pearls. The target study was good and, if you were ultra-low and lucky, it could have been done.

One progressive development was more discrimination from equipment scanning for threats."[746]

Prior became EW officer at Waddington and made a point of expressing his views on the quality of EW in the air force. Later, he became Wing EW instructor:

"New kit was coming in during the late 1970s. I could replicate most radars on this simulator equipment and this increased the value of EW training involving the whole team – pilots and rear crew. There was also a screen which gave an instant and accurate bearing of a threat. Of course, you might be able to see the threat, but you still had to interpret the audio."

Some things, however, didn't change. John Reeve, a Vulcan pilot with 27 Squadron, had Riga amongst his targets:

"Our ECM aerials remained positioned for high-level attack. They were still in the wrong place when the Vulcan left service in 1982. There always seemed to be a 'what's the point?' attitude to spending money on the V-bombers. They were initially planned to retire in 1974 and, after that, they were always about to go out of service."[747]

RENEWED INTEREST IN ECM

It would be wrong to suggest that absolutely nothing was done to upgrade ECM, but V-Force expenditures were subject to strict control during the 1960s. There was a natural tension between those charged with ensuring the V-bombers plugged the gap in operational capability until the arrival of Polaris and those responsible for financial decisions concerning a weapon system due to leave the strategic nuclear frontline in a relatively short period of years. ECM took a back seat and, somewhat ironically, this didn't change until the 1966 Defence White Paper and a shift in planning emphasis, from general war to limited war operations against an enemy with defensive weapons of the same vintage as the Vulcan's ECM.

Eventually, this led to a trial of ECM use and effectiveness at low level, for that part of the Vulcan force (i.e. freefall squadrons) with a *conventional* low-level commitment. This study was for war in a non-European context, against an enemy armed with C-Band or S-Band SA-2s, but unlikely to have capability against aircraft flying below 1,000 ft or during a brief pop-up. By night or IMC, the enemy defence threat included interceptors (Fishbed variants) fitted with Spin Scan AI radar and armed with Atoll IR missiles and/or guns. Radar-controlled AAA guns were assumed present. The day/VMC threat included day fighters (Fresco, Farmer, Fishbed) with gun-ranging radars (Scan Fix and High Fix), armed with guns or IR missiles (Atoll), plus visually-sighted AAA guns and small-arms fire.[748]

These Phase C trials were designed to determine the best defensive techniques. Tactics were required to meet three situations: attack by AI-equipped or day fighters with missiles and/or guns at 500 ft over land or sea; when flying at 500 ft, AEO recognition of illumination by radars; and radar tracking by air defence artillery (ADA) fire-control radars during the attack phase. The risk of use of the Vulcan force in a non-European theatre raised political questions, given the small size of the force, high unit cost, the inability to replace aircraft and the need to avoid situations where the risk includes loss from, for example, small-arms fire. In short, safety of the aircraft took precedence over weapons delivery.[749]

By late 1968, the latest penetration aids fitted to, or ordered for, the Vulcan freefall force included:

- ARI 18146: an active jammer with several different modes (including a receive facility, providing X-Band coverage to the rear).
- ARI 5952 (Red Steer Mk 2): a tail-warner differing from the Mk 1 mainly in its scan pattern (over which the operator had an element of control).
- Cartridge Discharger No. 3 Mk 1: a system to explosively discharge decoys in pre-set quantities and at pre-set rates.
- ARI 5959: terrain-following radar.[750]

The existing fit included Red Shrimp, Blue Saga, Blue Diver and an automatic Window dispenser. According to Roy Brocklebank, Red Steer Mk 2 was "far superior" to its predecessor:

"This had a conventional scan pattern +/- 20 degrees vertical and +/- 70 degrees horizontal … you could often see the fighter before he saw you. Then, based on his range and aspect, and listening for the Blue Saga lock, the AEO could switch the Red Steer to a narrow sector, +/- 5 degrees, and this could see a missile launch."[751]

In July 1966 AEO Martin Anscombe completed a five-year double tour on 50 Squadron's Vulcans at Waddington. The RAF had plans to further harness his electronics expertise:

"I was posted to a signals command station at RAF Watton in October 1966, where a new EW flying unit, No. 360 (RN/RAF) Squadron, was being formed to provide an airborne EW training platform for all three services, and which was to be crewed and serviced by air force and naval personnel on a 2:1 basis."[752]

Eventually, 360 Squadron was equipped with the Canberra T.17, a fully refurbished B.2 with its entire bomb bay filled with ECM. Some devices were designed to search for fighters, whilst others were powerful blast jammers directed against ground radars. There were devices capable of locking onto and jamming AI fighter radars:

"Our role was to train all aircrew and other system users who would expect to operate in a hostile electronic environment and training included evasive tactics using chaff … Evasive manoeuvres and spoofing were an important part of EW. We were given free range to come up with EW measures and countermeasures, including spoofing and testing Blue Force authentication procedures for fighters. On occasion, we flew with female fighter controllers in the third seat."

Wing Commander Rod Powell, a Vulcan AEO, arrived at Scampton in 1966, joining 83 Squadron, flying Blue Steel-armed Vulcan B.2s. Writing in 2003, Powell gave his views:

"On paper the Vulcan had an impressive defensive suite comprising powerful jammers, a radar warning receiver, a tail-warning radar, infrared flares and oodles of chaff. This kit provided a reasonable degree of situational awareness, even by today's standards, and the crew could therefore take the necessary action to avoid or evade the ground or air defences. Or could it? We will never know what the survivability rate of the V-Force would have been, but my guess is that many of the aircraft would have been shot down before they reached their missile-release point or, in the case of the freefallers, the targets because, to be honest, the EW suite that we had at the time was just not good enough … The change to low-level operations in 1963 should have been accompanied by a change in EW tactics and a re-appraisal of the system's capabilities. This simply did not happen, at least, not in any meaningful way."[753]

Rod Powell felt that the AEOs "should have been far more assertive" in pressing for improvements to enhance survivability. He blamed the training emphasis on electrical systems, with "very little time" spent on EW and tactics. One issue deserving attention, on the switch to low level, was the loss of "jamming support", as each aircraft now operated independently. As for the Red Shrimps, they had a low-level jamming 'footprint' about the same size as the aircraft!

Powell gave a blunt assessment of operational reality:

"The upshot of all this was that, while our jammers did have lots of power in theory, the combination of the 'lossy' transmission cables, barrage jamming and the generous antenna radiation pattern severely reduced the impact on a threat radar. We could have done something about this but we never did. When we adopted low-level tactics we did not change our ECM procedures, nor did we adjust our antennae. Our route plans still required us simply to switch on all of our jammers as we entered enemy airspace. In fact, I seem to recall that there was a red line drawn on the maps annotated 'ECM switch-on line.'"

Deep in the 'coal hole': a nav/radar at work. (Andy Leitch Collection)

It is interesting to speculate on how many outwardly compliant AEOs might have exercised common sense, had they been thrust into the ultimate emergency. In any event, Roy Brocklebank's recollections differ somewhat: "I remember the active jammers were only switched on at the FCP – the final climb point."[754] A freefall pop-up provided the cue for these aircraft to begin active jamming.

LATE IMPROVEMENTS

It was obvious that single low-level penetrators should be electronically silent – responding only to direct threats. All policies are subject to change over time, but it seems the pace of change on this front was very slow. Rod Powell insisted:

> "The brief was to leave the jammers on in enemy territory and switch them off when exiting – if we ever did. As I look back on this now, I simply cannot imagine why no-one seems to have commented on such a blinkered approach and, if anyone ever did, why nothing was done about it."[755]

Powell, however, did acknowledge some late ECM improvements:

> "To be fair, despite what I perceive to have been a general lack of application, some effort was made to provide some aircraft with a more effective jamming capability. About 30 late-production Vulcans were fitted with an X-Band jammer; that would be I-Band today. This had a selectable fore and aft directionality to its jamming pattern, its antenna being located on the centreline just forward of the ECM bulge on the lower rear fuselage. It also had a modulated jamming output against specific threats, a 26Hz modulated signal against the SA-3's Low Blow tracking radar from the forward antenna and a conical scan from the aft antenna to counter fighter AI radar."

Beyond the late 1960s ECM upgrade with operations in a non-European limited conventional war in mind, the parsimonious attitude continued, with purse strings pulled tight. In April 1970, less than a year after the Polaris handover, the VCAS, Air Marshal Sir Peter Fletcher, wrote to Strike Command AOC-in-C Sir Denis Spotswood, confirming that there would be no further updating of Vulcan ECM, to provide an active capability. There was no stomach for a fight for funding:

> "Although the operational arguments are strong, I have … reluctantly come to the conclusion that we should not press ahead with these proposals at this stage. The cost involved is very considerable – some £12.36 million – and we could not be confident of securing agreement to go ahead. The effect of an adverse decision could well be to put the whole future of the Vulcan force at risk."[756]

The CAS agreed with Fletcher's decision, albeit "with reluctance", as an attempt to proceed would almost certainly attract the attention of those who would argue that it would be wrong to put expensive equipment in ageing aircraft. It might even prompt the retirement of the V-bombers. The VCAS took the view that, even without modern ECM, Vulcans could still be used low level at night "for the specific purpose of a late nuclear strike …" He made no mention of what Vulcans and their crews should do if war began in the morning.

The bean counters held the reins and the operational impact in a hot war might have been considerable, even catastrophic. One example of neglect involved chaff, carried in large quantities by the Vulcan and held in 'window boxes' in the wing, just aft of the main undercarriage legs, as described by Rod Powell: "In all, we had 4,000 packets of chaff, each about nine inches long, three inches wide and half-an-inch thick. It was pre-cut to various lengths, giving us wideband frequency coverage."[757] Roy Brocklebank, however, cites different figures: "… the Vulcan Aircrew Manual states just 1,850 packets of chaff or Window and a flare dispenser with 264 cartridges."

On the matter of neglect, Air Vice-Marshal Nigel Baldwin recalled his 1978 visit to Nellis AFB, to participate in the first night Red Flag combat exercise:

"We were permitted to use all of our ECM and could, if necessary, use all our chaff. The first time the AEOs tried it, the dispensers jammed, after having discharged only 20% or so of their contents. On investigation, it was discovered from the date stamps on the remaining packages that they were 15 or more years old! The contents were so compressed that they defeated the mechanism …"[758]

In the interests of balance, however, Roy Brocklebank pointed out that RBW and IRD were "state of the art" and the X-Band jammer did eventually arrive.[759] Perhaps a last comment on the RAF and ECM should belong to former V-Force AEO Wing Commander Richard 'Dick' Turpin: "Like so many other military functions, the EW training role has now been put out to civilian contract."[760]

In summary, British air defence exercises exposed the vulnerabilities of V-bombers attempting high-altitude attacks in daylight. Studies and trials confirmed the advantages of low-level strike, with reduced exposure to SAMs and fighters. The oral evidence from former aircrew suggests that briefed minimum altitudes were often ignored by determined captains enjoying the confidence of their crews. The 1971 Air Force Department paper set out a highly favourable view of the ability of ultra-low-flying Vulcans to penetrate below the envelope of SAM and fighter engagement and, in the final analysis, this view was probably realistic, given the likely scale of degradation of the Soviet defences in a mass US missile strike. It is evident that more V-bombers would have survived to the point of weapon release had a war sortie been flown at night and/or in IMC. There is also compelling evidence of strong performance by Vulcans in Red Flag during the 1970s. Equally, there were significant missed opportunities in the area of ECM, notably cancellation of the comprehensive jammer and the failure to undertake a sweeping review of ECM outfit and tactics to accompany the switch to low level.

20
ATTACKING TARGETS

> ❝ *I had a target south of Moscow; it was up to you to decide what to do after you had dropped. Our plan was to continue at low level, hoping to land at a Turkish airfield. There was some harmless speculation about filling up and taking off for a cruise climb at 45,000–50,000 ft and a flight to South America. Unfortunately, calculations showed that we would run out of fuel whilst still around 150 miles from the coast.* ❞
>
> Dennis Martin, Vulcan captain, IX Squadron

THROUGH THE BALTIC DEFENCES

During the wait for Polaris, Britain became increasingly reliant on the willingness of V-Force crews to apply extreme combat tactics to overcome – to some extent at least – the inadequacies of aircraft and weapons. Given the high level of training and commitment, it is likely that, had a war sortie been flown, a few (perhaps a few more in a night operation) would have successfully put weapons on targets.

Generally, long odds did not disturb crews; they adopted an aura of fatalism. Many quietly 'wrote themselves off'. In this atmosphere, it becomes easier to understand why complaining about inappropriate ECM or the poor prospects for surviving a laydown attack with a hydrogen bomb hardly seemed worth the trouble. The prevailing view was that deterrence would hold and a war sortie would never be flown.

Had war come (and putting aside the inevitable heavy losses on and around the MBF airfields in a Soviet missile strike), V-bomber war sorties had been planned to the last detail. Those V-bombers with Kola targets were treated as a distinct group. Main force aircraft were also divided according to targets, grouped in central and southern Russia categories. Each bomber had a time on target (TOT), derived from the duration of the flight to the coast plus the sortie leg penetrating from coast to target. Routes were planned to avoid other targets and known defences. Roy Brocklebank explains: "The sum of the two times, airfield to coast and coast to target, would give the flight time to target. This would give the crews their TOT, based on the 'E-Hour.'"[761]

Should the crews' faith in the common sense underlying deterrence prove ill-placed, V-bombers fortunate enough to survive a Soviet missile strike would have crossed the North Sea and, if authorised by the POSREL (positive release) signal, would have attempted to penetrate the Soviet coastal defence belt, the area defences and, finally, in the case of the free-

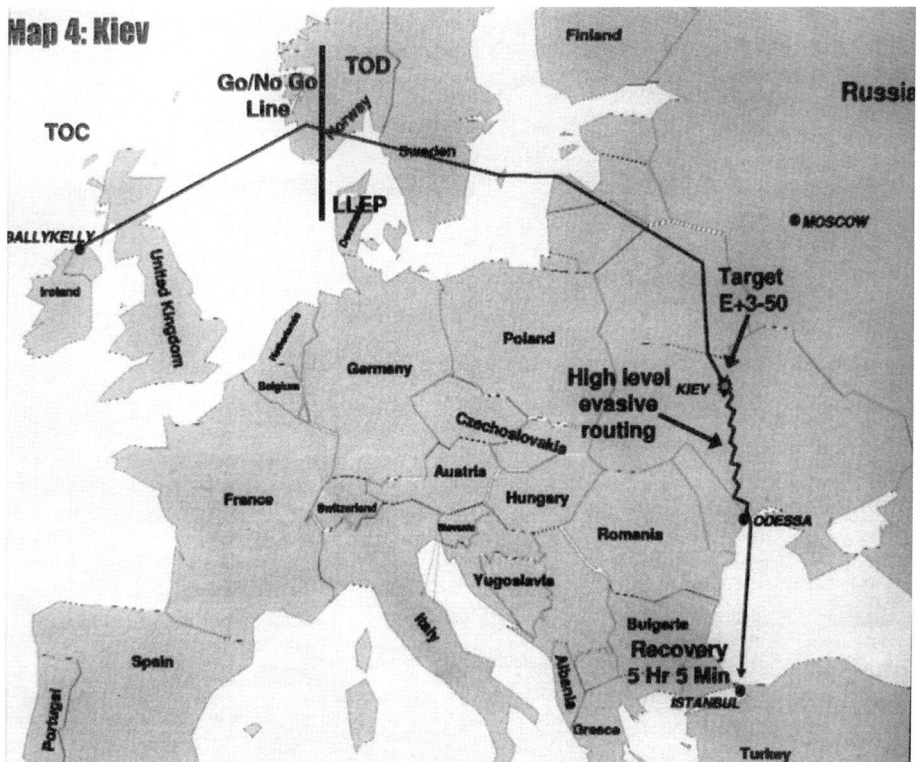

Plan of attack: a route plan for a deep penetration nuclear strike: Ballykelly to Kiev and then on to Turkey. (Paddy Langdown)

fallers point defences surrounding targets. A POSREL signal was required *before* reaching the Go/No Go line (8 degrees E). Assuming the go-ahead, the bombers would have crossed Norway, to begin their descent over Sweden in preparation for low-level penetration. Vulcan nav/radar Jim Walker expected POSREL at, or very shortly after, the scramble – otherwise "the whole system was flawed … electromagnetic pulse (EMP) would have surely blacked out radio transmissions."[762]

Some former tanker aircrew recall the airborne communications post (ACP) role given to the Valiant tanker force (and, subsequently, the Victors until around 1972). Heavy radio jamming was expected and most bomber aircrew assumed POSREL would be given at or shortly after scramble. Alan McLoughlin remembers the tanker crews' mission to ensure that vital signals were sent and received:

> "… we did a monthly session in the vault at Marham, where we refreshed the procedures, including codewords, frequencies and the locality of the 'racetrack' pattern off the Norwegian coast where we would establish ourselves in order to be able to relay signals to the main bomber force … we probably wouldn't have lasted long, since as well as having no defensive armament, we also had no ECM, so would have been sitting ducks for any Soviet fighters."[763]

The British airborne *communications* post role should not be confused with the American ACP (airborne *command* post) mission, as explained by Roy Brocklebank:

> "The Valiants were fulfilling the ACP communications role prior to their grounding. We had briefly considered the airborne command post role but, unlike SAC, we had insufficient senior officers to deploy to Marham. The role was therefore limited to communications."[764]

Andrew Brookes described how the bombers would have crossed the Baltic coast through two or three narrow 'gates' (each around two to three miles wide) in the high-level era. The plan was to penetrate Soviet-defended airspace in cells of six, flying at up to Mach 0.93, at heights exceeding 50,000 ft.[765] Reaching the targets would have required evasive routeing and the use of ECM (the latter subsequently largely confined, in low-level attack, to defend against direct threats to individual aircraft). The gate concept was abandoned with the switch to low-level penetration by single aircraft. Having crossed the coastal defence belt at ultra-low level, the survivors would have sought out their targets.

In the high-altitude period, entering Soviet airspace at three concentration points was intended to saturate local defences (although, in reality, V-Force survivors might well have lacked the numbers to achieve this effect). Then a switch of mission profile to single bombers crossing the coastal defences at ultra-low level and continuing low for extended periods would have meant much higher fuel consumption. Roy Brocklebank was targeting officer for Waddington's 24 Vulcans:

> "The deepest penetration targets were up to 700 miles, maybe a little more ... Some would require, for very deep penetration, Vulcan aircraft with bomb-bay fuel tanks. These could give up to 25% more fuel than the standard fuel fit, but only once we got WE.177B weapons."[766]

This is a reference to WE.177's extremely small size – similar to a 1,000-lb conventional bomb. The Vulcan's bomb bay, without tanks for extra fuel, was big enough to carry 21 of the latter! Beyond bomb-bay fuel, the other option for extending range was the selection of closer recovery bases.

Some aircrew, including 44 (Rhodesia) Squadron's Jim Walker, had concerns about getting as far as the Baltic coast: "We would be coming in over Sweden. Would the Swedes shoot us down? Had anyone told them we were going to do this? I understood they had a very effective air force."[767] Apparently, the Swedes were told. Richard Moore explains:

> "Swedish air defence was evidently not considered a threat to the V-Force. Despite its official neutrality, the Swedish government had made a series of secret arrangements to facilitate British and US use of Swedish airspace in wartime, including for the purposes of nuclear attack."[768]

It seems these understandings were extensive:

> "The Swedish Official Commission on Neutrality Policy of 1994 found that a number of Swedish air bases had been given longer and stronger runways, to accommodate very

heavy Allied aircraft, and concluded that they were intended for recovery landings of bombers damaged during a strike."

Roy Brocklebank remembers a friend recounting what a Swede had told him: "We are neutral, but we know who we are neutral against."

Some V-bombers and other British strike aircraft (including nuclear-capable Canberras and Buccaneers), in pursuing their missions, would have hit coastal defence targets – so opening the way for the MBF main force and, subsequently, waves of US-based SAC bombers. Roy Brocklebank reinforced the point that only a proportion of SAC's aircraft were routed over the Pole:

> "If you run out a line from Elgin AFB to Moscow, you enter the USSR exactly on the RAF penetration route. Barksdale is not far from Elgin; Loring, much further north, follows the same route. Fairchild, in Washington State, would also cross Greenland and a little further north in Norway but still enters the USSR through the Baltic States. However, shift the targets to Kola or Novaya Zemlya and they start to use polar routes."[769]

While RAF strike aircraft other than V-bombers would have been deployed to soften the Baltic defences, some RAF nuclear assets still had no defined war role as late as 1971, yet were ideal for attacking border/coastal defences. Mike Fazackerley noted that operational conversion unit (OCU) aircraft would have been generated for war sorties, including 237 OCU's Buccaneers at RAF Honington. This station had received 12 of the then new WE.177A low-yield tactical laydown weapons by April 1971 and was expecting an inventory totalling 35–40 bombs by the year-end. This OCU could provide a 'shadow squadron'.

It seems this capability had been missed, in terms of forward planning. In a note that April to the Senior Air Staff Officer (SASO) and Group Captain, Plans and Policy, Group Captain (Ops), M. M. J. Robinson, pointed to the oversight:

> "With SACLANT's reluctance to accept our Buccaneers in his pre-planned Strike Plan, the only use for these weapons is in the context of selective-release missions. While it will never be possible to predict the number of weapons required for selective release, it can be said with some confidence that 40 is more than enough. Therefore, unless we can make other arrangements for their use, some WE.177A weapons will remain in the armoury."[770]

Would 40 have been enough? Robinson was referring to a dimension of 'flexible response', the *selective release* of sufficient tactical nuclear weapons to halt a Soviet breakthrough with conventional forces. Roy Brocklebank suggests that SACEUR might have required more:

> "In one exercise (I cannot remember if it was Fallex or Wintex, but I favour Wintex and post-1974), the exercise ended after the implementation of White Dot Five which, I think, was a nuclear demonstration against 50 targets in the Central Region. We were told that SACEUR's logic was that if he was going to use nuclear he wanted a military benefit as well as a political demonstration. The exercise ended four minutes later."[771]

In any event, Robinson called for up to six OCU aircraft and crews to be earmarked for a NATO strike role. On the basis of two weapons per aircraft, this would commit up to 12 WE.177As on a pre-planned basis. Robinson had clear ideas on their potential targets:

"I have good reason to believe that insufficient attention has been made in the Priority Strike Plan to the greatly improved defences along the Baltic coast, and the SAM complexes and other air defence control centres in this area are well within the Buccaneer's capability."[772]

ATTACK PROFILES

V-Force crews trained in various weapon delivery formats, or 'attack profiles'. These changed over time, in response to evolving Soviet defences and the introduction of new British weapons and tactics. The original, high-level freefall attack was Type 2. This became 2A, an evasive attack run, after the loss of Gary Powers' U-2 in 1960. Roy Brocklebank described 2A:

"It began some 40 miles from target: the bomber pulled 1.5 g through 30 degrees, levelled wings for 15 seconds before turning 60 degrees in the opposite direction. Wings were levelled for 30 seconds before the evasive manoeuvre was repeated. The following steady leg was for 15 seconds, before the bomber rolled onto the attack heading around 15 miles out from the target and seven miles before weapon release."[773]

This profile was designed to defeat SA-2, which required at least 60 seconds' uninterrupted lock. It would allow three full weaves and take about three minutes 30 seconds. The aircraft would advance about 24 miles before rolling out at 15–16 miles.

The attack profiles changed when the V-Force went low level. The first British low-level nuclear-strike bombers were the SACEUR-assigned Valiants (aircraft initially armed with Blue Danube, the first UK nuclear weapon, which required release at high altitude). In the high-level days, John Muston's targets included an industrial city in the Ukraine with a population of over 300,000: "Looking back, I think our chances of success in a high-altitude attack would have been very poor. We would have been sitting ducks, cruising at Mach 0.72."[774]

Later, in the low-level NATO role, SACEUR Valiants carried American E weapons. These included Big E, the Mk 43 laydown bomb, for very low-level strike. The Valiant was slower than the Vulcan and Victor, but Roy Brocklebank notes that Mk 43 low-level delivery "suggests that the Valiant might have had as good survivability as the other aircraft that only had Yellow Sun 2 at this time."[775]

Some Valiant crews, however, were sceptical. Dick Fuller was a Valiant co-pilot with 49 Squadron during the 1959–63 period. Whilst at Marham, crews trained to deliver nuclear weapons, including the American laydown bomb, in a hi-lo-hi operational profile: "We would go out at height, then drop down to around 300 ft on crossing into enemy territory." On weapon release, they would put the aircraft into a very steep turn, in an effort to escape the shock wave:

"There was also the flash to worry about. When we were blacked out by screens, the captain and co-pilot had a sort of 'letterbox' to look through. Flying visually at 300 ft by peering through a letterbox leaves the probability of 'clobber' rather high. If the pilot was blinded by the flash, the co-pilot had to be ready to take over. I suppose most of us thought that war would be a one-way trip for the Valiants."[776]

Whilst Vulcan and Victor freefall bombers flew a hi-lo-hi mission profile from 1963–64 onwards, their Yellow Sun 2 bombs required a pop-up to 11,000 ft for successful release, so forcing them to enter SA-2's engagement zone. Yellow Sun Victor and Vulcan crews trained for 2E and 2H attacks. The 2E required a rapid pop-up climb to 11,000 ft about 12 miles from the target, with the aircraft steadying for weapon release in level flight. This demanded three miles straight and level before release. The 2H was a pull-up release in the climb. Bomber Command's Operational Research Branch had noted that crews participating in exercises tended to climb earlier than the desired 12-mile pull-up point. The average time from exposure to enemy SAMs to weapon release was about two minutes, but an alerted missile crew could achieve a successful engagement in 112 seconds. Roy Brocklebank described 2H, designed to overcome this by releasing in a climb rather than in level flight:

> "This was a precisely calculated approach to a pull-up, offset for wind effect, a timed rotation to the designated climb angle and release in the climb at 10,500 ft. This reduced exposure to enemy missile systems to the absolute minimum. In the case of the Vulcan Mk 2, the attack would begin about 30 miles out, when the initial point (IP) would be detectable on radar. At the IP, the aircraft would settle at its attack speed of 350 kts, aiming to get to the pop-up point 18,350 yards short of the target and 103 seconds before the desired TOT. At the pop, the nav/plotter would call the pop and count down five seconds. The pilot would rotate the aircraft smoothly into a 15-degree climb and fly a fixed heading until passing through 10,500 ft and climbing at about 10,000 ft per minute. The nav/radar and co-pilot would both press their bomb release buttons. This would be about 85 seconds after the pop and two miles from the target." [777]

It was estimated that the weapon would explode 9–17 seconds before the SA-2 could hit the bomber.

> "The attack was unaimed, the release point being determined by the height of the aircraft on the calculated heading. In training, with ballistic shapes, some impact points were as much as a mile in error. The Mk 1A Vulcan crews discovered that the NBS (Calc 3) could cope with the 10,000 ft per minute climb and steer the aircraft more accurately than the Mk 2's later Calc 3a. The Mk 2s were downgraded later to the Calc 3, so that they, too, could make low-altitude automatic attacks. Immediately after bomb release, the co-pilot would close the bomb-doors, the captain would bank the aircraft, and pull a 1.8 g turn through 140 degrees before levelling the wings and continuing the climb. The aircraft was now presenting its minimum profile to the target and the resultant light, heat and shock waves. Crews were told that the blast overpressure would not exceed 0.98 pounds per square inch ... Aircraft were expected to suffer structural damage with overpressures of one pound or more! After the escape turn, the aircraft would continue climbing and weaving to avoid SAMs, whilst maintaining a heading to the recovery airfield. Climbing and turning, the bombers would get to 48,000 ft before moderating the turns and continue climbing for height. It would take some 120 miles to reach 56,000 ft, the desired altitude overhead the recovery base."

The Valiant's principal attack profile was 2F – a low-altitude release of the American laydown bomb in level flight at about 320 kts and 500 ft. Roy Brocklebank says this was regarded as the safest, after a Blue Steel attack: "The aircraft would remain below the SAM cover but would be vulnerable to air defence artillery." Blue Steel crews did not have to enter the inner target area, provided their weapon 'agreed' to launch in the powered condition:

> "The Blue Steel missile could be fired at low level about 30 miles from the target ... The delivery aircraft would have safe separation from its own weapon's effects and had no need to penetrate the target defence zone. If the missile guidance or propulsion system failed, however, the crew would have to use the same delivery profile as for Yellow Sun."[778]

Early on, the Irish Sea was a regular venue for nuclear-release training, with Valiants dropping Blue Danube shapes over Jurby Range, just east of the Isle of Man. The splash was marked by radar. As for Yellow Sun, the 2E attack's fast climb from 500 ft to 11,000 ft was a high energy manoeuvre and the only free airspace was Newcastle, but there was competition from Newcastle Airport and a campaign to increase the civil airway structure in that area. Roy Brocklebank added: "With the advent of the 2H release in the climb we had much less freedom of approach and the continued climb after release needed more airspace." West Freugh Range, five miles south-east of Stranraer, was an obvious choice.[779] Brocklebank has clear memories of sorties including West Freugh radar bomb scoring unit (RBSU) 2H attacks:

> "All attacks were made off the low-level route against simulated targets around the north shore of Luce Bay. The three Vulcan types each had a discreet profile to reach 10,500 ft at the right distance from the target. The furthest out were the Mk 1A Vulcans; they would start their pull-up at about 21,700 yards. Next were the Mk 2s with 200 series engines and a pull-up at about 20,000 yards. Closest were the Mk 2s with 301 series engines and pulling up at 18,000 yards."[780]

For the Mk 2/301s the angle was 14 degrees. The pull-up data was recalculated on the results of simulated attacks, resulting in a pull-up at 18,350 yards and at a 15-degree climb angle:

> "The aircraft would approach the pull-up point on the designated track at the designated distance from the target, but that was in still air. This is where the 2H computer came in. If the guesstimated wind at 7,000 ft was a tailwind, the aircraft would have to start its climb earlier (if a headwind, it would start later). We would define the pull-up point as a radar position offset from a known radar feature, the same way as we did offset bombing."[781]

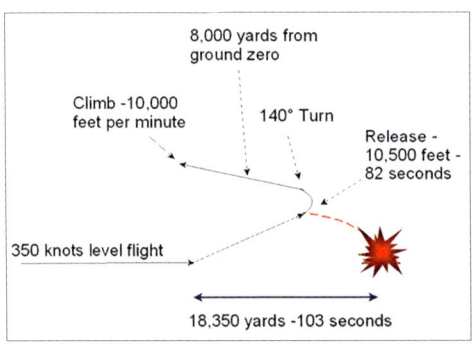

An attacking V-bomber could expect Russian attempts to jam the bombing system. Bomber Command tested the effects of a single H2S jammer over the January–April 1962 period. There were 269 bombing runs on jamming and on

Releasing 'sunshine': the 2H pop-up attack profile for Yellow Sun Mk 2 – with release in the climb. (Roy Brocklebank)

some 96% of occasions "fairly intense" jamming was generated on H2S displays. However, by the third attack, the average nav/radar "has ceased to be troubled by the H2S jamming from a single jammer and the bombing error thereafter was not markedly different from normal bombing runs." The main reason for this ineffectiveness was the counter countermeasure effect of the NBS long-range offset facility.[782] At the same time, of course, it must be pointed out that, in a hot war sortie each bomber would make *only the one attack*!

During autumn 1962 another Bomber Command report set out the results of a trial exploring the bombing of targets protected by multiple H2S jammers. This concluded that three ground jammers "do not destroy all the information content of the H2S display of an attacking bomber …" It was estimated that at least five jammers would be required to provide complete jamming around a target for an attack along a specified track. "Such jamming conditions would impose a very great problem to the nav/radar and the bombing accuracy would certainly suffer in consequence." The Operational Research Branch took refuge in a favourable assumption:

> "Since the full protection of a target by ground H2S jammers is a very expensive proposition, it is not unreasonable to assume that, in operations, jamming much more severe than that experienced in the trial with three jammers is unlikely."[783]

Was this a reasonable assumption? Was the provision of two extra jammers prohibitively expensive, in terms of protecting a large city? On the other hand, jamming capability would, in all probability, have been destroyed or severely degraded in the initial missile exchange opening general war. In reality for V-bomber crews, enemy jammers were likely to be the least of their worries.

The V-bombers' own jammers were tested for effectiveness in protecting the aircraft, both at high level and during a low-level pop-up for freefall Yellow Sun 2 (or unpowered Blue Steel) delivery. Exercise Blank Stare II examined Red Shrimp's ability to shield a solitary bomber, making a pop-up attack, from SA-2 S-Band radar. The trial, No. 457, was flown during April 1963 and sought to identify the optimum arrangement of Red Shrimp transmitters to counter simulated SA-2 batteries. Sorties were flown by Vulcan and Victor 1A aircraft operating from Seymour Johnson AFB, North Carolina, around 200 miles from the test radar location on Chesapeake Bay. The results were surprising: the aircraft could jam effectively during the pop-up, in contrast to theoretical studies suggesting negligible effects. Sorties were flown at high level (40,000 ft) and in the low-level/climb profile, testing modified transmitter and aerial configurations against Fan Song-type radars. In the initial low-level/climb tests, from 1,500 ft (lowest altitude permitted) to 12,000 ft:

> "Successful self-screening during the climb was achieved on 16 out of 22 occasions … A much superior self-screening capability was evident during climbs in front of the radar than in those behind the radar. However, in the latter climbs, the aircraft continuously exposed its upper surfaces to the radar yet the effectiveness of the jamming from that direction was greater than would have been expected."

Use of Window during the climb produced no advantage and "could be of direct assistance to the radar operator in determining the range of the aircraft".[784]

John Weller, a Vulcan nav/radar on IX Squadron, spent much time practising attack profiles, beginning with the high-altitude Type 2 and its evasive 2A variant:

> "The 2B was flown through jamming. We practised this with the RBSUs. Some had jammers that picked up our signal, amplified it and re-transmitted it. The challenge was to find the offsets beyond the jamming. The 2C profile was jammed/evasion, but we never flew that."[785]

Weller moved on to the 2E pop-up and the 2H pull-up variant for releasing Yellow Sun 2: "The 2H manoeuvre was thought up at Boscombe Down. It came in during March 1966."

System malfunction was always possible during the attack and crews trained to overcome such problems. Vic Bussereau recalled that, normally, the radar-generated markers were placed over the target or the offset in the stabilised mode, with the markers in the centre of the screen. If the markers didn't come up, the attack was made by pre-referenced chinagraph marks on the screen. The 'electronic centre' of the screen could be manipulated, depending on which way the target was approached. "If it proved impossible to get a stabilised mode, a plastic quadrant gave the nav/radar an allowance for drift."[786]

Each crew received a TOT, with three minutes' tolerance on either side. This was designed to provide a minimum separation between bursts during multiple strikes on a large target. Targeting officer Roy Brocklebank had concerns:

> "Clearly, having near simultaneous TOT would, if each aircraft got through, have catastrophic results in fratricide. I took this up with the Ops 1A at Bomber Command. He was the one who drew up the plans. He said he was aware of this and was trying to change the TOTs to improve the chances of actually getting bombs on targets. Obviously, against this was the advantage of saturating the target defences and that would be reduced by dissipating the concentration."[787]

In reality, the large-scale casualties on or near V-bomber bases, resulting from a Soviet missile strike, would almost certainly have removed this theoretical problem near and over the targets. There would have been no concentration, with the possible (but significant) exceptions of the first and second cities, Moscow and Leningrad. These cities appeared in Jim Walker's target folders: "We realised, of course, that the emphasis on TOT suggested there would be other strikes on the target – with the TOT giving some indication of when those strikes would happen."[788]

Blue Steel crews were beginning to train hard with their temperamental weapons, designed for high-altitude launch, when the decision to go low level was announced. In late 1963 Jeremy Mudford and crew collected the first B.2 modified for low-level launch of the stand-off bomb:

> "We had been expecting them. We had practised missile launches at high level and, suddenly, we were preparing for launches at 250 ft. We took it in our stride … There was a round-Britain route with low-level runs. There was a let-down over Dartmoor and a 250-ft run over the Bristol Channel and across Wales. We then headed up to Scotland, for a return along the east coast. However, low-flying time was limited, due to its adverse impact on airframe fatigue life."[789]

Nevertheless, time was found for the Mudford crew to fly at 300 kts at 250 ft over RAF Wittering on a press day introducing low-level Blue Steel aircraft.

Eventually, the pop-up era for freefall squadrons ended with the arrival of the new WE.177B laydown weapons in late 1966/early 1967. Vulcan nav/plotter James Vinales' crew planned to drop it from about 300 ft, flying at around 360 kts: "We would be around six miles away when hit by the shock wave. We were worried that the shock wave could put the aircraft in a nose-down attitude, so pilots were ready to pull up after release."[790]

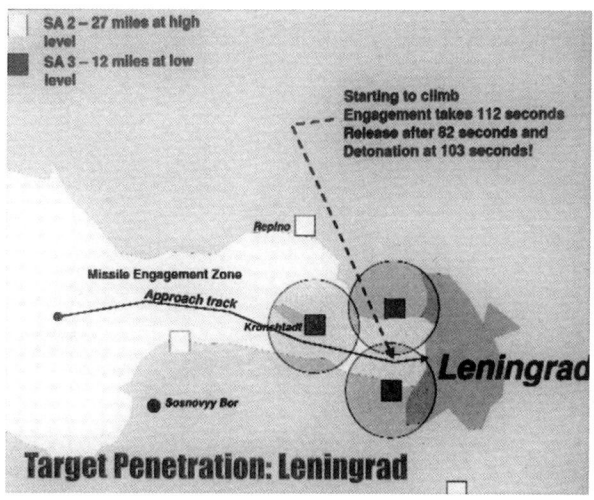

Mind the gap-fillers: final approach and attack on Leningrad. (Paddy Langdown)

It may have been freefall, but WE.177B was described by Mike Fazackerley as a complex and extremely sophisticated weapon:

> "…there were no less than 882 different combinations of delivery method and fusing in the A store and 435 in the B store. Some parameters taken into account when making selections were the intended drop height and speed of the delivery aircraft. The minimum height for the Vulcan to release a WE.177B in ballistic mode was 25,000 ft. In the parachute-retarded mode, the maximum drop height was 10,000 ft. For laydown, the minimum delivery height was 60 ft and the maximum 1,000 ft. The aim in the laydown mode was for the weapon to slap down tail-first, so the tail unit could absorb a lot of the impact. But the hard casing was designed and tested to hit a hard object head-on, with the radar fuse units acting as sacrificial shock absorbers, because typical target sets included buildings, armoured vehicles, etc., so a head-on collision was a possibility. The testing was done on the rocket sled at Porton Down."[791]

WEAPONS ON TARGETS

As the years progressed, V-Force capability and credibility became increasingly dependent on extreme combat tactics and the courage of crews willing to embrace these tactics. Reliance on hardware (aircraft and equipment) declined as new weapon systems were cancelled, so requiring crews to continue to plan for low-level deep penetration into increasingly hostile airspace. Blue Steel Mk 1, in its powered state, was a limited advance in capability, but most carrier aircraft would still be required to brave coastal and area defences, to launch on the outer fringe of point defences around the target. Victor nav/radar Norman Bonnor summarised events:

"Blue Steel Mk 2 was scrapped, as was the Blue Streak ballistic missile, in favour of Blue Steel Mk 1 and the promise of Skybolt – which had a range exceeding that of Blue Steel Mk 2. When Skybolt was cancelled, this left the squadrons with Blue Steel Mk 1 and freefall weapons, relying on "the skill of crews operating high-altitude bombers at extreme low level."[792]

Freefall crews were expected to close with and directly overfly their targets in a 2F laydown strike. Could aircraft dropping the parachute-retarded WE.177B weapon survive such an attack? Mike Fazackerley thought it could be done:

"...the RAF started taking the effects of nuclear blast on friendly aircraft and crews rather more seriously when the decision was taken that strike aircraft would have to operate at low level. The Weapons Development Committee (Nuclear Subcommittee) set up a Weapons Effects Study Group in 1966, with AWRE in the lead, to conduct studies and trials. Broadly, it concluded that the primary risks, depending on the nature and size of detonations, were blast, direct radiation effects and EMP. Thermal effects, flash blindness and fallout were judged to be of lesser concern.

"The fatal zone for aircraft originally designed for high-level operations (i.e. the Vulcan) was determined to be a blast overpressure greater than 4 psi or a direct radiation dose of 150 Rad. Damage could be expected above 1.5 psi but not sufficient to prevent the mission. For yields below about 30 kt radiation was the predominate risk factor. For larger weapons, blast was the predominate risk factor … for aircraft designed for low-level flight (e.g. Tornado and Jaguar) damage would not occur below 4 psi and lethality would be proportionately higher … The lethal (4 psi) zone for the Vulcan from a 450-kt detonation (e.g. WE177B) was calculated at 4.3 km or 2.3NM. The Vulcan's one-time-only speed over the target was 415 kts or 1NM every 8.7 seconds. So it follows that, in order to ensure survival, there needed to be a minimum of 20 seconds between release and detonation. To ensure no risk of some structural damage would require about twice that. Actually, the distance/times were probably lower than that because the studies were based on a worst case … a low airburst, which gives a greater blast overpressure because of reflected blast wave. A groundburst (e.g. WE177B) and/or the opportunity to climb higher would both have reduced the overpressure significantly … it would seem that the claimed 32 seconds would certainly have enabled survival and quite possibly have placed the aircraft beyond risk of damage." [793]

Roy Brocklebank gave his views on the 2F laydown attack:

"… our post-attack manoeuvre was not declared an escape manoeuvre but undoubtedly was. It was to maintain straight and level flight for ten miles. This would have ensured the tail was on the target. It would also have the effect of reducing the radar cross-section with respect to AAA and short-range SAMs … I calculated that the aircraft would be at about 5.5 miles from the target by the time the blast reached it and the blast decay would be below 1.5 psi. I don't believe the crew would have planned to fly higher post-release, though that might have been prudent. At the ten-mile point, most recovery profiles required a 180-degree turn and a parallel track. This track would have been about six miles displaced from the attack track. Abeam the target, the aircraft was to climb to its maximum altitude, activating the jammers and flying SAM evasive routeing … The advantage of the delayed climb was its proximity to destroyed defences on the ground. Once above 30,000 ft the only weapon, until the SA-5, that could catch us was the SA-2. At this stage of the war I would be surprised if there were many air defence fighters operable."[794]

Another explanation for the return to the target would be to act as a decoy, with the degraded defences unable to distinguish between a bomber now without a bomb and a bomber still with the weapon on board and on its attack run. This might make it more likely to get a second weapon on target, by encouraging any remaining defences to focus on an aircraft no longer representing a threat. A return to the target after release could double the *perceived* threat. Any reader who might doubt Bomber Command's willingness to deceive its own crews might consider the evidence (or, rather, lack of evidence) for the existence of German 'scarecrow shells' during World War 2. Despite Bomber Command's claims to the contrary, to reassure night-bomber crews, the vivid flashes of 'scarecrows' were, in fact, just what many crews thought they were: exploding British bombers (many the victims of night-fighters armed with *Schräge Musik* upward–firing cannons and positioned underneath, in the bombers' blind spot).

Returning to the V-bombers and the escape distance/time required to survive detonation of their own weapons, Roy Brocklebank maintains that Vulcan crews were told that the time between drop and detonation was 32 seconds. According to Mike Fazackerley, the weapon had no 32-second detonation setting. Yet, WE.177B did have a 32-second *arming* time available on the ground control unit:

> "…evidence points to the fact that the timer that was initiated on weapon release, and that first armed the weapon and then detonated it, was pre-set to a detonation time of 28 seconds in laydown mode, as long as the requisite safety breaks had been closed …

Low-level visual attack: the Vulcan had a detachable low-level bombsight, fitted at the co-pilot's position. (Andy Leitch Collection)

> The primary reason for minimising the time to detonation with laydown was because of concerns regarding weapon vulnerability whilst lying on the ground. The aim was to balance aircraft/crew survivability with minimum weapon time on the ground."[795]

The escape period was from release to detonation, plus the time required for the first shock wave to catch up with the aircraft. Roy Brocklebank did the sums:

> "… assuming a release speed of 415 kts and 32 seconds from release to bang, the aircraft would have travelled about 7,500 yards, or 3.7NM. The shock wave speed is around 1,000 yards per second. This gives an overtake speed of 766 yards per second … about ten seconds. Our aircraft would travel a further 2,300 yards in that time, a total of about 10,000 yards – or about 4.93 miles."[796]

Allowing for the potential decay of the shock wave speed, the total escape distance is "nearer the 5.5NM I calculated 50 years ago". Counterforce targets were often airfields largely free of obstructions but, in the case of countervalue targets (or counterforce targets within greater urban areas), the shock wave would be attenuated more quickly by buildings, so allowing additional time to escape.

Freefall Vulcans had a rather rudimentary visual bombsight at the co-pilot's station, for possible use in a daylight low-level laydown strike, in the event of radar failure. Andy Leitch recalls the sight, originally fitted to Canberras, was French-made, by SFOM (*Société Française d'Optique et de Mécanique*). "The detachable sight had an angled piece of glass which reflected a circle and crosshairs focused at infinity in the eye-line of the co-pilot." Roy Brocklebank recalls the earlier visual bombsight:

> "For a conventional laydown attack, the release point would be around 0.7 miles. For a nuclear laydown attack with a 450-yard forward throw (or less), blinds down, eyepatches on, and perhaps even the co-pilot incapacitated, it really had no role to play."

The credibility of the British deterrent threat hinged on a few V-bombers getting through. A successful V-bomber attack would have required luck and exceptional performance in combat: intelligent evasive routeing, prompt and effective countermeasures against direct threats, pinpoint navigation and timely arrival at the target/launch point, followed by faultless weapon release. There is a strong probability that, in war, a handful of surviving V-bombers would have put weapons on targets – even in a unilateral attack. *The challenge for the Soviets would be to kill every single penetrator prior to weapon release.*

There is anecdotal evidence that the Soviets themselves believed a few Vulcans could get through the defences. When John Huggins left the air force he joined the Territorial Army and spent 20 years as an infantry officer:

> "In the 1980s, just before the Berlin Wall came down, I was with a group of Soviet observers attending Exercise Lionheart, a brigade river crossing in Germany. One Soviet officer pointed to my wings and said: 'What's a pilot doing with the infantry?' Then I noticed that it was the same for him. I told him I had been a Vulcan pilot. He said: 'The Vulcan was the only one we feared.' I laughed but he insisted it was true: 'We feared it the most – we thought it would get through.' We shared some vodka together."[797]

During his time as a Vulcan captain, John Huggins was briefed to 'attack' American naval units in the Mediterranean. He took his Vulcan very low, dropped chaff to evade defending fighters and 'sank' the carrier USS *Roosevelt* off the Greek coast. "We were role-playing Soviet Badger bombers."[798]

When Polaris assumed the strategic nuclear lead, the British deterrent threat no longer relied on the survival of a handful of subsonic bombers. However Roger Dunsford points out that V-Force significance continued for another decade:

Are they looking up? Vulcan Captain John Huggins overflies an American aircraft carrier, having evaded the protecting fighters. (John Huggins)

> "The Soviet defences, particularly their SAM capabilities and numbers concentrated around their major centres, meant that the likelihood of manned aircraft getting through was diminishing rapidly ... By the second half of the 1960s, the days of the Vulcan and Victor as the primary deterrent were numbered. Polaris was used for the major strategic targets with the heaviest defences and we were assigned to less heavily defended, sub-strategic targets, such as regional command and control headquarters. We believed then, and I believe now, that this certainly did not mean the Soviet regime could ignore the threat from the V-Force – our targets were a very significant threat to their ability to retain overall control of the state machinery."[799]

RECOVERY AND CASUALTIES

Aircrew views on post-strike recovery often blended fatalism with black humour. Nav/plotter Bryan 'Monty' Montgomery talked in terms of acceptance:

> "Some targets were very long range, but why come back? We had our plans for the return, but it was all pie in the sky. We were briefed to return to an airfield at Aalborg, Denmark. For targets too far to allow recovery to such bases, due to fuel considerations, crews would continue flying east until, at a certain point over the Steppe of east Russia, they would abandon the aircraft and wait to be rescued by Allied forces. No-one thought much of this! Anyway, we didn't talk about it much as a crew."[800]

Nav/radar Barry Mullen's crew had operational orders to return to base:

> "We talked about it from time to time, but when we discussed 'what if' options, these were merely thoughts. On one occasion, someone asked whether we would have enough fuel to reach the Bahamas. There was plenty of black humour around. I remember a simulator session with a real hard bugger of an instructor. He gave me every possible kind of failure and then said: 'How are you going to get rid of the bomb?' In reply, I asked him: 'Where do you live?'"[801]

The 1971 Air Force Department submission to the Long Term Strategic Nuclear Working Party, proposing an air-delivered system as a Polaris successor, reviewed the then current air-delivered strike capabilities in a broad context, including emergent nuclear powers in receipt of extensive Soviet military aid – with air-defence weapons that would be encountered in a retaliatory strike against Russia, such as S-60 and ZSU guns and SA-3. It stated:

> "… the primary threat comprises guns and SA-3 which may be encountered randomly en route if their precise locations are not known, so that they cannot be avoided by tactical routeing. They may also be encountered as fixed deployments in defence of city targets comprising a typical five SA-3 site complex and an assumed deployment of five to ten S-60 gun batteries to provide all-round cover."[802]

Not surprisingly, the Tornado was judged to be the least vulnerable in this operational environment, with the Vulcan, "our largest, slowest and inherently most vulnerable aircraft", at greatest risk. Four encounters with S-60 Flap Wheel batteries by day would demand a force requirement of four aircraft "to ensure at least one survivor".

This is a statement of some significance, given that, in the 1960s, there would be very few V-bombers surviving a pre-emptive Soviet missile strike. Only a handful of bombers would have survived long enough to make an attack and, against this background, exclusive targeting of the two largest Soviet cities is logical in the context of maximised deterrence, despite the fact that in general war (as opposed to unilateral retaliation), Moscow and Leningrad would have been vaporised long before the few remaining V-bombers arrived. All V-Force crews, of course, were entirely familiar with tactics to attack Moscow and Leningrad, as these were QRA targets for all squadrons.

Taken overall, these themes suggest that a British retaliatory attack – making good the core deterrent threat – would see a handful of bombers successfully deliver two or three weapons on Moscow and Leningrad. The consequences, in terms of damage and casualties, would differ greatly between Plan A and Plan B. Under Plan A, of course, a small number of British weapons would add little to the destruction already inflicted by American missiles. Under Plan B, in the absence of a US missile strike, the damage and casualties inflicted by British megaton range weapons on the two leading Soviet cities would have been catastrophic. This outcome was judged by British planners to be sufficient to materially alter the balance of power between the USA and USSR. The focus on successful delivery of a few British weapons on the two largest Russian cities was entirely appropriate. It made both political and military sense, given the small number of surviving V-bombers likely to be in a position to make an attack, the desire to maximise the destructive potential of the few weapons actually delivered, the priority need to deter war by presenting the maximum deterrent threat and, finally, the inability of the Soviets to count on the destruction of all penetrators.

It would have been a lonely, terrifying and extremely brief war for V-bomber crews. The demands were extreme: penetrate the coastal belt, survive the area defences, and, in the case of the freefall bombers, push through the point defences by flying in at ultra-low level. V-Force training and exercises practised the attack profiles required for successful weapons delivery, followed by the escape manoeuvre. Timings suggest the bombers could survive blast, direct radiation and other effects from the detonation of their own weapons, but only with sufficient TOT separation. In general war, the Soviet defences would suffer severe degradation. Certainly, in both general and unilateral contexts, PVO-Strany's defences could offer *no absolute guarantee* that every surviving V-bomber would be destroyed before weapon release over, in all probability, Moscow and Leningrad.

Austin Long, in his 2008 review of 60 years of RAND research, provided admirable clarity on the true deterrent quality of megaton weapon threats against large cities:

> "Russian and Chinese nuclear forces exist almost exclusively to provide basic deterrence, which is inherently credible in intent. Given this highly credible intent to trade Moscow or Beijing for Washington, even a relatively small capability is very effective. What US president would undertake an operation with even a 5% chance of resulting in the destruction of one or two major US cities in any but the direst circumstances? A similar rationale underpinned the French and British nuclear force structure in the Cold War; the survival of even a handful of nuclear weapons would give even the most hardened Soviet pause in launching a first strike."[803]

21

TRAINING FOR A ONE-STRIKE WAR

> ❝ *The majority view amongst veterans is that they trained for a one-strike war, with very little chance of coming back if war came. Most were convinced that deterrence would hold, however, and that they would not be required to fly a war sortie.* ❞

THE 'GRAND TOUR'

Training, QRA, exercises and bombing/navigation competitions were the main themes of V-Force operational life. These activities shaped the preoccupations of operational crews, along with rigorous systems for checking competence and efficiency.

In their primary role, V-Force crews would fly only one war sortie: they trained for a one-strike nuclear war. This training had a global reach, from UK ranges such as Wainfleet and West Freugh and British cities 'destroyed' thousands of times in simulated attacks, to Goose Bay in Labrador, El Adem in Libya and China Rock, off Singapore. V-bomber training was intense, continuous and with the primary aim of successful delivery of a nuclear weapon during the first couple of hours of war.

Prior to the switch to low-level strike, a typical high-altitude flight profile involved a climb phase, followed by a cruise climb as weight reduced. A high-level flight of around six hours would include a 1,000NM Navex, simulated weapon release and either fighter affiliation or a descent for circuit work. Later, UK low-level routes were used.

V-bomber flying hours were precious and packed with training value. Sorties often involved a 'Grand Tour' of Britain, as recalled by Robin Woolven: "We kept to the UK low-level routes and avoided danger areas, active airfields and overflying the crowded south-east."[804] The low-level route could be joined from the English Channel by crossing the south Devon coast, then crossing Dartmoor and reaching the Bristol Channel, heading north and eventually returning down the east coast:

> "During the flight, the radar bomb scoring units put us to the test as we closed with our 'targets'. They were equally efficient at monitoring high-level and low-level attacks. One of our targets, the Runcorn Bridge – a large steel bridge in the Merseyside area – gave a very high quality radar return, much appreciated by the nav/radar."

Crews defended hard-won crew classification rankings – their place on the 'ladder of excellence'. Bryan Montgomery belonged to a crack select star crew. Each sortie counted in defence of their top status: "I remember flying as low as possible over the Welsh mountains and climbing to 10,000 ft to 'release' a weapon over Barrow." They had little information on Soviet defences at that time, but had begun to practise 2A manoeuvres, to evade SAMs: "Fox (the captain) would pull up left, go over in negative g, then climb to the right."[805]

RBSUs were modified anti-aircraft artillery (AAA) tracking radars (AA No. 3 Mk 7 [Blue Cedar], later succeeded by radar tracking system Mk 2). Norman Bonnor explained the procedures for use of RBSUs:

"They each covered a range of up to 40 targets of varying difficulty; crews could book attack times before take-off or call for an opportunity attack. Bomb release was simulated by the end of a tone transmitted by the aircraft on VHF, which automatically lifted a pen on the radar plotting table. The RBSU staff then used their tracking radar's values of track, speed and height to calculate the forward throw and trail of a simulated weapon and estimate the impact error."[806]

This was a 1kHz tone on VHF 100.0 MHz.[807]

One of Roy Brocklebank's targets was Haydock Park racecourse, Liverpool:

"We would run in on the bearing and the AA radar would lock on. This would be detected by our AEO, who would fire up Red Shrimp. He would then switch it off, to see if the missile lock had been broken. If they still had a lock, he'd have another go. In the USA, SAC bombers were tested against Nike SAM sites. Here, we used the gun-laying radars as Bloodhound SAM radars were not compatible with our systems, making it impossible to affiliate."[808]

Robin Woolven's first flight with 617 Squadron was on 6 July 1964:

"We were accompanied by Wing Commander Currell. This was a CO's check flight of five hours – a tactical profile sortie including navigational exercises and the use of ECM over the Western Isles' radar facilities. We flew with Currell once again on 15 July. This was a low-level check … I cannot be sure of the briefed minimum height but it was indeed 'low level' and we had no TFR. At that time there was no such thing as free-range flying at low level around the UK and access to the low-flying routes was controlled and monitored by the low-flying cell at RAF Uxbridge. We had to use one of the designated low-level routes. This flight was logged as UK LL Route 23 and included two simulated Blue Steel releases. By that stage we were checked out at high level, low level and at night (half of one of the flights took place during the hours of darkness)."[809]

Woolven's last flight with 617 Squadron was on 12 August 1966: "My logbook records three high-level Blue Steel attacks, over Lindholme and Kenley, during that sortie."

Crew efficiency was subject to constant monitoring. At this time, all pilots had regular checks on the Vulcan simulator at Coningsby. Navigators at Scampton had no need to travel to practise missile releases, as the Blue Steel training rig was housed in this station's operations block.[810]

Most V-Force aircrew had great confidence in their aircraft and systems. V-bomber captain Nick Dennis, in considering his Vulcan's defensive capabilities, had faith in its manoeuvrability but also wished for AAMs: "It seemed strange to train to attack the USSR in an aircraft without defensive weapons." He, for one, was happy with the ECM: "I was impressed – and quite surprised at what it could achieve."[811]

TRAINING SORTIES

At the same time, there was always a level of discontent amongst V-Force aircrew. Some complained about the lack of flying hours. Others wanted a different style of flying. Vulcan nav/radar John Weller, with IX Squadron, recalls morale in No. 1 Group at a low ebb in 1965:

"A lot of training seemed to be about boring holes in the sky just for the sake of it. Then there were the intelligence briefings. We were given the Soviet order of battle. On paper it looked horrendous. It was argued that, of the thousands of MiGs, only a third of them would work on the day. The defences would be weakened by a shortage of spares, lack of training and restrictions on flying hours. In contrast, we were demonstrating – as the deterrent – that we had the serviceability to put the aircraft in the air, but some sorties were a waste of time, particularly if aircraft unserviceability had delayed us until the ranges were closed."[812]

Vulcan captain Roger Smith provided more insights. In early 1963 he was engaged in advanced flying training in Vampires. This was at a time of V-Force expansion; 25 of the 27 course participants were posted to the V-Force:

"Our perception was that all the V-Force did was to fly in straight lines at 50,000 ft, dropping radar bombs on radar targets, a view largely gained from our mainly ex-Fighter Command instructors. Hence, those posted to the V-Force were devastated to think that a potentially exciting career flying Lightnings was not to be. In fact, the adverse reaction was so strong that the station commander wrote to the MoD, complaining about the situation. V-Force postings were reduced from 25 to 23!"[813]

Smith felt depressed on entering RAF Finningley's gates, to join 230 Vulcan OCU. Yet, his first close encounter with the bomber prompted second thoughts: "Wow! It was April 1964 and this Vulcan looked spectacular in its white anti-flash. It looked even better camouflaged, as our role changed from high to low level." He became a 12 Squadron co-pilot.

AEO Peter West gave a detailed account of a V-Force training flight:

"A normal sortie on any V-Force squadron consisted, usually, of a navigation phase, which took up about 70% of the flight, three radar bombing runs and either fighter affiliation or circuit training. The hardest working member of the crew was, invariably, the nav/plotter. He was the first into ops, to collect the Met forecast and prepare the flight plan. The rest of the crew arrived, generally, about an hour after the plotter, to carry out their pre-flight preparations. The captain briefed the crew, who then went for their pre-flight meal in what was popularly known as the 'aircrew feeder'. As we cleared the diner, the co-pilot carried out his most important task, that of collecting the in-flight rations. Out to the aircraft and a chat with the crew chief. The captain signed the Form 700 (aircraft log), accepting the aircraft as fit to fly.

"Into the cabin, AEO first, switching on the 28V electrical system which provided intercom, radio and lighting. When each crew member was strapped in, the AEO and captain went through the pre-flight checks. During this phase, the crew chief was also on the intercom, using an external lead. Once all was checked satisfactorily, the co-pilot called the tower for clearance to take off … this following our taxiing out to the runway. On take-off, we went straight into the nav phase which, sometimes post-1964, was flown over the low-level route around the UK. From time to time, the nav phase was over the Atlantic, limiting our navigation to Astro. The AEO spent his time monitoring the aircraft electrical systems and keeping an HF watch, sending position reports to Group HQ hourly.

"The next phase of the flight was to attack targets, where we were monitored by ground radar sites; they measured the results and passed these to us on the radio … After three such bombing runs the aircraft usually returned to base, to allow the pilots to practise landings and take-offs, this universally loathed by rear crews who had nothing to do but monitor flight instruments. If he was lucky, the AEO might be allowed a fighter affiliation instead of 'circuit and bumps'. This involved calling up a fighter control unit and asking for 'playmates'. These were usually forthcoming as the fighters were as keen as us. On my last sortie with 12 Squadron, in 1966, we had an all-out game with pairs of fighters over the North Sea. After ten attacks, they had to return to base low on fuel. The fighter controller broadcast: "I make that Christians ten, lions 0!" A great way to end my tour." [814]

The character of training changed after the Valiants were grounded in 1965. Punishing flying at low level was blamed but Tim McLelland observed: "… it seemed likely that it was the alloy that was the fundamental cause."[815] Cracks in a Victor fatigue specimen were also discovered. The training programme revisions, guided by caution, restricted low-level flying hours. Blue Steel Victor navigator Norman Bonnor remembers the switch in emphasis:

"Our training targets dramatically changed, from being based primarily on hours and sorties to new definitions based strictly on training value. We were allowed no more than four sorties a month and each one had to be packed with high value training. The senior staff at RAF Wittering thought this would lead to a drop in morale among crews, but far from it. We no longer flew without a missile, or had to carry unserviceabilities; we also had priority on range bookings over our colleagues in No. 1 Group, flying the Vulcan."[816]

Bonnor recalls the decision requiring each operational Blue Steel round on the station to be flown once every six months:

"When we flew with these wet missiles (without warheads, of course), rather than training rounds, high-test peroxide (HTP) temperatures were one of the items checked and logged every 30 minutes throughout the sortie. Should the HTP temperatures start to rise whilst airborne, the crew would divert immediately to the nearest Blue Steel diversion airfield, to offload the HTP into large tanks of water buried in the ground close to the operational readiness platform. There were several of these specially-equipped airfields around the country, apart from the main bases at Scampton and Wittering. The co-pilot and nav/radar formed the offload crew, who donned protective suits after landing and connected hoses to the missile. The offload kit was kept in the visual bomb-aiming position."

Vulcan crews enjoyed fighter affiliations, given that their aircraft was a bomber that thought it was a fighter. Vulcan captain Nick Dennis remembers the rivalry between V-bomber crews and the 'Lightning Boys':

"At that time, Lightnings had the Firestreak AAM – an infrared guided weapon. If it locked on, the fighter pilot would call 'Splash!', then ask for a vector back to Binbrook or another air defence base. Our aim was to avoid lock-on and we had all sorts of tricks up our sleeve. We would be at around 42,000–45,000 ft and the incoming Lightning would be at around 35,000 ft. We would see him – the AEO would get a positive from Red Steer. One tactic was to get over the top of him and lose speed, making it impossible for him to get behind us. If we could get behind the Lightning, we would call 'Splash!' The Lightning had a spectacular performance and was a wonderful interceptor, but it had to stay on your tail with Firestreak. The later Red Top was different. With this weapon, the fighter could attack head-on. It was game over – there was no counter."[817]

Nav/plotter Jim Milne said the Vulcan "could turn inside almost any opposing fighter of those days". He had confidence in the EW fit, in contrast to some:

"I was amazed at just how good the ECM was. We used to check out the kit over the Hebrides. When we got TFR, my skipper was prepared to have a go with it, but it made us a bit twitchy and we never used it at night."[818]

All crews did their share of simulator training, as described by Air Vice-Marshal Nigel Baldwin:

"Today, a substantial element of ground training is carried out in sophisticated, digital, three-axis, full-motion simulators. The V-bombers were firmly rooted in the analogue era. Nevertheless, there were flight simulators for the pilots, advanced for their time, a reasonable reproduction of the two-navigator station, complete with the radar, and an electrical trainer for the AEOs. But they were all located in separate buildings. Indeed, at one stage, there were only two Vulcan cockpit simulators, which meant that pilots at stations without one had to take a whole day every month to meet their training commitments. We never had one at Akrotiri in Cyprus, so the rules had to be changed. As the force contracted, however, we eventually finished up with a full set at each base and it proved possible to coordinate the three isolated crew positions, so that they could be made to work together, even if they were in different locations. It was a bit Heath Robinson, with complicated wiring looms linking the sites. Nevertheless, on a good day, it became possible to 'fly' a war sortie as a complete crew, with threats and battle damage. And an exhausting and thrilling experience it was too."[819]

Barry Mullen wanted Buccaneers but became a Vulcan nav/radar:

"The six-month ground course included lectures on aircraft systems and radar, together with simulator time. The analogue simulator presented a series of 'equipment failures'. We had to diagnose these failures and, somehow, still drop the weapon and complete the mission. We used offsets, taken from a good radar reflection, to aim our aircraft at the target. RAF Waddington had a simulator which allowed us to practise the switching for arming and dropping a nuclear weapon … The simulators at RAF Lindholme were designed for use by the nav/radar and nav/plotter. The system tracked the position on the map, using equipment such as the GPI (ground position indicator). System failures could be introduced and it was the job of the nav team to get to the target and drop the simulated weapon."[820]

Sortie prep: crew briefing in the ops room at RAF Waddington. (Barry Mullen)

If called upon to do so, it would have been Barry Mullen's lot to drop a weapon with the power to kill millions. V-Force aircrew underwent no psychological assessment:

> "We were shown a film of the effects of the atomic bombing of Hiroshima and Nagasaki and I thought that was pretty horrific. But we were just young lads at the time, all with a certain mindset. Our job was to protect our country, as a non-aggressor. We never got worked up over politics … I suppose pragmatism was the order of the day."

A ONE-SHOT SYSTEM

In the early years, the V-Force planned for up to three nuclear strikes. This changed with the dominance of missiles. There could be just one retaliatory attack, delivered by the survivors of a Soviet pre-emptive missile strike. Much later, under 'flexible response' and the concept of demonstrating resolve by possible limited first use of tactical nuclear weapons against an overwhelming Soviet conventional attack, some strike aircraft might have been tasked to undertake 'demonstration' missions – with the aim of terminating war, rather than provoking escalation. The potential need to resort to sparing early use of tactical nuclear weapons reflected NATO's persistent failure to hold adequate conventional war-fighting stocks. It was thought that the 30-day NATO standard stock of munitions and other consumables might evaporate in just one week of intense conventional battle. This suggests that stocks would be exhausted before the arrival of US reinforcements, so precipitating an early nuclear release decision.[821]

Such matters were beyond V-Force crews, who assumed they were training for a one-strike war, with nothing left to come home to. Their business was flying, rather than policy, and the buzz of low flying provided an outlet for many, including 'Monty' Montgomery: "Now the flying became more interesting. We would fly at around 250 ft over the Welsh mountains."[822] Dick Fuller remembers the aircraft being heavy on the controls: "The Valiant was a handful and there was plenty of turbulence over the hills."[823] Barry Mullen has vivid recollections of low flying:

> "Low meant low – from 500 ft down to 300 ft. My main screen was photographed to preserve our performance for later scrutiny. I set up the radar to scan directly in front of us. The black section visible on screen was what we were in danger of hitting. I then counted down the cut-off, from five to four and then three miles. It was at that point that I told the captain to pull up. I was an insurance for the automated system."[824]

According to Roy Brocklebank, TFR settings started at 100 ft and went up in 100 ft increments.[825] Vulcan AEO Hugh Prior was unconcerned when flying low: "That never worried me – if something happened at low level it would be over in an instant. I felt much the same about nuclear war."[826]

Innovations aimed at improving low-level navigation included a system relying on relief models. Vulcan nav/radar Jim Walker: "You could place a light in such a way that the shadows gave you an idea of what the radar picture would look like. By mid-1968, some of us were using this German-made system."[827]

THREATENING SOUTHERN RUSSIA

As the 1960s drew to a close, with Polaris now holding the UK's strategic nuclear frontline, two V-Force Vulcan squadrons – 35 and IX – moved from Cottesmore to RAF Akrotiri, Cyprus. This was a very welcome posting for aircrew and ground crew alike. It was less popular with the Russians. All aircraft were in Cyprus by mid-March 1969, replacing Near East Air Force (NEAF) Strike Wing Canberras. These Vulcans had three roles: provision of the UK nuclear contribution to the Central Treaty Organization (CENTO), provision of nuclear support to meet UK War Plan requirements and, thirdly, to contribute to UK conventional war plans in the region. In the nuclear role, these squadrons were required to generate 75% of available aircraft within 24 hours and the remainder as soon as possible (100% within 72 hours). Three armed aircraft would disperse to Muharraq (Bahrain) and six to Masirah Island, with the rest operating from Akrotiri. They would maintain NEAF strategic alert for up to 28 days.[828]

RAF Akrotiri had acquired nuclear weapons storage facilities some years previously, in 1961.[829] The Cyprus Vulcan squadrons were the only V-bomber units to have a permanent overseas base. Jim Walker was happy:

> "Cyprus was great – brilliant. In some ways it was like a flying club. By then, we knew the job inside out and the flying was routine. Our nuclear targets were in southern Russia; some were long-range, including Tashkent and Kiev."[830]

Barry Mullen was single, free and seized his opportunity for a sunshine tour. He joined the IX Squadron crew captained by Flight Lieutenant Fred Tiernan. Mullen was more than happy with his luck – which was better than some of the eight Cranwell cadets who had made up his intake. Three were to die in accidents. As a replacement nav/radar, Mullen's arrival was

All present and correct: IX Squadron at RAF Akrotiri, Cyprus. (Barry Mullen)

greeted with some uncertainty. However, on his first bombing sortie he managed to drop all 28-lb practice bombs within 50 ft of the bombing range target. The AEO passed judgement, saying: "He'll do!"[831]

The Cyprus Vulcans were armed with WE.177B hydrogen bombs but four WE.177A tactical weapons were sent out in October 1970 due to a shortage of high yield weapons. Mike Fazackerley explained:

"There was a gap – a period during which there were not enough WE.177Bs to go round. This was due to rotation of the Cyprus squadrons and some reorganisation following the retirement of Blue Steel. For a short period, there were 56 Vulcans and 52 WE.177Bs, including four spares. The situation resolved itself when 27 Squadron assumed its new role of long-range maritime reconnaissance."[832]

In the nuclear context, communication was a worry for retaliatory forces based in Cyprus. According to Roy Brocklebank, the planners allowed for communication problems or delay in the case of a war scramble:

"It was thought that headquarters in Cyprus would have to take the initiative, in order to get the force airborne. Unlike the UK, all 16 bombers were on one base and they had to make allowances for delayed communications with the UK. This led to new plans. They were based on how long you could afford to orbit over the sea between Cyprus and Turkey and still have adequate fuel reserves for completing the mission and landing back at base. For crews with Baku as their target, they had a couple of hours of flexibility. In contrast, those with targets as far away as Tashkent might have only minutes to tolerate a communications delay. When crews calculated their fuel plans, they would give two estimates; one was the time they could loiter and still recover with 4,000 lbs of fuel remaining. This was Delay 1. Delay 2 was the amount of time they could loiter, reach their target and fly on for a further ten minutes before baling out. You could have heard a pin drop when this plan was unveiled to the assembled crews. It was the first time we had been briefed for one-way missions."[833]

The bombs were flown to Cyprus by a series of special flights by transport aircraft. They arrived during the night hours and were disguised.[834] The Cyprus V-Force came to an end following the 1974 Turkish invasion, when the Vulcans returned to the UK. The resident squadrons of the NEAF Bomber Wing were succeeded by 'Detachment Squadrons', typically flights of four aircraft.

HEADING WEST

V-Bomber training programmes included Goose Rangers or Western Rangers – flying west to Goose Bay, Labrador, or USAF bases such as Offutt. British crews took part in USAF exercises and bombing competitions. Participation in a Strategic Air Command (SAC) bombing competition was always memorable. Vulcan co-pilot Keith Mans was struck by the high degree of confidence amongst V-Force aircrew:

"We thought we were better than them, but their aircraft had more modern ECM and inertial navigation. The competition was fierce and the participating V-bombers were always fitted with special equipment, to allow us to bomb more accurately. When comparing the B-52 and the V-bomber, the latter must have had a better chance on a war flight."[835]

Whilst on 100 Squadron, Norman Bonnor's Victor crew flew several Goose/Western Rangers:

"Most crews made at least two visits to Goose Bay during a tour and, occasionally, on to Omaha and SAC Headquarters. We always first flew north out of Goose Bay, allowing us to climb and cross the US border at over 50,000 ft. We flew against the American Nike SAM defences, although they did require us to warn them when we were 100–150 miles

Bound for Labrador: Crew 105 about to leave RAF Waddington for Goose Bay, on 9 January 1979. From left to right: 'Ossie' Ostridge (crew chief), Dave Carter (co-pilot), Dave Hartill (nav/plotter), Dennis Martin (captain), Mark Long (AEO) and Reg Brindley (nav/radar). (Dennis Martin)

out! We used our ECM and the Americans struggled. They had never encountered anything coming in at 57,000 ft. They were also impressed in other ways. For example, the Victor's weapons bay was almost as big as that of a B-52 … Our aircraft also looked very different. This always caught the eye of the Americans. In one instance, in 1990, a Victor tanker landed at a US base and the crew were asked: 'Is this your new stealth bomber?'"[836]

Going home: Crew 105 about to depart Goose Bay for RAF Waddington on 26 January 1979. (Dennis Martin)

Dennis Martin participated in exercises at Goose Bay in January 1979. Arriving on the 9th after a flight of five hours 30 minutes, his crew underwent the mandatory survival course the next day. On 11 January they flew two low-level sorties (two hours 10 minutes and two hours five minutes). On 12 January they departed Goose Bay, bound for Offutt AFB, Nebraska. A poor weather forecast prompted an en route decision to divert to Whiteman AFB, Missouri (a helicopter and missile station). On finals, they were warned to be aware of 'Prairie Chickens', a type of Grouse. The sortie lasted five hours.

As Dennis describes: "It was a Friday and we discovered there were no nearby towns and, over the weekend, there would be typical Mid-West freezing rain. Whiteman had no de-icing facilities and we could have been stuck there for days." All this prompted a change of plan. They refuelled and left for Barksdale in Louisiana – a short flight of one hour ten minutes. "We had a good weekend, with much eating and drinking. The USAF looked after us well, giving us a self-drive staff car as crew transport." They left Barksdale for Offutt on 15 January but went U/S there, requiring spares to be sent from the UK. The aircraft was grounded for seven days and the time was put to good use. They flew sorties on 22 and 23 January, leaving Offutt the following day for a return to Goose Bay.

A trip to America usually had its highlights. On leaving IX Squadron, Barry Mullen did a second tour as a 230 OCU instructor. He was also selected as a member of the Vulcan display crew. The 1978 display programme included a flight to Bergstrom AFB in Texas – where the crew were all made honorary citizens of Texas and invited to President Johnson's ranch, just outside Austin, where they met 'Ladybird' Johnson.[837]

V-bombers regularly tested American home defence fighters. They liked to dogfight. Vulcan captain Rob Williams, however, particularly enjoyed low levels over Goose Bay:

"This part of the world is empty. There are fewer people in this Canadian wilderness than there are in the North African desert. It may be a lonely place but it offers excellent low-level flying. The regulations were firm – no flying lower than 200 ft. We followed the rules but I know that some didn't."[838]

Survival training at Goose Bay: Vulcan captain Dennis Martin: "We built snowholes in a temperature of -35°C." From left to right: Dave Carter (co-pilot), survival instructor (unidentified), 'Nick' (another survival instructor), Dennis Martin (captain), Reg Brindley (nav/radar), Mark Long (AEO) and another unidentified survival instructor. Survival training at Goose Bay was mandatory. (Dennis Martin)

Goose Bay was not to everyone's taste. Vulcan captain Paul Millikin remembered the risk of being trapped on the ground by bad weather and snow:

> "The flying was good initially but became repetitive, with nothing but trees, lakes and snow as far as the eye could see. In the summer, the snow was replaced by millions of blackflies."[839]

Vulcan pilot Bill Taylor recalled the Vulcan's tendency to porpoise at speed when down to 100 ft: "Although the effect was not enough to destabilise the aeroplane, it was quite noticeable. This porpoising – due to the ground effect – disappeared when you flew over a snowfield."[840]

British bombers visiting Offutt AFB flew low-level attacks across the USA, using the USAF's 'oilburner' routes. One British visitor received a sharp lesson in the importance SAC attached to airborne command posts (ACPs). AEO Martin Anscombe never forgot the experience:

> "We burst a tyre on landing and asked for a tow (which was the standard operating procedure), rather than taxi in, but we were ordered to clear the runway immediately as the next ACP was about to take off. Nothing was allowed to interfere with an ACP. We realised the importance of this when two large bulldozers appeared, heading towards us. If we didn't move, they would move us."[841]

As for bombing and navigation competitions, the British did well in the American Giant Voice series. In 1974, Vulcans won three of the four trophies.

Vulcan captain Paddy Langdown's crew was selected for Giant Voice 1974. They won the Navigation Trophy. Langdown's nav/plotter was James Vinales, who received the Queen's Commendation in recognition of his efforts and, jointly with nav/radar Ed Candlish, the Guild of Air Pilots and Air Navigators Johnston Memorial Trophy for excellence in air navigation. The co-pilot was Anthony Dee and the AEO Colin Hinge. The regular nav/radar, Tony Thornthwaite, was ill at the time.

In competitions, as in love and war, all was fair. The 1967 Giant Voice, for example, was to include both high-level and low-level attacks, but there were differing interpretations of low level. During preparations, British crews understood that low level meant 2,500 ft, but target materials issued much later specified heights of between 4,000 ft and 7,100 ft, rendering the V-bombers' ultra-low-level offset practices inappropriate. At 5,000 ft the H2S reverted to the high-level pattern. So, final training sorties at low level had to switch to high-level offset procedures, with worse results. In effect, SAC's low-level bombing heights were high level for the V-Force.[842]

In the event, SAC cancelled the competition in late August. The British reciprocated. The rules for Bomber Command's Bombing and Navigation Competition were subject to constant change, leading to suggestions that this was to ensure visiting SAC crews couldn't win. The usefulness of competitions was questioned occasionally, but Air Vice-Marshal Nigel Baldwin came to recognise the broader purpose: "… looking back, I now realise the annual competition with SAC had a political importance way beyond our irritations in the crew room."[843]

A convincing win: Vulcan captain Paddy Langdown's crew won the Navigation Trophy in Giant Voice 1974. From left to right: Paddy Langdown (captain), Tony Dee (co-pilot), Ed Candlish (nav/radar), Jim Vinales (nav/plotter), Colin Hinge (AEO) and Des Sonley (crew chief). (Paddy Langdown)

That aside, the rivals kept a close eye on each other. Vulcan captain Dennis Martin participated in a Double Top RAF/USAF exercise: "I flew as an umpire in a B-52 making a low-level attack at 500 ft over East Anglia. My job was to ensure there was no cheating." His Americans missed the target – "another one in the weeds".[844]

The Americans devised what remains widely regarded as the most realistic battle experience available in peacetime. During the mid-1970s the USAF began Red Flag battle practice within a simulated Soviet air defence environment featuring early warning radars, SAM and AAA radars and aggressor squadron fighters using Soviet combat techniques. The tactical weapons and electronic warfare ranges had an area equal to the southern half of England and Wales. The ranges presented a group of 50 tactical targets and the 'frontline' included over 200 replica Soviet tanks. The Vulcans made radar attacks. The fast strike aircraft dropped live weapons. Geoff Lidbetter was AEO on Pete Crowe's Vulcan command crew. They flew out to Nellis in 1977, together with 21 x 1,000-lb bombs for the participating Buccaneers: "We found Red Flag very demanding. The sortie length was around 90 minutes, flying down 'missile alley'. It was all very realistic – the threats certainly sounded very real."[845] The attackers had to penetrate these defences and hit targets across the huge air-ground range north of Nellis.[846]

Vulcan pilot Steve Oddy took part in Red Flag 77/9 (that year's Red Flag was the first with non-US participants). The Vulcans soon discovered that their light grey undersurfaces glinted every time they turned. The undersides received a rush paint job – a finish in tan colours. In their favour, Vulcan combat tactics paid dividends. The aggressor fighters found it difficult to cope with Vulcans flying in at ultra-low level; they struggled to get a guns kill. Equally, the Vulcan's large and distinctive shadow was a giveaway: "We modified our routes to try and stay within the shadow of the mountain ranges as much as possible."[847]

No. 1 Group sent Vulcans to each Red Flag. The results showed the Vulcan to be a potent weapon in favourable circumstances, even into the late 1970s. Air Vice-Marshal Nigel Baldwin:

> "… by the late 1970s the Vulcan was rapidly becoming obsolescent (but) it still had one more shot in its locker … it proved possible to much enhance the aircraft's ability to operate at low level at night and in bad weather."

Vulcans flew in Red Flag 79/2 – the first all-night sortie exercise. Baldwin, commanding 50 Squadron at that time, was responsible for the work-up. There were no technical enhancements; they had to make do with the little-used basic TFR bought off the shelf ten years before:

> "We worked up both confidence and experience gradually and certainly impressed our American hosts at Nellis AFB when we flew through the mountainous Red Flag ranges, contour flying at night at 1,000 feet agl – well below the B-52s and most of the F-111s."[848]

The Vulcan could still surprise, as recounted by AEO Julian Grenfell. Its bite was discovered by an F-5 aggressor pilot who had been chasing one at low level for some time, unable to launch a missile or attack with guns. Suddenly, "the sky filled with silver". During debrief, the American fighter pilot described what happened:

> "He went on to say that he was so frightened by this sudden event that he pushed his throttles forward to maximum and climbed away. His aircraft was shaking violently (and so was he) and it was not until he had calmed down, at some 30,000 ft, that he realised his airbrakes were still out and that the silver was chaff! The Vulcan, by then, had long gone."[849]

Julian Grenfell recalls that Red Flag:

> "was monitored on a separate sensor system at Nellis AFB called Big Board. After each day's exercise, there was a debriefing at which all participants attended. Debriefs were made by 'package managers'. A package manager was the officer in charge of his flight's participation in the exercise … There would be some 400–500 participants in a day's exercise. Packages included bombers, fighters, AWACS, transport, forward air controllers, EW radars, acquisition radars, fire-control radars, umpires and assessors."

There can be no doubt that the generally excellent operational outcomes in Red Flag did much to counter concerns about obsolescence amongst V-Force crews, as made clear by Clive Richards, in discussing the success, in the late 1970s, of Vulcans flying at 200 ft agl in the Nellis high threat environment. He quoted detachment commander Group Captain J. E. Nevill:

> "The improvement in aircrew morale and enthusiasm were most noticeable on their return from successive sorties, particularly when debriefings disclosed the difficulties encountered by aggressor pilots in achieving 'kill' parameters during engagements with heat-seeking missiles and guns. It became apparent that even an aircraft of the Vulcan's size can, if flown skilfully and aggressively, deny 'gun-kill' parameters to a fighter following in close trail. The realisation of this fact came as a surprise to the RAF detachment, the Vulcan crews themselves and, most particularly, to the aggressors."[850]

Red Flag, however, also contributed to a growing awareness of the inadequacies of V-Force ECM. Wing AEO Julian Grenfell, on returning from Red Flag, spelt out the problems in a negative report for presentation at Strike Command HQ. He soon encountered pressure from senior officers attempting to dissuade him from tabling his findings. There was, however, no escaping reality. At high level, the three Red Shrimps represented considerable brute force jamming power, but at 100 ft "all you did was warm up the grass directly under the aircraft".[851]

Grenfell was blessed with considerable foresight. In 1970, whilst with the NEAF in Cyprus, he sent a paper to headquarters, arguing that Strike Command should 'strap' a Westinghouse AN/ALQ 101-8 ECM pod to a Vulcan for testing:

> "My reasoning was that the Vulcan's ECM was so poor that, in the event of an urgent need to upgrade Vulcan ECM, the HQ would have to use an ECM pod and, thereby, would understand the issues and problems involved in so doing. My paper was rejected out of hand! Fast forward to 1982 and what happened? The HQ Strike Command strapped on the AN/ALQ 101-10 pod to the Vulcans of Operation Black Buck."[852]

With the handover to Polaris and following the phase-out of Blue Steel, the Vulcan bomber force eventually declined to 48, four squadrons (32 aircraft) in the UK and 16 in Cyprus.[853] The remaining V-bombers were largely unchanged: there were no major upgrades, in contrast to the B-52. V-bomber pilot Philip Goodall had been seconded to the USAF and SAC. On returning to the UK he reported on the contrast between British policy regarding the Vulcan and American updating of the B-52 fleet – which gave positive results over Vietnam: "Certainly, modifications to the G and H models is continuing to ensure better penetration and survivability in the more demanding primary role."[854] Fortunately, V-Force aircrew were masters at getting the most from elderly aircraft and antiquated systems, as we have already seen.

GOING EAST

When V-bombers went east, to the Middle East or Far East, their trips were known as Lone Rangers. These flights underlined V-Force nuclear and conventional roles in support of CENTO and SEATO (Southeast Asia Treaty Organization). There were also longer detachments to bases such as Singapore. Furthermore, the Akrotiri Bomber Wing operated for five years, from 1969 until the 1974 Turkish invasion of Cyprus.

Lone Rangers reflected the very different political maps of the 1960s and 1970s. Low-level training, for example, included detachment to Luqa, Malta, or El Adem, to fly routes over

Gathering in the sun: Vulcans pictured at Luqa. (Andy Leitch Collection)

pre-Gaddafi Libya.[855] When V-bombers practised conventional bombing over the desert, the locals benefitted. Scrap metal dealers took risks to scavenge on the range. They were prepared to begin the search for debris even before the bombing had finished. There were also benefits when bombing practice involved sea targets. This provided a windfall for local fishermen, who would rush in to scoop up thousands of dead or stunned fish.

Iran was another V-Force destination. Peter West was the AEO in 12 Squadron commander Bob Tanner's crew:

> "My time with Bob included a fabulous trip to Iran, for a display. The Shah was so impressed that Bob was taken up for an introduction to the Peacock Throne. Bob had flown so low that it looked like we were taxiing without wheels!"[856]

V-bomber operations in Far East climatic conditions had been tested during the Malayan Emergency of the 1950s, with Valiants of 214 Squadron mobilised to Singapore in Exercise Profiteer. Detachments were hosted at Royal Australian Air Force base Butterworth. According to Roy Brocklebank, Far East readiness states were RS20 and RS10: "Due to the extreme heat and humidity, holding RS05 with the door closed and, on the Victor 1/1A, no air-ventilated suits, would not have been practicable. Crews outside, at RS10, in the shade and continuously hydrated, was more realistic." In 1959–1960, three Vulcan squadrons participated in Profiteer, testing the rapid reinforcement of the Far East Air Force. Vulcans visiting Butterworth on detachment continued their training sorties. Brocklebank recalled a fighter affiliation of unusual character: "We were in a turning fight with a Javelin. Nothing we did could shake him off our tail, five miles at seven o'clock." The fighter was on Red Steer and Brocklebank had him on H2S, in Fishpool mode. "Eventually, Bob Tanner said to knock it off; he was at 25,000 ft and we were still climbing through 48,000 ft."[857]

During the 1963–66 Indonesian Confrontation, V-bombers threatened the elimination of Indonesian air-strike capability. Initially, the detachment consisted of Victor Mk 1As. The Vulcan Mk 2s of the Coningsby Wing took over from September 1964. The situation deteriorated and the operational generation of both Victors and Vulcans began, with aircraft in the region bombed-up and dispersed. Crews were briefed on targets and issued with go-bags and sidearms. The crisis passed, the Victors returned to the UK and, eventually, the V-bomber detachments returned to Britain in August 1966.[858]

When mobilised for possible raids over Indonesia during the Confrontation, the Vulcans faced a strange mix of threats. Nav/radar John Weller:

> "There was danger from the guns and they were thought to have ZSU 23-4s protecting Jakarta – a nightmare, as discovered by the Americans over North Vietnam. The capital also had some Soviet SAMs. The Indonesian air force had P-51 Mustangs that could outfly us at low level!"[859]

Lone Rangers and detachments in the CENTO/SEATO regions reflected the underlying nuclear-strike role. Nuclear weapons were stored at Singapore. There were 48 Red Beard tactical weapons at Tengah (where they stayed until 1970). The planners had considered their eventual replacement with WE.177.[860] By 1973, however, Tengah had transferred to the Singapore Air Force. John Huggins remembered his targets in the Far East: "They included

Hot and humid: 101 Squadron on detachment at RAF Tengah, Singapore, in 1970. The turquoise tube fed cold air to the cabin whilst on the ground. (Anthony Wright)

the valley passes in Burma. Our job was to stop Chinese armies entering Burma, to invade India."[861]

Robin Woolven recalled some memorable CENTO air exercises over Greece, Turkey, Iran and Pakistan. On detachment from Cyprus during the early 1960s, he was in a low-level Canberra B.16, listening to a high-level attack on Karachi by a V-Force aircraft: "We had a laugh when a Pakistani fighter controller came on the air and moaned that a Vulcan was flying too high and too fast – 'the pilot should slow down!'"[862]

Other long-range 'playmates' included Australian Mirages. Dave Beane was an AEO with 10 Squadron at Cottesmore: "We flew against the Mirages over Darwin. They didn't do so well. Our Victors were more manoeuvrable than the fighters when at height. However, that was before the days of really sophisticated air-to-air missiles."[863]

BELIEF IN DETERRENCE

Flying V-bombers on the nuclear frontline meant buying into a wartime mentality during peacetime. It meant training to fight a war in the hope of never having to do so. Why start a war with no winners? The deeper issues surrounding deterrence were pushed aside by young men with other priorities. Vulcan captain John Huggins recalled the general lack of education about the Cold War:

"No-one talked to us about nuclear war or the theory of deterrence. Towering over everything was the concept of MAD, or mutually assured destruction. We knew a deterrent works only when an enemy believes the threat is real. This is the way to keep the peace. The Russians had to believe we could do it and, furthermore, were fully prepared to do it."[864]

When Robin Woolven joined 617 Squadron and its Blue Steel-armed Vulcans in 1964, he had no issues with his new role:

"I recall no arguments about the ethics or righteousness of our role on the nuclear frontline. Of course, it was over 50 years ago – that's the way the world was at that time. We lived through the Cold War and that's what we trained for."[865]

Nav/radar Alan McLoughlin was free of doubt: "I felt the same way as everyone else. I was entirely sold on the idea of deterrence. To my knowledge, no-one raised doubts."[866]

Vulcan AEO Barry Masefield had spent years flying maritime patrols and was a hardened Cold War warrior:

"Some people got quite excited about deterrence and the 'bucket of sunshine' in the Vulcan's bomb bay. This was not the case with me. I had been Cold War flying since 1965, locating Soviet surface vessels and submarines. Their behaviour was quite aggressive at times but, in my heart of hearts, I never thought deterrence would fail."[867]

However, no-one could be *absolutely* sure a war sortie would never happen – perhaps accidentally. Air Commodore Edward Jarron, a former Vulcan pilot, has another perspective on this issue:

"… I dispute the idea that most crews believed it would never happen. All the crews I knew had had conversations that faced up to the fact that we were training for a nuclear strike. However, we judged that we were in the business of deterring nuclear attacks against us. Although the likelihood of being scrambled on a war mission was low, that's quite different from convincing yourself that it will never happen. A credible deterrent requires everyone in the command chain, including the crews who will fly the missions, to sign up to the idea that they could be required to carry out a nuclear attack."[868]

Certainly, the retaliatory threat was real enough, as were the targets in Victor and Vulcan captain John Laycock's target folders:

"Target study was central to our lives and the capitals of the Baltic States were on the list. Tallinn was my primary target for a while. Archangel was another and Odesa a third. I had many targets over the years. I would have dropped the weapon – absolutely!"[869]

Nuclear deterrence (so far, at least) has an impeccable record. Vulcan co-pilot Keith Mans remains convinced:

"The history of warfare is not that complicated … most conflicts arise from misinterpretation of an opponent's intentions. We were successful in the Falklands, but only after we failed to deter Argentina. We also failed in Gulf War 1, by allowing Saddam to misinterpret the depth of our commitment to Kuwait. Deterrence relies on convincing the other side that you have both the commitment and resolve to respond. I've always thought that a central element of deterrence is the ability to signal clearly to the enemy the seriousness of your intentions. If you deploy and demonstrate effectively, deterrence can work in both conventional and nuclear environments. In contrast, any politician declaring a commitment *not* to retaliate undermines deterrence."[870]

Victor K Mk 1A tankers required replacement and the decision was taken to withdraw the Victor Mk 2s as bombers and convert these more powerful aircraft for the tanker role. With the disbandment of 100 and 139 Victor Squadrons on 30 September and 31 December 1968 respectively, the MBF became an all-Vulcan force. In 1969, work began to convert some Blue Steel Vulcans to the freefall role. The stand-off bomb was withdrawn from service.[871] During the mid-1970s, 'interim' arrangements were developed for the dispersal of 56 Vulcans, reflecting SACEUR's policy of a base loading of six strike aircraft. The Vulcans, at Scampton and Waddington, would be dispersed across ten airfields in an emergency.[872]

'Nuclear signalling', an important issue, does much to explain the longevity of the Vulcan Force following the handover to Polaris. Edward Jarron was Chief of Special Weapons at Supreme Headquarters, Allied Powers Europe (SHAPE) in the early 1990s:

> "The V-Force had a conventional-attack role and a tactical nuclear-deterrent role. Its most significant contribution, post-Polaris, was its visibility, in contrast to the submarines. This gave it an important nuclear-signalling role. In the world of flexible response, rather than tripwire, it was another means of keeping the enemy guessing."[873]

The V-Force preoccupation with excellence continued following the Polaris handover. Peter Moore joined 44 (Rhodesia) Squadron just as QRA ended and he progressed to command status:

> "… I arrived as a first tour co-pilot in July 1969, was selected for the intermediate co-pilot's course (a precursor to captaincy that enabled you to fly in the left-hand seat with a suitably-qualified captain), started my captain's course in April 1971, having been held back from an earlier course to fly in what was the winning crew for the 1971 STC Bombing Competition, and returned to 44 Squadron as a captain in July 1971. My tour ended in 1973 with a posting to Central Flying School."[874]

Target study remained a major focus for Vulcan crews post-QRA but, perhaps, the atmosphere became a little more relaxed with the strategic baton passing to the submarines. If so, this didn't last very long. It developed a renewed intensity with the arrival of TACEVAL (Tactical Evaluation) in 1970, as recalled by Peter Moore:

> "In my time as captain – 1971 to 1973 – we studied hard and were thoroughly tested on all aspects of the mission. As a captain, one of my targets was Zhukovsky Airport, near Moscow. Around 1996 I was sent to Russia by Marshall Aerospace to evaluate the Ilyushin 103 light trainer. Ilyushin's research centre was at Zhukovsky. On taxiing out with my Russian interpreter alongside, I began talking to him about the airfield layout. He was surprised at my apparent knowledge and deeply amused when I told him the origin of much of my information. After landing, we went up to the designer's office. My interpreter relayed my knowledge of Zhukovsky and the designer reached into his drawer to bring out a bottle of vodka. A couple of bear-hugs later, we started work on the bottle, followed by another and then half of another – shared between five or six people, including my driver for the return to Moscow!"

Later life occasionally threw surprises for former V-bomber aircrew. Vulcan captain Jon Tye was on holiday with his wife in Thailand when they decided to take a boat trip. During the cruise, he was engaged in conversation by a young blonde Russian eager to practise her English:

> "I asked her where she was from and she named one of my primary targets. This was such a shock that I couldn't talk to her anymore. Our targets were always barracks and rail centres. They never included pretty young blondes."[875]

Jon Tye was a Vulcan display pilot for five years, completing 69 displays. He had made a happy discovery: the Vulcan was very good at making a lot of noise and turning very tightly: "If you put the Vulcan in a spiral climb and climbed at 105 kts, which it would happily do, it would make an *immense* amount of noise for a long time!"

The Mick and Micky Finns of the QRA era were succeeded by the annual four-day no-notice TACEVAL. This did not require the dispersal of aircraft, although dispersal continued to be practised within four-day squadron-based exercises. Roger Dunsford flew Vulcans during the 1973–84 period, with three squadrons: 35, 617 and, finally, 44. He missed the "joys" of QRA but remembers TACEVAL call-outs in the middle of the night, "to exercise the squadron's capability to go through the process of preparation and launch of a full nuclear strike …"[876]

Intense preparations for a retaliatory attack on Kiev were imprinted on Roger Dunsford's mind:

> "… after the fall of the USSR I was part of an official RAF visit to Kiev, as guests of the newly-formed Ukrainian air force. We were in a coach when, on rounding a corner of a city centre block, I suddenly recognised the building in front of me from a photo I had studied many years before. Naturally, I kept my mouth shut as senior Ukrainian air force officers cordially greeted us. No doubt some of these same officers had been Soviet officers in this same building, when I had had reason to study the photo."

TACEVAL was a NATO programme to assess the operational capability of air units assigned to SACEUR but, in the UK case, it was decided to set up a British TACEVAL team at Strike Command Headquarters. TACEVAL exercises in the UK were attended by NATO observers. There were two parts to a TACEVAL assessment. Part 1 was a no-notice evaluation lasting around 12 hours, with the assessment team usually arriving in the early hours of the morning. Guardroom personnel were told to do nothing until all was ready. They were then ordered to sound the alert siren. Part 1 required the station to generate weapon systems within specified time periods. This was followed by Part 2, with tests of the ability to cope with a wide range of issues, including intruders, accidents, demonstrations, battle damage, deployments and aid to the civil power. Part 2 could last three or four days. Failure to meet standards would result in a prompt repeat of the exercise.[877]

On the security front, much had changed since the days of a man, a dog and a revolver. New measures to protect aircraft and facilities were tested by attack teams, provided by the army, including the SAS.

In the post-QRA era, aircraft states remained the key issue on every V-Force station. Tony Smith was a Vulcan crew chief with IX Squadron at RAF Waddington from 1976 to 1982. Bomber/Strike Command crew chiefs always had a special status – especially on the V-Force:

"Waddington was a brilliant station. The station commander, Eric Macey (later, Air Vice-Marshal) was magic. He knew virtually everyone by first name. The squadron had to have a least two aircraft on state (armed, at RS15 and signed over to the aircrew) at the end of every day. The working day didn't finish until that fact could be reported. We did a fair amount of servicing on line but major work was tackled in the hangar by the General Servicing Flight. Damp was the enemy of aircraft outside, particularly the equipment in the nosewheel bay. We had the habit of removing some of the boxes to the crew room, to keep them warm. We were always careful to remove the chaff and flare dispensers from an aircraft coming offline. If they fired inadvertently, there would be big problems." [878]

One thing that didn't change over the years was the bone-numbing cold of eastern England's winter months:

"We got used to it. We had all the winter gear and there were some creature comforts. We could get away for a warm-up break in the heated line hut. We even had a winter rum ration – tots for those working outside on the night shift. Ice and snow were the big challenges, given the Vulcan's huge wing area. Five or six inches of snow on that delta wing imposed a very heavy load. It was risky to climb up and attempt to brush it off. We tried using a rope to 'skid' the snow off the wing, but without much success. We had very heavy snowfalls and we couldn't brush it off fast enough."

Even post-QRA, the number of Vulcans available was central to SACEUR's plans, to the degree that aircraft were recalled if required to maintain strength. The daily briefing at Bomber Command Headquarters included a review of force location. Roy Brocklebank recalls an occasion when his crew's bombing exercise at El Adem was cancelled due to the AOC-in-C's concern over V-bomber numbers in the UK. Peter Moore remembers being ordered back from Labrador:

"I was recalled from Goose Bay one evening, which was most unusual because we never flew when daylight was failing at the Goose – survival options were limited enough without adding darkness. The recall codewords were 'White Cliffs', but I cannot remember if that was for operations or if it could be used for practice. We were just told by the wing commander CO to get our arses into the air ASAP."[879]

Most politicians and military chiefs, having recognised Polaris as a secure deterrent solution with a virtually guaranteed strike outcome, were content for the

Bone-numbing cold: a Vulcan in the snow at Waddington. (Andy Leitch Collection)

In the Arctic: 50 Squadron Vulcans on detachment at the Royal Norwegian Air Force base at Bodø, having flown in for Exercise Teamwork, 1980. (Anthony Wright)

post-1969 V-Force to continue as a secondary and usefully visible means of delivery. Vulcans excelled at nuclear signalling, which required no costly upgrades of war-fighting performance. Noisy public displays of the Vulcan were impressive and cost next to nothing. The background to these shrewd, pragmatic policies often involved unpalatable choices and sensitive decisions and, so, received little public profile. One obvious example is the low-key modification of Blue Steel Vulcans, restoring their freefall role post-Polaris handover.

The Vulcan threat to the Soviet Union remained in being until the early 1980s and was credible in a night/IMC attack scenario. Tim McLelland summed up V-Force positioning post-1969:

> "…with their arsenal of WE.177s, the Vulcan Force presented the East with a formidable presence. It was to assume a pseudo–tactical role that fitted neatly between the navy's Polaris long-range strike missiles and RAF Germany's tactical-strike Buccaneers (later replaced by Phantoms and Jaguars)."[880]

In 1999, Air Vice-Marshal Nigel Baldwin posed questions relating to V-Force capability and credibility: "Did the V-Force do the *right* training? Could we have done it?" He attempted an answer:

> "I suppose that all training turns out to be flawed to some degree when the system is actually put to the test. Operational experience would certainly have revealed that some of our techniques could have been improved – except, of course, that in World War 3 it would have been a one-shot system. My own view, given reinforcement by our experience on the night Red Flag and by subsequent night training, is that our training was essentially right and, remembering all the peacetime constraints, that we did about the right amount of it. We had both *quality* and *quantity* enough to ensure that a proportion of us *would* have been able to reach our targets … especially if we had been launched at night or in poor visibility by day."[881]

John Reeve gave a concise view: "I think we were in with a chance, but I would have been happier carrying half a dozen WE.177s rather than going through all that just to drop one."

With hindsight, Roy Brocklebank questioned whether the strict policy of isolating crews from sensitive and difficult issues was the best course:

"In retrospect, I think the absolute secrecy, with crews planning in isolation, created a level of amateurism. As targeting officer I knew the plans but as a second tourist I was relatively inexperienced – experience dilution was an on-going problem. At that time, the majority of aircrew only served to age 38 and there was little enthusiasm for the old to impart wisdom to youth or for youth to receive it."[882]

V-Force aircrew did their best with ground alert and they were supported by many measures to increase their chances of surviving a war scramble, with initiatives such as the provision of ORPs, Telescramble and simultaneous engine start. Yet, as we have seen, the many measures taken to improve scramble times contrast with failures to secure other improvements, achievable with relative ease and at modest cost. There was, of course, the command level failure to approve and steer through a larger QRA force. Certainly, the deployment of QRA aircraft could have been more creative. An atmosphere of competitive penny-pinching prevailed. Even the basics – sufficient RAF police to guard aircraft and enough telephones for rapid call-out – provoked heated debate and much hand-wringing. Funds should have been found to provide aircrew accommodation next to aircraft and to lay on reliable motor transport. V-bomber bases varied enormously in layout and facilities, but these differences were allowed to have an undue and disproportionate influence on QRA and alert and readiness.

There is strong oral evidence to show that V-Force crew classification did much to encourage the natural desire to excel in the various aircrew disciplines. Bombing and navigation competitions were another positive stimulus. These factors helped to offset negative pressures on morale, including resistance to a V-Force posting amongst those wanting fighters, restrictions on personal freedoms (freedoms taken for granted in a society at peace), the onerous alert and readiness regime and failures to provide the accommodation and other facilities commensurate with V-Force significance. Yet, in a very British way, these shortcomings were usually set aside, as part and parcel of service life.

British humour was in evidence when RAF Germany formally stood down the nuclear role of its Tornado squadrons on 31 March 1998. The officers of RAF Laarbruch held a dinner to mark the occasion. The menu included such delights a 'radiation plaice', 'sunshine steak' and 'meltdown moment'. Each diner was issued with a single anti-flash eyepatch.

22

SHOULD DETERRENCE FAIL ...

> *One can always devise surprise attack scenarios destroying much of the force on the ground. Yet Cold War responses were shaped by intelligence and the appreciation of intentions during periods of escalating tension. It was a matter for the leadership to react to intelligence and respond with an appropriate readiness state.*
>
> Keith Mans, Vulcan co-pilot

THE CLIFF EDGE

This is a brief glimpse of the end of the world as we know it, prepared with the help of former aircrew who contributed so much to this book (including Norman Bonnor, Roy Brocklebank, David Dinmore, John Huggins, Paddy Langdown and Dr Robin Woolven). Its purpose is to explain how a V-Force war sortie might have unfolded, had the order to scramble been given. It is not an attempt at alternative history but, rather, an outline offering operational details never before published for a wide audience. This overview concerns a retaliatory war flight flown c.1967. The context is an escalating crisis (in contrast to a 'bolt from the blue' attack), assuming sufficient strategic warning to allow maximum generation of aircraft, their dispersal and subsequent regeneration. This account makes some logical assumptions (as indicated in the text) where there is a lack of documentary evidence.

It soon became obvious that something very serious was going on. Training stopped as the crisis deepened. No-one now joked about the bucket of sunshine. There was no inclination to repeat past advice about what to do after a war sortie: "Continue flying east, bale out and settle down with a nice, warm Mongolian woman." The V-bombers were generated and loaded with live weapons. This was masked by declaring Exercise Mick, requiring force-wide generation of the maximum number of aircraft. Some bombers immediately flew to dispersal airfields – an unobtrusive trickle dispersal which broke a rigid taboo: flight over UK soil with a viable nuclear weapon. As the outbreak of war drew closer, AOC-in-C Bomber Command obtained political authorisation for Alert Condition 1, recognising an imminent missile threat to his airfields. The entire generated force split into small flights and dispersed. Work began, round-the-clock, to regenerate the bombers to combat status. Almost all available V-Force crews were involved in this maximum effort; even the 'new boys', yet to achieve full combat status, were told to take their place on the frontline.

ULTRA GROUND ALERT

Under Alert Condition 1 (which had been available to the AOC-in-C since 1961 but never called in peacetime – i.e. in the absence of imminent threat of war), flight alert (priority) targets were covered 24/7 by 24 dispersed aircraft, cockpit-manned by the most experienced crews. It is assumed they targeted Moscow and Leningrad exclusively. This was Bomber Command's near maximum retaliatory threat under ground alert. Indeed, this force of 24 bombers rapidly increased to 30, the absolute limit.

Whilst this author found no documentary evidence setting out detailed operational plans for implementing Alert Condition 1, such plans certainly existed and some inferences may be drawn with confidence: the planners would expect minimum warning – a low-trajectory IRBM strike on MBF airfields, giving a warning of just 3½ to 4½ minutes, plus up to two minutes extra, allowing for the spread of missile impact times. Secondly, aircraft at 24/7 cockpit readiness and with flight alert targets were dispersed across those airfields in the north and west receiving slightly more warning due to their geographical location. The 24/7 RS05 detachments ranged from four at Ballykelly, Northern Ireland, to a Somerset dispersal with just one flight alert-targeted bomber. Thirdly, up to 60 of the most experienced crews were allocated to the 30 24/7 RS05 bombers. These crews had a deep understanding of Moscow and Leningrad as targets – as the Soviet Union's two biggest cities had been primary QRA targets for over five years. Fourthly, the 24/7 RS05 bombers included Blue Steel missile carriers with desired ground zeros across Greater Moscow. Any minor shortfall in double crew availability could be met by arranging for, say, two out of three aircraft of a dispersed 24/7 flight to be cockpit-manned round the clock.

The crews of the 30 flight-alert RS05 bombers waited, all checks complete and poised for engine start/RS02 – wheels rolling. At this time, each of the 11 main force squadrons had around 10 crews available – 110 in total (most had an establishment of 11 crews, but this usually included one *ab initio* non-operational crew). Given around 60 crews required for 24/7 RS05 aircraft with flight-alert targets, this left around 50 crews available to single-crew all remaining bombers – dispersed, regenerated and held at RS07, with crews resting and sleeping next to the aircraft. The single-crewed bombers were held at RS05 during the 03.00-08.00 period, with all checks completed up to engine start. In a few cases, once again, this was enhanced by manning aircraft at the front of the queue round-the-clock, so increasing the total number of bombers at 24/7 RS05 to just over 30. Most of the aircraft had Moscow and Leningrad as targets, but a few had Kiev and other big cities, to spread the core retaliatory threat. All available bombers were at cockpit readiness, primed for engine start and instant response, during the early morning 'stand to' period.

The planners expected extremely heavy casualties in and around the airfields. In these circumstances, the mass targeting of Moscow and Leningrad maximised the deterrent threat of unacceptable damage, even without American participation. The Alert Condition 1 plans were designed to achieve some level of increase in war scramble survivors and, in turn, the number of weapons detonating on the enemy's most important countervalue assets.

Recognising the advantages of geography, it is assumed that the 30 24/7 cockpit-manned aircraft were distributed across 12 airfields:

Group 1	Ballykelly, Northern Ireland – four aircraft, eight crews.	
	St Mawgan, Cornwall – four aircraft, eight crews.	
	Brawdy, Pembrokeshire – four aircraft, eight crews.	
Group 2	Lossiemouth, Moray – three aircraft, six crews.	
	Machrihanish, Argyll – three aircraft, six crews.	
	Valley, Anglesey – three aircraft, six crews.	
Group 3	Leuchars, Fife – two aircraft, four crews.	
	Prestwick, South Ayrshire – two aircraft, four crews.	
	Llanbedr, Gwynedd – two aircraft, four crews.	
	Pershore, Worcestershire – one aircraft, two crews.	
	Boscombe Down, Wiltshire – one aircraft, two crews.	
	Yeovilton, Somerset – one aircraft, two crews.	

DISPERSED AND READY

War began with two days of conventional fighting in Western Europe. Alert Condition 1 dispersal was triggered by the codeword 'Prometheus'. A nav/radar remembers: "Crews flew to their dispersal airfields with weapons safe and radios off." This put them beyond reach of any 'conflicting messages'. There were conventional raids on Allied airfields in Western Europe, but none on UK bases.

Once inside the dispersed bombers, crews had a direct Telescramble connection to the bomber controller at Headquarters, High Wycombe. The go-bag was opened, to get the authentication envelopes. The folder with the JARIC low-level route could be left in the bag. The war SOP was handed to the AEO. The plotter opened the main route pack and got out his chart and the appropriate pre-prepared flight plan. He noted the first route heading, ready to pass to the pilots once airborne. Those aircraft with deep targets had been fitted with bomb-bay fuel tanks. With all checks complete, RS05 crews were left with their thoughts and the eerie 'confidence beep' on the Telescramble line. A nav/plotter in a 617 Squadron Vulcan was on the operational readiness platform at Lossiemouth. Underneath was a 1.1-mt Blue Steel powered bomb. From this Scottish airfield, he had been expecting to head north for a Kola target. Instead, he was handed a familiar QRA target – Moscow. The regeneration progressed well and in good time, for a Blue Steel system. An Argosy transport flew in the ground team from Scampton and they put pre-positioned equipment to good use.

One Vulcan captain reported to Waddington Ops, to check in. Once allocated his ALN he next visited the vault, in the ops block, to receive the target bag; the nav/radar received the weapon arming key. When the order came to disperse, this captain knew it was for real: "No aircraft ever flew with live nukes over the UK; the flight to the dispersal was a first."

When the dispersal order came, another Vulcan pilot had no doubt about the gravity of the situation. His 35 Squadron bomber now sat on the ORP at a dispersal in Scotland:

> "We prepared ourselves and our families for the worst. We had time to organise accommodation for our wives and children with relatives in rural areas or in the remotest locations we could find – and said our goodbyes. We had no doubt that our own chances of survival, if an attack on the UK was launched, were marginal. To be frank, we didn't rate our families' chances much higher either, but we had to do our best."

SCRAMBLE!

Just after 08.00 UK time the world fell off a cliff – with the order for RS02 (start engines and taxi), then:

> "Attention! Attention! This is the bomber controller for Bomblist Delta. Scramble! Authentication Echo Two Bravo E Hour 08.40 Zulu. For Bomblist Delta. Scramble! Authentication Echo Two Bravo E Hour 08.40 Zulu. For Bomblist Delta. Scramble! Authentication Echo Two Bravo E Hour 08.40 Zulu. For Bomblist Delta. Bomber controller out."

AEOs wrote down the message. Nav/radars verified correct format and checked authentication against the code in the SCRAM envelope. The code was authenticated and passed to the nav/plotter, who verified a valid message and authentication. A nav/radar recalled: "There wasn't a second to spare. The captain took off, with aircraft following in ten–15 seconds, rather than the 30 seconds in peacetime exercises."

The scramble message was not acknowledged:

> "… radio and radar use was minimised. There were to be no VHF/UHF or HF transmissions. All ECM was on standby. TACAN (tactical air navigation system) was on receive only. H2S was on sector scan only – as long as it took to get a radar fix. Doppler radar was on, as was the Radar Altimeter 6 and Radio Altimeter 7. TFR was on standby. The IFF was set for Area A and would be switched off on entering Area B."

One Victor nav/radar found he had plenty to do, as his aircraft carried Blue Steel: "After the scramble take-off, Blue Steel crews needed to start up and align the missile's inertial navigation system (INS), involving the NBS, the ground position indicator (GPI Mk 6) and other systems."

A Blue Steel Vulcan nav/plotter suddenly wished he'd made a final toilet visit. This soon went out of his mind as the bomber left the ORP. He and his crew continued to call out checks:

> "… we were well aware that we had left our families back at home – all within a few miles of obvious targets for the Soviets – to cope by themselves. I must admit I never briefed my wife, with (then) two small children, on anything approaching a survival plan."

The aircraft responded to rapid start. Four Olympus 301s burst into life and the bomber moved forward onto the runway, leading a flight of four. They turned onto their headings and climbed at full power to their briefed transit heights.

A fortunate few bombers escaped the wave of missiles now striking V-Force airfields. One Vulcan pilot remembered how his

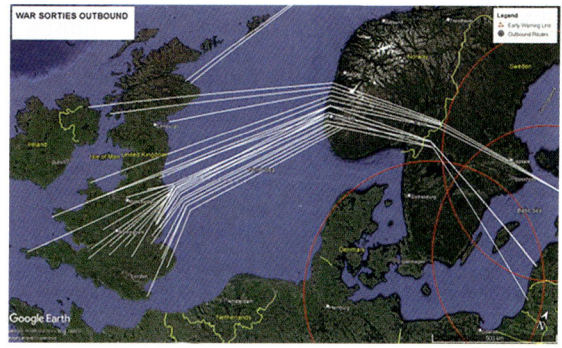

Routes to retaliation: across the North Sea, Norway and Sweden, with the enemy coast ahead. The arcs show Soviet radar cover. (Roy Brocklebank)

aircraft entered a steep climbing turn to port, with the blackout screens down to protect from flash. Within seconds the glare from a detonating weapon framed the screens. Several weapons detonated in his area. He recalled: "Everyone settled in, now on 100% oxygen." No-one said much.

Only ten V-bombers survived low-trajectory IRBM strikes on the airfields (all but two from the group of just over 30 24/7 cockpit-manned; almost all were first in the queue for take-off). The survivors reached the coast and began their North Sea crossing. This small group carried a warload totalling 7.1 mt. All but one aircraft had desired ground zeros in Moscow and Leningrad. Seventy V-bombers had been destroyed on the ground or in the air around their bases. More would have survived but they fell victim to reflected shock waves, as they tried to escape by flying close to the ground.

The survivors left behind an already ravaged country. They flew near parallel tracks to 5 degrees East, then parallel tracks towards 8 degrees East – the Go/No-Go line. The crews listened out for POSREL – positive release – the order to cross the Go/No-Go line and proceed with the retaliatory attack. The AEOs monitored command and group operational HF frequencies. VHF and UHF radios were tuned to briefed frequencies. Absolute radio silence was observed. Automatic direction-finders (ADF) were tuned to the BBC Light Programme.

Then it came, over the ADF: *"This is a special announcement. Plan A is now in force. D6F."* POSREL was received and the plan was SIOP (general war). The message was transmitted by high power HF transmitters over four frequencies, by the Fighter Command UHF forward relay transmitters and the BBC Wartime Broadcasting Service (the BBC Light Programme frequency). When POSREL was received, nav/radars opened their envelopes and verified the code, which was then checked by other crew members. As one Vulcan captain commented: "It was irrevocable … Armageddon was inevitable."

The route out was north-east and the Norwegian coast was the next navigational event. The outbound route was designed to avoid Central Europe's dense air defence environment. Once again, anti-flash screens were set up, cockpit windows were covered, as was the bomb-aimer's window. The curtains behind the pilots' seats and into the bomb-aimer's compartment were secured. The AEOs set up the ECM: Blue Saga to monitor S- and X-Band radars and the Red Steer tail-warner. The X-Band jammer was on auto-receive, ready to fire IR and RBW automatically if a threat was detected.

In the freefall aircraft, nav/radars set the target offsets on the CU 585 and the external offset box. A Vulcan nav/radar described the two offsets: "one well short of the target and outside the scope of any defensive jammers the enemy might deploy. The other offset was close to the target, to minimise compass errors." By placing the radar markers on the offset, the navigation system would be 'offset' to direct the aircraft to the target.

Navigators working hard in the four Blue Steel survivors focused on maintaining the briefed track. As the bombers reached the top of the descent point, they began a 5,000 ft per minute descent. A Vulcan pilot explained:

> "We needed to descend as quickly as possible to low level, to get under the radar. It didn't matter what the weather was like, we just had to get down to less than 250 ft and rely on the TFR, the radio altimeter and the nav/plotter to keep us below the radar and on course."

On crossing the boundary leaving Norway, the freefall bombers completed Position X checks – checking the weapon and enabling emergency safe release. Another Vulcan pilot recalled the need for adherence to strict emission controls, which would "hopefully hide us from the Soviet air defence system until we penetrated their long-range early warning line, based on the Tall King radar, with a range of about 250 miles."

A number of bombers went lower in the area of Linköping. The survivors flew over Sweden without incident at around 1,000–2,000 ft and began the Baltic crossing at ultra-low level – 200 ft–300 ft or lower. There was an opportunity for a final visual or radar update on Öland or the Gotland Islands, scanning backwards, towards the west. The islands screened their approach towards Lithuania and Latvia and prolonged the time before entering Soviet airspace. As they sped towards their penetration points, the last late runners in a wave of ICBMs and tactical weapons were still detonating on Russian targets, blinding more Soviet fighter pilots and degrading enemy air defence command and control systems. V-bomber crews switched off cabin ventilation and continued on 100% oxygen, to avoid breathing contaminated air. Eyepatches were worn. A nav/radar added: "Position Y checks were completed immediately prior to penetration of Soviet airspace. Thereafter, the weapon could be released in an armed (live) state and a nuclear yield ensue."

Soviet radar picket ships were the enemy's first line of defence in the Baltic, providing a forward early warning line. One Vulcan captain hoped to detect their emissions and "aim for the gaps". He continued: "We would not jam them as we might give away more by active jamming than gained by silence." The threats included forward-deployed fighters controlled by Bar Lock ground radars, with a low-level range of around 30 miles. The most serious fighter threat was the two-seat Firebar. The attackers made no attempt to jam Bar Lock as, in itself, it posed no threat, but crews were ready to frustrate any attacking Soviet fighter by breaking lock and deploying chaff and flares.

One nav/radar's crew had planned their low-level penetration at 325 kts, "but aircraft could cruise at up to 375 kts to make up time, perhaps necessary following evasive action". In another Vulcan, the captain took his bomber down to 150 ft at 350 kts for the crossing. The co-pilot recalled: "TFR became my main focus of attention … occasional changes of heading from the nav/plotter came through, but we continued almost due east for quite some time." The AEO repeatedly warned them that they had been detected by radar, "but the contacts lasted only a few seconds and there seemed no need to take evasive action".

If the AEO or co-pilot heard a radar searching on Blue Saga, they tried to identify the signature of the threat. Everyone was tensed for evasive action as the AEO watched Red Steer, to see if a fighter had slipped into the stern arc. If a fighter was closing, the AEO switched to narrow sector at the five-mile point, which meant he could see a missile launch. A nav/radar explained:

> "As soon as the missile was seen, the AEO would fire both IRD and RBW, as the X-Band radar tried to break missile lock. The pilot throttled back, to reduce the aircraft's IR signature, executed a rapid pull-up to 1,000–1,500 ft, rolled 90 degrees left or right (depending on the AEO's call) and rapidly dropped low again before making another 90-degree turn, back to parallel track."

The small force of surviving bombers squeezed through gaps in the SAM defences. The SA-2 sites were ten to 15 miles apart; these weapons were unable to engage at ultra-low level, but the low-level-capable SA-3, positioned as 'gap-fillers', were far more dangerous. As a nav/radar commented: "It was just hoped that the general confusion would help most of the bombers slip through." More importantly, the Baltic coastal defences were still reeling from a torrent of American missile strikes and air-dropped tactical weapons from British Canberras and Buccaneers. Two V-bombers were lost crossing the coast, leaving eight to proceed to their targets.

ATTACKING THE TARGETS

Once through the coastal belt, the main risk was from long-endurance area defence fighters. A Vulcan nav/plotter said his aircraft was flying well below safety height: "Both the pilots and rear crew were using JARIC's specially prepared large-scale topographical maps." These showed the known SAM sites and other defences. The V-bomber crews fought hard to stay alive, avoiding ground obstacles and SAM sites, attempting to break radar locks and dodging nuclear clouds. Nav/plotters gave a running commentary of the expected scene ahead from the prepared topos. Co-pilots on two aircraft lost eyes to flashes from weapon bursts. The anti-flash screens helped protect against thermal radiation – even quite low levels (such as reflections from clouds) could cause disabling burns.

Blue Steel carriers were approaching their missile release points. A Victor nav/radar described the final preparations for launch:

> "The last position fix was taken on a release point fix – the basis for defining the target position, or, rather, the airburst height above the target. I made the last corrections and the nav/plotter selected the missile INS to FREE."

The missile's bottom fin was unfolded and the locking pin on the missile release unit was withdrawn. The Blue Steel's fuel tanks were pressurised and the missile's auxiliary power unit was running. The captain and nav/plotter activated the final

Blue Steel attack: high-level and low-level stand-off bomb launches. (Norman Bonnor)

launch switch and the missile fell away. The motor fired and the weapon accelerated past the bomber's nose. The Red Snow warhead detonated on target two minutes later, with a yield of just over one megaton.

Freefall Vulcans carried a 450-kt WE.177B hydrogen bomb. When approaching the target, most freefall Vulcans increased speed to a once-only dash of 415 kts, commenced ten minutes out from DGZ. In one attacking Vulcan, the pilots heard the AEO's repeated assurances that he was detecting relatively few threats. The bomb run continued: "The final countdown began and the bomb-doors opened. The distance remaining wound down until the welcome announcement 'Bomb gone'. The bomb-doors closed as the bomber climbed and turned away, to escape the full force of the shock wave." With the detonation came the glare around the blinds and the AEO soon reported even fewer threats. One Vulcan captain always feared ramming:

> "There was a rumour that Lightning pilots had been ordered to ram Russian bombers once their Red Top missiles had gone. I believed the Soviets would do the same. It would be a small price to pay to stop a nuke on Moscow."

Nevertheless, his freefall Vulcan made a successful attack:

> "As we approached the initial point, about 25 miles out from the target, we went through the weapon checks. I had switched the bomb release safety lock to live at the Y position, aligning the gas ports to eject the weapon from the carrier."

WE.177B has been described as an engineering masterpiece but dropping it correctly required consummate skill. The speed was increased to 375 kts and the nav/radar guided the aircraft by using the offset aiming point. The bomb-doors opened automatically and the weapon was released around 450 yards from the target.

Thirty seconds after laydown, the bomb detonated with a yield close to the potential of 450 kt. "It blasted a hole 300 ft deep and half a mile wide, destroying what was left of the structures out to 15–20 miles. We were about eight miles away and at around 10,000 ft when the blast passed through us."

Another Vulcan made the dash over the target at 415 kts. The captain commented: "This speed was not based on scientific calculation but, rather, on a rough guess of how fast the Vulcan was travelling when it broke up over RAF Syerston during an air display in 1958. Not a comforting thought."

Six aircraft put their weapons on target: two on Leningrad and three on Moscow. The sixth aircraft caused another eruption across the burning rubble that was once the city of Kiev.

ATTEMPTING RECOVERY

Having made their successful attacks, the surviving crews broadcast their post-strike messages on UHF and HF. The heart of the message consisted of just two numbers: 1–3 to estimate yield and 4–7 to estimate accuracy. These numbers were encoded: 1 (full yield), 2 (partial yield), 3 (yield not observed), 4 (within 500 yards), 5 (as recollected – within 1,500 yards), 6 (as recollected – over 1,500 yards) and 7 (jettisoned away from the target area). The call sign was a trigraph associated with a block of ten ALNs and then three numbers representing the actual ALN. This was followed by the two three-letter groups representing the numbers from 1–7. All aircraft receiving a strike report were expected to log the message.

Now in the recovery phase, the AEOs switched on active jammers, the two Red Shrimps barrage jamming on S-Band (targeting Bar Lock fighter control radar and Fan Song SAM radar) and the third on L-Band. The two Blue Divers were jamming VHF radar and the bombers began dropping Window.

Once at height, anti-SAM manoeuvres were flown whilst within range of SA-2 sites. A nav/radar adds:

> "Once clear of the threat zone the aircraft would be headed straight to its designated recovery airfield, with IFF being switched back on once crossing the homebound switch-on line. Some might be in the UK but the majority were in Norway, Denmark or Turkey."

Some Vulcans were briefed to make for Norwegian airfields; one of the pilots reflected:

> "Would there be a serviceable airfield on which we could land? As unlikely as it seemed, we pressed on. We didn't hear much radio traffic, but we started our descent when the nav/plotter suggested and started calling on the airfield frequencies. To our great surprise, we eventually got an answer. It seemed that the runway had suffered in an attack with conventional bombs, but was still usable."

This Vulcan was one of four V-bombers to survive the war sortie.

SELECTED RESEARCH SOURCES AND BIBLIOGRAPHY

BOMBER COMMAND OPERATIONAL RESEARCH BRANCH MEMORANDA

AIR 14/4208, Memorandum No. 24, "The effect of tactical routeing on target coverage", March 1959
AIR 14/4283, 192, "The interception of Bomber Command day raids in Exercise Sunbeam", March 1959
AIR 14/4289, 201, "Exercise Mayflight, May 4–7 1959"
AIR 14/4286, 197, "Keeping a proportion of the Bomber Force airborne in an emergency", July 1959*
AIR 14/4287, 199, "The effect of delivery accuracy and target allocation on the effectiveness of a nuclear stockpile", c. September 1959*
AIR 14/4210, S.26 (hand-annotated revised number): "Target cover from remote dispersal bases overseas", October 1959*
AIR 14/4302, 219, "Analysis of Exercise Mayflight 3, July 1960," October 1960
AIR 14/4305, 222, "Calculations of the minimum warning times obtainable from the BMEWS, at Fylingdales Moor, of ballistic missile attacks on the United Kingdom," April 1961*
AIR 14/4306, 223, "Effectiveness of the Red Shrimp jammer in Exercises Spellbound 1, 2 and 3", April 1961
AIR 14/4211, 28, "Aircraft utilisation during a continuous airborne alert using freefall and stand-off weapons", March 1962
AIR 14/4311, 241, "The vulnerability of the MBF to ballistic missile attack", March 1962*
AIR 14/4315, 245, "Trial No. 441: An airborne alert, analysis of the aircraft servicing aspects", April 1962
AIR 14/4318, 249, "Performance of ECM in Exercise Spellbound 14", June 1962
AIR 14/4320, 251, "The use of H2S jammers in Bomber Command, January–April 1962", June 1962
AIR 14/4313, 243, "Performance of ECM in Exercise Spellbound", August 1962
AIR 14/4325, 256, "The bombing of targets protected by multiple H2S jammers", October 1962
AIR 14/4327, 258, "The Quick Reaction Alert in Bomber Command", October 1962*
AIR 14/4333, 264, "Exercise Matador 2", 8 February 1963
AIR 14/4341, 272, "Blue Steel and QRA", July 1963
AIR 14/4342, 273, "Generation of the 'Blue Steel' weapon system in Readiness exercises", August 1963
AIR 14/4343, 274, "Exercise Blank Stare II, Trial No. 457", August 1963
AIR 14/4344, 275, "The vulnerability of strike aircraft during low-level penetration of enemy defences", September 1963
AIR 14/4354, 285, "BMEWS and the QRA force", February 1964*
AIR 14/4356, 288, "A study of Blue Steel weapons system generation using computer simulation", April 1964
AIR 14/4359, 298, "Analysis of Exercise Nursemaid, April 14–15 1964", August 1964
AIR 14/4122, 301, "Air exercises and operational research in Bomber Command", August 1964
AIR 14/4368, 307, "Missile recovery from Exercise Mick at RAF Scampton", December 1964
AIR 14/4369, 308, "Missile recovery from Exercise Micky Finn 4 at RAF Scampton", February 1965
AIR 14/4374, 314, "The likely operational effectiveness of the freefall QRA force, May 1964–April 1965", 3 September 1965
AIR 14/4378, 319, "Analysis of Blue Steel System generation in Exercise Micky Finn 5", September 1965
AIR 14/4380, 321, "Analysis of Blue Steel generation in Exercise Mick, October 11 1965", December 1965
AIR 14/4385, 326, "The likely operational effectiveness of the Blue Steel QRA force, April-September 1965", March 1966
AIR 14/4387, 328, "Trial No. 512, Effectiveness of Window dispersal at low level against a fire control radar", April 1966
AIR 14/4389, 330, "Analysis of Blue Steel generation in Exercise 'Finnigan'", June 1966
AIR 14/4391, 332, "Review of Blue Steel system generation: March 1964–May 1966", July 1966
AIR 14/4401, 345, "An analysis of training for Exercise Giant Voice", October 1967

* Content of major interest

V-FORCE AIRCREW, GROUND CREW AND OTHER CONTRIBUTORS

Anscombe, Martin, Vulcan AEO, 50 Squadron
Beane, Dave, Victor/Valiant AEO, 10 Squadron, 27 Squadron, 101 Squadron
Bonnor, Air Commodore Norman, FRIN, FRAeS, Victor nav/radar, XV Squadron, 100 Squadron
Brocklebank, Squadron Leader Roy, Vulcan nav/radar, 12 Squadron; Wing targeting officer, RAF Waddington
Bussereau, Vic, Vulcan nav/radar, 35 Squadron, 50 Squadron
Cottingham, Tony, Valiant co-pilot, 49 Squadron; captain, 7 Squadron
Dennis, Nick, Vulcan co-pilot, 12 Squadron; captain, 44 (Rhodesia) Squadron

Dinmore, David, Vulcan co-pilot, 35 Squadron; captain, 44 (Rhodesia) Squadron
Doe, Cliff, Vulcan crew chief, 35 Squadron
Dunsford, Group Captain Roger, Vulcan co-pilot, 35 Squadron, 617 Squadron; captain 44 (Rhodesia) Squadron; captain and flight commander, 35 Squadron, 50 Squadron
Fazackerley, Mike, Canberra pilot and nuclear weapons historian
Flowerdew, Neil, Victor AEO, 214 Squadron
Frampton, Roger, Vulcan captain, 35 Squadron
Fulena, 'Woody', nav/radar, 35 Squadron
Fuller, Dick, Valiant co-pilot, 49 Squadron
Gaunt, Ray, air wireless fitter
Grenfell, Julian, Vulcan AEO, 27 Squadron, 617 Squadron
Hewitt, Len, Vulcan technician
Huggins, John, Vulcan co-pilot/first pilot, 101 Squadron; captain, 50 Squadron
Jarron, Air Commodore Edward, Vulcan pilot; assistant air attaché in Moscow during the mid-1970s; station commander, RAF Cranwell (1989–90); Chief of Special Weapons, SHAPE (1992)
Langdown, Paddy, Vulcan co-pilot/first pilot, 35 Squadron; captain, 50 Squadron, 101 Squadron
Lark, Lyle, air radar fitter
Laycock, John, Victor co-pilot and captain, XV Squadron; Vulcan captain and flight commander, 44 (Rhodesia) Squadron
Leitch, Andy, Vulcan pilot; test pilot
Lidbetter, Geoff, Vulcan AEO, 44 Squadron, 35 Squadron, 50 Squadron
MacGillivray, Bill, Vulcan captain, 101 Squadron, 35 Squadron
Mans, Keith, Vulcan co-pilot, 50 Squadron
Martin, Dennis, Vulcan co-pilot, 50 Squadron; captain, IX Squadron
Masefield, Barry, Vulcan AEO, 617 Squadron
McLoughlin, Alan, Victor tanker nav/radar, 214 Squadron
Millikin, Paul, Vulcan captain, 44 Squadron; Victor tanker captain 55 Squadron
Milne, Jim, Vulcan nav/plotter, 35 Squadron
Montgomery, Bryan 'Monty', Valiant nav/plotter, 148 Squadron
Moore, Peter, Vulcan co-pilot and captain, 44 (Rhodesia) Squadron
Mudford, Jeremy, Victor captain, 57 Squadron, 139 Squadron
Mullen, Barry, Vulcan nav/radar, IX Squadron, 50 Squadron
Muston, John, Valiant nav/radar, 49 Squadron
Prior, Hugh, Vulcan AEO, 44 (Rhodesia) Squadron
Reeve, John, Vulcan co-pilot, 27 Squadron; captain, IX Squadron
Sinclair, Bob, Vulcan nav/radar, 12 Squadron, 35 Squadron, IX Squadron
Smith, Roger, Vulcan co-pilot, 12 Squadron; captain, 35 Squadron
Smith, Tony, crew chief, IX Squadron
Taylor, Bill, Vulcan co-pilot, 27 Squadron; captain, 617 Squadron
Tye, Jon, Vulcan captain, 27 Squadron, IX Squadron, 44 Squadron
Vinales, James, Vulcan nav/plotter, 44 (Rhodesia) Squadron, 101 Squadron, 50 Squadron
Walker, Jim, Vulcan nav/radar, 44 (Rhodesia) Squadron, 35 Squadron
Weller, John, Vulcan nav/radar, IX Squadron
West, Gary, Victor co-pilot, 10 Squadron, 55 Squadron; captain, Victor tankers
West, Wing Commander Peter, MBE, Valiant/Vulcan AEO, 214 Squadron, 138 Squadron, 12 Squadron; AEO leader, 44 (Rhodesia) Squadron, 27 Squadron
Williams, Rob, Vulcan co-pilot, 12 Squadron; captain, IX Squadron
Woolven, Squadron Leader Robin, Vulcan nav/plotter, 617 Squadron
Wright, Anthony, Valiant nav/radar, 148 Squadron; Vulcan nav/radar, IX Squadron, 35 Squadron, 50 Squadron

BOOKS

Armitage, Michael, *The Royal Air Force: An Illustrated History*, Arms and Armour, 1993
Baylis, John, *Ambiguity and Deterrence: British Nuclear Strategy 1945–1964*, Clarendon Press, 1995
Baylis, John; Stoddart, Kristan, *The British Nuclear Experience: The Role of Beliefs, Culture and Identity*, Oxford University Press, 2015
Blackman, Tony and Wright, Anthony, *Valiant Boys*, Grub Street, 2017
Brookes Andrew, *RAF V-Force: Operations Manual*, Haynes Publishing, 2015
Brookes, Andrew, *V-Force: A History of Britain's Airborne Deterrent*, Jane's, 1982
Buttler, Tony, *British Secret Projects: Jet Bombers since 1949*, Midland Publishing (Ian Allan), 2003
Clarke, Dr Magnus, *The Nuclear Destruction of Britain*, Croon Helm, 1982

Cocroft, Wayne D. and Thomas, Roger J. C., ed. Barnwell, P. S., *Cold War: Building for Nuclear Confrontation 1946–1989*, Historic England, 2016
Freedman, Lawrence, *The Evolution of Nuclear Strategy* (Third Edition), Palgrave Macmillan, 2003
Galeotti, Mark, *Spetsnaz: Russia's Special Forces*, Osprey Publishing, 2015
Gibson, Chris, *Vulcan's Hammer: V-Force Projects and Weapons Since 1945*, Hikoki Publications, 2011
Goodall, Philip, *My Target was Leningrad: V-Force: Preserving Our Democracy*, Fonthill Media, 2015
Hennessy, Peter, *The Prime Minister: The Office and its Holders since 1945*, Penguin, 2001
Hennessy, Peter, *The Secret State* (Second Edition), Penguin, 2010
Hewson, Robert, "Soviet Threat and Countermeasures", *V-Force: Ready for the Unthinkable*, Newsdesk Communications, 2008
Jones, Matthew, *The Official History of the UK Strategic Nuclear Deterrent: Volume 1: From the V-Bomber Era to the Arrival of Polaris, 1945–1964*, Routledge, 2018
Lamb, Richard, *The Macmillan Years, 1957–1963*, John Murray, 1995
McLelland, Tim, *Britain's Cold War Bombers*, Fonthill Media, 2016
Menaul, Air Vice-Marshal Stewart, CB, CBE, DFC, AFC, *Countdown: Britain's Strategic Nuclear Forces*, Robert Hale, 1980
Moore, Richard, *Nuclear Illusion, Nuclear Reality: Britain, the United States and Nuclear Weapons, 1958–1964*, Palgrave Macmillan, 2010
Peacock, Lindsay, "Strategic Air Command." *V-Force: Ready for the Unthinkable*, Newsdesk Communications, 2008
Stoddart, Kristan, *Losing an Empire and Finding a Role: Britain, the USA, NATO and Nuclear Weapons, 1964–70*, Palgrave Macmillan, 2012
Twigge, Stephen and Scott, Len, *Planning Armageddon: Britain, the United States and the Command of Western Nuclear Forces, 1945–1964*, Routledge, 2014
White, Alan, *The King's Thunderbolts: No. 44 (Rhodesia) Squadron, Royal Air Force: An Operational Record and Roll of Honour, 1917–1982*, Tucann, 2007
Wilson, Jim, *Britain on the Brink: The Cold War's Most Dangerous Weekend, October 27–28 1962*, Pen & Sword, 2012
Wynn, Humphrey, *RAF Nuclear Deterrent Forces*, The Stationery Office, 1997
Young, Ken, *The American Bomb in Britain: US Air Forces' Strategic Presence, 1946–64*, Manchester University Press, 2016

DEPARTMENTAL PAPERS

AIR 20/7560, DCAS/1096, S.534, 30 January 1953
AIR 8/1858, "Warning of attack", briefing note for CAS, September 30 1953, COS 1588, 15 September 1953
AIR 8/1856, "Warning of attack", ACAS briefing note for CAS, 4 January 1955
AIR 20/11552, "The operational effectiveness of V-bombers", preliminary draft, 7 July 1955 (OR.16 [55] 5)
AIR 14/4198, "Extending the life of the V-bomber force", Bomber Command: TS Memorandum No. 14, 26 July 1955
AIR 8/1934, "Likely Soviet courses of action up to January 1 1957", ACAS briefing for Defence Committee meeting, 25 October 1955, (DC [55] 46)
AIR 20/11554, "A note on the dispersal and operation of the MBF", C.M.S.2518/D.D.Ops (B), referencing a CAS meeting on 23 November 1955
AIR 20/9729, Air Council, A.C.(56), "Deployment of the V-bomber force – Phase 1", note by AMSO, undated (probably Spring 1956)
AIR 6/124, "Future size and shape of the Royal Air Force", note by the VCAS to the Air Council Standing Committee, 7 June 1956 (SC [56] 16)
AIR 2/14578, "Valiant in the low-level altitude bombing role", D.Ops (B&R), Air Commodore B. K. Burnett, loose minute to ACAS (Ops), 27 June 1956
AIR 2/13717, "Study of the present ability of Bomber Command to come to an Alert State", 28 October 1957
AIR 20/11554, "V-bomber and PR force dispersal: completion of the V-bomber dispersal plan, dispersal of the PR force and implications of second and third bomber lifts", Air Council note by VCAS and AMSO, 4 February 1958
AIR 19/940, "Note on strike potential of MBF", DCAS to Secretary of State for Air, 19 February 1958
AIR 8/2238, "Readiness of Bomber Command", meeting of the Minister of Defence with the Secretary of State for Air, 21 July 1958
AIR 20/10530, "Readiness of Bomber Command", outcome of a meeting of, inter alia, CAS and the AOC-in-C Bomber Command with the Minister of Defence, 24 July 1958
AIR 2/14716, letter from Air Vice-Marshal J. N. T. Stephenson, ACAS (Policy), to AOC-in-Cs all RAF Commands, September 1958
AIR 2/17333, "Deliveries of Project E weapons", letter from Major General W. H. Blanchard, Commander, SAC 7th Air Division (headquartered at South Ruislip) to Air Ministry, 17 September 1958
AIR 20/10325, letter to VCAS, 10 March 1959
AIR 8/2238, "Progress report on the readiness of the MBF", 1 July 1959
AIR 19/632, "Disposal of aircrew who forfeit the confidence of their Commanding Officers", annex to Air Council letter A.301810/58/S.10 (d), 6 November 1959
AIR 20/10618, "Readiness of the MBF", letter from Air Marshal Sir Kenneth Cross, AOC-in-C Bomber Command, to CAS, 9 November 1959

AIR 20/10618, "Readiness of the MBF", letter from Air Marshal Sir Kenneth Cross, AOC-in-C Bomber Command, to CAS, 8 February 1960

AIR 14/3898, note from R. Bruce, Acting Chief Research Officer, Bomber Command, 6 May 1960 (BC/S.554/Res.)

AIR 2/18103, "Effectiveness of Bomber Command in the immediate future (i.e. until the beginning of 1965)", letter from Air Vice-Marshal John Grandy, ACAS (Ops), to AOC-in-C Bomber Command, 13 May 1960, (ACAS [Ops]), C.M.S. 2609/55/F.1351(S)/Ops 4020

AIR 2/17801, "Readiness of the MBF at weekends", letter from Group Captain A. H. C. Boxer, for AOC-in-C Bomber Command, to the Under Secretary of State, Air Ministry (D.Ops [BBM&R]), 20 July 1960

AIR 2/13717, "Notes on UK target selection and coordination, developments over the past 10–12 years", 26 August 1960

AIR 2/17801, "Essential Residential Telephones in Bomber Command", letter from Air Commodore C. G. Stowell to D.Ops (B&R), 16 December 1960

AIR 2/17801, letter from Group Captain A. D. Frank, for AOC-in-C Bomber Command, to the Under Secretary of State (D.Ops [B&R]), Air Ministry, 24 January 1961

AIR 20/11448, "Bomber dispersal", 6 June 1961

AIR 19/727, "The Deterrent Policy", Guidance Memorandum, Air Vice-Marshal T. O. Prickett, ACAS (Ops), 13 June 1961

AIR 8/2238, letter from Air Chief Marshal Sir Thomas Pike to the First Sea Lord, Admiral Sir Casper John, 11 July 1961

AIR 8/2238, "V-bombers – engine-starting systems", minute, Air Marshal R. B. Lees, DCAS, 19 July 1961

AIR 2/17801, "BCAR plan – Alert Conditions and Readiness States", Appendix A to letter from Group Captain A. Frank, for SASO, Bomber Command, to Headquarters No. 1 Group, 18 August 1961 (BC/S. 96237/Ops)

AIR 2/14578, "Trial No. 407 – low-level navigation in 'V aircraft'" (preliminary report), Bomber Command Development Unit, Report No.12/61, 3 October 1961

Air 2/14578, "Bomber Command Trial No. 407 – low-level navigation of 'V aircraft,'" letter from Squadron Leader A. D. Gibson, on behalf of the AOC-in-C Bomber Command, to the Under Secretary of State, Air Ministry (D.D.Ops [B]), 25 October 1961 (appended to BC/S.96737)

AIR 2/14578, "Bomber Command Trial No. 407 – low-level navigation of 'V aircraft,'" note on servicing personnel required for outstanding Valiant low-level flights in the Trial No. 407 programme, 25 October 1961 (appended to BC/S.96737)

AIR 8/2369, "Guard duties – Bomber Command Stations", 28 November 1961

AIR 8/2369, Air Council, conclusions of meeting 23 (61), 7 December 1961, Secret Annex

AIR 19/940, note by the Secretary of State for Air, 19 February 1962

AIR 20/11448, "The case for 36 dispersal airfields", Air Ministry, V-bomber dispersal, 11 September 1962; associated note, 13 September 1962

AIR 8/2201, "Strategic strike planning by Bomber Command" memorandum from T. O. Prickett, ACAS (Ops), to the CAS, 5 October 1962

AIR 25/1703, Operations Record Book, No. 1 Group, 27 October 1962

AIR 8/2369, "Increased Readiness - Bomber Command", letter from AOC-in-C, Air Marshal Sir Kenneth Cross, to CAS, Marshal of the Royal Air Force Sir Thomas G. Pike, 10 January 1963

AIR 2/16435, "Notes on Bomber Command plan to meet increased QRA commitment", draft, 17 January 1963

AIR 2/16435, "Allocation of dispersal airfields for MBF", loose minute from Air Commodore A. W. Heward, D.Ops (B&R), to ACAS (Ops), 1 March 1963

AIR 2/16435, "USAF request for information, RAF QRA status", loose minute from Wing Commander D. G. Evans, Air Plans 2, to D.Ops (B&R) and others, 5 April 1963

AIR 8/2369, note by W. H. Kyle, VCAS, 10 May 1963

AIR 14/3898, "The use of warning devices (Red Steer and Blue Saga) during attacks by fighter aircraft on bomber aircraft flying at high and low level", minute, Bomber Command Chief Research Officer T. H. Kerr, 4 July 1963

AIR 8/2369, minute to CAS from Air Vice-Marshal D. G. Smallwood, ACAS (Ops), 28 August 1963

AIR 2/16435, "Quick Reaction Alert", Air Plans 2/TS.1204, Group Captain J. R. L. Blount, 17 December 1963

AIR 8/2369, letter from VCAS to CAS (VCAS 7977), 24 December 1963

AIR 8/2369, Note to CAS from PS, 31 December 1963

AIR 8/2369, note of CAS meeting, Air Ministry, 15 January 1964

AIR 8/2369, letter from PS to VCAS to ACAS (Ops), 17 February 1964

AIR 8/2369, "Exercise Micky Finn – October 1964", draft minute from Air Vice-Marshal Smallwood, ACAS (Ops), subsequently sent to CAS for a possible minute from him to the Minister (RAF), November 1964

AIR 2/16435, D.Ops (B&R) (RAF), from HQ Bomber Command to MoD Air, subject: QRA (handwritten annotation), 20 January 1965

AIR 8/2369, note from M. E. Quinlan, PS to CAS, to PS to VCAS, 20 May 1965

AIR 8/2369, "Bomber Command, Exercise Micky Finn", note, Air Vice-Marshal L. M. Hodges, ACAS (Ops), to the PS to CAS, 13 July 1967

AIR 8/2572, letter from Air Marshal Sir Peter Fletcher, VCAS, to Air Chief Marshal Sir Denis Spotswood, AOC-in-C, Strike Command, 13 April 1970

AIR 2/19184, "Air-delivered strategic nuclear weapons systems", Air Force Department paper to the Long Term Strategic Nuclear Working Party, Interim Report, 30 September 1971

AIR 41/85, Wynn, Humphrey, Air Historical Branch (RAF), "The RAF in the postwar years: The bomber role 1945–70, 1984

AIR 14/86, James, T. C. G., Air Historical Branch (RAF), "The RAF in the postwar years: Defence Policy and the Royal Air Force, 1956–63", 1987
AVIA 65/43, "The development of the MBF: the place of the MBF in British strategy", 2 November 1954 (C.M.S. 2479/54)
AVIA 65/1114, "Serviceability of Blue Danube Mk 1 and Mk 2", note, Air Ministry, 29 November 1956 (File No. 407/090)
AVIA 65/818, "Note on nuclear weapons ordered for the RAF", 8 July 1959
CAB 21/4757, "Launching of strategic nuclear reprisal", Annex A, minute by J. M. Wilson, 3 February 1958
CAB 21/4756, "Nuclear retaliation procedures", letter from F. Cooper, Air Ministry, to J. S. Orme, Cabinet Office, 9 July 1959; note: "Procedures for authorising nuclear retaliation, RAF Bomber Command," attached to letter
CAB 21/4756, "Procedure for launching nuclear retaliation", informal meeting, Cabinet Office, 15 June 1960
CAB 21/4840, "Nuclear retaliation consultative procedures", draft memorandum for discussion with the US Government, 18 January 1962
DEFE 25/18, "The V-Force and the powered bomb", October 1958
DEFE 25/18, "The number of V-bomber aircraft which will reach their targets", note from Air Ministry to MoD, 10 October 1958
DEFE 25/18, note: "Bomber Command", 4 January 1960
DEFE 13/306, "Vulnerability of the V-bomber force", conclusions, meeting of the Defence Board; note by J. M. Wilson, Defence Board Secretariat; both 4 April 1960
DEFE 25/86, "V-bomber readiness", memorandum by the Chief of Defence Staff, 3 July 1961 (DRP/M [61]8, Item 4)
DEFE 25/86, minutes of the Defence Committee meeting, 12 January 1962
DEFE 13/849, AUS (AS), B.F. 20, note from Frank Cooper, 22 January 1965
DEFE 58/90, "Defence penetration techniques: the problem of defence penetration by Vulcan aircraft at low flight altitudes during a limited conventional conflict in a non-European area", Strike Command Development Unit Report No. 9/68 – Part 1: HQ STC Trial No. 549 Phase C, Annex L, 31 December 1968

REPORTS

Brodie, Bernard, "Strategy in the Missile Age", RAND, 1959; cited by Richards, "Time is No Longer Our Ally"
"Soviet Bloc Air and Missile Defense Capabilities through mid-1967", *National Intelligence Estimate Number 11-3-62*, submitted by the Director of Central Intelligence, 31 October 1962, released via the CIA Historical Review Program
"The Development of Soviet Air Defense Doctrine and Practice", Historical Evaluation & Research Organisation, for Sandia National Laboratories, SAND 80-7146/1, April 1981

JOURNAL ARTICLES

Alcock, Air Chief Marshal Sir Michael, GCB, KBE, DSc, FREng, "V-Force Development – Simultaneous Engine-Starting", article based on a paper to the RAF Historical Society, proceedings for 22 October 2013
Aylen, Jonathan, "First Waltz: Development and Deployment of Blue Danube, Britain's Post-War Atomic Bomb", *The International Journal for the History of Engineering & Technology*, Vol. 85, Issue 1, January 2015, pp. 31–59
Baldwin, Air Vice-Marshal Nigel, "Afternoon Discussion", RAF Historical Society, *Journal 28 – Seminar: Electronic Warfare*, 2003, pp. 104–110
Baldwin, Air Vice-Marshal Nigel, "Training the V-Force for Its Primary and Secondary Roles – Low-Level Tactics against the Soviet Bloc", RAF Historical Society, *Journal 20 – Seminar: Training in Peace for War*, 1999, pp. 24–33
Bonnor, Norman, "The V-Force: 1955-1966: Navigation at 50,000 and 500 ft", *V-Force Reunion*, Newark Air Museum, 17–18 May 2014
Boyes, John, "The Thor IRBM – the Cuban Missile Crisis and the Subsequent Run-Down of the Thor Force", RAF Historical Society, *Journal 42 – Misc Papers inc Thor Cuba 1962 – Arnhem Aircrew*, 2008, pp. 40–56
Brocklebank, Squadron Leader Roy, "How did Bomber Command prepare for war?", *Flypast*, 17 October 2008, based on a lecture to the Royal Institute of Navigation's History of Air Navigation Group, Tangmere
Brookes, Wing Commander Andrew, "V-Force Operational Deployment and Readiness", RAF Historical Society, *Journal 26 – Seminar: The RAF and Nuclear Weapons 1960–98*, 2001, pp. 54–66
Cooper GCB, CMG, PC, The Rt Hon. Sir Frank, "The Direction of Air Force Policy in the 1950s and 1960s", RAF Historical Society, *Journal 11*, 1993, pp. 10–21
Graham, Paul, "RAF Nuclear Deterrence in the Cold War", *Air Power Review*, Vol. 10, No. 1, Spring 2007, pp. 50–75
Hely, Squadron Leader Michael, "Afterthoughts", RAF Historical Society, *Journal 26 – Seminar: The RAF and Nuclear Weapons 1960–98*, 2001, pp. 105–112
Hudson, Peter, "A View from Whitehall", *Air Power Review (Deterrence Special Edition)*, Vol. 20, No. 2, Summer 2017, pp. 90–94
Jefford, Wing Commander 'Jeff', "EW in the Early Post-War Years – Lincolns to Valiants", RAF Historical Society, *Journal 28 – Seminar: Electronic Warfare*, 2003, pp. 58–69
Jones, Edgar, "LMF: The Use of Psychiatric Stigma in the Royal Air Force during the Second World War", *The Journal of Military History*, 70, January 2006, pp. 439–458
Leckenby, Phil, "QRA – A Personal Reminiscence", *655 Maintenance and Preservation Society Newsletter*, Issue 29, Spring 2013, pp. 14–18; originally published in the *44 (Rhodesia) Squadron Newsletter*

Norris, Robert S., Kristensen, Hans M., "The British Nuclear Stockpile, 1953–2013," *Bulletin of the Atomic Scientists*, 69:4, 2013, pp. 69–75, DOI: 10 1177/0096340213493260

Paton, Wing Commander David, assisted by Oliver, MAcr Derek, "Airborne Electronic Reconnaissance, 1948 to 1989", RAF Historical Society, *Journal 23 – Seminar: Cold War Intelligence Gathering*, 2001, pp. 59–68

Powell, Wing Commander Rod, "EW during the V-Force Era", RAF Historical Society, *Journal 28 – Seminar: Electronic Warfare*, 2003, pp. 70–85.

Richards, Clive, "'Time is No Longer Our Ally' RAF Bomber Command, Deterrence and the Transition to War, 1955–62", *Air Power Review*, Vol. 21, No. 2, Summer 2018, pp. 36–60

Robinson, Air Vice-Marshal Michael, "Summary of the Previous RAF Historical Society Seminar on the Origin and Development of the British Nuclear Deterrent 1945–60", RAF Historical Society, *Journal 26 – Seminar: The RAF and Nuclear Weapons 1960–98*, 2001, pp. 10–15

Sowrey, Air Marshal Sir Frederick, "Introduction by Seminar Chairman", RAF Historical Society, *Journal 28 – Seminar: Electronic Warfare*, 2003, pp. 13–14

Truelove, Air Commodore Owen, "Afternoon Discussion Period", RAF Historical Society, *Journal 26 – Seminar: The RAF and Nuclear Weapons 1960–98*, 2001, p. 96

Turpin, Wing Commander Richard 'Dick', "RAF EW training: 1966–94", RAF Historical Society, *Journal 28 – Seminar: Electronic Warfare*, 2003, pp. 88–91

PAPERS

Allen, Professor John E., "Blue Steel and Developments", The History of the UK Strategic Deterrent, Royal Aeronautical Society, 17 March 1999

Bonnor, Air Commodore Norman, FRIN, FRAeS, "Blue Steel – the V-Force's Stand-off Bomb" (undated)

Casteel, Major Burton A., USAF, "Spetsnaz: A Soviet Sabotage Threat", Report No. 86-0500, Air Command and Staff College, Air University, Maxwell AFB, April 1986

Fazackerley, Mike, "Weapon X: The Bomb with No Name: A Short History and Technical Description of WE.177" (unpublished)

Grenfell, Julian, "Vulcan Paper", note (undated)

Jones, Peter, CB, "The History of the UK Strategic Deterrent", Royal Aeronautical Society, London, 17 March 1999

Moore, Richard, "The Real Meaning of the Words: A Pedantic Glossary of British Nuclear Weapons", UK Nuclear History Working Paper No. 1, Mountbatten Centre for International Studies

Quinlivan, James T., "Soviet Strategic Air Defense: A Long Past and an Uncertain Future", AD-A228-306, paper, The RAND Corporation, September 1989

Wynn, Humphrey, "Early Air-Carried, Air-Launched Weapons", The History of the UK Strategic Deterrent, Royal Aeronautical Society, 17 March 1999

OTHER SOURCES

Brocklebank, Roy; Goodall, Philip; Hickley, Paul; West, Peter; Woolven, Robin; "Defence through Deterrence: British Policy during the 1960s and 1970s", Witness Seminar, Institute of Contemporary British History and Defence Studies Department, King's College, London, 10 September 2014

CIA (50X1-HUM), "Doctrine and Theory of Soviet Anti-Air Defense", 9 July 1958 (translation of Russian language original)

DASB/296/80, "UK Logistics Planning Policy", meeting of the Chiefs of Staff Committee, 6 May 1980

Langdown, Paddy, lecture notes: "The Vulcan Deterrent"

Owen, Robert, 617 Squadron Historian, Operations Record Book, 617 Squadron, August 1968; extract

Venables, Mark, "The Place of Air Power Doctrine in Postwar British Defence Planning and its Influence on the Genesis and Development of the Theory of Nuclear Deterrence, 1945–1952", doctoral thesis, King's College, London, 1985

NOTES TO CHAPTERS

1. BRITAIN'S AIRBORNE DETERRENT

1   Humphrey Wynn, "Early Air-Carried, Air-Launched weapons", The History of the UK Strategic Deterrent, Royal Aeronautical Society, 17 March 1999.
2   Chris Gibson, *Vulcan's Hammer: V-Force Projects and Weapons Since 1945*, Hikoki Publications, 2011, p. 10.
3   Paul Graham, "RAF Nuclear Deterrence in the Cold War", *Air Power Review*, Vol. 10, No. 1, Spring 2007, pp. 50-75.
4   AIR 20/7560, DCAS/1096, S.534, 30 January 1953.
5   Humphrey Wynn, *RAF Nuclear Deterrent Forces*, The Stationery Office, 1997, p. 71.
6   AIR 20/11552, "The operational effectiveness of the V-bombers", preliminary draft, OR.16 (55) 5, 7 July 1955.
7   Air Commodore Edward Jarron interviewed: 23/7/19.
8   Gibson, *Vulcan's Hammer*, pp. 12–13.
9   William W. Suit, historian, Air Force Materiel Command History Office, "The Transfer of B-29s to the RAF under the Military Defense Assistance Program," joint meeting, "Seeing off the Bear – Anglo-American Air Power Cooperation during the Cold War", RAF Historical Society and the Airforce Historical Foundation, 9–10 September 1993, Air Force History and Museums Program, USAF, 1995, 101-115.
10 Tony Blackman, *Vulcan Test Pilot*, Grub Street, 2007, p. 16.
11 Wynn, *RAF Nuclear Deterrent Forces*, pp. 582–609.
12 "Soviet Bloc Air and Missile Defense Capabilities through Mid-1967", *National Intelligence Estimate November 11-3-62*, 31 October 1962, pp. 7–9.
13 Squadron Leader Roy Brocklebank email: 22/3/21.
14 Clive Richards, "'Time is No Longer our Ally': RAF Bomber Command, deterrence and the transition to war, 1955-62", *Air Power Review*, Vol. 21, No. 2, Summer 2018, p. 36.
15 Dr Les Ruskell, former head of the Operational Analysis Cell at UK Joint Permanent Headquarters, Northwood; later at the Farnborough Air Sciences Trust (FAST), Farnborough; email: 24/6/19.
16 John Baylis and Kristan Stoddart, *The British Nuclear Experience: The Role of Beliefs, Culture and Identity*, Oxford University Press, 2015, pp. 142–3, 208.
17 AVM Stewart Menaul, CB, CBE, DFC, AFC, *Countdown: Britain's Strategic Nuclear Forces*, Robert Hale, 1980, pp. 31–2.
18 The Rt Hon. Sir Frank Cooper, GCB, CMG, PC, "The direction of Air Force policy in the 1950s and 1960s", RAF Historical Society, *Journal 11*, 1993, pp. 10–21.
19 Patrick E. Murray, Command Historian, Third Air Force, RAF Mildenhall, UK, "An initial response to the Cold War: the build-up of the USAF in the UK, 1948–1956", joint meeting, "Seeing off the Bear", RAF Historical Society and the Airforce Historical Foundation, 1995, pp. 15–24.
20 Ibid.
21 Ibid.
22 Ibid.
23 Matthew Jones, *The Official History of the UK Strategic Nuclear Deterrent: Volume 1: From the V-Bomber Era to the Arrival of Polaris, 1945–1964*, Routledge, 2018, p. 39.
24 *Hansard*, HC, vol. 537, Cols. 1896-7, 1 March 1955.
25 Jones, *The Official History of the UK Strategic Nuclear Deterrent*, p. 39.

2. SPECIAL WEAPONS

26 Richard Holmes, *The World at War*, Ebury Press, 2007, p. 376.
27 Richard Moore, *Nuclear Illusion, Nuclear Reality: Britain, the United States and Nuclear Weapons, 1958–1964*, Palgrave Macmillan, 2010, p. 78.
28 Gibson, *Vulcan's Hammer*, pp. 53–57.
29 Ibid, pp. 59, 63.
30 Wayne D. Cocroft, *"Fort Halstead, Dunton Green, Sevenoaks, Kent"*, English Heritage, Research Department Report Series, No. 49, 2010, pp. 3–16; "Britain's nuclear weapons: British nuclear testing." https://nuclearweaponarchive.org/Uk/UKTesting.html
31 Ibid.
32 Ibid.
33 Wynn, *RAF Nuclear Deterrent Forces*, p. 13.
34 Ibid, p. 27.
35 Jonathan Aylen, "First Waltz: Development and Deployment of Blue Danube, Britain's Post-war Atomic Bomb", *International Journal of Engineering and Technology*, Vol. 85, No. 1, January 2015, p. 37.
36 AIR 20/11554, Note to DCAS, CEE/1143, 16 March 1956.
37 AIR 20/11554, "Medium Bomber Airfields", letter to AMSO, 16 March 1956.
38 Aylen, "First Waltz: Development and Deployment of Blue Danube", p. 32.

39 Wynn, *RAF Nuclear Deterrent Forces*, p. 222.
40 Roy Brocklebank email: 2/4/20.
41 Wynn, *RAF Nuclear Deterrent Forces*, p. 570.
42 Tim McLelland, *Britain's Cold War Bombers*, Fonthill Media, 2016, p. 84.
43 John Muston interviewed: 18/2/19.
44 Kenneth Hubbard and Michael Simmons, *Dropping Britain's first H-Bomb: Story of Operation Grapple 1957/58*, Pen & Sword Aviation, 2008, pp. 73–74.
45 Gibson, *Vulcan's Hammer*, pp. 47–48.
46 Robert S. Norris and Hans M. Kristensen, "The British Nuclear Stockpile, 1953–2013", *Bulletin of the Atomic Scientists*, 69:4, 2013, pp. 69–75, DOI: 10.1177/0096340213493260.
47 Mike Fazackerley amongst documents/text provided: 15/11/20.
48 Gibson, *Vulcan's Hammer*, p. 47.
49 Lyle Lark interviewed: 27/3/18.
50 Moore, *Nuclear Illusion, Nuclear Reality*, p. 104.
51 Richard Moore, "The Real Meaning of the Words: A Pedantic Glossary of British Nuclear Weapons", Mountbatten Centre for International Studies, *UK Nuclear History Working Paper No. 1*, March 2004.
52 Mike Fazackerley, amongst documents/text provided: 15/11/20.
53 Gibson, *Vulcan's Hammer*, pp. 50–51.
54 Wynn, *RAF Nuclear Deterrent Forces*, p. 249.
55 Mike Fazackerley, amongst documents/text provided: 15/11/20.
56 Norris and Kristensen, "The British Nuclear Stockpile", pp. 69–75.
57 Moore, "The Real Meaning of the Words: A Pedantic Glossary of British Nuclear Weapons".
58 Air Commodore Owen Truelove, "Afternoon Discussion Period", RAF Historical Society, *Journal 26 – Seminar: The RAF and Nuclear Weapons 1960–98*, 2001, p. 96
59 AVIA 65/878, "Note on Nuclear Weapons ordered for the RAF," from the Ministry of Supply, 8 July 1959.
60 AIR 2/18103, Appendix "L" to Air Ministry letter C.80333/55, 26 July 1960, "Armament-Bomb, Aircraft, HE, 7,000 lb, HC Mk 1".
61 Gibson, *Vulcan's Hammer*, pp. 48–49.
62 Peter Moore email: 24/2/21.
63 AVIA 65/818, "Note on nuclear weapons ordered for the RAF", Ministry of Supply, 8 July 1959.
64 Norris and Kristensen, "The British Nuclear Stockpile", pp. 69–75.
65 Mike Fazackerley, amongst documents/text provided: 15/11/20.
66 AIR 2/17801, Headquarters, Bomber Command, Operation Order No. 5/62, "Quick Reaction Aircraft, MBF", BC/S.99162, January 1962; superseded by incorporation in Amendment No. 4, November 1962, Bomber Command Alert and Readiness Procedures.
67 Roy Brocklebank; documents/text provided: 25/6/20.
68 Dick Fuller; documents/text provided: 29/10/20.
69 Squadron Leader Michael Hely, "Nuclear Weapons Training – Ground Crew", RAF Historical Society, *Journal 26 – Seminar: The RAF and Nuclear Weapons 1960–98*, 2001, pp. 74–80
70 Roy Brocklebank; email: 5/4/20.
71 Air Commodore Mike Allisstone, "Nuclear Weapons and No. 94 MU, RAF Barnham", RAF Historical Society, *Journal 35*, 2005, pp. 54–61.
72 Aylen, "First Waltz: Development and Deployment of Blue Danube", p. 49.
73 Ibid.
74 Mike Allisstone; interviewed: 11/1/18; "Nuclear Weapons and No. 94 MU, RAF Barnham".
75 Hely, "Nuclear Weapons Training – Ground Crew", pp. 74–80.
76 Allisstone, "Nuclear Weapons and No. 94 MU, RAF Barnham", pp. 54–61.
77 Air Commodore Mike Allisstone interviewed: 11/1/18.
78 AWRE, notes, EOD warhead engineering specialist team, "Incident at RAF Brüggen – a viewpoint", 6 June 1984; Records, Board of Inquiry, RAF Brüggen, 3 May 1984.
79 Group Captain W. J. Taylor, "Engineering on a Nuclear Strike Squadron", RAF Historical Society, *Journal 26 – Seminar: The RAF and Nuclear Weapons 1960–98*, 2001, pp. 86–93.
80 Wynn, *RAF Nuclear Deterrent Forces*, pp. 97–98.
81 Hely, "Nuclear Weapons Training – Ground Crew", pp. 74–80.
82 Dr Stephen Twigge, Department of International Politics, The University College of Wales, "Anglo-American Air Force Collaboration and the Cuban Missile Crisis, a British perspective," proceedings of the second joint meeting, RAF Historical Society and the Airforce Historical Foundation, "Seeing off the Bear – Anglo-American Air Power Cooperation during the Cold War," 9–10 September 1993, Air Force History and Museums Program, USAF, 1995, 210.
83 Moore, "The Real Meaning of the Words: A Pedantic Glossary of British Nuclear Weapons".
84 AIR 2/17333, "Deliveries of Project E weapons", letter from Major-General W. H. Blanchard, Commander, SAC 7th Air Division (headquartered at South Ruislip), to Air Ministry, 17 September 1958.
85 Norris and Kristensen, "The British Nuclear Stockpile", pp. 69–75.
86 Bryan Montgomery interviewed: 27/2/18.

87 Stephen Twigge and Len Scott, *Planning Armageddon: Britain, the United States and the Command of Western Nuclear Forces, 1945–1964*, Routledge, 2014, p. 105.
88 John Huggins amongst documents/text provided: 26/10/20.
89 Wynn, *RAF Nuclear Deterrent Forces*, pp. 625–626.

3. POWERED BOMBS AND LAYDOWN BOMBS

90 Gibson, *Vulcan's Hammer*, p. 72.
91 Menaul, *Countdown*, p. 109.
92 Gibson, *Vulcan's Hammer*, p. 65.
93 Norris and Kristensen, "The British Nuclear Stockpile", pp. 69–75.
94 Menaul, *Countdown*, p. 110.
95 Wynn, *RAF Nuclear Deterrent Forces*, pp. 186-189.
96 Ibid., pp. 191–199.
97 Ibid., p. 202.
98 Ibid., pp. 328, 612, 620.
99 DEFE 25/86, minutes of the Defence Committee meeting, 12 January 1962.
100 Wynn, *RAF Nuclear Deterrent Forces*, pp. 209–210.
101 Ibid., pp. 210–211.
102 DEFE 25/86, meeting between Minister of Defence and departmental officials, 28 June 1960.
103 Gibson, *Vulcan's Hammer*, pp. 65–88.
104 DEFE 25/86, minute from the Secretary of State for Air to the Minister of Defence, 23 February 1961.
105 Gibson, *Vulcan's Hammer*, pp. 69–70.
106 John Baylis, *Ambiguity and Deterrence: British Nuclear Strategy 1945–1964*, Clarendon Press, 1995, p. 350.
107 Air Commodore Norman Bonnor, "The V-Force – 1955–1966: Navigation at 50,000 and 500 ft", V-Force Reunion, Newark Air Museum, 17–18 May 2014.
108 Wynn, *RAF Nuclear Deterrent Forces*, pp. 218–219.
109 Baylis, *Ambiguity and Deterrence*, p. 350.
110 Julian Grenfell interviewed: 10/12/18.
111 Mike Fazackerley; documents/text provided: 15/11/20.
112 Julian Grenfell interviewed: 10/12/18.
113 Norman Bonnor, FRIN, FRAeS, "General Notes", documents/text provided: 1/11/20.
114 Wynn, *RAF Nuclear Deterrent Forces*, p. 216.
115 Kristan Stoddart, *Losing an Empire and Finding a Role: Britain, the USA, NATO and Nuclear Weapons, 1964–70*, Palgrave Macmillan, 2012, p. 102.
116 AIR 14/4342, Bomber Command, Operational Research Branch, Memorandum No. 273, August 1963, "Generation of the 'Blue Steel' weapon system in Readiness exercises".
117 Norman Bonnor, "Blue Steel: the V-Force's stand-off bomb", undated.
118 Wynn, *RAF Nuclear Deterrent Forces*, p. 219.
119 Ibid., p. 220.
120 Professor John E. Allen, "Blue Steel and Developments", The History of the UK Strategic Deterrent, Royal Aeronautical Society, 17 March 1999, London.
121 AIR 41/85, Humphrey Wynn, "The RAF in the Post-war Years: The Bomber Role 1945–1970", 1984, p. 136.
122 Allen, "Blue Steel and Developments".
123 Rob Williams, documents/text provided, 27/10/20.
124 John Huggins, 26/10/20.
125 Peter Moore email: 24/2/21.
126 Norman Bonnor, documents/text provided: 1/11/20.
127 Bonnor, "Blue Steel: the V-Force's stand-off bomb".
128 Norman Bonnor, documents/text provided: 1/11/20.
129 Wynn, *RAF Nuclear Deterrent Forces*, pp. 460–461.
130 Norman Bonnor, "General Notes", documents/text provided: 1/11/20.
131 Bonnor, "The V-Force – 1955–1966: Navigation at 50,000 and 500 ft".
132 Bomber Command, Operational Research Branch, Memorandum No. 331, "First post-acceptance launch of Blue Steel", June 1966.
133 Norman Bonnor, "General Notes", documents/text provided: 1/11/20.
134 Wing Commander Jon Tye interviewed: 12/2/19.
135 Mike Fazackerley; documents/text provided: 15/11/20.
136 Roy Brocklebank email: 2/4/20.
137 Mike Fazackerley, "Weapon X: the bomb with no name: a short history and technical description of WE.177", unpublished; email: 20/2/21 – citing AIR 2/17330, 70a, para 3.
138 Mike Fazackerley, documents/text provided: 15/11/20.
139 Fazackerley, "Weapon X", p. 128.
140 Edward Jarron interviewed: 23/7/19.
141 Mike Fazackerley; documents/text provided: 15/11/20.

142 Ibid.
143 Ibid.
144 Humphrey Wynn, "The History of the UK Strategic Deterrent: Early Air-Carried, Air-Launched Weapons", 17 March 1999.
145 Fazackerley, "Weapon X", pp. 118–124.
146 Gibson, *Vulcan's Hammer*, p. 53.
147 Ibid., pp. 53–54.
148 Norris and Kristensen, "The British Nuclear Stockpile", pp. 69–75.
149 Fazackerley, "Weapon X", pp. 104–111.
150 Mike Fazackerley, documents/text provided: 15/11/20.
151 Ibid.
152 Wynn, *RAF Nuclear Deterrent Forces*, p. 423.
153 AIR 2/17330-86A.
154 Roy Brocklebank, documents/text provided: 25/6/20.
155 Tony Smith interviewed: 11/1/18.
156 Peter Moore email: 18/3/21.
157 Fazackerley, "Weapon X", pp. 76–88.
158 Roy Brocklebank email: 2/4/20.
159 Roy Brocklebank, documents/text provided: 25/6/20.
160 Fazackerley, "Weapon X", p. 77.
161 Wynn, *RAF Nuclear Deterrent Forces*, p. 553.
162 Ibid., p. 546.
163 Roy Brocklebank email: 2/4/20.
164 Fazackerley, "Weapon X", pp. 106–107.
165 Mike Fazackerley amongst documents/text provided: 15/11/20.
166 Fazackerley, "Weapon X", pp. 148–151.
167 Douglas Bateman, draft article, "The Royal Aircraft Establishment's Involvement in the Development of Nuclear Weapons"; https://en.wikipedia.org/wiki/Michael_John_Smith_(espionage)
168 Nigel West, *Historical Dictionary of Cold War Intelligence*, 2021, p. 273.
169 Mike Fazackerley; amongst documents/text provided: 15/11/20.
170 Ibid.

4. THE V-FORCE MISSION

171 Jones, *The Official History of the UK Strategic Nuclear Deterrent*, p. 42.
172 AIR 20/8574, "Comparative operational value of medium bombers", January 1953.
173 Minutes, Chiefs of Staff Committee meeting, 17 February 1953 (C.O.S. [53] 24th meeting), plus Confidential Annex.
174 Baylis and Stoddart, *The British Nuclear Experience*, p. 103.
175 Tony Blackman and Anthony Wright, *Valiant Boys*, Grub Street, 2017, p. 27.
176 Wynn, *RAF Nuclear Deterrent Forces*, p. 323.
177 AIR 41/85, p. 36.
178 Ibid.
179 Baylis, *Ambiguity and Deterrence*, p. 364.
180 Wynn, *RAF Nuclear Deterrent Forces*, p. 155.
181 Ibid., pp. 314–333.
182 Ibid; DEFE 25/18, "The V-bomber force and the powered bomb", memorandum from the Secretary of State for Air, George Ward, to the Defence Board, 29 October 1958 (DB (58)10).
183 DEFE 25/18.
184 Wynn, *RAF Nuclear Deterrent Forces*, pp. 79–80.
185 Ibid., pp. 144–151.
186 AVIA 65/43, "The development of the MBF: the place of the MBF in British strategy," note by VCAS, 2 November 1954 (C.M.S. 2479/54).
187 John Muston interviewed: 18/2/19.
188 Norman Bonnor, documents/text provided: 1/11/20.
189 Wing Commander Peter West MBE interviewed: 30/4/19.
190 Julian Grenfell interviewed: 10/12/18.
191 DEFE 25/18, note, "Bomber Command", 4 January 1960.
192 Wynn, "The RAF in the Postwar Years: The Bomber Role 1945–70", p. 91.
193 Wynn, *RAF Nuclear Deterrent Forces*, pp. 298–313.
194 Ibid, pp. 306–307, letter/list IIH1/243/2/2 RAF Wittering, BCAR Plan–Policy.
195 Ibid., pp. 307, 311.
196 Ibid., pp. 344–345.
197 John Boyes, "The Thor IRBM – the Cuban Missile Crisis and the subsequent rundown of the Thor force", RAF Historical Society, *Journal 42*, 2008, pp. 40–56.
198 AIR 20/10325, letter to VCAS, 10 March 1959.

199 Wynn, *RAF Nuclear Deterrent Forces*, pp. 344–345.
200 Twigge and Scott, *Planning Armageddon*, p. 113.
201 Boyes, "The Thor IRBM", pp. 40–56.
202 Ibid.
203 Wing Commander Colin Cummings, "Thor", RAF Historical Society, *Journal 26 – Seminar: The RAF and Nuclear Weapons 1960–98*, 2001, pp. 22–34.
204 Ibid.
205 Menaul, *Countdown,* pp. 100–101.
206 Roy Brocklebank, letter, amongst documents/text provided: 25/6/20.
207 Roy Brocklebank, "How did Bomber Command prepare for war?", *Flypast*, 17 October 2008, based on a lecture to the Royal Institute of Navigation's History of Air Navigation Group, Tangmere.
208 Wynn, *RAF Nuclear Deterrent Forces*, p. 314.
209 Stoddart, *Losing an Empire and Finding a Role*, p. 83.
210 Jeremy Mudford interviewed: 8/2/18.
211 Humphrey Wynn, "The RAF in the Post-war Years: The Bomber Role 1945–70", p. 89.
212 Roy Brocklebank email, 17/6/20.
213 Norman Bonnor, documents/text provided, 1/11/20.
214 Blackman and Wright, *Valiant Boys*, p. 167.
215 AIR 2/18103, Loose minute, "SACEUR Valiant force", from Group Captain R. McFarlane, D.D.L. (A.F), to D.D. Air Plans 1, 12 April 1962.
216 Martin Temperby, "V-Force in Bomber Command", *V-Force: Ready for the Unthinkable*, Newsdesk Communications, 2008, pp. 22–23.
217 Wynn, *RAF Nuclear Deterrent Forces*, p. 314.
218 DEFE 13/849, AUS (AS), B.F. 20, note from Frank Cooper, 22 January 1965.
219 DEFE 25/18, George Ward, Secretary of State for Air, "The V-Force and the powered bomb", Memorandum to the Defence Board, 29 October 1958.
220 AIR 8/1942, Cost of strategic deterrent, Annex to: "Nuclear sufficiency and Defence expenditure", 26 February 1958.
221 DEFE 13/849, "Directive for the Air Officer Commanding-in-Chief, Bomber Command, Royal Air Force, AF/W. 292/64.
222 CAB 21/4756, "Procedure for launching nuclear retaliation", informal meeting, Cabinet Office, 15 June 1960.
223 Twigge and Scott, *Planning Armageddon*, p. 205.
224 "Control after attack on UK", R.V. Alred (S.G. (61) 56), 11 December 1961; "Control and Communications" (S.G. (61) 42) (Revised).
225 Jones, *The Official History of the UK Strategic Nuclear Deterrent*, pp. 218–219.
226 "Control after attack on UK", R.V. Alred (S.G. (61) 56), 11 December 1961; "Control and Communications" (S.G. (61) 42) (Revised).
227 CAB 21/4756, "Procedure for launching nuclear retaliation", informal meeting, Cabinet Office, 15 June 1960.
228 Twigge and Scott, *Planning Armageddon*, pp. 87–89.
229 CAB 21/4757, see, for example, note from J. M. Wilson, 5 December 1957.
230 CAB 21/4756, "Nuclear retaliation procedures", letter of 9 July 1959 from F. Cooper, Air Ministry, to J. S. Orme, Cabinet Office; note: "Procedures for authorising nuclear retaliation, RAF Bomber Command" (attached to letter).
231 CAB 21/4840, "Nuclear retaliation consultative procedures", draft memorandum for discussion with the US Government, 18 January 1962.
232 DEFE 13/849, AUS, (AS) B.F. 20, note from Frank Cooper, 22 January 1965.
233 *Hansard*, 26 February 1959, Cols. 1414-1424.
234 Dr Les Ruskell email: 26/11/21.

5. DELIVERING THE MISSION

235 Roy Brocklebank, documents/text provided: 25/6/20.
236 DEFE 25/18, "The number of V-bomber aircraft which will reach their targets", note from Air Ministry to MoD, 10 October 1958.
237 Wynn, *RAF Nuclear Deterrent Forces*, pp. 300–302.
238 AIR 41/85, p. 44.
239 Wynn, *RAF Nuclear Deterrent Forces*, pp. 300–302.
240 Ibid., p. 303.
241 AIR 20/11448, "Bomber dispersals", note from VCAS, 6 June 1961.
242 Wynn, *RAF Nuclear Deterrent Forces*, pp. 304–306.
243 AIR 20/10618, letter from VCAS, Air Marshal E. G. Hudleston, Air Ministry, to Air Marshal Sir Kenneth Cross, AOC-in-C Bomber Command, 2 December 1960.
244 Wynn, *RAF Nuclear Deterrent Forces*, pp. 304–306.
245 AIR 41/86, T. C. G. James, "The RAF in the Post-war Years: Defence Policy and the Royal Air Force 1956–63", 1987, pp. 237, 241.
246 Peter Hennessy, *The Secret State* (Second Edition), Penguin, 2010, pp. 211–212; referring to Annex A, COS 1929/2/11/67.
247 AIR 41/86, pp. 104–105
248 AIR 20/9729, "Deployment of the V-bomber force – Phase 1" (Air Council, A.C. [56]), draft note by AMSO, 5 April 1956.

249 Twigge and Scott, *Planning Armageddon*, p. 53.
250 AIR 20/10530, "Readiness of Bomber Command", outcome of a 21 July 1958 meeting of, inter alia, CAS and the AOC-in-C Bomber Command with the Minister of Defence, 24 July 1958.
251 Lawrence Freedman, *The Evolution of Nuclear Strategy* (Third Edition), Palgrave Macmillan, 2003, pp. 232–233; citing Enthoven and Smith, *How Much is Enough?*, p. 174.
252 Tony Buttler, *British Secret Projects: Jet Bombers since 1949*, Midland Publishing (Ian Allan), 2003, p. 54.
253 Ibid., pp. 55, 61.
254 AIR 2/14578, Air Council, "The Valiant in the low-altitude bombing role", undated, note by DCAS.
255 AIR 2/14578, "Valiant in the low-level altitude bombing role", D.Ops (B&R), Air Commodore B. K. Burnett, loose minute to ACAS (Ops), 27 June 1956.
256 AIR 2/14578, "Bomber Command Trial No. 407 – low-level navigation of 'V' aircraft", letter from Squadron Leader A. D. Gibson, on behalf of the AOC-in-C Bomber Command, to the Under Secretary of State, Air Ministry (D.D.Ops [B]), 25 October 1961; appended to BC/S.96737.
257 AIR 2/14578, "Trial No. 407, low-level navigation in 'V' aircraft" (preliminary report), Bomber Command Development Unit, Report No. 12/61, 3 October 1961.
258 Roy Brocklebank emails: 2/4/20, 18/3/21.
259 AIR 2/14578, "Bomber Command Trial No. 407 – low-level navigation of 'V' aircraft", note on servicing personnel required for outstanding Valiant low-level flights in the Trial No. 407 programme, 25 October 1961, appended to BC/S.96737.
260 AIR 2/14578, HQ Bomber Command, Operation Order 30/61, 16 August 1961.
261 Menaul, *Countdown*, pp. 48–49.
262 Edward Jarron interviewed: 23/7/19.
263 Menaul, *Countdown*, p. 50.
264 Peter West MBE interviewed: 30/4/19.
265 Menaul, *Countdown*, pp. 50–51.
266 Wynn, *RAF Nuclear Deterrent Forces*, p. 74.
267 Ibid., pp. 321–322.
268 Peter Moore email: 18/3/21.

6. V-FORCE PILOTS

269 Wynn, *RAF Nuclear Deterrent Forces*, Introduction, vi–xii.
270 Ibid.
271 Gary West interviewed: 28/3/18.
272 Bonnor, "The V-Force: 1955–1966: Navigation at 50,000 and 500 ft".
273 John Huggins, amongst documents/text provided: 26/10/20.
274 Roger Smith interviewed: 11/12/18.
275 Jon Tye interviewed: 19/2/19.
276 Paul Millikin interviewed: 11/12/18.
277 Nick Dennis interviewed: 30/5/18.
278 Dennis Martin interviewed: 10/12/18.
279 John Huggins, amongst documents/text provided: 26/10/20.
280 Paul Millikin interviewed: 11/12/18.
281 Keith Mans, amongst documents/text provided: 17/11/20.
282 Group Captain Roger Dunsford, amongst documents/text provided: 19/11/20.
283 David Dinmore interviewed 1/5/19.
284 John Reeve interviewed: 29/5/18.
285 Roger Dunsford, amongst documents/text provided: 19/11/20.
286 Nick Dennis interviewed: 30/5/18.
287 David Dinmore interviewed: 1/5/19.
288 Bill MacGillivray interviewed: 5/6/18.
289 Peter Moore interviewed: 6/3/18.
290 Jon Tye interviewed: 19/2/19.
291 Roy Brocklebank, amongst documents/text provided: 25/6/20.
292 Dick Fuller, amongst documents/text provided: 29/10/20.
293 Tony Cottingham interviewed: 8/2/18.
294 Mike Fazackerley, amongst documents/text provided: 15/11/20.

7. NAVIGATORS, AEOS AND GROUND CREW

295   Roy Brocklebank, amongst documents/text provided: 25/6/20.
296   Barry Mullen, amongst documents/text provided: 29/10/20.
297   Wing Commander Vic Bussereau interviewed: 6/6/18.
298   John Weller interviewed: 1/8/18.
299   Udai 'Woody' P. N. Fulena interviewed: 26/6/18.
300   Flight Lieutenant Alan McLoughlin, amongst documents/text provided: 2/11/20.
301   John Laycock interviewed: 27/3/18.
302   Bonnor, "The V-Force: 1955–66: Navigation at 50,000 and 500 ft".
303   'Woody' Fulena interviewed: 26/6/18.
304   Anthony Wright interviewed: 26/3/19.
305   Jim Walker interviewed: 26/3/19.
306   Roy Brocklebank, amongst documents/text provided: 25/6/20.
307   Norman Bonnor, amongst documents/text provided: 1/11/20.
308   Bonnor, "The V-Force: 1955–1966: Navigation at 50,000 and 500 ft".
309   Vic Bussereau interviewed: 6/6/18.
310   Squadron Leader Bob Sinclair interviewed: 5/4/18.
311   Bryan 'Monty' Montgomery interviewed: 27/2/18.
312   Robin Woolven, amongst documents/text provided: 5/11/20.
313   James Vinales interviewed: 24/07/19.
314   Wing Commander Neil Flowerdew interviewed: 12/1/18.
315   Barry Masefield interviewed: 27/2/18.
316   Hugh Prior interviewed: 30/5/18.
317   Squadron Leader Geoff Lidbetter interviewed: 23/7/19.
318   Len Hewitt interviewed: 25/2/17.
319   Ray Gaunt interviewed: 4/4/18.
320   Cliff Doe interviewed: 25/3/19.
321   Lyle 'Taff' Lark interviewed: 27/3/18.

8. ON THE NUCLEAR FRONTLINE

322   DEFE 25/18, note: "Bomber Command", 4 January 1960.
323   AIR 2/17801, "Readiness of the MBF at weekends", letter from Group Captain A. H. C. Boxer, for the AOC-in-C Bomber Command, to the Under Secretary of State, Air Ministry (D.Ops [B.B.M. and R]), 20 July 1960.
324   AIR 41/85, p. 44.
325   AIR 20/10618, "Readiness of the MBF", report from ACAS (Ops) to VCAS on MBF Readiness, 8 February 1960; letter from AOC-in-C Bomber Command to CAS, 9 November 1959.
326   AIR 2/17801, letter, "Essential residential telephones in Bomber Command", from Air Commodore C. G. Stowell to D.Ops (B&R), 16 December 1960.
327   Dr Magnus Clarke, *The Nuclear Destruction of Britain*, Croon Helm, 1982, pp. 238–240.
328   Keith Mans, amongst documents/text provided: 17/11/20.
329   Roy Brocklebank email: 2/4/20.
330   Martin Anscombe interviewed: 28/2/18.
331   Robin Woolven, amongst documents/text provided: 5/11/20.
332   Norman Bonnor, amongst documents/text provided: 1/11/20.
333   Jeremy Mudford interviewed: 8/2/18.
334   John Huggins, amongst documents/text provided: 26/10/20.
335   Roy Brocklebank email: 6/4/20.
336   Clive Richards, "A Wasting Asset? The RAF's Medium Bomber Force in the Aftermath of the Nassau Agreement, 1962–1982".
337   AIR 2/18103, letter, "Effectiveness of Bomber Command in the immediate future (i.e. until the beginning of 1965)," from Air Vice-Marshal John Grandy, ACAS (Ops), to the AOC-in-C Bomber Command, 13 May 1960, ACAS (Ops) CMS.2609/55/F.1351 (S)/Ops 4020.
338   AIR 19/940, DCAS to Secretary of State for Air, "Note on strike potential of MBF", 19 February 1958.
339   Cooper, "The Direction of Air Force Policy in the 1950s and 1960s", pp. 10–21.
340   AIR 14/4208, Bomber Command, Operational Research Branch, Memorandum No. 24, "The effect of tactical routeing on target coverage", March 1959.
341   Wynn, *RAF Nuclear Deterrent Forces*, pp. 186–189.
342   Cooper, "The Direction of Air Force Policy in the 1950s and 1960s", pp. 10–21.
343   Wynn, *RAF Nuclear Deterrent Forces*, p. 198.
344   Gibson, *Vulcan's Hammer*, pp. 21–27.
345   AIR 14/4198, Bomber Command, Operational Research Branch, TS Memorandum No. 14, "Extending the life of the V-bomber force", 26 July 1955.
346   Menaul, *Countdown*, p. 105.

347 Wynn, *RAF Nuclear Deterrent Forces*, p. 605.
348 AVIA 65/1653, correspondence between A. S. Roger and the MoD, 1960.

9. DESTROYING THE TARGETS

349 Vic Bussereau interviewed: 6/6/18.
350 Stoddart, *Losing an Empire and Finding a Role*, p. 234.
351 Freedman, *The Evolution of Nuclear Strategy*, p. 121, citing Colonel T. F. Walkowicz, "Counterforce strategy: how we can exploit America's atomic advantage", *Air Force* Magazine, February 1955, p. 51.
352 Matthew Jones, *The Official History of the UK Strategic Nuclear Deterrent Volume 1*, pp. 35–36.
353 Roy Brocklebank email: 2/4/20.
354 Mark Venables, "The Place of Air Power Doctrine in Post-war British Defence Planning and Its Influence on the Genesis and Development of the Theory of Nuclear Deterrence, 1945–1952", King's College, London, 1985.
355 AIR 14/4287, Bomber Command, Operational Research Branch, Memorandum No. 199, "The effect of delivery accuracy and target allocation on the effectiveness of a nuclear stockpile", around August/ September 1959.
356 Roy Brocklebank note: 21/8/18.
357 Roy Brocklebank note: 22/8/22.
358 Dr Les Ruskell email: 26/4/21.
359 AIR 14/4287.
360 Norris and Kristensen, "The British Nuclear Stockpile", pp. 69–75.
361 AIR 14/4287.
362 Roy Brocklebank email: 10/8/18.
363 Roy Brocklebank note: 21/8/18.
364 Roy Brocklebank, amongst documents/text provided: 25/6/20.
365 Philip Goodall, *My Target was Leningrad: V-Force: Preserving Our Democracy*, Fonthill Media, 2015, p. 134.
366 Roy Brocklebank, letter, amongst documents/text provided: 25/6/20.
367 Roger Smith interviewed: 11/12/18.
368 Roy Brocklebank, amongst documents/text provided: 25/6/20.
369 Norman Bonnor email: 9/1/17.
370 Roy Brocklebank email: 2/4/20.
371 Norman Bonner email: 9/1/17.
372 Norman Bonner discussion with author: 6/11/16.
373 Norman Bonner email: 9/1/17.
374 Roy Brocklebank note: 2/4/20.
375 Roy Brocklebank; amongst documents/text provided: 25/6/20.
376 Roy Brocklebank; letter: 5/7/18.
377 John Reeve interviewed: 29/5/18.
378 Cooper, "The Direction of Air Force policy in the 1950s and 1960s", pp. 10–21.
379 AIR 2/13717, "Study of the present ability of Bomber Command to come to an Alert State", 28 October 1957.
380 Goodall, *My Target was Leningrad*, pp. 156–157.
381 Wynn, *RAF Nuclear Deterrent Forces*, pp. 273–274.
382 AIR 2/13717, Memorandum, the Chiefs of Staff Committee, "Strategic target policy for Bomber Command", 15 October 1957 (C.O.S. [57] 278).
383 Jones, *The Official History of the UK Strategic Nuclear Deterrent: Volume 1*, p. 51.
384 Twigge and Scott, *Planning Armageddon*, p. 71.
385 Jones, *The Official History of the UK Strategic Nuclear Deterrent: Volume 1*, p. 161.
386 Twigge and Scott, *Planning Armageddon*, p. 73.
387 Jones, *The Official History of the UK Strategic Nuclear Deterrent: Volume 1*, p. 164.
388 Ibid., pp. 293–295.
389 Twigge and Scott, *Planning Armageddon*, p. 72.
390 Ibid.
391 Baylis and Stoddart, *The British Nuclear Experience*, p. 128.
392 Ibid., p. 102.
393 Kristan Stoddart, *Losing an Empire and Finding a Role*, p. 10.
394 Ibid., p. 46.
395 Jones, *The Official History of the UK Strategic Nuclear Deterrent: Volume 1*, p. 306.
396 Ibid.
397 Ibid.
398 AIR 8/2201, "Strategic strike planning by Bomber Command", memorandum from T. O. Prickett, ACAS (Ops), to the CAS, 5 October 1962.
399 Ibid.
400 Ken Young, *The American Bomb in Britain: US Air Forces' Strategic Presence, 1946-64*, Manchester University Press, 2016, p. 263.
401 AIR 8/2201.
402 Anthony Wright interviewed: 26/3/19.

403 Roy Brocklebank, amongst documents/text provided: 25/6/20.
404 Brocklebank email: 13/4/20.
405 Brocklebank email: 2/4/20.
406 Peter Moore email: 24/2/21.
407 Brocklebank, "How did Bomber Command prepare for war?"; Roy Brocklebank, amongst documents/text provided: 25/6/20.
408 Dick Fuller, amongst documents/text provided: 29/10/20.
409 Nick Dennis interviewed: 30/5/18.
410 Roger Dunsford, amongst documents/text provided: 20/4/20.
411 Norman Bonnor, amongst documents/text provided: 1/11/20.
412 Bill MacGillivray interviewed: 5/6/18.
413 Roy Brocklebank email: 6/4/20.
414 Roy Brocklebank, amongst documents/text provided: 25/6/20.
415 Twigge and Scott, *Planning Armageddon*, pp. 70–71.
416 Wynn, *RAF Nuclear Deterrent Forces*, 313 (fn.).
417 "Target America", minute to the Prime Minister from the Secretary of State for Air, 11 January 1963; "Air defence – notes in reply to Minister's minute of January 7," Group Captain Hodgkinson; "Target America", minute from the Prime Minister to the Secretary of State for Air, 8 January 1963 (PM's personal minute, Serial No. M4/63).
418 Edward Jarron interviewed: 23/7/19.
419 John Huggins, documents/text provided: 26/10/20.
420 AIR 14/4333, Bomber Command, Operational Research Branch, Memorandum No. 264, "Exercise Matador 2", 8 February 1963.

10. THE THREAT TO THE AIRFIELDS

421 Andrew Brookes, *V-Force: A History of Britain's Airborne Deterrent*, Jane's, 1982, p. 143.
422 AIR 8/1934, "Likely Soviet courses of action up to January 1 1957", ACAS briefing for Defence Committee meeting, 28 October 1955, DC(55), 46.
423 Roy Brocklebank email: 18/3/21.
424 AIR 8/1858, "Warning of attack", briefing note for the CAS, 30 September 1953, COS 1588/15/9/53.
425 AIR 8/1858, "Warning of attack", ACAS briefing note for the CAS, 4 January 1955.
426 AIR 8/1942, "Future metropolitan fighter force", note for CAS.
427 Richard Lamb, *The Macmillan Years, 1957-1963*, John Murray, 1995, pp. 282–283.
428 Ibid., p. 284.
429 AIR 6/124, "Future size and shape of the Royal Air Force", note from the VCAS to the Air Council Standing Committee, 7 June 1956, SC (56) 16.
430 Michael Armitage, *The Royal Air Force: An Illustrated History*, Arms and Armour, 1993, p. 204.
431 AIR 2/16435, "USAF request for information of RAF QRA status", loose minute from Wing Commander D. G. Evans, Air Plans 2, to D.Ops (B&R) and others, 5 April 1963.
432 AIR 2/13717, "Study of the present ability of Bomber Command to come to an alert state", D.D.Ops (B), 28 October 1957.
433 Richards, "Time is No Longer Our Ally", pp. 39–40; CAB 21/4035, JPG/55/1, JIC (55) 12, 4 January 1955.
434 AIR 6/124.
435 Michael Hely, "Afterthoughts", RAF Historical Society, *Journal 26 – Seminar: The RAF and Nuclear Weapons 1960-98*, 2001, pp. 105–112.
436 Menaul, *Countdown*, p. 112.
437 AIR 14/4305, Bomber Command, Operational Research Branch, Memorandum No. 222, "Calculations of the minimum warning times obtainable from the BMEWS, at Fylingdales Moor, of ballistic missile attacks on the United Kingdom", April 1961.
438 AIR 14/4354, Bomber Command, Operational Research Branch, Memorandum No. 285, "BMEWS and the QRA force", February 1964.

11. QUICK REACTION ALERT

439 Richards, "Time is No Longer Our Ally", pp. 47–48.
440 Wynn, *RAF Nuclear Deterrent Forces*, pp. 363–372.
441 Anthony Wright interviewed: 26/3/19.
442 Dick Fuller, amongst documents/text provided: 29/10/20.
443 Tony Cottingham interviewed: 8/2/18.
444 Wynn, *RAF Nuclear Deterrent Forces*, pp. 467–497.
445 Ibid., pp. 363–367.
446 Ibid., p. 334.
447 AIR 8/2369, letter from Air Marshal Sir Kenneth Cross, AOC-in-C Bomber Command, to Air Chief Marshal Sir Edmund Hudleston, VCAS, 31 October 1961.
448 AIR 8/2369, Air Council, conclusions of meeting 23(61), 7 December 1961, item iv.
449 AIR 2/16435, "Notes on Bomber Command plan to meet increased QRA commitment", Ops B.2, draft, 17 January 1963.

450 Edward Jarron interviewed: 23/7/19.
451 Baylis, *Ambiguity and Deterrence,* p. 349.
452 Wynn, *RAF Nuclear Deterrent Forces,* p. 335.
453 Squadron Leader Robin Woolven, "Selected chronology of the RAF and the 1962 Cuban Missile Crisis, *Air Power Review,* Deterrence Special Edition, Vol. 20, No. 2, Summer 2017, pp. 140–41.
454 AIR 8/2639, "Increased Readiness – Bomber Command", letter from Bomber Command AOC-in-C, Air Marshal Sir Kenneth Cross, to the CAS, Marshal of the Royal Air Force Sir Thomas G. Pike, 10 January 1963.
455 AIR 8/2369, Air Council, conclusions of meeting 23(61), 7 December 1961, Secret Annex.
456 AIR 8/2369, "Guard duties – Bomber Command stations", 28 November 1961.
457 AIR 14/4354, Bomber Command, Operational Research Branch, Memorandum No. 285, "BMEWS and the QRA force", February 1964.
458 Moore, *Nuclear Illusion, Nuclear Reality,* p. 224.
459 Roy Brocklebank email: 21/4/20.
460 Roy Brocklebank email: 25/6/20.
461 AIR 2/16435, Air Plans 2/TS. 1204, "Quick Reaction Alert", loose minute and briefing document, Group Captain J. R. L. Blount, A/D Air Plans, 17 December 1963.

12. CUBA AND LIFE ON QRA

462 Nick Dennis interviewed: 30/5/18.
463 'Woody' Fulena interviewed: 26/6/18.
464 Alan White, *The King's Thunderbolts: No. 44 (Rhodesia) Squadron, Royal Air Force: An Operational Record and Roll of Honour, 1917–1982,* Tucann, 2007, p. 180.
465 AIR 2/16435, D.Ops (B&R) (RAF), from Headquarters, Bomber Command to MoD Air, Subject: QRA (handwritten annotation), 20 January 1965.
466 AIR 14/4327, Bomber Command, Operational Research Branch, Memorandum No. 258, "The Quick Reaction Alert in Bomber Command", October 1962, Appendix A.
467 Ibid., Appendix B.
468 Blackman and Wright, *Valiant Boys,* p. 147.
469 AIR 14/4327, Appendix B.
470 White, *The King's Thunderbolts,* p. 180.
471 Peter Moore email:18/3/21.
472 Peter Moore email: 24/2/21.
473 White, *The King's Thunderbolts,* p. 183.
474 Peter Moore email: 18/3/21.
475 Cliff Doe interviewed: 28/3/19.
476 AIR 14/4327, Appendix C.
477 Roy Brocklebank email 5/4/20.
478 Roy Brocklebank email: 22/3/21.
479 AIR 14/4327, Appendix C.
480 Ibid.
481 Ibid.
482 Roy Brocklebank email: 9/4/20.
483 Brookes, *V-Force – The History of Britain's Airborne Deterrent,* p. 82.
484 Young, *The American Bomb in Britain,* p. 94.
485 Goodall, *My Target was Leningrad,* p. 160.
486 AIR 14/4327.
487 Jim Wilson, *Britain on the Brink: The Cold War's Most Dangerous Weekend, October 27–28 1962,* Pen & Sword, 2012, p. 121.
488 Menaul, *Countdown,* p. 114.
489 Twigge and Scott, *Planning Armageddon,* p. 123; citing AIR 25/1703, Operations Record Book, Headquarters, No. 1 Group, 27 October 1962.
490 Wilson, *Britain on the Brink,* p. 130.
491 Twigge and Scott, *Planning Armageddon,* p. 123; citing AIR 25/1703, Operations Record Book, Headquarters, No. 1 Group, 27 October 1962.
492 Ibid.
493 Menaul, *Countdown,* p. 115.
494 Dr Les Ruskell email: 26/11/21.
495 Stewart Menaul, *Countdown,* pp. 116–117.
496 Martin Anscombe interviewed: 28/2/18.
497 White, *The King's Thunderbolts,* p. 183.
498 Air Vice-Marshal Michael Robinson, "Summary of the previous RAF Historical Society seminar on the origin and development of the British nuclear deterrent 1945–60", RAF Historical Society, *Journal 26 – Seminar: The RAF and Nuclear Weapons 1960–98,* 2001, pp. 10–15.
499 Twigge and Scott, *Planning Armageddon,* p. 127.

500 Dick Fuller, documents/text provided: 29/10/20.
501 Peter West interviewed: 30/4/19.
502 Dave Beane, amongst documents/text provided: 27/10/20.
503 Norman Bonnor, amongst documents/text provided: 1/11/20.
504 Roy Brocklebank email: 22/3/21.
505 AIR 8/2369, note of CAS meeting, Air Ministry, 15 January 1964.
506 AIR 8/2369, letter from VCAS to ACAS (Ops), 17 February 1964.
507 AIR 8/2369, note to CAS from PS, 31 December 1963.
508 AIR 8/2369, letter from the VCAS to the CAS, 24 December 1963.
509 AIR 8/2369, note from CAS to VCAS, 20 May 1965.

13. REDUCING EXPOSURE ON THE GROUND

510 Richards, "Time is No Longer Our Ally", p. 39 citing Bernard Bradie, "Strategy in the Missile Age", RAND, 1959, p. 283.
511 AIR 14/4286, Bomber Command, Operational Research Branch, Memorandum No. 197, "Keeping a proportion of the bomber force airborne in an emergency", 13 July 1959.
512 Richards, "Time is No Longer Our Ally", p. 48.
513 AIR 14/4211, Bomber Command, Operational Research Branch, Memorandum No. 28, "Aircraft utilisation during a continuous airborne alert using freefall and stand-off weapons", March 1962.
514 AIR 14/4315, Bomber Command, Operational Research Branch, Memorandum No. 245, "Trial No. 441: An airborne alert, analysis of the aircraft servicing aspects", April 1962.
515 AIR 14/4311, Bomber Command, Operational Research Branch, Memorandum No. 241, "The vulnerability of the MBF to ballistic missile attack", November 1961.
516 AIR 19/940, note by the Secretary of State for Air, 19 February 1962.
517 Peter Hudson, "A View from Whitehall", Deterrence Special Edition, *Air Power Review*, Vol. 20, No. 2, Summer 2017, p. 94.
518 AIR 14/4210, Bomber Command, Operational Research Branch, Memorandum No. S.26, "Target cover from remote dispersal bases overseas", October 1959.
519 Peter Moore email: 18/3/21.
520 AIR 14/4210.
521 Twigge and Scott, *Planning Armageddon*, p. 296.
522 Roger Dunsford, email, amongst documents/text provided: 19/11/20.
523 AIR 2/17801, "BCAR plan – Alert Conditions and Readiness States", Appendix A to a letter from Group Captain A. D. Frank, for SASO, Bomber Command, to Headquarters, No. 1 Group, 18 August 1961 (BC/S.96237/Ops).
524 Roy Brocklebank email: 15/4/19.
525 Wynn, *RAF Nuclear Deterrent Forces*, pp. 334–335.
526 Andrew Brookes, "V-Force Operational Deployment and Readiness", RAF Historical Society, *Journal 26 – Seminar: The RAF and Nuclear Weapons 1960–98*, 2001, pp. 54–66.
527 AIR 2/17801, "Effects of the missile threat to the deterrent", letter from Group Captain A. D. Frank, for AOC-in-C, Bomber Command, to the Under-Secretary of State (D.Ops [B&R]), Air Ministry, 24 January 1961.
528 Richards, "Time is No Longer Our Ally", p. 44.
529 AIR 8/2238, "Readiness of Bomber Command", meeting of the Minister of Defence with the Secretary of State for Air, 21 July 1958.
530 AIR 8/2238, "Progress report on the readiness of the MBF", 1 July 1959.
531 AIR 8/2238, letter from Air Chief Marshal Sir Thomas Pike to the First Sea Lord, Admiral Sir Caspar John, 11 July 1961.
532 AIR 20/11554, "A note on the dispersal and operation of the MBF", referencing a CAS meeting on 23 November 1955, C.M.S. 2518/D.D.Ops (B).
533 AIR 20/9729, "Deployment of the V-bomber force – Phase 1", note by AMSO, Air Council.
534 Roy Brocklebank email: 16/4/19.
535 AIR 41/86, p. 105.
536 AIR 20/11554, "V-bomber and PR force dispersal: Completion of the V-bomber dispersal plan, dispersal of the PR force and implications of second and third bomber lifts", Air Council note by VCAS and AMSO (A.C. (58) 7), 4 February 1958.
537 Roy Brocklebank email: 5/4/20.
538 AIR 2/16435, "Allocation of dispersal airfields for the MBF", loose minute from Air Commodore A. W. Heward, D.Ops (B&R), to ACAS (Ops), 1 March 1963.
539 Wayne D. Cocroft and Roger J. C. Thomas, ed. P. S. Barnwell, *Cold War: Building for Nuclear Confrontation 1946–1989*, Historic England, 2016, p. 27.
540 Roy Brocklebank email: 21/4/20.
541 Peter Moore email: 24/2/21.
542 Tony Cottingham interviewed 8/2/18.
543 Wynn, *RAF Nuclear Deterrent Forces*, pp. 262–263.
544 Ibid., pp. 263–264.
545 Ibid.
546 Roy Brocklebank, letter, amongst document/text provided: 25/6/20.
547 Gary West interviewed: 28/3/18.
548 Robin Woolven, amongst documents/text provided: 5/11/20.
549 Norman Bonnor, amongst documents/text provided: 1/11/20.

550 Roy Brocklebank, amongst documents/text provided: 25/6/20.
551 Roy Brocklebank email: 5/4/20.
552 Norman Bonnor, amongst documents/text provided: 1/11/20.
553 Roy Brocklebank email: 5/4/20; documents/text provided: 25/6/20.
554 Bob Sinclair interviewed: 5/4/18.

14. GENERATING WEAPON SYSTEMS

555 Freedman, *The Evolution of Nuclear Strategy*, pp. 232–233; citing Enthovan and Smith, "How much is enough?", p. 174.
556 DEFE 13/306, "Vulnerability of the V-bomber force", conclusions, meeting of the Defence Board, 4 April 1960.
557 Tom Kerr, *Always a Challenge: An RAF Scientist in the Cold War Years – A First-Hand Account*, self-published, 2002, p. 80.
558 DEFE 13/306. "Vulnerability of the V-bomber force", conclusions, meeting of the Defence Board, 4 April 1960.
559 Ibid.; note by J. M. Wilson, Defence Board Secretariat, 4 April 1960.
560 AIR 2/19184, "Air-delivered strategic nuclear weapons systems", Air Force Department paper to the Long Term Strategic Nuclear Working Party, Interim Report, 30 September 1971.
561 AIR 14/4327.
562 Roy Brocklebank email: 12/11/21.
563 Edward Jarron interviewed: 23/7/19.
564 Roy Brocklebank email: 4/12/19.
565 Roy Brocklebank email: 22/3/21.
566 Peter Moore email: 18/3/21.
567 AIR 8/2369, note by Air Marshal W. H. Kyle, VCAS, 10 May 1963.
568 AIR 8/2369, minute to CAS from Air Vice-Marshal D. G. Smallwood, ACAS (Ops), 28 August 1963.
569 AIR 14/4359, Bomber Command, Operational Research Branch, Memorandum No. 298, "Analysis of Exercise Nursemaid, 14–15 April 1964", August 1964.
570 Roy Brocklebank email, amongst documents/text provided: 25/6/20.
571 AIR 14/4385, Bomber Command, Operational Research Branch, Memorandum No. 326, "The likely operational effectiveness of the Blue Steel QRA force, April–September 1965", March 1966.
572 AIR 14/4374, Bomber Command, Operational Research Branch, Memorandum No. 314, "The likely operational effectiveness of the freefall QRA force, May 1964–April 1965", September 1965.
573 Bill Taylor interviewed: 19/2/19.
574 AIR 14/4341, Bomber Command, Operational Research Branch, Memorandum No. 272, "Blue Steel and QRA", July 1963.
575 AIR 14/4356, Bomber Command, Operational Research Branch, Memorandum No. 288, "A study of Blue Steel weapon system generation using computer simulation", April 1964.
576 Robin Woolven, "Defence through deterrence: British policy during the 1960s and 1970s", Witness Seminar, Institute of Contemporary British History and Defence Studies Department, King's College, London, 10 September 2014.
577 Robin Woolven amongst documents/text provided: 5/11/20.
578 Bonnor, "Blue Steel – the V-Force's stand-off bomb".
579 Norman Bonnor, "General Notes"; amongst documents/text provided: 1/11/20.
580 AIR 14/4368, Bomber Command, Operational Research Branch, Memorandum No. 307, "Missile recovery from Exercise Mick at RAF Scampton", December 1964.
581 AIR 14/4369, Bomber Command, Operational Research Branch, Memorandum No. 308, "Missile recovery from Exercise Micky Finn 4 at RAF Scampton", February 1965.
582 AIR 14/4380, Bomber Command, Operational Research Branch, Memorandum No. 321, "Analysis of Blue Steel system generation in Exercise Mick, October 11 1965", December 1965.
583 Moore, *Nuclear Illusion, Nuclear Reality*, p. 97.
584 AIR 8/2369, "Exercise Micky Finn – October 1964", draft minute from Air Vice-Marshal D. G. Smallwood, ACAS (Ops), November 1964, subsequently sent to CAS for a possible minute from him to the Minister (RAF).
585 AIR 14/4378, Bomber Command, Operational Research Branch, Memorandum No. 319, "Analysis of Blue Steel system generation in Exercise Micky Finn 5", September 1965.
586 AIR 14/4389, Bomber Command, Operational Research Branch, Memorandum No. 330, "Analysis of Blue Steel system generation in Exercise 'Finnigan'", June 1966.
587 AIR 14/4385, Bomber Command, Operational Research Branch, Memorandum No. 326, "The likely operational effectiveness of the Blue Steel QRA force: April-September 1965", March 1966.
588 AIR 14/4391, Bomber Command, Operational Research Branch, Memorandum No. 332 "Review of Blue Steel system generation: March 1964–May 1966", July 1966.
589 AIR 8/2369, "Bomber Command, Exercise Micky Finn", note, AVM L. M. Hodges, ACAS (Ops), to the PS to CAS, 13 July 1967.

15. SURVIVING A WAR SCRAMBLE

590 John Laycock interviewed: 27/3/18.
591 Roy Brocklebank, amongst documents/text provided: 25/6/20.
592 Phil Leckenby, "QRA – A Personal Reminiscence", *655 Maintenance and Preservation Society*, Issue 29, Spring 2013, originally published in the *44 (Rhodesia) Squadron Newsletter*.

593 Mark Galeotti, *Spetsnaz: Russia's Special Forces*, Osprey Publishing, 2015, pp. 5, 15, 19.
594 Robin Woolven email: 8/2/22.
595 Wikipedia, 2022 "Military Provost Guard Service". Last modified January 21 2022.
596 Major Burton A. Casteel Jr, USAF, "Spetsnaz: A Soviet Sabotage Threat", Report No. 86-0500, Air Command and Staff College, Air University, Maxwell AFB, April 1986.
597 AIR 2/14716, letter from Air Vice-Marshal J. N. T. Stephenson, ACAS (Policy), to AOC-in-Cs of all RAF Commands, September 1958.
598 Phil Leckenby, "QRA – A Personal Reminiscence".
599 Edward Jarron interviewed: 23/7/19.
600 John Huggins, "Vulcan War Flight", paper; amongst documents/text provided: 26/10/20.
601 Robin Woolven, amongst documents/text provided: 5/11/20.
602 Paddy Langdown, lecture notes: "The Vulcan deterrent".
603 AIR 14/4289, Bomber Command, Operational Research Branch, Memorandum No. 201, "Exercise Mayflight", 4–7 May 1959.
604 AIR 14/4302, Bomber Command, Operational Research Branch, Memorandum No. 219, "Analysis of Exercise Mayflight 3, July 1960", October 1960.
605 Tony Cottingham interviewed: 8/2/18.
606 Dick Fuller, amongst documents/text provided: 29/10/20.
607 Air Chief Marshal Sir Michael Alcock, GCB, KBE, DSc, FREng; "V-Force development – simultaneous engine starting", article based on a paper to the RAF Historical Society, proceedings for 22 October 2013.
608 Air Chief Marshal Sir Michael Alcock email: 20/5/19.
609 DEFE 25/86, memorandum by the Chief of the Defence Staff, "V-bomber readiness" (DRP/M [61]8, Item 4), 3 July 1961.
610 AIR 8/2238, "V-bombers – engine starting systems", minute, Air Marshal R. B. Lees, DCAS, 19 July 1961.
611 AIR 14/4305, Bomber Command, Operational Research Branch, Memorandum No. 222, "Calculations of the minimum warning times obtainable from the BMEWS at Fylingdales Moor, of ballistic missile attacks on the UK", April 1961.
612 John Huggins, amongst documents/text provided: 26/10/20.
613 Roy Brocklebank note: October 2018.
614 John Huggins, amongst documents/text provided: 26/10/20.
615 AIR 14/4311, Bomber Command, Operational Research Branch, Memorandum No. 241, "The vulnerability of the MBF to ballistic missile attack", March 1962.
616 Roy Brocklebank email: 20/4/19.
617 AIR 14/4311.
618 Roy Brocklebank email: 5/4/20.
619 AIR 14/4311.
620 Roy Brocklebank email:18/3/21.
621 AIR 14/4311.
622 Roy Brocklebank email: 5/4/20.
623 AIR 14/4311.
624 Roy Brocklebank email: 20/3/19.
625 AIR 14/4311.

16. LIVING ON YOUR NERVES

626 Edward Jarron interviewed: 23/7/19.
627 Rob Williams, amongst documents/text provided: 27/10/20.
628 John Huggins, amongst documents/text provided: 26/10/20.
629 Roy Brocklebank, amongst documents/text provided: 25/6/20.
630 Peter Moore email: 24/2/21.
631 Jim Milne interviewed: 5/4/18.
632 Roy Brocklebank email: 31/1/22.
633 Bob Sinclair interviewed: 5/4/18.
634 John Huggins, amongst documents/text provided: 26/10/20.
635 Jim Walker interviewed: 26/3/19.
636 Edgar Jones, "LMF: the use of psychiatric stigma in the Royal Air Force during the Second World War", *The Journal of Military History*, 70, April 2006, pp. 439–458.
637 AIR 19/632, Annex to Air Council Letter A. 301810/58/S.10 (d), "Disposal of aircrew who forfeit the confidence of their Commanding Officers", 6 November 1959.
638 Air Vice-Marshal Nigel Baldwin, "Morning Discussion", RAF Historical Society, *Journal 20 – Seminar: Training in Peace for War*, 1999, pp. 42–54.
639 Jeremy Mudford interviewed: 8/2/18.
640 Tony Smith interviewed: 11/11/18.
641 Roger Smith interviewed: 11/12/18.
642 David Dinmore interviewed: 1/5/19.
643 Goodall, *My Target was Leningrad*, p. 133.
644 John Weller interviewed: 1/8/18.
645 Ibid.

646 Ibid.
647 Roy Brocklebank email: 31/1/22.
648 Peter Moore email: 18/3/21.
649 Norman Bonnor, amongst documents/text provided: 1/11/20.
650 Roy Brocklebank email: 10/4/20.
651 Air Vice-Marshal Nigel Baldwin, "Afternoon Discussion Period", RAF Historical Society, *Journal 26 – Seminar: The RAF and Nuclear Weapons 1960–98*, 2001, pp. 93–97.
652 AIR 20/11448, Air Ministry, V-bomber dispersal: "The case for 36 dispersal airfields", 11 September 1962, and associated notes, 13 September 1962.
653 AIR 14/4122, Bomber Command, Operational Research Branch, Memorandum No. 301, "Air exercises and operational research in Bomber Command", August 1964.
654 John Laycock interviewed: 27/3/18.
655 Bill Taylor interviewed: 19/2/19.

17. SOVIET AIR DEFENCES

656 "Soviet Bloc Air and Missile Defense Capabilities Through Mid-1967", *National Intelligence Estimate Number 11-3-62*, submitted by the Director of Central Intelligence, 31 October 1962, released under the CIA Historical Review Program.
657 Robert Hewson, "Soviet Threat and Countermeasures", *V-Force: Ready for the Unthinkable*, pp. 16–17.
658 "The Development of Soviet Air Defense Doctrine and Practice", Historical Evaluation & Research Organization, for Sandia National Laboratories, SAND 80-7146/1, April 1981, 92.
659 Roy Brocklebank email: 22/3/21.
660 Roy Brocklebank email: 3/4/20.
661 "Soviet Bloc Air and Missile Defense Capabilities Through Mid-1967", *National Intelligence Estimate Number 11-3-62*.
662 AIR 2/19184, Air Force Department, "Air-delivered strategic nuclear weapon systems", September 1971.
663 Wing Commander David Paton, assisted by Master Aircrew Derek Oliver, "Airborne electronic reconnaissance, 1948-1989"; RAF Historical Society, *Journal 23 – Seminar: Cold War Intelligence Gathering*, 2001, pp. 59–68.
664 Ibid.
665 James T. Quinlivan, "Soviet Strategic Air Defense: A Long Past and an Uncertain Future", AD-A228-306, paper, The RAND Corporation, September 1989, 10.
666 Donald E. Walzenbach, "The Anglo-American origins of overflying the Soviet Union: the case of the 'invisible aircraft'", proceedings of the joint meeting, RAF Historical Society and the Airforce Historical Foundation, "Seeing off the Bear, Anglo-American Air Power Cooperation during the Cold War", 9–10 September 1993, Air Force History and Museums Program, USAF, 1995, pp. 191–207.
667 Ibid.
668 Squadron Leader John Crampton, "Afternoon Discussion Period", RAF Historical Society, *Journal 23 – Seminar: Cold War Intelligence Gathering*, 2001, pp. 97–99.
669 Quinlivan, "Soviet Strategic Air Defense: A Long Past and an Uncertain Future", pp. 10–12.
670 Wikipedia, 2021. "Surface-to-air missile". Last modified July 21 2021, en.wikipedia.org/wiki/surface-to-air_missile
671 Julian Grenfell email: 10/4/19.
672 Quinlivan, "Soviet Strategic Air Defense: A Long Past and an Uncertain Future", pp. 12–13.
673 Roy Brocklebank email: 5/4/20.
674 Quinlivan, "Soviet Strategic Air Defense: A Long Past and an Uncertain Future", pp. 15–16.
675 AIR 2/19184, Air Force Department, "Air-delivered strategic nuclear weapon systems", September 1971.
676 Ibid, Annex C.
677 Roy Brocklebank email: 6/4/20.
678 AIR 2/19184.
679 Julian Grenfell email: 14/4/19.
680 AIR 2/19184.
681 Kerr, *Always a Challenge: An RAF Scientist in the Cold War Years*, p. 74.
682 AIR 2/19184.
683 Julian Grenfell, "Vulcan Paper", notes, undated.
684 Julian Grenfell email: 14/4/19.
685 Quinlivan, "Soviet Strategic Air Defense: A Long Past and an Uncertain Future", p. 13.
686 Ibid, pp. 13–14.
687 Goodall, *My Target was Leningrad*, p. 164.
688 Julian Grenfell email: 14/4/19.
689 AIR 2/19184, Air Force Department, "Air-delivered strategic nuclear weapon systems", September 1971.
690 DEFE 58/90, Strike Command Development Unit Report No.9/68 – Part 1: HQ STC Trial No.549 Phase C – "Defence penetration techniques: the problem of defence penetration by Vulcan aircraft at low flight altitudes during a limited conventional conflict in a non-European area", Annex L, December 31 1968.
691 AIR 2/19184.
692 "The Development of Soviet Air Defense Doctrine and Practice", Historical Evaluation & Research Organization, for Sandia, April 1981, p. 81.
693 AIR 2/19184.
694 John Laycock interviewed: 27/3/18.

18. PENETRATING THE DEFENCES

695 AIR 14/4306, Bomber Command, Operational Research Branch, Memorandum No. 223, "Effectiveness of the Red Shrimp jammer in Exercises Spellbound 1, 2 and 3", April 1961.
696 AIR 14/4318, Bomber Command, Operational Research Branch, Memorandum No. 249, "Performance of ECM in Exercise Spellbound 14", June 1962.
697 Roy Brocklebank, amongst documents/text provided: 25/6/20.
698 AIR 14/4313, Bomber Command, Operational Research Branch, Memorandum No. 243, "Performance of ECM in Exercises Spellbound", August 1962.
699 Roy Brocklebank email: 6/4/20.
700 AIR 14/4344, Bomber Command, Operational Research Branch, Memorandum No. 275, "The vulnerability of strike aircraft during low-level penetration of enemy defences", September 1963.
701 Hudson, "A View from Whitehall", p. 94.
702 AIR 19/727, Air Vice-Marshal T. O. Prickett, ACAS (Ops), Guidance Memorandum, "The Deterrent Policy", 13 June 1961.
703 Bonnor, "Blue Steel – the V-Force's stand-off bomb".
704 Nick Dennis interviewed: 30/5/18.
705 John Weller interviewed: 1/8/18.
706 Peter West interviewed: 30/4/19.
707 Jim Walker interviewed: 26/3/19.
708 Roy Brocklebank emails: 3/4/20, 20/4/20.
709 AIR 14/4300, Bomber Command, Operational Research Branch, Memorandum No. 217, "PPI analysis for bombing assessment", Bombing Assessment Team, BC/S.553/RES., October 1960.
710 DEFE 58/90.
711 Paul Hickley, "Defence through Deterrence: British Policy during the 1960s and 1970s", Witness Seminar, Institute of Contemporary British History and Defence Studies Department, King's College, London, 10 September 2014.
712 AIR 14/4341, Bomber Command, Operational Research Branch, Memorandum No. 272, "Blue Steel and QRA", July 1963.
713 Julian Grenfell, "Vulcan Paper".
714 Dick Fuller, amongst documents/text provided: 29/10/20.
715 AIR 2/19184.
716 Ibid, Annex A, Appendix D.
717 Ibid, Annex A.
718 Ibid.
719 Quinlivan, "Soviet Strategic Air Defense: A Long Past and an Uncertain Future", p. 14.
720 AIR 2/19184.
721 AIR 14/4283, Bomber Command, Operational Research Branch, Memorandum No. 192, "The interception of Bomber Command day raids in Exercise Sunbeam", March 1959.
722 Peter West interviewed: 30/4/19.
723 Roy Brocklebank, amongst documents/text provided: 25/6/20.
724 Robert Owen, 617 Squadron Historian, Operations Record Book, 617 Squadron, August 1968; extract provided: 4/4/19.
725 "Doctrine and Theory of Soviet Anti-Air Defense", 9 July 1958, translation of Russian language original document, Central Intelligence Agency, 5OX1-HUM; https://www.cia.gov/library/readingroom/document/cia-rdp81-01043r002300240011-4
726 Roger Dunsford amongst documents/text provided: 20/4/20.

19. ECM AND OTHER COUNTERMEASURES

727 Air Marshal Sir Frederick Sowrey, KCB, CBE, AFC, "Introduction by Seminar Chairman", RAF Historical Society, *Journal 28 – Seminar: Electronic Warfare*, 2003, p. 13.
728 DEFE 58/90.
729 Wing Commander 'Jeff' Jefford, "EW in the early post-war years – Lincolns to Valiants", RAF Historical Society, *Journal 28 – Seminar: Electronic Warfare*, 2003, pp. 58–69; Wing Commander Rod Powell, "EW during the V-Force era", RAF Historical Society, *Journal 28 – Seminar: Electronic Warfare*, 2003, pp. 70–85.
730 Roy Brocklebank email: 6/4/20.
731 AIR 14/4122, Bomber Command, Operational Research Branch, Memorandum No. 301, "Air exercises and operational research in Bomber Command", R. Bruce and S. H. Hood, August 1964.
732 Wynn, *RAF Nuclear Deterrent Forces*, p. 322.
733 Roy Brocklebank email: 12/8/19.
734 Dick Fuller, amongst documents/text provided: 29/10/20.
735 DEFE 58/90.
736 AIR 14/4387, Bomber Command, Operational Research Branch, Memorandum No. 328, Trial No. 512, "Effectiveness of Window dispensed at low level against a fire control radar", April 1966.
737 Wing Commander Peter West, "Defence through deterrence: British policy during the 1960s and 1970s", Witness Seminar, Institute of Contemporary British History and Defence Studies Department, King's College, London, 10 September 2014.

738 AIR 14/3898, minute, Bomber Command Chief Research Officer T. H. Kerr, "The use of warning devices (Red Steer and Blue Saga) during attacks by fighter aircraft on bomber aircraft flying at high and low level", 4 July 1963.
739 Julian Grenfell interviewed: 10/12/18.
740 AIR 14/3898, BC/S.554/Res., note from R. Bruce, Acting Chief Research Officer, Bomber Command, 6 May 1960.
741 Dave Beane, amongst documents/text provided: 27/10/20.
742 Barry Masefield interviewed: 27/2/18.
743 Roger Dunsford, amongst documents/text provided: 20/4/20.
744 Hugh Prior interviewed: 30/5/18.
745 Roy Brocklebank email: 18/3/21.
746 Hugh Prior interviewed: 30/5/18.
747 John Reeve interviewed: 29/5/18.
748 DEFE 58/90.
749 Ibid., main report.
750 Ibid., Annex B.
751 Roy Brocklebank email: 6/4/20.
752 Martin Anscombe interviewed: 28/2/18.
753 Powell, "EW during the V-Force era", pp. 70–85.
754 Roy Brocklebank email: 22/3/21.
755 Powell, "EW during the V-Force era", pp. 70–85.
756 AIR 8/2572, letter from Air Marshal Sir Peter Fletcher, VCAS, to Air Chief Marshal Sir Denis Spotswood, AOC-in-C, Strike Command, 13 April 1970.
757 Powell, "EW during the V-Force era", pp. 70–85.
758 Baldwin, "Afternoon Discussion Period", pp. 104–110.
759 Roy Brocklebank email: 21/4/20.
760 Wing Commander Richard 'Dick' Turpin, "RAF EW training: 1966–94", RAF Historical Society, *Journal 28 – Seminar: Electronic Warfare*, 2003, p. 91.

20. ATTACKING TARGETS

761 Roy Brocklebank email: 17/6/20.
762 Jim Walker interviewed: 26/3/19.
763 Alan McLoughlin email: 12/11/20.
764 Roy Brocklebank email: 2/11/20.
765 Andrew Brookes, *RAF V-Force: Operations Manual*, Haynes Publishing, 2015, pp. 119–23.
766 Roy Brocklebank; "Defence through Deterrence", Witness Seminar, Institute of Contemporary British History and Defence Studies Department, King's College, London, 10 September 2014.
767 Jim Walker interviewed: 26/3/19.
768 Moore, *Nuclear Illusion, Nuclear Reality: Britain, the United States and Nuclear Weapons, 1958–1964*, pp. 207, 293 citing Robert Dalsjö, "Lifeline lost: the rise and fall of 'neutral' Sweden's secret reserve option of wartime help from the West", 2006, pp. 164–5.
769 Roy Brocklebank letter re: "Plan A": 9/8/18.
770 Loose minute, Group Captain (Ops), M. M. J. Robinson, to Group Captain, Plans and Policy, "Buccaneer OCU – assignment", 15 April 1971; cited by Mike Fazackerley email: 11/9/18.
771 Roy Brocklebank email: 18/3/21.
772 Loose minute, Group Captain (Ops) M. M. J. Robinson, "Buccaneer OCU – assignment", April 15 1971; cited by Mike Fazackerley email: 11/9/18.
773 Roy Brocklebank email: 4/6/19.
774 John Muston email 18/2/19.
775 Roy Brocklebank email: 4/6/19.
776 Dick Fuller, amongst documents/text provided: 29/10/20.
777 Brocklebank, "How did Bomber Command prepare for war?".
778 Ibid.
779 Roy Brocklebank email: 4/6/19.
780 Roy Brocklebank email: 28/1/21.
781 Ibid.
782 AIR 14/4320, Bomber Command, Operational Research Branch, Memorandum No. 251, "The use of H2S jammers in Bomber Command, January–April 1962", June 1962.
783 AIR 14/4325, Bomber Command, Operational Research Branch, Memorandum No. 256, "The bombing of targets protected by multiple H2S jammers", October 1962.
784 AIR 14/4343, Bomber Command, Operational Research Branch, Memorandum No. 274, "Exercise Blank Stare II, Trial No. 457", August 1963.
785 John Weller interviewed: 1/8/18.
786 Vic Bussereau interviewed: 6/6/18.
787 Roy Brocklebank letter: 16/8/18.
788 Jim Walker interviewed: 26/3/19.

789 Jeremy Mudford interviewed: 8/2/18.
790 James Vinales interviewed: 24/7/19.
791 Mike Fazackerley, notes: 16/11/20; 20/2/21.
792 Norman Bonnor, amongst documents/text provided: 1/11/20.
793 Mike Fazackerley email: 10/8/19; citing AIR 2/18150, WDC (NC).
794 Roy Brocklebank email: 10/8/19.
795 Mike Fazackerley emails: 29/7/19, 15/11/20.
796 Roy Brocklebank email: 12/8/19.
797 John Huggins, amongst documents/text provided: 26/11/20.
798 Ibid.
799 Roger Dunsford, amongst documents/text provided: 20/11/20.
800 Bryan 'Monty' Montgomery interviewed: 27/2/18.
801 Barry Mullen, amongst documents/text provided: 29/10/20.
802 AIR 2/19184.
803 Austin Long, *Deterrence – From Cold War to Long War: Lessons from Six Decades of RAND Research*, RAND Corporation, 2008, p. 64.

21. TRAINING FOR A ONE-STRIKE WAR

804 Robin Woolven, amongst documents/text provided: 5/11/20.
805 Bryan 'Monty' Montgomery interviewed: 27/2/18.
806 Bonnor, "The V-Force: 1955–1966: Navigation at 50,000 and 500 ft".
807 Roy Brocklebank email: 11/4/20.
808 Roy Brocklebank, amongst documents/text provided: 25/6/20.
809 Robin Woolven, amongst documents/text provided: 5/11/20.
810 Ibid.
811 Nick Dennis interviewed: 30/5/18.
812 John Weller interviewed: 1/8/18.
813 Roger Smith interviewed: 11/12/18.
814 Wing Commander Peter West, letter: 6/5/19.
815 McLelland, *Britain's Cold War Bombers*, p. 103.
816 Bonnor, "Blue Steel, the V-Force's stand-off bomb".
817 Nick Dennis interviewed: 30/5/18.
818 Jim Milne interviewed: 5/4/18.
819 Air Vice-Marshal Nigel Baldwin, "Training the V-Force for Its Primary and Secondary Roles – Low-Level Tactics against the Soviet Bloc", RAF Historical Society, *Journal 20 –Seminar: Training in Peace for War*, 1999, pp. 24–33.
820 Barry Mullen, amongst documents/text provided: 29/10/20.
821 DASB/296/80, "UK Logistic Planning Policy", meeting of the Chiefs of Staff Committee, 6 May 1980.
822 Bryan 'Monty' Montgomery interviewed: 27/2/18.
823 Dick Fuller, amongst documents/text provided: 29/10/20.
824 Barry Mullen, amongst documents/text provided: 29/10/20.
825 Roy Brocklebank email: 10/4/20.
826 Hugh Prior interviewed: 30/5/18.
827 Jim Walker interviewed: 26/3/19.
828 Wynn, *RAF Nuclear Deterrent Force*, p. 546.
829 AIR 41/85, p. 71.
830 Jim Walker interviewed: 26/3/19.
831 Barry Mullen, amongst document/text provided: 29/10/20.
832 Mike Fazackerley, amongst documents/text provided: 15/11/20.
833 Roy Brocklebank, amongst documents/text provided: 25/6/20.
834 Bob Sinclair interviewed: 5/4/18.
835 Keith Mans, amongst documents/text provided: 17/11/20.
836 Norman Bonnor, amongst documents/text provided: 1/11/20.
837 Barry Mullen, amongst documents/text provided: 29/10/20.
838 Rob Williams, amongst documents/text provided: 27/10/20.
839 Paul Millikin interviewed: 11/12/18.
840 Bill Taylor interviewed: 19/2/19.
841 Martin Anscombe interviewed: 28/2/18.
842 AIR 14/4401, Bomber Command, Operational Research Branch, Memorandum No. 345, "An analysis of training for Exercise Giant Voice", October 1967.
843 Baldwin, "Training the V-Force for Its Primary and Secondary Roles – Low-Level Tactics against the Soviet Bloc", pp. 24–33.
844 Dennis Martin interviewed: 10/12/18.
845 Geoff Lidbetter interviewed: 23/7/19.
846 White, *The King's Thunderbolts*, pp. 184–185.

847 Steve Oddy email: 25/1/23.
848 Baldwin, "Training the V-Force for Its Primary and Secondary Roles – Low-Level Tactics against the Soviet Bloc", pp. 24–33.
849 Julian Grenfell email: 20/4/19.
850 Clive Richards, "A Wasting Asset? The RAF's Medium Bomber Force in the aftermath of the Nassau Agreement, 1962–1982", RAF Historical Society, *Journal 78*, 2022, pp. 59–60; citing AIR 20/12698, Appendix G "Vulcan Operations", p. 12.
851 Julian Grenfell interviewed: 10/12/18.
852 Julian Grenfell email: 20/4/19.
853 Wynn, *RAF Nuclear Deterrent Forces*, p. 545.
854 Goodall, *My Target was Leningrad*, pp. 159–60.
855 Baldwin, "Training the V-Force for Its Primary and Secondary Roles – Low-Level Tactics against the Soviet Bloc", pp. 23–24.
856 Peter West interviewed: 30/4/19.
857 Roy Brocklebank email: 5/4/20.
858 Wynn, *RAF Nuclear Deterrent Forces*, pp. 442–48.
859 John Weller interviewed: 1/8/18.
860 Stoddart, *Losing an Empire and Finding a Role*, p. 99.
861 John Huggins, amongst documents/text provided: 26/10/20.
862 Robin Woolven, amongst documents/text provided: 5/11/20.
863 Dave Beane, amongst documents/text provided: 27/10/20.
864 John Huggins, amongst documents/text provided: 26/10/20.
865 Robin Woolven, amongst documents/text provided: 5/11/20.
866 Alan McLoughlin, amongst documents/text provided: 2/11/20.
867 Barry Masefield interviewed: 27/2/18.
868 Edward Jarron interviewed: 23/7/19.
869 John Laycock interviewed: 27/3/18.
870 Keith Mans, amongst documents/text provided: 17/11/20.
871 Clive Richards, "A Wasting Asset?", pp. 52–54.
872 DEFE 58/102, "Strike aircraft dispersal – interim arrangements", STC/1077/Plans, 9 June 1975.
873 Edward Jarron interviewed: 23/7/19.
874 Peter Moore email: 24/2/21.
875 Jon Tye interviewed: 19/2/19.
876 Roger Dunsford, amongst documents/text provided: 20/11/20.
877 White, *The King's Thunderbolts*, pp. 184–185.
878 Tony Smith interview: 11/1/20.
879 Peter Moore email: 18/3/21.
880 McLelland, *Britain's Cold War Bombers*, p. 175.
881 Baldwin, "Training the V-Force for Its Primary and Secondary Roles – Low-Level Tactics against the Soviet Bloc", pp. 24–33.
882 Roy Brocklebank email: 25/6/20.

INDEX

Allisstone, Air Cdre Mike 27–9
Anscombe, Martin 111, 172, 276, 306
Atomic Weapons Research Establishment (AWRE) 20, 24, 28, 46, 47, 49, 290
Avro Vulcan 8, 11–12, 18, 24, 26, 30–1, 34, 41–2, 45–7, 49, 51–2, 54–6, 58, 60, 66, 72–3, 78–80, 85, 96, 105–7, 116, 119, 124, 142–3, 152–4, 159, 166, 171–2, 180, 182–3, 192–3, 200, 204, 221, 225, 233, 237–9, 243, 245–6, 250–1, 254, 260, 264–5, 266–8, 270–1, 274–9, 282, 284–7, 289–94, 297–300, 302 16, 325–6
Baldwin, Nigel 235, 241–2, 279, 300, 307–8, 316
Ballistic Missile Early Warning Stations (BMEWS) 36, 56, 61, 67, 114, 116, 145, 150, 155–9, 161, 171, 175–7, 199–200, 220, 222, 225–30, 237–8
Beane, Dave 166, 174, 273, 311
Boeing:
  B-29 Superfortress 11, 15–16
  B-47 Stratojet 16, 76, 169, 216, 221, 238
  B-52 Stratofortress 132, 169, 182, 238, 249, 274, 304, 305, 307–9
Bomber Command Armament School (BCAS) 27, 28, 30, 88
Bomber Command Operations Centre (BCOC) 57, 114, 150, 151, 156, 170, 175, 176
Bonnor, Air Cdre Norman 36–8, 40–1, 54, 59, 75, 95, 97–8, 112, 131–2, 141, 174–5, 193–4, 208–9, 240, 259, 289–90, 297, 299, 304–5
Boyle, MRAF Sir Dermot 31, 50, 110
British Nuclear Deterrent Study Group (BNDSG) 68, 118, 134, 198, 258
Broadhurst, ACM Sir Harry 51, 57, 187
Brocklebank, Roy 8–9, 12, 21, 25, 26–7, 42, 46–7, 58, 59, 71–2, 88–9, 91, 96–7, 112, 113, 124–6, 130–2, 138–42, 155–6, 159–60, 166–9, 175, 186, 189, 191–5, 200–4, 211, 214–16, 223, 225–6, 228–30, 232–3, 238–9, 241, 245–6, 249–51, 255–6, 261–2, 266, 269, 270, 274, 276, 278–9, 280–8, 290–2, 297, 302–4, 310, 315, 317
Burnett, ACM B. K. 71
Bussereau, Vic 93, 98–9, 122, 288
Cooper, Sir Frank 15, 116, 117, 133,
Cottingham, Tony 54, 89–90, 152–3, 192, 220,
Cross, ACM Sir Kenneth 'Bing' 36, 38–9, 41, 66, 68, 110, 112–13, 153–5, 170, 186, 187, 189, 221

Cuban Missile Crisis 136, 154, 163, 170–5, 216
Cyprus 46, 47, 83, 99, 100, 110–11, 116–17, 126, 139, 183–4, 201, 238, 249, 302–4, 309, 311
D'Arcy, Mike 96, 234, 260
Dennis, Nick 77–8, 84, 141, 162, 259, 297, 299–300
Dinmore, David 82, 84–5, 237
Doe, Cliff 106–8, 165–6
Dunsford, Roger 81–2, 83–4, 141, 184–5, 267–8, 274, 293, 314
Electric countermeasures (ECM):
  Blue Diver 48, 72, 73, 269–70, 276, 326
  Blue Saga 73, 144, 239, 270, 272, 276, 322–3
  Green Palm 73, 239, 269–70, 274
  Green Satin 38, 72, 95, 98, 108
  IR 239, 243, 322, 323
  Red Shrimp 72, 73, 144, 239, 269, 270, 274, 276, 287, 297
  Red Steer 48, 73, 144, 239, 266, 270, 272, 276, 300, 310, 322–3
  Window (Chaff) 73, 118, 144, 252, 255–6, 266, 269–71, 273, 274, 276, 279, 287, 308, 315, 323, 326
Elworthy, MRAF Sir Charles 60
Exercises:
  Coop 261
  EDOM 157, 192–3, 215
  Finnigan 211
  Goose Ranger 68, 211, 260, 304–6
  Kinsman 68, 202, 214
  Lone Ranger 68, 309–11
  Mayflight 67, 202, 214, 219–20
  Mick 67, 159, 202, 209–11, 237, 314, 318
  Micky Finn 67–8, 159, 191, 202, 207, 209–12, 237, 314
  Red Flag 185, 267–8, 279, 307–9, 316
  Spellbound 255–6
  Sunbeam 265–6
  TACEVAL 216, 313–14
  Western Ranger 68, 111, 261, 304
Fazackerley, Mike 23–4, 26, 36–7, 42–5, 47–9, 90, 283, 289–92, 303
Flowerdew, Neil 101–2
Frampton, Roger 78
Fulena, 'Woody' 93–4, 96, 162–3,
Fuller, Dick 27, 89, 92, 141, 152–3, 162, 173, 220–1, 263, 270–1, 284, 302
Gaunt, Ray 106
Giant Voice 306–7
Goose Bay, Labrador 68, 71, 108, 111, 162, 168, 260–1, 268, 296, 304–6, 315

Grandy, MRAF Sir John 39, 114, 159
Grenfell, Julian 36–7, 54–5, 251–3, 263, 273, 308, 309
Handley Page Victor 10–12, 24, 26, 30, 31, 41–2, 46, 51–2, 54, 55, 58–60, 66, 74, 78, 94, 95, 102, 116, 152, 154, 173, 187, 192, 209, 221, 236, 238–9, 243, 247, 271, 281, 284–5, 287, 293, 299, 305, 310–11, 313
Hely, Michael 27, 28, 30, 150
Hewitt, Len 105–6
Hudleston, ACM Sir Edmund 66, 68, 186, 192
Huggins, John 31, 40, 75–6, 79–80, 89, 105, 113, 143–4, 218, 223–4, 232–5, 292–3, 310–11
Indonesian Confrontation 194, 261, 310
Ivelaw-Chapman, ACM Sir Ronald 10, 148, 150
Jarron, Air Cdre Edward 44, 72, 143, 154, 201, 218, 231, 312, 313
Kennedy, John F. 37, 61
Kerr, Tom 37, 144, 180, 197, 206–7, 251, 255, 270, 272
Kyle, ACM Sir Wallace 39, 60–1, 202
Langdown, Paddy 109, 219, 306
Lark, Lyle 23, 107–8
Laycock, John 94–5, 214–15, 243, 254, 312
Leckenby, Phil 96, 163, 164, 215–17
Leitch, Andy 54, 55, 69, 116, 141, 143, 153, 188, 191, 201, 226, 266, 292
Lidbetter, Geoff 104–5, 307
Lloyd, ACM Sir Hugh 18
Long Term Strategic Nuclear Working Party 199, 249–50, 263, 294
MacGillivray, Bill 85–6, 142, 201
Macmillan, Harold 37, 49, 50, 57, 61, 109, 143, 148, 170, 197
Mans, Keith 65, 80–1, 110, 272–3, 304, 312, 318
Martin, Dennis 78–9, 280, 305, 307
Masefield, Barry 102–4, 273–4, 312
McLoughlin, Alan 94, 281, 312
Menaul, AVM Stewart 14–15, 32, 33, 58, 72–3, 118–19, 170–2
Millikin, Paul 77, 80, 306
Mills, ACM Sir George 53, 123
Milne, Jim 232–3, 300
Montgomery, Bryan 'Monty' 31, 100, 255, 293, 296, 302,
Moore, Peter 26, 40, 46, 73, 86–7, 140, 164–5, 182, 191–2, 201–2, 232, 239–40, 313, 315
Mudford, Jeremy 58, 112–13, 236, 247, 288
Mullen, Barry 91–3, 294, 300–3, 305
Muston, John 21–2, 54, 284

NATO 11, 14, 30, 47, 51, 63, 65, 68, 124, 131, 136–7, 154, 160–1, 186, 216, 265, 270, 283–4, 301, 314
Near East Air Force (NEAF) 302, 304, 309
Nuclear weapons testing 19–22
Pike, MRAF Sir Thomas 36, 154, 188, 196
Powell, Rod 276–9
Prior, Hugh 104, 274–5, 302
Quick Reaction Alert (QRA) 152–61
RAF Squadrons and Units:
  9 (IX) 231, 238, 302, 314
  12 54, 84, 97, 141, 162, 173–4, 194–5, 299
  15 (XV) 95, 132, 166, 174–5, 194, 214
  27 36, 42, 106, 130, 205, 238, 303
  35 47, 83, 238, 302, 314
  44 (Rhodesia) 26, 40, 47, 86–7, 96, 107, 165, 181, 238, 267
  50 47, 107, 172, 181, 238
  100 36, 41, 194, 208, 240, 304, 313
  101 47, 86, 107, 165, 238
  148 100, 108, 152
  207 108, 152
  214 102, 108, 310
  617 33, 35, 36, 42, 47, 112, 238, 266, 314
  230 OCU 55, 58, 80, 84–6, 96, 97, 104, 245
  232 OCU 11, 53–55, 58
  No. 1 Air Navigation School 93
  No. 2 Air Navigation School 93
  No. 1 Group 58, 63, 170, 187, 298–9, 308
  No. 3 Group 58, 152, 187
RAF Stations:
  Akrotiri 48, 100, 300, 302, 309
  Barnham 27–9
  Brize Norton 16, 85, 216
  Coningsby 55, 58, 84, 96–7, 154, 162, 168, 190, 211, 216, 224, 235, 297
  Cottesmore 28, 55, 58, 99, 112, 130, 139, 154, 162, 166–8, 170, 174–5, 187, 190, 192–4, 215–16, 232, 241, 302
  Cranwell 56, 81–3, 92, 190–1
  Faldingworth 27, 28, 171
  Finningley 48, 55, 79, 92, 190, 192
  Gaydon 11, 53, 55, 58, 97, 108, 190, 231
  Honington 28, 31, 55, 58, 99, 154, 167–8, 170, 190, 192, 227, 383
  Hullavington 93–4
  Leeming 56, 66, 77, 92, 190
  Lindholme 91, 93, 94, 300
  Manston 56, 76, 86, 190
  Marham 15, 30–1, 55, 58, 67, 78, 90, 99–100, 108, 149, 152–3, 173, 186, 190, 192, 242, 281, 284
  North Luffenham 83, 88, 99

Oakington 78–80, 82, 86
Scampton 15, 36–7, 39–42, 47, 55, 58, 83–4, 96–7, 99, 106, 130–1, 154, 163, 168, 170, 190, 192–3, 202, 205, 207–12, 224, 238, 297, 299, 313
South Cerney 76–7, 79, 93, 94, 96, 102
Stradishall 91, 93–4, 99, 101
Topcliffe 102, 104–5
Valley 27, 56, 77, 80, 82, 86, 90, 190, 231, 320
Waddington 15, 26, 31, 40, 46–7, 55, 58, 79, 85, 86, 96, 99, 104–7, 111, 113, 130, 138–9, 142, 146, 154, 162–5, 170–2, 181, 190, 192–5, 204, 215–16, 232, 235, 237, 238, 241, 250, 266, 300, 313, 314–15
Wittering 22, 27, 28, 30, 36, 41–2, 51, 53, 55, 58–9, 88, 90, 92, 99, 108, 154, 168, 170, 173, 190, 192, 209–12
Wyton 55, 58, 102, 190, 247
Readiness states 69, 115, 149, 156–8, 161, 176–7, 185, 195, 198–200, 202, 217–19, 242, 229, 319, 231, 310
Reeve, John 82–3, 132, 240, 275, 316
Richards, Clive 13, 308
Robinson, AVM Michael 58, 173
Ruskell, Dr Les 13, 38, 64, 74, 126–7, 171, 244
Sandys, Duncan 64, 148–9, 187, 196–7
SIMSTART 115, 158, 170, 199, 218–22
Sinclair, Bob 99, 112, 195, 233
Singapore 99, 101, 103–5, 183–4, 296, 309–11
Smith, Roger 76, 131, 237, 298–9
Smith, Tony 46, 237, 314–15
Soviet Union:
  Defences 244–54
  PVO-Strany 244–9, 252–3, 264, 295
  Threat 117, 216–17, 246
Spetsnaz 216–17
Spies 19, 48
Strategic Air Command (SAC) 31, 53, 56, 63, 64, 108, 112, 119, 132–3, 136–7, 140, 143, 146, 150, 154, 168–9, 171, 176–7, 180, 187, 216, 238, 282–3, 297, 304, 306–7, 309
Supreme Allied Commander, Atlantic (SACLANT) 47, 283
Supreme Allied Commander, Europe (SACEUR) 18, 30–1, 45, 47, 51, 55, 59, 61, 63, 65, 90, 137, 144, 147, 152–5, 160, 186, 192, 242, 283, 284, 313–15
Surface-to-air missiles (SAMs):
  Bloodhound 57, 149, 189, 297
  Nike 111, 297, 304
  SA-1 12, 247, 249
  SA-2 12, 244, 246, 249–50, 258, 263, 274–5, 284–5, 287, 291, 324, 326
  SA-3 244–5, 249–51, 257, 263, 274, 278, 294, 324

  SA-8 273
  SA-10 249
Sweden 130, 132, 245, 281–2, 323
Taylor, Bill 205–6, 243, 306
Tedder, MRAF 1st Baron 14–15, 133
Truelove, Air Cdre Owen 24
Tye, Jon 42, 76–7, 87, 313–14
USAF 15–16, 56, 111, 133, 143, 149, 169, 173, 216–17, 221, 237, 247, 267–8, 279, 304–9
Vickers Valiant 8, 10, 12, 18–19, 21, 23, 30–1, 32, 43, 46, 51, 54–6, 58–9, 63–4, 70–3, 108, 116, 123, 139, 141, 152–4, 173, 180, 182, 184, 186, 220–1, 238, 242–3, 247–9, 263, 265, 281–2, 284–6, 299, 310
Vinales, James 101, 289, 306
Walker, Jim 96, 234, 260–1, 281, 282, 288, 302
WE.177 (all variants) 18, 26, 29–30, 40, 42–9, 89, 126, 203–4, 260–1, 282–3, 289–91, 303, 310, 316, 325
Weaponry:
  B43 laydown bomb 18, 31, 43, 152
  Blue Boar 18, 33, 117
  Blue Danube 18–25, 28, 30, 44, 49, 129, 175, 284, 286
  Blue Moon 11
  Blue Steel 18–19, 26, 30, 32–42, 46, 49, 52, 55, 58–60, 68, 70, 73, 96–7, 114–17, 118, 120, 130, 159, 180, 182–4, 193, 202–13, 239, 245–6, 248, 258, 263, 269, 285–90, 297, 299, 303, 309, 319–21, 324
  Hound Dog 26, 248
  Polaris 30, 34, 37, 43–9, 51, 60–1, 63, 66, 104, 121, 134–6, 144, 172, 178, 181–2, 199, 264, 268, 273–5, 278, 280, 293–4, 302, 309, 313, 315–16
  Project E 18, 31, 67, 133, 192
  Red Beard 18, 25–6, 30, 43, 44, 47, 49, 100–1, 137, 175, 310
  Skybolt 18–19, 26, 33–4, 37, 43–6, 49, 52, 60–1, 68–70, 73, 118–21, 135, 172, 180–2, 196–7, 259, 269–71, 290
  Thor 55–8, 60, 64, 136–7, 150, 154–5, 170, 172, 186, 181, 202
  Violet Club 18, 23–4, 48
  Yellow Sun Mk 1/2 18, 24, 26–7, 30–1, 35, 40, 43, 45–6, 48–9, 129, 165, 174–5, 192, 203–5, 239, 260–1, 284–8
Weller, John 93, 237–8, 259, 288, 298, 310
West, Gary 74, 193
West, Peter 54, 72–3, 84, 173–4, 260, 266, 269, 271–2, 298–9, 310
Williams, Rob 39, 231, 305
Woolven, Dr Robin 100–1, 112, 193, 208, 216, 218, 296–7, 311–12
Wright, Anthony 96, 137, 152